Risk Management and Financial Institutions

Founded in 1807, John Wiley & Sons is the oldest independent publishing company in the United States. With offices in North America, Europe, Australia and Asia, Wiley is globally committed to developing and marketing print and electronic products and services for our customers' professional and personal knowledge and understanding.

The Wiley Finance series contains books written specifically for finance and investment professionals as well as sophisticated individual investors and their financial advisors. Book topics range from portfolio management to e-commerce, risk management, financial engineering, valuation and financial instrument analysis, as well as much more.

For a list of available titles, visit our web site at www.WileyFinance.com.

Risk Management and Financial Institutions

Third Edition

JOHN C. HULL

WILEY

John Wiley & Sons, Inc.

Published by John Wiley & Sons, Inc., Hoboken, New Jersey.
Published simultaneously in Canada.

This book was previously published in two editions by Prentice Hall in 2006 and 2009.

For general information on our other products and services or for technical support, please contact our Customer Care Department within the United States at (800) 762-2974, outside the United States at (317) 572-3993 or fax (317) 572-4002.

Wiley also publishes its books in a variety of electronic formats. Some content that appears in print may not be available in electronic books. For more information about Wiley products, visit our web site at www.wiley.com.

Library of Congress Cataloging-in-Publication Data:

Hull, John, 1946–
    Risk management and financial institutions + website / John C. Hull. – 3rd ed.
        p. cm.
    Includes bibliographical references and index.
    ISBN 978-1-118-26903-9 (cloth); ISBN 978-1-118-28477-3 (ebk);
    ISBN 978-1-118-28291-5 (ebk); ISBN 978-1-118-28638-8
    1. Risk management.   2. Financial institutions–Management.   I. Title.
    HD61.H83 2012
    332.1068′1–dc23

                                                2012003579

Printed in the United States of America

10   9   8   7   6   5   4   3

To Michelle, Peter, and David

Contents

Business Snapshots   xvii

Preface   xix

CHAPTER 1
Introduction   1
1.1   Risk vs. Return for Investors   2
1.2   The Efficient Frontier   5
1.3   The Capital Asset Pricing Model   8
1.4   Arbitrage Pricing Theory   13
1.5   Risk vs. Return for Companies   13
1.6   Risk Management by Financial Institutions   16
1.7   Credit Ratings   18
     Summary   18
     Further Reading   19
     Practice Questions and Problems   19
     Further Questions   20

CHAPTER 2
Banks   21
2.1   Commercial Banking   22
2.2   The Capital Requirements of a Small Commercial Bank   24
2.3   Deposit Insurance   26
2.4   Investment Banking   27
2.5   Securities Trading   32
2.6   Potential Conflicts of Interest in Banking   33
2.7   Today's Large Banks   34
2.8   The Risks Facing Banks   37
     Summary   38
     Further Reading   38
     Practice Questions and Problems   38
     Further Questions   39

CHAPTER 3
Insurance Companies and Pension Plans   41
3.1   Life Insurance   41
3.2   Annuity Contracts   45
3.3   Mortality Tables   46
3.4   Longevity and Mortality Risk   50
3.5   Property-Casualty Insurance   51

3.6   Health Insurance   53
3.7   Moral Hazard and Adverse Selection   55
3.8   Reinsurance   56
3.9   Capital Requirements   56
3.10   The Risks Facing Insurance Companies   58
3.11   Regulation   58
3.12   Pension Plans   59
       Summary   62
       Further Reading   64
       Practice Questions and Problems   64
       Further Questions   65

CHAPTER 4
Mutual Funds and Hedge Funds   **67**
4.1   Mutual Funds   67
4.2   Hedge Funds   74
4.3   Hedge Fund Strategies   79
4.4   Hedge Fund Performance   83
       Summary   84
       Further Reading   85
       Practice Questions and Problems   85
       Further Questions   86

CHAPTER 5
Trading in Financial Markets   **89**
5.1   The Markets   89
5.2   Long and Short Positions in Assets   90
5.3   Derivatives Markets   92
5.4   Plain Vanilla Derivatives   93
5.5   Clearing Houses   103
5.6   Margin   104
5.7   Non-Traditional Derivatives   107
5.8   Exotic Options and Structured Products   111
5.9   Risk Management Challenges   114
       Summary   115
       Further Reading   115
       Practice Questions and Problems   116
       Further Questions   118

CHAPTER 6
The Credit Crisis of 2007   **121**
6.1   The U.S. Housing Market   121
6.2   Securitization   124
6.3   The Crisis   131
6.4   What Went Wrong?   131
6.5   Lessons from the Crisis   133
       Summary   134
       Further Reading   135

Practice Questions and Problems 136
Further Questions 136

CHAPTER 7
How Traders Manage Their Risks **137**
7.1 Delta 137
7.2 Gamma 144
7.3 Vega 146
7.4 Theta 148
7.5 Rho 149
7.6 Calculating Greek Letters 150
7.7 Taylor Series Expansions 151
7.8 The Realities of Hedging 152
7.9 Hedging Exotic Options 153
7.10 Scenario Analysis 154
Summary 156
Further Reading 156
Practice Questions and Problems 156
Further Questions 157

CHAPTER 8
Interest Rate Risk **159**
8.1 The Management of Net Interest Income 159
8.2 LIBOR and Swap Rates 162
8.3 Duration 164
8.4 Convexity 168
8.5 Generalization 169
8.6 Nonparallel Yield Curve Shifts 172
8.7 Interest Rate Deltas in Practice 174
8.8 Principal Components Analysis 176
8.9 Gamma and Vega 179
Summary 179
Further Reading 180
Practice Questions and Problems 181
Further Questions 181

CHAPTER 9
Value at Risk **183**
9.1 Definition of VaR 183
9.2 Examples of the Calculation of VaR 185
9.3 VaR vs. Expected Shortfall 186
9.4 VaR and Capital 188
9.5 Coherent Risk Measures 190
9.6 Choice of Parameters for VaR 191
9.7 Marginal VaR, Incremental VaR, and Component VaR 195
9.8 Euler's Theorem 196
9.9 Aggregating VaRs 197
9.10 Back-Testing 197

Summary   200
Further Reading   201
Practice Questions and Problems   201
Further Questions   202

CHAPTER 10
Volatility   **205**
10.1   Definition of Volatility   205
10.2   Implied Volatilities   208
10.3   Are Daily Percentage Changes in Financial
       Variables Normal?   209
10.4   The Power Law   211
10.5   Monitoring Daily Volatility   213
10.6   The Exponentially Weighted Moving Average Model   216
10.7   The GARCH(1,1) Model   218
10.8   Choosing Between the Models   220
10.9   Maximum Likelihood Methods   220
10.10 Using GARCH(1,1) to Forecast Future Volatility   225
       Summary   229
       Further Reading   229
       Practice Questions and Problems   230
       Further Questions   231

CHAPTER 11
Correlations and Copulas   **233**
11.1   Definition of Correlation   233
11.2   Monitoring Correlation   235
11.3   Multivariate Normal Distributions   238
11.4   Copulas   240
11.5   Application to Loan Portfolios: Vasicek's Model   246
       Summary   252
       Further Reading   253
       Practice Questions and Problems   253
       Further Questions   254

CHAPTER 12
Basel I, Basel II, and Solvency II   **257**
12.1   The Reasons for Regulating Banks   257
12.2   Bank Regulation Pre-1988   258
12.3   The 1988 BIS Accord   259
12.4   The G-30 Policy Recommendations   262
12.5   Netting   263
12.6   The 1996 Amendment   265
12.7   Basel II   268
12.8   Credit Risk Capital Under Basel II   269
12.9   Operational Risk Capital Under Basel II   277
12.10 Pillar 2: Supervisory Review   278
12.11 Pillar 3: Market Discipline   278

12.12   Solvency II   279
        Summary   280
        Further Reading   281
        Practice Questions and Problems   281
        Further Questions   283

CHAPTER 13
Basel 2.5, Basel III, and Dodd–Frank   **285**
13.1   Basel 2.5   285
13.2   Basel III   289
13.3   Contingent Convertible Bonds   295
13.4   Dodd–Frank Act   296
13.5   Legislation in Other Countries   298
        Summary   299
        Further Reading   300
        Practice Questions and Problems   300
        Further Questions   301

CHAPTER 14
Market Risk VaR: The Historical Simulation Approach   **303**
14.1   The Methodology   303
14.2   Accuracy   308
14.3   Extensions   309
14.4   Computational Issues   313
14.5   Extreme Value Theory   314
14.6   Applications of EVT   317
        Summary   319
        Further Reading   320
        Practice Questions and Problems   320
        Further Questions   321

CHAPTER 15
Market Risk VaR: The Model-Building Approach   **323**
15.1   The Basic Methodology   323
15.2   Generalization   326
15.3   Correlation and Covariance Matrices   327
15.4   Handling Interest Rates   330
15.5   Applications of the Linear Model   334
15.6   Linear Model and Options   335
15.7   Quadratic Model   338
15.8   Monte Carlo Simulation   340
15.9   Non-Normal Assumptions   341
15.10   Model-Building vs. Historical Simulation   342
        Summary   343
        Further Reading   343
        Practice Questions and Problems   343
        Further Questions   345

CHAPTER 16

Credit Risk: Estimating Default Probabilities   **347**

16.1   Credit Ratings   347
16.2   Historical Default Probabilities   349
16.3   Recovery Rates   351
16.4   Credit Default Swaps   352
16.5   Credit Spreads   357
16.6   Estimating Default Probabilities from Credit Spreads   360
16.7   Comparison of Default Probability Estimates   362
16.8   Using Equity Prices to Estimate Default Probabilities   367
       Summary   370
       Further Reading   371
       Practice Questions and Problems   371
       Further Questions   373

CHAPTER 17

Counterparty Credit Risk in Derivatives   **375**

17.1   Credit Exposure on Derivatives   375
17.2   Bilateral Clearing   376
17.3   Central Clearing   380
17.4   CVA   382
17.5   The Impact of a New Transaction   385
17.6   CVA Risk   387
17.7   Wrong Way Risk   388
17.8   DVA   389
17.9   Some Simple Examples   389
       Summary   394
       Further Reading   395
       Practice Questions and Problems   395
       Further Questions   396

CHAPTER 18

Credit Value at Risk   **399**

18.1   Ratings Transition Matrices   400
18.2   Vasicek's Model   402
18.3   Credit Risk Plus   403
18.4   CreditMetrics   405
18.5   Credit VaR in the Trading Book   406
       Summary   410
       Further Reading   410
       Practice Questions and Problems   411
       Further Questions   411

CHAPTER 19

Scenario Analysis and Stress Testing   **413**

19.1   Generating the Scenarios   413
19.2   Regulation   419

19.3	What to Do with the Results	423
	Summary	426
	Further Reading	426
	Practice Questions and Problems	427
	Further Questions	428

CHAPTER 20
Operational Risk   **429**

20.1	What is Operational Risk?	430
20.2	Determination of Regulatory Capital	431
20.3	Categorization of Operational Risks	433
20.4	Loss Severity and Loss Frequency	434
20.5	Implementation of AMA	435
20.6	Proactive Approaches	439
20.7	Allocation of Operational Risk Capital	440
20.8	Use of Power Law	441
20.9	Insurance	442
20.10	Sarbanes-Oxley	443
	Summary	444
	Further Reading	445
	Practice Questions and Problems	445
	Further Questions	446

CHAPTER 21
Liquidity Risk   **447**

21.1	Liquidity Trading Risk	447
21.2	Liquidity Funding Risk	454
21.3	Liquidity Black Holes	462
	Summary	468
	Further Reading	469
	Practice Questions and Problems	470
	Further Questions	470

CHAPTER 22
Model Risk   **473**

22.1	Marking to Market	473
22.2	Models for Linear Products	475
22.3	Physics vs. Finance	476
22.4	How Models are Used for Pricing Standard Products	478
22.5	Hedging	484
22.6	Models for Nonstandard Products	485
22.7	Dangers in Model Building	486
22.8	Detecting Model Problems	487
	Summary	488
	Further Reading	488
	Practice Questions and Problems	489
	Further Questions	489

CHAPTER 23

Economic Capital and RAROC   **491**

23.1   Definition of Economic Capital   491
23.2   Components of Economic Capital   493
23.3   Shapes of the Loss Distributions   495
23.4   Relative Importance of Risks   497
23.5   Aggregating Economic Capital   498
23.6   Allocation of Economic Capital   501
23.7   Deutsche Bank's Economic Capital   503
23.8   RAROC   503
       Summary   505
       Further Reading   506
       Practice Questions and Problems   506
       Further Questions   507

CHAPTER 24

Risk Management Mistakes to Avoid   **509**

24.1   Risk Limits   509
24.2   Managing the Trading Room   512
24.3   Liquidity Risk   514
24.4   Lessons for Nonfinancial Corporations   517
24.5   A Final Point   518
       Further Reading   519

Appendix A

Compounding Frequencies for Interest Rates   **521**

Appendix B

Zero Rates, Forward Rates, and Zero-Coupon Yield Curves   **525**

Appendix C

Valuing Forward and Futures Contracts   **529**

Appendix D

Valuing Swaps   **531**

Appendix E

Valuing European Options   **533**

Appendix F

Valuing American Options   **535**

Appendix G

Taylor Series Expansions   **539**

Appendix H

Eigenvectors and Eigenvalues   **543**

Appendix I
  Principal Components Analysis   547

Appendix J
  Manipulation of Credit Transition Matrices   549

Appendix K
  Valuation of Credit Default Swaps   551

Appendix L
  Synthetic CDOs and Their Valuation   555

Answers to Questions and Problems   559

Glossary   595

DerivaGem Software   615

Table for $N(x)$ **when** $x \leq 0$ 621

Table for $N(x)$ **when** $x \geq 0$ 623

Index   625

Business Snapshots

1.1	The Hidden Costs of Bankruptcy	15
2.1	Google's IPO	30
2.2	PeopleSoft's Poison Pill	31
2.3	How to Keep Loans Performing	36
3.1	Equitable Life	47
3.2	A Perfect Storm	61
4.1	Mutual Fund Returns Can Be Misleading	73
5.1	The Unanticipated Delivery of a Futures Contract	96
5.2	A System's Error?	97
5.3	Microsoft's Hedging	112
5.4	Procter and Gamble's Bizarre Deal	113
5.5	SocGen's Big Loss in 2008	114
6.1	All BBBs Are Not the Same	130
6.2	A Trading Opportunity?	134
7.1	Hedging By Gold Mining Companies	140
7.2	Dynamic Hedging in Practice	153
7.3	Is Delta Hedging Easier or More Difficult for Exotics?	154
9.1	Historical Perspectives on VaR	184
10.1	What Causes Volatility?	207
10.2	Making Money from Foreign Currency Options	210
12.1	Systemic Risk	258
13.1	Credit Suisse's CoCo Bond Issues	296
16.1	The CDS Market	353
16.2	Is the CDS Market a Fair Game?	355
16.3	Risk-Neutral Valuation	365
16.4	Contagion	367
17.1	Rehypothecation	379
19.1	Long-Term Capital Management's Big Loss	417
19.2	Traffic Light Options	423
20.1	The Hammersmith and Fulham Story	439
20.2	Rogue Trader Insurance	443
21.1	Northern Rock	455
21.2	Ashanti Goldfields	458
21.3	Metallgesellschaft	459
21.4	The Crash of 1987	464
22.1	Kidder Peabody's Embarrassing Mistake	476
22.2	Exploiting the Weaknesses of a Competitor's Model	477
22.3	Crashophobia	481
23.1	The EGT Fund	498
24.1	Big Losses	510

Preface

M uch has happened in financial markets since the second edition of this book was published. We have experienced the worst crisis in more than 70 years. Risk management has assumed more importance than ever before in financial institutions. Market participants are wrestling with initiatives such as Basel III and Dodd–Frank. Liquidity risk and scenario analysis are receiving much more attention.

Risk Management and Financial Institutions has been expanded and updated to reflect these market developments. Like my other popular text *Options, Futures, and Other Derivatives*, this book is designed to be useful to practicing managers as well as college students. Those studying for GARP and PRMIA qualifications will find the book particularly helpful.

The book is appropriate for elective courses in either risk management or financial institutions. It is not necessary for students to take a course on options and futures markets prior to taking a course based on this book. But if they have taken such a course, some of the material in the first eight chapters does not need to be covered.

The level of mathematical sophistication and the way material is presented has been managed carefully so that the book is accessible to as wide an audience as possible. For example, when covering copulas in Chapter 11, I present the intuition followed by a detailed numerical example; when covering maximum likelihood methods in Chapter 10 and extreme value theory in Chapter 14, I provide numerical examples and enough details for readers to develop their own Excel spreadsheets. I have also provided my own Excel spreadsheets for many applications on my website: www.rotman.utoronto.ca/~hull.

This is a book about risk management, so there is relatively very little material on the valuation of derivatives. (This is the main focus of my other two books *Options, Futures, and Other Derivatives* and *Fundamentals of Futures and Options Markets*.) The appendices at the end of the book include material that summarizes some of the key results that are important in risk management and the DerivaGem software can be downloaded from my website.

WHAT'S NEW

The third edition has been fully updated and contains much new material. In particular:

1. There is a new chapter on Basel 2.5, Basel III, and Dodd–Frank.
2. There is more material on counterparty credit risk.
3. There is more material on the calculation of credit VaR (for both the banking book and the trading book).

4. The chapter on the crisis has been updated and is now positioned earlier in the book.
5. There is more material on central clearing, collateralization, and the overnight indexed swap rate.
6. There is more material on Vasicek's model and other similar models. The use of maximum likelihood methods to estimate the parameters in Vasicek's model is now covered.
7. The software illustrating VaR calculations has been enhanced.
8. There is more material on the implementation of the AMA approach for operational risk.
9. Appendices explaining how CDSs and synthetic CDOs are valued have been included.
10. There are a number of enhancements to the DerivaGem software, which is available from my website: www.rotman.utoronto.ca/~hull.
11. New software for applications such as principal components analysis and the manipulation of credit transition matrices is now available on my website.

SLIDES

Several hundred PowerPoint slides can be downloaded from my website or from Wiley's Higher Education website. Adopting instructors are welcome to adapt the slides to meet their own needs.

QUESTIONS AND PROBLEMS

End-of-chapter problems are divided into two groups: "Practice Questions and Problems" and "Further Questions." Solutions to the former are at the end of the book. Solutions to the latter and accompanying software are available to adopting instructors from Wiley's Higher Education website.

INSTRUCTOR'S MANUAL

The instructor's manual is made available online to adopting instructors by Wiley. It contains solutions to "Further Questions" (with Excel spreadsheets), notes on the teaching of each chapter, and some suggestions on course organization.

ACKNOWLEDGMENTS

Many people have played a part in the production of this book. I have benefited from interactions with many academics and practicing risk managers. I would like to thank the students in my MBA and Master of Finance risk management courses at University of Toronto, many of whom have made suggestions as to how the material could be improved. Yoshit Rostogi provided excellent research assistance.

Alan White, a colleague at the University of Toronto, deserves a special acknowledgment. Alan and I have been carrying out joint research and consulting in the area of derivatives and risk management for over 25 years. During that time we have spent countless hours discussing key issues. Many of the new ideas in this book, and many of the new ways used to explain old ideas, are as much Alan's as mine. Alan has done most of the development work on the DerivaGem software.

Special thanks are due to many people at Wiley, particularly Evan Burton, Meg Freeborn, Vincent Nordhaus, and Mary Daniello for their enthusiasm, advice, and encouragement.

I welcome comments on the book from readers. My e-mail address is hull@rotman.utoronto.ca.

JOHN HULL
Joseph L. Rotman School of Management
University of Toronto

Risk Management
and Financial
Institutions

CHAPTER 1

Introduction

Imagine you are the Chief Risk Officer (CRO) of a major corporation. The CEO wants your views on a major new venture. You have been inundated with reports showing that the new venture has a positive net present value and will enhance shareholder value. What sort of analysis and ideas is the CEO looking for from you?

As CRO it is your job to consider how the new venture fits into the company's portfolio. What is the correlation of the performance of the new venture with the rest of the company's business? When the rest of the business is experiencing difficulties, will the new venture also provide poor returns, or will it have the effect of dampening the ups and downs in the rest of the business?

Companies must take risks if they are to survive and prosper. The risk management function's primary responsibility is to understand the portfolio of risks that the company is currently taking and the risks it plans to take in the future. It must decide whether the risks are acceptable and, if they are not acceptable, what action should be taken.

Most of this book is concerned with the ways risks are managed by banks and other financial institutions, but many of the ideas and approaches we will discuss are equally applicable to nonfinancial corporations. Risk management has become progressively more important for all corporations in the last few decades. Financial institutions in particular are finding they have to increase the resources they devote to risk management. Large "rogue trader" losses such as those at Barings Bank in 1995, Allied Irish Bank in 2002, Société Générale in 2007, and UBS in 2011 would have been avoided if procedures used by the banks for collecting data on trading positions had been more carefully developed. Huge "subprime" losses at banks such as Citigroup, UBS, and Merrill Lynch would have been less severe if risk management groups had been able to convince senior management that unacceptable risks were being taken.

This opening chapter sets the scene. It starts by reviewing the classical arguments concerning the risk-return trade-offs faced by an investor who is choosing a portfolio of stocks and bonds. It then considers whether the same arguments can be used by a company in choosing new projects and managing its risk exposure. The chapter concludes that there are reasons why companies—particularly financial institutions—should be concerned with the total risk they face, not just with the risk from the viewpoint of a well-diversified shareholder.

1.1 RISK VS. RETURN FOR INVESTORS

As all fund managers know, there is a trade-off between risk and return when money is invested. The greater the risks taken, the higher the return that can be realized. The trade-off is actually between risk and *expected return*, not between risk and actual return. The term "expected return" sometimes causes confusion. In everyday language an outcome that is "expected" is considered highly likely to occur. However, statisticians define the expected value of a variable as its average (or mean) value. Expected return is therefore a weighted average of the possible returns, where the weight applied to a particular return equals the probability of that return occurring. The possible returns and their probabilities can be either estimated from historical data or assessed subjectively.

Suppose, for example, that you have $100,000 to invest for one year. One alternative is to buy Treasury bills yielding 5% per annum. There is then no risk and the expected return is 5%. Another alternative is to invest the $100,000 in a stock. To simplify things, we suppose that the possible outcomes from this investment are as shown in Table 1.1. There is a 0.05 probability that the return will be +50%; there is a 0.25 probability that the return will be +30%; and so on. Expressing the returns in decimal form, the expected return per year is:

$$0.05 \times 0.50 + 0.25 \times 0.30 + 0.40 \times 0.10 + 0.25 \times (-0.10) + 0.05 \times (-0.30) = 0.10$$

This shows that in return for taking some risk you are able to increase your expected return per annum from the 5% offered by Treasury bills to 10%. If things work out well, your return per annum could be as high as 50%. But the worst-case outcome is a −30% return or a loss of $30,000.

One of the first attempts to understand the trade-off between risk and expected return was by Markowitz (1952). Later Sharpe (1964) and others carried the Markowitz analysis a stage further by developing what is known as the capital asset pricing model. This is a relationship between expected return and what is termed "systematic risk." In 1976, Ross developed arbitrage pricing theory which can be viewed as an extension of the capital asset pricing model to the situation where there are several sources of systematic risk. The key insights of these researchers have had a profound effect on the way portfolio managers think about and analyze the risk-return trade-offs that they face. In this section we review these insights.

TABLE 1.1 Return in One Year from Investing $100,000 in Equities

Probability	Return
0.05	+50%
0.25	+30%
0.40	+10%
0.25	−10%
0.05	−30%

Quantifying Risk

How do you quantify the risk you are taking when you choose an investment? A convenient measure that is often used is the standard deviation of return over one year. This is

$$\sqrt{E(R^2) - [E(R)]^2}$$

where R is the return per annum. The symbol E denotes expected value so that $E(R)$ is expected return per annum. In Table 1.1, as we have shown, $E(R) = 0.10$. To calculate $E(R^2)$ we must weight the alternative squared returns by their probabilities:

$$E(R^2) = 0.05 \times 0.50^2 + 0.25 \times 0.30^2 + 0.40 \times 0.10^2 + 0.25 \times (-0.10)^2$$
$$+ 0.05 \times (-0.30)^2 = 0.046$$

The standard deviation of returns is therefore $\sqrt{0.046 - 0.1^2} = 0.1897$ or 18.97%.

Investment Opportunities

Suppose we choose to characterize every investment opportunity by its expected return and standard deviation of return. We can plot available risky investments on a chart such as Figure 1.1 where the horizontal axis is the standard deviation of return and the vertical axis is the expected return.

Once we have identified the expected return and the standard deviation of the return for individual investments, it is natural to think about what happens when we combine investments to form a portfolio. Consider two investments with returns R_1

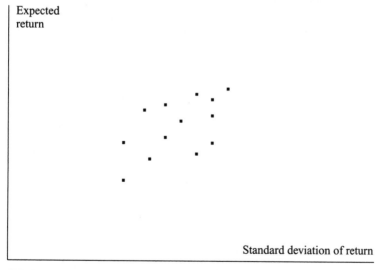

FIGURE 1.1 Alternative Risky Investments

and R_2. The return from putting a proportion w_1 of our money in the first investment and a proportion $w_2 = 1 - w_1$ in the second investment is

$$w_1 R_1 + w_2 R_2$$

The portfolio expected return is

$$\mu_P = w_1\mu_1 + w_2\mu_2 \tag{1.1}$$

where μ_1 is the expected return from the first investment and μ_2 is the expected return from the second investment. The standard deviation of the portfolio return is given by

$$\sigma_P = \sqrt{w_1^2\sigma_1^2 + w_2^2\sigma_2^2 + 2\rho w_1 w_2\sigma_1\sigma_2} \tag{1.2}$$

where σ_1 and σ_2 are the standard deviations of R_1 and R_2 and ρ is the coefficient of correlation between the two.

Suppose that μ_1 is 10% per annum and σ_1 is 16% per annum while μ_2 is 15% per annum and σ_2 is 24% per annum. Suppose also that the coefficient of correlation, ρ, between the returns is 0.2 or 20%. Table 1.2 shows the values of μ_P and σ_P for a number of different values of w_1 and w_2. The calculations show that by putting part of your money in the first investment and part in the second investment a wide range of risk-return combinations can be achieved. These are plotted in Figure 1.2.

Most investors are risk-averse. They want to increase expected return while reducing the standard deviation of return. This means that they want to move as far as they can in a "northwest" direction in Figures 1.1 and 1.2. Figure 1.2 shows that forming a portfolio of the two investments we have been considering helps them do this. For example, by putting 60% in the first investment and 40% in the second, a portfolio with an expected return of 12% and a standard deviation of return equal to 14.87% is obtained. This is an improvement over the risk-return trade-off for the

TABLE 1.2 Expected Return, μ_P, and Standard Deviation of Return, σ_P, from a Portfolio Consisting of Two Investments

w_1	w_2	μ_P	σ_P
0.0	1.0	15%	24.00%
0.2	0.8	14%	20.09%
0.4	0.6	13%	16.89%
0.6	0.4	12%	14.87%
0.8	0.2	11%	14.54%
1.0	0.0	10%	16.00%

The expected returns from the investments are 10% and 15%; the standard deviation of the returns are 16% and 24%; and the correlation between returns is 0.2.

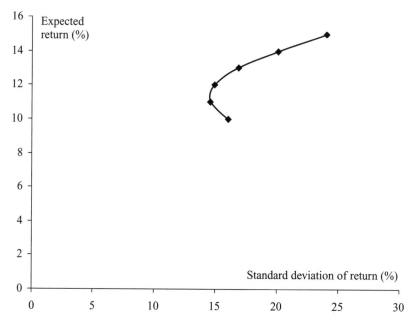

FIGURE 1.2   Alternative Risk-Return Combinations from Two Investments
(as Calculated in Table 1.2)

first investment. (The expected return is 2% higher and the standard deviation of the
return is 1.13% lower.)

1.2 THE EFFICIENT FRONTIER

Let us now bring a third investment into our analysis. The third investment can be
combined with any combination of the first two investments to produce new risk-
return combinations. This enables us to move further in the northwest direction. We
can then add a fourth investment. This can be combined with any combination of the
first three investments to produce yet more investment opportunities. As we continue
this process, considering every possible portfolio of the available risky investments,
we obtain what is known as an *efficient frontier*. This represents the limit of how
far we can move in a northwest direction and is illustrated in Figure 1.3. There is
no investment that dominates a point on the efficient frontier in the sense that it
has both a higher expected return and a lower standard deviation of return. The
area southeast of the efficient frontier represents the set of all investments that are
possible. For any point in this area that is not on the efficient frontier, there is a
point on the efficient frontier that has a higher expected return and lower standard
deviation of return.

In Figure 1.3 we have considered only risky investments. What does the efficient
frontier of all possible investments look like? Specifically, what happens when we
include the risk-free investment? Suppose that the risk-free investment yields a return
of R_F. In Figure 1.4 we have denoted the risk-free investment by point F and drawn a

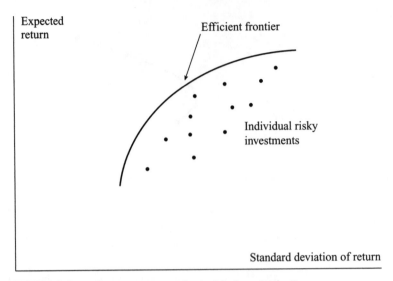

FIGURE 1.3   Efficient Frontier Obtainable from Risky Investments

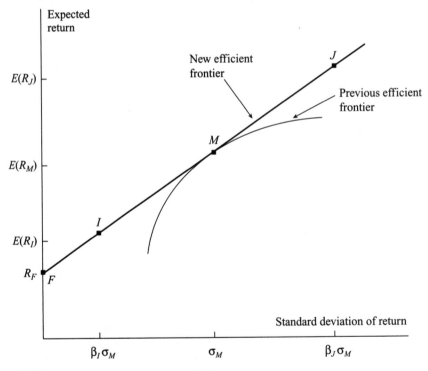

FIGURE 1.4   The Efficient Frontier of All Investments

Point I is achieved by investing a percentage β_I of available funds in portfolio M and the rest in a risk-free investment. Point J is achieved by borrowing $\beta_J - 1$ of available funds at the risk-free rate and investing everything in portfolio M.

tangent from point F to the efficient frontier of risky investments that was developed in Figure 1.3. M is the point of tangency. As we will now show, the line FJ is our new efficient frontier.

Consider what happens when we form an investment I by putting β_I of the funds we have available for investment in the risky portfolio, M, and $1 - \beta_I$ in the risk-free investment F ($0 < \beta_I < 1$). From equation (1.1) the expected return from the investment, $E(R_I)$, is given by

$$E(R_I) = (1 - \beta_I)R_F + \beta_I E(R_M)$$

and from equation (1.2), because the risk-free investment has zero standard deviation, the return R_I has standard deviation

$$\beta_I \sigma_M$$

where σ_M is the standard deviation of return for portfolio M. This risk-return combination corresponds to the point labeled I in Figure 1.4. From the perspective of both expected return and standard deviation of return, point I is β_I of the way from F to M.

All points on the line FM can be obtained by choosing a suitable combination of the investment represented by point F and the investment represented by point M. The points on this line dominate all the points on the previous efficient frontier because they give a better risk-return combination. The straight line FM is therefore part of the new efficient frontier.

If we make the simplifying assumption that we can borrow at the risk-free rate of R_F as well as invest at that rate, we can create investments that are on the continuation of FM beyond M. Suppose, for example, that we want to create the investment represented by the point J in Figure 1.4 where the distance of J from F is β_J times the distance of M from F ($\beta_J > 1$). We borrow $\beta_J - 1$ of the amount that we have available for investment at rate R_F and then invest everything (the original funds and the borrowed funds) in the investment represented by point M. After allowing for the interest paid, the new investment has an expected return, $E(R_J)$ given by

$$E(R_J) = \beta_J E(R_M) - (\beta_J - 1)R_F$$

and the standard deviation of the return is

$$\beta_J \sigma_M$$

This shows that the risk and expected return combination corresponds to point J.

The argument that we have presented shows that, when the risk-free investment is considered, the efficient frontier must be a straight line. To put this another way there should be linear trade-off between the expected return and the standard deviation of returns, as indicated in Figure 1.4. All investors should choose the same portfolio of risky assets. This is the portfolio represented by M. They should then reflect their appetite for risk by combining this risky investment with borrowing or lending at the risk-free rate.

It is a short step from here to argue that the portfolio of risky investments represented by M must be the portfolio of all risky investments. Suppose a particular investment is not in the portfolio. No investors would hold it and its price would have to go down so that its expected return increased and it became part of portfolio M. In fact, we can go further than this. To ensure a balance between the supply and demand for each investment, the price of each risky investment must adjust so that the amount of that investment in portfolio M is proportional to the amount of that investment available in the economy. The investment represented by point M is therefore usually referred to as the *market portfolio*.

1.3 THE CAPITAL ASSET PRICING MODEL

How do investors decide on the expected returns they require for individual investments? Based on the analysis we have presented, the market portfolio should play a key role. The expected return required on an investment should reflect the extent to which the investment contributes to the risks of the market portfolio.

A common procedure is to use historical data to determine a best-fit linear relationship between returns from an investment and returns from the market portfolio. This relationship has the form:

$$R = a + \beta R_M + \epsilon \tag{1.3}$$

where R is the return from the investment, R_M is the return from the market portfolio, a and β are constants, and ϵ is a random variable equal to the regression error.

Equation (1.3) shows that there are two uncertain components to the risk in the investment's return:

1. A component βR_M, which is a multiple of the return from the market portfolio.
2. A component ϵ, which is unrelated to the return from the market portfolio.

The first component is referred to as *systematic risk*. The second component is referred to as *nonsystematic risk*.

Consider first the nonsystematic risk. If we assume that the ϵs for different investments are independent of each other, the nonsystematic risk is almost completely diversified away in a large portfolio. An investor should not therefore be concerned about nonsystematic risk and should not require an extra return above the risk-free rate for bearing nonsystematic risk.

The systematic risk component is what should matter to an investor. When a large well-diversified portfolio is held, the systematic risk represented by βR_M does not disappear. An investor should require an expected return to compensate for this systematic risk.

We know how investors trade off systematic risk and expected return from Figure 1.4. When $\beta = 0$ there is no systematic risk and the expected return is R_F. When $\beta = 1$, we have the same systematic risk as the market portfolio, which is represented by point M, and the expected return should be $E(R_M)$. In general

$$E(R) = R_F + \beta[E(R_M) - R_F] \tag{1.4}$$

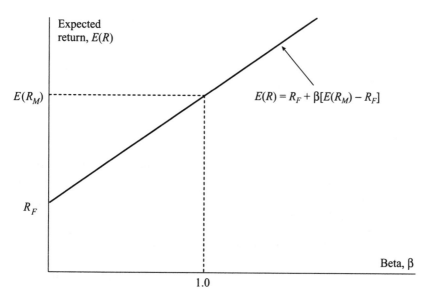

FIGURE 1.5   The Capital Asset Pricing Model

This is the *capital asset pricing model*. The excess expected return over the risk-free rate required on the investment is β times the excess expected return on the market portfolio. This relationship is plotted in Figure 1.5. The parameter β is the *beta* of the investment.

EXAMPLE 1.1

Suppose that the risk-free rate is 5% and the return on the market portfolio is 10%. An investment with a beta of 0 should have an expected return of 5%. This is because all of the risk in the investment can be diversified away. An investment with a beta of 0.5 should have an expected return of

$$0.05 + 0.5 \times (0.1 - 0.05) = 0.075$$

or 7.5%. An investment with a beta of 1.2 should have an expected return of

$$0.05 + 1.2 \times (0.1 - 0.05) = 0.11$$

or 11%.

The parameter, β, is equal to $\rho\sigma/\sigma_M$ where ρ is the correlation between the return from the investment and the return from the market portfolio, σ is the standard deviation of the return from the investment, and σ_M is the standard deviation of the return from the market portfolio. Beta measures the sensitivity of the return from the investment to the return from the market portfolio. We can define the beta of any investment portfolio as in equation (1.3) by regressing its returns against the returns from the market portfolio. The capital asset pricing model in equation (1.4) should then apply with the return R defined as the return from the portfolio. In Figure 1.4 the market portfolio represented by M has a beta of 1.0 and the riskless portfolio represented by F has a beta of zero. The portfolios represented by the points I and J have betas equal to β_I and β_J, respectively.

Assumptions

The analysis we have presented leads to the surprising conclusion that all investors want to hold the same portfolios of assets (the portfolio represented by M in Figure 1.4.) This is clearly not true. Indeed, if it were true, markets would not function well at all because investors would not want to trade with each other! In practice, different investors have different views on the attractiveness of stocks and other risky investment opportunities. This is what causes them to trade with each other and it is this trading that leads to the formation of prices in markets.

The reason why the analysis leads to conclusions that do not correspond with the realities of markets is that, in presenting the arguments, we implicitly made a number of assumptions. In particular:

1. We assumed that investors care only about the expected return and the standard deviation of return of their portfolio. Another way of saying this is that investors look only at the first two moments of the return distribution. If returns are normally distributed, it is reasonable for investors to do this. However, the returns from many portfolios are non-normal. They have *skewness* and *excess kurtosis*. Skewness is related to the third moment of the distribution and excess kurtosis is related to the fourth moment. In the case of positive skewness, very high returns are more likely and very low returns are less likely than the normal distribution would predict; in the case of negative skewness, very low returns are more likely and very high returns are less likely than the normal distribution would predict. Excess kurtosis leads to a distribution where both very high and very low returns are more likely than the normal distribution would predict. Most investors are concerned about the possibility of extreme negative outcomes. They are likely to want a higher expected return from investments with negative skewness or excess kurtosis.

2. We assumed that the ϵs for different investments in equation (1.3) are independent. Equivalently we assumed the returns from investments are correlated with each other only because of their correlation with the market portfolio. This is clearly not true. Ford and General Motors are both in the automotive sector. There is likely to be some correlation between their returns that does not arise from their correlation with the overall stock market. This means that their ϵs are not likely to be independent of each other.

3. We assumed that investors focus on returns over just one period and the length of this period is the same for all investors. This is also clearly not true. Some investors such as pension funds have very long time horizons. Others such as day traders have very short time horizons.

4. We assumed that investors can borrow and lend at the same risk-free rate. This is approximately true for a large financial institution in normal market conditions with a good credit rating. But it is not true for small investors.

5. We did not consider tax. In some jurisdictions, capital gains are taxed differently from dividends and other sources of income. Some investments get special tax treatment and not all investors are subject to the same tax rate. In practice, tax considerations have a part to play in the decisions of an investor. An investment that is appropriate for a pension fund that pays no tax might be quite inappropriate for a high-marginal-rate taxpayer living in New York, and vice versa.

6. Finally, we assumed that all investors make the same estimates of expected returns, standard deviations of returns, and correlations between returns for available investments. To put this another way, we assumed that investors have *homogeneous expectations*. This is clearly not true. Indeed, as indicated earlier, if we lived in a world of homogeneous expectations there would be no trading.

In spite of all this, the capital asset pricing model has proved to be a useful tool for portfolio managers. Estimates of the betas of stocks are readily available and the expected return on a portfolio estimated by the capital asset pricing model is a commonly used benchmark for assessing the performance of the portfolio manager, as we will now explain.

Alpha

When we observe a return of R_M on the market, what do we expect the return on a portfolio with a beta of β to be? The capital asset pricing model relates the expected return on a portfolio to the expected return on the market. But it can also be used to relate the expected return on a portfolio to the actual return on the market:

$$E(R_P) = R_F + \beta(R_M - R_F)$$

where R_F is the risk-free rate and R_P is the return on the portfolio.

EXAMPLE 1.2

Consider a portfolio with a beta of 0.6 when the risk-free interest rate is 4%. When the return from the market is 20%, the expected return on the portfolio is

$$0.04 + 0.6 \times (0.2 - 0.04) = 0.136$$

or 13.6%. When the return from the market is 10%, the expected return from the portfolio is

$$0.04 + 0.6 \times (0.1 - 0.04) = 0.076$$

or 7.6%. When the return from the market is −10%, the expected return from the portfolio is

$$0.04 + 0.6 \times (-0.1 - 0.04) = -0.044$$

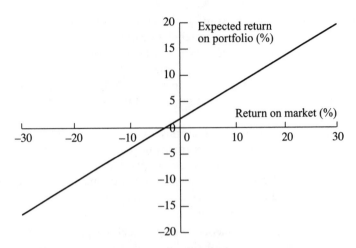

FIGURE 1.6   Relation between Expected Return on Portfolio
and the Actual Return on the Market When Portfolio Beta is 0.6
and Risk-Free Rate is 4%

or −4.4%. The relationship between the expected return on the portfolio and the
return on the market is shown in Figure 1.6.

Suppose that the actual return on the portfolio is greater than the expected
return:

$$R_P > R_F + \beta(R_M - R_F)$$

The portfolio manager has produced a superior return for the amount of systematic
risk being taken. The extra return is

$$\alpha = R_P - R_F - \beta(R_M - R_F)$$

This is commonly referred to as the *alpha* created by the portfolio manager.

EXAMPLE 1.3

A portfolio manager has a portfolio with a beta of 0.8. The one-year risk-free rate
of interest is 5%, the return on the market during the year is 7%, and the portfolio
manager's return is 9%. The manager's alpha is

$$\alpha = 0.09 - 0.05 - 0.8 \times (0.07 - 0.05) = 0.024$$

or 2.4%.

Portfolio managers are continually searching for ways of producing a positive
alpha. One way is by trying to pick stocks that outperform the market. Another is
by *market timing*. This involves trying to anticipate movements in the market as a

whole and moving funds from safe investments such as Treasury bills to the stock market when an upturn is anticipated and in the other direction when a downturn is anticipated. Chapter 4 explains other strategies used by hedge funds to try to create positive alpha.

Although the capital asset pricing model makes simplifying assumptions, the alpha and beta parameters that come out of the model are widely used to characterize investments. Beta describes the return obtained from taking systematic risk. The higher the value of beta, the greater the systematic risk being taken and the greater the extent to which returns are dependent on the performance of the market. Alpha represents the extra return made from superior portfolio management (or perhaps just good luck). An investor can make a positive alpha only at the expense of other investors who are making a negative alpha. The weighted average alpha of all investors is zero.

1.4 ARBITRAGE PRICING THEORY

Arbitrage pricing theory can be viewed as an extension of the capital asset pricing model. The return from an investment is assumed to depend on several factors. (These factors might involve variables such as the gross national product, the domestic interest rate, and the inflation rate.) By exploring ways in which investors can form portfolios that eliminate their exposure to the factors, arbitrage pricing theory shows that the expected return from an investment is linearly dependent on the factors.

The assumption that the ϵs for different investments are independent in the equation (1.3) ensures that there is just one factor driving expected returns (and therefore one source of systematic risk) in the capital asset pricing model. This is the return from the market portfolio. In arbitrage pricing theory there are several factors affecting investment returns. Each factor is a separate source of systematic risk. Unsystematic (i.e., diversifiable) risk in arbitrage pricing theory is the risk that is unrelated to all the factors.

1.5 RISK VS. RETURN FOR COMPANIES

We now move on to consider the trade-offs between risk and return made by a company. How should a company decide whether the expected return on a new investment project is sufficient compensation for its risks?

The ultimate owners of a company are its shareholders and a company should be managed in the best interests of its shareholders. It is therefore natural to argue that a new project undertaken by the company should be viewed as an addition to its shareholder's portfolio. The company should calculate the beta of the investment project and its expected return. If the expected return is greater than that given by the capital asset pricing model, it is a good deal for shareholders and the investment should be accepted. Otherwise it should be rejected.

The argument just given suggests that nonsystematic risks should not be considered when accept/reject decisions on new projects are taken. In practice of course, companies are concerned about nonsystematic as well as systematic risks. For example, most companies insure themselves against the risk of their buildings being burned down—even though this risk is entirely nonsystematic and can be diversified away by their shareholders. They try to avoid taking high risks and often hedge their exposures to exchange rates, interest rates, commodity prices, and other market variables.

Earnings stability and the survival of the company are important managerial objectives. Companies do try and ensure that their expected returns on new ventures are consistent with the risk-return trade-offs of their shareholders. But there is an overriding constraint that the total risks taken should not be allowed to get too large.

Most investors are also concerned about the overall risk of the companies they invest in. They do not like surprises and prefer to invest in companies that show solid growth and meet earnings forecasts. They like companies to manage risks carefully and limit the overall amount of risk—both systematic and nonsystematic—they are taking.

The theoretical arguments we presented in Sections 1.1 to 1.4 suggest that investors should not behave in this way. They should hold a well-diversified portfolio and encourage the companies they invest in to make high risk investments when the combination of expected return and systematic risk is favorable. Some of the companies in a shareholder's portfolio will go bankrupt, but others will do very well. The result should be an overall return to the shareholder that is satisfactory.

Are investors behaving suboptimally? Would their interests be better served if companies took more nonsystematic risks? There is an important argument to suggest that this is not necessarily the case. This argument is usually referred to as the "bankruptcy costs" argument. It is often used to explain why a company should restrict the amount of debt it takes on, but it can be extended to apply to a wider range of risk management decisions than this.

Bankruptcy Costs

In a perfect world, bankruptcy would be a fast affair where the company's assets (tangible and intangible) are sold at their fair market value and the proceeds are distributed to bondholders, shareholders, and other stake holders using well-defined rules. If we lived in such a perfect world, the bankruptcy process itself would not destroy value for shareholders. Unfortunately, the real world is far from perfect. By the time a company reaches the point of bankruptcy, it is likely that its assets have lost some value. The bankruptcy process itself invariably reduces the value of its assets further. This further reduction in value is referred to as *bankruptcy costs*.

What is the nature of bankruptcy costs? Once a bankruptcy has been announced customers and suppliers become less inclined to do business with the company; assets sometimes have to be sold quickly at prices well below those that would be realized in an orderly sale; the value of important intangible assets such as the company's brand name and its reputation in the market are often destroyed; the company is no longer run in the best interests of shareholders; large fees are often paid to accountants and lawyers; and so on. The story in Business Snapshot 1.1 is representative of what often happens in practice. It illustrates how, when a high risk decision works out badly, there can be disastrous bankruptcy costs.

BUSINESS SNAPSHOT 1.1

The Hidden Costs of Bankruptcy

Several years ago, a company had a market capitalization of $2 billion and $500 million of debt. The CEO decided to acquire a company in a related industry for $1 billion in cash. The cash was raised using a mixture of bank debt and bond issues. The price paid for the company was justified on the basis of potential synergies, but key threats to the profitability of the company were overlooked.

Many of the anticipated synergies were not realized. Furthermore, the company that was acquired was not profitable and proved to be a cash drain on the parent company. After three years the CEO resigned. The new CEO sold the acquisition for $100 million (10% of the price paid) and announced that the company would focus on its original core business. However, by then the company was highly leveraged. A temporary economic downturn made it impossible for the company to service its debt and it declared bankruptcy.

The offices of the company were soon filled with accountants and lawyers representing the interests of the various parties (banks, different categories of bondholders, equity holders, the company, and the board of directors). These people directly or indirectly billed the company about $10 million per month in fees. The company lost sales that it would normally have made because nobody wants to do business with a bankrupt company. Key senior executives left. The company experienced a dramatic reduction in its market share.

After two years and three reorganization attempts, an agreement was reached between the various parties and a new company with a market capitalization of $700,000 was incorporated to continue the remaining profitable parts of the business. The shares in the new company were entirely owned by the banks and the bondholders. The shareholders got nothing.

The largest bankruptcy in U.S. history was that of Lehman Brothers on September 15, 2008. Two years later on September 14, 2010, the *Financial Times* reported that the legal and accounting fees in the United States and Europe relating to the bankruptcy of all the subsidiaries of the Lehman holding company had almost reached $2 billion, even though some of the services had been provided at discounted rates.

We mentioned earlier that corporate survival is an important managerial objective and that shareholders like companies to avoid excessive risks. We now understand one reason why this is so. Bankruptcy laws vary widely from country to country, but they all have the effect of destroying value as lenders and other creditors vie with each other to get paid. This value has often been painstakingly built up by the company over many years. It makes sense for a company that is operating in the best interests of its shareholders to limit the probability of this value destruction occurring. It does this by limiting the total risk (systematic and nonsystematic) that it takes.

When a major new investment is being contemplated, it is important to consider how well it fits in with other risks taken by the company. Relatively small investments can often have the effect of reducing the overall risks taken because of their diversification benefits. However, a large investment can dramatically increase these risks. Many spectacular corporate failures (such as the one in Business Snapshot 1.1) can be traced to CEOs who made large acquisitions (often highly leveraged) that did not work out.

1.6 RISK MANAGEMENT BY FINANCIAL INSTITUTIONS

Most of the rest of this book is concerned with financial institutions such as banks and insurance companies. Like other companies, these are concerned with providing a good trade-off between return and systematic risk for their investors. Like other companies, they are also concerned with total risks (systematic plus nonsystematic) because the bankruptcy costs arguments given in the previous section apply to them. However, there is another reason why most financial institutions carefully monitor total risks. This is that regulators require them to do so.

Unlike other companies, most financial institutions are heavily regulated. Governments throughout the world want a stable financial sector. It is important that companies and private individuals have confidence in banks and insurance companies when they transact business. The regulations are designed to ensure that the probability of a large bank or an insurance company experiencing severe financial difficulties is low. The bail-outs of financial institutions in 2008 during the subprime crisis illustrate the reluctance of governments to let large financial institutions fail.

Bankruptcy often arises from losses being incurred. Regulators try to ensure that the capital held by a bank is sufficient to provide a cushion to absorb the losses with a high probability. Suppose for example that there is considered to be only a 0.1% probability that a financial institution will experience a loss of $2 billion or more in a year. Regulators might require the bank to hold equity capital equal to $2 billion. This would ensure that there is a 99.9% probability that the equity capital is sufficient to absorb the losses. The models used by regulators are discussed in more detail in later chapters.

The key point here is that regulators are concerned with total risks, not just systematic risks. Their goal is to make bankruptcy a highly unlikely event.

How Risks Are Managed

There are two broad risk management strategies open to a financial institution (or any other organization). One approach is to identify risks one by one and handle each one separately. This is sometimes referred to as *risk decomposition*. The other is to reduce risks by being well diversified. This is sometimes referred to as *risk aggregation*. Both approaches are typically used by financial institutions.

Consider, for example, the market risks incurred by the trading room of a U.S. bank. These risks depend on the future movements in a multitude of market variables (exchange rates, interest rates, stock prices, and so on). To implement the risk decomposition approach, the trading room is organized so that a trader is responsible for trades related to just one market variable (or perhaps a small group of market variables). For example, there could be one trader who is responsible for all trades involving the dollar-yen exchange rate. At the end of each day, the trader is required to ensure that certain risk measures are kept within limits specified by the bank. If the end of the day is approached and it looks as though one or more of the risk measures will be outside the specified limits, the trader must either get special permission to maintain the position or execute new hedging trades so that the limits are adhered to. (The risk measures and the way they are used are discussed in Chapter 7.)

The risk managers, working in what is termed the "middle office" of a bank, implement the risk aggregation approach for the market risks being taken. This involves calculating at the end of each day the total risk faced by the bank from movements in all market variables. Hopefully, the bank is well diversified so that its overall exposure to market movements is fairly small. If risks are unacceptably high, then the reasons must be determined and corrective action taken. The models used for the aggregation of market risks are given in Chapters 9, 14, and 15.

Risk aggregation is a key tool for insurance companies. Consider automobile insurance. The insurance company's payout on one particular automobile insurance policy is quite uncertain. However, the payout from 100,000 similar insurance policies can be predicted with reasonable accuracy.

Credit risks are also traditionally managed using risk aggregation. It is important for a financial institutions to be well diversified. If, for example, a bank lends 40% of its available funds to a single borrower, it is not well diversified and likely to be subject to unacceptable risks. If the borrower runs into financial difficulties and is unable to make interest and principal payments, the bank could become insolvent.

If the bank adopts a more diversified strategy of lending 0.01% of its available funds to each of 10,000 different borrowers, it is in a much safer position. Suppose that in an average year the probability of any one borrower defaulting is 1%. We can expect that close to 100 borrowers will default in the year and the losses on these borrowers will be more than offset by the profits earned on the 99% of loans that perform well. To maximize the benefits of diversification, borrowers should be in different geographical regions and different industries. A large international bank with different types of borrowers all over the world is likely to be much better diversified than a small bank in Texas that lends entirely to oil companies. But, however well diversified a bank is, it is still exposed to systematic risk, which creates variations in the probability of default for all borrowers from year to year. The 1% probability of default for borrowers in our example is for an average year. When the economy is doing well, the probability of default is less than this and when there is an economic downturn it is liable to be considerably more than this. Models for capturing this exposure are discussed in later chapters.

Since the late 1990s, we have seen the emergence of an active market for credit derivatives. Credit derivatives allow banks to handle credit risks one by one (risk decomposition) rather than relying solely on risk diversification. They also allow banks to buy protection against the overall level of defaults in the economy. However, for every buyer of credit protection there must be a seller. Many sellers of credit protection, whether on individual names or on portfolios, took huge losses during the credit crisis that started in 2007. The credit crisis is discussed further in Chapter 6.

1.7 CREDIT RATINGS

Credit ratings provide information that is widely used by financial market participants for the management of credit risks. A credit rating is a measure of the credit
quality of a debt instrument such as a bond. However, the rating of a corporate or
sovereign bond is often assumed to be an attribute of the bond issuer rather than of
the bond itself. Thus, if the bonds issued by a company have a rating of AAA, the
company is often referred to as having a rating of AAA.

The three major credit rating agencies are Moody's, S&P, and Fitch. The best
rating assigned by Moody's is Aaa. Bonds with this rating are considered to have
almost no chance of defaulting. The next best rating is Aa. Following that come A,
Baa, Ba, B, Caa, Ca, and C. The S&P ratings corresponding to Moody's Aaa, Aa,
A, Baa, Ba, B, Caa, Ca, and C are AAA, AA, A, BBB, BB, B, CCC, CC, and C,
respectively. To create finer rating measures Moody's divides the Aa rating category
into Aa1, Aa2, and Aa3; it divides A into A1, A2 and A3; and so on. Similarly
S&P divides its AA rating category into AA+, AA, and AA−; it divides its A rating
category into A+, A, and A−; and so on. Moody's Aaa rating category and S&P's
AAA rating are not subdivided, nor usually are the two lowest rating categories.
Fitch's rating categories are similar to those of S&P.

There is usually assumed to be an equivalence between the meanings of the
ratings assigned by the different agencies. For example, a BBB+ rating from S&P is
considered equivalent to a Baa1 rating from Moody's. Instruments with ratings of
BBB− (Baa3) or above are considered to be *investment grade*. Those with ratings
below BBB− (Baa3) are termed *noninvestment grade* or *speculative grade* or *junk
bonds*. In August 2012, S&P created a stir by downgrading the debt of the U.S.
government from AAA to AA+.

We will learn a lot more about credit ratings in later chapters of this book. For
example, Chapter 6 discusses the role of ratings in the credit crisis that started in
2007. Chapters 12 and 13 provide information on how ratings are used in regulation.
Chapter 16 provides statistics on the default rates of companies with different credit
ratings. Chapter 18 examines the extent to which the credit ratings of companies
change through time.

SUMMARY

An important general principle in finance is that there is a trade-off between risk and
return. Higher expected returns can usually be achieved only by taking higher risks.
In theory, shareholders should not be concerned with risks they can diversify away.
The expected return they require should reflect only the amount of systematic (i.e.,
non-diversifiable) risk they are bearing.

Companies, although sensitive to the risk-return trade-offs of their shareholders,
are concerned about total risks when they do risk management. They do not ignore
the unsystematic risk that their shareholders can diversify away. One valid reason
for this is the existence of bankruptcy costs, which are the costs to shareholders
resulting from the bankruptcy process itself.

For financial institutions such as banks and insurance companies there is another
important reason: regulation. The regulators of financial institutions are primarily

concerned with minimizing the probability that the institutions they regulate will fail. The probability of failure depends on the total risks being taken, not just the risks that cannot be diversified away by shareholders. As we will see later in this book, regulators aim to ensure that financial institutions keep enough capital for the total risks they are taking.

Two general approaches to risk management are risk decomposition and risk aggregation. Risk decomposition involves managing risks one by one. Risk aggregation involves relying on the power of diversification to reduce risks. Banks use both approaches to manage market risks. Credit risks have traditionally been managed using risk aggregation, but with the advent of credit derivatives the risk decomposition approach can be used.

FURTHER READING

Markowitz, H. "Portfolio Selection." *Journal of Finance* 7, no. 1 (March 1952): 77–91.

Ross, S. "The Arbitrage Theory of Capital Asset Pricing." *Journal of Economic Theory* 13, no. 3 (December 1976): 341–360.

Sharpe, W. "Capital Asset Prices: A Theory of Market Equilibrium." *Journal of Finance* 19, no. 3 (September 1964): 425–442.

Smith, C. W. and R. M. Stulz. "The Determinants of a Firm's Hedging Policy." *Journal of Financial and Quantitative Analysis* 20 (1985): 391–406.

Stulz, R. M. *Risk Management and Derivatives*. Southwestern, 2003.

PRACTICE QUESTIONS AND PROBLEMS (ANSWERS AT END OF BOOK)

1.1 An investment has probabilities of 0.1, 0.2, 0.35, 0.25, and 0.1 for giving returns equal to 40%, 30%, 15%, −5%, and −15%. What is the expected return and the standard deviation of returns?

1.2 Suppose that there are two investments with the same probability distribution of returns as in Problem 1.1. The correlation between the returns is 0.15. What is the expected return and standard deviation of return from a portfolio where money is divided equally between the investments?

1.3 For the two investments considered in Figure 1.2 and Table 1.2, what are the alternative risk-return combinations if the correlation is (a) 0.3, (b) 1.0, and (c) −1.0?

1.4 What is the difference between systematic and nonsystematic risk? Which is more important to an equity investor? Which can lead to the bankruptcy of a corporation?

1.5 Outline the arguments leading to the conclusion that all investors should choose the same portfolio of risky investments. What are the key assumptions?

1.6 The expected return on the market portfolio is 12% and the risk-free rate is 6%. What is the expected return on an investment with a beta of (a) 0.2, (b) 0.5, (c) 1.4?

1.7 "Arbitrage pricing theory is an extension of the capital asset pricing model." Explain this statement.

1.8 "The capital structure decision of a company is a trade-off between bankruptcy costs and the tax advantages of debt." Explain this statement.

1.9 What is meant by risk aggregation and risk decomposition? Which requires an in-depth understanding of individual risks? Which requires a detailed knowledge of the correlations between risks?

1.10 A bank's operational risk includes the risk of very large losses because of employee fraud, natural disasters, litigation, etc. Do you think operational risk best handled by risk decomposition or risk aggregation? (Operational risk will be discussed in Chapter 20.)

1.11 A bank's profit next year will be normally distributed with a mean of 0.6% of assets and a standard deviation of 1.5% of assets. The bank's equity is 4% of assets. What is the probability that the bank will have a positive equity at the end of the year? Ignore taxes.

1.12 Why do you think that banks are regulated to ensure that they do not take too much risk but most other companies (for example, those in manufacturing and retailing) are not?

1.13 List the bankruptcy costs incurred by the company in Business Snapshot 1.1.

1.14 The return from the market last year was 10% and the risk-free rate was 5%. A hedge fund manager with a beta of 0.6 has an alpha of 4%. What return did the hedge fund manager earn?

FURTHER QUESTIONS

1.15 Suppose that one investment has a mean return of 8% and a standard deviation of return of 14%. Another investment has a mean return of 12% and a standard deviation of return of 20%. The correlation between the returns is 0.3. Produce a chart similar to Figure 1.2 showing alternative risk-return combinations from the two investments.

1.16 The expected return on the market is 12% and the risk-free rate is 7%. The standard deviation of the return on the market is 15%. One investor creates a portfolio on the efficient frontier with an expected return of 10%. Another creates a portfolio on the efficient frontier with an expected return of 20%. What is the standard deviation of the returns of the two portfolios?

1.17 A bank estimates that its profit next year is normally distributed with a mean of 0.8% of assets and the standard deviation of 2% of assets. How much equity (as a percentage of assets) does the company need to be (a) 99% sure that it will have a positive equity at the end of the year and (b) 99.9% sure that it will have positive equity at the end of the year? Ignore taxes.

1.18 A portfolio manager has maintained an actively managed portfolio with a beta of 0.2. During the last year, the risk-free rate was 5% and major equity indices performed very badly, providing returns of about −30%. The portfolio manager produced a return of −10% and claims that in the circumstances it was good. Discuss this claim.

CHAPTER 2

Banks

The word "bank" originates from the Italian word "banco." This is a desk or bench, covered by a green tablecloth, that was used several hundred years ago by Florentine bankers. The traditional role of banks has been to take deposits and make loans. The interest charged on the loans is greater than the interest paid on deposits. The difference between the two has to cover administrative costs and loan losses (i.e., losses when borrowers fail to make the agreed payments of interest and principal), while providing a satisfactory return on equity.

Today, most large banks engage in both commercial and investment banking. Commercial banking involves, among other things, the deposit-taking and lending activities we have just mentioned. Investment banking is concerned with assisting companies in raising debt and equity, and providing advice on mergers and acquisitions, major corporate restructurings, and other corporate finance decisions. Large banks are also often involved in securities trading (e.g., by providing brokerage services).

Commercial banking can be classified as *retail banking* or *wholesale banking*. Retail banking, as its name implies, involves taking relatively small deposits from private individuals or small businesses and making relatively small loans to them. Wholesale banking involves the provision of banking services to medium and large corporate clients, fund managers, and other financial institutions. Both loans and deposits are much larger in wholesale banking than in retail banking. Sometimes banks fund their wholesale or retail lending by borrowing in financial markets themselves.

Typically the spread between the cost of funds and the lending rate is smaller for wholesale banking than for retail banking. However, this tends to be offset by lower costs. (When a certain dollar amount of wholesale lending is compared to the same dollar amount of retail lending, the expected loan losses and administrative costs are usually much less.) Banks that are heavily reliant on wholesale banking and fund their lending by borrowing in financial markets are often referred to as *money center banks*.

This chapter will review how commercial and investment banking have evolved over the last hundred years. It will examine the way the banks are regulated, consider the nature of the risks facing the banks, and look at the key role of capital in providing a cushion against losses.

2.1 COMMERCIAL BANKING

Commercial banking in virtually all countries has been subject to a great deal of regulation. This is because most national governments consider it important that individuals and companies have confidence in the banking system. Among the issues addressed by regulation is the capital that banks must keep, the activities they are allowed to engage in, deposit insurance, and the extent to which mergers and foreign ownership are allowed. The nature of bank regulation during the twentieth century has influenced the structure of commercial banking in different countries. To illustrate this, we consider the case of the United States.

The United States is unusual in that it has a large number of banks (6,530 in 2010). This leads to a relatively complicated payments system compared with those of other countries with fewer banks. There are a few large money center banks such as Citigroup and JPMorgan Chase. There are several hundred regional banks that engage in a mixture of wholesale and retail banking, and several thousand community banks that specialize in retail banking.

Table 2.1 summarizes the size distribution of banks in the United States in 1984 and 2010. The number of banks declined by over 50% between the two dates. In 2010, there were less small community banks and more large banks than in 1984. Although there were only 86 banks (1.3% of the total) with assets of $10 billion or more in 2010, they accounted for over 80% of the assets in the U.S. banking system.

The structure of banking in the United States is largely a result of regulatory restrictions on interstate banking. At the beginning of the twentieth century, most

TABLE 2.1   Bank Concentration in the United States in 1984 and 2010

| | | 1984 | | |
Size (Assets)	Number	Percent of Total	Assets ($ billions)	Percent of Total
Under $100 million	12,044	83.2	404.2	16.1
$100 million to $1 billion	2,161	14.9	513.9	20.5
$1 billion to $10 billion	254	1.7	725.9	28.9
Over $10 billion	24	0.2	864.8	34.5
Total	14,483		2,508.9	

| | | 2010 | | |
Size (Assets)	Number	Percent of Total	Assets ($ billions)	Percent of Total
Under $100 million	2,328	35.7	132.2	1.1
$100 million to $1 billion	3,693	56.6	1,059.0	8.8
$1 billion to $10 billion	423	6.5	1,089.0	9.0
Over $10 billion	86	1.3	9,786.2	81.1
Total	6,530		12,066.4	

Source: FDIC Quarterly Banking Profile, www.fdic.gov.

U.S. banks had a single branch from which they served customers. During the early part of the twentieth century, many of these banks expanded by opening more branches in order to serve their customers better. This ran into opposition from two quarters. First, small banks that still had only a single branch were concerned that they would lose market share. Second, large money center banks were concerned that the multibranch banks would be able to offer check-clearing and other payment services and erode the profits that they themselves made from offering these services. As a result, there was pressure to control the extent to which community banks could expand. Several states passed laws restricting the ability of banks to open more than one branch within a state.

The McFadden Act was passed in 1927 and amended in 1933. This act had the effect of restricting all banks from opening branches in more than one state. This restriction applied to nationally chartered as well as to state-chartered banks. One way of getting round the McFadden Act was to establish a *multibank holding company*. This is a company that acquires more than one bank as a subsidiary. By 1956, there were 47 multibank holding companies. This led to the Douglas Amendment to the Bank Holding Company Act. This did not allow a multibank holding company to acquire a bank in a state that prohibited out-of-state acquisitions. However, acquisitions prior to 1956 were grandfathered (that is, multibank holding companies did not have to dispose of acquisitions made prior to 1956).

Banks are creative in finding ways around regulations—particularly when it is profitable for them to do so. After 1956, one approach was to form a one-bank holding company. This is a holding company with just one bank as a subsidiary and a number of nonbank subsidiaries in different states from the bank. The nonbank subsidiaries offered financial services such as consumer finance, data processing, and leasing and were able to create a presence for the bank in other states.

The 1970 Bank Holding Companies Act restricted the activities of one-bank holding companies. They were only allowed to engage in activities that were closely related to banking, and acquisitions by them were subject to approval by the Federal Reserve. They had to divest themselves of acquisitions that did not conform to the act by 1980.

After 1970, the interstate banking restrictions started to disappear. Individual states passed laws allowing banks from other states to enter and acquire local banks. (Maine was the first to do so in 1978.) Some states allowed free entry of other banks. Some allowed banks from other states to enter only if there were reciprocal agreements. (This means that state A allowed banks from state B to enter only if state B allowed banks from state A to do so.) In some cases, groups of states developed regional banking pacts that allowed interstate banking.

In 1994, the U.S. Congress passed the Riegel-Neal Interstate Banking and Branching Efficiency Act. This Act led to full interstate banking becoming a reality. It permitted bank holding companies to acquire branches in other states. It invalidated state laws that allowed interstate banking on a reciprocal or regional basis. Starting in 1997, bank holding companies were allowed to convert out-of-state subsidiary banks into branches of a single bank. Many people argue that this type of consolidation is necessary to enable U.S. banks to be large enough to compete internationally. The Riegel-Neal Act prepared the way for a wave of consolidation in the U.S. banking system (for example, the acquisition by JPMorgan of banks formerly named Chemical, Chase, Bear Stearns, and Washington Mutual).

2.2 THE CAPITAL REQUIREMENTS OF A SMALL COMMERCIAL BANK

To illustrate the role of capital in banking, we consider a hypothetical small community bank named Deposits and Loans Corporation (DLC). DLC is primarily engaged
in the traditional banking activities of taking deposits and making loans. A summary
balance sheet for DLC at the end of 2012 is shown in Table 2.2 and a summary
income statement for 2012 is shown in Table 2.3.

Table 2.2 shows that the bank has $100 million of assets. Most of the assets
(80% of the total) are loans made by the bank to private individuals and small
corporations. Cash and marketable securities account for a further 15% of the
assets. The remaining 5% of the assets are fixed assets (i.e., buildings, equipment,
etc.). A total of 90% of the funding for the assets comes from deposits of one sort
or another from the bank's customers. A further 5% is financed by subordinated
long-term debt. (These are bonds issued by the bank to investors that rank below
deposits in the event of a liquidation.) The remaining 5% is financed by the bank's
shareholders in the form of equity capital. The equity capital consists of the original
cash investment of the shareholders and earnings retained in the bank.

Consider next the income statement for 2012 shown in Table 2.3. The first item
on the income statement is net interest income. This is the excess of the interest
earned over the interest paid and is 3% of the total assets in our example. It is
important for the bank to be managed so that net interest income remains roughly
constant regardless of movements in interest rates. We will discuss this in more detail
in Chapter 8.

The next item is loan losses. This is 0.8% for the year in question. Clearly it is
very important for management to quantify credit risks and manage them carefully.
But however carefully a bank assesses the financial health of its clients before making
a loan, it is inevitable that some borrowers will default. This is what leads to loan
losses. The percentage of loans that default will tend to fluctuate from year to year
with economic conditions. It is likely that in some years default rates will be quite
low, while in others they will be quite high.

The next item, non-interest income, consists of income from all the activities of a
bank other than lending money. This includes fees for the services the bank provides
for its clients. In the case of DLC non-interest income is 0.9% of assets.

The final item is non-interest expense and is 2.5% of assets in our example.
This consists of all expenses other than interest paid. It includes salaries, technology-
related costs, and other overheads. As in the case of all large businesses, these have
a tendency to increase over time unless they are managed carefully. Banks must try

TABLE 2.2 Summary Balance Sheet for DLC at End of 2012 ($ millions)

Assets		Liabilities and Net Worth	
Cash	5	Deposits	90
Marketable Securities	10	Subordinated Long-Term Debt	5
Loans	80	Equity Capital	5
Fixed Assets	5		
Total	100	Total	100

TABLE 2.3   Summary Income Statement for DLC in 2012 ($ millions)

Net Interest Income	3.00
Loan Losses	(0.80)
Non-Interest Income	0.90
Non-Interest Expense	(2.50)
Pre-Tax Operating Income	0.60

to avoid large losses from litigation, business disruption, employee fraud, and so on. The risk associated with these types of losses is known as *operational risk* and will be discussed in Chapter 20.

Capital Adequacy

One measure of the performance of a bank is return on equity (ROE). Tables 2.2 and 2.3 show that the DLC's before-tax ROE is 0.6/5 or 12%. If this is considered unsatisfactory, one way DLC might consider improving its ROE is by buying back its shares and replacing them with deposits so that equity financing is lower and ROE is higher. For example, if it moved to the balance sheet in Table 2.4 where equity is reduced to 1% of assets and deposits are increased to 94% of assets, its before-tax ROE would jump up to 60%.

How much equity capital does DLC need? One approach to answering this question is to hypothesize an extreme scenario and consider whether the bank will survive. Suppose that there is a severe recession and as a result the bank's loan losses rise by 3.2% of assets to 4% next year. (We assume that other items on the income statement in Table 2.3 are unaffected.) The result will be a pre-tax net operating loss of 2.6% of assets (0.6 − 3.2 = −2.6). Assuming a tax rate of 30%, this would result in an after-tax loss of about 1.8% of assets.

In Table 2.2, equity capital is 5% of assets and so an after-tax loss equal to 1.8% of assets, although not at all welcome, can be absorbed. It would result in a reduction of the equity capital to 3.2% of assets. Even a second bad year similar to the first would not totally wipe out the equity.

If DLC has moved to the more aggressive capital structure shown in Table 2.4, it is far less likely to survive. One year where the loan losses are 4% of assets would totally wipe out equity capital and the bank would find itself in serious financial difficulties. It would no doubt try to raise additional equity capital, but it is likely to find this difficult when in such a weak financial position. It is possible that there

TABLE 2.4   Alternative Balance Sheet for DLC at End of 2012 with Equity only 1% of Assets ($ Millions)

Assets		Liabilities and Net Worth	
Cash	5	Deposits	94
Marketable Securities	10	Subordinated Long-Term Debt	5
Loans	80	Equity Capital	1
Fixed Assets	5		
Total	100	Total	100

would be a run on the bank (where all depositors decide to withdraw funds at the same time) and the bank would be forced into liquidation. If all assets could be liquidated for book value (a big assumption), the long-term debt-holders would likely receive about $4.2 million rather than $5 million (they would in effect absorb the negative equity) and the depositors would be repaid in full.

Clearly, it is inadequate for a bank to have only 1% of assets funded by equity capital. Maintaining equity capital equal to 5% of assets is more reasonable. Note that equity and subordinated long-term debt are both sources of capital. Equity provides the best protection against adverse events. (In our example, when the bank has $5 million of equity capital rather than $1 million it stays solvent and is unlikely to be liquidated.) Subordinated long-term debt-holders rank below depositors in the event of default, but subordinated debt does not provide as good a cushion for the bank as equity because it does not prevent the bank's insolvency.

As we shall see in Chapters 12 and 13, bank regulators have tried to ensure that the capital a bank keeps is sufficient to cover the risks it takes. The risks include market risks, credit risks, and operational risks. Equity capital is categorized as "Tier 1 capital" while subordinated long-term debt is categorized as "Tier 2 capital."

2.3 DEPOSIT INSURANCE

To maintain confidence in banks, government regulators in many countries have introduced guaranty programs. These typically insure depositors against losses up to a certain level.

The United States with its large number of small banks is particularly prone to bank failures. After the stock market crash of 1929 the United States experienced a major recession and about 10,000 banks failed between 1930 and 1933. Runs on banks and panics were common. In 1933, the United States government created the Federal Deposit Insurance Corporation (FDIC) to provide protection for depositors. Originally, the maximum level of protection provided was $2,500. This has been increased several times and became $250,000 per depositor per bank in October 2008. Banks pay a premium that is a percentage of their domestic deposits. In 2007, a system was introduced where the premium depends on the risk of the bank (as measured by its capital ratios).

Up to 1980, the system worked well. There were no runs on banks and few bank failures. However, between 1980 and 1990, bank failures in the United States accelerated with the total number of failures during this decade being over 1,000 (larger than for the whole 1933 to 1979 period). There were several reasons for this. One was the way in which banks managed interest rate risk and we will talk about that in Chapter 8. Another reason was the reduction in oil and other commodity prices which led to many loans to oil, gas, and agricultural companies not being repaid.

A further reason for the bank failures was that the existence of deposit insurance allowed banks to follow risky strategies that would not otherwise be feasible. For example, they could increase their deposit base by offering high rates of interest to depositors and use the funds to make risky loans. Without deposit insurance, a bank could not follow this strategy because their depositors would see what they were doing, decide that the bank was too risky, and withdraw their funds. With deposit insurance, it can follow the strategy because depositors know that, if the worst happens, they are protected under FDIC. This is an example of what is known as *moral hazard*. We will talk about moral hazard further in Chapter 3. It can be defined as the possibility that the existence of insurance changes the behavior of the insured party. The introduction of risk-based premiums referred to earlier reduces moral hazard to some extent.

During the 1980s, the funds of FDIC became seriously depleted and it had to borrow $30 billion from the U.S. Treasury. In December 1991, Congress passed the FDIC Improvement Act to prevent any possibility of the fund becoming insolvent in the future. Between 1991 and 2006, bank failures in the United States were relatively rare and by 2006 the fund had reserves of about $50 billion. In 2008, the failure of banks such as IndyMac again depleted FDIC funds.

2.4 INVESTMENT BANKING

The main activity of investment banking is raising debt and equity financing for corporations or governments. This involves originating the securities, underwriting them, and then placing them with investors. In a typical arrangement a corporation approaches an investment bank indicating that it wants to raise a certain amount of finance in the form of debt, equity, or hybrid instruments such as convertible bonds. The securities are originated complete with legal documentation outlining the rights of the security holder. A prospectus is created outlining the company's past performance and future prospects. The risks faced by the company from such things as major lawsuits are itemized. There is a "road show" in which the investment bank and senior management from the company attempt to market the securities to large fund managers. A price for the securities is agreed between the bank and the corporation. The bank then sells the securities in the market.

There are a number of different types of arrangement between the investment bank and the corporation. Sometimes the financing takes the form of a *private placement* in which the securities are sold to a small number of large institutional investors such as life insurance companies or pension funds and the investment bank receives a fee. On other occasions it takes the form of a *public offering*, where securities are offered to the general public. A public offering may be on a *best efforts* or *firm commitment* basis. In the case of a best efforts public offering, the investment bank does as well as it can to place the securities with investors and is paid a fee that depends to some extent on its success. In the case of a firm commitment public offering, the investment bank agrees to buy the securities from the issuer at a particular price and then attempts to sell them in the market for a slightly higher price. It makes a profit equal to the difference between the price at which it sells the securities and the price it pays the issuer. If for any reason it is unable to sell the securities, it ends up owning them itself. The difference between the two types of deal is illustrated in Example 2.1.

EXAMPLE 2.1

A bank has agreed to underwrite an issue of 50 million shares by ABC Corporation. In negotiations between the bank and the corporation the target net price to be received by the corporation has been set at $30 per share. This means that the corporation is expecting to raise 30×50 million dollars or $1.5 billion in total. The bank can either offer the client a best efforts arrangement where it charges a fee of $0.30 per share sold so that, assuming all shares are sold, it obtains a total fee of $0.3 \times 50 = 15$ million dollars. Alternatively, it can offer a firm commitment where it agrees to buy the shares from ABC Corporation for $30 per share.

The bank is confident that it will be able to sell the shares, but is uncertain about the price. As part of its procedures for assessing risk, it considers two alternative scenarios. Under the first scenario, it can obtain a price of $32 per share; under the second scenario, it is able to obtain only $29 per share.

In a best-efforts deal, the bank obtains a fee of $15 million in both cases. In a firm commitment deal, its profit depends on the price it is able to obtain. If it sells the shares for $32, it makes a profit of $(32 - 30) \times 50 = \$100$ million because it has agreed to pay ABC Corporation $30 per share. However, if it can only sell the shares for $29 per share, it loses $(30 - 29) \times 50 = \$50$ million because it still has to pay ABC Corporation $30 per share. The situation is summarized in the table following. The decision taken is likely to depend on the probabilities assigned by the bank to different outcomes and what is referred to as its "risk appetite."

	Profits If Best Efforts	Profits If Firm Commitment
Can sell at $29	+$15 million	−$50 million
Can sell at $32	+$15 million	+$100 million

When equity financing is being raised and the company is already publicly traded, the investment bank can look at the prices at which the company's shares are trading a few days before the issue is to be sold as a guide to the issue price. Typically it will agree to attempt to issue new shares at a target price slightly below the current price. The main risk is then that the price of the company's shares will show a substantial decline before the new shares are sold.

IPOs

When the company wishing to issue shares is not publicly traded, the share issue is known as an *initial public offering* (IPO). These types of offering are typically made on a best efforts basis. The correct offering price is difficult to determine and depends on the investment bank's assessment of the company's value. The bank's best estimate of the market price is its estimate of the company's value divided by the number of shares currently outstanding. However, the bank will typically set the offering price below its best estimate of the market price. This is because it does not want to take the chance that the issue will not sell. (It typically earns the same fee per share sold regardless of the offering price.)

Often there is a substantial increase in the share price immediately after shares are sold in an IPO (sometimes as much as 40%), indicating that the company could have raised more money if the issue price had been higher. As a result, IPOs are considered attractive buys by many investors. Banks frequently offer IPOs to the fund managers that are their best customers and to senior executives of large companies in the hope that they will provide them with business. (The latter is known as "spinning" and is frowned upon by regulators.)

Dutch Auction Approach

A few companies have used a Dutch auction approach for their IPOs. As for a regular IPO, a prospectus is issued and usually there is a road show. Individuals and companies bid by indicating the number of shares they want and the price they are prepared to pay. Shares are first issued to the highest bidder, then to the next highest bidder, and so on, until all the shares have been sold. The price paid by all successful bidders is the lowest bid that leads to a share allocation. This is illustrated in Example 2.2.

EXAMPLE 2.2

A company wants to sell one million shares in an IPO. It decides to use the Dutch auction approach. The bidders are shown in the table following. In this case, shares are allocated first to C, then to F, then to E, then to H, then to A. At this point, 800,000 shares have been allocated. The next highest bidder is D who has bid for 300,000 shares. Because only 200,000 remain unallocated, D's order is only two-thirds filled. The price paid by all the investors to whom shares are allocated (A, C, D, E, F, and H) is the price bid by D, or $29.00.

Bidder	Number of Shares	Price
A	100,000	$30.00
B	200,000	$28.00
C	50,000	$33.00
D	300,000	$29.00
E	150,000	$30.50
F	300,000	$31.50
G	400,000	$25.00
H	200,000	$30.25

Dutch auctions potentially overcome two of the problems with a traditional IPO that we have mentioned. First, the price that clears the market ($29.00 in Example 2.2) should be the market price if all potential investors have participated in the bidding process. Second, the situations where investment banks offer IPOs only to their favored clients are avoided. However, the company does not take advantage of the relationships that investment bankers have developed with large investors that usually enable the investment bankers to sell an IPO very quickly. One high profile IPO that used a Dutch auction was the Google IPO in 2004. This is discussed in Business Snapshot 2.1.

Advisory Services

In addition to assisting companies with new issues of securities, investment banks offer advice to companies on mergers and acquisitions, divestments, major corporate restructurings, and so on. They will assist in finding merger partners and takeover targets or help companies find buyers for divisions or subsidiaries of which they want

BUSINESS SNAPSHOT 2.1

Google's IPO

Google, developer of the the well-known Internet search engine, decided to go public in 2004. It chose to use the Dutch auction approach. It was assisted by two investment banks, Morgan Stanley and Credit Suisse First Boston. The SEC gave approval for it to raise funds up to a maximum of $2,718,281,828. (Why the odd number? The mathematical constant e is 2.7182818...) The IPO method was not a pure Dutch auction because Google reserved the right to change the number of shares that would be issued and the percentage allocated to each bidder when it saw the bids.

Some investors expected the price of the shares to be as high as $120. But when Google saw the bids, it decided that the number of shares offered would be 19,605,052 at a price of $85. This meant that the total value of the offering was $19,605,052 \times 85$ or $1.67 billion. Investors who had bid $85 or above obtained 74.2% of the shares they had bid for. The date of the IPO was August 19, 2004. Most companies would have given investors who bid $85 or more 100% of the amount they bid for and raised $2.25 billion, instead of $1.67 billion. Perhaps Google (stock symbol: GOOG) correctly anticipated it would have no difficulty in selling further shares at a higher price later.

The initial market capitalization was $23.1 billion with over 90% of the shares being held by employees. These employees included the founders, Sergei Brin and Larry Page, and the CEO, Eric Schmidt. On the first day of trading, the shares closed at $100.34, 18% above the offer price and there was a further 7% increase on the second day. Google's issue therefore proved to be underpriced—but not as underpriced as some other IPOs of technology stocks where traditional IPO methods were used.

The cost of Google's IPO (fees paid to investment banks, etc.) was 2.8% of the amount raised. This compares with an average of about 4% for a regular IPO.

There were some mistakes made and Google was lucky that these did not prevent the IPO from going ahead as planned. Sergei Brin and Larry Page gave an interview to *Playboy* magazine in April 2004. The interview appeared in the September issue. This violated SEC requirements that there be a "quiet period" with no promoting of the company's stock in the period leading up to an IPO. To avoid SEC sanctions, Google had to include the *Playboy* interview (together with some factual corrections) in its SEC filings. Google also forgot to register 23.2 million shares and 5.6 million stock options.

Google's stock price rose rapidly in the period after the IPO. Approximately one year later (in September 2005) it was able to raise a further $4.18 billion by issuing an additional 14,159,265 shares at $295. (Why the odd number? The mathematical constant π is 3.14159265...)

BUSINESS SNAPSHOT 2.2

PeopleSoft's Poison Pill

In 2003, the management of PeopleSoft, Inc., a company that provided human resource management systems, was concerned about a takeover by Oracle, a company specializing in database management systems. It took the unusual step of guaranteeing to its customers that, if it were acquired within two years and product support was reduced within four years, its customers would receive a refund of between two and five times the fees paid for their software licenses. The hypothetical cost to Oracle was estimated at $1.5 billion. The guarantee was opposed by PeopleSoft's shareholders. (It was clearly not in their interests!) PeopleSoft discontinued the guarantee in April 2004.

Oracle did succeed in acquiring PeopleSoft in December 2004. Although some jobs at PeopleSoft were eliminated, Oracle maintained at least 90% of PeopleSoft's product development and support staff.

---

to divest themselves. They will also advise the management of companies which are themselves merger or takeover targets. Sometimes they suggest steps they should take to avoid a merger or takeover. These are known as *poison pills*. Examples of poison pills are:

1. A potential target adds to its charter a provision where, if another company acquires one third of the shares, other shareholders have the right to sell their shares to that company for twice the recent average share price.
2. A potential target grants to its key employees stock options that vest (i.e., can be exercised) in the event of a takeover. This is liable to create an exodus of key employees immediately after a takeover, leaving an empty shell for the new owner.
3. A potential target adds to its charter provisions making it impossible for a new owner to get rid of existing directors for one or two years after an acquisition.
4. A potential target issues preferred shares that automatically get converted to regular shares when there is a change in control.
5. A potential target adds a provision where existing shareholders have the right to purchase shares at a discounted price during or after a takeover.
6. A potential target changes the voting structure so that shares owned by management have more votes than those owned by others.

Poison pills, which are illegal in many countries outside the United States, have to be approved by a majority of shareholders. Often shareholders oppose poison pills because they see them as benefiting only management. An unusual poison pill, tried by PeopleSoft to fight a takeover by Oracle, is explained in Business Snapshot 2.2.

Valuation, strategy, and tactics are key aspects of the advisory services offered by an investment bank. For example, in advising Company A on a potential takeover of Company B, it is necessary for the investment bank to value Company B and help Company A assess possible synergies between the operations of the two companies. It must also consider whether it is better to offer Company B's shareholders cash or a share-for-share exchange (i.e., a certain number of shares in Company A in exchange for each share of Company B). What should the initial offer be? What does it expect the final offer that will close the deal to be? It must assess the best way to approach the senior managers of Company B and consider what the motivations of the managers will be. Will the takeover be a hostile one (opposed by the management of Company B) or friendly one (supported by the management of Company B)? In some instances there will be antitrust issues and approval from some branch of government may be required.

2.5 SECURITIES TRADING

Banks often get involved in securities trading, providing brokerage services, and making a market in individual securities. In doing so, they compete with smaller securities firms that do not offer other banking services.

A broker assists in the trading of securities by taking orders from clients and arranging for them to be carried out on an exchange. Some brokers operate nationally and some serve only a particular region. Some, known as full-service brokers, offer investment research and advice. Others, known as discount brokers, charge lower commissions, but provide no advice. Some offer online services and some such as E*TRADE provide a platform for customers to trade without a broker.

A market maker facilitates trading by always being prepared to quote a bid (price at which it is prepared to buy) and offer (price at which it is prepared to sell). When providing a quote, it does not know whether the person requesting the quote wants to buy or sell. The market maker makes a profit from the spread between the bid and the offer, but takes the risk that it will be left with an unacceptably high exposure.

Many exchanges on which stocks, options, and futures trade use market makers. Typically an exchange will specify a maximum level for the size of a market maker's bid-offer spread (the difference between the offer and the bid). Banks are often market makers for instruments such as forward contracts, swaps, and options trading in the over-the-counter (OTC) market. (See Chapter 5 for a discussion of these instruments and the over-the-counter market.)

Trading is closely related to market making. Most large investment and commercial banks have extensive trading activities. The counterparties in their trading activities are typically other banks, corporations, and fund managers. Banks trade for three main reasons:

1. To meet the needs of its counterparties. For example, a bank may sell a foreign currency option to a corporate client to help it reduce its foreign exchange risk or buy a credit derivative from a hedge fund to help it implement a trading strategy.
2. To reduce its own risks. This will be discussed further in Chapter 7.
3. To take a speculative position in the hope of making a profit. This is referred to as trading for its own account or proprietary ("prop") trading.

2.6 POTENTIAL CONFLICTS OF INTEREST IN BANKING

There are many potential conflicts of interest between commercial banking, securities services, and investment banking when they are all conducted under the same corporate umbrella. For example:

1. When asked for advice by an investor, a bank might be tempted to recommend securities that the investment banking part of its organization is trying to sell. When it has a fiduciary account (i.e., a customer account where the bank can choose trades for the customer), the bank can "stuff" difficult-to-sell securities into the account.
2. A bank, when it lends money to a company, often obtains confidential information about the company. It might be tempted to pass that information to the mergers and acquisitions arm of the investment bank to help it provide advice to one of its clients on potential takeover opportunities.
3. The research end of the securities business might be tempted to recommend a company's share as a "buy" in order to please the company's management and obtain investment banking business.
4. Suppose a commercial bank no longer wants a loan it has made to a company on its books because the confidential information it has obtained from the company leads it to believe that there is an increased chance of bankruptcy. It might be tempted to ask the investment bank to arrange a bond issue for the company, with the proceeds being used to pay off the loan. This would have the effect of replacing its loan with a loan made by investors who were less well-informed.

As a result of these types of conflict of interest, some countries have in the past attempted to separate commercial banking from investment banking. The Glass-Steagall Act of 1933 in the United States limited the ability of commercial banks and investment banks to engage in each other's activities. Commercial banks were allowed to continue underwriting Treasury instruments and some municipal bonds. They were also allowed to do private placements. But they were not allowed to engage in other activities such as public offerings. Similarly, investment banks were not allowed to take deposits and make commercial loans.

In 1987, the Federal Reserve Board relaxed the rules somewhat and allowed banks to establish holding companies with two subsidiaries, one in investment banking and the other in commercial banking. The revenue of the investment banking subsidiary was restricted to being a certain percentage of the group's total revenue.

In 1997, the rules were relaxed further so that commercial banks could acquire existing investment banks. Finally, in 1999, the Financial Services Modernization Act was passed. This effectively eliminated all restrictions on the operations of banks, insurance companies, and securities firms. In 2007, there were five large investment banks in the United States that had little or no commercial banking interests. These were Goldman Sachs, Morgan Stanley, Merrill Lynch, Bear Stearns, and Lehman Brothers. In 2008, the credit crisis led to Lehman Brothers going bankrupt, Bear Stearns being taken over by JPMorgan Chase, and Merrill Lynch being taken over by Bank of America. Goldman Sachs and Morgan Stanley became bank holding companies with both commercial and investment banking interests. (As a result, they had to maintain lower leverage ratios and subject themselves to more regulatory scrutiny.) The year 2008 therefore marked the end of an era for investment banking in the United States.

2.7 TODAY'S LARGE BANKS

Today's large banks operate globally and transact business in many different areas. They are still engaged in the traditional commercial banking activities of taking deposits, making loans, and clearing checks (both nationally and internationally). They offer retail customers credit cards, telephone banking, Internet banking, and automatic teller machines (ATMs). They provide payroll services to businesses and, as already mentioned, they have huge trading activities.

Banks offer lines of credit to businesses and individual customers. They provide a range of services to companies when they are exporting goods and services. Companies can enter into a variety of contracts with banks that are designed to hedge risks they face relating to foreign exchange, commodity prices, interest rates, and other market variables. These contracts will be discussed in later chapters. Even risks related to the weather can be hedged.

Banks undertake securities research and offer "buy," "sell," and "hold" recommendations on individual stocks. They offer brokerage services (discount and full service). They offer trust services where they are prepared to manage portfolios of assets for clients. They have economics departments that consider macroeconomic trends and actions likely to be taken by central banks. These departments produce forecasts on interest rates, exchange rates, commodity prices, and other variables. Banks offer a range of mutual funds and in some cases have their own hedge funds. Increasingly banks are offering insurance products.

The investment banking arm of a bank has complete freedom to underwrite securities for governments and corporations. It can provide advice to corporations on mergers and acquisitions and other topics relating to corporate finance.

How are the conflicts of interest outlined in Section 2.6 handled? There are internal barriers known as known as *Chinese walls*. These internal barriers prohibit the transfer of information from one part of the bank to another when this is not in the best interests of one or more of the bank's customers. There have been some well-publicized violations of conflict-of-interest rules by large banks. These have led to hefty fines and lawsuits. Top management has a big incentive to enforce Chinese walls. This is not only because of the fines and lawsuits. A bank's reputation is its most valuable asset. The adverse publicity associated with conflict-of-interest violations can lead to a loss of confidence in the bank and business being lost in many different areas.

Accounting

It is appropriate at this point to provide a brief discussion of how a bank calculates a profit or loss from its many diverse activities. Activities that generate fees, such as most investment banking activities, are straightforward. Accrual accounting rules similar to those that would be used by any other business apply.

For other banking activities, there is an important distinction between the "banking book" and the "trading book." As its name implies, the trading book includes all the contracts the bank enters into as part of its trading operations. The value of the assets and liabilities in the trading book are *marked to market* daily. This means that the value of the book is adjusted on an almost continual basis to reflect changes in market prices. If a bank trader buys an asset for $100 on one day and the price falls to $60 the next day, the bank records an immediate loss of $40—even if it has no intention of selling the asset in the immediate future. Sometimes it is not easy to estimate the value of a contract that has been entered into because there are no market prices for similar transactions. For example, there might be a lack of liquidity in the market or it might be the case that the transaction is a complex nonstandard derivative that does not trade sufficiently frequently for benchmark market prices to be available. Banks are nevertheless expected to come up with a market price in these circumstances. Often a model has to be assumed. The process of coming up with a "market price" is then sometimes termed *marking to model* because the banks must assume a model in determining the price. (Chapter 22 discusses model risk and accounting issues further.)

The banking book includes loans made to corporations and individuals. These are not marked to market. If a borrower is up-to-date on principal and interest payments on a loan, the loan is recorded in the bank's books at the principal amount owed plus accrued interest. If payments due from the borrower are more than 90 days past due, the loan is usually classified as a *nonperforming loan*. The bank does not then accrue interest on the loan when calculating its profit. When problems with the loan become more serious and it becomes likely that principal will not be repaid, the loan is classified as a loan loss.

A bank creates a reserve for loan losses. This is a charge against the income statement for an estimate of the loan losses that will be incurred. Periodically the reserve is increased or decreased. A bank can smooth out its income from one year to the next by overestimating reserves in good years and underestimating them in bad years. Actual loan losses are charged against reserves. Occasionally, as described in Business Snapshot 2.3, a bank resorts to artificial ways of avoiding the recognition of loan losses.

The Originate-to-Distribute Model

DLC, the small hypothetical bank we looked at in Tables 2.2 to 2.4, took deposits and used them to finance loans. In recent years, banks have increasingly assumed the role of originators of loans rather than keepers of loans. Typically pools of loans are packaged and tranches are sold to investors. This process is described in more detail in Chapter 6 and is referred to as the *originate-to-distribute model* for the operations of a bank.

The originate-to-distribute model has been used in the U.S. mortgage market for some time. In order to increase the liquidity of the U.S. mortgage market and facilitate the growth of home ownership, three government sponsored entities were created: the Government National Mortgage Association (GNMA) or "Ginnie Mae," the Federal National Mortgage Association (FNMA) or "Fannie Mae," and the Federal Home Loan Mortgage Corporation (FHLMC) or "Freddie Mac." These agencies buy pools of mortgages from banks and other mortgage originators, guarantee the timely

BUSINESS SNAPSHOT 2.3

How to Keep Loans Performing

When a borrower is experiencing financial difficulties and is unable to make interest and principal payments as they become due, it is sometimes tempting to lend more money to the borrower so that the payments on the old loans can be kept up to date. This is an accounting game, sometimes referred to as *debt rescheduling*. It allows interest on the loans to be accrued and avoids (or at least defers) the recognition of loan losses.

In the 1970s, banks in the United States and other countries lent huge amounts of money to Eastern European, Latin American, and other less developed countries (LDCs). Some of the loans were made to help countries develop their infrastructure, but others were less justifiable (e.g., one was to finance the coronation of a ruler in Africa). Sometimes the money found its way into the pockets of dictators. For example, the Marcos family in the Philippines allegedly transferred billions of dollars into its own bank accounts.

In the early 1980s, many LDCs were unable to service their loans. One option for them was *debt repudiation*, but a more attractive alternative was debt rescheduling. In effect, this leads to the interest on the loans being capitalized and bank funding requirements for the loans to increase. Well-informed LDCs were aware of the desire of banks to keep their LDC loans performing so that profits looked strong. They were therefore in a strong negotiating position as their loans became 90 days overdue and banks were close to having to produce their quarterly financial statements.

In 1987, Citicorp (now Citigroup) took the lead in refusing to reschedule LDC debt and increased its loan loss reserves by $3 billion in recognition of expected losses on the debt. Other banks with large LDC exposures followed suit.

repayment of interest and principal, and then package the cash flow streams and sell them to investors. The investors typically take what is known as prepayment risk. This is the risk that interest rates will decrease and mortgages will be paid off earlier than expected. However, they do not take any credit risk because the mortgages are guaranteed by GNMA, FNMA, or FHLMC. In 1999, FNMA and FHLMC started to guarantee subprime loans and as a result ran into serious financial difficulties.[1]

The originate-to-distribute model has—at least until the credit crisis that started in 2007—been used for many types of bank lending including student loans, commercial loans, commercial mortgages, residential mortgages, and credit card

---

[1] GNMA has always been government owned whereas FNMA and FHLMC used to be private corporations with shareholders. As a result of their financial difficulties in 2008, the U.S. government had to step in and assume complete control of FNMA and FHLMC.

receivables. Except in the case of the mortgages guaranteed by the agencies mentioned above, it is usually the investors that bear the credit risk when the loans are packaged and sold.

The originate-to-distribute model is also termed *securitization* because securities are created from cash flow streams originated by the bank. It is an attractive model for banks. By securitizing its loans it gets them off the balance sheet and frees up funds to enable it to make more loans. It also frees up capital that can be used to cover risks being taken elsewhere in the bank. (This is particularly attractive if the bank feels that the capital required by regulators for a loan is too high.) A bank earns a fee for originating a loan and a further fee if it services the loan after it has been sold.

As we will explain in Chapter 6, the originate-to-distribute model got out of control during the 2000 to 2006 period. Banks relaxed their mortgage lending standards and the credit quality of the instruments being originated declined sharply. This led to a severe credit crisis and a period during which the originate-to-distribute model could not be used by banks because investors had lost confidence in the securities that had been created.

2.8 THE RISKS FACING BANKS

A bank's operations give rise to many risks. Much of the rest of this book is devoted to considering these risks in detail.

Central bank regulators require banks to hold capital for the risks they are bearing. In 1988, international standards were developed for the determination of this capital. These standards and the way they have evolved since 1988 are discussed in Chapters 12 and 13. Capital is now required for each of three types of risk: credit risk, market risk, and operational risk.

Credit risk is the risk that counterparties in loan transactions and derivatives transactions will default. This has traditionally been the greatest risk facing a bank and is usually the one for which the most regulatory capital is required. Market risk arises primarily from the bank's trading operations. It is the risk relating to the possibility that instruments in the bank's trading book will decline in value. Operational risk is the risk that losses are made because internal systems fail to work as they are supposed to or because of external events. The time horizon for considering losses from credit risks and operational risks is one year, whereas the time horizon for considering losses from market risks is ten days. The objective of regulators is to keep the total capital of a bank sufficiently high that the chance of a bank failure is very low. For example, in the case of credit risk and operational risk, the capital is chosen so that the chance of unexpected losses exceeding the capital in a year is 0.1%.

In addition to calculating regulatory capital, most large banks have systems in place for calculating what is termed *economic capital* (see Chapter 23). This is the capital that the bank, using its own models rather than those prescribed by regulators, thinks it needs. Economic capital is often less than regulatory capital. However, banks have no choice but to maintain their capital above the regulatory capital level. The form the capital can take (equity, subordinated debt, etc.) is prescribed by regulators.

To avoid having to raise capital at short notice, banks try to keep their capital well above the regulatory minimum.

When banks announced huge losses on their subprime mortgage portfolios in 2007 and 2008, many had to raise new equity capital in a hurry. *Sovereign wealth funds*, which are investment funds controlled by the government of a country, have provided some of this capital. For example, Citigroup, which reported losses in the region of $40 billion, raised $7.5 billion in equity from the Abu Dhabi Investment Authority in November 2007 and $14.5 billion from investors that included the governments of Singapore and Kuwait in January 2008. Later, Citigroup and many other banks required capital injections from their own governments to survive.

SUMMARY

Banks are complex global organizations engaged in many different types of activities. The traditional separation of commercial and investment banking has largely disappeared. Today, the world's large banks are engaged in taking deposits, making loans, underwriting securities, trading, providing brokerage services, providing fiduciary services, advising on a range of corporate finance issues, offering mutual funds, providing services to hedge funds, and so on. There are potential conflicts of interest and banks develop internal rules to avoid them. It is important that senior managers are vigilant in ensuring that employees obey these rules. The cost in terms of reputation, lawsuits, and fines from inappropriate behavior where one client (or the bank) is advantaged at the expense of another client can be very large.

There are now international agreements on the regulation of banks. This means that the capital banks are required to keep for the risks they are bearing does not vary too much from one country to another. Many countries have guaranty programs that protect small depositors from losses arising from bank failures. This has the effect of maintaining confidence in the banking system and avoiding mass withdrawals of deposits when there is negative news (or perhaps just a rumor) about problems faced by a particular bank.

FURTHER READING

Saunders, A., and M. M. Cornett. *Financial Institutions Management: A Risk Management Approach*, 6th ed. New York: McGraw-Hill, 2008.

PRACTICE QUESTIONS AND PROBLEMS
(ANSWERS AT END OF BOOK)

2.1 How did concentration in the U.S. banking system change between 1984 and 2010?

2.2 What government policies led to the large number of small community banks in the United States?

2.3 What risks does a bank take if it funds long-term loans with short-term deposits?

2.4 Suppose that an out-of-control trader working for DLC bank (see Tables 2.2 and 2.3) loses $7 million trading foreign exchange. What do you think would happen?

2.5 What is meant by net interest income?

2.6 Which items on the income statement of DLC bank in Section 2.2 are most likely to be affected by (a) credit risk, (b) market risk, and (c) operational risk

2.7 Explain the terms "private placement" and "public offering." What is the difference between "best efforts" and "firm commitment" for a public offering?

2.8 The bidders in a Dutch auction are as follows:

Bidder	Number of Shares	Price
A	20,000	$100.00
B	30,000	$93.00
C	50,000	$110.00
D	70,000	$88.00
E	60,000	$80.00
F	10,000	$105.00
G	90,000	$70.00
H	80,000	$125.00

The number of shares being auctioned is 150,000. What is the price paid by investors? How many shares does each investor receive?

2.9 What is the attraction of a Dutch auction over the normal procedure for an IPO? In what ways was Google's IPO different from a standard Dutch auction?

2.10 Management sometimes argues that poison pills are in the best interests of shareholders because they enable management to extract a higher price from would-be acquirers. Discuss this argument.

2.11 Give three examples of the conflicts of interest in a large bank. How are conflicts of interest handled?

2.12 A loan for $10 million that pays 8% interest is classified as nonperforming. What is the impact of this on the income statement?

2.13 Explain how the loan loss provision account works.

2.14 What is the originate-to-distribute model? Why was it not used in the period following July 2007?

FURTHER QUESTIONS

2.15 Regulators calculate that DLC bank (see Section 2.2) will report a profit that is normally distributed with a mean of $0.6 million and a standard deviation of $2.0 million. How much equity capital in addition to that in Table 2.2 should regulators require for there to be a 99.9% chance of the capital not being wiped out by losses?

2.16 Explain the moral hazard problems with deposit insurance. How can they be overcome?

2.17 The bidders in a Dutch auction are as follows:

Bidder	Number of Shares	Price
A	60,000	$50.00
B	20,000	$80.00
C	30,000	$55.00
D	40,000	$38.00
E	40,000	$42.00
F	40,000	$42.00
G	50,000	$35.00
H	50,000	$60.00

The number of shares being auctioned is 210,000. What is the price paid by investors? How many shares does each investor receive?

2.18 An investment bank has been asked to underwrite an issue of 10 million shares by a company. It is trying to decide between a firm commitment where it buys the shares for $10 per share and a best efforts where it charges a fee of 20 cents for each share sold. Explain the pros and cons of the two alternatives.

CHAPTER 3

Insurance Companies and Pension Plans

The role of insurance companies is to provide protection against adverse events. The company or individual seeking protection is referred to as the *policyholder*. The policyholder makes regular payments, known as *premiums*, and receives payments from the insurance company if certain specified events occur. Insurance is usually classified as *life insurance* and *nonlife insurance*, with health insurance often being considered to be a separate category. Nonlife insurance is also referred to as *property-casualty insurance* and this is the terminology we will use here.

A life insurance contract typically lasts a long time and provides payments to the policyholder that depend on when he or she dies. A property-casualty insurance contract typically lasts one year (although it may be renewed) and provides compensation for losses from accidents, fire, theft, and so on.

Insurance has existed for many years. As long ago as 200 BC, there was a form of life insurance in ancient Greece where an individual could make a lump sum payment (the amount dependent on his or her age) and obtain a monthly income for life. The Romans had a different sort of life insurance where an individual could purchase a contract that would provide a payment to relatives on his or her death. In ancient China, a form of property-casualty insurance existed between merchants where, if the ship of one merchant sank, the rest of the merchants would provide compensation.

A pension plan is a form of insurance arranged by a company for its employees. It is designed to provide the employees with income for the rest of their lives once they have retired. Typically both the company and its employees make regular monthly contributions to the plan and the funds in the plan are invested to provide income for current and future retirees.

This chapter describes how the contracts offered by insurance companies work. It explains the risks that insurance companies face and the way they are regulated. It also discusses key issues associated with pension plans.

3.1 LIFE INSURANCE

In life insurance contracts, the payments to the policyholder depend—at least to some extent—on when the policyholder dies. Outside the United States, the term *life assurance* is often used to describe a contract where the event being insured against is certain to happen at some future time (e.g., a contract that will pay $100,000 on the policyholder's death). Life insurance is used to describe a contract where the event being insured against may never happen (for example, a contract that provides a payoff in the event of the accidental death of the policyholder.)[1] In the United States, all types of life policies are referred to as life insurance and this is the terminology that will be adopted here.

There are many different types of life insurance products. The products available vary from country to country. We will now describe some of the more common ones.

Term Life Insurance

Term life insurance (sometimes referred to as *temporary life insurance*) lasts a pre-determined number of years. If the policyholder dies during the life of the policy, the insurance company makes a payment to the specified beneficiaries equal to the face amount of the policy. If the policyholder does not die during the term of the policy, no payments are made by the insurance company. The policyholder is required to make regular monthly or annual premium payments to the insurance company for the life of the policy or until the policyholder's death (whichever is earlier). The face amount of the policy typically stays the same or declines with the passage of time. One type of policy is an *annual renewable term* policy. In this, the insurance company guarantees to renew the policy from one year to the next at a rate reflecting the policyholder's age without regard to the policyholder's health.

A common reason for term life insurance is a mortgage. For example, a person aged 35 with a 25-year mortgage might choose to buy 25-year term insurance (with a declining face amount) to provide dependents with the funds to pay off the mortgage in the event of his or her death.

Whole Life Insurance

Whole life insurance (sometimes referred to as *permanent life insurance*) provides protection over the whole life of the policyholder. The policyholder is required to make regular monthly or annual payments until his or her death. The face value of the policy is then paid to the designated beneficiary. In the case of term life insurance, there is no certainty that there will be a payout, but in the case of whole life insurance, a payout is certain to happen providing the policyholder continues to make the agreed premium payments. The only uncertainty is when the payout will occur. Not surprisingly, whole life insurance requires considerably higher premiums than term life insurance policies. Usually, the payments and the face value of the policy both remain constant through time.

Policyholders can often redeem (surrender) whole life policies early or use the policies as collateral for loans. When a policyholder wants to redeem a whole life

---

[1] In theory, for a contract to be referred to as life assurance, it is the event being insured against that must be certain to occur. It does not need to be the case that a payout is certain. Thus a policy that pays out if the policyholder dies in the next 10 years is life assurance. In practice, this distinction is sometimes blurred.

policy early, it is sometimes the case that an investor will buy the policy from the policyholder for more than the surrender value offered by the insurance company. The investor will then make the premium payments and collect the face value from the insurance company when the policyholder dies.

The annual premium for a year can be compared with the cost of providing term life insurance for that year. Consider a man who buys a $1 million whole life policy at the age of 40. Suppose that the premium is $20,000 per year. As we will see later, the probability of a male aged 40 dying within one year is about 0.0023 suggesting that a fair premium for one-year insurance is about $2,300. This means that there is a *surplus premium* of $17,700 available for investment from the first year's premium. The probability of a man aged 41 dying in one year is about 0.0025 suggesting that a fair premium for insurance during the second year is $2,500. This means that there is a $17,500 surplus premium available for investment from the second year's premium. The cost of a one-year policy continues to rise as the individual get older so that at some stage it is greater than the annual premium. In our example, this would have happened by the 30th year because the probability of a man aged 70 dying in one year is 0.0256. (A fair premium for the 30th year is $25,600, which is more than the $20,000 received.) The situation is illustrated in Figure 3.1. During the early years, the insurance company invests the surplus premiums to make up the premium shortfall later on. Figure 3.1 shows that there is a savings element to whole life insurance. In the early years, the part of the premium not needed to cover the risk of a payout is invested on behalf of the policyholder by the insurance company.

There are tax advantages associated with life insurance policies in many countries. If the policyholder invested the surplus premiums, tax would normally be payable on the income as it was earned. But, when the surplus premiums are invested within the insurance policy, the tax treatment is often better. In the United States, for example, tax on the investment income is payable only when the policyholder

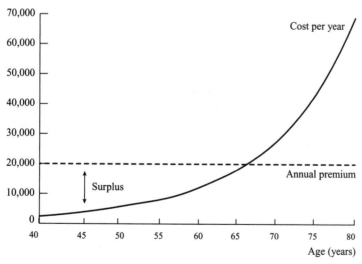

FIGURE 3.1 Cost of Life Insurance per Year Compared with the Annual Premium in a Whole Life Contract

dies and cash is received by the policyholder's beneficiaries.[2] Life insurance policies therefore lead to a deferral of taxes. This is beneficial to the policyholder. The later taxes are paid, the lower their present value. In Canada, the situation is even more favorable to the policyholder than in the United States because no taxes have to be paid by beneficiaries on the payouts from life insurance policies.

Variable Life Insurance

Given that a whole life insurance policy involves funds being invested for the policyholder, a natural development is to allow the policyholder to specify how the funds are invested. Variable life (VL) insurance is a form of whole life insurance where the surplus premiums discussed earlier are invested in a fund chosen by the policyholder. This could be an equity fund, a bond fund, or a money market fund. A minimum guaranteed payout on death is usually specified, but the payout can be more if the fund does well. Income earned from the investments can be applied toward the premiums, if desired. The policyholder can usually switch from one fund to another at any time.

Universal Life

Universal life (UL) insurance is also a form of whole life insurance. The policyholder can reduce the premium down to a specified minimum without the policy lapsing. The surplus premiums are invested by the insurance company in fixed income products such as bonds, mortgages, and money market instruments. The insurance company guarantees a certain minimum return, say 4%, on these funds. The policyholder can choose between two options. Under the first option, a fixed benefit is paid on death; under the second option, the policyholder's beneficiaries receive more than the fixed benefit if the investment return is greater than the guaranteed minimum. Needless to say, premiums are lower for the first option.

Variable-Universal Life Insurance

Variable-universal life (VUL) insurance blends the features found in variable life insurance and universal life insurance. The policyholder can choose between a number of alternatives for the investment of surplus premiums. The insurance company guarantees a certain minimum death benefit and interest on the investments can be applied toward premiums. Premiums can be reduced down to a specified minimum without the policy lapsing.

Endowment Life Insurance

Endowment life insurance lasts for a specified period and pays a lump sum either when the policyholder dies or at the end of the period, whichever is first. There are

---

[2] If the policyholder dies early, very little income has been earned from surpluses and very little tax is payable by the policyholder's beneficiaries. If the policyholder lives for a long time, a much larger part of the cash received from the insurance company is taxable.

many different types of endowment life insurance contracts. The amount that is paid out can be specified in advance as the same regardless of whether the policyholder dies or survives to the end of the policy. Sometimes the payout is also made if the policyholder has a critical illness. In a *with-profits* endowment life insurance policy, the insurance company declares periodic bonuses that depend on the performance of the insurance company's investments. These bonuses accumulate to increase the amount paid out to the policyholder assuming the policyholder lives beyond the end of the life of the policy. In a unit-linked endowment, the amount paid out at maturity depends on the performance of a fund chosen by the policyholder. A *pure endowment* policy has the policy that a payout occurs only if the policyholder survives to the end of the life of the policy.

Group Life Insurance

Group life insurance covers many people under a single policy. It is often purchased by a company for its employees. The policy may be *contributory* where the premium payments are shared by the employer and employee or *noncontributory* where the employer pays the whole of the cost. There are economies of scale in group life insurance. The selling and administration costs are lower. Whereas an individual is usually required to undergo medical tests when purchasing life insurance in the usual way, this may not be necessary for group life insurance. The insurance company knows that it will be taking on some better-than-average risks and some worse-than-average risks.

3.2 ANNUITY CONTRACTS

Many life insurance companies also offer annuity contracts. Whereas a life insurance contract has the effect of converting regular payments into a lump sum, an annuity contract has the opposite effect: that of converting a lump sum into regular payments. In a typical arrangement, the policyholder makes a lump sum payment to the insurance company and the insurance company agrees to provide the policyholder with an annuity that starts at a particular date and lasts for the rest of the policyholder's life. In a *fixed annuity* contract the payments to be received by the policyholder every month are specified in advance. In some instances, the annuity starts immediately after the lump sum payment by the policyholder. More usually, the lump sum payment is made by the policyholder several years ahead of the time when the annuity is to start and the insurance company invests the funds to create the annuity. (This is referred to as a *deferred annuity*.) Instead of a lump sum, the policyholder sometimes saves for the annuity by making regular monthly, quarterly, or annual payments to the insurance company. At a specified future date (e.g., when the policyholder is 65 years old), the funds that have accumulated are converted to a lifetime annuity.

A *variable annuity* (VA) contract is a deferred annuity contract where the insurance company invests in equities, bonds, or other instruments chosen by the policyholder and the annual payments received by the policyholder are not fixed in advance. Typically they depend on the performance of the investments and the level of interest rates at the time the annuity starts.

As with life insurance, there can be tax deferral advantages to the policyholder. This is because taxes usually have to be paid only when the annuity income is received. The value to which the funds invested by the insurance company on behalf of the policyholder have grown is referred to as the *accumulated value*. Funds can usually be withdrawn early, but there are liable to be penalties. In other words, the surrender value of an annuity contract is typically less than the accumulated value. This is because the insurance company has to recover selling and administration costs. Policies sometimes allow *penalty-free withdrawals* where a certain percentage of the accumulated value or a certain percentage of the original investment can be withdrawn in a year without penalty. In the event that the policyholder dies before the start of the annuity (and sometimes in other circumstances such as when the policyholder is admitted to a nursing home), the full accumulated value can often be withdrawn without penalty.

Some deferred annuity contracts in the United States have embedded options. The accumulated value is sometimes calculated so that it tracks a particular equity index such as the S&P 500. Lower and upper limits are specified. If the growth in the index in a year is less than the lower limit, the accumulated value grows at the lower limit rate; if it is greater than the upper limit, the accumulated value grows at the upper limit rate; otherwise it grows at the same rate as the S&P 500. Suppose that the lower limit is 2% and the upper limit is 8%. The policyholder is assured that the accumulated value will always grow by at least 2% in a year, but index growth rates in excess of 8% are given up. In this type of arrangement, the policyholder is typically not compensated for dividends that would be received from an investment in the stocks underlying the index and the insurance company may be able to change parameters such as the lower limit and the upper limit from one year to the next. These types of contracts appeal to investors who want an exposure to the equity market but are reluctant to risk a decline in their accumulated value. Sometimes, the way the accumulated value grows from one year to the next is a quite complicated function of the performance of the index during the year.

In the United Kingdom, the annuity contracts offered by insurance companies used to guarantee a minimum level for the interest rate used for the calculation of the size of the annuity payments. Many insurance companies regarded this guarantee—an interest rate option granted to the policyholder—as a necessary marketing cost and did not calculate the cost of the option or hedge their risks. As interest rates declined and life expectancies increased, many insurance companies found themselves in financial difficulties and, as described in Business Snapshot 3.1, one of them went bankrupt.

3.3 MORTALITY TABLES

Mortality tables are the key to valuing life insurance contracts. Table 3.1 shows an extract from the mortality rates estimated by the U.S. Department of Social Security for 2007. To understand the table, consider the row corresponding to age 31. The second column shows that the probability of a man who has just reached age 31 dying within the next year is 0.001453 (or 0.1453%). The third column shows that the probability of a man surviving to age 31 is 0.97009 (or 97.009%). The fourth

BUSINESS SNAPSHOT 3.1

Equitable Life

Equitable Life was a British life insurance company founded in 1762 that at its peak had 1.5 million policyholders. Starting in the 1950s, Equitable Life sold annuity products where it guaranteed that the interest rate used to calculate the size of the annuity payments would be above a certain level. (This is known as a Guaranteed Annuity Option, GAO.) The guaranteed interest rate was gradually increased in response to competitive pressures and increasing interest rates. Toward the end of 1993, interest rates started to fall. Also, life expectancies were rising so that the insurance companies had to make increasingly high provisions for future payouts on contracts. Equitable Life did not take action. Instead, it grew by selling new products. In 2000, it was forced to close its doors to new business. A report issued by Ann Abraham in July 2008 was highly critical of regulators and urged compensation for policyholders.

An interesting aside to this is that regulators did at one point urge insurance companies that offered GAOs to hedge their exposures to an interest rate decline. As a result, many insurance companies scrambled to enter into contracts with banks that paid off if long-term interest rates declined. The banks in turn hedged their risk by buying instruments such as bonds that increased in price when rates fell. This was done on such a massive scale that the extra demand for bonds caused long-term interest rates in the UK to decline sharply (increasing losses for insurance companies on the unhedged part of their exposures). This shows that, when large numbers of different companies have similar exposures, problems are created if they all decide to hedge at the same time. There are not likely to be enough investors willing to take on their risks without market prices changing.

column shows that a man aged 31 has a remaining life expectancy of 46.20 years. This means than on average he will live to age 77.20. The remaining three columns show similar statistics for a woman. The probability of a 31-year-old woman dying within one year is 0.000678 (0.0678%), the probability of a woman surviving to age 31 is 0.98403 (98.403%), and the remaining life expectancy for a 31-year-old woman is 50.53 years.

The full table shows that the probability of death during the following year is a decreasing function of age for the first 10 years of life and then starts to increase. Mortality statistics for women are a little more favorable than for men. If a man is lucky enough to reach age 90, the probability of death in the next year is 17.4%. The full table shows this probability is 36.2% at age 100 and 58.4% at age 110. For women, the corresponding probabilities are 13.6%, 31.2%, and 55.8%, respectively.

Some numbers in the table can be calculated from other numbers. The third column of the table shows that the probability of a man surviving to 90 is 0.15722.

TABLE 3.1 Mortality Table

	Male			Female		
Age (Years)	Probability of Death within 1 Year	Survival Probability	Life Expectancy	Probability of Death within 1 Year	Survival Probability	Life Expectancy
0	0.007379	1.00000	75.38	0.006096	1.00000	80.43
1	0.000494	0.99262	74.94	0.000434	0.99390	79.92
2	0.000317	0.99213	73.98	0.000256	0.99347	78.95
3	0.000241	0.99182	73.00	0.000192	0.99322	77.97
...	...	...	...	...	...	...
30	0.001428	0.97147	47.13	0.000642	0.98466	51.50
31	0.001453	0.97009	46.20	0.000678	0.98403	50.53
32	0.001487	0.96868	45.27	0.000721	0.98336	49.56
33	0.001529	0.96724	44.33	0.000771	0.98266	48.60
...	...	...	...	...	...	...
40	0.002323	0.95525	37.84	0.001377	0.97586	41.91
41	0.002526	0.95303	36.93	0.001506	0.97452	40.97
42	0.002750	0.95062	36.02	0.001650	0.97305	40.03
43	0.002993	0.94800	35.12	0.001810	0.97144	39.10
...	...	...	...	...	...	...
50	0.005512	0.92224	28.99	0.003255	0.95530	32.69
51	0.006008	0.91716	28.15	0.003517	0.95219	31.80
52	0.006500	0.91165	27.32	0.003782	0.94885	30.91
53	0.006977	0.90572	26.49	0.004045	0.94526	30.02
...	...	...	...	...	...	...
60	0.011407	0.85227	20.92	0.006961	0.91220	23.97
61	0.012315	0.84254	20.16	0.007624	0.90585	23.14
62	0.013289	0.83217	19.40	0.008322	0.89895	22.31
63	0.014326	0.82111	18.66	0.009046	0.89147	21.49
...	...	...	...	...	...	...
70	0.025579	0.72066	13.73	0.017163	0.81944	16.05
71	0.028032	0.70223	13.08	0.018987	0.80537	15.32
72	0.030665	0.68254	12.44	0.020922	0.79008	14.61
73	0.033467	0.66161	11.82	0.022951	0.77355	13.91
...	...	...	...	...	...	...
80	0.064457	0.47974	7.90	0.045561	0.61930	9.43
81	0.071259	0.44882	7.41	0.050698	0.59109	8.86
82	0.078741	0.41683	6.94	0.056486	0.56112	8.31
83	0.086923	0.38401	6.49	0.062971	0.52942	7.77
...	...	...	...	...	...	...
90	0.174013	0.15722	3.92	0.136190	0.27333	4.69
91	0.191354	0.12986	3.64	0.151300	0.23610	4.36
92	0.209867	0.10501	3.38	0.167602	0.20038	4.04
93	0.229502	0.08297	3.15	0.185078	0.16680	3.76

Source: U.S. Department of Social Security, www.ssa.gov/OACT/STATS/table4c6.html.

The probability of the man surviving to 91 is 0.12986. It follows that the probability of a man dying between his 90th and 91st birthday is $0.15722 - 0.12986 = 0.02736$. Conditional on a man reaching the age of 90, the probability that he will die in the course of the following year is therefore

$$\frac{0.02736}{0.15722} = 0.1740$$

This is consistent with the number given in the second column of the table.

The probability of a man aged 90 dying in the second year (between ages 91 and 92) is the probability that he does not die in the first year multiplied by the probability that he does die in the second year. From the numbers in the second column of the table, this is

$$(1 - 0.174013) \times 0.191354 = 0.158056$$

Similarly, the probability that he dies in the third year (between ages 92 and 93) is

$$(1 - 0.174013) \times (1 - 0.191354) \times 0.209867 = 0.140177$$

Assuming that death occurs on average halfway though a year, the life expectancy of a man aged 90 is

$$0.5 \times 0.174013 + 1.5 \times 0.158056 + 2.5 \times 0.140177 + \cdots$$

EXAMPLE 3.1

Assume that interest rates for all maturities are 4% per annum with semiannual compounding and premiums are paid once a year at the beginning of the year. What is an insurance company's break-even premium for $100,000 of term life insurance for a man of average health aged 90? If the term insurance lasts one year, the expected payout is $0.174013 \times 100,000$ or $17,401. Assume that the payout occurs halfway through the year. (This is likely to be approximately true on average.) The premium is $17,401 discounted for six months. This is $17,401/1.02$ or $17,060.

Suppose next that the term insurance lasts two years. In this case, the present value of expected payouts in the first year is $17,060 as before. The probability that the policyholder dies during the second year is $(1 - 0.174013) \times 0.191354 = 0.158056$ so that there is also an expected payout of $0.158056 \times 100,000$ or $15,806 during the second year. Assuming this happens at 18 months, the present value of the payout is $15,806/(1.02^3)$ or $14,894. The total present value of the payout is $17,060 + 14,894$ or $31,954.

Consider next the premium payments. We are certain that the first premium will be paid. The probability of the second premium payment being made at the beginning of the second year is the probability that the man does not die during the first year. This is $1 - 0.174013 = 0.825987$. When the premium is X dollars per year, the present value of the premium payments is

$$X + \frac{0.825987 \times X}{(1.02)^2} = 1.793913X$$

The break-even annual premium is given by the value of X that equates the present value of the expected premium payments to the present value of the expected payout. This is the value of X that solves

$$1.793913X = 31,954$$

or $X = 17,812$. The break-even premium payment is therefore $17,812.

3.4 LONGEVITY AND MORTALITY RISK

Longevity risk is the risk that advances in medical sciences and lifestyle changes will lead to people living longer. Increases in longevity adversely affect the profitability of most types of annuity contracts (because the annuity has to be paid for longer), but increases the profitability of most life insurance contracts (because the final payout is either delayed or, in the case of term insurance, less likely to happen). Life expectancy has been steadily increasing in most parts of the world. Average life expectancy of a child born in the United States in 2007 is estimated to be about 20 years higher than for a child born in 1929. Life expectancy varies from country to country.

Mortality risk is the risk that wars, epidemics such as AIDS, or pandemics such as Spanish flu will lead to people living a shorter time than expected. This adversely affects the payouts on most types of life insurance contracts (because the insured amount has to be paid earlier than expected), but should increase the profitability of annuity contracts (because the annuity is not paid out for as long). In calculating the impact of mortality risk, it is important to consider the age groups within the population that are likely to be most affected by a particular event.

To some extent, the longevity and mortality risks in the annuity business of a life insurance company offset those in its regular life insurance contracts. Actuaries must carefully assess the insurance company's net exposure under different scenarios. If the exposure is unacceptable, they may decide to enter into reinsurance contracts for some of the risks. Reinsurance is discussed later in this chapter.

Longevity Derivatives

A longevity derivative provides payoffs that are potentially attractive to insurance companies when they are concerned about their longevity exposure on annuity contracts and to pension funds. A typical contract is a *longevity bond*, also known as a *survivor bond*, which first traded in the late 1990s. A population group is defined and the coupon on the bond at any given time is defined as being proportional to the number of individuals in the population that are still alive. Who will sell such bonds? The answer is some speculators find the bonds attractive because they have very little systematic risk. (See Section 1.3 for a discussion of systematic risk.) The bond payments depend on how long people live and this is largely uncorrelated with returns from the market.

3.5 PROPERTY-CASUALTY INSURANCE

Property-casualty insurance can be subdivided into property insurance and casualty insurance. Property insurance provides protection against loss of or damage to property (from fire, theft, water damage, etc.). Casualty insurance provides protection against legal liability exposures (from, for example, injuries caused to third parties). Casualty insurance might more accurately be referred to as liability insurance. Sometimes both types of insurance are included in a single policy. For example, a home owner might buy insurance that provides protection against various types of loss such as property damage and theft as well as legal liabilities if others are injured while on the property. Similarly, car insurance typically provides protection against theft of, or damage to, one's own vehicle as well as protection against claims brought by others.

Typically property-casualty policies are renewed from year to year and the insurance company will increase the premium if its assessment of the expected payout increases. (This is in contrast to life insurance, where premiums are typically set in advance for many years.) Because property-casualty insurance companies get involved in many different types of insurance there is some natural risk diversification. For some risks, the "law of large numbers" applies. For example, if an insurance company has written policies protecting 250,000 home owners against losses from theft and fire damage, the expected payout can be predicted reasonably accurately. This is because the policies provide protection against a large number of (almost) independent events. (Of course, there are liable to be trends in the number of losses and the insurance company should keep track of these trends in determining year-to-year changes in the premiums.)

Property damage arising from natural disasters such as hurricanes give rise to payouts for an insurance company that are much less easy to predict. For example, Hurricane Katrina in the United States in the summer of 2005 and the heavy storm in north west Europe in January 2007 that measured 12 on the Beaufort scale proved to be very expensive. These are termed *catastrophic risks*. The problem with them is that the claims made by different policyholders are not independent. Either a hurricane happens in a year and the insurance company has to deal with a large number of claims for hurricane-related damage or there is no hurricane in the year and therefore no claims are made. Most large insurers have models based on geographical, seismographical, and meteorological information to estimate the probabilities of catastrophes and the losses resulting therefrom. This provides a basis for setting premiums, but it does not alter the "all-or-nothing" nature of these risks for insurance companies.

Liability insurance, like catastrophe insurance, gives rise to total payouts that vary from year to year and are difficult to predict. For example, claims arising from asbestos-related damages to workers' health have proved very expensive for insurance companies in the United States. A feature of liability insurance is what is known as *long-tail risk*. This is the possibility of claims being made several years after the insured period is over. In the case of asbestos, for example, the health risks were not realized until some time after exposure. As a result, the claims, when they were made, were under policies that had been in force several years previously. This creates a complication for actuaries and accountants. They cannot close the books soon after the end of each year and calculate a profit or loss. They must allow for the cost of claims that have not yet been made, but may be made some time in the future.

Claims made under property-casualty policies can be characterized, from the perspective of the insurance company, by their frequency and their severity. A general principle is that the total cost per year of high-frequency, low-severity claims (such as claims arising from theft) is relatively easy to predict. By contrast, the total cost per year of low-frequency, high-severity claims (such as those arising from catastrophic risks and liability insurance) are much less easy to predict.

CAT Bonds

The derivatives market has come up with a number of products for hedging catastrophic risk. The most popular is a CAT bond. This is a bond issued by a subsidiary of an insurance company that pays a higher-than-normal interest rate. In exchange for the extra interest, the holder of the bond agrees to cover payouts on a particular type of catastrophic risk that are in a certain range. Depending on the terms of the CAT bond, the interest or principal (or both) can be used to meet claims.

Suppose an insurance company has a $70 million exposure to California earthquake losses and wants protection for losses over $40 million. The insurance company could issue CAT bonds with a total principal of $30 million. In the event that the insurance company's California earthquake losses exceeded $40 million, bondholders would lose some or all of their principal. As an alternative, the insurance company could cover the same losses by making a much bigger bond issue where only the bondholders' interest is at risk. Yet another alternative is to make three separate bond issues covering losses in the range $40 to $50 million, $50 to $60 million, and $60 to $70 million, respectively.

CAT bonds typically give a high probability of an above-normal rate of interest and a low-probability of a high loss. Why would investors be interested in such instruments? The answer is that the return on CAT bonds, like the longevity bonds considered earlier, have no statistically significant correlations with market returns.[3] CAT bonds are therefore an attractive addition to an investor's portfolio. Their total risk can be completely diversified away in a large portfolio. If a CAT bond's expected return is greater than the risk-free interest rate (and typically it is), it has the potential to improve risk-return trade-offs.

Ratios Calculated by Property-Casualty Insurers

Insurance companies calculate a *loss ratio* for different types of insurance. This is the ratio of payouts made to premiums earned in a year. Loss ratios are typically

---

[3] See R. H. Litzenberger, D. R. Beaglehole, and C. E. Reynolds, "Assessing Catastrophe Reinsurance-Linked Securities as a New Asset Class," *Journal of Portfolio Management* (Winter 1996): 76–86.

TABLE 3.2   Example Showing Calculation of Operating
Ratio for a Property-Casualty Insurance Company

Loss ratio	75%
Expense ratio	30%
Combined ratio	105%
Dividends	1%
Combined ratio after dividends	106%
Investment income	(9%)
Operating ratio	97%

in the 60% to 80% range. Statistics published by A. M. Best show that loss ratios in the United States have tended to increase through time. The *expense ratio* for an insurance company is the ratio of expenses to premiums earned in a year. The two major sources of expenses are loss adjustment expenses and selling expenses. Loss adjustment expenses are those expenses related to determining the validity of a claim and how much the policyholder should be paid. Selling expenses include the commissions paid to brokers and other expenses concerned with the acquisition of business. Expense ratios in the United States are typically in the 25% to 30% range and have tended to decrease through time.

The *combined ratio* is the sum of the loss ratio and the expense ratio. Suppose that for a particular category of policies in a particular year the loss ratio is 75% and the expense ratio is 30%. The combined ratio is then 105%. Sometimes a small dividend is paid to policyholders. Suppose that this is 1% of premiums. When this is taken into account we obtain what is referred to as the *combined ratio after dividends*. This is 106% in our example. This number suggests that the insurance company has lost 6% before tax on the policies being considered. In fact, this may not be the case. Premiums are generally paid by policyholders at the beginning of a year and payouts on claims are made during the year, or after the end of the year. The insurance company is therefore able to earn interest on the premiums during the time that elapses between the receipt of premiums and payouts. Suppose that, in our example, investment income is 9% of premiums received. When the investment income is taken into account, a ratio of $106 - 9 = 97\%$ is obtained. This is referred to as the *operating ratio*. Table 3.2 summarizes the example.

3.6   HEALTH INSURANCE

Health insurance has some of the attributes of property-casualty insurance and some of the attributes of life insurance. It is sometimes considered to be a totally separate category of insurance. The extent to which health care is provided by the government varies from country to country. In the United States publicly funded health care has traditionally been limited and health insurance has therefore been an important consideration for most people. Canada is at the other extreme: nearly all health care needs are provided by a publicly funded system. Doctors are not allowed to offer most services privately. The main role of health insurance in Canada is to cover prescription costs and dental care, which are not funded publicly. In most other countries, there is a mixture of public and private health care. The United Kingdom, for example, has a publicly funded health care system, but some individuals buy insurance to have access to a private system that operates side by side with the public system. (The main advantage of private health insurance is a reduction in waiting times for routine elective surgery.)

In 2010, President Obama signed into law the Patient Protection and Affordable Care Act in an attempt to reform health care in the United States and increase the number of people with medical coverage. The eligibility for Medicaid (a program for low income individuals) was expanded and subsidies were provided for low and middle income families to help them buy insurance. The act prevents health insurers from taking pre-existing medical conditions into account and requires employers to provide coverage to their employees or pay additional taxes. One difference between the United States and many other countries continues to be that health is largely provided by the private rather than the public sector.

In health insurance, as in other forms of insurance, the policyholder makes regular premium payments and payouts are triggered by events. Examples of such events are the policyholder needing an examination by a doctor, the policyholder requiring treatment at a hospital, and the policyholder requiring prescription medication. Typically the premiums increase because of overall increases in the costs of providing health care. However, they usually cannot increase because the health of the policyholder deteriorates. It is interesting to compare health insurance with auto insurance and life insurance in this respect. An auto insurance premium can increase (and usually does) if the policyholder's driving record indicates that expected payouts have increased and if the costs of repairs to automobiles have increased. Life insurance premiums do not increase—even if the policyholder is diagnosed with a health problem that significantly reduces life expectancy. Health insurance premiums are like life insurance premiums in that changes to the insurance company's assessment of the risk of a payout do not lead to an increase in premiums. However, it is like auto insurance in that increases in the overall costs of meeting claims do lead to premium increases.

Of course, when a policy is first issued, an insurance company does its best to determine the risks it is taking on. In the case of life insurance, questions concerning the policyholder's health have to be answered, pre-existing medical conditions have to be declared, and physical examinations may be required. In the case of auto insurance, the policyholder's driving record is investigated. In both of these cases, insurance can be refused. In the case of health insurance, legislation sometimes determines the circumstances under which insurance can be refused. As indicated earlier, the Patient Protection and Affordable Health Care Act makes it very difficult for insurance companies in the United States to refuse applications because of pre-existing medical conditions.

Health insurance is often provided by the *group health insurance plans* of employers. These plans typically cover the employee and the employee's family. Usually, the employee cannot be refused insurance because of pre-existing medical conditions and the cost of the health insurance is often split between the employer and employee. The expenses that are covered vary from plan to plan. In the United States, most plans cover basic medical needs such as medical check-ups, physicals, treatments for common disorders, surgery, and hospital stays. Pregnancy costs may or may not be covered. Procedures such as cosmetic surgery are usually not covered.

3.7 MORAL HAZARD AND ADVERSE SELECTION

We now consider two key risks facing insurance companies: moral hazard and adverse selection.

Moral Hazard

Moral hazard is the risk that the existence of insurance will cause the policyholder to behave differently than he or she would without the insurance. This different behavior increases the risks and the expected payouts of the insurance company. Examples of moral hazard are:

1. A car owner buys insurance to protect against the car being stolen. As a result of the insurance, he or she becomes less likely to lock the car.
2. An individual purchases health insurance. As a result of the existence of the policy, more health care is demanded than previously.
3. As a result of a government-sponsored deposit insurance plan, a bank takes more risks because it knows that it is less likely to lose depositors because of this strategy. (This was discussed in Section 2.3)

Moral hazard is not a big problem in life insurance. Insurance companies have traditionally dealt with moral hazard in property-casualty and health insurance in a number of ways. Typically there is a *deductible*. This means that the policyholder is responsible for bearing the first part of any loss. Sometimes there is a *co-insurance provision* in a policy. The insurance company then pays a predetermined percentage (less than 100%) of losses in excess of the deductible. In addition there is nearly always a *policy limit* (i.e., an upper limit to the payout). The effect of these provisions is to align the interests of the policyholder more closely with those of the insurance company.

Adverse Selection

Adverse selection is the phrase used to describe the problems an insurance company has when it cannot distinguish between good and bad risks. It offers the same price to everyone and inadvertently attracts more of the bad risks. If an insurance company is not able to distinguish good drivers from bad drivers and offers the same auto insurance premium to both, it is likely to attract more bad drivers. If it is not able to distinguish healthy from unhealthy people and offers the same life insurance premiums to both, it is likely to attract more unhealthy people.

To lessen the impact of adverse selection, an insurance company tries to find out as much as possible about the policyholder before committing itself. Before offering life insurance, it often requires the policyholder to undergo a physical examination by an approved doctor. Before offering auto insurance to an individual, it will try to obtain as much information as possible about the individual's driving record. In the case of auto insurance, it will continue to collect information on the driver's risk (number of accidents, number of speeding tickets, etc.) and make year-to-year changes to the premium to reflect this.

Adverse selection can never be completely overcome. It is interesting that, in spite of the physical examinations that are required, individuals buying life insurance tend to die earlier than mortality tables would suggest. But individuals who purchase annuities tend to live longer than mortality tables would suggest.

3.8 REINSURANCE

Reinsurance is an important way in which an insurance company can protect itself against large losses by entering into contracts with another insurance company. For a fee, the second insurance company agrees to be responsible for some of the risks that have been insured by the first company. Reinsurance allows insurance companies to write more policies than they would otherwise be able to do. Some of the counterparties in reinsurance contracts are other insurance companies or rich private individuals; others are companies that specialize in reinsurance such as Swiss Re and Warren Buffett's company, Berkshire Hathaway.

Reinsurance contracts can take a number of forms. Suppose that an insurance company has an exposure of $100 million to hurricanes in Florida and wants to limit this to $50 million. One alternative is to enter into annual reinsurance contracts that cover on a pro rata basis 50% of its exposure. (The reinsurer would then probably receive 50% of the premiums.) If hurricane claims in a particular year total $70 million, the costs to the insurance company would be only $0.5 \times \$70$ or $35 million, and the reinsurance company would pay the other $35 million.

Another more popular alternative, involving lower reinsurance premiums, is to buy a series of reinsurance contracts covering what are known as *excess cost layers*. The first layer might provide indemnification for losses between $50 million and $60 million, the next layer might cover losses between $60 million and $70 million, and so on. Each reinsurance contract is known as an *excess-of-loss reinsurance contract*.

3.9 CAPITAL REQUIREMENTS

The balance sheets for life insurance and property-casualty insurance companies are different because the risks taken and reserves that must be set aside for future payouts are different.

Life Insurance Companies

Table 3.3 shows an abbreviated balance sheet for a life insurance company. Most of the life insurance company's investments are in corporate bonds. The insurance company tries to match the maturity of its assets with the maturity of liabilities.

TABLE 3.3   Abbreviated Balance Sheet for Life Insurance Company

Assets		Liabilities and Net Worth	
Investments	90	Policy reserves	80
Other assets	10	Subordinated long-term debt	10
		Equity capital	10
Total	100	Total	100

However, it takes on credit risk because the default rate on the bonds may be higher than expected.

Unlike a bank, an insurance company has exposure on the liability side of the balance sheet as well as on the asset side. The policy reserves (80% of assets in this case) are estimates (usually conservative) of actuaries for the payouts on the policies that have been written. The estimates may prove to be low if the holders of life insurance policies die earlier than expected or the holders of annuity contracts live longer than expected. The 10% equity on the balance sheet includes the original equity contributed and retained earnings and provides a cushion. If payouts are greater than loss reserves by an amount equal to 5% of assets, equity will decline, but the life insurance company will survive.

Property-Casualty Insurance Companies

Table 3.4 shows an abbreviated balance sheet for a property-casualty life insurance company. A key difference between Table 3.3 and Table 3.4 is that the equity in Table 3.4 is much higher. This reflects the differences in the risks taken by the two sorts of insurance companies. The payouts for a property-casualty company are much less easy to predict than those for a life insurance company. Who knows when a hurricane will hit Miami or how large payouts will be for the next asbestos-like liability problem? The unearned premiums item on the liability side represents premiums that have been received, but apply to future time periods. If a policyholder pays $2,500 for house insurance on June 30 of a year, only $1,250 has been earned by December 31 of the year. The investments in Table 3.4 consist largely of liquid bonds with shorter maturities than the bonds in Table 3.3.

TABLE 3.4   Abbreviated Balance Sheet for Property-Casualty Insurance Company

Assets		Liabilities and Net Worth	
Investments	90	Policy reserves	45
Other assets	10	Unearned premiums	15
		Subordinated long-term debt	10
		Equity capital	30
Total	100	Total	100

3.10 THE RISKS FACING INSURANCE COMPANIES

The most obvious risk for an insurance company is that the policy reserves are not sufficient to meet the claims of policyholders. Although the calculations of actuaries are usually fairly conservative, there is always the chance that payouts much higher than anticipated will be required. Insurance companies also face risks concerned with the performance of their investments. Many of these investments are in corporate bonds. If defaults on corporate bonds are above average, the profitability of the insurance company will suffer. It is important that an insurance company's bond portfolio be diversified by business sector and geographical region. An insurance company also needs to monitor the liquidity risks associated with its investments. Illiquid bonds (e.g., those the insurance company might buy in a private placement) tend to provide higher yields than bonds that are publicly owned and actively traded. However, they cannot be as readily converted into cash to meet unexpectedly high claims. Insurance companies enter into transactions with banks and reinsurance companies. This exposes them to credit risk. Like banks, insurance companies are also exposed to operational risks and business risks.

Regulators specify minimum capital requirements for an insurance company to provide a cushion against losses. Insurance companies, like banks, have also developed their own procedures for calculating economic capital. This is their own internal estimate of required capital (see Chapter 23).

3.11 REGULATION

The ways in which insurance companies are regulated in the United States and Europe are quite different.

The United States

In the United States, the McCarran-Ferguson Act of 1945 confirmed that insurance companies are regulated at the state level rather than the federal level. (Banks, by contrast, are regulated at the federal level.) This means that a large insurance company that operates throughout the United States has to deal with 50 different regulatory authorities. From time to time there have been suggestions that a federal regulatory body be set up. The National Association of Insurance Commissioners (NAIC) provides some services to state regulatory commissions. For example, it provides statistics on the loss ratios of property-casualty insurers. This helps state regulators identify those insurers for which the ratios are outside normal ranges. The Dodd-Frank Act of 2010 set up the Federal Insurance Office, which is housed in the Department of the Treasury. It is tasked with monitoring the insurance industry and identifying gaps in regulation.

Insurance companies are required to file detailed annual financial statements with state regulators, and the state regulators conduct periodic on-site reviews. Capital requirements are determined by regulators using risk-based capital standards determined by NAIC. These capital levels reflect the risk that policy reserves are inadequate, that counterparties in transactions default, and that the income on investments is less than expected.

The policyholder is protected against an insurance company becoming insolvent (and therefore unable to make payouts on claims) by insurance guaranty associations. An insurer is required to be a member of the guaranty association in a state as a condition of being licensed to conduct business in the state. When there is an insolvency by another insurance company operating in the state, each insurance company operating in the state has to contribute an amount to the state guaranty fund that is dependent on the premium income it collects in the state. The fund is used to pay the small policyholders of the insolvent insurance company. (The definition of a small policyholder varies from state to state.) There may be a cap on the amount the insurance company has to contribute to the state guaranty fund in a year. This can lead to the policyholder having to wait several years before the guaranty fund is in a position to make a full payout on its claims. In the case of life insurance, where policies last for many years, the policyholders of insolvent companies are usually taken over by other insurance companies. However, there may be some change to the terms of the policy so that the policyholder is somewhat worse off than before.

The guaranty system for insurance companies in the United States is therefore different from that for banks. In the case of banks, there is a permanent fund created from premiums paid by banks on their domestic deposits. In the case of insurance companies, there is no permanent fund. Insurance companies have to make contributions after an insolvency has occurred. An exception to this is property-casualty companies in New York State where a permanent fund does exist.

Europe

In Europe, insurance companies are regulated by the European Union. This means that in theory the same regulatory framework applies to insurance companies throughout Europe. The framework that has existed since the 1970s is now known as Solvency I. It was heavily influenced by research carried out by Professor Campagne from the Netherlands who showed that, with a capital equal to 4% of policy provisions, life insurance companies have a 95% chance of surviving. Investment risks are not explicitly considered by Solvency I.

A number of countries, such as the UK, the Netherlands, and Switzerland, have developed their own plans to overcome some of the weaknesses in Solvency I. The European Union is working on Solvency II which assigns capital for a wider set of risks than Solvency I. Both Solvency I and Solvency II are discussed further in Chapter 12.

3.12 PENSION PLANS

Pension plans are set up by companies for their employees. Typically, contributions are made to a pension plan by both the employee and the employer while the employee is working. When the employee retires, he or she receives a pension until death. A pension fund therefore involves the creation of a lifetime annuity from regular contributions and has similarities to some of the products offered by life insurance companies. There are two types of pension plans: defined benefit and defined contribution.

In a *defined benefit plan*, the pension that the employee will receive on retirement is defined by the plan. Typically it is calculated by a formula that is based on the number of years of employment and the employee's salary. For example, the pension per year might equal the employee's average earnings per year during the last three years of employment multiplied the number of years of employment multiplied by 2%. The employee's spouse may continue to receive a (usually reduced) pension if the employee dies before the spouse. In the event of the employee's death while still employed, a lump sum is often payable to dependents and a monthly income may be payable to a spouse or dependent children. Sometimes pensions are adjusted for inflation. This is known as indexation. For example, the indexation in a defined benefit plan might lead to pensions being increased each year by 75% of the increase in the consumer price index.

In a *defined contribution plan* the employer and employee contributions are invested on behalf of the employee. When employees retire there are typically a number of options open to them. The amount to which the contributions have grown can be converted to a lifetime annuity. In some cases, the employee can opt to receive a lump sum instead of an annuity. The key difference between a defined contribution and a defined benefit plan is that, in the former, the funds are identified with individual employees. An account is set up for each employee and the pension is calculated only from the funds contributed to that account. By contrast, in a defined benefit plan, all contributions are pooled and payments to retirees are made out of the pool. In the United States, a 401(k) plan is a form of defined contribution plan where the employee elects to have some portion of his or her income directed to the plan (with possibly some employer matching) and can choose between a number of investment alternatives (e.g., stocks, bonds, and money market instruments).

A key aspect of both defined benefit and defined contribution plans is the fact that income tax is deferred. No taxes are payable on money contributed to the plan by the employee and contributions by a company are deductible. Taxes are payable only when pension income is received.

Defined contribution plans involve very little risk for employers. If the performance of the plan's investments is less than anticipated, the employee bears the cost. By contrast, defined benefit plans impose significant risks on employers because they are ultimately responsible for paying the promised benefits. Let us suppose that the assets of a defined benefit plan total $100 million and that actuaries calculate the present value of the obligations to be $120 million. The plan is $20 million underfunded and the employer is required to make up the shortfall (usually over a number of years). The risks posed by defined benefit plans have led some companies to convert defined benefit plans to defined contribution plans.

Estimating the present value of the liabilities in defined benefit plans is not easy. An important issue is the discount rate used. The higher the discount rate, the lower is the present value of the pension plan liabilities. It used to be common to use the average rate of return on the assets of the pension plan as the discount rate. This encourages the pension plan to invest in equities because the average return on equities is higher than the average return on bonds, making the value of the liabilities look low. Accounting standards now recognize that the liabilities of pension plans are obligations similar to bonds and require the liabilities of the pension plans of private companies to be discounted at AA-rated bond yields. The difference between the value of the assets of a defined benefit plan and that of its liabilities must be

---

BUSINESS SNAPSHOT 3.2

A Perfect Storm

During the period December 31, 1999, to December 31, 2002, the S&P 500 declined by about 40% from 1469.25 to 879.82 and 20-year Treasury rates in the United States declined by 200 basis points from 6.83% to 4.83%. The impact of the first of these events was that the market value of the assets of pension plans declined sharply. The impact of the second of the two events was that the discount rate used by defined benefit plans for their liabilities decreased so that the fair value of the liabilities calculated by actuaries increased. This created a "perfect storm" for defined benefit pension plans. Many funds that had been overfunded became underfunded. Funds that had been slightly underfunded became much more seriously underfunded. A combination of negative equity returns and declining interest rates, such as occurred during the three-year period just considered, is a nightmare for all managers of defined benefit plans.

Accounting rules requiring pension plan overfunding (underfunding) to be recorded as an asset (liability) on the balance sheet make the impact of perfect storms much more transparent. It is not surprising that many companies have tried to replace defined benefit pension plans with defined contribution plans.

---

recorded as an asset or liability on the balance sheet of the company. Thus, if a company's defined benefit plan is underfunded the company's shareholder equity is reduced. A "perfect storm" is created when the assets of a pension plan decline sharply in value and the discount rate for its liabilities decreases sharply (see Business Snapshot 3.2).

Are Defined Benefit Plans Viable?

A typical defined benefit plan provides the employee with about 70% of final salary as a pension and includes some indexation for inflation. What percentage of the employee's income during his or her working life should be set aside for providing the pension? The answer depends on assumptions about interest rates, how fast the employee's income rises during the employee's working life, and so on. But, if an insurance company were asked to provide a quote for the sort of defined benefit plan we are considering, the required contribution rate would be about 25% of income each year. (Problems 3.15 and 3.19 provide an indication of calculations that can be carried out.) The insurance company would invest the premiums in corporate bonds (in the same way that it does the premiums for life insurance and annuity contracts) because this provides the best way of matching the investment income with the payouts.

The contributions to defined benefit plans (employer plus employee) are much less than 25% of income. In a typical defined benefit plan, the employer and employee each contribute around 5%. The total contribution is therefore only 40% of what an insurance actuary would calculate the required premium to be. It is therefore not surprising that many pension plans are underfunded.

Unlike insurance companies, pension funds choose to invest a significant proportion of their assets in equities. (A typical portfolio mix for a pension plan is 60% equity and 40% debt.) By investing in equities, the pension fund is creating the situation where there is some chance that the pension plan will be fully funded. But there is also some chance of severe underfunding. If equity markets do well, as they have done from 1960 to 2000 in many parts of the world, defined benefit plans find they can afford their liabilities. But if equity markets perform badly, and since 2000 the performance has been less than stellar, there are likely to be problems.

This raises an interesting question: who is responsible for underfunding in defined benefit plans? In the first instance, it is the company's shareholders that bear the cost. If the company declares bankruptcy, the cost may be borne by the government via insurance that is offered.[4] In either case there is a transfer of wealth to retirees from the next generation.

A similar issue applies to the pension plans that are sponsored by governments (such as Social Security in the United States). These are similar to defined benefit plans in that they require regular contributions and provide lifetime pensions.

Many people argue that wealth transfers from one generation to another are not acceptable. A 25% contribution rate to pension plans is probably not feasible. If defined benefit plans are to continue, there must be modifications to the terms of the plan so that there is some risk sharing between retirees and the next generation. If equity markets perform badly during their working life, retirees must be prepared to accept a lower pension and receive only modest help from the next generation. If equity markets perform well, retirees can receive a full pension and some of the benefits can be passed on to the next generation.

Longevity risk is a major concern for pension plans. We mentioned earlier that life expectancy increased by 20 years between 1929 and 2004. If this trend continues and life expectancy increases by a further 4.25 years by 2020, the underfunding problems of defined benefit plans (both those administered by companies and those administered by national governments) will become more severe. It is not surprising that, in many jurisdictions, individuals have the right to work past the normal retirement age. This helps solve the problems faced by pension plans. An individual who retires at 70 rather than 65 makes an extra five years of pension contributions and the period of time for which the pension is received is shorter by five years.

SUMMARY

There are two main types of insurance companies: life and property-casualty. Life insurance companies offer a number of products that provide a payoff when the policyholder dies. Term life insurance provides a payoff only if the policyholder dies

---

[4] For example, in the United States, the Pension Benefit Guaranty Corporation (PBGC) insures private defined benefit plans. If the premiums the PBGC receives from plans are not sufficient to meet claims, presumably the government would have to step in.

during a certain period. Whole life insurance provides a payoff on the death on the insured, regardless of when this is. There is a savings element to whole life insurance. Typically, the portion of the premium not required to meet expected payouts in the early years of the policy is invested and this is used to finance expected payouts in later years. Whole life insurance policies can give rise to tax benefits because tax is deferred on the investment returns until there is a payout on the policy.

Life insurance companies also offer annuity contracts. These are contracts that, in return for a lump sum payment, provide the policyholder with an annual income from a certain date for the rest of his or her life. Mortality tables provide important information for the valuation of the life insurance contracts and annuities. However, actuaries must consider (a) longevity risk (the possibility that people will live longer than expected) and (b) mortality risk (the possibility that epidemics such as AIDS or Spanish flu will reduce life expectancy for some segments of the population).

Property-casualty insurance is concerned with providing protection against a loss of, or damage to, property. It also protects individuals and companies from legal liabilities. The most difficult payouts to predict are those where the same event is liable to trigger claims by many policyholders at about the same time. Examples of such events are hurricanes or earthquakes. Payouts arising from legal liabilities are also difficult to predict.

Health insurance has some of the features of life insurance and some of the features of property-casualty insurance. Health insurance premiums are like life insurance premiums in that changes to the company's assessment of the risk of payouts do not lead to an increase in premiums. However, it is like property-casualty insurance in that increases in the overall costs of providing health care can lead to increases in premiums.

Two key risks in insurance are moral hazard and adverse selection. Moral hazard is the risk that the behavior of an individual or corporation with an insurance contract will be different from the behavior without the insurance contract. Adverse selection is the risk that the individuals and companies who buy a certain type of policy are those for which expected payouts are relatively high. Insurance companies take steps to reduce these two types of risk, but they cannot eliminate them altogether.

Insurance companies are different from banks in that their liabilities as well as their assets are subject to risk. A property-casualty insurance company must typically keep more equity capital, as a percent of total assets, than a life insurance company. In the United States, insurance companies are regulated at the state level rather than at the federal level. In Europe, insurance companies are regulated by the European Union and by national governments. The European Union is currently working on a new set of capital requirements known as Solvency II.

There are two types of pension plans: defined benefit plans and defined contribution plans. Defined contribution plans are straightforward. Contributions made by an employee and contributions made by the company on behalf of the employee are kept in a separate account, invested on behalf of the employee, and converted into a lifetime annuity when the employee retires. In a defined benefit plan, contributions from all employees and the company are pooled and invested. Retirees receive a pension that is based on the salary they earned while working. The viability of defined benefit plans is questionable. Many are underfunded and need superior returns from equity markets to pay promised pensions to both current retirees and future retirees.

FURTHER READING

Ambachtsheer, K. P. *Pension Revolution: A Solution to the Pensions Crisis.* Hoboken, NJ: John Wiley & Sons, 2007.

Canter, M. S., J. B. Cole, and R. L. Sandor. "Insurance Derivatives: A New Asset Class for the Capital Markets and a New Hedging Tool for the Insurance Industry." *Journal of Applied Corporate Finance* (Autumn 1997): 69–83.

Doff, R. *Risk Management for Insurers: Risk Control, Economic Capital, and Solvency II.* London: Risk Books, 2007.

Froot, K.A. "The Market for Catastrophe Risk: A Clinical Examination." *Journal of Financial Economics* 60 (2001): 529–571.

Litzenberger, R. H., D. R. Beaglehole, and C. E. Reynolds, "Assessing Catastrophe Reinsurance-Linked Securities as a New Asset Class." Journal of Portfolio Management (Winter 1996): 76–86.

PRACTICE QUESTIONS AND PROBLEMS
(ANSWERS AT END OF BOOK)

3.1 What is the difference between term life insurance and whole life insurance? Explain the tax advantages of whole life insurance.

3.2 Explain the meaning of variable life insurance and universal life insurance.

3.3 A life insurance company offers whole life and annuity contracts. In which contracts does it have exposure to (a) longevity risk, (b) mortality risk?

3.4 "Equitable Life gave its policyholders a free option." Explain the nature of the option.

3.5 Use Table 3.1 to calculate the minimum premium an insurance company should charge for a $1 million two-year term life insurance policy issued to a woman aged 50. Assume that the premium is paid at the beginning of each year and that the interest rate is zero.

3.6 From Table 3.1, what is the probability that a man aged 30 will live to 90? What is the same probability for a woman aged 30?

3.7 What features of the policies written by a property-casualty insurance company give rise to the most risk?

3.8 Explain how CAT bonds work.

3.9 Consider two bonds that have the same coupon, time to maturity and price. One is a B-rated corporate bond. The other is a CAT bond. An analysis based on historical data shows that the expected losses on the two bonds in each year of their life is the same. Which bond would you advise a portfolio manager to buy and why?

3.10 How does health insurance in the United States differ from that in Canada and the United Kingdom?

3.11 An insurance company decides to offer individuals insurance against losing their jobs. What problems is it likely to encounter?

3.12 Why do property-casualty insurance companies hold more capital than life insurance companies?

3.13 Explain what is meant by "loss ratio" and "expense ratio" for a property-casualty insurance company. "If an insurance company is profitable, it must be the case that the loss ratio plus the expense ratio is less than 100%." Discuss this statement.

3.14 What is the difference between a defined benefit and a defined contribution pension plan?

3.15 Suppose that in a certain defined benefit pension plan

(a) Employees work for 40 years earning wages that increase with inflation

(b) They retire with a pension equal to 75% of their final salary. This pension also increases with inflation

(c) The pension is received for 20 years

(d) The pension fund's income is invested in bonds which earn the inflation rate.

Estimate the percentage of an employee's salary that must be contributed to the pension plan if it is to remain solvent. (*Hint*: Do all calculations in real rather than nominal dollars.)

FURTHER QUESTIONS

3.16 Use Table 3.1 to calculate the minimum premium an insurance company should charge for a $5 million three-year term life insurance contract issued to a man aged 60. Assume that the premium is paid at the beginning of each year and death always takes place halfway through a year. The risk-free interest rate is 6% per annum (with semiannual compounding).

3.17 An insurance company's losses of a particular type per year are to a reasonable approximation normally distributed with a mean of $150 million and a standard deviation of $50 million. (Assume that the risks taken on by the insurance company are entirely nonsystematic.) The one-year risk-free rate is 5% per annum with annual compounding. Estimate the cost of the following:

(a) A contract that will pay in one-year's time 60% of the insurance company's costs on a pro rata basis

(b) A contract that pays $100 million in one-year's time if losses exceed $200 million.

3.18 During a certain year, interest rates fall by 200 basis points (2%) and equity prices are flat. Discuss the effect of this on a defined benefit pension plan that is 60% invested in equities and 40% invested in bonds.

3.19 Suppose that in a certain defined benefit pension plan

(a) Employees work for 45 years earning wages that increase at a real rate of 2%

(b) They retire with a pension equal to 70% of their final salary. This pension increases at the rate of inflation minus 1%.

(c) The pension is received for 18 years.

(d) The pension fund's income is invested in bonds which earn the inflation rate plus 1.5%.

Estimate the percentage of an employee's salary that must be contributed to the pension plan if it is to remain solvent. (*Hint*: Do all calculations in real rather than nominal dollars.)

CHAPTER 4

Mutual Funds and Hedge Funds

Mutual funds and hedge funds invest cash on behalf of individuals and companies. The funds from different investors are pooled and investments are chosen by the fund manager in an attempt to meet specified objectives. Mutual funds, which are called "unit trusts" in some countries, serve the needs of relatively small investors, while hedge funds seek to attract funds from wealthy individuals and large investors such as pension funds. Hedge funds are subject to much less regulation than mutual funds. They are free to use a wider range of trading strategies than mutual funds and are usually more secretive about what they do.

This chapter describes the types of mutual fund and hedge fund that exist. It examines how they are regulated and the fees they charge. It also looks at how successful they have been at producing good returns for investors.

4.1 MUTUAL FUNDS

One of the attractions of mutual funds for the small investor is the diversification opportunities they offer. As we saw in Chapter 1, diversification improves an investor's risk-return trade-off. However, it can be difficult for a small investor to hold enough stocks to be well diversified. In addition, maintaining a well-diversified portfolio can lead to high transaction costs. A mutual fund provides a way in which the resources of many small investors are pooled so that the benefits of diversification are realized at a relatively low cost.

Mutual funds have grown very fast since the Second World War. Table 4.1 shows estimates of the assets managed by mutual funds in the United States since 1940. These assets were over $12 trillion by 2011. About 50% of U.S. households own mutual funds. Some mutual funds are offered by firms that specialize in asset management, such as Fidelity. Others are offered by banks such as JPMorgan Chase. Some insurance companies also offer mutual funds. For example, in 2001 the large U.S. insurance company, State Farm, began offering 10 mutual funds throughout the United States. They can be purchased on the Internet or over the phone or through State Farm agents.

Mutual funds are regulated by the SEC in the U.S. They are required to state their objectives in a prospectus that is available to potential investors. A number of different types of funds have been created, such as:

1. Bond funds that invest in fixed income securities with a life of more than one year.

TABLE 4.1   Growth of Assets of
Mutual Funds in United States

Year	Assets ($ billions)
1940	0.5
1960	17.0
1980	134.8
2000	6,964.6
2011	12,224.3

Source: Investment Company Institute.

2. Equity funds that invest in common and preferred stock.
3. Hybrid funds that invest in stocks, bonds, and other securities.
4. Money market funds that invest in interest-bearing instruments with a life of less than one year.
5. Index funds that are passively managed and designed to match the performance of a market index such as the S&P 500.

An investor in a mutual fund owns a certain number of shares in the fund. The most common type of mutual fund is an *open-end fund*. This means that the total number of shares outstanding goes up as investors buy more shares and down as shares are redeemed. Mutual funds are valued at 4 P.M. each day. This involves the mutual fund manager calculating the market value of each asset in the portfolio so that the total value of the fund is determined. This total value is divided by the number of shares outstanding to obtain the value of each share. The latter is referred to as the *net asset value* (NAV) of the fund. Shares in the fund can be bought from the fund or sold back to the fund at any time. When an investor issues instructions to buy or sell shares, it is the next-calculated NAV that applies to the transaction. For example, if an investor decides to buy at 2 P.M. on a particular business day, the NAV at 4 P.M. on that day determines the amount paid by the investor.

The investor usually pays tax as though he or she owned the securities in which the fund has invested. Thus, when the fund receives a dividend, an investor in the fund has to pay tax on the investor's share of the dividend, even if the dividend is reinvested in the fund for the investor. When the fund sells securities, the investor is deemed to have realized an immediate capital gain or loss, even if the investor has not sold any of his or her shares in the fund. Suppose the investor buys shares at $100 and the trading by the fund leads to a capital gain of $20 per share in the first year and a capital loss of $25 per share in the second year. The investor has to declare a capital gain of $20 in the first year and a loss of $25 in the second year. When the investor sells the shares, there is also a capital gain or loss. To avoid double counting, the purchase price of the shares is adjusted to reflect the capital gains and losses that have already accrued to the investor. Thus, if in our example the investor sold shares in the fund after the end of the first year, the purchase price would be assumed to be $120 for the purpose of calculating capital gains or losses on the transaction; if the investor sold the shares in the fund after the end of the second year, the purchase price would be assumed to be $95 for the purpose of calculating capital gains or losses on the transaction.

Index Funds

Some funds are designed to track a particular equity index such as the S&P 500 and the FTSE 100. The tracking can most simply be achieved by buying all the shares in the index in amounts that reflect their weight. For example, if IBM has 1% weight in a particular index, 1% of the tracking portfolio for the index would be invested in IBM stock. Another way of achieving tracking is to choose a smaller portfolio of representative shares that has been shown by research to track the chosen portfolio closely. Yet another way is to use index futures.

One of the first index funds was launched in the United States on December 31, 1975, by John Bogle to track the S&P 500. It started with only $11 million of assets and was initially ridiculed as being "un-American" and "Bogle's folly." However, it was later renamed the Vanguard 500 Index Fund and the assets under administration reached $100 billion in November 1999.

How accurately do index funds track the index? Two relevant measures are the *tracking error* and the *expense ratio*. The tracking error of a fund is usually defined as the standard deviation of the difference between the fund's return per year and the index return per year. The expense ratio is the fee charged per year, as a percentage of assets, for administering the fund. A survey in 2010 by the organization Morningstar, which monitors mutual funds, found that index funds had tracking errors that averaged 0.29% and expense ratios than averaged 0.38%.

Costs

Mutual funds incur a number of different costs. These include management expenses, sales commissions, accounting and other administrative costs, transactions costs on trades, and so on. To recoup these costs, and to make a profit, fees are charged to investors. A *front-end load* is a fee charged when an investor first buys shares in a mutual fund. Not all funds charge this type of fee. Those that do are referred to as front-end loaded. In the United States, front-end loads are restricted to being less than 8.5% of the investment. Some funds charge fees when an investor sells shares. These are referred to as a *back-end load*. Typically the back-end load declines with the length of time the shares in the fund have been held. All funds charge an annual fee. There may be separate fees to cover management expenses, distribution costs, and so on. The *total expense ratio* is the total of the annual fees charged per share divided by the value of the share.

Khorana et al. (2009) compared the mutual fund fees in 18 different countries.[1] They assumed in their analysis that a fund is kept for five years. The "total shareholder cost" per year is calculated as

$$\text{Total expense ratio} + \frac{\text{Front-end load}}{5} + \frac{\text{Back-end load}}{5}$$

Their results are summarized in Table 4.2. The average fees for equity funds vary from 1.41% in Australia to 3.00% in Canada. Fees for equity funds are on average

---

[1] See A. Khorana, H. Servaes, and P. Tufano, "Mutual Fund Fees Around the World," *Review of Financial Studies* 22 (March 2009): 1279–1310.

TABLE 4.2   Average Total Cost per Year When Mutual
Fund is Held for Five Years (% of Assets)

Country	Bond Funds	Equity Funds
Australia	0.75	1.41
Austria	1.55	2.37
Belgium	1.60	2.27
Canada	1.84	3.00
Denmark	1.91	2.62
Finland	1.76	2.77
France	1.57	2.31
Germany	1.48	2.29
Italy	1.56	2.58
Luxembourg	1.62	2.43
Netherlands	1.73	2.46
Norway	1.77	2.67
Spain	1.58	2.70
Sweden	1.67	2.47
Switzerland	1.61	2.40
United Kingdom	1.73	2.48
United States	<u>1.05</u>	<u>1.53</u>
Average	1.39	2.09

Source: Khorana, Servaes, and Tufano, "Mutual Fund Fees
Around the World," *Review of Financial Studies* 22 (March
2009): 1279–1310.

about 50% higher than for bond funds. Index funds tend to have lower fees than
regular funds because no highly paid stock pickers or analysts are required. For some
index funds in the United States, fees are as low as 0.15% per year.

Closed-End Funds

The funds we have talked about so far are open-end funds. These are by far the most
common type of fund. The number of shares outstanding varies from day to day
as individuals choose to invest in the fund or redeem their shares. Closed-end funds
are like regular corporations and have a fixed number of shares outstanding. The
shares of the fund are traded on a stock exchange. For closed-end funds, two NAVs
can be calculated. One is the price at which the shares of the fund are trading. The
other is the market value of the fund's portfolio divided by the number of shares
outstanding. The latter can be referred to as the fair market value. Usually a closed-
end fund's share price is less than its fair market value. A number of researchers have
investigated the reason for this. Research by Ross (2002) suggests that the fees paid
to fund managers provide the explanation.[2]

---

[2] See S. Ross, "Neoclassical Finance, Alternative Finance, and the Closed End Fund
Puzzle,"*European Financial Management* 8 (2002): 129–137.

ETFs

Exchange-traded funds (ETFs) have existed in the United States since 1993 and in Europe since 1999. They usually track an index and so are an alternative to an index mutual fund for investors who are comfortable earning a return that is designed to mirror the index. One of the most widely known ETFs, called the Spider, tracks the S&P 500 and trades under the symbol SPY. In a survey of investment professionals conducted in March 2008, 67% called ETFs the most innovative investment vehicle of the last two decades and 60% reported that ETFs have fundamentally changed the way they construct investment portfolios. In 2008, the SEC in the United States authorized the creation of actively managed ETFs. ETFs came under scrutiny in 2011 because of their role in the trading activities of Kweku Adoboli, who lost $2.3 billion for UBS.

ETFs are created by institutional investors. Typically an institutional investor deposits a block of securities with the ETF and obtains shares in the ETF (known as *creation units*) in return. Some or all of the shares in the ETF are then traded on a stock exchange. This gives ETFs the characteristics of a closed-end fund rather than an open-end fund. However, a key feature of ETFs is that institutional investors can exchange large blocks of shares in the ETF for the assets underlying the shares at that time. They can give up shares they hold in the ETF and receive the assets or they can deposit new assets and receive new shares. This ensures that there is never any appreciable difference between the price at which shares in the ETF are trading on the stock exchange and their fair market value. This is a key difference between ETFs and closed-end funds and makes ETFs more attractive to investors than closed-end funds.

ETFs have a number of advantages over open-end mutual funds. ETFs can be bought or sold at any time of the day. They can be shorted in the same way that shares in any stock are shorted. (See Chapter 5 for a discussion of short selling.) ETF holdings are disclosed twice a day, giving investors full knowledge of the assets underlying the fund. Mutual funds by contrast only have to disclose their holdings relatively infrequently. When shares in a mutual fund are sold, managers often have to sell the stocks in which the fund has invested to raise the cash that is paid to the investor. When shares in the ETF are sold, this is not necessary as another investor is providing the cash. This means that transactions costs are saved and there are less unplanned capital gains and losses passed on to shareholders. Finally, the expense ratios of ETFs tend to be less than those of mutual funds.

Mutual Fund Returns

Do actively managed mutual funds outperform stock indices such as the S&P 500? Some funds in some years do very well, but this could be the result of good luck rather than good investment management. Two key questions for researchers are:

1. Do actively managed funds outperform stock indices on average?
2. Do funds that outperform the market in one year continue to do so?

The answer to both questions appears to be no. In a classic study, Jensen (1969) performed tests on mutual fund performance using 10 years of data on 115 funds.[3]

---

[3] See M. C. Jensen, "Risk, the Pricing of Capital Assets and the Evaluation of Investment Portfolios," *Journal of Business* 42 (April 1969): 167–247.

TABLE 4.3 Consistency of Good Performance By
Mutual Funds

Number of Consecutive Years of Positive Alpha	Number of Observations	Percentage of Observations When Next Alpha Is Positive
1	574	50.4
2	312	52.0
3	161	53.4
4	79	55.8
5	41	46.4
6	17	35.3

He calculated the alpha for each fund in each year. (As explained in Section 1.3, alpha is the return earned in excess of that predicted by the capital asset pricing model.) The average alpha of all funds was slightly negative, even before management costs were taken into account. Jensen tested whether funds with positive alphas tended to continue to earn positive alphas. His results are summarized in Table 4.3. The first row shows that 574 positive alphas were observed from the 1,150 observations (close to 50%). Of these positive alphas, 50.4% were followed by another year of positive alpha. Row two shows that, when two years of positive alphas have been observed, there is a 52% chance that the next year will have a positive alpha, and so on. The results show that, when a manager has achieved above average returns for one year (or several years in a row), there is still only a probability of about 50% of achieving above average returns the next year. The results suggest that managers who obtain positive alphas do so because of luck rather than skill. It is possible that there are some managers who are able to perform consistently above average, but they are a very small percentage of the total. More recent studies have confirmed Jensen's conclusions. On average, mutual fund managers do not beat the market and past performance is not a good guide to future performance. The success of index funds shows that this research has influenced the views of many investors.

Mutual funds frequently advertise impressive returns. However, the fund being featured might be one fund out of many offered by the same organization that happens to have produced returns well above the average for the market. Distinguishing between good luck and good performance is always tricky. Suppose an asset management company has 32 funds following different trading strategies and assume that the fund managers have no particular skills, so that the return of each fund has a 50% chance of being greater than the market each year. The probability of a particular fund beating the market every year for the next five years is $(1/2)^5$ or 1/32. This means that by chance one out of the 32 funds will show a great performance over the five-year period!

One point should be made about the way returns over several years are expressed. One mutual fund might advertise "The average of the returns per year that we have achieved over the last five years is 15%." Another might say "If you had invested your money in our mutual fund for the last five years your money would have grown at 15% per year." These statements sound the same, but are actually different, as illustrated by Business Snapshot 4.1. In many countries, regulators have strict rules to ensure that mutual fund returns are not reported in a misleading way.

BUSINESS SNAPSHOT 4.1

Mutual Fund Returns Can Be Misleading

Suppose that the following is a sequence of returns per annum reported by a mutual fund manager over the last five years (measured using annual compounding):

$$15\%, \quad 20\%, \quad 30\%, \quad -20\%, \quad 25\%$$

The arithmetic mean of the returns, calculated by taking the sum of the returns and dividing by 5, is 14%. However, an investor would actually earn less than 14% per annum by leaving the money invested in the fund for five years. The dollar value of $100 at the end of the five years would be

$$100 \times 1.15 \times 1.20 \times 1.30 \times 0.80 \times 1.25 = \$179.40$$

By contrast, a 14% return (with annual compounding) would give

$$100 \times 1.14^5 = \$192.54$$

The return that gives $179.40 at the end of five years is 12.4%. This is because

$$100 \times (1.124)^5 = 179.40$$

What average return should the fund manager report? It is tempting for the manager to make a statement such as: "The average of the returns per year that we have realized in the last five years is 14%." Although true, this is misleading. It is much less misleading to say: "The average return realized by someone who invested with us for the last five years is 12.4% per year." In some jurisdictions, regulations require fund managers to report returns the second way.

This phenomenon is an example of a result that is well known by mathematicians. The geometric mean of a set of numbers (not all the same) is always less than the arithmetic mean. In our example, the return multipliers each year are 1.15, 1.20, 1.30, 0.80, and 1.25. The arithmetic mean of these numbers is 1.140, but the geometric mean is only 1.124. An investor who keeps an investment for several years earns the geometric mean of the returns per year, not the arithmetic mean.

Regulation and Mutual Fund Scandals

Because they solicit funds from small retail customers, many of whom are unsophisticated, mutual funds are heavily regulated. The SEC is the primary regulator of mutual funds in the United States. Mutual funds must file a registration document with the SEC. Full and accurate financial information must be provided to prospective fund purchasers in a prospectus. There are rules to prevent conflicts of interest, fraud, and excessive fees.

Despite the regulations, there have been a number of scandals involving mutual funds. One of these involves *late trading*. As mentioned earlier in this chapter, if a request to buy or sell mutual fund shares is placed by an investor with a broker by 4 P.M. on any given business day, it is the NAV of the fund at 4 P.M. that determines the price that is paid or received by the investor. In practice, for various reasons, an order to buy or sell is sometimes not passed from a broker to a mutual fund until later than 4 P.M. This allows brokers to collude with investors and submit new orders or change existing orders after 4 P.M. The NAV of the fund at 4 P.M. still applies to the investors—even though they may be using information on market movements (particularly movements in overseas markets) after 4 P.M. Late trading is not permitted under SEC regulations and there were a number of prosecutions in the early 2000s that led to multi-million-dollar payments and employees being fired.

Another scandal is known as *market timing*. This is a practice where favored clients are allowed to buy and sell mutual funds shares frequently (e.g., every few days) without penalty. One reason why they might want to do this is because they are indulging in the illegal practice of late trading. Another reason is that they are analyzing the impact of stocks whose prices have not been updated recently on the fund's NAV. Suppose that the price of a stock has not been updated for several hours. (This could be because it does not trade frequently or because it trades on an exchange in a country in a different time zone.) If the U.S. market has gone up (down) in the last few hours, the calculated NAV is likely to understate (overstate) the value of the underlying portfolio and there is a short-term trading opportunity. Taking advantage of this is not necessarily illegal. However, it may be illegal for the mutual fund to offer special trading privileges to favored customers because the costs (such as those associated with providing the liquidity necessary to accommodate frequent redemptions) are borne by all customers.

Other scandals have involved *front running* and *directed brokerage*. Front running occurs when a mutual fund is planning a big trade that is expected to move the market. It informs favored customers or partners before executing the trade, allowing them to trade for their own account first. Directed brokerage involves an improper arrangement between a mutual fund and a brokerage house where the brokerage house recommends the mutual fund to clients in return for receiving orders from the mutual fund for stock and bond purchases.

4.2 HEDGE FUNDS

Hedge funds are different from mutual funds in that they are subject to very little regulation. This is because they only accept funds from financially sophisticated individuals and organizations. Examples of the regulations that affect mutual funds are the requirements that:

1. Shares be redeemable at any time
2. NAV be calculated daily
3. Investment policies be disclosed
4. The use of leverage be limited

Hedge funds are largely free from these regulations. This gives them a great deal of freedom to develop sophisticated, unconventional, and proprietary investment strategies. Hedge funds are sometimes referred to as *alternative investments*.

The first hedge fund, A. W. Jones & Co., was created by Alfred Winslow Jones in the United States in 1949. It was structured as a general partnership to avoid SEC regulations. Jones combined long positions in stocks considered to be undervalued with short positions in stocks considered to be overvalued. He used leverage to magnify returns. A performance fee equal to 20% of profits was charged to investors. The fund performed well and the term "hedge fund" was coined in a newspaper article written about A. W. Jones & Co. by Carol Loomis in 1966. The article showed that the fund's performance after allowing for fees was better than the most successful mutual funds. Not surprisingly, the article led to a great deal of interest in hedge funds and their investment approach. Other hedge fund pioneers were George Soros, Walter J. Schloss, and Julian Robertson.[4]

The term "hedge fund" implies that risks are being hedged. The trading strategy of Jones did involve hedging. He had little exposure to the overall direction of the market because his long position (in stocks considered to be undervalued) at any given time was about the same size as his short position (in stocks considered to be overvalued). However, for some hedge funds, the word "hedge" is inappropriate because they take aggressive bets on the future direction of the market with no particular hedging policy.

Hedge funds have grown in popularity over the years. The year 2008 was not a good year for hedge fund returns, but it is estimated that at the end of the year over $1 trillion was still invested with hedge fund managers throughout the world. Many hedge funds are registered in tax-favorable jurisdictions. For example, over 30% of hedge funds are domiciled in the Cayman Islands. *Funds of funds* have been set up to allocate funds to different hedge funds. Hedge funds are difficult to ignore. It has been estimated that they account for 40% to 50% of the daily turnover on the New York and London stock exchanges, 70% of the volume of convertible bond trading, 20% to 30% of the volume of credit default swap trading, 82% of the volume of trading in U.S. distressed debt, 33% of the trading in non-investment grade bonds. They are also very active participants in the ETF market, often taking short positions.

Fees

One characteristic of hedge funds that distinguishes them from mutual funds is that fees are higher and dependent on performance. An annual management fee that is usually between 1% and 3% of assets under management is charged. This is designed to meet operating costs—but there may be an additional fee for such things as audits, account administration, and trader bonuses. Moreover, an incentive fee that

---

[4] The famous Warren Buffett of Omaha can also be considered to be a hedge fund pioneer. In 1956, he started Buffett partnership LP with seven limited partners and $100,100. Buffett charged his partners 25% of profits above a hurdle rate of 25%. He specialized in special situations, merger arbitrage, spin offs, and distressed debt opportunities and earned an average of 29.5% per year. The partnership was disbanded 1969 and Berkshire Hathaway (a holding company, not a hedge fund) was formed.

is usually between 15% and 30% of realized profits (if any) after management fees are charged. This fee structure is designed to attract the most talented and sophisticated investment managers. Thus, a typical hedge fund fee schedule might be expressed as "2 plus 20%" indicating that the fund charges 2% per year of assets under management and 20% of profit. On top of high fees there is usually a lock up period of at least one year during which invested funds cannot be withdrawn. Some hedge funds with good track records have sometimes charged much more than the average. Steve Cohen's SAC Capital Partners has charged as much as "3 plus 35%" and Jim Simons' Renaissance Technologies Corp. has charged as much as "5 plus 44%."

The agreements offered by hedge funds may include clauses that make the incentive fees more palatable. For example:

1. There is sometimes a *hurdle rate*. This is the minimum return necessary for the incentive fee to be applicable.
2. There is sometimes a *high-water mark clause*. This states that any previous losses must be recouped by new profits before an incentive fee applies. Because different investors place money with the fund at different times, the high-water mark is not necessarily the same for all investors. There may be a *proportional adjustment clause* stating that, if funds are withdrawn by investors, the amount of previous losses that has to be recouped is adjusted proportionally. Suppose a fund worth $200 million loses $40 million and $80 million of funds are withdrawn. The high-water mark clause on its own would require $40 million of profits on the remaining $80 million to be achieved before the incentive fee applied. The proportional adjustment clause would reduce this to $20 million because the fund is only half as big as it was when the loss was incurred.
3. There is sometimes a *clawback clause* that allows investors to apply part or all of previous incentive fees to current losses. A portion of the incentive fees paid by the investor each year is then retained in a *recovery account*. This account is used to compensate investors for a percentage of any future losses.

Some hedge fund managers have become very rich from the generous fee schedules. In 2010, hedge fund managers reported as earning over $1 billion were John Paulson of Paulson and Co., Ray Dalio of Bridgewater Associates, Jim Simons of Renaissance Technologies (a former math professor), David Tepper of Appaloosa Management, Steve Cohen of SAC Capital, and Eddie Lampert of ESL Investments.

If an investor has a portfolio of investments in hedge funds, the fees paid can be quite high. As a simple example, suppose that an investment is divided equally between two funds, A and B. Both funds charge 2 plus 20%. In the first year, Fund A earns 20% while Fund B earns −10%. The investor's average return on investment before fees is 0.5 × 20% + 0.5 × (−10%) or 5%. The fees paid to fund A are 2% + 0.2 × (20 − 2)% or 5.6%. The fees paid to Fund B are 2%. The average fee paid on the investment in the hedge funds is therefore 3.8%. The investor is left with a 1.2% return. This is half what the investor would get if 2 plus 20% were applied to the overall 5% return.

When a fund of funds is involved, there is an extra layer of fees and the investor's return after fees is even worse. A typical fee charged by a fund of hedge funds used to be 1% of assets under management plus 10% of the net (after incentive fees and management fees) profits of the hedge funds they invest in. Suppose a fund of hedge funds divides its money equally between 10 hedge funds. All charge 2 plus 20% and the fund of hedge funds charges 1 plus 10%. It sounds as though the investor pays 3 plus 30%—but it can be much more than this. Suppose that five of the hedge funds lose 40% and the other five make 40%. An incentive fee of 20% of 38% or 7.6% has to be paid to each of the profitable hedge funds. The total incentive fee paid to all hedge funds is therefore 3.8% of the funds invested. In addition there is a 2% annual fee paid to the hedge funds and 1% annual fee paid to the fund of funds. The investor's net return is −6.8% of the amount invested. (This is 6.8% less than the return on the underlying assets before fees.) The fees charged by funds of hedge funds have declined sharply as a result of poor performance in 2008 and 2011.

Incentives of Hedge Fund Managers

The fee structure gives hedge fund managers an incentive to make a profit. But it also encourages them to take risks. The hedge fund manager has a call option on the assets of the fund. As is well known, the value of a call option increases as the volatility of the underlying assets increases. This means that the hedge fund manager can increase the value of the option by taking risks that increase the volatility of the fund's assets.

Suppose that a hedge fund manager is presented with an opportunity where there is a 0.4 probability of a 60% profit and a 0.6 probability of a 60% loss with the fees earned by the hedge fund manager being 2 plus 20%. The expected return of the investment is

$$0.4 \times 60 + 0.6 \times (-60)$$

or −12%.

Even though this is a terrible expected return, the hedge fund manager might be tempted to accept the investment. If the investment produces a 60% profit, the hedge fund's fee is $2 + 0.2 \times 58$ or 13.6%. If the investment produces a 60% loss, the hedge fund's fee is 2%. The expected fee to the hedge fund is therefore

$$0.4 \times 13.6 + 0.6 \times 2 = 6.64$$

or 6.64% of the funds under administration. The expected management fee is 2% and the expected incentive fee is 4.64%.

To the investors in the hedge fund, the expected return is

$$0.4 \times (0.8 \times 58) + 0.6 \times (-60 - 2) = -18.64$$

or −18.64%.

The example is summarized in Table 4.4. It shows that the fee structure of a hedge fund gives its managers an incentive to take high risks even when expected returns are negative. The incentives may be reduced by hurdle rates, high-water mark clauses, and clawback clauses. However, these clauses are not always as useful to investors as they sound. One reason is that investors have to continue to invest with the fund to take advantage of them. Another is that, as losses mount up for a hedge fund, the managers have an incentive to wind up the hedge fund and start a new one.

TABLE 4.4   Return from a High Risk Investment where
Returns of +60% and –60% Have Probabilities of 0.4 and
0.6, Respectively

Expected return to hedge fund	6.64%
Expected return to investors	−18.64%
Overall expected return	−12.00%

The Hedge Fund Charges 2 plus 20%.

The incentives we are talking about here are real. Imagine how you would feel as an investor in the hedge fund, Amaranth. One of its traders, Brian Hunter, liked to make huge bets on the price of natural gas. Until 2006, his bets were largely right and as a result he was regarded as a star trader. His remuneration including bonuses is reputed to have been close to $100 million in 2005. During 2006, his bets proved wrong and Amaranth, which had about $9 billion of assets under administration, lost a massive $6.5 billion. (This was even more than the loss of Long-Term Capital Management in 1998.) Brian Hunter did not have to return the bonuses he had previously earned. Instead, he left Amaranth and tried to start his own hedge fund.

It is interesting to note that, in theory, two individuals can create a money machine as follows. One starts a hedge fund with a certain high risk (and secret) investment strategy. The other starts a hedge fund with an investment strategy that is the opposite of that followed by the first hedge fund. For example, if the first hedge fund decides to buy $1 million of silver, the second hedge fund shorts this amount of silver. At the time they start the funds, the two individuals enter into an agreement to share the incentive fees. One hedge fund (we do not know which one) will do well and earn good incentive fees. The other will do badly and earn no incentive fees. Provided that they can find investors for their funds, they have a money machine!

Prime Brokers

Prime brokers are the banks that offer services to hedge funds. Typically a hedge fund, when it is first started, will choose a particular bank as its prime broker. This bank handles the hedge fund's trades (which may be with itself or with other financial institutions), carries out calculations each day to determine the collateral the hedge fund has to provide, borrows securities for the hedge fund when it wants to take short positions, provides cash management and portfolio reporting services, and makes loans to the hedge fund. In some cases, the prime broker provides risk management and consulting services and introduces the hedge fund to potential investors. The prime broker has a good understanding of the hedge fund's portfolio and will typically carry out stress tests on the portfolio to decide how much leverage it is prepared to offer the fund.

As a hedge fund gets larger, it is likely to use more than one prime broker. This means that no one bank sees all its trades and has a complete understanding of its portfolio. The opportunity of transacting business with more than one prime broker gives a hedge fund more negotiating clout to reduce the fees it pays. Goldman Sachs,

Morgan Stanley, and many other large banks offer prime broker services to hedge funds and find them to be an important contributor to their profits.[5]

Although hedge funds are not heavily regulated, they do have to answer to their prime brokers. A hedge fund is often highly leveraged and has to post collateral with its prime brokers. When it loses money, more collateral has to be posted. If it cannot post more collateral, it has no choice but to close out its trades. One thing the hedge fund has to think about is the possibility that it will enter into a trade that is correct in the long term, but loses money in the short term. Consider a hedge fund that in early 2008 thinks credit spreads are too high. It might be tempted to take a highly leveraged position where BBB-rated bonds are bought and Treasury bonds are shorted. However, there is the danger that credit spreads will increase before they decrease. In this case, the hedge fund might run out of collateral and be forced to close out its position at a huge loss.

4.3 HEDGE FUND STRATEGIES

In this section we will discuss some of the strategies followed by hedge funds. Our classification is similar to the one used by Dow Jones Credit Suisse, which provides indices tracking hedge fund performance. Not all hedge funds can be classified in the way indicated. Some follow more than one of the strategies mentioned and some follow strategies that are not listed. (For example, there are funds specializing in weather derivatives.)

Long/Short Equity

As described earlier, long/short equity strategies were used by hedge fund pioneer Alfred Winslow Jones. They continue to be among the most popular of hedge fund strategies. The hedge fund manager identifies a set of stocks that are considered to be undervalued by the market and a set that are considered to be overvalued. The manager takes a long position in the first set and a short position in the second set. Typically, the hedge fund has to pay the prime broker 1% per year to rent the shares that are borrowed for the short position. (See Chapter 5 for a discussion of short selling.)

Long/short equity strategies are all about stock picking. If the overvalued and undervalued stocks have been picked well, the strategies should give good returns in both bull and bear markets. Hedge fund managers often concentrate on smaller stocks that are not well covered by analysts and research the stocks extensively using fundamental analysis, as pioneered by Benjamin Graham. The hedge fund manager may choose to maintain a net long bias where the shorts are of smaller magnitude than the longs or a net short bias where the reverse is true. Alfred Winslow Jones maintained a net long bias in his successful use of long/short equity strategies.

---

[5] Although a bank is taking some risks when it lends to a hedge fund, it is also true that a hedge fund is taking some risks when it chooses a prime broker. Many hedge funds that chose Lehman Brothers as their prime broker found that they could not access their assets when Lehman Brothers went bankrupt in 2008.

An *equity-market-neutral* fund uses a long/short strategy, but has no net long or net short bias. A *dollar-neutral* fund is an equity-market-neutral fund where the dollar amount of the long position equals the dollar amount of the short position. A *beta-neutral fund* is a more sophisticated equity-market-neutral fund where the weighted average beta of the shares in the long portfolio equals the weighted average beta of the shares in the short portfolio so that the overall beta of the portfolio is zero. If the capital asset pricing model is true, the beta-neutral fund should be totally insensitive to market movements. Long and short positions in index futures are sometimes used to maintain a beta-neutral position.

Sometimes equity market neutral funds go one step further. They maintain *sector neutrality* where long and short positions are balanced by industry sectors or *factor neutrality* where the exposure to factors such as the price of oil, the level of interest rates, or the rate of inflation is neutralized.

Dedicated Short

Managers of dedicated short funds look exclusively for overvalued companies and sell them short. They are attempting to take advantage of the fact that brokers and analysts are reluctant to issue sell recommendations—even though one might reasonably expect the number of companies overvalued by the stock market to be approximately the same as the number of companies undervalued at any given time. Typically, the companies chosen are those with weak financials, those that change their auditors regularly, those that delay filing reports with the SEC, companies in industries with overcapacity, companies suing or attempting to silence their short sellers, and so on.

Distressed Securities

Bonds with credit ratings of BB or lower are known as "non-investment-grade" or "junk" bonds. Those with a credit rating of CCC are referred to as "distressed" and those with a credit rating of D are in default. Typically, distressed bonds sell at a big discount to their par value and provide a yield that is over 1,000 basis points (10%) more than the yield on Treasury bonds. Of course, an investor only earns this yield if the required interest and principal payments are actually made.

The managers of funds specializing in distressed securities calculate carefully a fair value for distressed securities by considering possible future scenarios and their probabilities. Distressed debt cannot usually be shorted and so they are searching for debt that is undervalued by the market. Bankruptcy proceedings usually lead to a reorganization or liquidation of a company. The fund managers understand the legal system, know priorities in the event of liquidation, estimate recovery rates, consider actions likely to be taken by management, and so on.

Some funds are passive investors. They buy distressed debt when the price is below its fair value and wait. Other hedge funds adopt an active approach. They might purchase a sufficiently large position in outstanding debt claims so that they have the right to influence a reorganization proposal. In Chapter 11 reorganizations in the United States, each class of claims must approve a reorganization proposal with a two-thirds majority. This means that one-third of an outstanding issue can be sufficent to stop a reorganization proposed by management or other stakeholders.

In a reorganization of a company, the equity is often worthless and the outstanding debt is converted into new equity. Sometimes, the goal of an active manager is to buy more than one-third of the debt, obtain control of a target company, and then find a way to extract wealth from it.

Merger Arbitrage

Merger arbitrage involves trading after a merger or acquisition is announced in the hope that the announced deal will take place. There are two main types of deals: cash deals and share-for-share exchanges.

Consider first cash deals. Suppose that Company A announces that it is prepared to acquire all the shares of Company B for $30 per share. Suppose the shares of Company B were trading at $20 prior to the announcement. Immediately after the announcement its share price might jump to $28. It does not jump immediately to $30 because (a) there is some chance that the deal will not go through and (b) it may take some time for the full impact of the deal to be reflected in market prices. Merger-arbitrage hedge funds buy the shares in company B for $28 and wait. If the acquisition goes through at $30, the fund makes a profit of $2 per share. If it goes through at a higher price, the profit is bigger. However, if for any reason the deal does not go through, the hedge fund will take a loss.

Consider next a share-for-share exchange. Suppose that Company A announces that it is willing to exchange one of its shares for four of Company B's shares. Assume that Company B's shares were trading at 15% of the price of Company A's shares prior to the announcement. After the announcement, Company B's share price might rise to 22% of Company A's share price. A merger-arbitrage hedge fund would buy a certain amount of Company B's stock and at the same time short a quarter as much of Company A's stock. This strategy generates a profit if the deal goes ahead at the announced share-for-share exchange ratio or one that is more favorable to Company B.

Merger-arbitrage hedge funds can generate steady, but not stellar, returns. It is important to distinguish merger arbitrage from the activities of Ivan Boesky and others who used inside information to trade before mergers became public knowledge.[6] Trading on inside information is illegal. Ivan Boesky was sentenced to three years in prison and fined $100 million.

Convertible Arbitrage

Convertible bonds are bonds that can be converted into the equity of the bond issuer at certain specified future times with the number of shares received in exchange for a bond possibly depending on the time of the conversion. The issuer usually has the right to call the bond (i.e., buy it back a prespecified price) in certain circumstances. Usually, the issuer announces its intention to call the bond as a way of forcing the holder to convert the bond into equity immediately. (If the bond is not called, the holder is likely to postpone the decision to convert it into equity for as long as possible.)

---

[6] The Michael Douglas character of Gordon Gekko in the award winning movie *Wall Street* was based on Ivan Boesky.

A convertible arbitrage hedge fund has typically developed a sophisticated model for valuing convertible bonds. The convertible bond price depends in a complex way on the price of the underlying equity, its volatility, the level of interest rates, and the chance of the issuer defaulting. Many convertible bonds trade at prices below their fair value. Hedge fund managers buy the bond and then hedge their risks by shorting the stock. (This is an application of delta hedging that will be discussed in Chapter 7.) Interest rate risk and credit risk can be hedged by shorting nonconvertible bonds that are issued by the company that issued the convertible bond. Alternatively, the managers can take positions in interest rate futures contracts, asset swaps, and credit default swaps to accomplish this hedging.

Fixed Income Arbitrage

The basic tool of fixed income trading is the zero-coupon yield curve, the construction of which is discussed in Appendix B. One strategy followed by hedge funds that engage in fixed income arbitrage is a *relative value* strategy, where they buy bonds that the zero-coupon yield curve indicates are undervalued by the market and sell bonds that it indicates are overvalued. *Market-neutral* strategies are similar to relative value strategies except that the hedge fund manager tries to ensure that the fund has no exposure to interest rate movements.

Some fixed-income hedge fund managers follow directional strategies where they take a position based on a belief that a certain spread between interest rates, or interest rates themselves, will move in a certain direction. Usually they have a lot of leverage and have to post collateral. They are therefore taking the risk that they are right in the long term, but that the market moves against them in the short term so that they cannot post collateral and are forced to close out their positions at a loss. This is what happened to Long-Term Capital Management (see Business Snapshot 19.1).

Emerging Markets

Emerging market hedge funds specialize in investments associated with developing countries. Some of these funds focus on equity investments. They screen emerging market companies looking for shares that are overvalued or undervalued. They gather information by traveling, attending conferences, meeting with analysts, talking to management, and employing consultants. Usually they invest in securities trading on the local exchange, but sometimes they use American Depository Receipts (ADRs). ADRs are certificates issued in the United States and traded on a U.S. exchange. They are backed by shares of a foreign company. ADRs may have better liquidity and lower transactions costs than the underlying foreign shares. Sometimes there are price discrepancies between ADRs and the underlying shares giving rise to arbitrage opportunities.

Another type of investment is debt issued by an emerging market country. Eurobonds are bonds issued by the country and denominated in a hard currency such as the U.S. dollar or the euro. Brady bonds are dollar-denominated bonds backed by the U.S. Treasury. Local currency bonds are bonds denominated in the local currency. Hedge funds invest in all three types of bond. Both Eurobonds and local currency bonds are risky. Countries such as Russia, Argentina, Brazil, and Venezuela have defaulted many times on their debt.

Global Macro

Global macro is the hedge fund strategy use by star managers such as George Soros and Julian Robertson. Global macro hedge fund managers carry out trades that reflect global macroeconomic trends. They look for situations where markets have, for whatever reason, moved away from equilibrium and place large bets that they will move back into equilibrium. Often the bets are on exchange rates and interest rates. A global macro strategy was used in 1992 when George Soros's Quantum Fund gained $1 billion by betting that the British pound would decrease in value. More recently, hedge funds have (with mixed results) placed bets that the huge U.S. balance of payments would cause the value of the U.S. dollar to decline. The main problem for global macro funds is that they do not know when equilibrium will be restored. World markets can for various reasons be in disequilibrium for long periods of time.

Managed Futures

Hedge fund managers that use managed futures strategies attempt to predict future movements in commodity prices. Some rely on the manager's judgment; others use computer programs to generate trades. Some managers base their trading on technical analysis, which analyzes past price patterns to predict the future. Others use fundamental analysis, which involves calculating a fair value for the commodity from economic, political, and other relevant factors.

When technical analysis is used, trading rules are usually first tested on historical data. This is known as back-testing. If (as is often the case) a trading rule has come from an analysis of past data, trading rules should be tested out of sample (that is, on data that are different from the data used to generate the rules). Analysts should be aware of the perils of data mining. Analysts have been known to generate thousands of different trading rules and then test them on historical data. Just by chance a few of the trading rules will perform very well—but this does not mean that they will perform well in the future.

4.4 HEDGE FUND PERFORMANCE

It is not as easy to assess hedge fund performance as it is to assess mutual fund performance. There is no data set that records the returns of all hedge funds. For the Tass hedge funds database, which is available to researchers, participation by hedge funds is voluntary. Small hedge funds and those with poor track records often do not report their returns and are therefore not included in the data set. When returns are reported by a hedge fund, the database is usually backfilled with the fund's previous returns. This creates a bias in the returns that are in the data set because, as just mentioned, the hedge funds that decide to start providing data are likely to be the ones doing well. When this bias is removed, some researchers have argued, hedge fund returns are no better than mutual fund returns, particularly when fees are taken into account.

Arguably, hedge funds can improve the risk-return trade-offs available to pension plans. This is because pension plans cannot (or choose not to) take short positions, obtain leverage, invest in derivatives, and engage in many of the complex trades that

TABLE 4.5 Hedge Fund Performance

Category	2010 Return per Annum	2004–2010 Return per Annum	Standard Deviation of Monthly Returns (Annualized)	Sharpe Ratio
Convertible arbitrage	10.95%	7.87%	7.08%	0.63
Dedicated short bias	−22.47%	−3.81%	17.05%	−0.42
Emerging markets	11.34%	8.22%	15.22%	0.32
Equity market neutral	−0.85%	5.09%	10.64%	0.16
Event driven	12.63%	10.38%	6.11%	1.15
Fixed income arbitrage	12.51%	5.26%	5.93%	0.32
Global macro	13.47%	12.47%	10.03%	0.91
Long/short equity	9.28%	10.24%	9.97%	0.69
Managed futures	12.22%	6.63%	11.80%	0.28
Multi-strategy	9.29%	8.22%	5.45%	0.89
Hedge fund index	10.95%	9.42%	7.70%	0.78

Source: Dow Jones Credit Suisse.
The Sharpe ratio is the ratio of the mean of $r - r_f$ to its standard deviation where r is the realized return and r_f is the risk-free rate.

are favored by hedge funds. Investing in a hedge fund is a simple way in which a pension fund can (for a fee) expand the scope of its investing. This may improve its efficient frontier. (See Section 1.2 for a discussion of efficient frontiers.)

It is not uncommon for hedge funds to report good returns for a few years and then "blow up." Long-Term Capital Management reported returns (before fees) of 28%, 59%, 57%, and 17% in 1994, 1995, 1996, and 1997, respectively. In 1998, it lost virtually all its capital. Some people have argued that hedge fund returns are like the returns from writing out-of-the-money options. Most of the time, the options cost nothing, but every so often they are very expensive.

This may be unfair. Advocates of hedge funds would argue that hedge fund managers search for profitable opportunities that other investors do not have the resources or expertise to find. They would point out that the top hedge fund managers have been very successful at finding these opportunities.

The performance of different types of hedge funds, as given by Dow Jones Credit Suisse, is shown in Table 4.5. Over the seven-year period, 2004 to 2010, the average annual return was 9.42%. This compares with about 1.8% for the S&P 500 index during this period. However, the statistics do not include results for the year 2011 during which the hedge fund index lost 7.40% while the S&P 500 was flat. Also, the statistics do not take account of dividends on the S&P 500 and as already explained there may be biases in the hedge fund data.

SUMMARY

Mutual funds offer a way small investors can capture the benefits of diversification. Overall, the evidence is that actively managed funds do not outperform the market and this has led many investors to choose funds that are designed to track a market index such as the S&P 500. Mutual funds are highly regulated. They cannot take short positions or use leverage and must allow investors to redeem their shares in the mutual fund at any time. Most mutual funds are open-end funds, so that the number of shares in the fund increases (decreases) as investors contribute (withdraw) funds. An open-end mutual fund calculates the net asset value of shares in the fund at 4 P.M. each business day and this is the price used for all buy and sell orders placed in the previous 24 hours. A closed-end fund has a fixed number of shares that trade in the same way as the shares of any other corporation.

Exchange-traded funds (ETFs) are proving to be popular alternatives to open- and closed-ended funds. The shares held by the fund are known at any given time. Large institutional investors can exchange shares in the fund at any time for the assets underlying the shares, and vice versa. This ensures that the shares in the ETF (unlike shares in a closed-end fund) trade at a price very close to the funds's net asset value. Shares in an ETF can be traded at any time (not just at 4 P.M.) and shares in an ETF (unlike shares in an open-end mutual fund) can be shorted.

Hedge funds cater to the needs of large investors. Compared to mutual funds, they are subject to very few regulations and restrictions. Hedge funds charge investors much higher fees than mutual funds. The fee for a typical fund is "2 plus 20%." This means that the fund charges a management fee of 2% per year and receives 20% of the profits (if any) generated by the fund. Hedge fund managers have a call option on the assets of the fund and, as a result, may have an incentive to take high risks.

Among the strategies followed by hedge funds are long/short equity, dedicated short, distressed securities, merger arbitrage, convertible arbitrage, fixed income arbitrage, emerging markets, global macro, and managed futures. The jury is still out on whether hedge funds on average provide superior risk-return trade-offs to index funds after fees. There is a tendency for hedge funds to provide excellent returns for a number of years and then report a disastrous loss.

FURTHER READING

Khorana, A., H. Servaes, and P. Tufano. "Mutual Fund Fees Around the World." *Review of Financial Studies* 22 (March 2009): 1279–1310.

Jensen, M. C. "Risk, the Pricing of Capital Assets, and the Evaluation of Investment Portfolios." *Journal of Business* 42, no. 2 (April 1969): 167–247.

Lhabitant, F.-S. *Handbook of Hedge Funds*. Chichester: John Wiley & Sons, 2006.

Ross, S. "Neoclassical Finance, Alternative Finance, and the Closed End Fund Puzzle." *European Financial Management* 8 (2002): 1291–1237.

PRACTICE QUESTIONS AND PROBLEMS (ANSWERS AT END OF BOOK)

4.1 What is the difference between an open-end and closed-end mutual fund?

4.2 How is the NAV of an open-end mutual fund calculated? When is it calculated?

4.3 An investor buys 100 shares in a mutual fund on January 1, 2012, for $30 each. The fund makes capital gains in 2012 and 2013 of $3 per share and $1 per share, respectively, and earns no dividends. The investor sells the shares in the fund during 2014 for $32 per share. What capital gains or losses is the investor deemed to have made in 2012, 2013, and 2014?

4.4 What is an index fund? How is it created?

4.5 What is a mutual fund's (a) front-end load and (b) back-end load?

4.6 Explain how an exchange-traded fund that tracks an index works. What is the advantage of an exchange-traded fund (a) over an open-end mutual fund and (b) a closed-end mutual fund?

4.7 What is the difference between the geometric mean and the arithmetic mean of a set of numbers? Why is the difference relevant to the reporting of mutual fund returns?

4.8 Explain the meaning of (a) late trading, (b) market timing, (c) front running, and (d) directed brokerage.

4.9 Give three examples of the rules that apply to mutual funds, but not to hedge funds.

4.10 "If 70% of convertible bond trading is by hedge funds, I would expect the profitability of that strategy to decline." Discuss this viewpoint.

4.11 Explain the meanings of the terms hurdle rate, high-water mark clause, and clawback clause when used in connection with the incentive fees of hedge funds.

4.12 A hedge fund charges 2 plus 20%. Investors want a return after fees of 20%. How much does the hedge fund have to earn, before fees, to provide investors with this return? Assume that the incentive fee is paid on the net return after management fees have been subtracted.

4.13 "It is important for a hedge fund to be right in the long term. Short-term gains and losses do not matter." Discuss this statement.

4.14 "The risks that hedge funds take are regulated by their prime brokers." Discuss this statement.

FURTHER QUESTIONS

4.15 An investor buys 100 shares in a mutual fund on January 1, 2012, for $50 each. The fund earns dividends of $2 and $3 per share during 2012 and 2013. These are reinvested in the fund. Its realized capital gains in 2012 and 2013 are $5 per share and $3 per share, respectively. The investor sells the shares in the fund during 2014 for $59 per share. Explain how the investor is taxed.

4.16 Good years are followed by equally bad years for a mutual fund. It earns +8%, –8%, +12%, –12% in successive years. What is the investor's overall return for the four years?

4.17 A fund of funds divides its money between five hedge funds that earn –5%, 1%, 10%, 15%, and 20% before fees in a particular year. The fund of funds charges 1 plus 10% and the hedge funds charge 2 plus 20%. The hedge funds' incentive fees are calculated on the return after management fees. The fund of funds incentive fee is calculated on the net (after management fees and incentive fees) average return of the hedge funds in which it invests and after its own management fee has been subtracted. What is the overall return on the investments? How is it divided between the fund of funds, the hedge funds, and investors in the fund of funds?

4.18 A hedge fund charges 2 plus 20%. A pension fund invests in the hedge fund. Plot the return to the pension fund as a function of the return to the hedge fund.

CHAPTER 5

Trading in Financial Markets

Financial institutions do a huge volume of trading in a wide range of different financial instruments. There are a number of reasons for this. Some trades are designed to satisfy the needs of their clients, some are to manage their own risks, some are to exploit arbitrage opportunities, and some are to reflect their own views on the direction in which market prices will move.

We will discuss the approaches a financial institution uses to manage its trading risks in later chapters. The purpose of this chapter is to set the scene by describing the instruments that trade, how they trade, and the ways they are used.

5.1 THE MARKETS

There are two markets for trading financial instruments. These are the *exchange-traded market* and the *over-the-counter* (or OTC) *market*.

Exchange-Traded Markets

Exchanges have been used to trade financial products for many years. Some exchanges such as the New York Stock Exchange (NYSE; www.nyse.com) focus on the trading of stocks. Others such as the CME Group (www.cmegroup.com) and the Chicago Board Options Exchange (CBOE; www.cboe.com) are concerned with the trading of derivatives such as futures and options.

The role of the exchange is to define the contracts that trade and organize trading so that market participants can be sure that the trades they agree to will be honored. Traditionally individuals have met at the exchange and agreed on the prices for trades, often by using an elaborate system of hand signals. Most exchanges have now moved wholly or partly to *electronic trading*. This involves traders entering their desired trades at a keyboard and a computer being used to match buyers and sellers. Not everyone agrees that the shift to electronic trading is desirable. Electronic trading is less physically demanding than traditional floor trading. However, in some ways, it is also less exciting. Traders do not have the opportunity to attempt to predict short-term market trends from the behavior and body language of other traders.

Sometimes trading is facilitated with market makers. These are individuals or companies who are always prepared to quote both a *bid price* (price at which they are prepared to buy) and an *offer price* (price at which they are prepared to sell). For example, at the request of a trader, a market maker might quote "bid 30.30, offer 30.50" for a particular share indicating a willingness to buy at \$30.30 and sell at \$30.50. At the time quotes are provided to the trader, the market maker does not know whether the trader wishes to buy or sell. Typically the exchange will specify an upper bound for the spread between a market maker's bid and offer prices. The market maker earns its profit from this spread, but must manage its inventories carefully to limit its exposure to price changes.

Over-the-Counter Markets

The OTC market is a huge telephone- and computer-linked network of traders who work for financial institutions, large corporations, or fund managers. It is used for trading many different products including bonds, foreign currencies, and derivatives. Banks are very active participants in the market and often act as market makers for the more commonly traded instruments. For example, most banks are prepared to provide bid and offer quotes on a range of different exchange rates.

A key advantage of the over-the-counter market is that the terms of a contract do not have to be those specified by an exchange. Market participants are free to negotiate any mutually attractive deal. Phone conversations in the over-the-counter market are usually taped. If there is a dispute over what was agreed, the tapes are replayed to resolve the issue. Trades in the over-the-counter market are typically much larger than trades in the exchange-traded market.

5.2 LONG AND SHORT POSITIONS IN ASSETS

The simplest type of trade is the purchase of an asset for cash or the sale of an asset that is owned for cash. Examples of such trades are:

1. The purchase of 100 IBM shares
2. The sale of 1 million British pounds for dollars
3. The purchase of 1,000 ounces of gold
4. The sale of \$1 million worth of bonds issued by General Motors

The first of these trades would typically be done on an exchange; the other three would be done in the over-the-counter market. The trades are sometimes referred to as *spot trades* because they lead to almost immediate (on the spot) delivery of the asset.

Short Sales

In some markets, it is possible to sell an asset that you do not own with the intention of buying it back later. This is referred to as shorting the asset. We will illustrate how it works by considering a short sale of shares of a stock.

Suppose an investor instructs a broker to short 500 shares of a certain stock. The broker will carry out the instructions by borrowing the shares from another client and selling them on an exchange in the usual way. (A small fee may be charged for the borrowed shares.) The investor can maintain the short position for as long as desired, provided there are always shares available for the broker to borrow. At some stage, however, the investor will close out the position by purchasing 500 shares. These are then replaced in the account of the client from whom the shares were borrowed. The investor takes a profit if the stock price has declined and a loss if it has risen. If, at any time while the contract is open, the broker runs out of shares to borrow, the investor is *short-squeezed* and is forced to close out the position immediately, even if not ready to do so.

An investor with a short position must pay to the broker any income, such as dividends or interest, that would normally be received on the asset that has been shorted. The broker will transfer this to the client account from which the asset was borrowed. Suppose a trader shorts 500 shares in April when the price per share is $120 and closes out the position by buying them back in July when the price per share is $100. Suppose further that a dividend of $1 per share is paid in May. The investor receives $500 \times \$120 = \$60,000$ in April when the short position is initiated. The dividend leads to a payment by the investor of $500 \times \$1 = \$500$ in May. The investor also pays $500 \times \$100 = \$50,000$ for shares when the position is closed out in July. The net gain is, therefore,

$$\$60,000 - \$500 - \$50,000 = \$9,500$$

Table 5.1 illustrates this example and shows that (assuming no fee is charged for borrowing the shares) the cash flows from the short sale are the mirror image of the cash flows from purchasing the shares in April and selling them in July.

An investor entering into a short position is required to maintain a *margin account* with the broker to guarantee that future obligations will be met. Margin accounts are discussed later in the chapter.

From time to time, regulations are changed on short selling. The SEC abolished the uptick rule in the United States in July 2007 and reintroduced it in April 2009. (The effect of this rule is to allow shorting only when the most recent movement in

TABLE 5.1   Cash Flows from Short Sale and Purchase of Shares

Purchase of Shares	
April: Purchase 500 shares for $120	−$60,000
May: Receive Dividend	+$500
July: Sell 500 shares for $100 per share	+$50,000
Net Profit = −$9,500	

Short Sale of Shares	
April: Borrow 500 shares and sell them for $120	+$60,000
May: Pay Dividend	−$500
July: Buy 500 shares for $100 per share	−$50,000
Replace borrowed shares to close short position	
Net Profit = +$9,500	

the price of the stock is an increase.) On September 19, 2008, in an attempt to halt the slide in bank stock prices, the SEC imposed a temporary ban on the short selling of 799 financial companies. This was similar to a ban imposed by the UK Financial Services Authority (FSA) the day before.

5.3 DERIVATIVES MARKETS

A derivative is an instrument whose value depends on (or derives from) other more basic market variables. A stock option, for example, is a derivative whose value is dependent on the price of a stock.

Derivatives trade in both the exchange-traded and OTC markets. Both markets are huge. Although the statistics that are collected for the two markets are not exactly comparable, it is clear that the over-the-counter derivatives market is much larger than the exchange-traded derivatives market. The Bank for International Settlements (www.bis.org) started collecting statistics on the markets in 1998. Figure 5.1 compares (a) the estimated total principal amounts underlying transactions that were outstanding in the over-the-counter markets between June 1998 and December 2010 and (b) the estimated total value of the assets underlying exchange-traded contracts during the same period. Using these measures, in December 2010, the over-the-counter market was $601.0 trillion and the exchange-traded market was $67.9 trillion.

In interpreting these numbers, we should bear in mind that the principal (or value of assets) underlying a derivatives transaction is not the same as its value. An example of an over-the-counter contract is an agreement to buy 100 million U.S. dollars with British pounds at a predetermined exchange rate in one year. The total principal amount underlying this transaction is $100 million. However, the value of the contract might be only $1 million. The Bank for International Settlements

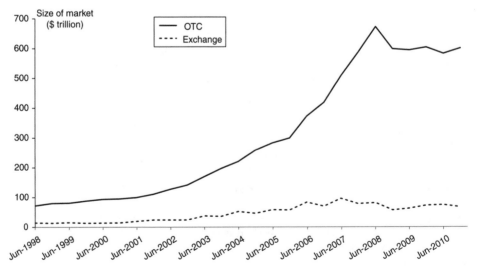

FIGURE 5.1   Size of Over-the-Counter and Exchange-Traded Derivatives Markets

TABLE 5.2 Spot and Forward Quotes for the USD/GBP Exchange Rate, August 24, 2011 (GBP = British pound; USD = U.S. dollar; quote is number of USD per GBP)

	Bid	Offer
Spot	1.6398	1.6402
1-month forward	1.6392	1.6397
3-month forward	1.6382	1.6387
1-year forward	1.6328	1.6334

estimates the gross market value of all OTC contracts outstanding in December 2010 to be about $21.1 trillion.[1]

5.4 PLAIN VANILLA DERIVATIVES

This section discusses the standard, or commonly traded, contracts in derivatives markets: forwards, futures, swaps, and derivatives. They are sometimes referred to as *plain vanilla* products.

Forward Contracts

A forward contract is an agreement to buy an asset in the future for a certain price. Forward contracts trade in the over-the-counter market. One of the parties to a forward contract assumes a *long position* and agrees to buy the underlying asset on a certain specified future date for a certain specified price. The other party assumes a *short position* and agrees to sell the asset on the same date for the same price.

Forward contracts on foreign exchange are very popular. Table 5.2 provides quotes on the exchange rate between the British pound (GBP) and the U.S. dollar (USD) that might be provided by a large international bank on August 24, 2011. The quotes are for the number of USD per GBP. The first row indicates that the bank is prepared to buy GBP (also known as sterling) in the spot market (i.e., for virtually immediate delivery) at the rate of $1.6398 per GBP and sell sterling in the spot market at $1.6402 per GBP; the second row indicates that the bank is prepared to buy sterling in one month at $1.6392 per GBP and sell sterling in one month at $1.6397 per GBP; and so on.

Forward contracts can be used to hedge foreign currency risk. Suppose that on August 24, 2011, the treasurer of a U.S. corporation knows that the corporation will pay £1 million in one year (on August 24, 2012) and wants to hedge against exchange rate moves. The treasurer can agree to buy £1 million one-year forward

---

[1] A contract that is worth $1 million to one side and –$1 million to the other side would be counted as having a gross market value of $1 million.

at an exchange rate of 1.6334 by trading with the bank providing the quotes in Table 5.2. The corporation then has a long forward contract on GBP. It has agreed that on August 24, 2012, it will buy £1 million from the bank for $1.6334 million. The bank has a short forward contract on GBP. It has agreed that on August 24, 2012, it will sell £1 million for $1.6334 million. Both the corporation and the bank have made a binding commitment.

What are the possible outcomes in the trade we have just described? The forward contract obligates the corporation to purchase 1 million pounds at an exchange rate of 1.6334 in one year. If the spot exchange rate applicable to the corporation when buying pounds rose to, say, 1.8000 at the end of one year the forward contract leads to 1 million pounds being purchased by the corporation for an exchange rate of 1.6334 rather than at the spot exchange rate of 1.8000. This is worth $166,600 (= (1.8000 − 1.6334) × $1,000,000) to the corporation. Of course, it may also happen that the contract will have a negative final value to the corporation. If the exchange rate falls to 1.5000 by the end of the year, the forward contract leads to 1 million pounds being purchased by the corporation for an exchange rate of 1.6334 rather than at the 1.5000 available in the market. This costs the corporation $133,400 (= (1.6334 − 1.5000) × $1,000,000). This example shows that a long forward contract can lead to a payoff that is a gain or loss. The payoff is the spot price of the assets underlying the forward contract minus the agreed delivery price for the assets and is shown in Figure 5.2(a).

The bank in our example has entered into a short forward contract. Its position is the mirror image of that of the corporation. It has agreed to sell 1 million pounds for an exchange rate of 1.6334 in one year. If the spot exchange rate applicable to the bank rose to 1.8000, at the end of the year the forward contract leads to

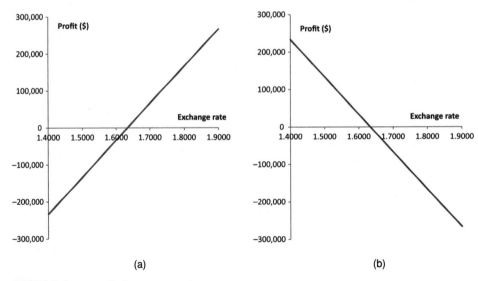

(a)   (b)

FIGURE 5.2   Payoffs from Forward Contracts
(a) Long position to buy 1 million British pounds, (b) Short position to sell 1 million British pounds.

1 million pounds being sold by the bank for an exchange rate of 1.6334 rather than at the spot exchange rate of 1.8000. This costs the bank $166,600. If the exchange rate falls to 1.5000 by the end of the year the forward contract leads to 1 million pounds being sold by the bank for an exchange rate of 1.6334 rather than 1.5000. This is worth $133,400 to the bank. The payoff is the agreed delivery price for the assets underlying the forward contract minus spot price and is shown in Figure 5.2(b).

Futures Contracts

Futures contracts, like forward contracts, are agreements to buy an asset at a future time. Unlike forward contracts, futures are traded on an exchange. This means that the contracts that trade are standardized. The exchange defines the amount of the asset underlying one contract, when delivery can be made, exactly what can be delivered, and so on. Contracts are referred to by their delivery month. For example, the September 2013 gold futures is a contract where delivery is made in September 2013. Whereas only one delivery day is usually specified for a forward contract, a futures contract can often be delivered on several days during the delivery month. Alternative delivery times, delivery locations, and so on, are defined by the exchange. It is nearly always the party with the short position that has the right to initiate the delivery process and choose between the alternatives.

Most futures contracts trade actively with the futures price at any given time being determined by supply and demand. If there are more buyers than sellers at a time when the September 2013 price of gold is $1,680 per ounce, the price goes up. Similarly, if there are more sellers than buyers, the price goes down.

One of the attractive features of exchange-traded contracts such as futures is that it is easy to close out a position. If you buy (i.e., take a long position in) a September 2013 gold futures contract in March 2012, you can exit in June 2012 by selling (i.e., taking a short position in) the same contract. Closing out a position in a forward contract is not as easy as closing out a position in a futures contract. As a result, forward contracts usually lead to final delivery of the underlying assets, whereas futures contracts are usually closed out before the delivery month is reached. Business Snapshot 5.1 is an amusing story showing that the assets underlying futures contracts do get delivered if mistakes are made in the close out.

The futures price of an asset is usually very similar to its forward price. Appendix C at the end of the book gives the relationship between the futures or forward price of an asset and its spot price. One difference between a futures and a forward contract is that a futures is settled daily whereas a forward is settled at the end of its life. For example, if a futures price increases during a day, money flows from traders with short positions to traders with long positions at the end of the day. Similarly, if a futures price decreases during a day, money flows in the other direction. The way this happens is described in Section 5.6. Because a futures contract is settled daily whereas a forward contract is settled at the end of its life, the timing of the realization of gains and losses is different for the two contracts. This sometimes causes confusion, as indicated in Business Snapshot 5.2. Table 5.3 summarizes the difference between forward and futures contracts.

BUSINESS SNAPSHOT 5.1

The Unanticipated Delivery of a Futures Contract

This story (which may well be apocryphal) was told to the author of this book many years ago by a senior executive of a financial institution. It concerns a new employee of the financial institution who had not previously worked in the financial sector. One of the clients of the financial institution regularly entered into a long futures contract on live cattle for hedging purposes and issued instructions to close out the position on the last day of trading. (Live cattle futures contracts trade on the Chicago Mercantile Exchange and each contract is on 40,000 pounds of cattle.) The new employee was given responsibility for handling the account.

When the time came to close out a contract, the employee noted that the client was long one contract and instructed a trader at the exchange go long (not short) one contract. The result of this mistake was that the financial institution ended up with a long position in two live cattle futures contracts. By the time the mistake was spotted, trading in the contract had ceased.

The financial institution (not the client) was responsible for the mistake. As a result it started to look into the details of the delivery arrangements for live cattle futures contracts—something it had never done before. Under the terms of the contract, cattle could be delivered by the party with the short position to a number of different locations in the United States during the delivery month. Because it was long, the financial institution could do nothing but wait for a party with a short position to issue a *notice of intention to deliver* to the exchange and for the exchange to assign that notice to the financial institution.

It eventually received a notice from the exchange and found that it would receive live cattle at a location 2,000 miles away the following Tuesday. The new employee was dispatched to the location to handle things. It turned out that the location had a cattle auction every Tuesday. The party with the short position that was making delivery bought cattle at the auction and then immediately delivered them. Unfortunately the cattle could not be resold until the next cattle auction the following Tuesday. The employee was therefore faced with the problem of making arrangements for the cattle to be housed and fed for a week. This was a great start to a first job in the financial sector!

Swaps

The first swap contracts were negotiated in the early 1980s. Since then, the market has seen phenomenal growth. Swaps now occupy a position of central importance in the over-the-counter derivatives market.

A swap is an agreement between two companies to exchange cash flows in the future. The agreement defines the dates when the cash flows are to be paid and the way in which they are to be calculated. Usually the calculation of the cash flows involves the future values of interest rates, exchange rates, or other market variables.

BUSINESS SNAPSHOT 5.2

A System's Error?

A foreign exchange trader working for a bank enters into a long forward contract to buy one million pounds sterling at an exchange rate of 1.6000 in three months. At the same time, another trader on the next desk takes a long position in 16 three-month futures contracts on sterling. The futures price is 1.6000 and each contract is on 62,500 pounds. The positions taken by the forward and futures traders are therefore the same. Within minutes of the positions being taken, the forward and the futures prices both increase to 1.6040. The bank's systems show that the futures trader has made a profit of $4,000 while the forward trader has made a profit of only $3,900. The forward trader immediately calls the bank's systems department to complain. Does the forward trader have a valid complaint?

The answer is no! The daily settlement of futures contracts ensures that the futures trader realizes an almost immediate profit corresponding to the increase in the futures price. If the forward trader closed out the position by entering into a short contract at 1.6040, the forward trader would have contracted to buy 1 million pounds at 1.6000 in three months and sell 1 million pounds at 1.6040 in three months. This would lead to a $4,000 profit—but in three months, not today. The forward trader's profit is the present value of $4,000.

The forward trader can gain some consolation from the fact that gains and losses are treated symmetrically. If the forward/futures prices dropped to 1.5960 instead of rising to 1.6040, the futures trader would take a loss of $4,000 while the forward trader would take a loss of only $3,900. Also, over the three-month contract life, the total gain or loss from the futures contract and the forward contract will be the same.

TABLE 5.3   Comparison of Forward and Futures Contracts

Forward	Futures
Private contract between two parties	Traded on an exchange
Not standardized	Standardized contract
Usually one specified delivery date	Range of delivery dates
Settled at end of contract	Settled daily
Delivery or final cash settlement usually takes place	Contract is usually closed out prior to maturity
Some credit risk	Virtually no credit risk

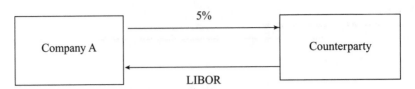

FIGURE 5.3   A Plain Vanilla Interest Rate Swap

A forward contract can be viewed as a simple example of a swap. Suppose it is March 1, 2013, and a company enters into a forward contract to buy 100 ounces of gold for $1,600 per ounce in one year. The company can sell the gold in one year as soon as it is received. The forward contract is therefore equivalent to a swap where the company agrees that on March 1, 2014, it will swap 100 times the spot price of gold for $160,000.

Whereas a forward contract is equivalent to the exchange of cash flows on just one future date, swaps typically lead to cash flow exchanges taking place on several future dates. The most common swap is a "plain vanilla" interest rate swap where a fixed rate of interest is exchanged for LIBOR.[2] Both interest rates are applied to the same notional principal. A swap where Company A pays a fixed rate of interest of 5% and receives LIBOR is shown in Figure 5.3. Suppose that in this contract interest rates are reset every six months, the notional principal is $100 million, and the swap lasts for three years. Table 5.4 shows the cash flows to Company A if six-month LIBOR interest rates prove to be those shown in the second column of the table. The swap is entered into on March 5, 2013. The six-month interest rate on that date is 4.2% per year or 2.1% per six months. As a result, the floating-rate cash flow received six months later on September 5, 2013, is 0.021 × 100 or $2.1 million. Similarly the six-month interest rate of 4.8% per annum (or 2.4% per six months) on September 5, 2013, leads to the floating cash flow received six months later (on March 5, 2014) being $2.4 million; and so on. The fixed-rate cash flow paid is always $2.5 million (5% of $100 million applied to a six-month period).[3] Note that the timing of cash flows corresponds to the usual way interest rates such as LIBOR work. The interest is observed at the beginning of the period to which it applies and paid at the end of the period.

Plain vanilla interest rate swaps are very popular because they can be used for many purposes. For example, the swap in Figure 5.3 could be used by Company A to transform borrowings at a floating rate of LIBOR plus 1% to borrowings at a fixed rate of 6%. The combination of

1. Pay interest at LIBOR plus 1% under loan agreement;
2. Receive LIBOR under swap agreement; and
3. Pay 5% under the swap agreement

---

[2] LIBOR is the London Interbank Offered Rate. It is the rate at which a bank offers to make large wholesale deposits with another bank and is discussed in Chapter 8.
[3] Note that we have not taken account of day count conventions, holidays calendars, and so on in Table 5.4.

TABLE 5.4 Example of Cash Flows ($ millions) to Company A in Swap

Date	6-Month LIBOR Rate (%)	Floating Cash Flow Received	Fixed Cash Flow Paid	Net Cash Flow
Mar. 5, 2013	4.20			
Sep. 5, 2013	4.80	+2.10	−2.50	−0.40
Mar. 5, 2014	5.30	+2.40	−2.50	−0.10
Sep. 5, 2014	5.50	+2.65	−2.50	+0.15
Mar. 5, 2015	5.60	+2.75	−2.50	+0.25
Sep. 5, 2015	5.90	+2.80	−2.50	+0.30
Mar. 5, 2016	6.40	+2.95	−2.50	+0.45

As shown in Figure 5.3, swap lasts three years and has a principal of $100 million.

nets out to a fixed payment of 6%. It can also be used by Company A to transform an investment earning a fixed rate of 4.5% to an investment earning LIBOR minus 0.5%. The combination of

1. Receive 4.5% on the investment;
2. Receive LIBOR under swap agreement; and
3. Pay 5% under the swap agreement

nets out to a floating income at the rate of LIBOR minus 0.5%.

EXAMPLE 5.1

Suppose a bank has floating-rate deposits and five-year fixed-rate loans. As will be discussed in Chapter 8, this exposes the bank to significant risks. If rates rise, the deposits will be rolled over at high rates and the bank's net interest income will contract. The bank can hedge its risks by entering into the interest rate swap in Figure 5.3 (taking the role of Company A). The swap can be viewed as transforming the floating-rate deposits to fixed-rate deposits. Alternatively, it can be viewed as transforming the fixed-rate loans to floating-rate loans.

Many banks are market makers in swaps. Table 5.5 shows quotes for U.S. dollar swaps that might be posted by a bank.[4] The first row shows that the bank is prepared to enter into a two-year swap where it pays a fixed rate of 6.03% and receives LIBOR. It is also prepared to enter into a swap where it receives 6.06% and pays LIBOR. The bid–offer spread in Table 5.5 is 3 or 4 basis points. The average of the bid and offered fixed rates are known as the *swap rate*. This is shown in the final column of the table.

The valuation of plain vanilla interest rate swaps is discussed in Appendix D at the end of this book. The trading of swaps and other over-the-counter derivatives

---

[4] The standard swap in the United States is one where fixed payments made every six months are exchanged for floating LIBOR payments made every three months. In Table 5.4, we assumed that fixed and floating payments are exchanged every six months.

TABLE 5.5 Swap Quotes Made by a Market Maker (percent per annum)

Maturity (years)	Bid	Offer	Swap Rate
2	6.03	6.06	6.045
3	6.21	6.24	6.225
4	6.35	6.39	6.370
5	6.47	6.51	6.490
7	6.65	6.68	6.665
10	6.83	6.87	6.850

has traditionally been facilitated by ISDA, the International Swaps and Derivatives Association. This organization has developed standard contracts that are widely used by market participants. Swaps can be designed so that the periodic cash flows depend on the future value of any well-defined variable. Swaps dependent on interest rates, exchange rates, commodity prices, and equity indices are popular. Sometimes there are embedded options in a swap. For example, one side might have the option to terminate a swap early or to choose between a number of different ways of calculating cash flows. One bizarre swap entered into between Bankers Trust and Procter and Gamble will be discussed later in the chapter. (See Business Snapshot 5.4.)

Options

Options are traded both on exchanges and in the over-the-counter market. There are two basic types of option. A *call option* gives the holder the right to buy the underlying asset by a certain date for a certain price. A *put option* gives the holder the right to sell the underlying asset by a certain date for a certain price. The price in the contract is known as the *exercise price* or *strike price*; the date in the contract is known as the *expiration date* or *maturity date*. *American options* can be exercised at any time up to the expiration date. *European options* can be exercised only on the expiration date itself.[5] Most of the options that are traded on exchanges are American. In the exchange-traded equity option market, one contract is usually an agreement to buy or sell 100 shares. European options are generally easier to analyze than American options, and some of the properties of an American option are frequently deduced from those of its European counterpart.

An *at-the-money option* is an option where the strike price is close to the price of the underlying asset. An *out-of-the-money option* is a call option where the strike price is above the price of the underlying asset or a put option where the strike price is below this price. An *in-the-money option* is a call option where the strike price is below the price of the underlying asset or a put option where the strike price is above this price.

It should be emphasized that an option gives the holder the right to do something. The holder does not have to exercise this right. By contrast, in a forward and futures contract, the holder is obligated to buy or sell the underlying asset. Note that whereas

---

[5] Note that the terms *American* and *European* do not refer to the location of the option or the exchange. Some options trading on North American exchanges are European.

TABLE 5.6 Prices of Options on Intel, August 25, 2011 (stock price = $19.58)

Strike Price ($)	Calls			Puts		
	Sept. 11	Oct. 11	Jan. 12	Sept. 11	Oct. 11	Jan. 12
18	1.70	2.14	n.a.	0.09	0.57	n.a.
19	0.82	1.44	1.87	0.24	0.86	1.48
20	0.25	0.87	1.34	0.68	1.29	1.95
21	0.04	0.48	0.92	1.46	1.89	2.53

it costs nothing to enter into a forward or futures contract, there is a cost to acquiring an option. This cost is referred to as the *option premium*.

The largest exchange in the world for trading stock options is the Chicago Board Options Exchange (CBOE; www.cboe.com). Table 5.6 gives the closing mid-market prices of some of the American options trading on Intel (ticker INTC) on August 25, 2011. The option strike prices are $18, $19, $20, and $21. The maturities are September 2011, October 2011, and January 2012. The September options have an expiration date of September 17, 2011; the October options have an expiration date of October 22, 2011; and the January options have an expiration date of January 21, 2012.[6] Intel's stock price at the close of trading on August 25, 2011, was $19.58.

Suppose an investor instructs a broker to buy one October call option contract on Intel with a strike price of $20. The broker will relay these instructions to a trader at the CBOE. This trader will then find another trader who wants to sell one October call contract on Intel with a strike price of $20, and a price will be agreed upon. We assume that the price is $0.87, as indicated in Table 5.6. This is the price for an option to buy one share. In the United States, one stock option contract is a contract to buy or sell 100 shares. Therefore, the investor must arrange for $87 to be remitted to the exchange through the broker. The exchange will then arrange for this amount to be passed on to the party on the other side of the transaction.

In our example, the investor has obtained at a cost of $87 the right to buy 100 Intel shares for $20 each. The party on the other side of the transaction has received $87 and has agreed to sell 100 Intel shares for $20 per share if the investor chooses to exercise the option. If the price of Intel does not rise above $20 before October 22, 2011, the option is not exercised and the investor loses $87. But if the Intel share price does well and the option is exercised when it is $30, the investor is able to buy 100 shares at $20 per share when they are worth $30 per share. This leads to a gain of $1,000, or $913 when the initial cost of the options is taken into account.

If the investor is bearish on Intel, an alternative trade would be the purchase of one January put option contract with a strike price of $20. From Table 5.6, we see that this would cost 100 × $1.95 or $195. The investor would obtain at a cost of $195 the right to sell 100 Intel shares for $20 per share prior to January, 2012. If the Intel share price moves above $20 the option is not exercised and the investor loses $195. But if the investor exercises when the stock price is $15, the investor makes

---

[6] The exchange chooses the expiration date as the Saturday following the third Friday of the delivery month.

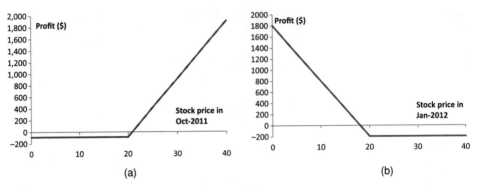

FIGURE 5.4 Net Profit from Long Position in an Option Contract on Intel Assuming No Early Exercise. (a) October Call with a Strike Price of $20 and (b) January Put with a Strike Price of $20.00

a gain of $500 by buying 100 Intel shares at $20 and selling them for $15. The net profit after the cost of the options is taken into account is $305.

The options trading on the CBOE are American. If we assume for simplicity that they are European so that they can be exercised only at maturity, the investor's profit as a function of the final stock price for the Intel options we have been considering is shown in Figure 5.4.

There are four types of trades in options markets:

1. Buying a call
2. Selling a call
3. Buying a put
4. Selling a put

Buyers are referred to as having *long positions*; sellers are referred to as having *short positions*. Selling an option is also known as *writing an option*.

Options trade very actively in the over-the-counter market as well as on exchanges. The underlying assets include stocks, currencies, and stock indices. Indeed the over-the-counter market for options is now larger than the exchange-traded market. Whereas exchange-traded options tend to be American, options trading in the over-the-counter market are frequently European. The advantage of the over-the-counter market is that maturity dates, strike prices, and contract sizes can be tailored to meet the precise needs of a client. They do not have to correspond to those specified by the exchange. The sizes of option trades in the over-the-counter are usually much greater than those on exchanges.

Valuation formulas and numerical procedures for options on a variety of assets are in Appendices E and F at the end of this book.

Interest Rate Options

Important interest rate options that trade in the over-the-counter market are *caps*, *floors*, and *swap options* (also known as *swaptions*). Whereas a swap exchanges a sequence of floating rates for a fixed rate, as indicated in Table 5.4, a cap, as its name implies, caps the floating rate. It is a series of call options on a floating rate (usually LIBOR). If the floating rate is greater than the strike rate (also known cap rate), there is a payoff equal to the excess of the floating rate over the cap rate; if the floating rate is less than the cap rate, there is no payoff. As in the case of swaps, payoffs are made at the end of the period covered by an interest rate.

There is usually no payoff for the first period covered, because the rate for that period is known when the contract is entered into. Consider a trader who on March 5, 2013, buys a three-year cap on six-month LIBOR with a cap rate of 5.2% and a principal of $100 million. If rates proved to be those indicated in the second column of Table 5.4, there would be no payoff on March 5, 2014. The payoff on September 5, 2014, would be $0.5 \times (0.0530 - 0.0520) \times 100$ or $0.05 million. Similarly there would be payoffs of $0.15 million, $0.20 million, and $0.35 million on March 5, 2015, September 5, 2015, and March 5, 2016, respectively.

A floor is similarly a series of put options on floating rates. If the instrument we have just been considering were a floor rather than a cap, the payoff would be $0.5 \times (0.0520 - 0.0480) \times 100$ or $0.20 million on March 5, 2014, and zero on the other dates.

A swap option is an option to enter into a swap at some future time where the fixed rate is the strike rate. There are two types of swap options. One option is to pay the strike rate and receive LIBOR; the other is the option to pay LIBOR and receive the strike rate.

5.5 CLEARING HOUSES

Exchange-traded derivatives contracts are administered by a clearing house. The clearing house has a number of members and trades by non-members have to be channeled through members for clearing. The members of the clearing house contribute to a guarantee fund that is managed by the clearing house.

Suppose that, in a particular exchange-traded market, Trader X agrees to sell one contract to Trader Y. The clearing house in effect stands between the two traders so that Trader X is selling the contract to the clearing house and Trader Y is buying the contract from the clearing house. The advantage of this is that Trader X does not need to worry about the creditworthiness of Trader Y, and vice versa. Both traders deal only with the clearing house. If a trader is a clearing house member, the trader deals directly with the clearing house. Otherwise, the trader deals with the clearing house through a clearing house member.

When a trader has potential future liabilities from a trade (e.g., when the trader is entering into a futures contract or selling an option), the clearing house requires the trader to provide cash or marketable securities as collateral. This collateral is referred to as *margin*. Different circumstances under which margin is required and the procedures that are used are discussed in the next section. Without margin, the clearing house is taking the risk that the market will move against the trader and the trader will then walk away from his or her commitments. The clearing house aims to set margin requirements sufficiently high that it is over 99% certain that this will not happen. On those few occasions where it does happen, the guarantee fund is used. As a result, failures by clearing houses are extremely rare.

The OTC Market and Central Clearing

Some OTC trades have been cleared through clearing houses (which in this context are usually referred to as central clearing parties or CCPs) for many years. Following the 2007 to 2009 credit crisis, regulators have required the use of central clearing for "standard" OTC derivatives. This is changing the character of the OTC market. Prior to the crisis, the majority of OTC trades between two parties were cleared bilaterally and governed by an agreement (usually an ISDA agreement) between the two sides. Following the crisis, the majority of trades are being handled by CCPs. This is discussed further in the next section and in Chapter 17.

5.6 MARGIN

Many trades in financial markets involve credit risk. If Party B buys an asset from Party A for cash, there is little or no credit risk. But if Party A lends money to Party B so that Party B can buy the asset, Party A is obviously subject to credit risk. Derivatives transactions involve credit risk because they invariably involve at least one party agreeing to make payments to the other on future dates under certain circumstances.

Margin, which is collateral deposited by a trader, is a way of dealing with credit risk. There are two main reasons for margin:

1. The trader is borrowing money to buy an asset. This is referred to as *buying on margin*. The margin is the amount provided by the trader toward the cost of the assets.
2. The trader is entering into a contract that could lead to the trader owing money in the future. In this case, the margin can be regarded as collateral for the trade. By posting margin, the trader is saying "I am good for this trade. The margin I have posted can be used to cover any losses."

Trades involving margin are monitored daily. Sometimes an *initial margin* has to be posted. If the market moves against the trader, there may be a *margin call* requesting that additional margin, known as *variation margin*, be posted to bring the balance up to a *maintenance margin* level. If the margin is not posted, the trader's position is closed out. The most common type of margin is cash. However, securities that are owned by the trader are sometimes used. For example, Treasury bills might be marginable at 90% of their value. (This means that they are credited to the trader's margin account at 90% of their value.) Shares of a stock might be marginable at 50% of their value.

There are many different ways in which margin accounts operate. This section gives a few examples.

Buying on Margin

Many assets can be bought on margin. As an example, we consider the situation where a trader buys 1,000 shares for $120 per share on margin using a broker. The broker states that the initial margin is 50% and the maintenance margin is 25%.

The initial margin is the minimum percentage of the cost of the trade that has to be provided by trader. Therefore, in this case, the trader has to deposit at least $60,000 in cash or in the form of marginable securities with the broker. We suppose that the trader deposits $60,000 in cash. The remaining $60,000 that is required to buy the shares is borrowed from the broker (with the broker keeping the shares as collateral). The balance in the margin account is calculated as the value of the shares minus the amount owed to the broker. Initially, therefore, the balance in the margin account is $60,000 and the amount borrowed is $60,000. Gains and losses on the shares (as well as interest charged by the broker) are reflected in the margin account balance, which can also be viewed as the trader's equity in the position.

The *maintenance margin* (25% in this case) is the minimum margin balance as a percentage of the value of the shares purchased. If the margin balance drops below this minimum, there is a margin call requiring the trader to provide additional margin bringing the balance up to the maintenance margin level.

Suppose that the price of the share declines by $10. The balance in the margin account falls to $50,000 and the value of the shares purchased is $110,000. The amount borrowed from the broker remains at $60,000. The margin as a percent of the value of the shares purchased is 50,000/110,000. This is more than 25% and so there is no margin call. (The calculations here ignore the interest that would be charged by the broker.) Suppose that, a short time later, the price of the share falls to $78. The loss on the position is 120,000 − 78,000 or $42,000. The balance in the margin account falls to $60,000 − $42,000 = $18,000 and the value of the shares is $78,000. The balance in the margin account has now fallen to 18,000/78,000 = 23.1% of the value of the shares. Because this is less than 25%, there is a margin call. This requires the trader to bring the margin balance up to 25% of the value of the shares. This means that 0.25 × 78,000 − 18,000 = $1,500 of additional margin must be provided. If it is not provided, the broker sells the shares. If it is provided, the position is maintained and the amount borrowed from the broker falls to $58,500.

Margin for Short Sales

When sales are shorted, a typical initial margin is 150% of the value of the shares. Suppose that a trader shorts 100 shares when the price is $60. As explained in Section 5.2, the shares are borrowed and sold in the market. The proceeds of the sale, $6,000, belong to the trader. However, the margin that must be initially posted is 150% of $6,000, or $9,000 in total. The trader must therefore post margin equal to the proceeds of the sale plus an additional $3,000. In this case, when the value of the shares declines, the balance in the margin account increases. When the value of the shares increases, the balance in the margin account decreases.

Suppose that the maintenance margin is 125%. This means that, when the balance in the margin account falls below 125% of the value of the shares, there is a margin call requiring that the balance be brought up to 125% of the value of the shares. Suppose that the share price rises to $70. The value of the shares that have been shorted is $7,000 and the maintenance margin is 1.25 × 7,000 or $8,750. The $9,000 initial margin covers this. However, if the share price rises again to $80, the maintenance margin is 1.25 × 8,000 or $10,000. There is a $1,000 margin call. If it is not met, the position is closed out.

Note one important difference between this example and the earlier one. In the earlier example, $60,000 was borrowed from the broker and the trader has to pay interest to the broker on it. In this example, the initial margin, and any additional margin contributed, belongs to the trader and, if the trader has a good broker, interest will be paid on the funds by the broker.

Margin for Futures Trades

Consider a trader who buys one contract (100 ounces) of September gold for $1,680. Suppose that the initial margin is $6,000 per contract and the maintenance margin is $4,500 per contract. The trader must post $6,000 of margin with the broker at the time of the trade. Losses on the futures contract are charged to the margin account daily. This is the daily settlement process referred to earlier. Suppose the price of gold falls to $1,670. The trader loses $1,000. (Gold which the trader agreed to buy for $1,680 can now only be sold for $1,670.) The balance in the margin account is reduced from $6,000 to $5,000. Because the maintenance margin has not been reached, there is no margin call. If the next day the price of gold falls to $1,660, the trader loses a further $1,000 and the balance in the margin account is reduced to $4,000. This is below the maintenance margin level. The trader is then required to bring the balance in the margin account up to the initial margin level. The margin call is therefore $2,000. If the margin is not provided within 24 hours, the broker will close out the position. Note a difference between this arrangement and the arrangements discussed above for buying on margin and short sales. Here the trader has to bring the balance in the margin account up to the initial margin level. In the other cases, it is sufficient for the trader to bring the balance up to the maintenance margin level.

The initial margin and maintenance margin for futures traders who are selling are the same as those for futures traders who are buying. Traders earn interest on the balance in their margin accounts. As indicated earlier, the daily settlement procedures mean that funds flow from the margin accounts of traders with short positions to the margin accounts of traders with long positions when the futures price increases and in the other direction when it decreases.

Margin for Option Trading

When a trader purchases options for cash, there are no margin requirements because there are no circumstances under which the trader will have a liability in the future. Options on stocks and stock indices that last longer than nine months can be bought on margin in the United States. The initial and maintenance margin is 75% of the value of the option.

When options are sold, there are potential future liabilities and margin must be posted. When a call option on a stock has been written, the initial and maintenance margin in the United States is the greater of

1. 100% of the value of the option plus 20% of the underlying share price less the amount, if any, by which the option is out-of-the-money
2. 100% of the value of the option plus 10% of the share price

When a put option has been written, it is the greater of

1. 100% of the value of the option plus 20% of the underlying share price less the amount if any which the option is out-of-the-money
2. 100% of the value of the option plus 10% of the exercise price

These margin requirements may be reduced if the trader has other positions in the stock. For example, if the trader has a fully covered position (where the trader has sold call options on a certain number of shares and owns the same number of shares), there is no margin requirement on the short option position.

Unlike futures, options are not settled daily and so the whole margin balance belongs to the trader and earns interest.

OTC Trades

As mentioned in Section 5.5, there is now a requirement that central clearing parties (CCPs) be used for standard OTC derivatives. When a company has cleared trades through a CCP, it is required to post initial margin and variation margin with the CCP. The size of the initial margin required from a company at a particular time depends on the CCP's assessment of the volatility of the value of the trades of the company that are being cleared with the CCP. Similarly to an exchange clearing house, the CCP wants to be sure that the initial margin will nearly always be sufficient to cover losses in the event that positions have to be closed out because the company does not respond to a margin call.

In trades that are cleared bilaterally rather than centrally, an ISDA agreement between two market participants usually defines how the trades will be handled. Often margin has to be posted. In this context, margin is usually referred to as "collateral." An initial margin is referred to as an "independent amount." Often there is no independent amount and a "threshold" is specified. This is the amount by which the outstanding contracts can move in favor of one side before the other side has to post collateral. The collateral (margin) requirements when trades are cleared bilaterally are therefore often not as great as they would be if the trades were cleared centrally or done on an exchange. This poses more risk for the financial institutions that operate in the OTC market—and potentially for the financial system as a whole. There is a danger that a default by one financial institution can lead to losses by other financial institutions. This in turn can lead to further defaults and further losses. The possibility of this sort of scenario is the reason why legislators have insisted on central clearing for standard OTC transactions. Collateral agreements and the quantification of counterparty credit risk is discussed further in Chapter 17.

5.7 NON-TRADITIONAL DERIVATIVES

Whenever there are risks in the economy, financial engineers have attempted to devise derivatives to allow entities with exposures to manage their risks. Financial institutions typically act as intermediaries and arrange for the risks to be passed on to either (a) entities that have opposite exposures or (b) speculators who are willing to assume the risks. This section gives examples of derivatives that have been developed to meet specific needs.

Weather Derivatives

Many companies are in the position where their performance is liable to be adversely affected by the weather.[7] It makes sense for these companies to consider hedging their weather risk in much the same way as they hedge foreign exchange or interest rate risks.

The first over-the-counter weather derivatives were introduced in 1997. To understand how they work, we explain two variables:

HDD: Heating degree days

CDD: Cooling degree days

A day's HDD is defined as

$$HDD = \max(0, 65 - A)$$

and a day's CDD is defined as

$$CDD = \max(0, A - 65)$$

where A is the average of the highest and lowest temperature during the day at a specified weather station, measured in degrees Fahrenheit. For example, if the maximum temperature during a day (midnight to midnight) is 68° Fahrenheit and the minimum temperature is 44° Fahrenheit, $A = 56$. The daily HDD is then 9 and the daily CDD is 0.

A typical over-the-counter product is a forward or option contract providing a payoff dependent on the cumulative HDD or CDD during a month (that is, the total of the HDDs or CDDs for every day in the month). For example, a dealer could in January 2012 sell a client a call option on the cumulative HDD during February 2013 at the Chicago O'Hare Airport weather station with a strike price of 700 and a payment rate of $10,000 per degree day. If the actual cumulative HDD is 820, the payoff is $1.2 million. Often contracts include a payment cap. If the cap in our example is $1.5 million, the client's position is equivalent to a long call option on cumulative HDD with a strike price of 700 and a short call option on cumulative HDD with a strike price of 850.

A day's HDD is a measure of the volume of energy required for heating during the day. A day's CDD is a measure of the volume of energy required for cooling during the day. Most weather derivative contracts are entered into by energy producers and energy consumers. But retailers, supermarket chains, food and drink manufacturers, health service companies, agriculture companies, and companies in

---

[7] The U.S. Department of Energy has estimated that one-seventh of the U.S. economy is subject to weather risk.

the leisure industry are also potential users of weather derivatives. The Weather Risk Management Association (www.wrma.org) has been formed to serve the interests of the weather risk management industry.

In September 1999, the Chicago Mercantile Exchange began trading weather futures and European options on weather futures. The contracts are on the cumulative HDD and CDD for a month observed at a weather station.[8] The contracts are settled in cash just after the end of the month once the HDD and CDD are known. One futures contract is $100 times the cumulative HDD or CDD. The HDD and CDD are calculated by a company, Earth Satellite Corporation, using automated data collection equipment.

Oil Derivatives

Crude oil is one of the most important commodities in the world. Global demand in 2010 was estimated by the United States Energy Information Administration (www.eia.gov) to be about 85 million barrels per day. Ten-year fixed-price supply contracts have been commonplace in the over-the-counter market for many years. These are swaps where oil at a fixed price is exchanged for oil at a floating price.

In the 1970s, the price of oil was highly volatile. The 1973 war in the Middle East led to a tripling of oil prices. Following the fall of the Shah of Iran in the late 1970s, oil prices again increased. These events led oil producers and users to a realization that they needed more sophisticated tools for managing oil price risk. In the 1980s, both the over-the-counter market and the exchange-traded market developed products to meet this need. Oil prices have been very volatile since 2007 making the derivatives very useful to market participants.

In the over-the-counter market, virtually any derivative that is available on common stocks or stock indices is now available with oil as the underlying asset. Swaps, forward contracts, and options are popular. Contracts sometimes require settlement in cash and sometimes require settlement by physical delivery (i.e., by delivery of the oil).

Exchange-traded contracts on oil are also popular. The New York Mercantile Exchange (NYMEX) and the International Petroleum Exchange (IPE) trade a number of oil futures and futures options contracts. Some of the futures contracts are settled in cash; others are settled by physical delivery. For example, the Brent crude oil futures traded on the IPE has cash settlement based on the Brent index price; the light sweet crude oil futures traded on NYMEX require physical delivery. In both cases, the amount of oil underlying one contract is 1,000 barrels. NYMEX also trades popular contracts on two refined products: heating oil and gasoline. In both cases, one contract is for the delivery of 42,000 gallons.

Natural Gas Derivatives

The natural gas industry throughout the world has been going through a period of deregulation and the elimination of government monopolies. The supplier of natural

---

[8] The CME has introduced contracts for 10 different weather stations (Atlanta, Chicago, Cincinnati, Dallas, Des Moines, Las Vegas, New York, Philadelphia, Portland, and Tucson).

gas is now not necessarily the same company as the producer of the gas. Suppliers are faced with the problem of meeting daily demand.

A typical over-the-counter contract is for the delivery of a specified amount of natural gas at a roughly uniform rate over a one-month period. Forward contracts, options, and swaps are available in the over-the-counter market. The seller of gas is usually responsible for moving the gas through pipelines to the specified location.

NYMEX trades a contract for the delivery of 10,000 million British thermal units of natural gas. The contract, if not closed out, requires physical delivery to be made during the delivery month at a roughly uniform rate to a particular hub in Louisiana. The IPE trades a similar contract in London.

Electricity Derivatives

Electricity is an unusual commodity because it cannot easily be stored.[9] The maximum supply of electricity in a region at any moment is determined by the maximum capacity of all the electricity-producing plants in the region. In the United States there are 140 regions known as *control areas*. Demand and supply are first matched within a control area, and any excess power is sold to other control areas. It is this excess power that constitutes the wholesale market for electricity. The ability of one control area to sell power to another control area depends on the transmission capacity of the lines between the two areas. Transmission from one area to another involves a transmission cost, charged by the owner of the line, and there are generally some energy transmission losses.

A major use of electricity is for air-conditioning systems. As a result, the demand for electricity, and therefore its price, is much greater in the summer months than in the winter months. The nonstorability of electricity causes occasional very large movements in the spot price. Heat waves have been known to increase the spot price by as much as 1,000% for short periods of time.

Like natural gas, electricity has been going through a period of deregulation and the elimination of government monopolies. This has been accompanied by the development of an electricity derivatives market. NYMEX now trades a futures contract on the price of electricity, and there is an active over-the-counter market in forward contracts, options, and swaps. A typical contract (exchange-traded or over-the-counter) allows one side to receive a specified number of megawatt hours for a specified price at a specified location during a particular month. In a 5×8 contract, power is received for five days a week (Monday to Friday) during the off-peak period (11 P.M. to 7 A.M.) for the specified month. In a 5×16 contract, power is received five days a week during the on-peak period (7 A.M. to 11 P.M.) for the specified month. In a 7×24 contract, it is received around the clock every day during the month. Option contracts have either daily exercise or monthly exercise. In the case of daily exercise, the option holder can choose on each day of the month (by giving one day's notice) to receive the specified amount of power at the specified strike price. When there is monthly exercise, a single decision on whether to receive

---

[9] Electricity producers with spare capacity sometimes use it to pump water to the top of their hydroelectric plants so that it can be used to produce electricity at a later time. This is the closest they can get to storing this commodity.

power for the whole month at the specified strike price is made at the beginning of the month.

An interesting contract in electricity and natural gas markets is what is known as a *swing option* or *take-and-pay option*. In this contract, a minimum and maximum for the amount of power that must be purchased at a certain price by the option holder is specified for each day during a month and for the month in total. The option holder can change (or swing) the rate at which the power is purchased during the month, but usually there is a limit on the total number of changes that can be made.

5.8 EXOTIC OPTIONS AND STRUCTURED PRODUCTS

Many different types of exotic options and structured products trade in the over-the-counter market. Although the amount of trading in them is small when compared with the trading in the plain vanilla derivatives discussed in Section 5.4, they are important to a bank because the profit on trades in exotic options and structured products tends to be much higher than on plain vanilla options or swaps.

Here are a few examples of exotic options:

Asian options: Whereas regular options provide a payoff based on the final price of the underlying asset at the time of exercise, Asian options provide a payoff based on the average of the price of the underlying asset over some specified period. An example is an *average price call option* that provides a payoff in one year equal to $\max(\overline{S} - K, 0)$ where $\overline{S}$ is the average asset price during the year and K is the strike price.

Barrier options: These are options that come into existence or disappear when the price of the underlying asset reaches a certain barrier. For example, a knock-out call option with a strike price of $30 and a barrier of $20 is a regular call option that ceases to exist if the asset price falls below $20.

Basket options: These are options on a portfolio of assets rather than options on a single asset.

Binary options: These are options that provide a fixed dollar payoff, or a certain amount of the underlying asset, if some condition is satisfied. An example is an option that provides a payoff in one year of $1,000 if a stock price is greater than $20.

Compound options: These are options on options. There are four types: a call on a call, a call on a put, a put on a call, and a put on a put. An example of a compound option is an option to buy an option on a stock currently worth $15. The first option expires in one year and has a strike price of $1. The second option expires in three years and has a strike price of $20.

Lookback options: These are options that provide a payoff based on the maximum or minimum price of the underlying asset over some period. An example is an option that provides a payoff in one year equal to $S_T - S_{min}$ where S_T is the asset price at the end of the year and S_{min} is the minimum asset price during the year.

BUSINESS SNAPSHOT 5.3

Microsoft's Hedging

Microsoft actively manages its foreign exchange exposure. In some countries (e.g., Europe, Japan, and Australia), it bills in the local currency and converts its net revenue to U.S. dollars monthly. For these currencies, there is a clear exposure to exchange rate movements. In other countries (e.g., those in Latin America, Eastern Europe, and Southeast Asia), it bills in U.S. dollars. The latter appears to avoid any foreign exchange exposure—but it does not.

Suppose the U.S. dollar strengthens against the currency of a country in which it is billing in U.S. dollars. People in the country will find Microsoft's products more expensive because it takes more of the local currency to buy $1. As a result, Microsoft is likely to find it necessary to reduce its (U.S. dollar) price in the country or face a decline in sales. Microsoft therefore has a foreign exchange exposure—both when it bills in U.S. dollars and when it bills in the local currency. (This shows that it is important for a company to consider the big picture when assessing its exposure.)

Microsoft likes to use options for hedging. Suppose it chooses a one-year time horizon. Microsoft recognizes that its exposure to an exchange rate (say, the Japanese yen–U.S. dollar exchange rate) is an exposure to the average of the exchange rates at the end of each month during the year. This is because approximately the same amount of Japanese yen is converted to U.S. dollars each month. Asian options rather than regular options are appropriate to hedge its exposure. What is more, Microsoft's total foreign exchange exposure is a a weighted average of the exchange rates in all the countries in which it does business. This means that a basket option, where the option is on a portfolio of currencies, is an appropriate tool for hedging. A contract it likes to negotiate with banks is therefore an Asian basket option. The cost of this option is much less than a portfolio of put options, one for each month and each exchange rate (see Problem 5.23), but it gives Microsoft exactly the protection it wants.

Microsoft faces other financial risks. For example, it is exposed to interest rate risk on its bond portfolio. (When rates rise the portfolio loses money.) It also has two sorts of exposure to equity prices. It is exposed to the equity prices of the companies in which it invests. It is also exposed to its own equity price because it regularly repurchases its own shares as part of its stock awards program. It sometimes uses sophisticated option strategies to hedge these risks.

Exotic options are sometimes more appropriate for hedging than plain vanilla options. As explained in Business Snapshot 5.3, Microsoft uses Asian options on a basket for some of its foreign currency hedging.

Structured products are products created by banks to meet the needs of investors or corporate treasurers. One example of a structured product is a principal protected

BUSINESS SNAPSHOT 5.4

Procter & Gamble's Bizarre Deal

A particularly bizarre swap is the so-called "5/30" swap entered into between Bankers Trust (BT) and Procter & Gamble (P&G) on November 2, 1993. This was a five-year swap with semiannual payments. The notional principal was $200 million. BT paid P&G 5.30% per annum. P&G paid BT the average 30-day CP (commercial paper) rate minus 75 basis points plus a spread. The average commercial paper rate was calculated by taking observations on the 30-day commercial paper rate each day during the preceding accrual period and averaging them.

The spread was zero for the first payment date (May 2, 1994). For the remaining nine payment dates, it was

$$\max\left[0, \frac{98.5\left(\frac{\text{5-yr CMT\%}}{5.78\%}\right) - (\text{30-yr TSY Price})}{100}\right]$$

In this, five-year CMT is the constant maturity Treasury yield (that is, the yield on a five-year Treasury note, as reported by the U.S. Federal Reserve). The 30-year TSY price is the midpoint of the bid and offer cash bond prices for the 6.25% Treasury bond maturing on August 2023. Note that the spread calculated from the formula is a decimal interest rate. It is not measured in basis points. If the formula gives 0.1 and the CP rate is 6%, the rate paid by P&G is 15.25%.

P&G were hoping that the spread would be zero and the deal would enable it to exchange fixed-rate funding at 5.30% for funding at 75 basis points less than the commercial paper rate. In fact, interest rates rose sharply in early 1994, bond prices fell, and the swap proved very, very expensive. (See Problem 5.36.)

note, where a bank offers an investor the opportunity to earn a certain percentage of the return provided by the S&P 500 with a guarantee that the return will not be negative. Another example of a (highly) structured product is the 5/30 transaction described in Business Snapshot 5.4.[10] (In the case of this product, it is debatable whether Bankers Trust was meeting a client need or selling the client a product it did not need!)

---

[10] The details of this transaction are in the public domain because it later became the subject of litigation. See D. J. Smith, "Aggressive Corporate Finance: A Close Look at the Procter and Gamble–Bankers Trust Leveraged Swap," *Journal of Derivatives* 4, no. 4 (Summer 1997): 67–79.

BUSINESS SNAPSHOT 5.5

SocGen's Big Loss in 2008

Derivatives are very versatile instruments. They can be used for hedging, speculation, and arbitrage. One of the risks faced by a company that trades derivatives is that an employee who has a mandate to hedge or to look for arbitrage opportunities may become a speculator.

Jérôme Kerviel joined Société Générale (SocGen) in 2000 to work in the compliance area. In 2005, he was promoted and became a junior trader in the bank's Delta One products team. He traded equity indices such as the German DAX index, the French CAC 40, and the Euro Stoxx 50. His job was to look for arbitrage opportunities. These might arise if a futures contract on an equity index was trading for a different price on two different exchanges. They might also arise if equity index futures prices were not consistent with the prices of the shares constituting the index.

Kerviel used his knowledge of the bank's procedures to speculate while giving the appearance of arbitraging. He took big positions in equity indices and created fictitious trades to make it appear that he was hedged. In reality, he had large bets on the direction in which the indices would move. The size of his unhedged position grew over time to tens of billions of euros.

In January 2008, his unauthorized trading was uncovered by SocGen. Over a three-day period, the bank unwound his position for a loss of 4.9 billion euros. This was at the time the biggest loss created by fraudulent activity in the history of finance. (Later in the year, much bigger losses from Bernard Madoff's Ponzi scheme came to light.)

Rogue trader losses were not unknown at banks prior to 2008. For example, in the 1990s Nick Leeson, who worked at Barings Bank, had a similar mandate to Jérôme Kerviel. His job was to arbitrage between Nikkei 225 futures quotes in Singapore and Osaka. Instead he found a way to make big bets on the direction of the Nikkei 225 using futures and options, losing $1 billion and destroying the 200-year old bank. In 2002, it was found that John Rusnak at Allied Irish Bank had lost $700 million from unauthorized foreign exchange trading. In 2011, Kweku Adoboli, a member of UBS's Delta One team, lost $2.3 billion by engaging in activities very similar to those of Jérôme Kerviel. The lesson from these losses is that it is important to define unambiguous risk limits for traders and then be very careful when monitoring what they do to make sure that the limits are adhered to.

5.9 RISK MANAGEMENT CHALLENGES

Instruments such as futures, forwards, swaps, options, and structured products are versatile. They can be used for hedging, for speculation, and for arbitrage. (Hedging involves reducing risks; speculation involves taking risks; and arbitrage involves attempting to lock in a profit by simultaneously trading in two or more markets.) It is this very versatility that can cause problems. Sometimes traders who have a mandate to hedge risks or follow an arbitrage strategy become (consciously or unconsciously) speculators. The results can be disastrous. One example of this is provided by the activities of Jérôme Kerviel at Société Générale (see Business Snapshot 5.5).

To avoid the type of problems Société Générale encountered is an important risk management challenge. Both financial and nonfinancial corporations must set up controls to ensure that derivatives are being used for their intended purpose. Risk limits should be set and the activities of traders should be monitored daily to ensure that the risk limits are adhered to. We will be discussing this in later chapters.

SUMMARY

There are two types of market in which financial products trade: the exchange-traded market and the over-the-counter market. This chapter has reviewed spot trades, forwards, futures, swaps, and options contracts. A forward or futures contract involves an obligation to buy or sell an asset at a certain time in the future for a certain price. A swap is an agreement to exchange cash flows in the future in amounts dependent on the values of one or more market variables. There are two types of option: calls and puts. A call option gives the holder the right to buy an asset by a certain date for a certain price. A put option gives the holder the right to sell an asset by a certain date for a certain price.

Forward, futures, and swap contracts have the effect of locking in the prices that will apply to future transactions. Options by contrast provide insurance. They ensure that the price applicable to a future transaction will not be worse than a certain level. Exotic options and structured products are tailored to the particular needs of corporate treasurers. For example, as shown in Business Snapshot 5.3, Asian basket options can allow a company such as Microsoft to hedge its net exposure to several risks over a period of time.

Margin is cash or marketable securities deposited by a trader in a margin account with either a broker or a counterparty. Margin accounts are used when a trader wishes to borrow money for trading or when the trading may give rise to future liabilities. The trader's position is monitored daily and there may be margin calls requesting further margin. If the trader does not satisfy a margin call within 24 hours, the trader's position is usually closed out.

Derivatives now trade on a wide variety of variables. This chapter has reviewed those that provide payoffs dependent on the weather, oil, natural gas, and electricity. It has also discussed exotic options and structured products.

FURTHER READING

Boyle, P. and F. Boyle. *Derivatives: The Tools That Changed Finance*. London: Risk Books, 2001.

Flavell, R. *Swaps and Other Instruments*. Chichester: John Wiley & Sons, 2002.

Geczy, C., B. A. Minton, and C. Schrand. "Why Firms Use Currency Derivatives." *Journal of Finance 52*, no. 4 (1997): 1323–1354.

Litzenberger, R. H. "Swaps: Plain and Fanciful." *Journal of Finance* 47, no. 3 (1992): 831–850.

Miller, M. H. "Financial Innovation: Achievements and Prospects." *Journal of Applied Corporate Finance* 4 (Winter 1992): 4–11.

Warwick B., F. J. Jones, and R. J. Teweles. *The Futures Games*, 3rd ed. New York: McGraw-Hill, 1998.

PRACTICE QUESTIONS AND PROBLEMS
(ANSWERS AT END OF BOOK)

5.1 What is the difference between a long forward position and a short forward position?

5.2 Explain carefully the difference between hedging, speculation, and arbitrage.

5.3 What is the difference between entering into a long forward contract when the forward price is $50 and taking a long position in a call option with a strike price of $50?

5.4 Explain carefully the difference between selling a call option and buying a put option.

5.5 An investor enters into a short forward contract to sell 100,000 British pounds for U.S. dollars at an exchange rate of 1.7000 U.S. dollars per pound. How much does the investor gain or lose if the exchange rate at the end of the contract is (a) 1.6900 and (b) 1.7200?

5.6 A trader enters into a short cotton futures contract when the futures price is 50 cents per pound. The contract is for the delivery of 50,000 pounds. How much does the trader gain or lose if the cotton price at the end of the contract is (a) 48.20 cents per pound and (b) 51.30 cents per pound?

5.7 Suppose you write a put contract with a strike price of $40 and an expiration date in three months. The current stock price is $41 and the contract is on 100 shares. What have you committed yourself to? How much could you gain or lose?

5.8 What is the difference between the over-the-counter market and the exchange-traded market? Which of the two markets do the following trade in: (a) a forward contract, (b) a futures contract, (c) an option, (d) a swap, and (e) an exotic option?

5.9 You would like to speculate on a rise in the price of a certain stock. The current stock price is $29, and a three-month call with a strike of $30 costs $2.90. You have $5,800 to invest. Identify two alternative strategies, one involving an investment in the stock and the other involving investment in the option. What are the potential gains and losses from each?

5.10 Suppose that you own 5,000 shares worth $25 each. How can put options be used to provide you with insurance against a decline in the value of your holding over the next four months?

5.11 When first issued, a stock provides funds for a company. Is the same true of a stock option? Discuss.

5.12 Suppose that a March call option to buy a share for $50 costs $2.50 and is held until March. Under what circumstances will the holder of the option make a profit? Under what circumstances will the option be exercised?

5.13 Suppose that a June put option to sell a share for $60 costs $4 and is held until June. Under what circumstances will the seller of the option (i.e., the party with the short position) make a profit? Under what circumstances will the option be exercised?

5.14 A company knows that it is due to receive a certain amount of a foreign currency in four months. What type of option contract is appropriate for hedging?

5.15 A United States company expects to have to pay 1 million Canadian dollars in six months. Explain how the exchange rate risk can be hedged using (a) a forward contract and (b) an option.

5.16 In the 1980s, Bankers Trust developed index currency option notes (ICONs). These are bonds in which the amount received by the holder at maturity varies with a foreign exchange rate. One example was its trade with the Long-Term Credit Bank of Japan. The ICON specified that if the yen–U.S. dollar exchange rate, S_T, is greater than 169 yen per dollar at maturity (in 1995), the holder of the bond receives $1,000. If it is less than 169 yen per dollar, the amount received by the holder of the bond is

$$1,000 - \max\left[0, 1,000\left(\frac{169}{S_T} - 1\right)\right]$$

When the exchange rate is below 84.5, nothing is received by the holder at maturity. Show that this ICON is a combination of a regular bond and two options.

5.17 Suppose that USD-sterling spot and forward exchange rates are as follows:

Spot	1.6080
90-day forward	1.6056
180-day forward	1.6018

What opportunities are open to an arbitrageur in the following situations?
(a) A 180-day European call option to buy $1 for $1.57 costs 2 cents.
(b) A 90-day European put option to sell $1 for $1.64 costs 2 cents.

5.18 A company has money invested at 5% for five years. It wishes to use the swap quotes in Table 5.5 to convert its investment to a floating-rate investment. Explain how it can do this.

5.19 A company has borrowed money for five years at 7%. Explain how it can use the quotes in Table 5.5 to convert this to a floating-rate liability.

5.20 A company has a floating-rate liability that costs LIBOR plus 1%. Explain how it can use the quotes in Table 5.5 to convert this to a three-year fixed-rate liability.

5.21 A corn farmer argues "I do not use futures contracts for hedging. My real risk is not the price of corn. It is that my whole crop gets wiped out by the weather." Discuss this viewpoint. Should the farmer estimate his or her expected production of corn and hedge to try to lock in a price for expected production?

5.22 An airline executive has argued: "There is no point in our hedging the price of jet fuel. There is just as much chance that we will lose from doing this as that we will gain." Discuss the executive's viewpoint.

5.23 Why is the cost of an Asian basket put option to Microsoft considerably less that the cost of a portfolio of put options, one for each currency and each maturity (see Business Snapshot 5.3)?

5.24 A United States investor writes five call option contracts. The option price is $3.50, the strike price is $60, and the stock price is $57. What is the initial margin requirement?

5.25 "Oil, gas, and electricity prices tend to exhibit mean reversion." What do you think is meant by this statement? Which energy source is likely to have the highest rate of mean reversion? Which is likely to have the lowest?

5.26 Does a knock-out barrier call option become more or less valuable as the frequency with which the barrier is observed is increased?

5.27 Suppose that each day during July the minimum temperature is 68° Fahrenheit and the maximum temperature is 82° Fahrenheit. What is the payoff from a call option on the cumulative CDD during July with a strike of 250 and a payment rate of $5,000 per degree day?

5.28 Explain how a 5×8 option contract on electricity for May 2013 with daily exercise works. Explain how a 5×8 option contract on electricity for May 2013 with monthly exercise works. Which is worth more?

5.29 A trader shorts 500 shares of a stock when the price is $50. The initial margin is 160% and the maintenance margin is 130%. How much margin is required from the investor initially? How high does the price of the stock have to rise for there to be a margin call?

FURTHER QUESTIONS

5.30 A company enters into a short futures contract to sell 5,000 bushels of wheat for 25 cents per bushel. The initial margin is $3,000 and the maintenance margin is $2,000. What price change would lead to a margin call? Under what circumstances could $1,500 be withdrawn from the margin account?

5.31 The current price of a stock is $94, and three-month European call options with a strike price of $95 currently sell for $4.70. An investor who feels that the price of the stock will increase is trying to decide between buying 100 shares and buying 2,000 call options (= 20 contracts). Both strategies involve an investment of $9,400. What advice would you give? How high does the stock price have to rise for the option strategy to be more profitable?

5.32 A bond issued by Standard Oil worked as follows. The holder received no interest. At the bond's maturity the company promised to pay $1,000 plus an additional amount based on the price of oil at that time. The additional amount was equal to the product of 170 and the excess (if any) of the price of a barrel of oil at maturity over $25. The maximum additional amount paid was $2,550 (which corresponds to a price of $40 per barrel). Show that the bond is a combination of a regular bond, a long position in call options on oil with a strike price of $25, and a short position in call options on oil with a strike price of $40.

5.33 The price of gold is currently $1,500 per ounce. The forward price for delivery in one year is $1,700. An arbitrageur can borrow money at 10% per annum.

What should the arbitrageur do? Assume that the cost of storing gold is zero and that gold provides no income.

5.34 A company's investments earn LIBOR minus 0.5%. Explain how it can use the quotes in Table 5.5 to convert them to (a) three-, (b) five-, and (c) ten-year fixed-rate investments.

5.35 What position is equivalent to a long forward contract to buy an asset at K on a certain date and a long position in a European put option to sell it for K on that date?

5.36 Estimate the interest rate paid by P&G on the 5/30 swap in Business Snapshot 5.4 if (a) the CP rate is 6.5% and the Treasury yield curve is flat at 6% and (b) the CP rate is 7.5% and the Treasury yield curve is flat at 7% with semiannual compounding.

5.37 A trader buys 200 shares of a stock on margin. The price of the stock is $20. The initial margin is 60% and the maintenance margin is 30%. How much money does the trader have to provide initially? For what share price is there a margin call?

CHAPTER 6

The Credit Crisis of 2007

Starting in 2007, the United States experienced the worst financial crisis since the 1930s. The crisis spread rapidly from the United States to other countries and from financial markets to the real economy. Some financial institutions failed. Many more had to be bailed out by national governments. The first decade of the twenty-first century has been disastrous for the financial sector, and the risk management practices of financial institutions have been subjected to a great deal of criticism. As we will see in later chapters, the crisis has led to a major overhaul of the way financial institutions are regulated.

This chapter examines the origins of the crisis, what went wrong, why it went wrong, and the lessons that can be learned. In the course of the chapter, we will find out about the U.S. housing market, asset-backed securities, and collateralized debt obligations.

6.1 THE U.S. HOUSING MARKET

A natural starting point for a discussion of the credit crisis of 2007 is the U.S. housing market. Figure 6.1 shows the S&P/Case-Shiller composite-10 index for house prices in the United States between January 1987 and July 2011. This tracks house prices for ten major metropolitan areas in the United States. In about the year 2000, house prices started to rise much faster than they had in the previous decade. The very low level of interest rates between 2002 and 2005 was an important contributory factor, but the bubble in house prices was largely fueled by mortgage lending practices.

The 2000 to 2006 period was characterized by a huge increase in what is termed subprime mortgage lending. Subprime mortgages are mortgages that are considered to be significantly more risky than average. Before 2000, most mortgages classified as subprime were second mortgages. After 2000, this changed as financial institutions became more comfortable with the notion of a subprime first mortgage.

The Relaxation of Lending Standards

Mortgage lenders started to relax their lending standards in about 2000. This made house purchases possible for many families that had previously been considered to be not sufficiently creditworthy to qualify for a mortgage. These families increased the demand for real estate and prices rose. To mortgage brokers and mortgage lenders,

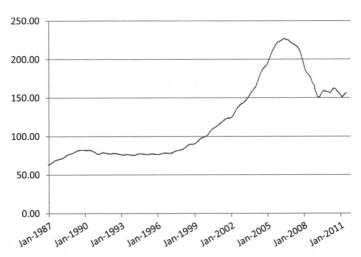

FIGURE 6.1 The S&P/Case-Shiller Composite-10 Index of U.S. Real Estate Prices, 1987 to 2011

the combination of more lending and rising house prices was attractive. More lending meant bigger profits. Rising house prices meant that the lending was well covered by the underlying collateral. If the borrower defaulted, the resulting foreclosure would lead to little or no loss.

How could mortgage brokers and mortgage lenders keep increasing their profits? Their problem was that, as house prices rose, it was more difficult for first-time buyers to afford a house. In order to continue to attract new entrants to the housing market, they had to find ways to relax their lending standards even more—and this is exactly what they did. The amount lent as a percentage of the house price increased. Adjustable rate mortgages (ARMs) were developed where there was a low "teaser" rate of interest that would last for two or three years and be followed by a rate that was much higher.[1] A typical teaser rate was about 6% and the rate after the end of the teaser-rate period was typically six-month LIBOR plus 6%.[2] However, teaser rates as low as 1% or 2% have been reported. Lenders also became more cavalier in the way they reviewed mortgage applications. Indeed, the applicant's income and other information reported on the application were frequently not checked.

Why was the government not regulating the behavior of mortgage lenders? The answer is that the U.S. government had since the 1990s been trying to expand home ownership, and had been applying pressure to mortgage lenders to increase loans to low and moderate income households. Some state legislators (such as those

---

[1] If real estate prices increased, lenders expected the borrowers to prepay and take out a new mortgage at the end of the teaser rate period. However, prepayments penalties, often zero on prime mortgages, were quite high on subprime mortgages.

[2] A "2/28" ARM, for example, is an ARM where the rate is fixed for two years and then floats for the remaining 28 years.

in Ohio and Georgia) were concerned about what was going on and wanted to curtail predatory lending.[3] However, the courts decided that national standards should prevail.

A number of terms have been used to describe mortgage lending during the period leading up to the credit crisis. One is "liar loans" because individuals applying for a mortgage, knowing that no checks would be carried out, sometimes chose to lie on the application form. Another term used to describe some borrowers is "NINJA" (no income, no job, no assets). Some analysts realized that the mortgages were risky, but pricing in the market for securities created from the mortgages suggests that the full extent of the risks and their potential impact on markets was not appreciated until well into 2007.

Mian and Sufi (2009) have carried out research confirming that there was a relaxation of the criteria used for mortgage lending.[4] Their research defines "high denial zip codes" as zip codes where a high proportion of mortgage applicants had been turned down in 1996, and shows that mortgage origination grew particularly fast for these zip codes between 2000 to 2007. Moreover, their research shows that lending criteria were relaxed progressively through time rather than all at once because originations in high denial zip codes are an increasing function of time during the 2000 to 2007 period. Zimmerman (2007) provides some confirmation of this.[5] He shows that subsequent default experience indicates that mortgages made in 2006 were of a lower quality than those made in 2005 and these were in turn of lower quality than the mortgages made in 2004. Standard & Poor's has estimated that subprime mortgage origination in 2006 alone totaled $421 billion. AMP Capital Investors estimate that there was a total of $1.4 trillion of subprime mortgages outstanding in July 2007.

The Bubble Bursts

The result of the relaxation of lending standards was a bubble in house prices. Prices increased very fast during the 2000 to 2006 period. All bubbles burst eventually and this one was no exception. In the second half of 2006, house prices started to edge down. One reason was that, as house prices increased, demand for houses declined. Another was that some borrowers with teaser rates found that they could no longer afford their mortgages when the teaser rates ended. This led to foreclosures and an increase in the supply of houses for sale. The decline in house price fed on itself. Individuals who had borrowed 100%, or close to 100%, of the cost of a house found that they had negative equity (i.e., the amount owing on the mortgage was greater than the value of the house). Some of these individuals chose to default. This

---

[3] Predatory lending describes the situation where a lender deceptively convinces borrowers to agree to unfair and abusive loan terms.

[4] See A. Mian and A. Sufi, "The Consequences of Mortgage Credit Expansion: Evidence from the US Mortgage Default Crisis," *Quarterly Journal of Economics* 124, no. 4 (November 2009): 1449–1496.

[5] See T. Zimmerman, "The Great Subprime Meltdown," *Journal of Structured Finance* (Fall 2007): 7–20.

led to more foreclosures, a further increase in the supply of houses for sale, and a further decline in house prices.

One of the features of the U.S. housing market is that mortgages are non-recourse in some states. This means that, when there is a default, the lender is able to take possession of the house, but other assets of the borrower are off-limits.[6] Consequently, the borrower has a free American-style put option. He or she can at any time sell the house to the lender for the principal outstanding on the mortgage.[7] (During the teaser-interest-rate period this principal typically increased, making the option more valuable.) Market participants realized belatedly how costly the put option could be. If the borrower had negative equity, the optimal decision was to exchange the house for the outstanding principal on the mortgage. The house was then sold, adding to the downward pressure on house prices.

It would be a mistake to assume that all mortgage defaulters were in the same position. Some were unable to meet mortgage payments and suffered greatly when they had to give up their homes. But many of the defaulters were speculators who bought multiple homes as rental properties and chose to exercise their put options. It was their tenants who suffered. There are also reports that some house owners (who were not speculators) were quite creative in extracting value from their put options. After handing the keys to their house to the lender, they turned around and bought (sometimes at a bargain price) another house that was in foreclosure. Imagine two people owning identical houses next to each other. Both have mortgages of $250,000. Both houses are worth $200,000 and in foreclosure can be expected to sell for $170,000. What is the owners' optimal strategy? The answer is that each person should exercise the put option and buy the neighbor's house.

The United States was not alone in having declining real estate prices. Prices declined in many other countries as well. Real estate in the United Kingdom was particularly badly affected.

As foreclosures increased, the losses on mortgages also increased. Losses were high because houses in foreclosure were often surrounded by other houses that were also for sale. They were sometimes in poor condition. In addition, banks faced legal and other fees. In normal market conditions, a lender can expect to recover 75% of the amount owing in a foreclosure. In 2008 and 2009, recovery rates as low as 25% were experienced in some areas.

6.2 SECURITIZATION

The originators of mortgages did not in many cases keep the mortgages themselves. They sold portfolios of mortgages to companies that created products for investors from them. This process is known as *securitization*. Securitization has been an

---

[6] In some other states, mortgages are not non-recourse but there is legislation making it difficult for lenders to take possession of other assets besides the house.

[7] In some states, the bank owned the house, but had no rights to use it in any way as long as payments were made on the mortgage. Title was transferred to the borrower only when the mortgage was finally paid off. Strictly speaking, the borrower did not have a put option in this situation because he or she did not own the house. However, the borrower had effective ownership and had the equivalent of a put option to give up this effective ownership.

important and useful tool for transferring risk in financial markets for many years. It underlies the originate-to-distribute model that was widely used by banks prior to 2007 and is discussed in Chapter 2.

Securitization played a part in the creation of the housing bubble. The behavior of mortgage originators was influenced by their knowledge that mortgages would be securitized.[8] When considering new mortgage applications, the question was not: "Is this a credit we want to assume?" Instead it was: "Is this a mortgage we can make money from by selling it to someone else?"

When mortgages were securitized, the only information received about the mortgages by the buyers of the products that were created from them was the loan-to-value ratio (i.e the ratio of the size of the loan to the assessed value of the house) and the borrower's FICO (credit) score.[9] The reason why lenders did not check information on things such as the applicant's income, the number of years the applicant had lived at his or her current address, and so on, was that this information was considered irrelevant. The most important thing for the lender was whether the mortgage could be sold to others—and this depended primarily on the loan-to-value ratio and the applicant's FICO score.

It is interesting to note in passing that both the loan-to-value ratio and the FICO score were of doubtful quality. The property assessors who determined the value of a house at the time of a mortgage application sometimes inflated valuations because they knew that the lender wanted a low loan-to-value ratio. Potential borrowers were sometimes counseled to take certain actions that would improve their FICO scores.[10]

We now consider the products that were created from the mortgages and sold in the market.

Asset-Backed Securities

An *asset-backed security* (ABS) is a security created from the cash flows of financial assets such as loans, bonds, credit card receivables, mortgages, auto loans, and aircraft leases. Sometimes, cash flow streams such as royalties from the future sales of a piece of music are even used. The way the security works is illustrated by Figure 6.2. A portfolio of assets (such as subprime mortgages) is sold by the originators of the assets to a special purpose vehicle (SPV) and the cash flows from the assets are allocated to tranches. In Figure 6.2, there are three tranches. These are the senior tranche, the mezzanine tranche, and the equity tranche. The portfolio has a principal of $100 million. This is divided as follows: $75 million to the senior tranche, $20 million to the mezzanine tranche, and $5 million to the equity tranche. The senior tranche is promised a return of 6%, the mezzanine tranche is promised a return of 10%, and the equity tranche is promised a return of 30%.

---

[8] Research by Keys et al. shows that there was a link between securitization and the lax screening of mortgages. See B. J. Keys, T. Mukherjee, A. Seru, and V. Vig, "Did Securitization Lead to Lax Screening? Evidence from Subprime Loans," *Quarterly Journal of Economics* 125, no. 1 (February 2010): 307–362.

[9] FICO is a credit score developed by the Fair Isaac Corporation and is widely used in the United States. It ranges from 300 to 850.

[10] One such action might be to make regular payments on a credit card for a few months.

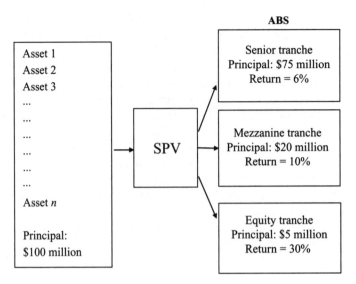

FIGURE 6.2   Creation of an ABS from a Portfolio of Assets (simplified)

It sounds as though the equity tranche has the best deal, but this is not necessarily the case. The equity tranche is much less likely to realize its return than the other two tranches. Cash flows are allocated to tranches by specifying what is known as a waterfall. An approximation to the way a waterfall works is in Figure 6.3. There is a separate waterfall for interest and principal cash flows. Interest cash flows from the assets are allocated to the senior tranche until the senior tranche has received its promised return on its outstanding principal. Assuming that the promised return to the senior tranche can be made, cash flows are then allocated to the mezzanine tranche. If the promised return to the mezzanine tranche on its outstanding principal can be made and interest cash flows are left over, they are allocated to the equity tranche. Principal cash flows are used first to repay the principal of the senior tranche, then the mezzanine tranche, and finally the equity tranche.[11]

The structure in Figure 6.2 typically lasts several years. The extent to which the tranches get their principal back depends on losses on the underlying assets. The first 5% of losses are borne by the principal of the equity tranche. If losses exceed 5%, the equity tranche loses all its principal and some losses are borne by the principal of the mezzanine tranche. If losses exceed 25%, the mezzanine tranche loses all its principal and some losses are borne by the principal of the senior tranche.

There are therefore two ways of looking at an ABS. One is with reference to the waterfall in Figure 6.3. Cash flows go first to the senior tranche, then to the mezzanine tranche, and then to the equity tranche. The other is in terms of losses. Losses of principal are first borne by the equity tranche, then by the mezzanine tranche, and then by the senior tranche.

---

[11] The priority rule described here is a simplification. The precise waterfall rules are somewhat more complicated and outlined in a legal document several hundred pages long.

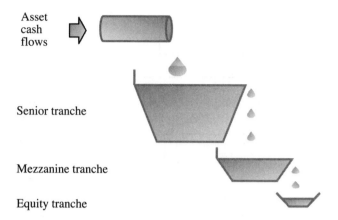

FIGURE 6.3 The Waterfall in an Asset-Backed Security

The ABS is designed so that the senior tranche is rated AAA. The mezzanine tranche is typically rated BBB. The equity tranche is typically unrated. Unlike the ratings assigned to bonds, the ratings assigned to the tranches of an ABS are what might be termed "negotiated ratings." The objective of the creator of the ABS is to make the senior tranche as big as possible without losing its AAA credit rating. (This maximizes the profitability of the structure.) The ABS creator examines information published by rating agencies on how tranches are rated and may present several structures to rating agencies for a preliminary evaluation before choosing the final one. The creator of the ABS makes a profit because the weighted average return on the assets in the underlying portfolio is greater than the weighted average return offered to the tranches.

A particular type of ABS is a *collateralized debt obligation* (CDO). This is an ABS where the underlying assets are fixed-income securities. The procedures used by the market to value a CDO are outlined in Appendix L.

ABS CDOs

Finding investors to buy the senior AAA-rated tranches created from subprime mortgages was not difficult. Equity tranches were typically retained by the originator of the mortgages or sold to a hedge fund. Finding investors for the mezzanine tranches was more difficult. This led financial engineers to be creative (arguably too creative). Financial engineers created an ABS from the mezzanine tranches of ABSs that were created from subprime mortgages. This is known as an *ABS CDO* or *Mezz ABS CDO* and is illustrated in Figure 6.4. The senior tranche of the ABS CDO is rated AAA. This means that the total of the AAA-rated instruments created in the example that is considered here is 90% (75% plus 75% of 20%) of the principal of the underlying mortgage portfolios. This seems high but, if the securitization were carried further with an ABS being created from the mezzanine tranches of ABS CDOs (and this did happen), the percentage would be pushed even higher.

In the example in Figure 6.4, the AAA-rated tranche of the ABS would probably be downgraded in the second half of 2007. However, it would receive the

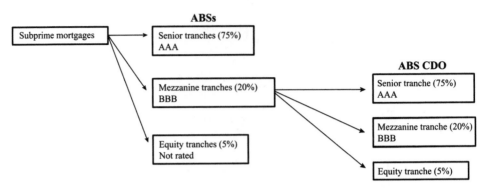

FIGURE 6.4   Creation of ABSs and an ABS CDO from Subprime Mortgages (simplified)

promised return if losses on the underlying mortgage portfolios were less than 25% because all losses of principal would then be absorbed by the more junior tranches. The AAA-rated tranche of the ABS CDO in Figure 6.4 is much more risky. It will get paid the promised return if losses on the underlying portfolios are 10% or less because in that case mezzanine tranches of ABSs have to absorb losses equal to 5% of the ABS principal or less. As they have a total principal of 20% of the ABS principal, their loss is at most 5/20 or 25%. At worst this wipes out the equity tranche and mezzanine tranche of the ABS CDO but leaves the senior tranche unscathed.

The senior tranche of the ABS CDO suffers losses if losses on the underlying portfolios are more than 10%. Consider, for example, the situation where losses are 20% on the underlying portfolios. In this case, losses on the mezzanine tranches of the ABSs are 15/20 or 75% of their principal. The first 25% is absorbed by the equity and mezzanine tranches of the ABS CDO. The senior tranche of the ABS CDO therefore loses 50/75 or 67% of its value. These and other results are summarized in Table 6.1.

Many banks have lost money investing in the senior tranches of ABS CDOs. The investments typically promised a return quite a bit higher than the bank's funding cost. Because they were rated AAA, the capital requirements were minimal. Merrill Lynch is an example of a bank that lost a great deal of money from investments in

TABLE 6.1   Losses to AAA-Rated Tranches of ABS CDO

Losses to Subprime Portfolios	Losses to Mezzanine Tranche of ABS	Losses to Equity Tranche of ABS CDO	Losses to Mezzanine Tranche of ABS CDO	Losses to Senior Tranche of ABS CDO
10%	25%	100%	100%	0%
15%	50%	100%	100%	33%
20%	75%	100%	100%	67%
25%	100%	100%	100%	100%

(as shown in Figure 6.4)

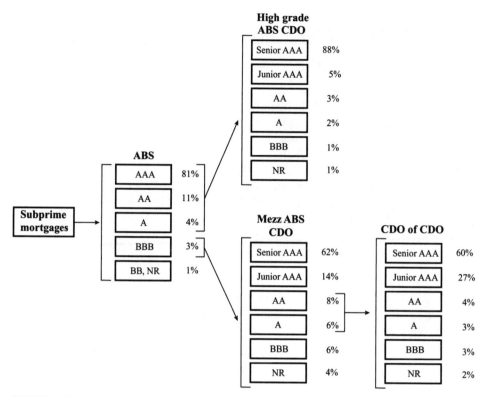

FIGURE 6.5 More Realistic Example of Subprime Securitizations with ABS, ABS CDOs, and a CDO of CDO Being Created

ABS CDOs. In July 2008, Merrill Lynch agreed to sell senior tranches of ABS CDOs, that had previously been rated AAA and had a principal of $30.6 billion, to Lone Star Funds for 22 cents on the dollar.[12]

CDOs and ABS CDOs in Practice

Figures 6.2 and 6.4 illustrate the nature of the securitizations that were done. In practice, many more tranches were created than those shown in Figures 6.2 and 6.4 and many of the tranches were thinner (i.e., corresponded to a narrower range of losses). Figure 6.5 shows a more realistic example of the structures that were created. This is adapted from an illustration by Gorton, which was taken from an article by UBS.[13]

---

[12] In fact the deal was worse than it sounds for Merrill Lynch because Merrill Lynch agreed to finance 75% of the purchase price. If the value of the tranches fell below 16.5 cents on the dollar, Merrill Lynch might find itself owning the assets again.

[13] G. Gorton, "The Subprime Panic," *European Financial Management* 15, no. 1 (2008): 10–46.

BUSINESS SNAPSHOT 6.1

Not All BBBs Are the Same

Analysts tended to assume that the mezzanine tranche of an ABS, when rated BBB, can be considered to be identical to a BBB bond for the purposes of evaluating a CDO created from the mezzanine tranches. This is not a good assumption. The rating agency models attempted to ensure that the BBB tranche of an ABS had the same probability of loss, or the same expected loss, as a BBB bond. But the probability distribution of the loss is very different. For example, it is much more likely that an investor in the BBB tranche of an ABS will lose everything, than that this will happen for a BBB-rated bond. (This is sometimes referred to as "cliff risk.") This means that the risk characteristics of ABS CDO tranches are quite different from the risk characteristics of similar CDO tranches created from bonds. This difference becomes more pronounced as tranches become thinner.

One lesson from this is that it is dangerous to interpret ratings for tranches of an ABS—or any other structured product—in the same way that ratings for bonds are interpreted. For similarly rated bonds and structured products, the probability distribution of losses are markedly different.

It can be seen that two ABS CDOs might be created. One is created from the BBB rated tranches of ABSs (similarly to the ABS CDO in Figure 6.4); the other is from the AAA, AA, and A tranches of ABSs. The figure shows a third level of securitization based on the A and AA tranches of the Mezz ABS CDO. There was typically a small amount of *overcollateralization* with the face value of the mortgages being greater (by 1% or 2%) than the total face value of the ABS tranches. This created a cushion for investors, but by carrying out a similar analysis to that in Table 6.1 it is not difficult to see that investors in many of the tranches created will lose principal in many situations.

The risks in the AAA-rated tranches of ABSs and ABS CDOs were higher than either investors or rating agencies realized. One of the reasons for this involves correlation. The values of the tranches of ABSs depend on the default correlation of the underlying mortgages. The tranches of ABS CDOs are even more heavily dependent on these default correlations. If mortgages exhibit a fairly low default correlation (as they do in normal times), there is very little chance of a high overall default rate and the AAA-rated tranches of both ABSs and ABS CDOs are safe. But, many analysts overlooked the fact that correlations always increase in stressed market conditions. In 2005 to 2006, the models used by investors and rating agencies assumed correlations that were too low for the upheavals in the U.S. housing market that were considered likely by many observers. As explained in Business Snapshot 6.1, another mistake made by analysts was to assume that the BBB-rated tranches of an ABS were equivalent in risk to BBB-rated bonds. There are important differences between the two and these differences can have a big effect on the valuation of the tranches of ABS CDOs.

6.3   THE CRISIS

The defaults on mortgages in the United States had a number of consequences. Financial institutions and other investors who had bought the tranches of ABSs and ABS CDOs lost money. Losses were also incurred by some mortgage originators because they had provided guarantees as to the quality of the mortgages that were securitized and because they faced lawsuits over their lending practices.

As often happens when losses are experienced in one segment of the debt market there was a "flight to quality." Investors became reluctant to take any credit risk and preferred to buy Treasury instruments and similarly safe investments. Credit spreads (the extra return required for taking credit risks) increased sharply. It was difficult for many nonfinancial companies to obtain loans from banks. Indeed, banks became reluctant to lend to each other and interbank lending rates increased sharply.

The tranches of ABSs and ABS CDOs were downgraded by rating agencies in the second half of 2007. The market for these tranches became very illiquid. Investors realized that they did not understand the tranches as well as they had previously thought and that they had placed too much reliance on credit ratings. This emphasizes the importance of transparency in financial markets. The products created during the period leading up to the crisis were very complicated.[14] Investors did not worry about this until problems emerged. They then found that the liquidity of the market was such that they could only trade at fire-sale prices.

Banks such as Citigroup, UBS, and Merrill Lynch suffered huge losses. There were many government bailouts of financial institutions. Lehman Brothers was allowed to fail. The world experienced the worst recession since the 1930s. Unemployment increased. Even people in remote parts of the world that had no connection with U.S. financial institutions were affected.

Banks are now paying a price for the crisis. As we will see in Chapter 13, they are required to keep more capital than before. They are also required to maintain certain liquidity ratios. Legislation such as Dodd–Frank in the U.S. increases the oversight of financial institutions and restricts their activities in areas such as proprietary trading and derivatives trading.

6.4   WHAT WENT WRONG?

"Irrational exuberance" is a phrase coined by Alan Greenspan, Chairman of the Federal Reserve Board, to describe the behavior of investors during the bull market of the 1990s. It can also be applied to the period leading up the credit crisis. Mortgage lenders, the investors in tranches of ABSs and ABS CDOs that were created from residential mortgages, and the companies that sold protection on the tranches assumed that the "good times" would last for ever. They thought that U.S. house prices would continue to increase. There might be declines in one or two areas, but

---

[14] Some of the products that were created were even more complicated than the description in Section 6.2. For example, sometimes ABS CDO tranches were included in the portfolios used to created other ABS CDOs.

the possibility of the widespread decline shown in Figure 6.1 was a scenario not considered by most people.

Many factors contributed to the crisis that started in 2007. Mortgage originators used lax lending standards. Products were developed to enable mortgage originators to profitably transfer credit risk to investors. Rating agencies moved from their traditional business of rating bonds, where they had a great deal of experience, to rating structured products, which were relatively new and for which there were relatively little historical data. The products bought by investors were complex and in many instances investors and rating agencies had inaccurate or incomplete information about the quality of the underlying assets. Investors in the structured products that were created thought they had found a money machine and chose to rely on rating agencies rather than forming their own opinions about the underlying risks. The return promised on the structured products rated AAA was high compared with the returns promised on bonds rated AAA.

Regulatory Arbitrage

Many of the mortgages were originated by banks and it was banks that were the main investors in the tranches that were created from the mortgages. Why would banks choose to securitize mortgages and then buy the securitized products that were created? The answer concerns what is termed *regulatory arbitrage*. The regulatory capital banks were required to keep for the tranches created from a portfolio of mortgages was much less than the regulatory capital that would be required for the mortgages themselves. This is because the mortgages were kept in what is referred to as the "banking book" whereas the tranches were kept is what is referred to as the "trading book." Capital requirements were different for the banking book and the trading book. We will discuss this point further in Chapters 12 and 13.

Incentives

Economists use the term "agency costs" to describe the situation where incentives are such that the interests of two parties in a business relationship are not perfectly aligned. The process by which mortgages were originated, securitized, and sold to investors was unfortunately riddled with agency costs.

The incentive of the originators of mortgages was to make loans that would be acceptable to the creators of the ABS and ABS CDO tranches. The incentive of the individuals who valued houses on which the mortgages were written was to please the lender by providing as high a valuation as possible so that the loan-to-value ratio was as low as possible. (Pleasing the lender was likely to lead to more business from that lender.) The main concern of the creators of ABSs and ABS CDOs was the profitability of the structures (i.e., the excess of the weighted average inflows over the weighted average outflows). They wanted the volume of AAA-rated tranches that they created to be as high as possible and found ways of using the published criteria of rating agencies to achieve this. The rating agencies were paid by the issuers of the securities they rated and about half their income came from structured products.

Another source of agency costs concerns financial institutions and their employees. Employee compensation falls into three categories: regular salary, the end-of-year bonus, and stock or stock options. Many employees at all levels of seniority in financial institutions, particularly traders, receive much of their compensation in the form of end-of-year bonuses. This form of compensation is focused on a short-term performance. If an employee generates huge profits one year and is responsible for severe losses the next year, the employee will receive a big bonus the first year and will not have to return it the following year. The employee might lose his or her job as a result of the second year losses, but even that is not a disaster. Financial institutions seem to be surprisingly willing to recruit individuals with losses on their resumes.

Imagine you are an employee of a financial institution investing in ABS CDOs in 2006. Almost certainly you would have recognized that there was a bubble in the U.S. housing market and would expect that bubble to burst sooner or later. However, it is possible that you would decide to continue with your ABS CDO investments. If the bubble did not burst until after December 31, 2006, you would still get a nice bonus at the end of 2006!

6.5 LESSONS FROM THE CRISIS

Some of the lessons for risk managers from the crisis are as follows:

1. Risk managers should be watching for situations where there is irrational exuberance and make sure that senior management recognize that the "good times" will not last for ever.
2. Correlations always increase in stressed markets. In considering how bad things might get, risk managers should not use correlations that are estimated from normal market conditions.
3. Recovery rates decline when default rates increase (see Section 16.3). This is true for almost all debt instruments, not just mortgages. In considering how bad things might get, risk managers should not use recovery rates that are estimated during normal market conditions.
4. Risk managers should ensure that the incentives of traders and other personnel encourage them to make decisions that are in the interests of the organization they work for. Many financial institutions have revised their compensation policies as a result of the crisis. Bonuses are now often spread out over several years rather than all being paid at once. If good performance in one year is followed by bad performance in the next, part of the bonus for the good-performance year that has not yet been paid may be clawed back.
5. If a deal seems too good to be true, it probably is. AAA-rated tranches of structured products promised returns that were higher than the returns promised on AAA bonds by 100 basis points, or more. A sensible conclusion from this for an investor would be that further analysis is needed because there are likely to be risks in the tranches that are not considered by rating agencies.
6. Investors should not rely on ratings. They should understand the assumptions made by rating agencies and carry out their own analyses.
7. Transparency is important in financial markets. If there is a lack of transparency (as there was for ABS CDOs), markets are liable to dry up when there is negative news.

BUSINESS SNAPSHOT 6.2

A Trading Opportunity?

Some traders made a huge amount of money betting against the subprime mortgage market. Suppose that you are analyzing markets in 2005 and 2006, but are uncertain about how subprime mortgages will perform. Is there a trading opportunity open to you?

The answer is that Mezz ABS CDOs do present a trading opportunity. Figure 6.5 is a simplification of how tranches were actually created. In practice, there were usually three ABS tranches rated BBB+, BBB, and BBB–. Each was very thin, about 1% wide. Separate Mezz ABS CDOs were created from each of the three types of tranches. Consider the Mezz ABS CDO created from BBB+ tranches. A trader might reasonably conclude that the BBB+ tranche created from different pools of mortgages would either all be safe (because there would be no real estate crisis) or would all be wiped out. (Because the tranches are only 1% wide, it is unlikely that they would be only partially wiped out.) This means that all the Mezz ABS CDO tranches created from ABS tranches rated BBB+ are either safe or wiped out. The Mezz ABS CDO tranches are therefore much the same as each other and should have the same rating (BBB+ in the case we are considering).

Having recognized this, what should the trader do? He or she should buy junior ABS CDO tranches (which are inexpensive because of their rating) and short senior ABS CDO tranches (which are relatively expensive). If the underlying principal is the same for both trades, the trader can then relax knowing that a profit has been locked in.

This emphasizes the point in Business Snapshot 6.1 that BBB tranches (particularly very thin BBB tranches) should not be considered equivalent to BBB bonds.

8. Re-securitization, which led to the creation of ABS CDOs and CDOs of CDOs, was a badly flawed idea. The assets used to create ABSs in the first leg of the securitization should be as well diversified as possible. There is then nothing to be gained from further securitization.

Business Snapshot 6.1 makes the point that many market participants considered ABS tranches rated BBB to be equivalent to BBB bonds. Business Snapshot 6.2 suggests a trading strategy that could be followed by people who realized that this was not so.

SUMMARY

The credit crisis starting in 2007 had a devastating effect on financial markets throughout the world. Its origins can be found in the U.S. housing market. The

U.S. government was keen to encourage home ownership. Interest rates were low. Mortgage brokers and mortgage lenders found it attractive to do more business by relaxing their lending standards. Products for securitizing mortgages had been developed so that the investors bearing the credit risk were not necessarily the same as the original lenders. Rating agencies were prepared to give a AAA rating to senior tranches that were created by securitization. There was no shortage of buyers for these AAA-rated tranches because their yields were higher than the yields on AAA-rated bonds. Banks thought the "good times" would continue and, because compensation plans focused their attention on short-term profits, chose to ignore the housing bubble and its potential impact on some very complicated products they were trading.

House prices rose as both first-time buyers and speculators entered the market. Some mortgages had included a low "teaser rate" for two or three years. After the teaser rate ended, some borrowers faced higher interest rates that they could not afford and had no choice but to default. This led to foreclosures and an increase in the supply of houses being sold. The price increases between 2000 and 2006 began to be reversed. Speculators and others who found that the amount owing on their mortgages was greater than the value of their houses (i.e., they had negative equity) defaulted. This accentuated the price decline.

Many factors played a part in creating the U.S. housing bubble and resulting recession. These include irrational exuberance on the part of market particpants, poor incentives, too much reliance on rating agencies, not enough analysis by investors, and the complexity of the products that were created. The crisis has provided a number of lessons for risk managers. As we will see later in this book, it has also led to a major overhaul of bank regulation and bank legislation.

FURTHER READING

Gorton, G. "The Panic of 2007." Working Paper, Yale School of Management, 2008.

Hull, J. C. "The Financial Crisis of 2007: Another Case of Irrational Exuberance." In *The Finance Crisis and Rescue: What Went Wrong? Why? What Lessons Can be Learned?* University of Toronto Press, 2008.

Hull, J. C. and A. White. "The Risk of Tranches Created from Mortgages." *Financial Analysts Journal*, 66, no. 5 (Sept/Oct 2010): 54–67.

Keys, B. J., T. Mukherjee, A. Seru, and V. Vig. "Did Securitization Lead to Lax Screening? Evidence from Subprime Loans." *Quarterly Journal of Economics* 125, no. 1 (February 2010): 307–362.

Krinsman, A. N. "Subprime Mortgage Meltdown: How Did it Happen and How Will It End?" *Journal of Structured Finance* (Summer 2007): 13–19.

Lewis, M. *The Big Short: Inside the Doomsday Machine.* New York: W. W. Norton and Co., 2010.

Mian, A. and A. Sufi. "The Consequences of Mortgage Credit Expansion: Evidence from the US Mortgage Default Crisis." *Quarterly Journal of Economics* 124, no. 4 (November 2009): 1449–1496.

Sorkin, A. R. *Too Big to Fail.* New York: Penguin, 2009.

Tett, G. *Fool's Gold: How the Bold Dream of a Small Tribe at JPMorgan Was Corrupted by Wall Street Greed and Unleashed a Catastrophe.* New York: Free Press, 2009.

Zimmerman, T. "The Great Subprime Meltdown." *The Journal of Structured Finance* (Fall 2007): 7–20.

PRACTICE QUESTIONS AND PROBLEMS (ANSWERS AT END OF BOOK)

6.1 Why did mortgage lenders frequently not check on information in the mortgage application during the 2000 to 2007 period?

6.2 Why do you think the increase in house prices during the 2000 to 2007 period is referred to as a bubble?

6.3 What are the numbers in Table 6.1 for a loss rate of (a) 5% and (b) 12%?

6.4 In what ways are the risks in the tranche of an ABS different from the risks in a similarly rated bond?

6.5 Explain the difference between (a) an ABS, and (b) an ABS CDO.

6.6 How were the risks in ABS CDOs misjudged by the market?

6.7 What is meant by the term "agency costs"?

6.8 What is a waterfall in a securitization?

6.9 How is an ABS CDO created? What was the motivation to create ABS CDOs?

6.10 How did Mian and Sufi show that mortgage lenders relaxed their lending criteria during the 2000 to 2006 period?

6.11 What is a mezzanine tranche?

6.12 Explain the influence of an increase in default correlation on (a) the risks in the equity tranche of an ABS and (b) the risks in the senior tranches of an ABS.

6.13 Explain why the end-of-year bonus is regarded as short-term compensation.

FURTHER QUESTIONS

6.14 Suppose that the principals assigned to the senior, mezzanine, and equity tranches for the ABSs and ABS CDO in Figure 6.4 are 70%, 20%, and 10% instead of 75%, 20% and 5%. How are the results in Table 6.1 affected?

6.15 Investigate what happens as the width of the mezzanine tranche of the ABS in Figure 6.4 is decreased, with the reduction in the mezzanine tranche principal being divided equally between the equity and senior tranches. In particular, what is the effect on Table 6.1?

CHAPTER 7

How Traders Manage Their Risks

The trading function within a financial institution is referred to as the *front office*; the part of the financial institution that is concerned with the overall level of the risks being taken, capital adequacy, and regulatory compliance is referred to as the *middle office*; the record keeping function is referred to as the *back office*. As explained in Section 1.6, there are two levels within a financial institution at which trading risks are managed. First, the front office hedges risks by ensuring that exposures to individual market variables are not too great. Second, the middle office aggregates the exposures of all traders to determine whether the total risk is acceptable. In this chapter we focus on the hedging activities of the front office. In later chapters we will consider how risks are aggregated in the middle office.

This chapter explains what are termed the "Greek letters" or simply the Greeks. Each of the Greeks measures a different aspect of the risk in a trading position. Traders calculate their Greeks at the end of each day and are required to take action if the internal risk limits of the financial institution they work for are exceeded. Failure to take this action is liable to lead to immediate dismissal.

7.1 DELTA

Imagine that you are a trader working for a U.S. bank and responsible for all trades involving gold. The current price of gold is $1,800 per ounce. Table 7.1 shows a summary of your portfolio (known as your "book"). How can you manage your risks?

The value of your portfolio is currently $117,000. One way of investigating the risks you face is to revalue the portfolio on the assumption that there is a small increase in the price of gold from $1,800 per ounce to $1,800.10 per ounce. Suppose that the $0.10 increase in the price of gold decreases the value of your portfolio by $100 from $117,000 to $116,900. This means that the sensitivity of the portfolio to the price of gold is

$$\frac{-100}{0.1} = -1,000$$

This is referred to as the *delta* of the portfolio. The portfolio loses value at a rate of about $1,000 per $1 increase in the price of gold. Similarly, it gains value at a rate of about $1,000 per $1 decrease in the price of gold.

TABLE 7.1   Summary of Gold Portfolio

Position	Value ($)
Spot Gold	180,000
Forward Contracts	–60,000
Futures Contracts	2,000
Swaps	80,000
Options	–110,000
Exotics	25,000
Total	117,000

In general, the *delta* of a portfolio with respect to a market variable is

$$\frac{\Delta P}{\Delta S}$$

where ΔS is a small increase in the value of the variable and ΔP is the resultant change in the value of the portfolio. Using calculus terminology, delta is the partial derivative of the portfolio value with respect to the value of the variable:

$$\text{Delta} = \frac{\partial P}{\partial S}$$

In our example, the trader can eliminate the delta exposure by buying 1,000 ounces of gold. This is because the delta of a long position in 1,000 ounces of gold is 1,000. (The position gains value at the rate of $1,000 per $1 increase in the price of gold.) This is known as *delta hedging*. When the hedging trade is combined with the existing portfolio the resultant portfolio has a delta of zero. Such a portfolio is referred to as *delta neutral*.

Linear Products

A linear product is one whose value at any given time is linearly dependent on the value of an underlying market variable (see Figure 7.1). Forward contracts are linear products; options are not.

A linear product can be hedged relatively easily. As a simple example, consider a U.S. bank that has entered into a forward contract with a corporate client where it agreed to sell the client 1 million euros for $1.3 million in one year. Assume that the euro and dollar interest rates are 4% and 3% with annual compounding. This means that the present value of a 1 million euro cash flow in one year is 1,000,000/1.04 = 961,538 euros. The present value of 1.3 million dollars in one year is 1,300,000/1.03 = 1,262,136 dollars. Suppose that S is the value of one euro in dollars today. The value of the contract today in dollars is[1]

$$1,262,136 - 961,538S$$

----
[1] See Appendix C for more information on the valuation of forward contracts.

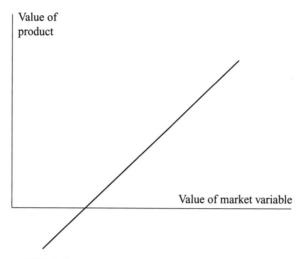

FIGURE 7.1 A Linear Product

This shows that the value of the contract is linearly related to the exchange rate, S. The delta of the contract is $-961,538$. It can be hedged by buying 961,538 euros. Because of the linearity, the hedge provides protection against both small and large movements in S.

When the bank enters into the opposite transaction and agrees to buy one million euros in one year, the value of the contract is also linear in S

$$961,538S - 1,262,136$$

The bank has a delta of $+961,538$. It must hedge by shorting 961,538 euros. It does this by borrowing the euros today at 4% and immediately converting them to U.S. dollars. The one million euros received in one year are used to repay the loan.

Shorting assets to hedge forward contracts is sometimes tricky. Gold is an interesting case in point. Financial institutions often find that they enter into very large forward contracts to buy gold from gold producers. This means that they need to borrow large quantities of gold to create a short position for hedging. As outlined in Business Snapshot 7.1, central banks are the source of the borrowed gold. A fee known as the gold lease rate is charged by central banks for lending the gold.

Linear products have the attractive property that hedges protect against large changes as well as small ones in the value of the underlying asset. They also tend to have another attractive property: the hedge, once it has been set up, never needs to be changed. (This is sometimes referred to as the "hedge and forget" property.) For an illustration of this, consider again the first forward contract we considered where a bank agrees to sell a client 1.3 million euros for 1 million dollars. A total of 961,538 euros are purchased to hedge the position. These can be invested at 4% for one year so that they grow to exactly 1 million euros in one year. This is exactly what the bank needs to complete the forward transaction in one year so that there is no need to adjust the hedge during the year.

BUSINESS SNAPSHOT 7.1

Hedging By Gold Mining Companies

It is natural for a gold mining company to consider hedging against changes in the price of gold. Typically it takes several years to extract all the gold from a mine. Once a gold mining company decides to go ahead with production at a particular mine, it has a big exposure to the price of gold. Indeed a mine that looks profitable at the outset could become unprofitable if the price of gold plunges.

Gold mining companies are careful to explain their hedging strategies to potential shareholders. Some gold mining companies do not hedge. They tend to attract shareholders who buy gold stocks because they want to benefit when the price of gold increases and are prepared to accept the risk of a loss from a decrease in the price of gold. Other companies choose to hedge. They estimate the number of ounces they will produce each month for the next few years and enter into futures or forward contracts to lock in the price that will be received.

Suppose you are Goldman Sachs and have just entered into a forward contract with a gold mining company where you agree to buy a large amount of gold at a fixed price. How do you hedge your risk? The answer is that you borrow gold from a central bank and sell it at the current market price. (The central banks of some of the countries that hold large amounts of gold are prepared to lend gold for a fee known as the gold lease rate.) At the end of the life of the forward contract, you buy gold from the gold mining company under the terms of the forward contract and use it to repay the central bank.

Nonlinear Products

Options to buy or sell assets and other more complex derivatives are nonlinear products. The relationship between the value of the product and the underlying asset price at any given time is nonlinear. This nonlinearity makes them more difficult to hedge for two reasons. First, making a nonlinear portfolio delta neutral only protects against small movements in the price of the underlying asset. Second, we are not in a hedge-and-forget situation. The hedge needs to be changed frequently. This is known as *dynamic hedging*. Consider as an example a trader who sells 100,000 European call options on a non-dividend-paying stock when

1. Stock price is $49
2. Strike price is $50
3. Risk-free interest rate is 5%
4. Stock price volatility is 20% per annum
5. Time to option maturity is 20 weeks

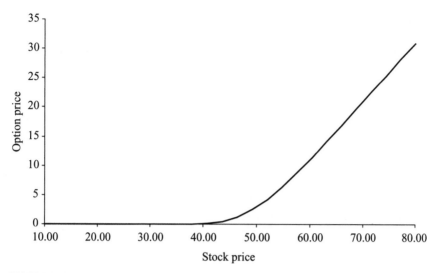

FIGURE 7.2 Value of Option as a Function of Stock Price

We suppose that the amount received for the options is $300,000 and that the trader has no other positions dependent on the stock.

The value of one option as a function of the underlying stock price is shown in Figure 7.2. The delta of one option changes with the stock price in the way shown in Figure 7.3.[2] At the time of the trade, the value of an option to buy one share of the stock is $2.40 and the delta of the option is 0.522. Because the trader is short 100,000 options, the value of the trader's portfolio is –$240,000 and the delta of the portfolio is –$52,200. The trader can feel pleased that the options have been sold for $60,000 more than their theoretical value, but is faced with the problem of hedging the risk in the portfolio.

Immediately after the trade, the trader's portfolio can be made delta neutral by buying 52,200 shares of the underlying stock. If there is a small decrease (increase) in the stock price, the gain (loss) to the trader of the short option position should be offset by the loss (gain) on the shares. For example, if the stock price increases from $49 to $49.10, the value of the options will decrease by about 52,200 × 0.10 = $5,220, while the value of the shares will increase by this amount.

In the case of linear products, once the hedge has been set up it does not need to be changed. This is not the case for nonlinear products. To preserve delta neutrality, the hedge has to be adjusted periodically. This is known as *rebalancing*.

Tables 7.2 and 7.3 provide two examples of how rebalancing might work in our example. Rebalancing is assumed to be done weekly. As mentioned, the the initial value of delta for a single option is 0.522 and the delta of the portfolio is –52,200.

---

[2] Figures 7.2 and 7.3 were produced with the DerivaGem software that can be down-loaded from the author's website. The Black–Scholes–Merton model is selected by choosing "Black–Scholes-European" as the option type.

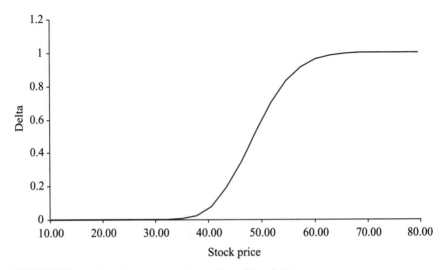

FIGURE 7.3   Delta of Option as a Function of Stock Price

TABLE 7.2   Simulation of Delta Hedging (Option closes in-the-money and cost of hedging is $263,300.)

Week	Stock Price	Delta	Shares Purchased	Cost of Shares Purchased ($000)	Cumulative Cash Outflow ($000)	Interest Cost ($000)
0	49.00	0.522	52,200	2,557.8	2,557.8	2.5
1	48.12	0.458	(6,400)	(308.0)	2,252.3	2.2
2	47.37	0.400	(5,800)	(274.7)	1,979.8	1.9
3	50.25	0.596	19,600	984.9	2,966.6	2.9
4	51.75	0.693	9,700	502.0	3,471.5	3.3
5	53.12	0.774	8,100	430.3	3,905.1	3.8
6	53.00	0.771	(300)	(15.9)	3,893.0	3.7
7	51.87	0.706	(6,500)	(337.2)	3,559.5	3.4
8	51.38	0.674	(3,200)	(164.4)	3,398.5	3.3
9	53.00	0.787	11,300	598.9	4,000.7	3.8
10	49.88	0.550	(23,700)	(1,182.2)	2,822.3	2.7
11	48.50	0.413	(13,700)	(664.4)	2,160.6	2.1
12	49.88	0.542	12,900	643.5	2,806.2	2.7
13	50.37	0.591	4,900	246.8	3,055.7	2.9
14	52.13	0.768	17,700	922.7	3,981.3	3.8
15	51.88	0.759	(900)	(46.7)	3,938.4	3.8
16	52.87	0.865	10,600	560.4	4,502.6	4.3
17	54.87	0.978	11,300	620.0	5,126.9	4.9
18	54.62	0.990	1,200	65.5	5,197.3	5.0
19	55.87	1.000	1,000	55.9	5,258.2	5.1
20	57.25	1.000	0	0.0	5,263.3	

TABLE 7.3 Simulation of Delta Hedging (Option closes out-of-the-money and cost of hedging = $256,600)

Week	Stock Price	Delta	Shares Purchased	Cost of Shares Purchased ($000)	Cumulative Cash Outflow ($000)	Interest Cost ($000)
0	49.00	0.522	52,200	2,557.8	2,557.8	2.5
1	49.75	0.568	4,600	228.9	2,789.2	2.7
2	52.00	0.705	13,700	712.4	3,504.3	3.4
3	50.00	0.579	(12,600)	(630.0)	2,877.7	2.8
4	48.38	0.459	(12,000)	(580.6)	2,299.9	2.2
5	48.25	0.443	(1,600)	(77.2)	2,224.9	2.1
6	48.75	0.475	3,200	156.0	2,383.0	2.3
7	49.63	0.540	6,500	322.6	2,707.9	2.6
8	48.25	0.420	(12,000)	(579.0)	2,131.5	2.1
9	48.25	0.410	(1,000)	(48.2)	2,085.4	2.0
10	51.12	0.658	24,800	1,267.8	3,355.2	3.2
11	51.50	0.692	3,400	175.1	3,533.5	3.4
12	49.88	0.542	(15,000)	(748.2)	2,788.7	2.7
13	49.88	0.538	(400)	(20.0)	2,771.4	2.7
14	48.75	0.400	(13,800)	(672.7)	2,101.4	2.0
15	47.50	0.236	(16,400)	(779.0)	1,324.4	1.3
16	48.00	0.261	2,500	120.0	1,445.7	1.4
17	46.25	0.062	(19,900)	(920.4)	526.7	0.5
18	48.13	0.183	12,100	582.4	1,109.6	1.1
19	46.63	0.007	(17,600)	(820.7)	290.0	0.3
20	48.12	0.000	(700)	(33.7)	256.6	

This means that, as soon as the option is written, $2,557,800 must be borrowed to buy 52,200 shares at a price of $49. The rate of interest is 5%. An interest cost of approximately $2,500 is therefore incurred in the first week.

In Table 7.2, the stock price falls by the end of the first week to $48.12. The delta declines to 0.458. A long position in 45,800 shares is now required to hedge the option position. Sixty-four hundred (= 52,200 − 45,800) shares are therefore sold to maintain the delta neutrality of the hedge. The strategy realizes $308,000 in cash, and the cumulative borrowings at the end of week 1 are reduced to $2,252,300. During the second week the stock price reduces to $47.37 and delta declines again. This leads to 5,800 shares being sold at the end of the second week. During the third week, the stock price increases to over $50 and delta increases. This leads to 19,600 shares being purchased at the end of the third week. Toward the end of the life of the option, it becomes apparent that the option will be exercised and delta approaches 1.0. By week 20, therefore, the hedger owns 100,000 shares. The hedger receives $5 million (= 100,000 × $50) for these shares when the option is exercised so that the total cost of writing the option and hedging it is $263,300.

Table 7.3 illustrates an alternative sequence of events where the option closes out-of-the-money. As it becomes clear that the option will not be exercised, delta approaches zero. By week 20, the hedger therefore has no position in the underlying stock. The total costs incurred are $256,600.

In Tables 7.2 and 7.3, the costs of hedging the option, when discounted to the beginning of the period, are close to, but not exactly, the same as the theoretical (Black–Scholes–Merton) price of $240,000. If the hedging scheme worked perfectly, the cost of hedging would, after discounting, be exactly equal to the Black–Scholes–Merton price for every simulated stock price path. The reason for the variation in the cost of delta hedging is that the hedge is rebalanced only once a week. As rebalancing takes place more frequently, the variation in the cost of hedging is reduced. Of course, the examples in Tables 7.2 and 7.3 are idealized in that they assume the model underlying the Black–Scholes–Merton formula is exactly correct and there are no transaction costs.

Delta hedging aims to keep the value of the financial institution's position as close to unchanged as possible. Initially, the value of the written option is $240,000. In the situation depicted in Table 7.2, the value of the option can be calculated as $414,500 in week 9. Thus, the financial institution has lost $414,500 - 240,000 = $174,500$ on its short option position. Its cash position, as measured by the cumulative cost, is $1,442,900 worse in week 9 than in week 0. The value of the shares held has increased from $2,557,800 to $4,171,100 for a gain of $1,613,300. The net effect is that the value of the financial institution's position has changed by only $4,100 during the nine-week period.

Where the Cost Comes From

The delta-hedging procedure in Tables 7.2 and 7.3 in effect creates a long position in the option synthetically to neutralize the trader's short option position. As the tables illustrate, the scheme tends to involve selling stock just after the price has gone down and buying stock just after the price has gone up. It might be termed a buy-high, sell-low scheme! The cost of $240,000 comes from the average difference between the price paid for the stock and the price realized for it.

Transaction Costs

Maintaining a delta-neutral position in a single option and the underlying asset, in the way that has just been described, is liable to be prohibitively expensive because of the transaction costs incurred on trades. Maintaining delta neutrality is more feasible for a large portfolio of derivatives dependent on a single asset because only one trade in the underlying asset is necessary to zero out delta for the whole portfolio. The hedging transactions costs are absorbed by the profits on many different trades.

7.2 GAMMA

As mentioned, for a nonlinear portfolio, delta neutrality only provides protection against small changes in the price of the underlying asset.

The *gamma*, Γ, of a portfolio measures the extent to which large changes cause problems. Gamma is the rate of change of the portfolio's delta with respect to the

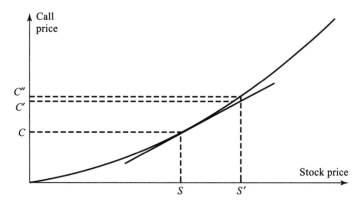

FIGURE 7.4 Hedging Error Introduced by Nonlinearity

price of the underlying asset. It is the second partial derivative of the portfolio with respect to asset price:

$$\text{Gamma} = \frac{\partial^2 P}{\partial S^2}$$

If gamma is small, delta changes slowly, and adjustments to keep a portfolio delta neutral need to be made only relatively infrequently. However, if gamma is large in absolute terms, delta is highly sensitive to the price of the underlying asset. It is then quite risky to leave a delta-neutral portfolio unchanged for any length of time. Figure 7.4 illustrates this point for an option on a stock. When the stock price moves from S to S', delta hedging assumes that the option price moves from C to C', when in fact it moves from C to C''. The difference between C' and C'' leads to a hedging error. This error depends on the curvature of the relationship between the option price and the stock price. Gamma measures this curvature.[3]

Gamma is positive for a long position in an option. The general way in which gamma varies with the price of the underlying stock is shown in Figure 7.5. Gamma is greatest for options where the stock price is close to the strike price K.

Making a Portfolio Gamma Neutral

A linear product has zero gamma and cannot be used to change the gamma of a portfolio. What is required is a position in an instrument, such as an option, that is not linearly dependent on the underlying asset price.

Suppose that a delta-neutral portfolio has a gamma equal to Γ, and a traded option has a gamma equal to Γ_T. If the number of traded options added to the portfolio is w_T, the gamma of the portfolio is

$$w_T \Gamma_T + \Gamma$$

---

[3] Indeed, the gamma of an option is sometimes referred to as its *curvature* by practitioners

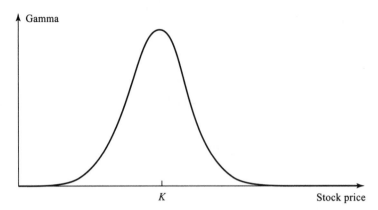

FIGURE 7.5 Relationship between Gamma of an Option and Price
of Underlying Stock where K is the Option's Strike Price

Hence, the position in the traded option necessary to make the portfolio gamma
neutral is $w_T = -\Gamma/\Gamma_T$. Including the traded option is likely to change the delta
of the portfolio, so the position in the underlying asset then has to be changed to
maintain delta neutrality. Note that the portfolio is gamma neutral only for a short
period of time. As time passes, gamma neutrality can be maintained only if the
position in the traded option is adjusted so that it is always equal to $-\Gamma/\Gamma_T$.

Making a delta-neutral portfolio gamma neutral can be regarded as a first correction for the fact that the position in the underlying asset cannot be changed continuously when delta hedging is used. Delta neutrality provides protection against
relatively small asset price moves between rebalancing. Gamma neutrality provides
protection against larger movements in the asset price between hedge rebalancing. Suppose that a portfolio is delta neutral and has a gamma of −3,000. The
delta and gamma of a particular traded call option are 0.62 and 1.50, respectively.
The portfolio can be made gamma neutral by including in the portfolio a long
position of

$$\frac{3,000}{1.5} = 2,000$$

in the call option. (The gamma of the portfolio is then $-3,000 + 1.5 \times 2,000 = 0$.)
However, the delta of the portfolio will then change from zero to $2,000 \times 0.62 = 1,240$. A quantity, 1,240, of the underlying asset must therefore be sold to keep it
delta neutral.

7.3 VEGA

Another source of risk in derivatives trading is the possibility that volatility will
change. The volatility of a market variable measures our uncertainty about the
future value of the variable. (It will be discussed more fully in Chapter 10.) In option
valuation models, volatilities are often assumed to be constant, but in practice they

do change through time. Spot positions and forwards do not depend on the volatility of asset prices but options and more complicated derivatives do. Their values are liable to change because of movements in volatility as well as because of changes in the asset price and the passage of time.

The *vega* of a portfolio, V, is the rate of change of the value of the portfolio with respect to the volatility, σ, of the underlying asset price.[4]

$$V = \frac{\partial P}{\partial \sigma}$$

If vega is high in absolute terms, the portfolio's value is very sensitive to small changes in volatility. If vega is low in absolute terms, volatility changes have relatively little impact on the value of the portfolio.

The vega of a portfolio can be changed by adding a position in a traded option. If V is the vega of the portfolio and V_T is the vega of a traded option, a position of $-V/V_T$ in the traded option makes the portfolio instantaneously vega neutral. Unfortunately, a portfolio that is gamma neutral will not, in general, be vega neutral, and vice versa. If a hedger requires a portfolio to be both gamma and vega neutral, at least two traded derivatives dependent on the underlying asset must usually be used.

EXAMPLE 7.1

Consider a portfolio dependent on the price of an asset that is delta neutral, with a gamma of $-5,000$ and a vega of $-8,000$. The options shown in the table below can be traded. The portfolio could be made vega neutral by including a long position in 4,000 of Option 1. This would increase delta to 2,400 and require that 2,400 units of the asset be sold to maintain delta neutrality. The gamma of the portfolio would change from $-5,000$ to $-3,000$.

	Delta	Gamma	Vega
Portfolio	0	−5,000	−8,000
Option 1	0.6	0.5	2.0
Option 2	0.5	0.8	1.2

To make the portfolio gamma and vega neutral, both Option 1 and Option 2 can be used. If w_1 and w_2 are the quantities of Option 1 and Option 2 that are added to the portfolio, we require that

$$-5,000 + 0.5w_1 + 0.8w_2 = 0$$

$$-8,000 + 2.0w_1 + 1.2w_2 = 0$$

---

[4] Vega is the name given to one of the "Greek letters" in option pricing, but it is not one of the letters in the Greek alphabet

The solution to these equations is $w_1 = 400$, $w_2 = 6,000$. The portfolio can therefore be made gamma and vega neutral by including 400 of Option 1 and 6,000 of Option 2. The delta of the portfolio after the addition of the positions in the two traded options is $400 \times 0.6 + 6,000 \times 0.5 = 3,240$. Hence, 3,240 units of the underlying asset would have to be sold to maintain delta neutrality.

The vega of a long position in an option is positive. The variation of vega with the price of the underlying asset is similar to that of gamma and is shown in Figure 7.6. Gamma neutrality protects against large changes in the price of the underlying asset between hedge rebalancing. Vega neutrality protects against variations in volatility.

The volatilities of short-dated options tend to be more variable than the volatilities of long-dated options. The vega of a portfolio is therefore often calculated by changing the volatilities of short-dated options by more than that of long-dated options. One way of doing this is discussed in Section 10.10.

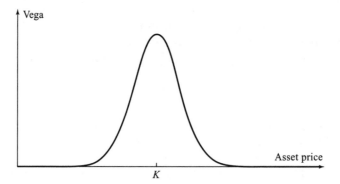

FIGURE 7.6 Variation of Vega of an Option with Price of Underlying Asset where K is Option's Strike Price

7.4 THETA

The *theta* of a portfolio, Θ, is the rate of change of the value of the portfolio with respect to the passage of time, with all else remaining the same. Theta is sometimes referred to as the *time decay* of the portfolio.

Theta is usually negative for an option.[5] This is because as the time to maturity decreases with all else remaining the same, the option tends to become less valuable. The general way in which Θ varies with stock price for a call option on a stock is shown in Figure 7.7. When the stock price is very low, theta is close to zero. For an at-the-money call option, theta is large and negative. Figure 7.8 shows typical patterns for the variation of Θ with the time to maturity for in-the-money, at-the-money, and out-of-the-money call options.

---

[5] An exception to this could be an in-the-money European put option on a non-dividend-paying stock or an in-the-money European call option on a currency with a very high interest rate.

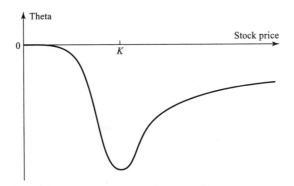

FIGURE 7.7 Variation of Theta of a European Call Option with Stock Price where K is Option's Strike Price

Theta is not the same type of Greek letter as delta. There is uncertainty about a future asset price, but there is no uncertainty about the passage of time. It makes sense to hedge against changes in the price of an underlying asset, but it does not make any sense to hedge against the effect of the passage of time on an option portfolio. In spite of this, many traders regard theta as a useful descriptive statistic for a portfolio. In a delta-neutral portfolio, when theta is large and positive, gamma tends to be large and negative and vice versa.

7.5 RHO

The final Greek letter we consider is rho. Rho is the rate of change of a portfolio with respect to the level of interest rates. Currency options have two rhos, one for the

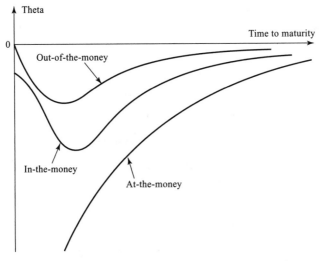

FIGURE 7.8 Typical Patterns for Variation of Theta of a European Call Option with Time to Maturity

domestic interest rate and one for the foreign interest rate. When bonds and interest rate derivatives are part of the portfolio, traders usually consider carefully the ways in which the whole term structure of interest rates can change. We discuss this in the next chapter.

7.6 CALCULATING GREEK LETTERS

Appendices E and F explain how Greek letters can be calculated. The software DerivaGem, which can be downloaded from the author's website, can be used for European and American options. Consider again the European call option in Section 7.1. The stock price is $49, the strike price is $50, the risk-free rate is 5%, the stock price volatility is 20% and the time to exercise is 20 weeks or 20/52 year. Table 7.4 shows delta, gamma, vega, theta, and rho for the option (i.e., for a long position in one option) and for a short position in 100,000 options, which was the position considered in Tables 7.2 and 7.3.

Here are some examples of how these numbers can be interpreted:

1. When there is an increase of $0.1 in the stock price with no other changes, the option price increases by about 0.522×0.1 or $0.0522. The value of a short position in 100,000 options decreases by $5,220.
2. When there is an increase $0.1 in the stock price with no other changes, the delta of the option increases by about 0.066×0.1 or 0.0066. The delta of a short position in 100,000 options decreases by 660.
3. When there is an increase in volatility of 0.5% (from 20% to 20.5%) with no other changes, the option price increases by about 0.121×0.5 or $0.0605. The value of a short position in 100,000 options decreases by $6,050.
4. When one day goes by with no changes to the stock price or its volatility, the option price decreases by about $0.012. The value of a short position in 100,000 options increases by $1,200.
5. When interest rates increase by 1% (or 100 basis points) with no other changes, the option price increases by $0.089. The value of a short position in 100,000 options decreases by $8,900.

TABLE 7.4 Greek Letters Calculated Using DerivaGem

	Single Option	Short Position in 100,000 Options
Value ($)	2.40	−240,000
Delta (per $)	0.522	−52,200
Gamma (per $)	0.066	−6,600
Vega (per %)	0.121	−12,100
Theta (per day)	−0.012	1,200
Rho (per %)	0.089	−8,900

$S = 49, K = 50, r = 5\%, \sigma = 20\%$, and $T = 20$ weeks.

7.7 TAYLOR SERIES EXPANSIONS

Taylor series expansions are explained in Appendix G. They can be used to show how the change in the portfolio value in a short period of time depends on the Greek letters. Consider a portfolio dependent on a single asset price, S. If the volatility of the underlying asset and interest rates are assumed to be constant, the value of the portfolio, P, is a function of S, and time t. The Taylor series expansion gives

$$\Delta P = \frac{\partial P}{\partial S}\Delta S + \frac{\partial P}{\partial t}\Delta t + \frac{1}{2}\frac{\partial^2 P}{\partial S^2}\Delta S^2 + \frac{1}{2}\frac{\partial^2 P}{\partial t^2}\Delta t^2 + \frac{\partial^2 P}{\partial S \partial t}\Delta S \Delta t + \cdots \qquad (7.1)$$

where ΔP and ΔS are the change in P and S in a small time interval Δt. The first term is delta times ΔS and is eliminated by delta hedging. The second term, which is theta times Δt is non-stochastic. The third term can be made zero by ensuring that the portfolio is gamma neutral as well as delta neutral. Arguments from stochastic calculus show that ΔS is of order $\sqrt{\Delta t}$. This means that third term on the right-hand side is of order Δt. Later terms in the Taylor series expansion are of higher order than Δt.

For a delta-neutral portfolio, the first term on the right-hand side of equation (7.1) is zero, so that

$$\Delta P = \Theta \Delta t + \frac{1}{2}\Gamma \Delta S^2 \qquad (7.2)$$

when terms of higher order than Δt are ignored. The relationship between the change in the portfolio value and the change in the stock price is quadratic as shown in Figure 7.9. When gamma is positive, the holder of the portfolio gains from large movements in the asset price and loses when there is little or no movement. When gamma is negative, the reverse is true so that a large positive or negative movement in the asset price leads to severe losses.

EXAMPLE 7.2

Suppose that the gamma of a delta-neutral portfolio of options on an asset is $-10{,}000$. Suppose that a change of $+2$ in the price of the asset occurs over a short period of time (for which Δt can be assumed to be zero). Equation (7.2) shows that there is an unexpected decrease in the value of the portfolio of approximately $0.5 \times 10{,}000 \times 2^2 = \$20{,}000$. Note that the same unexpected decrease would occur if there were a change of -2.

When the volatility of the underlying asset is uncertain, P is a function of σ, S, and t. Equation (7.1) then becomes

$$\Delta P = \frac{\partial P}{\partial S}\Delta S + \frac{\partial P}{\partial \sigma}\Delta \sigma + \frac{\partial P}{\partial t}\Delta t + \frac{1}{2}\frac{\partial^2 P}{\partial S^2}\Delta S^2 + \frac{1}{2}\frac{\partial^2 P}{\partial \sigma^2}\Delta \sigma^2 + \cdots$$

where $\Delta \sigma$ is the change in σ in time Δt. In this case, delta hedging eliminates the first term on the right-hand side. The second term is eliminated by making the portfolio

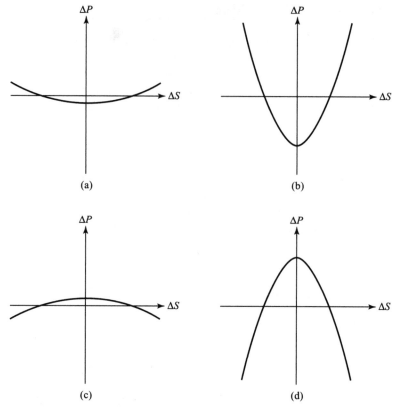

FIGURE 7.9 Alternative Relationships between ΔP and ΔS for a Delta-Neutral Portfolio
(a) Slightly positive gamma, (b) large positive gamma, (c) slightly negative gamma, and (d) large negative gamma

vega neutral. The third term is non-stochastic. The fourth term is eliminated by making the portfolio gamma neutral.

Traders often define other "Greek letters" to correspond to higher-order terms in the Taylor series expansion. For example, $\partial^2 P/\partial \sigma^2$ is sometimes referred to as "gamma of vega."

7.8 THE REALITIES OF HEDGING

In an ideal world, traders working for financial institutions would be able to rebalance their portfolios very frequently in order to maintain a zero delta, a zero gamma, a zero vega, and so on. In practice, this is not possible. When managing a large portfolio dependent on a single underlying asset, traders usually make delta zero, or close to zero at least once a day by trading the underlying asset. Unfortunately a zero gamma and a zero vega are less easy to achieve because it is difficult to find options or other nonlinear derivatives that can be traded in the volume required at competitive prices (see discussion of dynamic hedging in Business Snapshot 7.2).

BUSINESS SNAPSHOT 7.2

Dynamic Hedging in Practice

In a typical arrangement at a financial institution, the responsibility for a portfolio of derivatives dependent on a particular underlying asset is assigned to one trader or to a group of traders working together. For example, one trader at Goldman Sachs might be assigned responsibility for all derivatives dependent on the value of the Australian dollar. A computer system calculates the value of the portfolio and Greek letters for the portfolio. Limits are defined for each Greek letter and special permission is required if a trader wants to exceed a limit at the end of a trading day.

The delta limit is often expressed as the equivalent maximum position in the underlying asset. For example, the delta limit of Goldman Sachs on Microsoft might be $10 million. If the Microsoft stock price is $50, this means that the absolute value of delta as we have calculated it can be no more that 200,000. The vega limit is usually expressed as a maximum dollar exposure per 1% change in the volatility.

As a matter of course, options traders make themselves delta neutral—or close to delta neutral—at the end of each day. Gamma and vega are monitored, but are not usually managed on a daily basis. Financial institutions often find that their business with clients involves writing options and that as a result they accumulate negative gamma and vega. They are then always looking out for opportunities to manage their gamma and vega risks by buying options at competitive prices.

There is one aspect of an options portfolio that mitigates problems of managing gamma and vega somewhat. Options are often close to the money when they are first sold so that they have relatively high gammas and vegas. But after some time has elapsed, the underlying asset price has often changed enough for them to become deep out-of-the-money or deep in-the-money. Their gammas and vegas are then very small and of little consequence. The nightmare scenario for an options trader is where written options remain very close to the money as the maturity date is approached.

There are large economies of scale in being an options trader. As noted earlier, maintaining delta neutrality for an individual option on an asset by trading the asset daily would be prohibitively expensive. But it is realistic to do this for a portfolio of several hundred options on the asset. This is because the cost of daily rebalancing is covered by the profit on many different trades.

7.9 HEDGING EXOTIC OPTIONS

Exotic options (see Section 5.8) can often be hedged using the approach we have outlined. As explained in Business Snapshot 7.3, delta hedging is sometimes easier

BUSINESS SNAPSHOT 7.3

Is Delta Hedging Easier or More Difficult for Exotics?

We can approach the hedging of exotic options by creating a delta-neutral position and rebalancing frequently to maintain delta neutrality. When we do this, we find that some exotic options are easier to hedge than plain vanilla options and some are more difficult.

An example of an exotic option that is relatively easy to hedge is an average price call option (see Asian options in Section 5.8). As time passes, we observe more of the asset prices that will be used in calculating the final average. This means that our uncertainty about the payoff decreases with the passage of time. As a result, the option becomes progressively easier to hedge. In the final few days, the delta of the option always approaches zero because price movements during this time have very little impact on the payoff.

By contrast, barrier options (see Section 5.8) are relatively difficult to hedge. Consider a knock-out call option on a currency when the exchange rate is 0.0005 above the barrier. If the barrier is hit, the option is worth nothing. If the barrier is not hit, the option may prove to be quite valuable. The delta of the option is discontinuous at the barrier, making conventional hedging very difficult.

for exotics and sometimes more difficult. When delta hedging is not feasible for a portfolio of exotic options an alternative approach known as *static options replication* is sometimes used. This is illustrated in Figure 7.10. Suppose that S denotes the asset price and t denotes time with the current ($t = 0$) value of S being S_0. Static options replication involves choosing a boundary in $\{S, t\}$ space that will eventually be reached and then finding a portfolio of regular options that is worth the same as the portfolio of exotic options at a number of points on the boundary. The portfolio of exotic options is hedged by shorting this portfolio of regular options. Once the boundary is reached, the hedge is unwound. A new hedge can then be created with static options replication if desired.

The theory underlying static options replication is that, if two portfolios are worth the same at all $\{S, t\}$ points on the boundary, they must be worth the same at all the $\{S, t\}$ points that can be reached prior to the boundary. In practice, values of the original portfolio of exotic options and the replicating portfolio of regular options are matched at some, but not all, points on the boundary. The procedure therefore relies on the idea that if two portfolios have the same value at a reasonably large number of points on the boundary, their values are likely to be close at other points on the boundary.

7.10 SCENARIO ANALYSIS

In addition to monitoring risks such as delta, gamma, and vega, option traders often also carry out a scenario analysis. The analysis involves calculating the gain or loss on

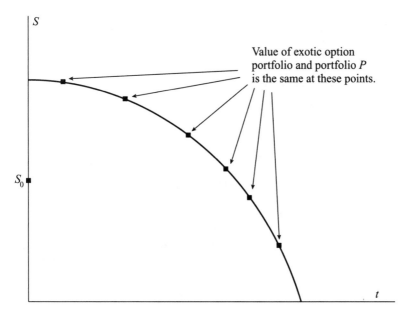

FIGURE 7.10 Static Options Replication
A replicating portfolio, P is chosen so that it has the same value as the
exotic option portfolio at a number of points on a boundary.

their portfolio over a specified period under a variety of different scenarios. The time
period chosen is likely to depend on the liquidity of the instruments. The scenarios
can be either chosen by management or generated by a model.

Consider a trader with a portfolio of options on a particular foreign currency.
There are two main variables on which the value of the portfolio depends. These are
the exchange rate and the exchange rate volatility. Suppose that the exchange rate
is currently 1.0000 and its volatility is 10% per annum. The bank could calculate
a table such as Table 7.5 showing the profit or loss experienced during a two-week
period under different scenarios. This table considers seven different exchange rates
and three different volatilities.

In Table 7.5, the greatest loss is in the lower-right corner of the table. The loss
corresponds to the volatility increasing to 12% and the exchange rate moving up to
1.06. Usually the greatest loss in a table such as 7.5 occurs at one of the corners, but
this is not always so. For example, as we saw in Figure 7.9, when gamma is positive,
the greatest loss is experienced when the underlying asset price stays where it is.

TABLE 7.5 Profit or Loss Realized in Two Weeks under Different Scenarios ($ millions)

	Exchange Rate						
Volatility	0.94	0.96	0.98	1.00	1.02	1.04	1.06
8%	+102	+55	+25	+6	−10	−34	−80
10%	+80	+40	+17	+2	−14	−38	−85
12%	+60	+25	+9	−2	−18	−42	−90

SUMMARY

A trader working for a bank, who is responsible for all the trades involving a particular asset, monitors a number of Greek letters and ensures that they are kept within the limits specified by the bank.

The delta, Δ, of a portfolio is the rate of change, of its value with respect to the price of the underlying asset. Delta hedging involves creating a position with zero delta (sometimes referred to as a delta-neutral position). Because the delta of the underlying asset is 1.0, one way of hedging the portfolio is to take a position of $-\Delta$ in the underlying asset. For portfolios involving options and more complex derivatives, the position taken in the underlying asset has to be changed periodically. This is known as rebalancing.

Once a portfolio has been made delta neutral, the next stage is often to look at its gamma. The gamma of a portfolio is the rate of change of its delta with respect to the price of the underlying asset. It is a measure of the curvature of the relationship between the portfolio and the asset price. Another important hedge statistic is vega. This measures the rate of change of the value of the portfolio with respect to changes in the volatility of the underlying asset. Gamma and vega can be changed by trading options on the underlying asset.

In practice, derivatives traders usually rebalance their portfolios at least once a day to maintain delta neutrality. It is usually not feasible to maintain gamma and vega neutrality on a regular basis. Typically a trader monitors these measures. If they get too large, either corrective action is taken or trading is curtailed.

FURTHER READING

Derman, E., D. Ergener, and I. Kani. "Static Options Replication." *Journal of Derivatives* 2, no. 4 (Summer 1995): 78–95.
Taleb, N. N., *Dynamic Hedging: Managing Vanilla and Exotic Options*. New York: John Wiley & Sons, 1996

PRACTICE QUESTIONS AND PROBLEMS
(ANSWERS AT END OF BOOK)

7.1 The delta of a derivatives portfolio dependent on the S&P 500 index is –2,100. The S&P 500 index is currently 1,000. Estimate what happens to the value of the portfolio when the index increases to 1,005.

7.2 The vega of a derivatives portfolio dependent on the dollar-sterling exchange rate is 200 ($ per %). Estimate the effect on the portfolio of an increase in the volatility of the exchange rate from 12% to 14%.

7.3 The gamma of a delta-neutral portfolio is 30 (per $). Estimate what happens to the value of the portfolio when the price of the underlying asset (a) suddenly increases by $2 and (b) suddenly decreases by $2.

7.4 What does it mean to assert that the delta of a call option is 0.7? How can a short position in 1,000 options be made delta neutral when the delta of a long position in each option is 0.7?

7.5 What does it mean to assert that the theta of an option position is −100 per day? If a trader feels that neither a stock price nor its implied volatility will change, what type of option position is appropriate?

7.6 What is meant by the gamma of an option position? What are the risks in the situation where the gamma of a position is large and negative and the delta is zero?

7.7 "The procedure for creating an option position synthetically is the reverse of the procedure for hedging the option position." Explain this statement.

7.8 A company uses delta hedging to hedge a portfolio of long positions in put and call options on a currency. Which of the following would lead to the most favorable result?
(a) A virtually constant spot rate
(b) Wild movements in the spot rate
How does your answer change if the portfolio contains short option positions?

7.9 A bank's position in options on the dollar–euro exchange rate has a delta of 30,000 and a gamma of −80,000. Explain how these numbers can be interpreted. The exchange rate (dollars per euro) is 0.90. What position would you take to make the position delta neutral? After a short period of time, the exchange rate moves to 0.93. Estimate the new delta. What additional trade is necessary to keep the position delta neutral? Assuming the bank did set up a delta-neutral position originally, has it gained or lost money from the exchange-rate movement?

7.10 "Static options replication assumes that the volatility of the underlying asset will be constant." Explain this statement.

7.11 Suppose that a trader using the static options replication technique wants to match the value of a portfolio of exotic derivatives with the value of a portfolio of regular options at 10 points on a boundary. How many regular options are likely to be needed? Explain your answer.

7.12 Why is an Asian option easier to hedge than a regular option?

7.13 Explain why there are economies of scale in hedging options.

7.14 Consider a six-month American put option on a foreign currency when the exchange rate (domestic currency per foreign currency) is 0.75, the strike price is 0.74, the domestic risk-free rate is 5%, the foreign risk-free rate is 3%, and the exchange-rate volatility is 14% per annum. Use the DerivaGem software (binomial tree with 100 steps) to calculate the price, delta, gamma, vega, theta, and rho of the option. Verify that delta is correct by changing the exchange rate to 0.751 and recomputing the option price.

FURTHER QUESTIONS

7.15 The gamma and vega of a delta-neutral portfolio are 50 per $ and 25 per %, respectively. Estimate what happens to the value of the portfolio when there is a shock to the market causing the underlying asset price to decrease by $3 and its volatility to increase by 4%.

7.16 Consider a one-year European call option on a stock when the stock price is $30, the strike price is $30, the risk-free rate is 5%, and the volatility is 25% per annum. Use the DerivaGem software to calculate the price, delta, gamma, vega, theta, and rho of the option. Verify that delta is correct by changing the stock price to $30.1 and recomputing the option price. Verify that gamma is correct by recomputing the delta for the situation where the stock price is $30.1. Carry out similar calculations to verify that vega, theta, and rho are correct.

7.17 A financial institution has the following portfolio of over-the-counter options on sterling:

Type	Position	Delta of Option	Gamma of Option	Vega of Option
Call	−1,000	0.50	2.2	1.8
Call	−500	0.80	0.6	0.2
Put	−2,000	−0.40	1.3	0.7
Call	−500	0.70	1.8	1.4

A traded option is available with a delta of 0.6, a gamma of 1.5, and a vega of 0.8.

(a) What position in the traded option and in sterling would make the portfolio both gamma neutral and delta neutral?

(b) What position in the traded option and in sterling would make the portfolio both vega neutral and delta neutral?

7.18 Consider again the situation in Problem 7.17. Suppose that a second traded option with a delta of 0.1, a gamma of 0.5, and a vega of 0.6 is available. How could the portfolio be made delta, gamma, and vega neutral?

7.19 Reproduce Table 7.2. (In Table 7.2, the stock position is rounded to the nearest 100 shares.) Calculate the gamma and theta of the position each week. Using the DerivaGem Applications Builders to calculate the change in the value of the portfolio each week (before the rebalancing at the end of the week) and check whether equation (7.2) is approximately satisfied. (*Note:* DerivaGem produces a value of theta "per calendar day." The theta in equation 7.2 is "per year.")

CHAPTER **8**

Interest Rate Risk

Interest rate risk is more difficult to manage than the risk arising from market variables such as equity prices, exchange rates, and commodity prices. One complication is that there are many different interest rates in any given currency (Treasury rates, interbank borrowing and lending rates, swap rates, mortgage rates, deposit rates, prime borrowing rates, and so on). Although these tend to move together, they are not perfectly correlated. Another complication is that we need more than a single number to describe the interest rate environment. We need a function describing the variation of the rate with maturity. This is known as the *term structure of interest rates* or the *yield curve*.

Consider, for example, the situation of a U.S. government bond trader. The trader's portfolio is likely to consist of many bonds with different maturities. There is an exposure to movements in the one-year rate, the two-year rate, the three-year rate, and so on. The trader's delta exposure is therefore more complicated than that of the gold trader in Table 7.1. He or she must be concerned with all the different ways in which the U.S. Treasury yield curve can change its shape through time.

This chapter starts with a description of traditional approaches used by a financial institution to manage interest rate risk. It explains the importance of LIBOR and swap rates to financial institutions. It then covers duration and convexity measures. These can be regarded as the interest rate equivalents of the delta and gamma measures considered in the previous chapter. A number of different approaches to managing the risks of nonparallel shifts are then presented. These include the use of partial durations, the calculation of multiple deltas, and the use of principal components analysis.

8.1 THE MANAGEMENT OF NET INTEREST INCOME

A key risk management activity for a bank is the management of net interest income. This is the excess of interest received over interest paid. It is the role of the asset-liability management function within the bank to ensure that *net interest margin*, which is net interest income divided by income producing assets remains roughly constant through time. This section considers how this is done.

How can fluctuations in net interest margin occur? Consider a simple situation where a bank offers consumers a one-year and a five-year deposit rate as well as a one-year and five-year mortgage rate. The rates are shown in Table 8.1. We make the simplifying assumption that market participants expect the one-year interest rate

TABLE 8.1   Example of Rates Offered by a
Bank to Its Customers

Maturity (years)	Deposit Rate	Mortgage Rate
1	3%	6%
5	3%	6%

for future time periods to equal the one-year rates prevailing in the market today. Loosely speaking, this means that the market considers interest rate increases to be just as likely as interest rate decreases. As a result, the rates in Table 8.1 are "fair" in that they reflect the market's expectations. Investing money for one year and reinvesting for four further one-year periods leads to an uncertain return. But, given our assumptions, the expected overall return is the same as a single five-year investment. Similarly, borrowing money for one year and refinancing each year for the next four years leads to the same expected financing costs as a single five-year loan.

Suppose you have money to deposit and agree with the prevailing view that interest rate increases are just as likely as interest rate decreases. Would you choose to deposit your money for one year at 3% per annum or for five years at 3% per annum? The chances are that you would choose one year because this gives you more financial flexibility. It ties up your funds for a shorter period of time.

Now suppose that you want a mortgage. Again you agree with the prevailing view that interest rate increases are just as likely as interest rate decreases. Would you choose a one-year mortgage at 6% or a five-year mortgage at 6%? The chances are that you would choose a five-year mortgage because it fixes your borrowing rate for the next five years and subjects you to less refinancing risk.

When the bank posts the rates shown in Table 8.1, it is likely to find that the majority of its depositors opt for a one-year maturity and the majority of the customers seeking mortgages opt for a five-year maturity. This creates an asset/liability mismatch for the bank and subjects its net interest income to risks. The deposits that are financing the five-year 6% mortgages are rolled over every year. There is no problem if interest rates fall. After one year, the bank will find itself financing the five-year 6% mortgages with deposits that cost less than 3% and net interest income will increase. However, if interest rates rise, the deposits that are financing the 6% mortgages will cost more than 3% and net interest income will decline. Suppose that there is a 3% rise in interest rates during the first two years. This would reduce net interest income for the third year to zero.

It is the job of the asset-liability management group to ensure that this type of interest rate risk is minimized. One way of doing this is to ensure that the maturities of the assets on which interest is earned and the maturities of the liabilities on which interest is paid are matched. In our example, the matching can be achieved by increasing the five-year rate on both deposits and mortgages. For example, the bank could move to the situation in Table 8.2 where the five-year deposit rate is 4% and the five-year mortgage rate is 7%. This would make five-year deposits relatively more attractive and one-year mortgages relatively more attractive. Some customers

TABLE 8.2   Five-Year Rates Are Increased in an
Attempt to Match Maturities of Assets and Liabilities

Maturity (years)	Deposit Rate	Mortgage Rate
1	3%	6%
5	4%	7%

who chose one-year deposits when the rates were as in Table 8.1 will choose five-year deposits when rates are as in Table 8.2. Some customers who chose five-year mortgages when the rates were as in Table 8.1 will choose one-year mortgages. This may lead to the maturities of assets and liabilities being matched. If there is still an imbalance with depositors tending to choose a one-year maturity and borrowers a five-year maturity, five-year deposit and mortgage rates could be increased even further. Eventually the imbalance will disappear.

The net result of all banks behaving in the way we have just described is that long-term rates tend to be higher than those predicted by expected future short-term rates. This phenomenon is referred to as *liquidity preference theory*. It leads to long-term rates being higher than short-term rates most of the time. Even when the market expects a small decline in short-term rates, liquidity preference theory is likely to cause long-term rates to be higher than short-term rates. Only when a steep decline in interest rates is expected will long-term rates be less than short-term rates.

Many banks now have sophisticated systems for monitoring the decisions being made by customers so that, when they detect small differences between the maturities of the assets and liabilities being chosen, they can fine-tune the rates they offer. Often derivatives such as interest rate swaps are used to manage their exposures (see Example 5.1 in Section 5.4). The result of all this is that net interest margin is usually very stable and does not lead to significant risks. This has not always been the case. In the 1980s in the United States, the failures of savings and loans companies and Continental Illinois were largely a result of their failure to match maturities for assets and liabilities.

Liquidity

In addition to eroding net interest margin, a mismatch of assets and liabilities can lead to liquidity problems. A bank that funds long-term loans with short-term deposits has to replace maturing deposits with new deposits on a regular basis. (This is sometimes referred to as *rolling over* the deposits.) If depositors lose confidence in the bank, it might find it difficult to do this. A well-known example of a financial institution that failed because of liquidity problems is Northern Rock in the United Kingdom. It chose to finance much of its mortgage portfolio with wholesale deposits, some lasting only three months. Starting in September 2007, the depositors became nervous because of the problems surfacing in the United States. As a result, Northern Rock was unable to finance its assets and was taken over by the UK government in early 2008 (see Business Snapshot 21.1). In the United States Bear Stearns and Lehman Brothers experienced similar problems in rolling over their wholesale deposits.

Many of the problems during the credit crisis that started in 2007 were caused by a shortage of liquidity. As often happens during stressed market conditions, there was a flight to quality where investors looked for very safe investments and were not prepared to take credit risks. Bank regulators have now recognized the need to set liquidity requirements, as well as capital requirements, for banks. Chapter 13 explains the Basel III liquidity requirements and Chapter 21 discusses liquidity issues in more detail.

8.2 LIBOR AND SWAP RATES

A key interest rate for banks is LIBOR, the *London interbank offered rate*. This is the rate at which a bank is prepared to lend to another bank.[1] Many loans to corporations and governments, as well as some mortgages, have floating rates that are reset to LIBOR periodically. For example, a loan in sterling to a corporation might be quoted as "three-month LIBOR plus 40 basis points." The rate of interest would then be set equal to three-month sterling LIBOR plus 40 basis points every three months. The British Bankers Association (BBA; www.bba.org.uk) provides LIBOR in different currencies for maturities ranging from overnight to 12-months at 11 A.M. every business day. In total, 15 maturities for each of 10 different currencies are provided. The rates are based on information provided to the BBA by large banks when they answer the question: "At what rate could you borrow funds, were you to do so by asking for and then accepting interbank offers in a reasonable market size just prior to 11 A.M.?" The LIBOR rate provided by the BBA is the average of the responses from banks after the rates in the lowest quartile and highest quartile have been discarded.

A bank must satisfy certain creditworthiness criteria to qualify for receiving LIBOR deposits (i.e, a LIBOR loan) from another bank. Typically it must have a AA credit rating. LIBOR rates are therefore the one-month to twelve-month borrowing rates for banks that have AA credit ratings.

How can the LIBOR yield curve be extended beyond one year? There are two possible approaches:

1. Create a yield curve to represent the rates at which AA-rated companies can today borrow funds for periods of time longer than one year.
2. Create a yield curve to represent the future short-term borrowing rates for AA-rated companies.

It is important to understand the difference. Suppose that the yield curve is 4% for all maturities. If the yield curve is created in the first way, this means that companies rated AA today can lock in an interest rate of 4% regardless of how long they want to borrow. If the yield curve is created in the second way, the forward interest rate that the market assigns to the short-term borrowing rates of companies that will be

---

[1] Banks also quote LIBID, the London interbank bid rate. The is the rate at which a bank is prepared to accept deposits from another bank. The LIBOR quote is slightly higher than the LIBID quote, reflecting the bank's bid–offer spread.

rated AA at a future time is 4%. (See Appendix B for how forward rates are defined and calculated.) When the yield curve is created in the first way, it gives the forward short-term borrowing rate for a company that is AA-rated today. When it is created in the second way, it gives the forward short-term borrowing rate for a company that will be AA at the beginning of the period covered by the forward contract.

In practice, the LIBOR yield curve is extended using the second approach. Swap rates (see Table 5.5.) are used to extend the LIBOR yield curve, as described in Appendix B.[2] The resulting yield curve is sometimes called the LIBOR yield curve, sometimes the swap yield curve, and sometimes the LIBOR/swap yield curve. To understand why swap rates can be used to extend the LIBOR yield curve when the second approach is used, note that a bank can convert a series of short term LIBOR loans to a swap rate using the swap market. For example, it can

1. Lend a certain principal for six months to a AA borrower and relend it for nine successive six-month periods to AA borrowers; and
2. Enter into a swap to exchange the LIBOR for the five-year swap rate

This means that the swap rate represents what the bank can expect to earn from a series of short-term loans to AA-rated borrowers at LIBOR. It is sometimes referred to as a "continually refreshed" rate.

LIBOR vs. Treasury Rates

The risk-free rate is important in the pricing of financial contracts. Traditionally financial institutions have assumed that the LIBOR/swap yield curve provides the risk-free rate. Treasury rates are regarded as too low to be used as risk-free rates because:

1. Treasury bills and Treasury bonds must be purchased by financial institutions to fulfill a variety of regulatory requirements. This increases demand for these Treasury instruments, driving their prices up and their yields down.
2. The amount of capital a bank is required to hold to support an investment in Treasury bills and bonds is substantially smaller than the capital required to support a similar investment in other very-low-risk instruments.
3. In the United States, Treasury instruments are given a favorable tax treatment compared with most other fixed-income investments because they are not taxed at the state level.

The OIS Rate

An overnight indexed swap is a swap where a fixed rate for a period (e.g., one month, three months, one year, or two years) is exchanged for the geometric average of overnight rates during the period. The relevant overnight rates are the rates in the

---

[2] Eurodollar futures, which are contracts on the future value of LIBOR, can also be used to extend the LIBOR yield curve.

government-organized interbank market where banks with excess reserves lend to banks that need to borrow to meet their reserve requirements.[3] In the United States, the overnight borrowing rate in this market is known as the fed funds rate. The effective fed funds rate on a particular day is the weighted average of the overnight rates paid by borrowing banks to lending banks on that day. This is what is used in the OIS geometric average calculations. Many other countries have similar overnight markets. For example, the Eonia (Euro OverNight Index Average) is the European equivalent to the effective fed funds rate; the SONIA (Sterling OverNight Index Average) is the British equivalent; and so on.

If during a certain period a bank borrows at the overnight rate (rolling the loan and interest forward each day) it pays the geometric average of the overnight interest rates for the period. Similarly, if it lends at the overnight rate every day, it receives the geometric average of the overnight rates for the period. An OIS therefore allows overnight borrowing or lending to be swapped for borrowing or lending at a fixed rate. The fixed rate is referred to as the OIS swap rate.

The OIS swap rate is often assumed to be a better proxy for the risk-free rate than LIBOR. A key indicator of stress in the banking system is the LIBOR-OIS spread. This is the amount by which the three-month London Interbank Offered Rate (LIBOR) exceeds the three-month overnight indexed swap (OIS) rate. As discussed, the former is the rate of interest at which a bank will extend unsecured credit to a AA-rated bank for a term of three months. The latter is the rate of interest at which funds can be borrowed by a bank for three months by using overnight borrowings at the fed funds rate of interest in conjunction with a swap which converts the overnight borrowing to three-month borrowing. Banks can in theory borrow at the three-month OIS rate and lend the funds to a AA-rated bank at the three-month LIBOR rate of interest. The LIBOR-OIS spread is therefore a credit spread that compensates lenders for the possibility that a AA-rated bank might default during a three-month period. In normal market conditions, the LIBOR-OIS spread is less than 10 basis points (annualized). The larger the LIBOR-OIS spread, the greater the reluctance of banks to lend to each other because of perceptions about counterparty credit.

Prior to August 2007, the LIBOR-OIS spread was less than 10 basis points. In August 2007, as problems in the U.S. housing market became apparent and banks became increasingly reluctant to lend to each other, it started to increase. It reached a peak of 364 basis points in early October 2008. By a year later, it had returned to more normal levels. (Later it rose again as a result of concerns about the financial health of Greece and a few other European countries.)

8.3 DURATION

Duration is a widely used measure of a portfolio's exposure to yield curve movements. Suppose y is a bond's yield and B is its market price. The duration D of the

---

[3] Central banks require commercial banks to keep a certain percentage of customer deposits as "reserves" that cannot be lent out. The reserves can take the form of cash or deposits with the central bank.

bond is given by

$$\frac{\Delta B}{B} = -D\Delta y$$

or equivalently

$$\Delta B = -DB\Delta y \qquad (8.1)$$

where Δy is a small change in the bond's yield and ΔB is the corresponding change in its price. Duration measures the sensitivity of percentage changes in the bond's price to changes in its yield. Using calculus notation, we can write

$$D = -\frac{1}{B}\frac{dB}{dy} \qquad (8.2)$$

Consider a bond that provides cash flows $c_1, c_2, \ldots, c_n$ at times $t_1, t_2, \ldots, t_n$. (The cash flows consist of the coupon and principal payments on the bond.) The bond yield, y, is defined as the discount rate that equates the bond's theoretical price to its market price. If the yield on the bond is measured with continuous compounding (see Appendix A), it follows that the relationship between the price B of the bond and its yield y is

$$B = \sum_{i=1}^{n} c_i e^{-yt_i}$$

From this, it follows that

$$D = \sum_{i=1}^{n} t_i \left(\frac{c_i e^{-yt_i}}{B} \right) \qquad (8.3)$$

The term in parentheses in equation (8.3) is the ratio of the present value of the cash flow at time t_i to the bond price. The bond price is the present value of all the cash flows. The duration is therefore a weighted average of the times when payments are made, with the weight applied to time t_i being equal to the proportion of the bond's total present value provided by the cash flow at time t_i. (The sum of the weights is 1.0.) This explains where the term "duration" comes from. Duration is a measure of how long the bondholder has to wait for cash flows. A zero-coupon bond that lasts n years has a duration of n years. However, a coupon-bearing bond lasting n years has a duration of less than n years, because the holder receives some of the cash payments prior to year n.

Consider a three-year 10% coupon bond with a face value of $100. Suppose that the yield on the bond is 12% per annum with continuous compounding. This means that $y = 0.12$. Coupon payments of $5 are made every six months. Table 8.3 shows the calculations necessary to determine the bond's duration. The present values of the bond's cash flows, using the yield as the discount rate, are shown in column 3. (For example, the present value of the first cash flow is $5e^{-0.12\times0.5} = 4.709$.) The

TABLE 8.3 Calculation of Duration

Time (years)	Cash Flow ($)	Present Value	Weight	Time x Weight
0.5	5	4.709	0.050	0.025
1.0	5	4.435	0.047	0.047
1.5	5	4.176	0.044	0.066
2.0	5	3.933	0.042	0.083
2.5	5	3.704	0.039	0.098
3.0	105	73.256	0.778	2.333
Total	130	94.213	1.000	2.653

sum of the numbers in column 3 is the bond's market price, 94.213. The weights are calculated by dividing the numbers in column 3 by 94.213. The sum of the numbers in column 5 gives the duration as 2.653 years.

Small changes in interest rates are often measured in *basis points*. A basis point is 0.01% per annum. The following example investigates the accuracy of the duration relationship in equation (8.1).

EXAMPLE 8.1

For the bond in Table 8.3, the bond price, B, is 94.213 and the duration, D, is 2.653 so that equation (8.1) gives

$$\Delta B = -94.213 \times 2.653 \Delta y$$

or

$$\Delta B = -249.95 \Delta y$$

When the yield on the bond increases by 10 basis points ($= 0.1\%$), $\Delta y = +0.001$. The duration relationship predicts that $\Delta B = -249.95 \times 0.001 = -0.250$ so that the bond price goes down to $94.213 - 0.250 = 93.963$. How accurate is this? When the bond yield increases by 10 basis points to 12.1%, the bond price is

$$5e^{-0.121 \times 0.5} + 5e^{-0.121 \times 1.0} + 5e^{-0.121 \times 1.5} + 5e^{-0.121 \times 2.0}$$
$$+ 5e^{-0.121 \times 2.5} + 105e^{-0.121 \times 3.0} = 93.963$$

which is (to three decimal places) the same as that predicted by the duration relationship.

Modified Duration

The definition of duration in equation (8.3) was suggested by Frederick Macaulay in 1938. It is referred to as *Macaulay's duration*. When the yield y on the bond is measured with continuous compounding, it is equivalent to the definition in equation (8.1) or (8.2). When duration is defined using equations (8.1) or (8.2) and other compounding frequencies are used for y, a small adjustment is necessary to Macaulay's duration. When y is measured with annual compounding, it can be shown that the expression for D in equation (8.3) must be divided by $1 + y$. More generally, when y is expressed with a compounding frequency of m times per year, it must be divided by $1 + y/m$. Duration defined with these adjustments to equation (8.3) is referred to as *modified duration*.

EXAMPLE 8.2

The bond in Table 8.3 has a price of 94.213 and a duration of 2.653. The yield, expressed with semiannual compounding is 12.3673%. (See Appendix A.) The (modified) duration appropriate for calculating sensitivity to the yield when it is expressed with semiannual compounding is

$$\frac{2.653}{1 + 0.123673/2} = 2.4985$$

From equation (8.1),

$$\Delta B = -94.213 \times 2.4985 \Delta y$$

or

$$\Delta B = -235.39 \Delta y$$

When the yield (semiannually compounded) increases by 10 basis points ($= 0.1\%$), $\Delta y = +0.001$. The duration relationship predicts that we expect ΔB to be $-235.39 \times 0.001 = -0.235$ so that the bond price goes down to $94.213 - 0.235 = 93.978$. How accurate is this? When the bond yield (semiannually compounded) increases by 10 basis points to 12.4673% (or to 12.0941% with continuous compounding), an exact calculation similar to that in the previous example shows that the bond price becomes 93.978. This shows that the modified duration is accurate for small yield changes.

Dollar Duration

The dollar duration of a bond is defined as the product of its duration and its price. If $D_\$$ is dollar duration, it follows from equation (8.1) that

$$\Delta B = -D_\$ \Delta y$$

or using calculus notation

$$D_\$ = -\frac{dB}{dy}$$

Whereas duration relates proportional changes in a bond's price to its yield, dollar duration relates actual changes in the bond's price to its yield. Dollar duration is similar to the delta measure discussed in Chapter 7.

8.4 CONVEXITY

The duration relationship measures exposure to small changes in yields. This is illustrated in Figure 8.1, which shows the relationship between the percentage change in value and change in yield for two bonds with the same duration. The gradients of the two curves are the same at the origin. This means that both portfolios change in value by the same percentage for small yield changes, as predicted by equation (8.1). For large yield changes, the bonds behave differently. Bond X has more curvature in its relationship with yields than bond Y. A factor known as *convexity* measures this curvature and can be used to improve the relationship between bond prices and yields.

The convexity for a bond is

$$C = \frac{1}{B}\frac{d^2 B}{dy^2} = \frac{\sum_{i=1}^{n} c_i t_i^2 e^{-y t_i}}{B}$$

where y is the bond's yield measured with continuous compounding. This is the weighted average of the square of the time to the receipt of cash flows. From

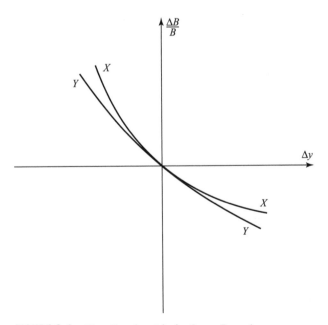

FIGURE 8.1 Two Bonds with the Same Duration

Appendix G, a second order approximation to the change in the bond price is

$$\Delta B = \frac{dB}{dy}\Delta y + \frac{1}{2}\frac{d^2 B}{dy^2}\Delta y^2$$

This leads to

$$\frac{\Delta B}{B} = -D\Delta y + \frac{1}{2}C(\Delta y)^2 \qquad (8.4)$$

EXAMPLE 8.3

Consider again the bond in Table 8.3. The bond price, B, is 94.213 and the duration, D, is 2.653. The convexity is

$$0.05 \times 0.5^2 + 0.047 \times 1.0^2 + 0.044 \times 1.5^2 + 0.042 \times 2.0^2 + 0.039 \times 2.5^2$$
$$+ 0.779 \times 3.0^2 = 7.570$$

The convexity relationship in equation (8.4) is therefore

$$\frac{\Delta B}{B} = -2.653\Delta y + \frac{1}{2} \times 7.570 \times (\Delta y)^2$$

Consider a 2% change in the bond yield from 12% to 14%. The duration relationship predicts that the dollar change in the value of the bond will be $-94.213 \times 2.653 \times 0.02 = -4.999$. The convexity relationship predicts that it will be

$$-94.213 \times 2.653 \times 0.02 + 0.5 \times 94.213 \times 7.570 \times 0.02^2 = -4.856$$

The actual change in the value of the bond is -4.859. This shows that the convexity relationship gives much more accurate results than duration for a large change in the bond yield.

Dollar Convexity

The *dollar convexity* of a bond, $C_\$$, can be defined analogously to dollar duration as the product of convexity and the value of the portfolio. This means that

$$C_\$ = \frac{d^2 B}{dy^2}$$

and shows that dollar convexity is similar to the gamma measure introduced in Chapter 7.

8.5 GENERALIZATION

So far we have used duration and convexity to measure the sensitivity of the price of a single bond to interest rates. The definitions of duration and convexity can

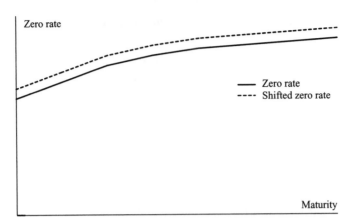

FIGURE 8.2   A Parallel Shift in Zero Rates

be generalized so that they apply to a portfolio of bonds—or to any portfolio of interest-rate-dependent instruments. We define a parallel shift in the zero-coupon yield curve as a shift where all zero-coupon interest rates change by the same amount, as indicated in Figure 8.2.

Suppose that P is the value of the portfolio of interest-rate-dependent securities. We can make a small parallel shift in the zero-coupon yield curve and observe the change ΔP in P. Duration is defined as

$$D = -\frac{1}{P}\frac{\Delta P}{\Delta y} \tag{8.5}$$

where Δy is the size of the small parallel shift.[4] Equation (8.5) is equivalent to

$$\frac{\Delta P}{P} = -D\Delta y \tag{8.6}$$

Suppose a portfolio consists of a number of interest-rate dependent assets. The ith asset is worth X_i and has a duration D_i ($i = 1, 2, \ldots, n$). Define ΔX_i as the change in the value of X_i arising from the yield curve shift Δy. It follows that $P = \sum_{i=1}^{n} X_i$ and $\Delta P = \sum_{i=1}^{n} \Delta X_i$ so that from equation (8.5) the duration of the portfolio is given by

$$D = -\frac{1}{P}\sum_{i=1}^{n}\frac{\Delta X_i}{\Delta y}$$

The duration of the ith asset is

$$D_i = -\frac{1}{X_i}\frac{\Delta X_i}{\Delta y}$$

---

[4] A small parallel shift of Δy in the zero-coupon yield curve leads to the yield of all bonds changing by approximately Δy.

Hence

$$D = \sum_{i=1}^{n} \frac{X_i}{P} D_i$$

This shows that the duration D of a portfolio is the weighted average of the durations of the individual assets comprising the portfolio with the weight assigned to an asset being proportional to the value of the asset.

The dollar duration $D_\$$ of a portfolio can be defined as duration of the portfolio times the value of the portfolio:

$$D_\$ = -\frac{\Delta P}{\Delta y}$$

This is a measure of the delta of the portfolio with respect to interest rates. The dollar duration of a portfolio consisting of a number of interest-rate-dependent assets is the sum of the dollar durations of the individual assets.

The convexity measure can be generalized in the same way as duration. For any interest-rate-dependent portfolio whose value is P we define the convexity C as $1/P$ times the second partial derivative of the value of the portfolio with respect to a parallel shift in the zero-coupon yield curve. Equation (8.4) is correct with B replaced by P:

$$\frac{\Delta P}{P} = -D\Delta y + \frac{1}{2}C(\Delta y)^2 \tag{8.7}$$

The relationship between the convexity of a portfolio and the convexity of the assets comprising the portfolio is similar to that for duration: the convexity of the portfolio is the weighted average of the convexities of the assets with the weights being proportional to the value of the assets. For a portfolio with a particular duration, convexity tends to be greatest when the portfolio provides payments evenly over a long period of time. It is least when the payments are concentrated around one particular point in time.

The dollar convexity for a portfolio worth P can be defined as P times the convexity. This a measure of the gamma of the portfolio with respect to interest rates. The dollar convexity of a portfolio consisting of a number of interest-rate-dependent positions is the sum of the dollar convexities of the individual assets.

Portfolio Immunization

A portfolio consisting of long and short positions in interest-rate-dependent assets can be protected against relatively small parallel shifts in the yield curve by ensuring that its duration is zero. It can be protected against relatively large parallel shifts in the yield curve by ensuring that its duration and convexity are both zero or close to zero.

8.6 NONPARALLEL YIELD CURVE SHIFTS

Unfortunately the basic duration relationship in equation (8.6) only quantifies exposure to parallel yield curve shifts. The duration plus convexity relationship in equation (8.7) allows the shift to be relatively large, but it is still a parallel shift.

Some researchers have extended duration measures so that nonparallel shifts can be considered. Reitano (1992) suggests a partial duration measure where just one point on the zero-coupon yield curve is shifted and all other points remain the same.[5] Suppose that the zero curve is as shown in Table 8.4 and Figure 8.3. Shifting the five-year point involves changing the zero curve as indicated in Figure 8.4. In general, the partial duration of the portfolio for the ith point on the zero curve is

$$D_i = -\frac{1}{P}\frac{\Delta P_i}{\Delta y_i}$$

where Δy_i is the size of the small change made to the ith point on the yield curve and ΔP_i is the resulting change in the portfolio value. The sum of all the partial duration measures equals the usual duration measure.[6] The percentage change in the portfolio value arising from Δy_i is $-D_i \Delta y_i$.

Suppose that the partial durations for a particular portfolio are as shown in Table 8.5. The duration of the portfolio (sum of the partial durations) is only 0.2. This means that the portfolio is relatively insensitive to parallel shifts in the yield curve. However, the durations for short maturities are positive while those for long maturities are negative. This means that the portfolio loses (gains) in value when short rates rise (fall). It gains (loses) in value when long rates rise (fall).

We are now in a position to go one step further and calculate the sensitivity of a portfolio value to any nonparallel shifts. Suppose that, in the case of the yield curve shown in Figure 8.3, we define a rotation where the changes to the 1-year, 2-year, 3-year, 4-year 5-year, 7-year and 10-year are $-3e$, $-2e$, $-e$, 0, e, $3e$, and $6e$ for some small e. This is illustrated in Figure 8.5. From the partial durations in Table 8.5, the percentage change in the value of the portfolio arising from the rotation is

$$-[0.2 \times (-3e) + 0.6 \times (-2e) + 0.9 \times (-e) + 1.6 \times 0 + 2.0 \times e$$
$$-2.1 \times 3e - 3.0 \times 6e] = 25.0e$$

For a parallel shift of e in the yield curve, the percentage change in the value of the portfolio is $-0.2e$. This shows that a portfolio that gives rise to the partial durations in Table 8.5 is much more heavily exposed to a rotation of the yield curve than to a parallel shift.

---

[5] See R. Reitano, "Nonparallel Yield Curve Shifts and Immunization," *Journal of Portfolio Management* (Spring 1992): 36–43.
[6] When the ith point on the zero curve is shifted, the other points are not shifted and rates on the shifted yield curve are calculated using linear interpolation as indicated in Figure 8.4.

TABLE 8.4   Zero-Coupon Yield Curve (rates continuously compounded)

Maturity (years)	1	2	3	4	5	7	10
Rate (%)	4.0	4.5	4.8	5.0	5.1	5.2	5.3

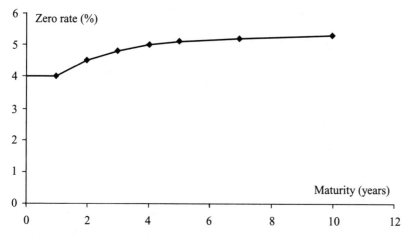

FIGURE 8.3   The Zero-Coupon Yield Curve (as shown in Table 8.4)

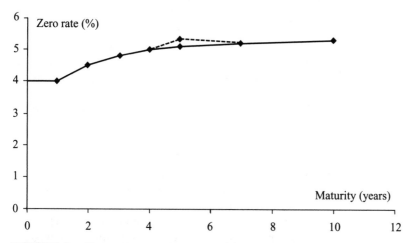

FIGURE 8.4   Change in Zero-Coupon Yield Curve When One Point Is Shifted

TABLE 8.5   Partial Durations for a Portfolio

Maturity (years)	1	2	3	4	5	7	10	Total
Duration	0.2	0.6	0.9	1.6	2.0	−2.1	−3.0	0.2

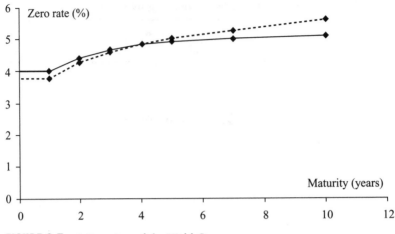

FIGURE 8.5 A Rotation of the Yield Curve

8.7 INTEREST RATE DELTAS IN PRACTICE

In practice, a number of different approaches are used to calculate interest rate deltas. One approach is to define delta as the dollar duration. This is the sensitivity of the portfolio to a parallel shift in the zero-coupon yield curve. A measure related to this definition of delta is DV01. This is the impact of a one-basis-point increase in all rates. It is the dollar duration multiplied by 0.0001. Alternatively, it is the duration of the portfolio multiplied by the value of the portfolio multiplied by 0.0001.

In practice, analysts like to calculate several deltas to reflect their exposures to all the different ways in which the yield curve can move. There are a number of different ways this can be done. One approach corresponds to the partial duration approach that we outlined in the previous section. It involves computing the impact of a one-basis-point change similar to the one illustrated in Figure 8.4 for each point on the zero-coupon yield curve. This delta is the partial duration calculated in Table 8.5 multiplied by the value of the portfolio multiplied by 0.0001. The sum of the deltas for all the points on the yield curve equals the DV01. Suppose that the portfolio in Table 8.5 is worth $1 million. The deltas are shown in Table 8.6.

A variation on this approach is to divide the yield curve into a number of segments or "buckets" and calculate for each bucket the impact of changing all the zero rates corresponding to the bucket by one basis point while keeping all other zero rates unchanged. This approach is often used in asset-liability management (see Section 8.1) and is referred to as *GAP management*. Figure 8.6 shows the type of

TABLE 8.6 Deltas for Portfolio in Table 8.5.

Maturity (yrs)	1	2	3	4	5	7	10	Total
Delta	−20	−60	−90	−160	−200	210	300	−20

Value of portfolio is $1 million. The dollar impact of a one-basis-point increase in points on the zero curve is shown.

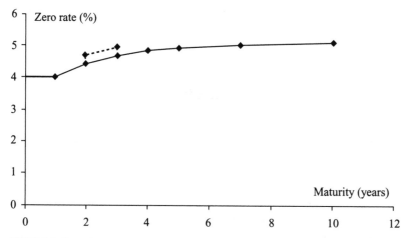

FIGURE 8.6 Change Considered to Yield Curve When Bucketing Approach
Is Used

change that would be considered for the segment of the zero curve between 2.0 and
3.0 years in Figure 8.3. As with the partial duration approach, the sum of the deltas
for all the segments equals the DV01.

Calculating Deltas to Facilitate Hedging

One of the problems with the delta measures that we have considered so far is that
they are not designed to make hedging easy. Consider the deltas in Table 8.6. If we
plan to hedge our portfolio with zero-coupon bonds, we can calculate the position
in a one-year zero coupon bond to zero out the $200 per basis point exposure to the
one-year rate, the position in a two-year zero-coupon bond to zero out the exposure
to the two-year rate, and so on. But, if other instruments are used, a much more
complicated analysis is necessary.

In practice, traders tend to use positions in the instruments that have been used
to construct the zero curve to hedge their exposure. For example, a government
bond trader is likely to take positions in the actively traded government bonds that
were used to construct the Treasury zero curve when hedging. A trader of instruments
dependent on the LIBOR/swap yield curve is likely take a position in LIBOR deposits,
Eurodollar futures, and swaps when hedging.

To facilitate hedging, traders therefore often calculate the impact of small
changes in the quotes for each of the instruments used to construct the zero curve.
The quote for the instrument is changed by a small amount, the zero-coupon yield
curve is recomputed, and the portfolio revalued. Consider a trader responsible for
interest rate caps and swap options. Suppose that, when there is a one-basis-point
change in a Eurodollar futures quote, the portfolio value increases by $500. Each
Eurodollar futures contract changes in value by $25 for a one-basis-point change in
the Eurodollar futures quote. It follows that the traders exposure can be hedged with
20 contracts. Suppose that the exposure to a one-basis-point change in the five-year
swap rate is $4,000 and that a five-year swap with a notional principal of $1 million

changes in value by $400 for a one-basis-point change in the five-year swap rate. The exposure can be hedged by trading swaps with a notional principal of $10 million.

8.8 PRINCIPAL COMPONENTS ANALYSIS

The approaches we have just outlined can lead to analysts calculating 10 to 15 different deltas for every zero curve. This seems like overkill because the variables being considered are quite highly correlated with each other. For example, when the yield on a five-year bond moves up by a few basis points, most of the time the yield on a ten-year bond moves in a similar way. Arguably a trader should not be worried when a portfolio has a large positive exposure to the five-year rate and a similar large negative exposure to the ten-year rate.

One approach to handling the risk arising from groups of highly correlated market variables is principal components analysis. This is a standard statistical tool with many applications in risk management. It takes historical data on daily changes in the market variables and attempts to define a set of components or factors that explain the movements.

The approach is best illustrated with an example. The market variables we will consider are swap rates with maturities of 1 year, 2 years, 3 years, 4 years, 5 years, 7 years, 10 years, and 30 years. Tables 8.7 and 8.8 show results produced for these market variables using 2,780 daily observations between 2000 and 2011. The first column in Table 8.7 shows the maturities of the rates that were considered. The remaining eight columns in the table show the eight factors (or principal components) describing the rate moves. The first factor, shown in the column labeled PC1, corresponds to a roughly parallel shift in the yield curve. When we have one unit of that factor, the one-year rate increases by 0.216 basis points, the two-year rate increases by 0.331 basis points, and so on. The second factor is shown in the column labeled PC2. It corresponds to a "twist" or change of slope of the yield curve. Rates between 1 year and 4 years move in one direction; rates between 5 years and 30 years move in the other direction. The third factor corresponds to a "bowing" of the yield curve. Relatively short (1-year and 2-year) and relatively long (10-year and 30-year) rates move in one direction; the intermediate rates move in the other direction. The

TABLE 8.7　Factor Loadings for Swap Data

	PC1	PC2	PC3	PC4	PC5	PC6	PC7	PC8
1-year	0.216	−0.501	0.627	−0.487	0.122	0.237	0.011	−0.034
2-year	0.331	−0.429	0.129	0.354	−0.212	−0.674	−0.100	0.236
3-year	0.372	−0.267	−0.157	0.414	−0.096	0.311	0.413	−0.564
4-year	0.392	−0.110	−0.256	0.174	−0.019	0.551	−0.416	0.512
5-year	0.404	0.019	−0.355	−0.269	0.595	−0.278	−0.316	−0.327
7-year	0.394	0.194	−0.195	−0.336	0.007	−0.100	0.685	0.422
10-year	0.376	0.371	0.068	−0.305	−0.684	−0.039	−0.278	−0.279
30-year	0.305	0.554	0.575	0.398	0.331	0.022	0.007	0.032

TABLE 8.8   Standard Deviation of Factor Scores

PC1	PC2	PC3	PC4	PC5	PC6	PC7	PC8
17.55	4.77	2.08	1.29	0.91	0.73	0.56	0.53

interest rate move for a particular factor is known as *factor loading*. In our example, the first factor's loading for the one-year rate is 0.216.[7]

Because there are eight rates and eight factors, the interest rate changes observed on any given day can always be expressed as a linear sum of the factors by solving a set of eight simultaneous equations. The quantity of a particular factor in the interest rate changes on a particular day is known as the *factor score* for that day.

The importance of a factor is measured by the standard deviation of its factor score. The standard deviations of the factor scores in our example are shown in Table 8.8 and the factors are listed in order of their importance. In carrying out the analysis, interest rate movements were measured in basis points. A quantity of the first factor equal to one standard deviation, therefore, corresponds to the one-year rate moving by $0.216 \times 17.55 = 3.78$ basis points, the two-year rate moving by $0.331 \times 17.55 = 5.81$ basis points, and so on.

Software for carrying out the calculations underlying Tables 8.7 and 8.8 is on the author's website. The calculations are explained in Appendix I at the end of the book. Principal components analysis is a standard statistical tool. To implement principal components analysis, it is first necessary to calculate a variance-covariance matrix from the observations (see Chapter 15 for a discussion of variance–covariance matrices). In our example, the variance-covariance matrix would be a matrix with eight rows and eight columns with the first element of the first row being the variance of the daily changes in the one-year rate, the second element of the first row being the covariance between the daily changes in the one-year rate and the daily changes in the two-year rate, and so on. The factor loadings are the eigenvectors calculated from this matrix and the variance of the factor scores are the eigenvalues calculated from the matrix. (Eigenvectors and eigenvalues are explained in Appendix H.)

The factors have the property that the factor scores are uncorrelated across the data. For instance, in our example, the first factor score (amount of parallel shift) is uncorrelated with the second factor score (amount of twist) across the 2,780 days. The variances of the factor scores have the property that they add up to the total variance of the data. From Table 8.8, the total variance of the original data (that is, sum of the variance of the observations on the one-year rate, the variance of the observations on the two-year rate, and so on) is

$$17.55^2 + 4.77^2 + 2.08^2 + \ldots + 0.53^2 = 338.8$$

From this it can be seen that the first factor accounts for $17.55^2/338.8 = 90.9\%$ of the variance in the original data; the first two factors account for

$$(17.55^2 + 4.77^2)/338.8 = 97.7\%$$

---

[7] The factor loadings have the property that the sum of their squares for each factor is 1.0. Also, note that a factor is not changed if the signs of all its factor loadings are reversed.

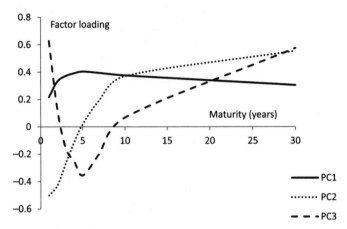

FIGURE 8.7 The Three Most Important Factors Driving
Movements in Swap Rates

of the variance in the data; the third factor accounts for a further 1.3% of the
variance. This shows that most of the risk in interest rate moves are accounted for
by the first two or three factors. It suggests that we can relate the risks in a portfolio
of interest rate dependent instruments to movements in these factors instead of
considering all eight interest rates. The three most important factors from Table 8.7
are plotted in Figure 8.7.[8]

Using Principal Components Analysis to Calculate Deltas

To illustrate how a principal components analysis can provide an alternative way of
calculating deltas, suppose we have a portfolio with the exposures to interest rate
moves shown in Table 8.9. A one-basis-point change in the three-year rate causes the
portfolio value to increase by $10 million; a one-basis-point change in the four-year
rate causes it to increase by $4 million; and so on. We use the first two factors to
model rate moves. (As mentioned earlier, this captures over 97% of the variance
in rate moves.) Using the data in Table 8.7, our delta exposure to the first factor
(measured in millions of dollars per unit of the factor with the factor loadings being
assumed to be in basis points) is

$$10 \times 0.372 + 4 \times 0.392 - 8 \times 0.404 - 7 \times 0.394 + 2 \times 0.376 = -0.05$$

and our delta exposure to the second factor is

$$10 \times (-0.267) + 4 \times (-0.110) - 8 \times 0.019 - 7 \times 0.194 + 2 \times 0.371 = -3.87$$

---

[8] Results similar to those described here, concerning the nature of the factors and the amount
of the total risk they account for, are obtained when a principal components analysis is used
to explain the movements in almost any yield curve in any country.

TABLE 8.9 Change in Portfolio Value for a 1-Basis-Point Rate Move ($ millions)

3-Year Rate	4-Year Rate	5-Year Rate	7-Year Rate	10-Year Rate
+10	+4	−8	−7	+2

The approach being used here is similar to the approach described in Section 8.6 where partial durations were used to estimate the impact of a particular type of shift in the yield curve. The advantage of using a principal components analysis is that it tells you which are the most appropriate shifts to consider. It also provides information on the relative importance of different shifts. In the example we have considered, the exposure to the second shift is almost 80 times greater than our exposure to the first shift. However, from Table 8.8 the standard deviation first shift is about 3.7 times as great as the standard deviation of the second shift. The importance of a factor for a particular portfolio can be measured as the product of the delta exposure and the standard deviation of the factor score. Using this measure, the second factor is over 20 times as important as the first factor for the portfolio in Table 8.9.

8.9 GAMMA AND VEGA

When several delta measures are calculated for interest rates, there are many possible gamma measures. Suppose that 10 instruments are used to compute the zero curve and that we measure deltas with respect to changes in the quotes for each of these. Gamma is a second partial derivative of the form $\partial^2 P / \partial x_i \partial x_j$ where P is the portfolio value. We have 10 choices for x_i and 10 choices for x_j and a total of 55 different gamma measures. This may be "information overload." One approach is to ignore cross-gammas and focus on the 10 partial derivatives where $i = j$. Another is to calculate a single gamma measure as the second partial derivative of the value of the portfolio with respect to a parallel shift in the zero curve. (This is dollar convexity.) A further possibility is to calculate gammas with respect to the first two factors in a principal components analysis.

The vega of a portfolio of interest rate derivatives measures its exposure to volatility changes. Different volatilities are used to price different interest rate derivatives. One approach is to make the same small change to all volatilities and calculate the effect on the value of the portfolio. Another is to carry out a principal components analysis to calculate factors that reflect the patterns of volatility changes across different instruments (caps, swaps, bond options, etc.) that are traded. Vega measures can then be calculated for the first two or three factors.

SUMMARY

A bank's net interest margin is a measure of the excess of the interest rate it earns over the interest rate it pays. There are now well-established asset/liability management procedures to ensure that this remains roughly constant from year to year.

LIBOR is an important interest rate that governs the rates paid on many floating-rate loans throughout the world. The LIBOR rate is a short-term borrowing rate for AA-rated financial institutions. A complete LIBOR term structure of interest rates is constructed from LIBOR rates, Eurodollar futures, and swap rates. Forward interest rates calculated from this term structure are the forward borrowing rates for companies that will be AA-rated at the beginning of the period covered by the forward contract—not companies that are AA-rated today. The LIBOR/swap term structure of interest rates has traditionally been used as a proxy for the term structure of risk-free interest rates by most financial institutions.

An important concept in interest rate markets is duration. Duration measures the sensitivity of the value of a portfolio to a small parallel shift in the zero-coupon yield curve. The relationship is

$$\Delta P = -PD\Delta y$$

where P is the value of the portfolio, D is the duration of the portfolio, Δy is the size of a small parallel shift in the zero curve, and ΔP is the resultant effect on the value of the portfolio. A more precise relationship is

$$\Delta P = -PD\Delta y + \frac{1}{2}PC(\Delta y)^2$$

where C is the convexity of the portfolio. This relationship is accurate for relatively large parallel shifts in the yield curve but does not quantify the exposure to nonparallel shifts.

To quantify exposure to all the different ways the yield curve can change through time, several duration or delta measures are necessary. There are a number of ways these can be defined. A principal components analysis can be a useful alternative to calculating multiple deltas. It shows that the yield curve shifts that occur in practice are to a large extent a linear sum of two or three standard shifts. If a portfolio manager is hedged against these standard shifts he or she is therefore also well hedged against the shifts that occur in practice.

FURTHER READING

Duffie, D. "Debt Management and Interest Rate Risk." In *Risk Management: Challenges and Solutions*, edited by W. Beaver and G. Parker. New York: McGraw-Hill, 1994.

Fabozzi, F. J. *Duration, Convexity, and Other Bond Risk Measures*. Frank J. Fabozzi Associates, 1999.

Frye, J. "Principals of Risk: Finding VAR through Factor-Based Interest Rate Scenarios." In *VAR: Understanding and Applying Value at Risk*. London: Risk Publications, 1997, 275–288.

Jorion, P. *Big Bets Gone Bad: Derivatives and Bankruptcy in Orange County*. New York: Academic Press, 1995.

Reitano, R. "Nonparallel Yield Curve Shifts and Immunization." *Journal of Portfolio Management* (Spring 1992), 36–43.

PRACTICE QUESTIONS AND PROBLEMS (ANSWERS AT END OF BOOK)

8.1 Suppose that a bank has $5 billion of one-year loans and $20 billion of five-year loans. These are financed by $15 billion of one-year deposits and $10 billion of five-year deposits. Explain the impact on the bank's net interest income of interest rates increasing by 1% every year for the next three years.

8.2 Explain why long-term rates are higher than short-term rates most of the time. Under what circumstances would you expect long-term rates to be lower than short-term rates?

8.3 Why are U.S. Treasury rates significantly lower than other rates that are close to risk free?

8.4 Explain how an overnight indexed swap works.

8.5 Explain why the LIBOR-OIS spread is a measure of stress in financial markets.

8.6 What does duration tell you about the sensitivity of a bond portfolio to interest rates? What are the limitations of the duration measure?

8.7 A five-year bond with a yield of 11% (continuously compounded) pays an 8% coupon at the end of each year.
   (a) What is the bond's price?
   (b) What is the bond's duration?
   (c) Use the duration to calculate the effect on the bond's price of a 0.2% decrease in its yield.
   (d) Recalculate the bond's price on the basis of a 10.8% per annum yield and verify that the result is in agreement with your answer to (c).

8.8 Repeat Problem 8.7 on the assumption that the yield is compounded annually. Use modified durations.

8.9 A six-year bond with a continuously compounded yield of 4% provides a 5% coupon at the end of each year. Use duration and convexity to estimate the effect of a 1% increase in the yield on the price of the bond. How accurate is the estimate?

8.10 Explain three ways in which multiple deltas can be calculated to manage non-parallel yield curve shifts.

8.11 Estimate the delta of the portfolio in Table 8.6 with respect to the first two factors in Table 8.7.

8.12 Use the partial durations in Table 8.5 to calculate the impact of a shift in the yield curve on a $10 million portfolio where the 1-, 2-, 3-, 4-, 5-, 7-, and 10-year rates increase by 10, 8, 7, 6, 5, 3, and 1 basis points respectively.

8.13 How are "dollar duration" and "dollar convexity" defined?

8.14 What is the relationship between (a) the duration, (b) the partial durations, and (c) the DV01 of a portfolio?

FURTHER QUESTIONS

8.15 Suppose that a bank has $10 billion of one-year loans and $30 billion of five-year loans. These are financed by $35 billion of one-year deposits and $5 billion of five-year deposits. The bank has equity totaling $2 billion and its return on equity is currently 12%. Estimate what change in interest rates next year would lead to the bank's return on equity being reduced to zero. Assume that the bank is subject to a tax rate of 30%.

8.16 Portfolio A consists of a one-year zero-coupon bond with a face value of $2,000 and a 10-year zero-coupon bond with a face value of $6,000. Portfolio B consists of a 5.95-year zero-coupon bond with a face value of $5,000. The current yield on all bonds is 10% per annum (continuously compounded).

   (a) Show that both portfolios have the same duration.

   (b) Show that the percentage changes in the values of the two portfolios for a 0.1% per annum increase in yields are the same.

   (c) What are the percentage changes in the values of the two portfolios for a 5% per annum increase in yields?

8.17 What are the convexities of the portfolios in Problem 8.16? To what extent does (a) duration and (b) convexity explain the difference between the percentage changes calculated in part (c) of Problem 8.16?

8.18 When the partial durations are as in Table 8.5, estimate the effect of a shift in the yield curve where the ten-year rate stays the same, the one-year rate moves up by $9e$, and the movements in intermediate rates are calculated by interpolation between $9e$ and 0. How could your answer be calculated from the results for the rotation calculated in Section 8.6?

8.19 Suppose that the change in a portfolio value for a one-basis-point shift in the 1-, 2-, 3-, 4-, 5-, 7-, 10-, and 30-year rates are (in $ million) $+5, -3, -1, +2, +5, +7, +8$, and $+1$, respectively. Estimate the delta of the portfolio with respect to the first three factors in Table 8.7. Quantify the relative importance of the three factors for this portfolio.

CHAPTER 9

Value at Risk

Chapters 7 and 8 describe how a trader responsible for a financial institution's exposure to a particular market variable (e.g., an equity index, an interest rate, or a commodity price) quantifies and manages risks by calculating measures such as delta, gamma, and vega. Often a financial institution's portfolio depends on hundreds, or even thousands, of market variables. A huge number of these types of risk measures are therefore produced each day. While very useful to traders, the risk measures do not provide senior management and the individuals that regulate financial institutions with a measure of the total risk to which a financial institution is exposed.

Value at risk (VaR) is an attempt to provide a single number that summarizes the total risk in a portfolio. It was pioneered by JPMorgan (see Business Snapshot 9.1.) and has become widely used by corporate treasurers and fund managers as well as by financial institutions. As we shall see in Chapter 12, it is the measure regulators have chosen to use for many of the calculations they carry out concerned with the setting of capital requirements for market risk, credit risk, and operational risk.

This chapter introduces the VaR measure and discusses its strengths and weaknesses. Chapters 14 and 15 discuss how VaR is calculated for market risk while Chapter 18 does the same for credit risk.

9.1 DEFINITION OF VaR

When using the value at risk measure, we are interested in making a statement of the following form:

"We are X percent certain that we will not lose more than V dollars in time T."

The variable V is the VaR of the portfolio. It is a function of two parameters: the time horizon, T, and the confidence level, X percent. It is the loss level during a time period of length T that we are $X\%$ certain will not be exceeded.

VaR can be calculated from either the probability distribution of gains during time T or the probability distribution of losses during time T. (In the former case, losses are negative gains; in the latter case, gains are negative losses.) When the distribution of gains is used, VaR is equal to minus the gain at the $(100 - X)$th percentile of the distribution as illustrated in Figure 9.1. When the distribution of

---

BUSINESS SNAPSHOT 9.1

Historical Perspectives on VaR

JPMorgan is credited with helping to make VaR a widely used measure. The Chairman, Dennis Weatherstone, was dissatisfied with the long-risk reports he received every day. These contained a huge amount of detail on the Greek letters for different exposures, but very little that was really useful to top management. He asked for something simpler that focused on the bank's total exposure over the next 24 hours measured across the bank's entire trading portfolio. At first his subordinates said this was impossible, but eventually they adapted the Markowitz portfolio theory (see Section 1.1) to develop a VaR report. This became known as the 4:15 report because it was placed on the chairman's desk at 4:15 P.M. every day after the close of trading.

Producing the report entailed a huge amount of work involving the collection of data daily on the positions held by the bank around the world, the handling of different time zones, the estimation of correlations and volatilities, and the development of computer systems. The work was completed in about 1990. The main benefit of the new system was that senior management had a better understanding of the risks being taken by the bank and were better able to allocate capital within the bank. Other banks had been working on similar approaches for aggregating risks and by 1993 VaR was established as an important risk measure.

Banks usually keep the details about the models they develop internally a secret. However, in 1994 JPMorgan made a simplified version of their own system, which they called RiskMetrics, available on the Internet. RiskMetrics included variances and covariances for a very large number of different market variables. This attracted a lot of attention and led to debates about the pros and cons of different VaR models. Software firms started offering their own VaR models, some of which used the RiskMetrics database. After that, VaR was rapidly adopted as a standard by financial institutions and some nonfinancial corporations. The BIS Amendment, which was based on VaR (see Section 12.6), was announced in 1996 and implemented in 1998. Later the RiskMetrics group within JPMorgan was spun off as a separate company. This company developed CreditMetrics for handling credit risks in 1997 and CorporateMetrics for handling the risks faced by non-financial corporations in 1999.

---

losses is used, VaR is equal to the loss at the Xth percentile of the distribution as indicated in Figure 9.2. For example, when T is five days and $X = 97$, VaR is minus the third percentile of the distribution of gains in the value of the portfolio over the next five days. Alternatively, it is the 97th percentile of the distribution of losses in the value of the portfolio over the next five days.

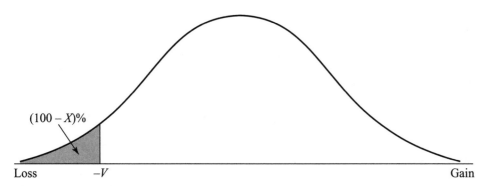

FIGURE 9.1   Calculation of VaR from the Probability Distribution of the Gain in the Portfolio Value

Losses are negative gains; confidence level is X%; VaR level is V.

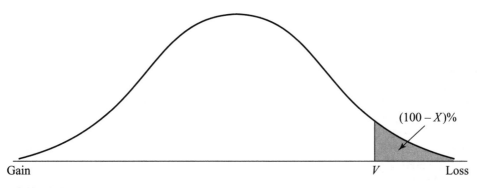

FIGURE 9.2   Calculation of VaR from the Probability Distribution of the Loss in the Portfolio Value

Gains are negative losses; confidence level is X%; VaR level is V.

9.2   EXAMPLES OF THE CALCULATION OF VaR

This section provides four simple examples to illustrate the calculation of VaR. In the first two examples, the probability distribution of the gain (or loss) is a continuous distribution. In the last two examples, it is a discrete distribution.

EXAMPLE 9.1

Suppose that the gain from a portfolio during six months is normally distributed with a mean of $2 million and a standard deviation of $10 million. From the properties of the normal distribution, the one-percentile point of this distribution is $2 - 2.33 \times 10$ or −$21.3 million. The VaR for the portfolio with a time horizon of six months and confidence level of 99% is therefore $21.3 million.

EXAMPLE 9.2

Suppose that for a one-year project all outcomes between a loss of $50 million and a gain of $50 million are considered equally likely. In this case, the loss from the project has a uniform distribution extending from –$50 million to +$50 million. There is a 1% chance that there will be a loss greater than $49 million. The VaR with a one-year time horizon and a 99% confidence level is therefore $49 million.

EXAMPLE 9.3

A one-year project has a 98% chance of leading to a gain of $2 million, a 1.5% chance of leading to a loss of $4 million and a 0.5% chance of leading to a loss of $10 million. The cumulative loss distribution is shown in Figure 9.3. The point on this cumulative distribution that corresponds to a cumulative probability of 99% is $4 million. It follows that VaR with a confidence level of 99% and a one-year time horizon is $4 million.

EXAMPLE 9.4

Consider again the situation in Example 9.3. Suppose that we are interested in calculating a VaR using a confidence level of 99.5%. In this case, Figure 9.3 shows that all losses between $4 and $10 million have a probability of 99.5% of not being exceeded. Equivalently, there is a probability of 0.5% of any specified loss level between $4 and $10 million being exceeded. VaR is therefore not uniquely defined. A sensible convention in this type of situation is to set VaR equal to the midpoint of the range of possible VaR values. This means that, in this case, VaR would equal $7 million.

9.3 VaR vs. EXPECTED SHORTFALL

VaR is an attractive measure because it is easy to understand. In essence, it asks the simple question "How bad can things get?" This is the question all senior managers

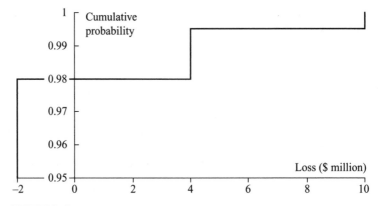

FIGURE 9.3   Cumulative Loss Distribution for Examples 9.3 and 9.4

want answered. They are very comfortable with the idea of compressing all the Greek letters for all the market variables underlying a portfolio into a single number. VaR is also fairly easy to back-test as we will see later in this chapter.

However, when VaR is used in an attempt to limit the risks taken by a trader, it can lead to undesirable results. Suppose that a bank tells a trader that the one-day 99% VaR of the trader's portfolio must be kept at less than $10 million. The trader can construct a portfolio where there is a 99.1% chance that the daily loss is less than $10 million and a 0.9% chance that it is $500 million. The trader is satisfying the risk limits imposed by the bank but is clearly taking unacceptable risks.

This type of behavior by a trader is not as unlikely as it seems. Many traders like taking high risks in the hope of realizing high returns. If they can find ways of taking high risks without violating risk limits, they will do so. To quote one trader the author has talked to: "I have never met a risk control system that I cannot trade around." The sort of probability distribution of gains that the trader might aim for is shown in Figure 9.4. The VaR in Figure 9.4 is the same as the VaR in Figure 9.1. However, the portfolio in Figure 9.4 is much riskier than the portfolio in Figure 9.1 because a large loss is more likely.

Expected Shortfall

A measure that can produce better incentives for traders than VaR is *expected shortfall*. This is also sometimes referred to as *conditional value at risk*, *conditional tail expectation*, or *expected tail loss*. Whereas VaR asks the question: "How bad can things get?" expected shortfall asks: "If things do get bad, what is the expected loss?" Expected shortfall, like VaR, is a function of two parameters: T (the time horizon) and X (the confidence level). It is the expected loss during time T conditional on the loss being greater than the Xth percentile of the loss distribution. For example, suppose that $X = 99$, T is 10 days, and the VaR is $64 million. The expected shortfall is the average amount lost over a 10-day period assuming that the loss is greater than $64 million.

As shown in the next section, expected shortfall has better properties than VaR in that it encourages diversification. One disadvantage is that it does not have the

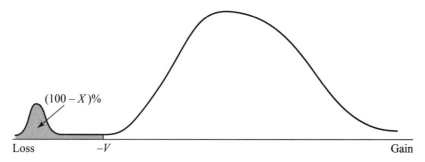

FIGURE 9.4 Probability Distribution for Gain in Portfolio Value During Time T

Confidence level is X%. Portfolio has the same VaR level, V, as in Figure 9.1, but a large loss is more likely.

simplicity of VaR and as a result is more difficult to understand. Another is that it is more difficult to back-test a procedure for calculating expected shortfall than it is to back-test a procedure for calculating VaR. (Back-testing, as will be explained later, is a way of looking at historical data to test the reliability of a particular methodology for calculating a risk measure.)

In spite of its weaknesses, VaR has become the most popular measure of risk among both regulators and risk managers. Therefore, in most of our discussions in this chapter and the chapters that follow, we will focus on how VaR can be measured and used. Many of the points we make apply equally to expected shortfall and other risk measures.

9.4 VaR AND CAPITAL

As we will describe in later chapters, VaR is used by regulators of financial institutions and by financial institutions themselves to determine the amount of capital they should keep. Regulators calculate the capital required for market risk as a multiple of the VaR calculated using a 10-day time horizon and a 99% confidence level. They calculate capital for credit risk and operational risk as the VaR using a one-year time horizon and a 99.9% confidence level.

Suppose that the VaR of a portfolio for a confidence level of 99.9% and a time horizon of one year is $50 million. This means that in extreme circumstances (theoretically, once every thousand years) the financial institution will lose more than $50 million in a year. It also means that if it keeps $50 million in capital it will have a 99.9% probability of not running out of capital in the course of one year.

Suppose we are trying to design a risk measure that will equal the capital a financial institution is required to keep. Is VaR (with an appropriate time horizon and an appropriate confidence level) the best measure? Artzner et al. have examined this question. They first proposed a number of properties that such a risk measure should have.[1] These are:

1. *Monotonicity*: If a portfolio produces a worse result than another portfolio for every state of the world, its risk measure should be greater.
2. *Translation Invariance*: If an amount of cash (K) is added to a portfolio, its risk measure should go down by K.
3. *Homogeneity*: Changing the size of a portfolio by a factor λ while keeping the relative amounts of different items in the portfolio the same, should result in the risk measure being multiplied by λ.
4. *Subadditivity*: The risk measure for two portfolios after they have been merged should be no greater than the sum of their risk measures before they were merged.

The first condition is straightforward. If one portfolio always performs worse than another portfolio, it clearly should be viewed as more risky and require more

---

[1] See P. Artzner, F. Delbaen, J.-M. Eber, and D. Heath, "Coherent Measures of Risk," *Mathematical Finance* 9 (1999): 203–228.

capital. The second condition is also reasonable. If we add an amount of cash equal to K to a portfolio this provides a buffer against losses and should reduce the capital requirement by K. The third condition is also reasonable. If we double the size of a portfolio, presumably we should require twice as much capital. The fourth condition states that diversification helps reduce risks. When we aggregate two portfolios, the total risk measure should either decrease or stay the same.

VaR satisfies the first three conditions. However, it does not always satisfy the fourth one, as is illustrated by the following two examples.

EXAMPLE 9.5

Suppose each of two independent projects has a probability of 0.02 of a loss of $10 million and a probability of 0.98 of a loss of $1 million during a one-year period. The one-year, 97.5% VaR for each project is $1 million. When the projects are put in the same portfolio, there is a $0.02 \times 0.02 = 0.0004$ probability of a loss of $20 million, a $2 \times 0.02 \times 0.98 = 0.0392$ probability of a loss of $11 million, and a $0.98 \times 0.98 = 0.9604$ probability of a loss of $2 million. The one-year 97.5% VaR for the portfolio is $11 million. The total of the VaRs of the projects considered separately is $2 million. The VaR of the portfolio is therefore greater than the sum of the VaRs of the projects by $9 million. This violates the subadditivity condition.

EXAMPLE 9.6

A bank has two $10 million one-year loans. The probabilities of default are as indicated in the following table.

Outcome	Probability
Neither loan defaults	97.50%
Loan 1 defaults; Loan 2 does not default	1.25%
Loan 2 defaults; Loan 1 does not default	1.25%
Both loans default	0.00%

If a default occurs, all losses between 0% and 100% of the principal are equally likely. If the loan does not default, a profit of $0.2 million is made.

Consider first Loan 1. This has a 1.25% chance of defaulting. When a default occurs the loss experienced is evenly distributed between zero and $10 million. This means that there is a 1.25% chance that a loss greater than zero will be incurred; there is a 0.625% chance that a loss greater than $5 million is incurred; there is no chance of a loss greater than $10 million. The loss level that has a probability of 1% of being exceeded is $2 million. (Conditional on a loss being made, there is an 80% or 0.8 chance that the loss will be greater than $2 million. Because the probability of a loss is 1.25% or 0.0125, the unconditional probability of a loss greater than $2 million is $0.8 \times 0.0125 = 0.01$ or 1%.) The one-year 99% VaR is therefore $2 million. The same applies to Loan 2.

Consider next a portfolio of the two loans. There is a 2.5% probability that a default will occur. As before, the loss experienced on a defaulting loan is evenly distributed between zero and $10 million. The VaR in this case turns out to be $5.8 million. This is because there is a 2.5% (0.025) chance of one of the loans defaulting and conditional on this event is a 40% (0.4) chance that the loss on the loan that defaults is greater than $6 million. The unconditional probability of a loss from a default being greater than $6 million is therefore $0.4 \times 0.025 = 0.01$ or 1%. In the event that one loan defaults, a profit of $0.2 million is made on the other loan, showing that the one-year 99% VaR is $5.8 million.

The total VaR of the loans considered separately is $2 + 2 = \$4$ million. The total VaR after they have been combined in the portfolio is $1.8 million greater at $5.8 million. This shows that the subadditivity condition is violated. (This is in spite of the fact that there are clearly very attractive diversification benefits from combining the loans into a single portfolio—particularly because they cannot default together.)

9.5 COHERENT RISK MEASURES

Risk measures satisfying all four conditions given above are referred to as coherent. Examples 9.5 and 9.6 illustrate that VaR is not coherent. It can be shown that the expected shortfall measure is always coherent. The following examples illustrate this.

EXAMPLE 9.7

Consider again the situation in Example 9.5. The VaR for one of the projects considered on its own is $1 million. To calculate the expected shortfall for a 97.5% confidence level we note that, of the 2.5% tail of the loss distribution, 2% corresponds to a $10 million loss and 0.5% to a $1 million loss. (Note that the other 97.5% of the distribution also corresponds to a loss of $1 million.) Conditional that we are in the 2.5% tail of the loss distribution, there is therefore an 80% probability of a loss of $10 million and a 20% probability of a loss of $1 million. The expected loss is $0.8 \times 10 + 0.2 \times 1$ or $8.2 million. This is the expected shortfall.

When the two projects are combined, of the 2.5% tail of the loss distribution, 0.04% corresponds to a loss of $20 million and 2.46% corresponds to a loss of $11 million. Conditional that we are in the 2.5% tail of the loss distribution, the expected loss is therefore $(0.04/2.5) \times 20 + (2.46/2.5) \times 11$ or $11.144 million.

Because $8.2 + 8.2 > 11.144$, the expected shortfall measure does satisfy the subadditivity condition for this example.

EXAMPLE 9.8

Consider again the situation in Example 9.6. We showed that the VaR for a single loan is $2 million. The expected shortfall from a single loan when the time horizon is one year and the confidence level is 99% is therefore the expected loss on the loan conditional on a loss greater than $2 million. Given that losses are uniformly distributed between zero and $10 million, the expected loss conditional on a loss greater than $2 million is halfway between $2 million and $10 million, or $6 million. The VaR for a portfolio consisting of the two loans was calculated in

Example 9.6 as $5.8 million. The expected shortfall from the portfolio is therefore the expected loss on the portfolio conditional on the loss being greater than $5.8 million. When one loan defaults, the other (by assumption) does not and outcomes are uniformly distributed between a gain of $0.2 million and a loss of $9.8 million. The expected loss, given that we are in the part of the distribution between $5.8 million and $9.8 million, is $7.8 million. This is therefore the expected shortfall of the portfolio.

Because $7.8 million is less than 2 × $6 million, the expected shortfall measure does satisfy the subadditivity condition.

The subadditivity condition is not of purely theoretical interest. It is not unknown for a bank to find that, when it combines two portfolios (e.g., its equity portfolio and its fixed income portfolio), the total VaR goes up.

A risk measure can be characterized by the weights it assigns to quantiles of the loss distribution.[2] VaR gives a 100% weighting to the Xth quantile and zero to other quantiles. Expected shortfall gives equal weight to all quantiles greater than the Xth quantile and zero weight to all quantiles below the Xth quantile. We can define what is known as a *spectral risk measure* by making other assumptions about the weights assigned to quantiles. A general result is that a spectral risk measure is coherent (i.e., it satisfies the subadditivity condition) if the weight assigned to the qth quantile of the loss distribution is a nondecreasing function of q. Expected shortfall satisfies this condition. However, VaR does not, because the weights assigned to quantiles greater than X are less than the weight assigned to the Xth quantile. Some researchers have proposed measures where the weights assigned to the qth quantile of the loss distribution increase relatively fast with q. One idea is to make the weight assigned to the qth quantile proportional to $e^{-(1-q)/\gamma}$ where γ is a constant. This is referred to as the *exponential spectral risk measure*. Figure 9.5 shows the weights assigned to loss quantiles for expected shortfall and for the exponential spectral risk measure when γ has two different values.

9.6 CHOICE OF PARAMETERS FOR VaR

We now return to considering VaR. The user must choose two parameters: the time horizon and the confidence level. A common (though not very good) assumption is that the change in the portfolio value over the time horizon is normally distributed. The mean change in the portfolio value is usually assumed to be zero. These assumptions are convenient because they lead to a simple formula for VaR

$$\text{VaR} = \sigma N^{-1}(X) \tag{9.1}$$

where X is the confidence level, σ is the standard deviation of the portfolio change over the time horizon, and N^{-1} is the inverse cumulative normal distribution (which can be calculated using NORMSINV in Excel). This equation shows that, regardless of the time horizon, VaR for a particular confidence level is proportional to σ.

---

[2] Quantiles are also referred to as percentiles or fractiles.

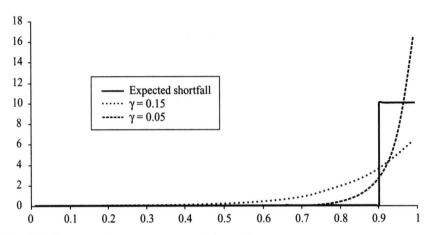

FIGURE 9.5   Weights as a Function of Quantiles

(a) Expected shortfall when $X = 90\%$, (b) exponential spectral risk measure with $\gamma = 0.15$, and (c) exponential spectral risk measure with $\gamma = 0.05$

EXAMPLE 9.9

Suppose that the change in the value of a portfolio over a 10-day time horizon is normal with a mean of zero and a standard deviation of \$20 million. The 10-day 99% VaR is

$$20N^{-1}(0.99) = 46.5$$

or \$46.5 million.

The Time Horizon

An appropriate choice for the time horizon depends on the application. The trading desks of banks calculate the profit and loss daily. When their positions are fairly liquid and actively managed, it therefore makes sense to calculate a VaR over a time horizon of one trading day. If the VaR turns out to be unacceptable, the portfolio can be adjusted fairly quickly. Also, a VaR with a longer time horizon might not be meaningful because of changes in the composition of the portfolio.

For an investment portfolio held by a pension fund, a time horizon of one month is often chosen. This is because the portfolio is traded less actively and some of the instruments in the portfolio are less liquid. Also the performance of pension fund portfolios is often monitored monthly.

Whatever the application, when market risks are being considered, analysts almost invariably start by calculating VaR for a time horizon of one day. The usual assumption is

$$T\text{-day VaR} = 1\text{-day VaR} \times \sqrt{T} \tag{9.2}$$

This formula is exactly true when the changes in the value of the portfolio on successive days have independent identical normal distributions with mean zero. In other cases, it is an approximation. The formula follows from equation (9.1) and the following results.

1. The standard deviation of the sum on T independent identical distributions is $\sqrt{T}$ times the standard deviation of each distribution.
2. The sum of independent normal distributions is normal.

Impact of Autocorrelation

In practice, the changes in the value of a portfolio from one day to the next are not always totally independent. Define ΔP_i as the change in the value of a portfolio on day i. A simple assumption is first-order autocorrelation where the correlation between ΔP_i and ΔP_{i-1} is ρ for all i. Suppose that the variance of ΔP_i is σ^2 for all i. Using the usual formula for the variance of the sum of two variables, the variance of $\Delta P_{i-1} + \Delta P_i$ is

$$\sigma^2 + \sigma^2 + 2\rho\sigma^2 = 2(1+\rho)\sigma^2$$

The correlation between ΔP_{i-j} and ΔP_i is ρ^j. This leads to the following formula for the variance of $\sum_{i=1}^{T} \Delta P_i$ (see Problem 9.11):

$$\sigma^2[T + 2(T-1)\rho + 2(T-2)\rho^2 + 2(T-3)\rho^3 + \ldots 2\rho^{T-1}] \tag{9.3}$$

Table 9.1 shows the impact of autocorrelation on the relationship between the T-day VaR and the one-day VaR. It assumes that the distribution of daily changes in the portfolio are identical normals with mean zero. Note that the ratio of the T-day VaR to the one-day VaR does not depend on the daily standard deviation, σ, or the confidence level. This follows from the result in equation (9.1) and the property of equation (9.3) that the T-day standard deviation is proportional to the one-day standard deviation. Comparing the $\rho = 0$ row in Table 9.1 with the other rows shows that the existence of autocorrelation results in the VaR estimates calculated from equation (9.1) being too low.

TABLE 9.1   Ratio of T-day VaR to One-day VaR for Different Values of T When There Is First-Order Correlation

	$T = 1$	$T = 2$	$T = 5$	$T = 10$	$T = 50$	$T = 250$
$\rho = 0$	1.00	1.41	2.24	3.16	7.07	15.81
$\rho = 0.05$	1.00	1.45	2.33	3.31	7.43	16.62
$\rho = 0.1$	1.00	1.48	2.42	3.46	7.80	17.47
$\rho = 0.2$	1.00	1.55	2.62	3.79	8.62	19.35

Distribution of change in portfolio value each day is assumed to have the same normal distribution with mean zero; ρ is the autocorrelation parameter.

EXAMPLE 9.10

Suppose that the standard deviation of daily changes in the portfolio value is $3 million and the first-order autocorrelation of daily changes is 0.1. From equation (9.3), the variance of the change in the portfolio value over five days is

$$3^2[5 + 2 \times 4 \times 0.1 + 2 \times 3 \times 0.1^2 + 2 \times 2 \times 0.1^3 + 2 \times 1 \times 0.1^4] = 52.7778$$

The standard deviation of the change in the value of the portfolio over five days is $\sqrt{52.7778}$ or 7.265. The five-day 95% VaR is therefore $7.265 \times N^{-1}(0.95) = 11.95$ or $11.95 million. Note that the ratio of the five-day standard deviation of portfolio changes to the one-day standard deviation is $7.265/3 = 2.42$. Because VaRs are proportional to standard deviations under the assumptions we are making, this is the number in Table 9.1 for $\rho = 0.1$ and $T = 5$.

Confidence Level

The confidence level chosen for VaR is likely to depend on a number of factors. Suppose that a bank wants to maintain a AA credit rating and calculates that companies with this credit rating have a 0.03% chance of defaulting over a one-year period. It might choose to use a 99.97% confidence level in conjunction with a one-year time horizon for internal risk management purposes. Suppose that the one-year 99.97% VaR across all exposures is $5 billion. This means that with $5 billion of capital the bank will have a 0.03% chance of becoming insolvent (i.e., running out of equity) during one year. This type of analysis might be communicated by banks to rating agencies in an attempt to convince the rating agency that the bank deserves its AA rating.

The confidence level that is actually used for the first VaR calculation is often much less than the one that is eventually reported. This is because it is very difficult to estimate a VaR directly when the confidence level is very high. If daily portfolio changes are assumed to be normally distributed with zero mean, we can use equation (9.1) to convert a VaR calculated with one confidence level to a VaR with another confidence level. Suppose that σ is the standard deviation of the change in the portfolio value over a certain time horizon and that the expected change in the portfolio value is zero. Denote VaR for a confidence level of X by VaR(X). From equation (9.1)

$$\text{VaR}(X) = \sigma N^{-1}(X)$$

for all confidence levels X. It follows that a VaR with a confidence level of X^* can be calculated from a VaR with a lower confidence level of X using

$$\text{VaR}(X^*) = \text{VaR}(X)\frac{N^{-1}(X^*)}{N^{-1}(X)} \tag{9.4}$$

Unfortunately this formula is critically dependent on the shape of the tails of the loss distribution being normal. When the distribution is not normal, the formula may be quite a bad approximation. Extreme value theory, which will be covered in Chapter 14, provides an alternative way of extrapolating tails of loss distributions.

Equation (9.4) assumes that the two VaR measures have the same time horizon. If we want to change the time horizon and are prepared to assume a normal distribution, we can use equation (9.4) in conjunction with equation (9.2) or (9.3).

EXAMPLE 9.11

Suppose that the one-day VaR with a confidence level of 95% is $1.5 million. Using the assumption that the distribution of changes in the portfolio value is normal with mean zero, equation (9.4) gives the one-day 99% VaR as

$$1.5 \times \frac{2.326}{1.645} = 2.12$$

or $2.12 million. If we assume daily changes are independent the 10-day 99% VaR is $\sqrt{10}$ times this, or $6.71 million, and the 250-day VaR is $\sqrt{250}$ times this, or $33.54 million.

9.7 MARGINAL VaR, INCREMENTAL VaR, AND COMPONENT VaR

Analysts often calculate additional measures in order to understand VaR. Consider a portfolio that is composed of a number of subportfolios. The subportfolios could correspond to asset classes (e.g., domestic equities, foreign equities, fixed income, and derivatives). They could correspond to the different business units (e.g, retail banking, investment banking, and proprietary trading). They could even correspond to individual trades. Suppose that the amount invested in ith subportfolio is x_i.

The *marginal value at risk* for the ith subportfolio is the sensitivity of VaR to the amount invested in the ith subportfolio. It is

$$\frac{\partial \text{VaR}}{\partial x_i}$$

To estimate marginal VaR, we can increase x_i to $x_i + \Delta x_i$ for a small Δx_i and recalculate VaR. If ΔVaR is the increase in VaR, the estimate of marginal VaR is $\Delta \text{VaR}/\Delta x_i$. For a well-diversified investment portfolio, marginal VaR is closely related to the capital asset pricing model's beta (see Section 1.3). If an asset's beta is high, its marginal VaR will tend to be high. If its beta is low, the marginal VaR tends to be low. In some circumstances, marginal VaR is negative indicating that increasing the weighting of a particular subportfolio reduces the risk of the portfolio.

The *incremental value at risk* for the ith subportfolio is the incremental effect of the ith subportfolio on VaR. It is the difference between VaR with the subportfolio and VaR without the subportfolio. Traders are often interested in the incremental VaR for a new trade.

The *component value at risk* for the ith subportfolio is

$$\frac{\partial \text{VaR}}{\partial x_i} x_i \qquad (9.5)$$

This can be calculated by making a small percentage change $y_i = \Delta x_i / x_i$ in the amount invested in the ith subportfolio and recalculating VaR. If Δ VaR is the increase in VaR, the estimate of component VaR is Δ VaR$/y_i$. In many situations this is a reasonable approximation to incremental VaR. This is because, if a subportfolio is small in relation to the size of the whole portfolio, it can be assumed that the marginal VaR remains constant as x_i is reduced all the way to zero. When this assumption is made, the impact of reducing x_i to zero is x_i times the marginal VaR—which is the component VaR.

Marginal VaR, incremental VaR, and component VaR can be defined similarly for other risk measures such as expected shortfall.

9.8 EULER'S THEOREM

A result produced by the great mathematician, Leonhard Euler, many years ago turns out to be very important when a risk measure for a whole portfolio is allocated to subportfolios. Suppose that V is a risk measure for a portfolio and x_i is a measure of the size of the ith subportfolio ($1 \leq i \leq M$). Assume that, when x_i is changed to λx_i for all x_i (so that the size of the portfolio is multiplied by λ), V changes to λV. This corresponds to third condition in Section 9.4 and is known as linear homogeneity. It is true for most risk measures.[3]

Euler's theorem shows that it is then true that

$$V = \sum_{i=1}^{M} \frac{\partial V}{\partial x_i} x_i \tag{9.6}$$

This result provides a way of allocating V to the subportfolios.

When the risk measure is VaR, Euler's theorem gives

$$\text{VaR} = \sum_{i=1}^{M} C_i$$

where C_i is the component VaR for the ith subportfolio. This is defined in Section 9.7 as

$$C_i = \frac{\partial \text{VaR}}{\partial x_i} x_i$$

This shows that the total VaR for a portfolio is the sum of the component VaRs for the subportfolios. Component VaRs are therefore a convenient way of allocating a total VaR to subportfolios. As explained in the previous section, component VaRs also have the attractive property that the ith component VaR for a large portfolio is approximately equal to the incremental VaR for that component.

---

[3] An exception could be a risk measure that incorporates liquidity. As a portfolio becomes larger, its liquidity declines.

Euler's theorem can be used to allocate other risk measures to subportfolios. For example, we can define component expected shortfall by equation (9.5) with VaR replaced by expected shortfall. The total expected shortfall is then the sum of component expected shortfalls.

In Chapter 23, we will show how Euler's theorem is used to allocate a bank's economic capital to its business units.

9.9 AGGREGATING VaRs

Sometimes a business has calculated VaRs, with the same confidence level and time horizon, for several different segments of its operations and is interested in aggregating them to calculate a total VaR. A formula for doing this is

$$\text{VaR}_{\text{total}} = \sqrt{\sum_i \sum_j \text{VaR}_i \text{VaR}_j \rho_{ij}} \qquad (9.7)$$

where VaR_i is the VaR for the ith segment, $\text{VaR}_{\text{total}}$ is the total VaR, and ρ_{ij} is the correlation between losses from segment i and segment j. This is exactly true when the losses (gains) have zero-mean normal distributions and provides a good approximation in many other situations.

EXAMPLE 9.12

Suppose the VaRs calculated for two segments of a business are $60 million and $100 million. The correlation between the losses is estimated as 0.4. An estimate of the total VaR is

$$\sqrt{60^2 + 100^2 + 2 \times 60 \times 100 \times 0.4} = 135.6$$

9.10 BACK-TESTING

Whatever the method used for calculating VaR, an important reality check is *back-testing*. This is a test of how well the current procedure for estimating VaR would have performed if it had been used in the past. It involves looking at how often the loss in a day would have exceeded the one-day 99% VaR when the latter is calculated using the current procedure. Days when the actual loss exceeds VaR are referred to as *exceptions*. If exceptions happen on about 1% of the days, we can feel reasonably comfortable with the current methodology for calculating VaR. If they happen on, say, 7% of days, the methodology is suspect and it is likely that VaR is underestimated. From a regulatory perspective, the capital calculated using the current VaR estimation procedure is then too low. On the other hand, if exceptions happen on, say, 0.3% of days it is likely that the current procedure is overestimating VaR and the capital calculated is too high.

One issue in back-testing a one-day VaR is whether we consider changes made in the portfolio during a day. There are two possibilities. The first is to compare VaR with the hypothetical change in the portfolio value calculated on the assumption that the composition of the portfolio remains unchanged during the day. The other is to compare VaR to the actual change in the value of the portfolio during the day. The assumption underlying the calculation of VaR is that the portfolio will remain unchanged during the day and so the first comparison based on hypothetical changes is more logical. However, it is actual changes in the portfolio value that we are ultimately interested in. In practice, risk managers usually compare VaR to both hypothetical portfolio changes and actual portfolio changes (and regulators insist on seeing the results of back-testing using actual changes as well as hypothetical changes). The actual changes are adjusted for items unrelated to the market risk, such as fee income and profits from trades carried out at prices different from the mid-market.

Suppose that the confidence level for a one-day VaR is $X\%$. If the VaR model used is accurate, the probability of the VaR being exceeded on any given day is $p = 1 - X/100$. Suppose that we look at a total of n days and we observe that the VaR level is exceeded on m of the days where $m/n > p$. Should we reject the model for producing values of VaR that are too low? Expressed formally, we can consider two alternative hypotheses:

1. The probability of an exception on any given day is p.
2. The probability of an exception on any given day is greater than p.

From the properties of the binomial distribution, the probability of the VaR level being exceeded on m or more days is

$$\sum_{k=m}^{n} \frac{n!}{k!(n-k)!} p^k (1-p)^{n-k}$$

This can be calculated using the BINOMDIST function in Excel. An often-used confidence level in statistical tests is 5%. If the probability of the VaR level being exceeded on m or more days is less than 5%, we reject the first hypothesis that the probability of an exception is p. If the probability of the VaR level being exceeded on m or more days is greater than 5%, the hypothesis is not rejected.

EXAMPLE 9.13

Suppose that we back-test a VaR model using 600 days of data. The VaR confidence level is 99% and we observe nine exceptions. The expected number of exceptions is six. Should we reject the model? The probability of nine or more exceptions can be calculated in Excel as $1 - \text{BINOMDIST}(8,600,0.01,\text{TRUE})$. It is 0.152. At a 5% confidence level we should not therefore reject the model. However, if the number of exceptions had been 12 we would have calculated the probability of 12 or more exceptions as 0.019 and rejected the model. The model is rejected when the number of exceptions is 11 or more. (The probability of 10 or more exceptions is greater than 5%, but the probability of 11 or more is less than 5%.)

When the number of exceptions, m, is lower than the expected number of exceptions, we can similarly test whether the true probability of an exception is 1%. (In this case, our alternative hypothesis is that the true probability of an exception is less than 1%.) The probability of m or fewer exceptions is

$$\sum_{k=0}^{m} \frac{n!}{k!(n-k)!} p^k (1-p)^{n-k}$$

and this is compared with the 5% threshold.

EXAMPLE 9.14

Suppose again that we back-test a VaR model using 600 days of data when the VaR confidence level is 99% and we observe one exception, well below the expected number of six. Should we reject the model? The probability of one or zero exceptions can be calculated in Excel as BINOMDIST(1,600,0.01,TRUE). It is 0.017. At a 5% confidence level, we should therefore reject the model. However, if the number of exceptions had been two or more, we would not have rejected the model.

The tests we have considered so far have been one-tailed tests. In Example 9.13, we assumed that the true probability of an exception was either 1% or greater than 1%. In Example 9.14, we assumed that it was 1% or less than 1%. Kupiec (1995) has proposed a relatively powerful two-tailed test.[4] If the probability of an exception under the VaR model is p and m exceptions are observed in n trials, then

$$-2\ln[(1-p)^{n-m}p^m] + 2\ln[(1-m/n)^{n-m}(m/n)^m] \tag{9.8}$$

should have a chi-square distribution with one degree of freedom. Values of the statistic are high for either very low or very high numbers of exceptions. There is a probability of 5% that the value of a chi-square variable with one degree of freedom will be greater than 3.84. It follows that we should reject the model whenever the expression in equation (9.8) is greater than 3.84.

EXAMPLE 9.15

Suppose that, as in the previous two examples we back-test a VaR model using 600 days of data when the VaR confidence level is 99%. The value of the statistic in equation (9.8) is greater than 3.84 when the number of exceptions, m, is one or less and when the number of exceptions is 12 or more. We therefore accept the VaR model when $2 \leq m \leq 11$ and reject it otherwise.

---

[4] See P. Kupiec, "Techniques for Verifying the Accuracy of Risk Management Models," *Journal of Derivatives* 3 (1995): 73–84.

Generally speaking, the difficulty of back-testing a VaR model increases as the VaR confidence level increases. This is an argument in favor of using a fairly low confidence level in conjunction with extreme value theory (see Chapter 14).

Bunching

A separate issue from the number of exceptions is *bunching*. If daily portfolio changes are independent, exceptions should be spread evenly throughout the period used for back-testing. In practice, they are often bunched together suggesting that losses on successive days are not independent. One approach to testing for bunching is to use the following statistic suggested by Christoffersen[5]

$$-2\ln[(1-\pi)^{u_{00}+u_{10}}\pi^{u_{01}+u_{11}} + 2\ln[(1-\pi_{01})^{u_{00}}\pi_{01}^{u_{01}}(1-\pi_{11})^{u_{10}}\pi_{11}^{u_{11}}]$$

where u_{ij} is the number of observations in which we go from a day where we are in state i to a day where we are in state j. This statistic is chi-square with one degree of freedom if there is no bunching. State 0 is a day where there is no exception while state 1 is a day where there is an exception. Also,

$$\pi = \frac{u_{01} + u_{11}}{u_{00} + u_{01} + u_{10} + u_{11}}$$

$$\pi_{01} = \frac{u_{01}}{u_{00} + u_{01}}$$

$$\pi_{11} = \frac{u_{11}}{u_{10} + u_{11}}$$

SUMMARY

A value at risk (VaR) calculation is aimed at making a statement of the form: "We are X percent certain that we will not lose more than V dollars in time T." The variable V is the VaR, X percent is the confidence level, and T is the time horizon. It has become a very popular risk measure. An alternative measure that has rather better theoretical properties is expected shortfall. This is the expected loss conditional on the loss being greater than the VaR level.

When changes in a portfolio value are normally distributed, a VaR estimate with one confidence level can be used to calculate a VaR level with another confidence level. Also, if one-day changes have independent normal distributions, an T-day VaR equals the one-day VaR multiplied by $\sqrt{T}$. When the independence assumption is relaxed, other somewhat more complicated formulas can be used to go from the one-day VaR to the T-day VaR.

Consider the situation where a portfolio has a number of subportfolios. The marginal VaR with respect to the ith subportfolio is the partial derivative of VaR

---

[5] See P. F. Christoffersen, "Evaluating Interval Forecasts," *International Economic Review* 39 (1998): 841–862.

with respect to the size of the subportfolio. The incremental VaR with respect to a particular subportfolio is the incremental effect of that subportfolio on VaR. There is a formula that can be used for dividing VaR into components that correspond to the positions taken in the subportfolios. The component VaRs sum to VaR and each component is, for a large portfolio of relatively small positions, approximately equal to the corresponding incremental VaR.

Back-testing is an important part of a VaR system. It examines how well the VaR model would have performed in the past. There are two ways in which back-testing may indicate weaknesses in a VaR model. One is in the percentage of exceptions, that is, the percentage of times the actual loss exceeds VaR. The other is in the extent to which exceptions are bunched. There are statistical tests to determine whether a VaR model should be rejected because of the percentage of exceptions or the amount of bunching. As we will see in Chapter 12, regulators have rules for increasing the VaR multiplier when market risk capital is calculated if they consider the results from back-testing over 250 days to be unsatisfactory.

FURTHER READING

Artzner P., F. Delbaen, J.-M. Eber, and D. Heath. "Coherent Measures of Risk." *Mathematical Finance* 9 (1999): 203–228.

Basak, S. and A. Shapiro. "Value-at-Risk-Based Risk Management: Optimal Policies and Asset Prices." *Review of Financial Studies* 14, no. 2 (2001): 371–405.

Beder, T. "VaR: Seductive But Dangerous." *Financial Analysts Journal* 51, no. 5 (1995): 12–24.

Boudoukh, J., M. Richardson, and R. Whitelaw. "The Best of Both Worlds." *Risk* (May 1998): 64–67.

Dowd, K. *Measuring Market Risk*, 2nd ed. New York: John Wiley and Sons, 2005.

Duffie, D. and J. Pan. "An Overview of Value at Risk." *Journal of Derivatives* 4, no. 3 (Spring 1997): 7–49.

Hopper, G. "Value at Risk: A New Methodology for Measuring Portfolio Risk." *Business Review*, Federal Reserve Bank of Philadelphia (July-August 1996): 19–29.

Hua P., and P. Wilmot. "Crash Courses." *Risk* (June 1997): 64–67.

Jackson, P., D. J. Maude, and W. Perraudin. "Bank Capital and Value at Risk." *Journal of Derivatives* 4, no. 3 (Spring 1997): 73–90.

Jorion, P. *Value at Risk*, 2nd ed. New York: McGraw-Hill, 2001.

Longin, F. M. "Beyond the VaR." *Journal of Derivatives* 8, no. 4 (Summer 2001): 36–48.

Marshall, C. and M. Siegel. "Value at Risk: Implementing a Risk Measurement Standard." *Journal of Derivatives* 4, no. 3 (Spring 1997): 91–111.

PRACTICE QUESTIONS AND PROBLEMS
(ANSWERS AT END OF BOOK)

9.1 What is the difference between expected shortfall and VaR? What is the theoretical advantage of expected shortfall over VaR?

9.2 What is a spectral risk measure? What conditions must be satisfied by a spectral risk measure for the subadditivity condition in Section 9.4 to be satisfied?

9.3 A fund manager announces that the fund's one-month 95% VaR is 6% of the size of the portfolio being managed. You have an investment of $100,000 in the fund. How do you interpret the portfolio manager's announcement?

9.4 A fund manager announces that the fund's one-month 95% expected shortfall is 6% of the size of the portfolio being managed. You have an investment of $100,000 in the fund. How do you interpret the portfolio manager's announcement?

9.5 Suppose that each of two investments has a 0.9% chance of a loss of $10 million, a 99.1% of a loss of $1 million. The investments are independent of each other.

  (a) What is the VaR for one of the investments when the confidence level is 99%?

  (b) What is the expected shortfall for one of the investments when the confidence level is 99%?

  (c) What is the VaR for a portfolio consisting of the two investments when the confidence level is 99%?

  (d) What is the expected shortfall for a portfolio consisting of the two investments when the confidence level is 99%?

  (e) Show that in this example VaR does not satisfy the subadditivity condition whereas expected shortfall does.

9.6 Suppose that the change in the value of a portfolio over a one-day time period is normal with a mean of zero and a standard deviation of $2 million, what is (a) the one-day 97.5% VaR, (b) the five-day 97.5% VaR, and (c) the five-day 99% VaR?

9.7 What difference does it make to your answer to Problem 9.6 if there is first-order daily autocorrelation with a correlation parameter equal to 0.16?

9.8 Explain carefully the differences between marginal VaR, incremental VaR, and component VaR for a portfolio consisting of a number of assets.

9.9 Suppose that we back-test a VaR model using 1,000 days of data. The VaR confidence level is 99% and we observe 17 exceptions. Should we reject the model at the 5% confidence level? Use a one-tailed test.

9.10 Explain what is meant by bunching.

9.11 Prove equation 9.3.

FURTHER QUESTIONS

9.12 Suppose that each of two investments has a 4% chance of a loss of $10 million, a 2% chance of a loss of $1 million, and a 94% chance of a profit of $1 million. They are independent of each other.

  (a) What is the VaR for one of the investments when the confidence level is 95%?

  (b) What is the expected shortfall when the confidence level is 95%?

  (c) What is the VaR for a portfolio consisting of the two investments when the confidence level is 95%?

  (d) What is the expected shortfall for a portfolio consisting of the two investments when the confidence level is 95%?

(e) Show that, in this example, VaR does not satisfy the subadditivity condition whereas expected shortfall does.

9.13 Suppose that daily changes for a portfolio have first-order correlation with correlation parameter 0.12. The 10-day VaR, calculated by multiplying the one-day VaR by $\sqrt{10}$, is \$2 million. What is a better estimate of the VaR that takes account of autocorrelation?

9.14 Suppose that we back-test a VaR model using 1,000 days of data. The VaR confidence level is 99% and we observe 15 exceptions. Should we reject the model at the 5% confidence level? Use Kupiec's two-tailed test.

CHAPTER 10

Volatility

It is important for a financial institution to monitor the volatilities of the market variables (interest rates, exchange rates, equity prices, commodity prices, etc.) on which the value of its portfolio depends. This chapter describes the procedures it can use to do this.

The chapter starts by explaining how volatility is defined. It then examines the common assumption that percentage returns from market variables are normally distributed and presents the power law as an alternative. After that it moves on to consider models with imposing names such as exponentially weighted moving average (EWMA), autoregressive conditional heteroscedasticity (ARCH), and generalized autoregressive conditional heteroscedasticity (GARCH). The distinctive feature of these models is that they recognize that volatility is not constant. During some periods, volatility is relatively low, while during other periods it is relatively high. The models attempt to keep track of variations in volatility through time.

10.1 DEFINITION OF VOLATILITY

A variable's volatility, σ, is defined as the standard deviation of the return provided by the variable per unit of time when the return is expressed using continuous compounding. (See Appendix A for a discussion of compounding frequencies.) When volatility is used for option pricing, the unit of time is usually one year, so that volatility is the standard deviation of the continuously compounded return per year. When volatility is used for risk management, the unit of time is usually one day so that volatility is the standard deviation of the continuously compounded return per day.

Define S_i as the value of a variable at the end of day i. The continuously compounded return per day for the variable on day i is

$$\ln \frac{S_i}{S_{i-1}}$$

This is almost exactly the same as

$$\frac{S_i - S_{i-1}}{S_{i-1}}$$

An alternative definition of daily volatility of a variable is therefore the standard deviation of the proportional change in the variable during a day. This is the definition that is usually used in risk management.

EXAMPLE 10.1

Suppose that an asset price is $60 and that its daily volatility is 2%. This means that a one-standard-deviation move in the asset price over one day would be 60×0.02 or $1.20. If we assume that the change in the asset price is normally distributed, we can be 95% certain that the asset price will be between $60 - 1.96 \times 1.2 = \$57.65$ and $60 + 1.96 \times 1.2 = \$62.35$ at the end of the day.

If we assume that the returns each day are independent with the same variance, the variance of the return over T days is T times the variance of the return over one day. This means that the standard deviation of the return over T days is $\sqrt{T}$ times the standard deviation of the return over one day. This is consistent with the adage "uncertainty increases with the square root of time."

EXAMPLE 10.2

Assume as in Example 10.1 that an asset price is $60 and the volatility per day is 2%. The standard deviation of the continuously compounded return over five days is $\sqrt{5} \times 2$ or 4.47%. Because five days is a short period of time, this can be assumed to be the same as the standard deviation of the proportional change over five days. A one-standard-deviation move would be $60 \times 0.0447 = 2.68$. If we assume that the change in the asset price is normally distributed, we can be 95% certain that the asset price will be between $60 - 1.96 \times 2.68 = \$54.74$ and $60 + 1.96 \times 2.68 = \$65.26$ at the end of the five days.

Variance Rate

Risk managers often focus on the variance rate rather than the volatility. The *variance rate* is defined as the square of the volatility. The variance rate per day is the variance of the return in one day. Whereas the standard deviation of the return in time T increases with the square root of time, the variance of this return increases linearly with time. If we wanted to be pedantic, we could say that it is correct to talk about the variance rate per day, but volatility is "per square root of day."

Business Days vs. Calendar Days

One issue is whether time should be measured in calendar days or business days. As shown in Business Snapshot 10.1, research shows that volatility is much higher on business days than on non-business days. As a result, analysts tend to ignore weekends and holidays when calculating and using volatilities. The usual assumption is that there are 252 days per year.

BUSINESS SNAPSHOT 10.1

What Causes Volatility?

It is natural to assume that the volatility of a stock or other asset is caused by new information reaching the market. This new information causes people to revise their opinions about the value of the asset. The price of the asset changes and volatility results. However, this view of what causes volatility is not supported by research.

With several years of daily data on an asset price, researchers can calculate:

1. The variance of the asset's returns between the close of trading on one day and the close of trading on the next day when there are no intervening nontrading days.
2. The variance of the asset's return between the close of trading on Friday and the close of trading on Monday.

The second is the variance of returns over a three-day period. The first is a variance over a one-day period. We might reasonably expect the second variance to be three times as great as the first variance. Fama (1965), French (1980), and French and Roll (1986) show that this is not the case. For the assets considered, the three research studies estimate the second variance to be 22%, 19%, and 10.7% higher than the first variance, respectively.

At this stage you might be tempted to argue that these results are explained by more news reaching the market when the market is open for trading. But research by Roll (1984) does not support this explanation. Roll looked at the prices of orange juice futures. By far the most important news for orange juice futures is news about the weather and this is equally likely to arrive at any time. When Roll compared the two variances for orange juice futures, he found that the second (Friday-to-Monday) variance is only 1.54 times the first (one-day) variance.

The only reasonable conclusion from all this is that volatility is to a large extent caused by trading itself. (Traders usually have no difficulty accepting this conclusion!)

Assuming that the returns on successive days are independent and have the same standard deviation, this means that

$$\sigma_{yr} = \sigma_{day} \sqrt{252}$$

or

$$\sigma_{day} = \frac{\sigma_{yr}}{\sqrt{252}}$$

showing that the daily volatility is about 6% of annual volatility.

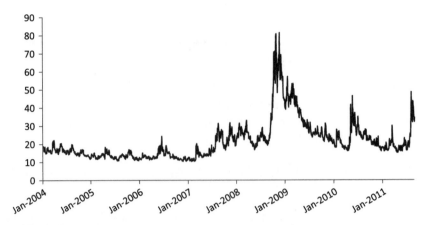

FIGURE 10.1   The VIX Index, January 2004 to September 2011

10.2 IMPLIED VOLATILITIES

Although risk managers usually calculate volatilities from historical data, they also try and keep track of what are known as *implied volatilities*. The one parameter in the Black–Scholes–Merton option pricing model that cannot be observed directly is the volatility of the underlying asset price (see Appendix E). The implied volatility of an option is the volatility that gives the market price of the option when it is substituted into the pricing model.

The VIX Index

The CBOE publishes indices of implied volatility. The most popular index, the VIX, is an index of the implied volatility of 30-day options on the S&P 500 calculated from a wide range of calls and puts.[1] Trading in futures on the VIX started in 2004 and trading in options on the VIX started in 2006. A trade involving options on the S&P 500 is a bet on both the future level of the S&P 500 and the volatility of the S&P 500. By contrast, a futures or options contract on the VIX is a bet only on volatility. One contract is on 1,000 times the index.

EXAMPLE 10.3

Suppose that a trader buys an April futures contract on the VIX when the futures price is $18.5 (corresponding to a 30-day S&P 500 volatility of 18.5%) and closes out the contract when the futures price is $19.3 (corresponding to an S&P 500 volatility of 19.3%). The trader makes a gain of $800.

Figure 10.1 shows the VIX index between January 2004 and September 2011. Between 2004 and mid-2007, it tended to stay between 10 and 20. It reached 30

---

[1] Similarly, the VXN is an index of the volatility of the NASDAQ 100 index and the VXD is an index of the volatility of the Dow Jones Industrial Average.

TABLE 10.1 Percentage of Days When Absolute Size of Daily Exchange Rate Moves Is Greater Than One, Two, ..., Six Standard Deviations (S.D. = standard deviation of percentage daily change)

	Real World (%)	Normal Model (%)
> 1 S.D.	25.04	31.73
> 2 S.D.	5.27	4.55
> 3 S.D.	1.34	0.27
> 4 S.D.	0.29	0.01
> 5 S.D.	0.08	0.00
> 6 S.D.	0.03	0.00

during the second half of 2007 and a record 80 in October and November 2008 after the failure of Lehman Brothers. By early 2010, it had returned to more normal levels, but in May 2010 it spiked at over 45 because of the European sovereign debt crisis. In August 2011, it increased again because of market uncertainties. Sometimes market participants refer to the VIX index as the "fear index."

10.3 ARE DAILY PERCENTAGE CHANGES IN FINANCIAL VARIABLES NORMAL?

A common assumption is that market variables are normal so that we can calculate a confidence interval from daily volatilities, as indicated in Examples 10.1 and 10.2. In practice, most financial variables are more likely to experience big moves than the normal distribution would suggest. Table 10.1 shows the results of a test of normality using daily movements in 12 different exchange rates over a 10-year period.[2] The first step in the production of the table is to calculate the standard deviation of daily percentage changes in each exchange rate. The next stage is to note how often the actual percentage changes exceeded one standard deviation, two standard deviations, and so on. These numbers are then compared with the corresponding numbers for the normal distribution.

Daily percentage changes exceed three standard deviations on 1.34% of the days. The normal model for returns predicts that this should happen on only 0.27% of days. Daily percentage changes exceed four, five, and six standard deviations on 0.29%, 0.08%, and 0.03% of days, respectively. The normal model predicts that we should hardly ever observe this happening. The table, therefore, provides evidence to support the existence of the fact that the probability distributions of changes in exchange rates have heavier tails than the normal distribution. Business Snapshot 10.2

---

[2] This table is based on J. C. Hull and A. White, "Value at Risk When Daily Changes in Market Variables Are Not Normally Distributed." *Journal of Derivatives 5*, no. 3 (Spring 1998): 9–19.

BUSINESS SNAPSHOT 10.2

Making Money from Foreign Currency Options

Black, Scholes, and Merton in their option pricing model assume that the underlying asset's price has a lognormal distribution at a future time. This is equivalent to the assumption that asset price changes over short periods, such as one day, are normally distributed. Suppose that most market participants are comfortable with the assumptions made by Black, Scholes, and Merton. You have just done the analysis in Table 10.1 and know that the normal/lognormal assumption is not a good one for exchange rates. What should
you do?

The answer is that you should buy deep-out-of-the-money call and put options on a variety of different currencies—and wait. These options will be relatively inexpensive and more of them will close in-the-money than the Black–Scholes–Merton model predicts. The present value of your payoffs will on average be much greater than the cost of the options.

In the mid-1980s, a few traders knew about the heavy tails of foreign exchange probability distributions. Everyone else thought that the lognormal assumption of the Black–Scholes–Merton was reasonable. The few traders who were well informed followed the strategy we have described—and made lots of money. By the late 1980s, most traders understood the heavy tails and the trading opportunities had disappeared.

---

shows how you could have made money if you had done an analysis similar to that in Table 10.1 in 1985!

Figure 10.2 compares a typical heavy tailed distribution (such as the one for foreign exchange) with a normal distribution that has the same mean and standard deviation.[3] The heavy-tailed distribution is more peaked than the normal distribution. In Figure 10.2, we can distinguish three parts of the distribution: the middle, the tails, and the intermediate parts (between the middle and the tails). When we move from the normal distribution to the heavy-tailed distribution, probability mass shifts from the intermediate parts of the distribution to both the tails and the middle. If we are considering the percentage change in a market variable, the heavy-tailed distribution has the property that small and large changes in the variable are more likely than they would be if a normal distribution were assumed. Intermediate changes are less likely.

---

[3] *Kurtosis* measures the size of a distribution's tails. A *leptokurtic distribution* has heavier tails than the normal distribution. A *platykurtic distribution* has less heavy tails than the normal distribution; a distribution with the same sized tails as the normal distribution is termed *mesokurtic*.

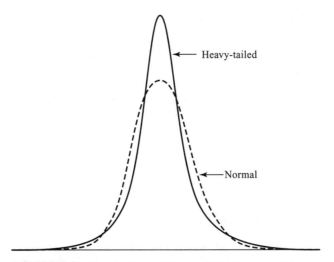

FIGURE 10.2 Comparison of Normal Distribution with a
Heavy-Tailed Distribution
The two distributions have the same mean and standard deviation.

10.4 THE POWER LAW

The power law provides an alternative to assuming normal distributions. The law asserts that, for many variables that are encountered in practice, it is approximately true that the value of the variable, v, has the property that when x is large

$$\text{Prob}(v > x) = Kx^{-\alpha} \tag{10.1}$$

where K and α are constants. The equation has been found to be approximately true for variables v as diverse as the income of an individual, the size of a city, and the number of visits to a website in a day.

EXAMPLE 10.4

Suppose that we know from experience that $\alpha = 3$ for a particular financial variable and we observe that the probability that $v > 10$ is 0.05. Equation (10.1) gives

$$0.05 = K \times 10^{-3}$$

so that $K = 50$. The probability that $v > 20$ can now be calculated as

$$50 \times 20^{-3} = 0.00625$$

The probability that $v > 30$ is

$$50 \times 30^{-3} = 0.0019$$

and so on.

TABLE 10.2   Values Calculated from Table 10.1

x	ln(x)	ln[Prob(v > x)]	ln[Prob(v > x)]
1	0.000	0.12520	−2.078
2	0.693	0.02635	−3.636
3	1.099	0.00670	−5.006
4	1.386	0.00145	−6.536
5	1.609	0.00040	−7.824
6	1.792	0.00015	−8.805

Equation (10.1) implies that

$$\ln[\text{Prob}(v > x)] = \ln K - \alpha \ln x$$

We can therefore do a quick test of whether it holds by plotting $\ln[\text{Prob}(v > x)]$ against $\ln x$. In order to do this for the data in Table 10.1, define the v as the number of standard deviations by which an exchange rate increases in one day. We assume that the probabilities reported in Table 10.1 come from observations that are evenly divided between positive and negative exchange rate moves. (For example, we assume that the 0.08% probability of an exchange rate move of more than five standard deviations is a result of a probability of 0.04% of the daily move being more that +5 standard deviations and a probability of 0.04% of the daily move being less than −5 standard deviations.)

The values of $\ln(x)$ and $\ln[\text{Prob}(v > x)]$ are calculated in Table 10.2. The data in Table 10.2 is plotted in Figure 10.3. This shows that the logarithm of the probability

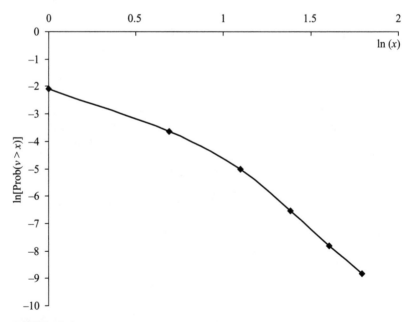

FIGURE 10.3   Log-Log Plot for Exchange Rate Increases
v is the exchange rate increase measured in standard deviations.

of the exchange rate increasing by more than x standard deviations is approximately linearly dependent on $\ln x$ for $x > 3$. This is evidence that the power law holds for this data. Using data for $x = 3, 4, 5,$ and 6, a regression analysis gives the best-fit relationship as

$$\ln[\text{Prob}(v > x)] = 1.06 - 5.51 \ln(x)$$

showing that estimates for K and α are as follows: $K = e^{1.06} = 2.88$ and $\alpha = 5.51$. An estimate for the probability of an increase greater than 4.5 standard deviations is

$$2.88 \times 4.5^{-5.51} = 0.00073$$

This means there is a probability of $2 \times 0.00073 = 0.00146$ that there will be a change (positive or negative) of more than 4.5 standard deviations. An estimate for the probability of an increase greater than seven standard deviations is

$$2.88 \times 7^{-5.51} = 0.000064$$

This means there is a probability of $2 \times 0.000064 = 0.000128$ that there will be a change (positive or negative) of more than seven standard deviations.

We examine the power law more formally and explain better procedures for estimating the parameters when we consider extreme value theory in Chapter 14. We also explain how it can be used in the assessment of operational risk in Chapter 20.

10.5 MONITORING DAILY VOLATILITY

Define σ_n as the volatility per day of a market variable on day n, as estimated at the end of day $n - 1$. The *variance rate*, which as mentioned earlier is defined as the square of the volatility is σ_n^2. Suppose that the value of the market variable at the end of day i is S_i. Define u_i as the continuously compounded return during day i (between the end of day $i - 1$ and the end of day i) so that

$$u_i = \ln \frac{S_i}{S_{i-1}}$$

One approach to estimating σ_n is to set it equal to the standard deviation of the u_i's. With the most recent m observations on the u_i in conjunction with the usual formula for standard deviation, this approach gives:

$$\sigma_n^2 = \frac{1}{m-1} \sum_{i=1}^{m} (u_{n-i} - \bar{u})^2 \tag{10.2}$$

where $\bar{u}$ is the mean of the u_i's:

$$\bar{u} = \frac{1}{m} \sum_{i=1}^{m} u_{n-i}$$

TABLE 10.3   Data for Computation of Volatility

Day	Closing Stock Price (dollars)	Price Relative S_i/S_{i-1}	Daily Return $u_i = \ln(S_i/S_{i-1})$
0	20.00		
1	20.10	1.00500	0.00499
2	19.90	0.99005	−0.01000
3	20.00	1.00503	0.00501
4	20.50	1.02500	0.02469
5	20.25	0.98780	−0.01227
6	20.90	1.03210	0.03159
7	20.90	1.00000	0.00000
8	20.90	1.00000	0.00000
9	20.60	0.98565	−0.01446
10	20.50	0.99515	−0.00487
11	21.00	1.02439	0.02410
12	21.10	1.00476	0.00475
13	20.70	0.98104	−0.01914
14	20.50	0.99034	−0.00971
15	20.70	1.00976	0.00971
16	20.90	1.00966	0.00962
17	20.40	0.97608	−0.02421
18	20.50	1.00490	0.00489
19	20.60	1.00488	0.00487
20	20.30	0.98544	−0.01467

EXAMPLE 10.5

Table 10.3 shows a possible sequence of stock prices. Suppose that we are interested in estimating the volatility for day 21 using 20 observations on the u_i so that $n = 21$ and $m = 20$. In this case,

$$\sum_{i=1}^{m} u_{n-i} = 0.01489$$

so that $\bar{u} = 0.00074$. The estimate of the standard deviation of the daily return calculated using equation (10.2) is 1.49%.

For risk management purposes, the formula in equation (10.2) is usually changed in a number of ways:

1. As explained in Section 10.1, u_i is defined as the percentage change in the market variable between the end of day $i - 1$ and the end of day i so that

$$u_i = \frac{S_i - S_{i-1}}{S_{i-1}} \tag{10.3}$$

This makes very little difference to the values of u_i that are computed.
2. $\bar{u}$ is assumed to be zero. The justification for this is that the expected change in a variable in one day is very small when compared with the standard deviation of changes.[4]
3. $m - 1$ is replaced by m. This moves us from an unbiased estimate of the volatility to a maximum likelihood estimate, as we explain in Section 10.9.

These three changes allow the formula for the variance rate to be simplified to

$$\sigma_n^2 = \frac{1}{m} \sum_{i=1}^{m} u_{n-i}^2 \tag{10.4}$$

where u_i is given by equation (10.3).

EXAMPLE 10.6

Consider again Example 10.5.

$$\sum u_i^2 = 0.00424$$

so that equation (10.4) gives

$$\sigma_n^2 = 0.00424/20 = 0.000214$$

and $\sigma_n = 0.014618$ or 1.46%. There is only a little difference from the result in Example 10.5.

Weighting Schemes

Equation (10.4) gives equal weight to all $u_{n-1}^2, u_{n-2}^2, \ldots, u_{n-m}^2$. Our objective is to estimate σ_n, the volatility on day n. It therefore makes sense to give more weight to recent data. A model that does this is

$$\sigma_n^2 = \sum_{i=1}^{m} \alpha_i u_{n-i}^2 \tag{10.5}$$

The variable α_i is the amount of weight given to the observation i days ago. The α's are positive. If we choose them so that $\alpha_i < \alpha_j$ when $i > j$, less weight is given to older observations. The weights must sum to unity, so that

$$\sum_{i=1}^{m} \alpha_i = 1$$

---

[4] This is likely to be the case even if the variable happened to increase or decrease quite fast during the m days of our data.

An extension of the idea in equation (10.5) is to assume that there is a long-run average variance rate and that this should be given some weight. This leads to the model that takes the form

$$\sigma_n^2 = \gamma V_L + \sum_{i=1}^{m} \alpha_i u_{n-i}^2 \tag{10.6}$$

where V_L is the long-run variance rate and γ is the weight assigned to V_L. Because the weights must sum to unity, we have

$$\gamma + \sum_{i=1}^{m} \alpha_i = 1$$

This is known as an ARCH(m) model. It was first suggested by Engle.[5] The estimate of the variance is based on a long-run average variance and m observations. The older an observation, the less weight it is given. Defining $\omega = \gamma V_L$, the model in equation (10.6) can be written

$$\sigma_n^2 = \omega + \sum_{i=1}^{m} \alpha_i u_{n-i}^2 \tag{10.7}$$

In the next two sections, we discuss two important approaches to monitoring volatility using the ideas in equations (10.5) and (10.6).

10.6 THE EXPONENTIALLY WEIGHTED MOVING AVERAGE MODEL

The exponentially weighted moving average (EWMA) model is a particular case of the model in equation (10.5) where the weights, α_i, decrease exponentially as we move back through time. Specifically, $\alpha_{i+1} = \lambda \alpha_i$ where λ is a constant between zero and one.

It turns out that this weighting scheme leads to a particularly simple formula for updating volatility estimates. The formula is

$$\sigma_n^2 = \lambda \sigma_{n-1}^2 + (1 - \lambda) u_{n-1}^2 \tag{10.8}$$

The estimate, σ_n, of the volatility for day n (made at the end of day $n - 1$) is calculated from σ_{n-1} (the estimate that was made at the end of day $n - 2$ of the volatility for day $n - 1$) and u_{n-1} (the most recent daily percentage change).

---

[5] See R. F. Engle, "Autoregressive Conditional Heteroscedasticity with Estimates of the Variance of U.K. Inflation," *Econometrica* 50 (1982): 987–1008. Robert Engle won the Nobel Prize for Economics in 2003 for his work on ARCH models.

To understand why equation (10.8) corresponds to weights that decrease exponentially, we substitute for σ_{n-1}^2 to get

$$\sigma_n^2 = \lambda[\lambda\sigma_{n-2}^2 + (1-\lambda)u_{n-2}^2] + (1-\lambda)u_{n-1}^2$$

or

$$\sigma_n^2 = (1-\lambda)(u_{n-1}^2 + \lambda u_{n-2}^2) + \lambda^2\sigma_{n-2}^2$$

Substituting in a similar way for σ_{n-2}^2 gives

$$\sigma_n^2 = (1-\lambda)(u_{n-1}^2 + \lambda u_{n-2}^2 + \lambda^2 u_{n-3}^2) + \lambda^3\sigma_{n-3}^2$$

Continuing in this way, we see that

$$\sigma_n^2 = (1-\lambda)\sum_{i=1}^{m}\lambda^{i-1}u_{n-i}^2 + \lambda^m\sigma_{n-m}^2$$

For a large m, the term $\lambda^m\sigma_{n-m}^2$ is sufficiently small to be ignored so that equation (10.8) is the same as equation (10.5) with $\alpha_i = (1-\lambda)\lambda^{i-1}$. The weights for the u_i decline at rate λ as we move back through time. Each weight is λ times the previous weight.

EXAMPLE 10.7

Suppose that λ is 0.90, the volatility estimated for a market variable for day $n-1$ is 1% per day, and during day $n-1$ the market variable increased by 2%. This means that $\sigma_{n-1}^2 = 0.01^2 = 0.0001$ and $u_{n-1}^2 = 0.02^2 = 0.0004$. Equation (10.8) gives

$$\sigma_n^2 = 0.9 \times 0.0001 + 0.1 \times 0.0004 = 0.00013$$

The estimate of the volatility for day n, σ_n, is, therefore, $\sqrt{0.00013}$ or 1.14% per day. Note that the expected value of u_{n-1}^2 is σ_{n-1}^2 or 0.0001. In this example, the realized value of u_{n-1}^2 is greater than the expected value, and as a result our volatility estimate increases. If the realized value of u_{n-1}^2 had been less than its expected value, our estimate of the volatility would have decreased.

The EWMA approach has the attractive feature that the data storage requirements are modest. At any given time, we need to remember only the current estimate of the variance rate and the most recent observation on the value of the market variable. When we get a new observation on the value of the market variable, we calculate a new daily percentage change and use equation (10.8) to update our estimate of the variance rate. The old estimate of the variance rate and the old value of the market variable can then be discarded.

The EWMA approach is designed to track changes in the volatility. Suppose there is a big move in the market variable on day $n-1$ so that u_{n-1}^2 is large. From equation (10.8) this causes our estimate of the current volatility to move upward. The value of λ governs how responsive the estimate of the daily volatility is to the most recent daily percentage change. A low value of λ leads to a great deal of weight being given to the u_{n-1}^2 when σ_n is calculated. In this case, the estimates produced for the volatility on successive days are themselves highly volatile. A high value of λ (i.e., a value close to 1.0) produces estimates of the daily volatility that respond relatively slowly to new information provided by the daily percentage change.

The RiskMetrics database, which was originally created by JPMorgan and made publicly available in 1994, used the EWMA model with $\lambda = 0.94$ for updating daily volatility estimates in its RiskMetrics database. The company found that, across a range of different market variables, this value of λ gives forecasts of the variance rate that come closest to the realized variance rate.[6]

10.7 THE GARCH(1,1) MODEL

We now move on to discuss what is known as the GARCH(1,1) model proposed by Bollerslev in 1986.[7] The difference between the EWMA model and the GARCH(1,1) model is analogous to the difference between equation (10.5) and equation (10.6). In GARCH(1,1), σ_n^2 is calculated from a long-run average variance rate, V_L, as well as from σ_{n-1} and u_{n-1}. The equation for GARCH(1,1) is

$$\sigma_n^2 = \gamma V_L + \alpha u_{n-1}^2 + \beta \sigma_{n-1}^2 \qquad (10.9)$$

where γ is the weight assigned to V_L, α is the weight assigned to u_{n-1}^2, and β is the weight assigned to σ_{n-1}^2. Because the weights must sum to one:

$$\gamma + \alpha + \beta = 1$$

The EWMA model is a particular case of GARCH(1,1) where $\gamma = 0$, $\alpha = 1 - \lambda$, and $\beta = \lambda$.

The "(1,1)" in GARCH(1,1) indicates that σ_n^2 is based on the most recent observation of u^2 and the most recent estimate of the variance rate. The more general GARCH(p, q) model calculates σ_n^2 from the most recent p observations on u^2 and the most recent q estimates of the variance rate.[8] GARCH(1,1) is by far the most popular of the GARCH models.

---

[6] See JPMorgan, *RiskMetrics Monitor*, Fourth Quarter, 1995. We will explain an alternative (maximum likelihood) approach to estimating parameters later in the chapter. The realized variance rate on a particular day was calculated as an equally weighted average of the u_i^2 on the subsequent 25 days. (See Problem 10.20.)

[7] See T. Bollerslev, "Generalized Autoregressive Conditional Heteroscedasticity," *Journal of Econometrics* 31 (1986): 307–327.

[8] Other GARCH models have been proposed that incorporate asymmetric news. These models are designed so that σ_n depends on the sign of u_{n-1}. Arguably, the models are more appropriate than GARCH(1,1) for equities. This is because the volatility of an equity's price tends to be inversely related to the price so that a negative u_{n-1} should have a bigger effect on σ_n than the same positive u_{n-1}. For a discussion of models for handling asymmetric news, see D. Nelson,

Setting $\omega = \gamma V_L$, the GARCH(1,1) model can also be written

$$\sigma_n^2 = \omega + \alpha u_{n-1}^2 + \beta \sigma_{n-1}^2 \qquad (10.10)$$

This is the form of the model that is usually used for the purposes of estimating the parameters. Once ω, α, and β have been estimated, we can calculate γ as $1 - \alpha - \beta$. The long-term variance V_L can then be calculated as ω/γ. For a stable GARCH(1,1) process, we require $\alpha + \beta < 1$. Otherwise the weight applied to the long-term variance is negative.

EXAMPLE 10.8

Suppose that a GARCH(1,1) model is estimated from daily data as

$$\sigma_n^2 = 0.000002 + 0.13 u_{n-1}^2 + 0.86 \sigma_{n-1}^2$$

This corresponds to $\alpha = 0.13$, $\beta = 0.86$, and $\omega = 0.000002$. Because $\gamma = 1 - \alpha - \beta$, it follows that $\gamma = 0.01$ and because $\omega = \gamma V_L$, it follows that $V_L = 0.0002$. In other words, the long-run average variance per day implied by the model is 0.0002. This corresponds to a volatility of $\sqrt{0.0002} = 0.014$ or 1.4% per day.

Suppose that the estimate of the volatility on day $n - 1$ is 1.6% per day so that $\sigma_{n-1}^2 = 0.016^2 = 0.000256$ and that on day $n - 1$ the market variable decreased by 1% so that $u_{n-1}^2 = 0.01^2 = 0.0001$. Then:

$$\sigma_n^2 = 0.000002 + 0.13 \times 0.0001 + 0.86 \times 0.000256 = 0.00023516$$

The new estimate of the volatility is, therefore, $\sqrt{0.00023516} = 0.0153$ or 1.53% per day.

The Weights

Substituting for σ_{n-1}^2 in equation (10.10) we obtain

$$\sigma_n^2 = \omega + \alpha u_{n-1}^2 + \beta(\omega + \alpha u_{n-2}^2 + \beta \sigma_{n-2}^2)$$

or

$$\sigma_n^2 = \omega + \beta\omega + \alpha u_{n-1}^2 + \alpha\beta u_{n-2}^2 + \beta^2 \sigma_{n-2}^2$$

Substituting for σ_{n-2}^2 we get

$$\sigma_n^2 = \omega + \beta\omega + \beta^2\omega + \alpha u_{n-1}^2 + \alpha\beta u_{n-2}^2 + \alpha\beta^2 u_{n-3}^2 + \beta^3 \sigma_{n-3}^2$$

"Conditional Heteroscedasticity and Asset Returns: A New Approach," *Econometrica* 59 (1990): 347–370 and R. F. Engle and V. Ng, "Measuring and Testing the Impact of News on Volatility," *Journal of Finance* 48 (1993): 1749–1778.

Continuing in this way, we see that the weight applied to u_{n-i}^2 is $\alpha\beta^{i-1}$. The weights decline exponentially at rate β. The parameter β can be interpreted as a "decay rate." It is similar to λ in the EWMA model. It defines the relative importance of the observations on the u_i in determining the current variance rate. For example, if $\beta = 0.9$, u_{n-2}^2 is only 90% as important as u_{n-1}^2; u_{n-3}^2 is 81% as important as u_{n-1}; and so on. The GARCH(1,1) model is the same as the EWMA model except that, in addition to assigning weights that decline exponentially to past u_i^2, it also assigns some weight to the long-run average variance rate.

10.8 CHOOSING BETWEEN THE MODELS

In practice, variance rates do tend to be pulled back to a long-run average level. This is known as *mean reversion*. The GARCH(1,1) model incorporates mean reversion whereas the EWMA model does not. GARCH(1,1) is, therefore, theoretically more appealing than the EWMA model.

In the next section, we will discuss how best-fit parameters ω, α, and β in GARCH(1,1) can be estimated. When the parameter ω is zero, the GARCH(1,1) reduces to EWMA. In circumstances where the best-fit value of ω turns out to be negative, the GARCH(1,1) model is not stable and it makes sense to switch to the EWMA model.

10.9 MAXIMUM LIKELIHOOD METHODS

It is now appropriate to discuss how the parameters in the models we have been considering are estimated from historical data. The approach used is known as the *maximum likelihood method*. It involves choosing values for the parameters that maximize the chance (or likelihood) of the data occurring.

We start with a very simple example. Suppose that we sample 10 stocks at random on a certain day and find that the price of one of them declined and the prices of the other nine either remained the same or increased. What is our best estimate of the proportion of stock prices that declined on the day? The natural answer is 0.1. Let us see if this is the result given by maximum likelihood methods.

Suppose that the probability of a price decline is p. The probability that one particular stock declines in price and the other nine do not is $p(1-p)^9$. (There is a probability p that it will decline and $1-p$ that each of the other nine will not.) Using the maximum likelihood approach, the best estimate of p is the one that maximizes $p(1-p)^9$. Differentiating this expression with respect to p and setting the result equal to zero, we find that $p = 0.1$ maximizes the expression. This shows that the maximum likelihood estimate of p is 0.1, as expected.

Estimating a Constant Variance

In our next example of maximum likelihood methods, we consider the problem of estimating a variance of a variable X from m observations on X when the underlying distribution is normal. We assume that the observations are $u_1, u_2, \ldots, u_m$ and that the mean of the underlying normal distribution is zero. Denote the variance by v. The likelihood of u_i being observed is the probability density function for X when $X = u_i$. This is

$$\frac{1}{\sqrt{2\pi v}} \exp\left(\frac{-u_i^2}{2v}\right)$$

The likelihood of m observations occurring in the order in which they are observed is

$$\prod_{i=1}^{m} \left[\frac{1}{\sqrt{2\pi v}} \exp\left(\frac{-u_i^2}{2v}\right) \right] \tag{10.11}$$

Using the maximum likelihood method, the best estimate of v is the value that maximizes this expression.

Maximizing an expression is equivalent to maximizing the logarithm of the expression. Taking logarithms of the expression in equation (10.11) and ignoring constant multiplicative factors, it can be seen that we wish to maximize

$$\sum_{i=1}^{m} \left[-\ln(v) - \frac{u_i^2}{v} \right] \tag{10.12}$$

or

$$-m \ln(v) - \sum_{i=1}^{m} \frac{u_i^2}{v}$$

Differentiating this expression with respect to v and setting the result equation to zero, we see that the maximum likelihood estimator of v is

$$\frac{1}{m} \sum_{i=1}^{m} u_i^2$$

This maximum likelihood estimator is the one we used in equation (10.4). The corresponding unbiased estimator is the same with m replaced by $m - 1$.

Estimating GARCH(1,1) or EWMA Parameters

We now consider how the maximum likelihood method can be used to estimate the parameters when GARCH(1,1) or some other volatility updating scheme is used. Define $v_i = \sigma_i^2$ as the estimate of the variance for day i. We assume that the probability distribution of u_i conditional on the variance is normal. A similar analysis to the one just given shows the best parameters are the ones that maximize

$$\prod_{i=1}^{m} \left[\frac{1}{\sqrt{2\pi v_i}} \exp\left(\frac{-u_i^2}{2v_i}\right) \right]$$

TABLE 10.4   Estimation of Parameters in GARCH(1,1) Model

Date	Day i	S_i	u_i	$v_i = \sigma_i^2$	$-\ln(v_i) - u_i^2/v_i$
06-Jan-88	1	0.007728			
07-Jan-88	2	0.007779	0.006599		
08-Jan-88	3	0.007746	−0.004242	0.00004355	9.6283
11-Jan-88	4	0.007816	0.009037	0.00004198	8.1329
12-Jan-88	5	0.007837	0.002687	0.00004455	9.8568
13-Jan-88	6	0.007924	0.011101	0.00004220	7.1529
...	...	...	...	...	...
...	...	...	...	...	...
13-Aug-97	2,421	0.008643	0.003374	0.00007626	9.3321
14-Aug-97	2,422	0.008493	−0.017309	0.00007092	5.3294
15-Aug-97	2,423	0.008495	0.000144	0.00008417	9.3824
					22,063.5833

Trial Estimates of GARCH parameters

ω	α	β
0.0000017528	0.061827	0.89855

Taking logarithms we see that this is equivalent to maximizing

$$\sum_{i=1}^{m} \left[-\ln(v_i) - \frac{u_i^2}{v_i} \right] \qquad (10.13)$$

This is the same as the expression in equation (10.12), except that v is replaced by v_i. We search iteratively to find the parameters in the model that maximize the expression in equation (10.13).

The spreadsheet in Table 10.4 indicates how the calculations could be organized for the GARCH(1,1) model. The table analyzes data on the Japanese yen exchange rate between January 6, 1988, and August 15, 1997. The numbers in the table are based on trial estimates of the three GARCH(1,1) parameters: ω, α, and β. The first column in the table records the date. The second column counts the days. The third column shows the exchange rate, S_i, at the end of day i. The fourth column shows the proportional change in the exchange rate between the end of day $i - 1$ and the end of day i. This is $u_i = (S_i - S_{i-1})/S_{i-1}$. The fifth column shows the estimate of the variance rate, $v_i = \sigma_i^2$, for day i made at the end of day $i - 1$. On day three, we start things off by setting the variance equal to u_2^2. On subsequent days equation (10.10) is used. The sixth column tabulates the likelihood measure, $-\ln(v_i) - u_i^2/v_i$. The values in the fifth and sixth columns are based on the current trial estimates of ω, α, and β. We are interested in choosing ω, α, and β to maximize the sum of the numbers in the sixth column. This involves an iterative search procedure.[9]

---

[9] As discussed later, a general purpose algorithm such as Solver in Microsoft's Excel can be used. Alternatively, a special purpose algorithm, such as Levenberg–Marquardt, can be used. The calculations using Solver that produced Table 10.4 are on the author's website: www.rotman.utoronto.ca/~hull.

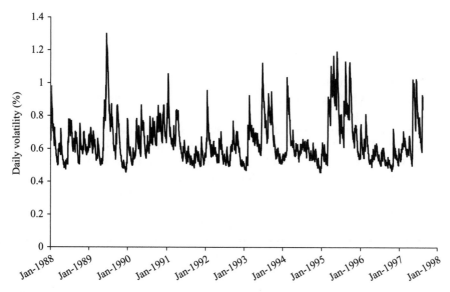

FIGURE 10.4 Daily Volatility of the Yen-USD Exchange Rate, 1988–1997

In our example, the optimal values of the parameters turn out to be

$$\omega = 0.0000017528$$
$$\alpha = 0.061827$$
$$\beta = 0.89855$$

and the maximum value of the function in equation (10.13) is 22,063.5833. (The numbers shown in Table 10.4 are actually those calculated on the final iteration of the search for the optimal ω, α, and β.)

The long-term variance rate, V_L, in our example is

$$\frac{\omega}{1 - \alpha - \beta} = \frac{0.0000017528}{0.039624} = 0.0000442$$

The long-term volatility is $\sqrt{0.0000442}$ or 0.665% per day.

Figure 10.4 shows the way in which the GARCH(1,1) volatility for the Japanese yen changed over the 10-year period covered by the data. Most of the time, the volatility was between 0.4% and 0.8% per day, but volatilities over 1% were experienced during some periods.

An alternative more robust approach to estimating parameters in GARCH(1,1) is known as *variance targeting*.[10] This involves setting the long-run average variance rate, V_L, equal to the sample variance calculated from the data (or to some other value that is believed to be reasonable). The value of ω then equals $V_L(1 - \alpha - \beta)$ and only two parameters have to be estimated. For the data in Table 10.4, the sample

---

[10] See R. Engle and J. Mezrich, "GARCH for Groups," *Risk* (August 1996): 36–40.

variance is 0.00004341, which gives a daily volatility of 0.659%. Setting V_L equal to the sample variance, the values of α and β that maximize the objective function in equation (10.13) are 0.0607 and 0.899, respectively. The value of the objective function is 22,063.5274, only marginally below the value of 22,063.5833 obtained using the earlier procedure.

When the EWMA model is used, the estimation procedure is relatively simple. We set $\omega = 0$, $\alpha = 1 - \lambda$, and $\beta = \lambda$, and only one parameter has to be estimated. In the data in Table 10.4, the value of λ that maximizes the objective function in equation (10.13) is 0.9686 and the value of the objective function is 21,995.8377.

Both GARCH(1,1) and the EWMA method can be implemented by using the Solver routine in Excel to search for the values of the parameters that maximize the likelihood function. The routine works well provided we structure our spreadsheet so that the parameters we are searching for have roughly equal values. For example, in GARCH(1,1) we could let cells A1, A2, and A3 contain $\omega \times 10^5$, α, and 0.1β. We could then set B1 = A1/100000, B2 = A2, and B3 = 10*A3. We would then use B1, B2, and B3 to calculate the likelihood function, but we would ask Solver to calculate the values of A1, A2, and A3 that maximize the likelihood function. Occasionally Solver gives a local maximum, so a number of different starting values for the parameter should be tested.

How Good Is the Model?

The assumption underlying a GARCH model is that volatility changes with the passage of time. During some periods, volatility is relatively high; during other periods, it is relatively low. To put this another way, when u_i^2 is high, there is a tendency for $u_{i+1}^2, u_{i+2}^2, \ldots$ to be high; when u_i^2 is low there is a tendency for u_{i+1}^2, $u_{i+2}^2, \ldots$ to be low. We can test how true this is by examining the autocorrelation structure of the u_i^2.

Let us assume that the u_i^2 do exhibit autocorrelation. If a GARCH model is working well, it should remove the autocorrelation. We can test whether it has done this by considering the autocorrelation structure for the variables u_i^2/σ_i^2. If these show very little autocorrelation, our model for σ_i has succeeded in explaining autocorrelations in the u_i^2.

Table 10.5 shows results for the yen-dollar exchange rate data referred to earlier. The first column shows the lags considered when the autocorrelation is calculated. The second column shows autocorrelations for u_i^2; the third column shows autocorrelations for u_i^2/σ_i^2.[11] The table shows that the autocorrelations are positive for u_i^2 for all lags between 1 and 15. In the case of u_i^2/σ_i^2, some of the autocorrelations are positive and some are negative. They are nearly always much smaller in magnitude than the autocorrelations for u_i^2.

The GARCH model appears to have done a good job in explaining the data. For a more scientific test, we can use what is known as the Ljung-Box statistic.[12] If

---

[11] For a series x_i, the autocorrelation with a lag of k is the coefficient of correlation between x_i and x_{i+k}.
[12] See G. M. Ljung and G. E. P. Box, "On a Measure of Lack of Fit in Time Series Models," *Biometrica* 65 (1978): 297–303.

TABLE 10.5 Autocorrelations Before and After the Use of a GARCH Model

Time Lag	Autocorr for u_i^2	Autocorr for u_i^2/σ_i^2
1	0.072	0.000
2	0.041	−0.010
3	0.057	0.005
4	0.107	0.000
5	0.075	0.011
6	0.066	0.009
7	0.019	−0.034
8	0.085	0.015
9	0.054	0.009
10	0.030	−0.022
11	0.038	−0.004
12	0.038	−0.021
13	0.057	−0.001
14	0.040	0.004
15	0.007	−0.026

a certain series has m observations the Ljung-Box statistic is

$$m \sum_{k=1}^{K} w_k c_k^2$$

where c_k is the autocorrelation for a lag of k, K is the number of lags considered, and

$$w_k = \frac{m+2}{m-k}$$

For $K = 15$, zero autocorrelation can be rejected with 95% confidence when the Ljung-Box statistic is greater than 25.

From Table 10.5, the Ljung-Box Statistic for the u_i^2 series is about 123. This is strong evidence of autocorrelation. For the u_i^2/σ_i^2 series, the Ljung-Box statistic is 8.2, suggesting that the autocorrelation has been largely removed by the GARCH model.

10.10 USING GARCH(1,1) TO FORECAST FUTURE VOLATILITY

The variance rate estimated at the end of day $n-1$ for day n, when GARCH(1,1) is used, is

$$\sigma_n^2 = (1 - \alpha - \beta)V_L + \alpha u_{n-1}^2 + \beta \sigma_{n-1}^2$$

so that

$$\sigma_n^2 - V_L = \alpha(u_{n-1}^2 - V_L) + \beta(\sigma_{n-1}^2 - V_L)$$

On day $n + t$ in the future, we have

$$\sigma_{n+t}^2 - V_L = \alpha(u_{n+t-1}^2 - V_L) + \beta(\sigma_{n+t-1}^2 - V_L)$$

The expected value of u_{n+t-1}^2 is σ_{n+t-1}^2. Hence,

$$E[\sigma_{n+t}^2 - V_L] = (\alpha + \beta)E[\sigma_{n+t-1}^2 - V_L]$$

where E denotes expected value. Using this equation repeatedly yields

$$E[\sigma_{n+t}^2 - V_L] = (\alpha + \beta)^t(\sigma_n^2 - V_L)$$

or

$$E[\sigma_{n+t}^2] = V_L + (\alpha + \beta)^t(\sigma_n^2 - V_L) \tag{10.14}$$

This equation forecasts the volatility on day $n + t$ using the information available at the end of day $n - 1$. In the EWMA model, $\alpha + \beta = 1$ and equation (10.14) shows that the expected future variance rate equals the current variance rate. When $\alpha + \beta < 1$, the final term in the equation becomes progressively smaller as t increases. Figure 10.5 shows the expected path followed by the variance rate for situations where the current variance rate is different from V_L. As mentioned earlier, the variance rate exhibits mean reversion with a reversion level of V_L and a reversion rate of $1 - \alpha - \beta$. Our forecast of the future variance rate tends toward V_L as we look

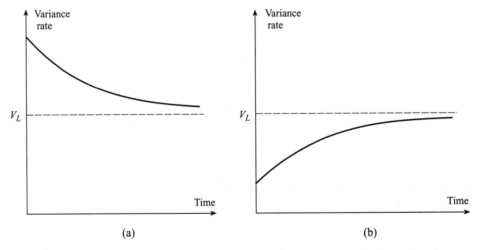

FIGURE 10.5 Expected Path for the Variance Rate when (a) Current Variance Rate Is above Long-Term Variance Rate and (b) Current Variance Rate Is below Long-Term Variance Rate

further and further ahead. This analysis emphasizes the point that we must have $\alpha + \beta < 1$ for a stable GARCH(1,1) process. When $\alpha + \beta > 1$, the weight given to the long-term average variance is negative and the process is "mean fleeing" rather than "mean reverting."

In the yen-dollar exchange rate example considered earlier, $\alpha + \beta = 0.9604$ and $V_L = 0.0000442$. Suppose that our estimate of the current variance rate per day is 0.00006. (This corresponds to a volatility of 0.77% per day.) In 10 days, the expected variance rate is

$$0.0000442 + 0.9604^{10}(0.00006 - 0.0000442) = 0.00005476$$

The expected volatility per day is $\sqrt{0.00005476}$ or 0.74%, still well above the long-term volatility of 0.665% per day. However, the expected variance rate in 100 days is

$$0.0000442 + 0.9604^{100}(0.00006 - 0.0000442) = 0.00004451$$

and the expected volatility per day is 0.667%, very close the long-term volatility.

Volatility Term Structures

Suppose it is day n. Define

$$V(t) = E(\sigma_{n+t}^2)$$

and

$$a = \ln \frac{1}{\alpha + \beta}$$

so that equation (10.14) becomes

$$V(t) = V_L + e^{-at}[V(0) - V_L]$$

$V(t)$ is an estimate of the instantaneous variance rate in t days. The average variance rate per day between today and time T is

$$\frac{1}{T}\int_0^T V(t)dt = V_L + \frac{1 - e^{-aT}}{aT}[V(0) - V_L]$$

The longer the life of the option, the closer this is to V_L. Define $\sigma(T)$ as the volatility per annum that should be used to price a T-day option under GARCH(1,1). Assuming 252 days per year, $\sigma(T)^2$ is 252 times the average variance rate per day, so that

$$\sigma(T)^2 = 252\left\{V_L + \frac{1 - e^{-aT}}{aT}[V(0) - V_L]\right\} \tag{10.15}$$

TABLE 10.6   Yen–Dollar Volatility Term Structure Predicted from GARCH(1,1)

Option life (days)	10	30	50	100	500
Option volatility (% per annum)	12.01	11.60	11.34	11.01	10.65

The relationship between the volatilities of options and their maturities is referred to as the *volatility term structure*. The volatility term structure is usually calculated from implied volatilities, but equation (10.15) provides an alternative approach for estimating it from the GARCH(1,1) model. Although the volatility term structure estimated from GARCH(1,1) is not the same as that calculated from implied volatilities, it is often used to predict the way that the actual volatility term structure will respond to volatility changes.

When the current volatility is above the long-term volatility, the GARCH(1,1) model estimates a downward-sloping volatility term structure. When the current volatility is below the long-term volatility, it estimates an upward-sloping volatility term structure. In the case of the yen-dollar exchange rate, $a = \ln(1/0.9604) = 0.0404$ and $V_L = 0.0000442$. Suppose that the current variance rate per day, $V(0)$, is estimated as 0.00006 per day. It follows from equation (10.15) that

$$\sigma(T)^2 = 252\left[0.0000442 + \frac{1 - e^{-0.0404T}}{0.0404T}(0.00006 - 0.0000442)\right]$$

where T is measured in days. Table 10.6 shows the volatility per year for different values of T.

Impact of Volatility Changes

Equation (10.15) can be written as

$$\sigma(T)^2 = 252\left\{V_L + \frac{1 - e^{-aT}}{aT}\left(\frac{\sigma(0)^2}{252} - V_L\right)\right\}$$

When $\sigma(0)$ changes by $\Delta\sigma(0)$, $\sigma(T)$ changes by approximately

$$\frac{1 - e^{-aT}}{aT}\frac{\sigma(0)}{\sigma(T)}\Delta\sigma(0) \tag{10.16}$$

Table 10.7 shows the effect of a volatility change on options of varying maturities for our yen-dollar exchange rate example. We assume as before that $V(0) = 0.00006$ so that the daily volatility is $\sqrt{0.00006} = 0.0077$ or 0.77% and

TABLE 10.7   Impact of 1% Change in the Instantaneous Volatility Predicted from GARCH(1,1)

Option life (days)	10	30	50	100	500
Increase in volatility (%)	0.84	0.61	0.47	0.27	0.06

$\sigma(0) = \sqrt{252} \times 0.77\% = 12.30\%$. The table considers a 100-basis-point change in the instantaneous volatility from 12.30% per year to 13.30% per year. This means that $\Delta\sigma(0) = 0.01$ or 1%.

Many financial institutions use analyses such as this when determining the exposure of their books to volatility changes. Rather than consider an across-the-board increase of 1% in implied volatilities when calculating vega, they relate the size of the volatility increase that is considered to the maturity of the option. Based on Table 10.7, a 0.84% volatility increase would be considered for a 10-day option, a 0.61% increase for a 30-day option, a 0.47% increase for a 50-day option, and so on.

SUMMARY

In risk management, the daily volatility of a market variable is defined as the standard deviation of the percentage daily change in the market variable. The daily variance rate is the square of the daily volatility. Volatility tends to be much higher on trading days than on nontrading days. As a result, nontrading days are ignored in volatility calculations. It is tempting to assume that daily changes in market variables are normally distributed. In fact, this is far from true. Most market variables have distributions for percentage daily changes with much heavier tails than the normal distribution. The power law has been found to be a good description of the tails of many distributions that are encountered in practice.

This chapter has discussed methods for attempting to keep track of the current level of volatility. Define u_i as the percentage change in a market variable between the end of day $i - 1$ and the end of day i. The variance rate of the market variable (that is, the square of its volatility) is calculated as a weighted average of the u_i^2. The key feature of the methods that have been discussed here is that they do not give equal weight to the observations on the u_i^2. The more recent an observation, the greater the weight assigned to it. In the EWMA model and the GARCH(1,1) model, the weights assigned to observations decrease exponentially as the observations become older. The GARCH(1,1) model differs from the EWMA model in that some weight is also assigned to the long-run average variance rate. Both the EWMA and GARCH(1,1) models have structures that enable forecasts of the future level of variance rate to be produced relatively easily.

Maximum likelihood methods are usually used to estimate parameters in GARCH(1,1) and similar models from historical data. These methods involve using an iterative procedure to determine the parameter values that maximize the chance or likelihood that the historical data will occur. Once its parameters have been determined, a model can be judged by how well it removes autocorrelation from the u_i^2.

The GARCH(1,1) model can be used to estimate a volatility for options from historical data. This analysis is often used to calculate the impact of a shock to volatility on the implied volatilities of options of different maturities.

FURTHER READING

On the Causes of Volatility

Fama, E. F. "The Behavior of Stock Market Prices," *Journal of Business* 38 (January 1965): 34–105.

French, K. R. "Stock Returns and the Weekend Effect," *Journal of Financial Economics* 8 (March 1980): 55–69.

French, K. R, and R. Roll. "Stock Return Variances: The Arrival of Information and the Reaction of Traders," *Journal of Financial Economics* 17 (September 1986): 5–26.

Roll, R. "Orange Juice and Weather," *American Economic Review* 74, no. 5 (December 1984): 861–80.

On GARCH

Bollerslev, T. "Generalized Autoregressive Conditional Heteroscedasticity," *Journal of Econometrics* 31 (1986): 307–327.

Cumby, R., S. Figlewski, and J. Hasbrook. "Forecasting Volatilities and Correlations with EGARCH Models," *Journal of Derivatives* 1, no. 2 (Winter 1993): 51–63.

Engle, R. F. "Autoregressive Conditional Heteroscedasticity with Estimates of the Variance of U.K. Inflation," *Econometrica* 50 (1982): 987–1008.

Engle, R. F. and J. Mezrich. "Grappling with GARCH," *Risk* (September 1995): 112–117.

Engle, R. F. and V. Ng. "Measuring and Testing the Impact of News on Volatility," *Journal of Finance* 48 (1993): 1749–1778.

Nelson, D. "Conditional Heteroscedasticity and Asset Returns; A New Approach," *Econometrica* 59 (1990): 347–370.

Noh, J., R. F. Engle, and A. Kane. "Forecasting Volatility and Option Prices of the S&P 500 Index," *Journal of Derivatives* 2 (1994): 17–30.

PRACTICE QUESTIONS AND PROBLEMS (ANSWERS AT END OF BOOK)

10.1 The volatility of an asset is 2% per day. What is the standard deviation of the percentage price change in three days?

10.2 The volatility of an asset is 25% per annum. What is the standard deviation of the percentage price change in one trading day? Assuming a normal distribution with zero mean, estimate 95% confidence limits for the percentage price change in one day.

10.3 Why do traders assume 252 rather than 365 days in a year when using volatilities?

10.4 What is implied volatility? What does it mean if different options on the same asset have different implied volatilities?

10.5 Suppose that observations on an exchange rate at the end of the last 11 days have been 0.7000, 0.7010, 0.7070, 0.6999, 0.6970, 0.7003, 0.6951, 0.6953, 0.6934, 0.6923, 0.6922. Estimate the daily volatility using both approaches in Section 10.5.

10.6 The number of visitors to websites follows the power law in equation (10.1) with $\alpha = 2$. Suppose that 1% of sites get 500 or more visitors per day. What percentage of sites get (a) 1,000 and (b) 2,000 or more visitors per day?

10.7 Explain the exponentially weighted moving average (EWMA) model for estimating volatility from historical data.

10.8 What is the difference between the exponentially weighted moving average model and the GARCH(1,1) model for updating volatilities?

10.9 The most recent estimate of the daily volatility of an asset is 1.5% and the price of the asset at the close of trading yesterday was $30.00. The parameter λ in the EWMA model is 0.94. Suppose that the price of the asset at the close of trading today is \$30.50. How will this cause the volatility to be updated by the EWMA model?

10.10 A company uses an EWMA model for forecasting volatility. It decides to change the parameter λ from 0.95 to 0.85. Explain the likely impact on the forecasts.

10.11 Assume that the S&P 500 at close of trading yesterday was 1,040 and the daily volatility of the index was estimated as 1% per day at that time. The parameters in a GARCH(1,1) model are $\omega = 0.000002$, $\alpha = 0.06$, and $\beta = 0.92$. If the level of the index at close of trading today is 1,060, what is the new volatility estimate?

10.12 The most recent estimate of the daily volatility of the dollar–sterling exchange rate is 0.6% and the exchange rate at 4:00 P.M. yesterday was 1.5000. The parameter λ in the EWMA model is 0.9. Suppose that the exchange rate at 4:00 P.M. today proves to be 1.4950. How would the estimate of the daily volatility be updated?

10.13 A company uses the GARCH(1,1) model for updating volatility. The three parameters are ω, α, and β. Describe the impact of making a small increase in each of the parameters while keeping the others fixed.

10.14 The parameters of a GARCH(1,1) model are estimated as $\omega = 0.000004$, $\alpha = 0.05$, and $\beta = 0.92$. What is the long-run average volatility and what is the equation describing the way that the variance rate reverts to its long-run average? If the current volatility is 20% per year, what is the expected volatility in 20 days?

10.15 Suppose that the daily volatility of the FTSE 100 stock index (measured in pounds sterling) is 1.8% and the daily volatility of the dollar–sterling exchange rate is 0.9%. Suppose further that the correlation between the FTSE 100 and the dollar/sterling exchange rate is 0.4. What is the volatility of the FTSE 100 when it is translated to U.S. dollars? Assume that the dollar/sterling exchange rate is expressed as the number of U.S. dollars per pound sterling. (*Hint:* When $Z = XY$, the percentage daily change in Z is approximately equal to the percentage daily change in X plus the percentage daily change in Y.)

10.16 Suppose that GARCH(1,1) parameters have been estimated as $\omega = 0.000003$, $\alpha = 0.04$, and $\beta = 0.94$. The current daily volatility is estimated to be 1%. Estimate the daily volatility in 30 days.

10.17 Suppose that GARCH(1,1) parameters have been estimated as $\omega = 0.000002$, $\alpha = 0.04$, and $\beta = 0.94$. The current daily volatility is estimated to be 1.3%. Estimate the volatility per annum that should be used to price a 20-day option.

FURTHER QUESTIONS

10.18 Suppose that observations on a stock price (in dollars) at the end of each of 15 consecutive days are as follows:

30.2, 32.0, 31.1, 30.1, 30.2, 30.3, 30.6, 30.9, 30.5, 31.1, 31.3, 30.8, 30.3, 29.9, 29.8

Estimate the daily volatility using both approaches in Section 10.5.

10.19 Suppose that the price of an asset at close of trading yesterday was $300 and its volatility was estimated as 1.3% per day. The price at the close of trading today is $298. Update the volatility estimate using
(a) The EWMA model with $\lambda = 0.94$
(b) The GARCH(1,1) model with $\omega = 0.000002$, $\alpha = 0.04$, and $\beta = 0.94$.

10.20 An Excel spreadsheet containing over 900 days of daily data on a number of different exchange rates and stock indices can be downloaded from the author's website: www.rotman.utoronto.ca/~hull/data. Choose one exchange rate and one stock index. Estimate the value of λ in the EWMA model that minimizes the value of

$$\sum_i (v_i - \beta_i)^2$$

where v_i is the variance forecast made at the end of day $i - 1$ and β_i is the variance calculated from data between day i and day $i + 25$. Use the Solver tool in Excel. To start the EWMA calculations, set the variance forecast at the end of the first day equal to the square of the return on that day.

10.21 Suppose that the parameters in a GARCH(1,1) model are $\alpha = 0.03$, $\beta = 0.95$ and $\omega = 0.000002$.
(a) What is the long-run average volatility?
(b) If the current volatility is 1.5% per day, what is your estimate of the volatility in 20, 40, and 60 days?
(c) What volatility should be used to price 20-, 40-, and 60-day options?
(d) Suppose that there is an event that increases the volatility from 1.5% per day to 2% per day. Estimate the effect on the volatility in 20, 40, and 60 days.
(e) Estimate by how much the event increases the volatilities used to price 20-, 40-, and 60-day options.

10.22 Estimate parameters for the EWMA and GARCH(1,1) model on the euro-USD exchange rate data between July 27, 2005, and July 27, 2010. This data can be found on the author's website:

www.rotman.utoronto.ca/~hull/data

10.23 The probability that the loss from a portfolio will be greater than $10 million in one month is estimated to be 5%.
(a) What is the one-month 99% VaR assuming the change in value of the portfolio is normally distributed with zero mean?
(b) What is the one-month 99% VaR assuming that the power law applies with $\alpha = 3$?

CHAPTER 11

Correlations and Copulas

Suppose that a company has an exposure to two different market variables. In the case of each variable, it gains $10 million if there is a one-standard-deviation increase and loses $10 million if there is a one-standard-deviation decrease. If changes in the two variables have a high positive correlation, the company's total exposure is very high; if they have a correlation of zero, the exposure is less but still quite large; if they have a high negative correlation, the exposure is quite low because a loss on one of the variables is likely to be offset by a gain on the other. This example shows that it is important for a risk manager to estimate correlations between the changes in market variables as well as their volatilities when assessing risk exposures.

This chapter explains how correlations can be monitored in a similar way to volatilities. It also covers what are known as copulas. These are tools that provide a way of defining a correlation structure between two or more variables, regardless of the shapes of their probability distributions. Copulas have a number of applications in risk management. They are a convenient way of modeling default correlation and, as we will show in this chapter, can be used to develop a relatively simple model for estimating the value at risk on a portfolio of loans. (The Basel II capital requirements, which will be discussed in the next chapter, use this model.) Copulas are also used to value credit derivatives and for the calculation of economic capital.

11.1 DEFINITION OF CORRELATION

The coefficient of correlation, ρ, between two variables V_1 and V_2 is defined as

$$\rho = \frac{E(V_1 V_2) - E(V_1)E(V_2)}{SD(V_1)SD(V_2)} \tag{11.1}$$

where E (.) denotes expected value and SD (.) denotes standard deviation. If there is no correlation between the variables, $E(V_1 V_2) = E(V_1)E(V_2)$ and $\rho = 0$. If $V_1 = V_2$, both the numerator and the denominator in the expression for ρ equal the variance of V_1. As we would expect, $\rho = 1$ in this case.

The *covariance* between V_1 and V_2 is defined as

$$\text{cov}(V_1, V_2) = E(V_1 V_2) - E(V_1)E(V_2) \tag{11.2}$$

so that the correlation can be written

$$\rho = \frac{\text{cov}(V_1, V_2)}{SD(V_1)SD(V_2)}$$

Although it is easier to develop intuition about the meaning of a correlation than a covariance, it is covariances that will prove to be the fundamental variables of our analysis. An analogy here is that variance rates were the fundamental variables for the EWMA and GARCH methods in Chapter 10, even though it is easier to develop intuition about volatilities.

Correlation vs. Dependence

Two variables are defined as statistically independent if knowledge about one of them does not affect the probability distribution for the other. Formally, V_1 and V_2 are independent if:

$$f(V_2 | V_1 = x) = f(V_2)$$

for all x where $f(.)$ denotes the probability density function.

If the coefficient of correlation between two variables is zero, does this mean that there is no dependence between the variables? The answer is no. We can illustrate this with a simple example. Suppose that there are three equally likely values for V_1: -1, 0, and $+1$. If $V_1 = -1$ or $V_1 = +1$ then $V_2 = 1$. If $V_1 = 0$ then $V_2 = 0$. In this case, there is clearly a dependence between V_1 and V_2. If we observe the value of V_1, we know the value of V_2. Also, a knowledge of the value of V_2 will cause us to change our probability distribution for V_1. However, the coefficient of correlation between V_1 and V_2 is zero.

This example emphasizes the point that the coefficient of correlation measures one particular type of dependence between two variables. This is linear dependence. There are many other ways in which two variables can be related. We can characterize the nature of the dependence between V_1 and V_2 by plotting $E(V_2)$ against V_1. Three examples are shown in Figure 11.1. Figure 11.1(a) shows linear dependence where the expected value of V_2 depends linearly on V_1. Figure 11.1(b) shows a V-shaped relationship between the expected value of V_2 and V_1. (This is similar to the example we have just considered; a symmetrical V-shaped relationship, however strong, leads to zero coefficient of correlation.) Figure 11.1(c) shows a type of dependence that is often seen when V_1 and V_2 are percentage changes in financial variables. For the values of V_1 normally encountered, there is very little relation between V_1 and V_2. However, extreme values of V_1 tend to lead to extreme values of V_2. (This could be consistent with correlations increasing in stressed market conditions.)

Another aspect of the way in which V_2 depends on V_1 is found by examining the standard deviation of V_2 conditional on V_1. As we will see later, this is constant when V_1 and V_2 have a bivariate normal distribution. But, in other situations, the standard deviation of V_2 is liable to depend on the value of V_1.

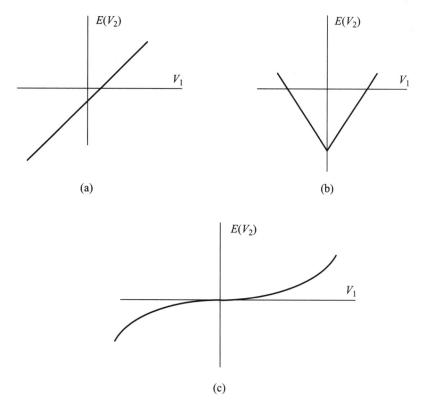

(a)

(b)

(c)

FIGURE 11.1 Examples of Ways in Which V_2 Can Be Dependent on V_1

11.2 MONITORING CORRELATION

Chapter 10 explained how exponentially weighted moving average and GARCH methods can be developed to monitor the variance rate of a variable. Similar approaches can be used to monitor the covariance rate between two variables. The variance rate per day of a variable is the variance of daily returns. Similarly the *covariance rate* per day between two variables is defined as the covariance between the daily returns of the variables.

Suppose that X_i and Y_i are the values of two variables, X and Y, at the end of day i. The returns on the variables on day i are

$$x_i = \frac{X_i - X_{i-1}}{X_{i-1}} \qquad y_i = \frac{Y_i - Y_{i-1}}{Y_{i-1}}$$

The covariance rate between X and Y on day n is from equation (11.2)

$$\text{cov}_n = E(x_n y_n) - E(x_n)E(y_n)$$

In Section 10.5, we explained that risk managers assume that expected daily returns are zero when the variance rate per day is calculated. They do the same when calculating the covariance rate per day. This means that the covariance rate per day between X and Y on day n is assumed to be

$$\text{cov}_n = E(x_n y_n)$$

Using equal weights for the last m observations on x_i and y_i gives the estimate

$$\text{cov}_n = \frac{1}{m} \sum_{i=1}^{m} x_{n-i} y_{n-i} \tag{11.3}$$

A similar weighting scheme for variances gives an estimate for the variance rate on day n for variable X as

$$\text{var}_{x,n} = \frac{1}{m} \sum_{i=1}^{m} x_{n-i}^2$$

and for variable Y as

$$\text{var}_{y,n} = \frac{1}{m} \sum_{i=1}^{m} y_{n-i}^2$$

The correlation estimate on day n is

$$\frac{\text{cov}_n}{\sqrt{\text{var}_{x,n}\text{var}_{y,n}}}$$

EWMA

Most risk managers would agree that observations from long ago should not have as much weight as recent observations. In Chapter 10, we discussed the use of the exponentially weighted moving average (EWMA) model for variances. We saw that it leads to weights that decline exponentially as we move back through time. A similar weighting scheme can be used for covariances. The formula for updating a covariance estimate in the EWMA model is similar to that in equation (10.8) for variances:

$$\text{cov}_n = \lambda \text{cov}_{n-1} + (1 - \lambda)x_{n-1}y_{n-1}$$

A similar analysis to that presented for the EWMA volatility model shows that the weight given to $x_{n-i}y_{n-i}$ declines as i increases (i.e., as we move back through time). The lower the value of λ, the greater the weight that is given to recent observations.

EXAMPLE 11.1

Suppose that $\lambda = 0.95$ and that the estimate of the correlation between two variables X and Y on day $n - 1$ is 0.6. Suppose further that the estimate of the volatilities for X and Y on day $n - 1$ are 1% and 2%, respectively. From the relationship between correlation and covariance, the estimate of the covariance rate between X and Y on day $n - 1$ is

$$0.6 \times 0.01 \times 0.02 = 0.00012$$

Suppose that the percentage changes in X and Y on day $n - 1$ are 0.5% and 2.5%, respectively. The variance rates and covariance rate for day n would be updated as follows:

$$\sigma_{x,n}^2 = 0.95 \times 0.01^2 + 0.05 \times 0.005^2 = 0.00009625$$

$$\sigma_{y,n}^2 = 0.95 \times 0.02^2 + 0.05 \times 0.025^2 = 0.00041125$$

$$\text{cov}_n = 0.95 \times 0.00012 + 0.05 \times 0.005 \times 0.025 = 0.00012025$$

The new volatility of X is $\sqrt{0.00009625} = 0.981$ % and the new volatility of Y is $\sqrt{0.00041125} = 2.028$ %. The new correlation between X and Y is

$$\frac{0.00012025}{0.00981 \times 0.02028} = 0.6044$$

Garch

GARCH models can also be used for updating covariance rate estimates and forecasting the future level of covariance rates. For example, the GARCH(1,1) model for updating a covariance rate between X and Y is

$$\text{cov}_n = \omega + \alpha x_{n-1} y_{n-1} + \beta \text{cov}_{n-1}$$

This formula, like its counterpart in equation (10.10) for updating variances, gives some weight to a long-run average covariance, some to the most recent covariance estimate, and some to the most recent observation on covariance (which is $x_{n-1} y_{n-1}$). The long-term average covariance rate is $\omega/(1 - \alpha - \beta)$. Formulas similar to those in equations (10.14) and (10.15) can be developed for forecasting future covariance rates and calculating the average covariance rate during a future time period.

Consistency Condition for Covariances

Once variance and covariance rates have been calculated for a set of market variables, a variance-covariance matrix can be constructed. When $i \neq j$, the (i, j) element of this matrix shows the covariance rate between variable i and variable j. When $i = j$ it shows the variance rate of variable i. (See Section 15.3.)

Not all variance-covariance matrices are internally consistent. The condition for an $N \times N$ variance-covariance matrix, Ω, to be internally consistent is

$$w^{\mathrm{T}} \Omega w \geq 0 \qquad (11.4)$$

for all $N \times 1$ vectors w where w^{T} is the transpose of w. A matrix that satisfies this property is known as *positive-semidefinite*.

To understand why the condition in equation (11.4) must hold, suppose that w is the (column) vector $(w_1, w_2, \ldots, w_N)$. The expression $w^{\mathrm{T}} \Omega w$ is the variance rate of $w_1z_1 + w_2z_2 + \ldots + w_Nz_N$ where z_i is the value of variable i. As such, it cannot be negative.

To ensure that a positive-semidefinite matrix is produced, variances and covariances should be calculated consistently. For example, if variance rates are calculated by giving equal weight to the last m data items, the same should be done for covariance rates. If variance rates are updated using an EWMA model with $\lambda = 0.94$, the same should be done for covariance rates. Using a GARCH model to update a variance-covariance matrix in a consistent way is trickier and requires a multivariate GARCH model.[1]

An example of a variance-covariance matrix that is not internally consistent is

$$\begin{pmatrix} 1 & 0 & 0.9 \\ 0 & 1 & 0.9 \\ 0.9 & 0.9 & 1 \end{pmatrix}$$

The variance of each variable is 1.0 and so the covariances are also coefficients of correlation in this case. The first variable is highly correlated with the third variable and the second variable is also highly correlated with the third variable. However, there is no correlation at all between the first and second variables. This seems strange. When we set w^T equal to $(1, 1, -1)$ we find that the condition in equation (11.4) is not satisfied, proving that the matrix is not positive-semidefinite.[2]

If we make a small change to a positive-semidefinite matrix that is calculated from observations on three variables (e.g., for the purposes of doing a sensitivity analysis), it is likely that the matrix will remain positive-semidefinite. However, if we do the same thing for observations on 1,000 variables, we have to be much more careful. An arbitrary small change to a positive-semidefinite $1,000 \times 1,000$ matrix is quite likely to lead to it no longer being positive-semidefinite.

11.3 MULTIVARIATE NORMAL DISTRIBUTIONS

Multivariate normal distributions are well understood and relatively easy to deal with. As we will explain in the next section, they can be useful tools for specifying the correlation structure between variables, even when the distributions of the variables are not normal.

We start by considering a bivariate normal distribution where there are only two variables, V_1 and V_2. Suppose that we know V_1. Conditional on this, the value of V_2 is normal with mean

$$\mu_2 + \rho\sigma_2 \frac{V_1 - \mu_1}{\sigma_1}$$

---

[1] See R. Engle and J. Mezrich, "GARCH for Groups," *Risk* (August 1996): 36–40, for a discussion of alternative approaches.

[2] It can be shown that the condition for a 3×3 matrix of correlations to be internally consistent is

$$\rho_{12}^2 + \rho_{13}^2 + \rho_{23}^2 - 2\rho_{12}\rho_{13}\rho_{23} \leq 1$$

where ρ_{ij} is the coefficient of correlation between variables i and j.

and standard deviation

$$\sigma_2\sqrt{1-\rho^2}$$

Here μ_1 and μ_2 are the unconditional means of V_1 and V_2, σ_1 and σ_2 are their unconditional standard deviations, and ρ is the coefficient of correlation between V_1 and V_2. Note that the expected value of V_2 conditional on V_1 is linearly dependent on the value of V_1. This corresponds to Figure 11.1(a). Also the standard deviation of V_2 conditional on the value of V_1 is the same for all values of V_1.

Generating Random Samples from Normal Distributions

Most programming languages have routines for sampling a random number between zero and one, and many have routines for sampling from a normal distribution.[3]

When samples ε_1 and ε_2 from a bivariate normal distribution (where both variables have mean zero and standard deviation one) are required, an appropriate procedure is as follows. Independent samples z_1 and z_2 from a univariate standardized normal distribution are obtained. The required samples ε_1 and ε_2 are then calculated as follows:

$$\varepsilon_1 = z_1$$

$$\varepsilon_2 = \rho z_1 + z_2\sqrt{1-\rho^2}$$

where ρ is the coefficient of correlation in the bivariate normal distribution.

Consider next the situation where we require samples from a multivariate normal distribution (where all variables have mean zero and standard deviation one) and the coefficient of correlation between variable i and variable j is ρ_{ij}. We first sample n independent variables $z_i (1 \le i \le n)$ from univariate standardized normal distributions. The required samples are $\varepsilon_i (1 \le i \le n)$, where

$$\varepsilon_i = \sum_{k=1}^{i} \alpha_{ik} z_k \tag{11.5}$$

and the α_{ik} are parameters chosen to give the correct variances and the correct correlations for the ε_i. For $1 \le j < i$, we must have

$$\sum_{k=1}^{i} \alpha_{ik}^2 = 1$$

and, for all $j < i$,

$$\sum_{k=1}^{j} \alpha_{ik} \alpha_{jk} = \rho_{ij}$$

---

[3] In Excel, the instruction = NORMSINV(RAND()) gives a random sample from a normal distribution.

The first sample, ε_1, is set equal to z_1. These equations can be solved so that ε_2 is calculated from z_1 and z_2, ε_3 is calculated from z_1, z_2, and z_3, and so on. The procedure is known as the *Cholesky decomposition*.

If we find ourselves trying to take the square root of a negative number when using the Cholesky decomposition, the variance-covariance matrix assumed for the variables is not internally consistent. As explained in Section 11.2, this is equivalent to saying that the matrix is not positive-semidefinite.

Factor Models

Sometimes the correlations between normally distributed variables are defined using a factor model. Suppose that U_1, U_2, ..., U_N have standard normal distributions (i.e., normal distributions with mean zero and standard deviation 1). In a one-factor model, each U_i has a component dependent on a common factor, F, and a component that is uncorrelated with the other variables. Formally

$$U_i = a_i F + \sqrt{1 - a_i^2} \, Z_i \tag{11.6}$$

where F and the Z_i have standard normal distributions and a_i is a constant between -1 and $+1$. The Z_i are uncorrelated with each other and uncorrelated with F. In this model, all the correlation between U_i and U_j arises from their dependence on the common factor, F. The coefficient of correlation between U_i and U_j is $a_i a_j$.

A one-factor model imposes some structure on the correlations and has the advantage that the resulting covariance matrix is always positive-semidefinite. Without assuming a factor model, the number of correlations that have to be estimated for the N variables is $N(N-1)/2$. With the one-factor model, we need only estimate N parameters: $a_1, a_2, \ldots, a_N$. An example of a one-factor model from the world of investments is the capital asset pricing model where the return on a stock has a component dependent on the return from the market and an idiosyncratic (nonsystematic) component that is independent of the return on other stocks (see Section 1.3).

The one-factor model can be extended to a two-factor, three-factor, or M-factor model. In the M-factor model

$$U_i = a_{i1} F_1 + a_{i2} F_2 + \ldots + a_{iM} F_M + \sqrt{1 - a_{i1}^2 - a_{i2}^2 - \ldots - a_{iM}^2} \, Z_i \tag{11.7}$$

The factors, $F_1, F_2, \ldots F_M$ have uncorrelated standard normal distributions and the Z_i are uncorrelated both with each other and with the factors. In this case, the correlation between U_i and U_j is

$$\sum_{m=1}^{M} a_{im} a_{jm}$$

11.4 COPULAS

Consider two correlated variables, V_1 and V_2. The *marginal distribution* of V_1 (sometimes also referred to as the unconditional distribution) is its distribution assuming

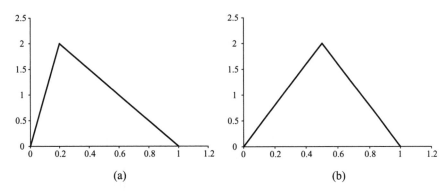

FIGURE 11.2 Triangular Distributions for V_1 and V_2

we know nothing about V_2; similarly, the marginal distribution of V_2 is its distribution assuming we know nothing about V_1. Suppose we have estimated the marginal distributions of V_1 and V_2. How can we make an assumption about the correlation structure between the two variables to define their joint distribution?

If the marginal distributions of V_1 and V_2 are normal, a convenient and easy-to-work-with assumption is that the joint distribution of the variables is bivariate normal.[4] (The correlation structure between the variables is then as described in Section 11.3.) Similar assumptions are possible for some other marginal distributions. But often there is no natural way of defining a correlation structure between two marginal distributions. This is where copulas come in.

As an example of the application of copulas, suppose that variables V_1 and V_2 have the triangular probability density functions shown in Figure 11.2. Both variables have values between 0 and 1. The density function for V_1 peaks at 0.2. The density function for V_2 peaks at 0.5. For both density functions, the maximum height is 2.0. To use what is known as a *Gaussian copula*, we map V_1 and V_2 into new variables U_1 and U_2 that have standard normal distributions. (A standard normal distribution is a normal distribution with mean zero and standard deviation 1.) The mapping is accomplished on a percentile-to-percentile basis. The one-percentile point of the V_1 distribution is mapped to the one-percentile point of the U_1 distribution. The 10-percentile point of the V_1 distribution is mapped to the ten-percentile point of the U_1 distribution, and so on. V_2 is mapped into U_2 in a similar way. Table 11.1 shows how values of V_1 are mapped into values of U_1. Table 11.2 similarly shows how values of V_2 are mapped into values of U_2. Consider the $V_1 = 0.1$ calculation in Table 11.1. The cumulative probability that V_1 is less than 0.1 is (by calculating areas of triangles) $0.5 \times 0.1 \times 1 = 0.05$ or 5%. The value 0.1 for V_1 therefore gets mapped to the five-percentile point of the standard normal distribution. This is -1.64.[5]

The variables U_1 and U_2 have normal distributions. We assume that they are jointly bivariate normal. This in turn implies a joint distribution and a correlation

---

[4] Although the bivariate normal assumption is a convenient one, it is not the only one that can be made. There are many other ways in which two normally distributed variables can be dependent on each other. For example, we could have $V_2 = V_1$ for $-k \le V_1 \le k$ and $V_2 = -V_1$ otherwise. See also Problem 11.11.

[5] It can be calculated using Excel: NORMSINV(0.05) = -1.64.

TABLE 11.1   Mapping of V_1 Which Has the Triangular Distribution in Figure 11.2(a) to U_1 Which Has a Standard Normal Distribution

V_1 Value	Percentile of Distribution	U_1 Value
0.1	5.00	−1.64
0.2	20.00	−0.84
0.3	38.75	−0.29
0.4	55.00	0.13
0.5	68.75	0.49
0.6	80.00	0.84
0.7	88.75	1.21
0.8	95.00	1.64
0.9	98.75	2.24

TABLE 11.2   Mapping of V_2 Which Has the Triangular Distribution in Figure 11.2(b) to U_2 Which Has a Standard Normal Distribution

V_2 Value	Percentile of Distribution	U_2 Value
0.1	2.00	−2.05
0.2	8.00	−1.41
0.3	18.00	−0.92
0.4	32.00	−0.47
0.5	50.00	0.00
0.6	68.00	0.47
0.7	82.00	0.92
0.8	92.00	1.41
0.9	98.00	2.05

structure between V_1 and V_2. The essence of copula is therefore that, instead of defining a correlation structure between V_1 and V_2 directly, we do so indirectly. We map V_1 and V_2 into other variables which have "well-behaved" distributions and for which it is easy to define a correlation structure.

Suppose that we assume the correlation between U_1 and U_2 is 0.5. The joint cumulative probability distribution between V_1 and V_2 is shown in Table 11.3. To illustrate the calculations, consider the first one where we are calculating the probability that $V_1 < 0.1$ and $V_2 < 0.1$. From Tables 11.1 and 11.2, this is the same as the probability that $U_1 < -1.64$ and $U_2 < -2.05$. From the cumulative bivariate normal distribution, this is 0.006 when $\rho = 0.5$.[6] (Note that the probability would be only $0.02 \times 0.05 = 0.001$ if $\rho = 0$.)

---

[6] An Excel function for calculating the cumulative bivariate normal distribution is on the author's website: www.rotman.utoronto.ca/~hull.

TABLE 11.3 Cumulative Joint Probability Distribution for V_1 and V_2 in the Gaussian Copula Model

V_1	V_2								
	0.1	0.2	0.3	0.4	0.5	0.6	0.7	0.8	0.9
0.1	0.006	0.017	0.028	0.037	0.044	0.048	0.049	0.050	0.050
0.2	0.013	0.043	0.081	0.120	0.156	0.181	0.193	0.198	0.200
0.3	0.017	0.061	0.124	0.197	0.273	0.331	0.364	0.381	0.387
0.4	0.019	0.071	0.149	0.248	0.358	0.449	0.505	0.535	0.548
0.5	0.019	0.076	0.164	0.281	0.417	0.537	0.616	0.663	0.683
0.6	0.020	0.078	0.173	0.301	0.456	0.600	0.701	0.763	0.793
0.7	0.020	0.079	0.177	0.312	0.481	0.642	0.760	0.837	0.877
0.8	0.020	0.080	0.179	0.318	0.494	0.667	0.798	0.887	0.936
0.9	0.020	0.080	0.180	0.320	0.499	0.678	0.816	0.913	0.970

(Correlation parameter = 0.5. Table shows the joint probability that V_1 and V_2 are less than the specified values.)

The correlation between U_1 and U_2 is referred to as the *copula correlation*. This is not, in general, the same as the correlation between V_1 and V_2. Because U_1 and U_2 are bivariate normal, the conditional mean of U_2 is linearly dependent on U_1 and the conditional standard deviation of U_2 is constant (as discussed in Section 11.3). However, a similar result does not in general apply to V_1 and V_2.

Expressing the Approach Algebraically

The way in which a Gaussian copula defines a joint distribution is illustrated in Figure 11.3. For a more formal description of the model, suppose that G_1 and G_2 are the cumulative marginal probability distribution of V_1 and V_2. We map $V_1 = v_1$ to $U_1 = u_1$ and $V_2 = v_2$ to $U_2 = u_2$ where

$$G_1(v_1) = N(u_1)$$

and

$$G_2(v_2) = N(u_2)$$

and N is the cumulative normal distribution function. This means that

$$u_1 = N^{-1}[G_1(v_1)] \qquad u_2 = N^{-1}[G_2(v_2)]$$
$$v_1 = G_1^{-1}[N(u_1)] \qquad v_2 = G_2^{-1}[N(u_2)]$$

The variables U_1 and U_2 are then assumed to be bivariate normal. The key property of a copula model is that it preserves the marginal distributions of V_1 and V_2 (however unusual these may be) while defining a correlation structure between them.

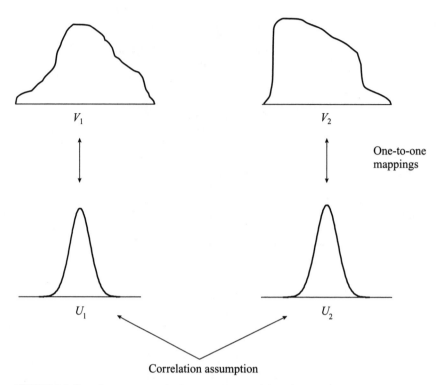

One-to-one
mappings

Correlation assumption

FIGURE 11.3   The Way in Which a Copula Model Defines a Joint Distribution

Other Copulas

The Gaussian copula is just one copula that can be used to define a correlation structure between V_1 and V_2. There are many other copulas leading to many other correlation structures. One that is sometimes used is the *Student t-copula*. This works in the same way as the Gaussian copula except that the variables U_1 and U_2 are assumed to have a bivariate Student t-distribution instead of a bivariate normal distribution. To sample from a bivariate Student t-distribution with f degrees of freedom and correlation ρ, the steps are:

1. Sample from the inverse chi-square distribution to get a value χ. (In Excel, the CHIINV function can be used. The first argument is RAND() and the second is f.)
2. Sample from a bivariate normal distribution with correlation ρ as described in Section 11.3.
3. Multiply the normally distributed samples by $\sqrt{f/\chi}$.

Tail Dependence

Figure 11.4 shows plots of 5,000 random samples from a bivariate normal while Figure 11.5 does the same for the bivariate Student t. The correlation parameter is 0.5 and the number of degrees of freedom for the Student t is 4. Define a "tail value"

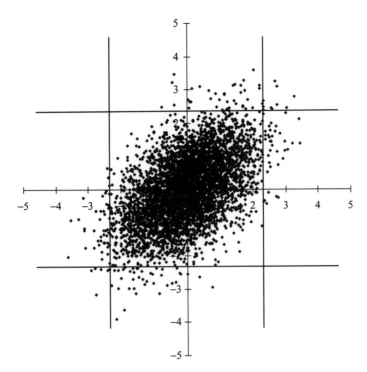

FIGURE 11.4   5,000 Random Samples from a Bivariate Normal Distribution

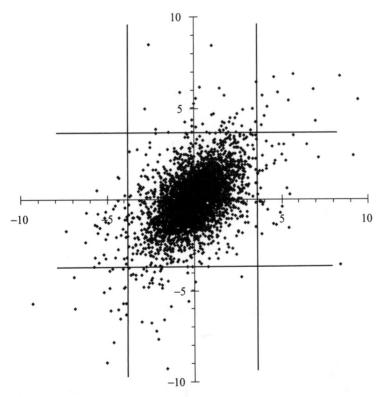

FIGURE 11.5   5,000 Random Samples from a Bivariate Student t-distribution with Four Degrees of Freedom

of a distribution as a value in the left or right 1% tail of the distribution. There is a tail value for the normal distribution when the variable is greater than 2.33 or less than −2.33. Similarly, there is a tail value in the t-distribution when the value of the variable is greater than 3.75 or less than −3.75. Vertical and horizontal lines in the figures indicate when tail values occur. The figures illustrate that it is more common for the two variables to have tail values at the same time in the bivariate Student t distribution than in the bivariate normal distribution. To put this another way, the *tail dependence* is higher in a bivariate Student t-distribution than in a bivariate normal distribution. We made the point earlier that correlations between market variables tend to increase in extreme market conditions, so that Figure 11.1(c) is sometimes a better description of the correlation structure between two variables than Figure 11.1(a). This has led some researchers to argue that the Student t-copula. provides a better description of the joint behavior of market variables than the Gaussian copula.

Multivariate Copulas

Copulas can be used to define a correlation structure between more than two variables. The simplest example of this is the multivariate Gaussian copula. Suppose that there are N variables, $V_1, V_2, \ldots, V_N$ and that we know the marginal distribution of each variable. For each i ($1 \leq i \leq N$), we transform V_i into U_i where U_i has a standard normal distribution. (As described earlier, the transformation is accomplished on a percentile-to-percentile basis.) We then assume that the U_i have a multivariate normal distribution.

A Factor Copula Model

In multivariate copula models, analysts often assume a factor model for the correlation structure between the Us. When there is only one factor, equation (11.6) gives

$$U_i = a_i F + \sqrt{1 - a_i^2} Z_i \tag{11.8}$$

where F and the Z_i have standard normal distributions. The Z_i are uncorrelated with each other and with F. Other factor copula models are obtained by choosing F and the Z_i to have other zero-mean unit-variance distributions. For example, if Z_i is normal and F has a Student t-distribution, we obtain a multivariate Student t-distribution for U_i. These distributional choices affect the nature of the dependence between the U-variables and therefore that between the V-variables.

11.5 APPLICATION TO LOAN PORTFOLIOS: VASICEK'S MODEL

We now present an application of the one-factor Gaussian copula that will prove useful in understanding the Basel II capital requirements, which are discussed in Chapter 12. Suppose a bank has a large portfolio of loans where the probability of default per year for each loan is 1%. If the loans default independently of each other, we would expect the default rate to be almost exactly 1% every year. In

TABLE 11.4 Annual Percentage Default Rate for All Rated Companies, 1970–2010

Year	Default Rate	Year	Default Rate	Year	Default Rate
1970	2.641	1984	0.927	1998	1.255
1971	0.285	1985	0.950	1999	2.214
1972	0.455	1986	1.855	2000	2.622
1973	0.454	1987	1.558	2001	3.978
1974	0.275	1988	1.365	2002	3.059
1975	0.360	1989	2.361	2003	1.844
1976	0.175	1990	3.588	2004	0.855
1977	0.351	1991	3.009	2005	0.674
1978	0.352	1992	1.434	2006	0.654
1979	0.087	1993	0.836	2007	0.367
1980	0.343	1994	0.614	2008	2.028
1981	0.163	1995	0.935	2009	5.422
1982	1.036	1996	0.533	2010	1.283
1983	0.967	1997	0.698		

Source: Moody's.

practice, loans do not default independently of each other. They are all influenced by macroeconomic conditions. As a result, in some years the default rate is high while in others it is low. This is illustrated by Table 11.4 which shows the default rate for all rated companies between 1970 and 2010. The default rate varies from a low of 0.087% in 1979 to a high of 5.422% in 2009. Other high-default-rate years were 1970, 1989, 1990, 1991, 1999, 2000, 2001, 2002, and 2008.

To model the defaults of the loans in a portfolio, we define T_i as the time when company i defaults. (There is an implicit assumption that all companies will default eventually—but the default may happen a long time, perhaps even hundreds of years, in the future.) We make the simplifying assumption that all loans have the same cumulative probability distribution for the time to default. We will denote this distribution by Q.

The Gaussian copula model can be used to define a correlation structure between the T_is. For each i, T_i is mapped to a variable U_i that has a standard normal distribution on a percentile-to-percentile basis. We assume the factor model in equation (11.8) for the correlation structure between the U_is and make the simplifying assumption that the a_is are all the same and equal to a so that:

$$U_i = aF + \sqrt{1 - a^2}\, Z_i$$

As in equation (11.8), the variables F and Z_i have independent standard normal distributions. The copula correlation between each pair of loans is in this case the same. It is

$$\rho = a^2$$

so that the expression for U_i can be written

$$U_i = \sqrt{\rho}\, F + \sqrt{1 - \rho}\, Z_i \qquad (11.9)$$

Suppose we are interested in the probability of default by some time T. (In many applications T will be one year.) This means that we are interested in the probability that $T_i < T$. If $N(U) = Q(T)$ so that

$$U = N^{-1}[Q(T)] \tag{11.10}$$

the value, T, on the probability distribution for a T_i gets mapped to the value, U, on the distribution for the U_i and

$$\text{Prob}(T_i < T) = \text{Prob}(U_i < U)$$

The probability of default by time T depends on the value of the factor, F. The factor can be thought of as an index of macroeconomic conditions. If F is high, macroeconomic conditions are good. Each U_i will then tend to be high so that $\text{Prob}(U_i < U)$ is low and therefore $\text{Prob}(T_i < T)$ is low. If F is low, macroeconomic conditions are bad. Each U_i will then tend to be low so that $\text{Prob}(U_i < U)$ is high and therefore $\text{Prob}(T_i < T)$ is high. To explore this further, we consider the probability of default conditional on F.

From equation (11.9)

$$Z_i = \frac{U_i - \sqrt{\rho}\,F}{\sqrt{1-\rho}}$$

The probability that $U_i < U$ conditional on the factor value, F, is

$$\text{Prob}(U_i < U|F) = \text{Prob}\left(Z_i < \frac{U - \sqrt{\rho}\,F}{\sqrt{1-\rho}}\right) = N\left(\frac{U - \sqrt{\rho}\,F}{\sqrt{1-\rho}}\right)$$

This is also $\text{Prob}(T_i < T|F)$ so that

$$\text{Prob}(T_i < T|F) = N\left(\frac{U - \sqrt{\rho}\,F}{\sqrt{1-\rho}}\right) \tag{11.11}$$

From equation (11.10)

$$U = N^{-1}[Q(T)]$$

The variable, $Q(T)$ is the unconditional probability that a loan will default by time T. We denote this by PD (short for probability of default) so that $U = N^{-1}(\text{PD})$ and equation (11.11) becomes

$$\text{Prob}(T_i < T|F) = N\left(\frac{N^{-1}(\text{PD}) - \sqrt{\rho}\,F}{\sqrt{1-\rho}}\right) \tag{11.12}$$

For a large portfolio of loans with the same PD, where the copula correlation for each pair of loans is ρ, this equation provides a good estimate of the percentage of loans defaulting by time T conditional on F. We will refer to this as the default rate.

As F decreases, the default rate increases. How bad can the default rate become? Because F has a normal distribution, the probability that F will be less than $N^{-1}(Y)$ is Y. There is therefore a probability of Y that the default rate will be greater than

$$N\left(\frac{N^{-1}(\text{PD}) - \sqrt{\rho}\,N^{-1}(Y)}{\sqrt{1-\rho}}\right)$$

Define WCDR(T, X) as the "worst case default rate" for a time horizon T and a confidence level X. This is the default rate that we are X % certain will not be exceeded in time T. It is obtained by substituting $Y = 1 - X$ into the above expression. Because $N^{-1}(X) = -N^{-1}(1 - X)$, we obtain

$$\text{WCDR}(T, X) = N\left(\frac{N^{-1}(\text{PD}) + \sqrt{\rho}\,N^{-1}(X)}{\sqrt{1-\rho}}\right) \tag{11.13}$$

This result was first developed by Vasicek in 1987.[7] The right hand side of the equation can easily be calculated using the NORMSDIST and NORMSINV functions in Excel.

If we have a portfolio of loans where each loan has the same size and the same probability of default, Vasicek's result can be used to calculate the value at risk for a confidence level of X and a time horizon of T as:

$$\text{VaR}(T, X) = L \times \text{LGD} \times \text{WCDR}(T, X)$$

where LGD is the loss given default (defined as the expected loss, as percent of principal, when a loan defaults) and L is the total loan principal.

In an important paper, Gordy shows that this result can be extended.[8] In a large portfolio of M loans where each loan is small in relation to the size of the portfolio, it is approximately true that

$$\text{VaR}(T, X) = \sum_{i=1}^{M} L_i \times \text{LGD}_i \times \text{WCDR}_i(T, X)$$

where L_i is the size of the ith loan, LGD_i is loss given default for the ith loan, and $\text{WCDR}_i(T, X)$ is the worst case default rate for the ith loan (i.e., it is the value of WCDR in equation (11.12) when PD is set equal to the probability of default for the ith loan).

---

[7] See O. Vasicek, "Probability of Loss on a Loan Portfolio" (Working Paper, KMV, 1987). Vasicek's results were published in *Risk* in December 2002 under the title "Loan Portfolio Value."

[8] See M. B. Gordy, "A Risk-Factor Model Foundation for Ratings-Based Bank Capital Ratios," *Journal of Financial Intermediation* 12 (2003): 199–232.

EXAMPLE 11.2

Suppose that a bank has a total of $100 million of retail exposures of varying sizes with each exposure being small in relation to the total exposure. The one-year probability of default for each loan is 2% and the loss given default for each loan is 40%. The copula correlation parameter, ρ, is estimated as 0.1. In this case,

$$\text{WCDR}(1, 0.999) = N\left(\frac{N^{-1}(0.02) + \sqrt{0.1}\,N^{-1}(0.999)}{\sqrt{1 - 0.1}}\right) = 0.128$$

showing that the 99.9% worst case default rate is 12.8%. Losses when this worst case loss rate occurs are $100 \times 0.128 \times 0.4$ or $5.13 million. This is an estimate of the value at risk with a one-year time horizon and a 99.9% confidence level.

Estimating PD and ρ

The maximum likelihood methods explained in Chapter 10 can be used to estimate PD and ρ from historical data on default rates. We used equation (11.13) to calculate a high percentile of the default rate distribution, but it is actually true for all percentiles. If DR is the default rate and G(DR) is the cumulative probability distribution function for DR, equation (11.13) shows that

$$\text{DR} = N\left(\frac{N^{-1}(\text{PD}) + \sqrt{\rho}\,N^{-1}(G(\text{DR}))}{\sqrt{1 - \rho}}\right)$$

Rearranging this equation

$$G(\text{DR}) = N\left(\frac{\sqrt{1 - \rho}\,N^{-1}(\text{DR}) - N^{-1}(\text{PD})}{\sqrt{\rho}}\right) \tag{11.14}$$

Differentiating this, the probability density function for the default rate is

$$g(\text{DR}) = \sqrt{\frac{1 - \rho}{\rho}}\,\exp\left\{\frac{1}{2}\left[(N^{-1}(\text{DR}))^2 - \left(\frac{\sqrt{1 - \rho}\,N^{-1}(\text{DR}) - N^{-1}(\text{PD})}{\sqrt{\rho}}\right)^2\right]\right\}$$

$$\tag{11.15}$$

The procedure for calculating maximum likelihood estimates for PD and ρ from historical data is as follows:

1. Choose trial values for PD and ρ.
2. Calculate the logarithm of the probability density in equation (11.15) for each of the observations on DR.
3. Use Solver to search for the values of PD and ρ that maximize the sum of the values in 2.

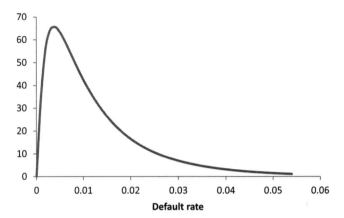

FIGURE 11.6 Probability Distribution of Default Rate When Parameters Are Estimated Using the Data in Table 11.4

One application of this is to the data in Table 11.4. The maximum likelihood estimates for ρ and PD are 0.110 and 1.34%, respectively. (See worksheet on the author's website for the calculations.) The probability distribution for the default rate is shown in Figure 11.6. The 99.9% worst case default rate is

$$N\left(\frac{N^{-1}(0.0134) + \sqrt{0.110}\,N^{-1}(0.999)}{\sqrt{1 - 0.110}}\right) = 0.104$$

or 10.4%.

Alternatives to the Gaussian Copula

The one-factor Gaussian copula model has its limitations. As Figure 11.4 illustrates, it leads to very little tail dependence. This means that an unusually early default for one company does not often happen at the same time as an unusually early default time for another company. It can be difficult to find a ρ to fit data. For example, there is no ρ that is consistent with a PD of 1% and the situation where one year in ten the default rate is greater than 3%. Other one-factor copula models with more tail dependence can provide a better fit to data. One approach to developing other one-factor copulas is to choose F or Z_i, or both, as distributions with heavier tails than the normal distribution in equation (11.9). (They have to be scaled so that they have a mean of zero and standard deviation of one.) The distribution of U_i is then determined (possibly numerically) from the distributions of F and Z_i. Equation (18.1) becomes

$$\text{WCDR}(T, X) = \Phi\left(\frac{\Psi^{-1}(\text{PD}) + \sqrt{\rho}\,\Theta^{-1}(X)}{\sqrt{1 - \rho}}\right)$$

where Φ, Θ, and Ψ are the cumulative probability distributions of Z_i, F, and U_i and equation (11.14) becomes[9]

$$G(\mathrm{DR}) = \Theta\left(\frac{\sqrt{1-\rho}\,\Phi^{-1}(\mathrm{DR}) - \Psi^{-1}(\mathrm{PD})}{\sqrt{\rho}}\right)$$

SUMMARY

Risk managers use correlations or covariances to describe the relationship between two variables. The daily covariance rate is the correlation between the daily returns on the variables multiplied by the product of their daily volatilities. The methods for monitoring a covariance rate are similar to those described in Chapter 10 for monitoring a variance rate. Risk managers often try to keep track of a variance–covariance matrix for all the variables to which they are exposed.

The marginal distribution of a variable is the unconditional distribution of the variable. Very often an analyst is in a situation where he or she has estimated the marginal distributions of a set of variables and wants to make an assumption about their correlation structure. If the marginal distributions of the variables happen to be normal, it is natural to assume that the variables have a multivariate normal distribution. In other situations, copulas are used. The marginal distributions are transformed on a percentile-to-percentile basis to normal distributions (or to some other distribution for which there is a multivariate counterpart). The correlation structure between the variables of interest is then defined indirectly from an assumed correlation structure between the transformed variables.

When there are many variables, analysts often use a factor model. This is a way of reducing the number of correlation estimates that have to be made. The correlation between any two variables is assumed to derive solely from their correlations with the factors. The default correlation between different companies can be modeled using a factor-based Gaussian copula model of their times to default.

An important application of copulas for risk managers is to the calculation of value at risk for loan portfolios. Analysts often assume that a one-factor copula model relates the probability distributions of the times to default for different loans. The percentiles of the distribution of the number of defaults on a large portfolio can then be calculated from the percentiles of the probability distribution of the factor. As we will see in the next chapter, this is the approach used in determining credit risk capital requirements for banks under Basel II.

---

[9] This approach is applied to evaluating the risk of tranches created from mortgages in J. Hull and A. White, "The Risk of Tranches Created from Mortgages," *Financial Analysts Journal* 66, no. 5 (September/October 2010): 54–67. It provides a better fit to historical data in many situations. Its main disadvantage is that the distributions used are not as easy to deal with as the normal distribution and numerical analysis may be necessary to determine Ψ and $g(\mathrm{DR})$.

FURTHER READING

Cherubini, U., E. Luciano, and W. Vecchiato. *Copula Methods in Finance.* Hoboken, NJ: John Wiley & Sons, 2004.

Demarta, S., and A. J. McNeil. "The *t*-Copula and Related Copulas." Working paper, Department of Mathematics, ETH Zentrum, Zurich, Switzerland.

Engle, R. F., and J. Mezrich. "GARCH for Groups," *Risk* (August 1996): 36–40.

Gordy, M. B. "A Risk-Factor Model Foundation for Ratings-Based Bank Capital Ratios," *Journal of Financial Intermediation* 12 (2003): 199–232.

Vasicek, O. "Probability of Loss on a Loan Portfolio." Working Paper, KMV, 1987. (Published in *Risk* in December 2002 under the title "Loan Portfolio Value.")

PRACTICE QUESTIONS AND PROBLEMS
(ANSWERS AT END OF BOOK)

11.1 If you know the correlation between two variables, what extra information do you need to calculate the covariance?

11.2 What is the difference between correlation and dependence? Suppose that $y = x^2$ and x is normally distributed with mean zero and standard deviation one. What is the correlation between x and y?

11.3 What is a factor model? Why are factor models useful when defining a correlation structure between large numbers of variables?

11.4 What is meant by a positive-semidefinite matrix? What are the implications of a correlation matrix not being positive-semidefinite?

11.5 Suppose that the current daily volatilities of asset A and asset B are 1.6% and 2.5%, respectively. The prices of the assets at close of trading yesterday were $20 and $40 and the estimate of the coefficient of correlation between the returns on the two assets made at that time was 0.25. The parameter λ used in the EWMA model is 0.95.

(a) Calculate the current estimate of the covariance between the assets.

(b) On the assumption that the prices of the assets at close of trading today are $20.50 and $40.50, update the correlation estimate.

11.6 Suppose that the current daily volatilities of asset X and asset Y are 1.0% and 1.2%, respectively. The prices of the assets at close of trading yesterday were $30 and $50 and the estimate of the coefficient of correlation between the returns on the two assets made at this time was 0.50. Correlations and volatilities are updated using a GARCH(1,1) model. The estimates of the model's parameters are $\alpha = 0.04$ and $\beta = 0.94$. For the correlation $\omega = 0.000001$ and for the volatilities $\omega = 0.000003$. If the prices of the two assets at close of trading today are $31 and $51, how is the correlation estimate updated?

11.7 Suppose that in Problem 10.15 the correlation between the S&P 500 index (measured in dollars) and the FTSE 100 index (measured in sterling) is 0.7, the correlation between the S&P 500 index (measured in dollars) and the dollar-sterling exchange rate is 0.3, and the daily volatility of the S&P 500 Index is 1.6%. What is the correlation between the S&P 500 index (measured in dollars) and the FTSE 100 index when it is translated to dollars? (*Hint:* For three variables X, Y, and Z, the covariance between $X + Y$ and Z equals the covariance between X and Z plus the covariance between Y and Z.)

11.8 Suppose that two variables V_1 and V_2 have uniform distributions where all values between 0 and 1 are equally likely. Use a Gaussian copula to define the correlation structure between V_1 and V_2 with a copula correlation of 0.3. Produce a table similar to Table 11.3 considering values of 0.25, 0.50, and 0.75 for V_1 and V_2. A spreadsheet for calculating the cumulative bivariate normal distribution is on the author's website: www.rotman.utoronto.ca/~hull.

11.9 Assume that you have independent random samples z_1, z_2, and z_3 from a standard normal distribution and want to convert them to samples ε_1, ε_2, and ε_3 from a trivariate normal distribution using the Cholesky decomposition. Derive three formulas expressing ε_1, ε_2, and ε_3 in terms of z_1, z_2, and z_3 and the three correlations that are needed to define the trivariate normal distribution.

11.10 Explain what is meant by tail dependence. How can you vary tail dependence by the choice of copula?

11.11 Suppose that the marginal distributions of V_1 and V_2 are standard normal distributions but that a Student t-copula with four degrees of freedom and a correlation parameter of 0.5 is used to define the correlation between the variables. How would you obtain samples from the joint distribution?

11.12 In Table 11.3, what is the probability density function of V_2 conditional on $V_1 < 0.1$? Compare it with the unconditional distribution of V_2.

11.13 What is the median of the distribution of V_2 when V_1 equals 0.2 in the example in Tables 11.1 and 11.2?

11.14 Suppose that a bank has made a large number of loans of a certain type. The total amount lent is $500 million. The one-year probability of default on each loan is 1.5% and the recovery rate is 30%. The bank uses a Gaussian copula for time to default. The copula correlation parameter is 0.2. Estimate the value at risk for the portfolio with a one-year time horizon and a confidence level of 99.5%.

11.15 Suppose that the default rate for a portfolio of consumer loans over the last 10 years has been 1%, 9%, 2%, 3%, 5%, 1%, 6%, 7%, 4%, and 1%. What are the maximum likelihood estimates of the parameters in Vasicek's model?

FURTHER QUESTIONS

11.16 Suppose that the price of Asset X at close of trading yesterday was $300 and its volatility was estimated as 1.3% per day. The price of X at the close of trading today is $298. Suppose further that the price of Asset Y at the close of trading yesterday was $8, its volatility was estimated as 1.5% per day, and its correlation with X was estimated as 0.8. The price of Y at the close of trading today is unchanged at $8. Update the volatility of X and Y and the correlation between X and Y using

(a) The EWMA model with $\lambda = 0.94$

(b) The GARCH(1,1) model with $\omega = 0.000002$, $\alpha = 0.04$, and $\beta = 0.94$. In practice, is the ω parameter likely to be the same for X and Y?

11.17 The probability density function for an exponential distribution is $\lambda e^{-\lambda x}$ where x is the value of the variable and λ is a parameter. The cumulative probability distribution is $1 - e^{-\lambda x}$. Suppose that two variables V_1 and V_2 have exponential distributions with λ parameters of 1.0 and 2.0, respectively. Use a Gaussian copula to define the correlation structure between V_1 and V_2 with a copula correlation of –0.2. Produce a table similar to Table 11.3 using values of 0.25, 0.5, 0.75, 1, 1.25, and 1.5 for V_1 and V_2. A spreadsheet for calculating the cumulative bivariate normal distribution is on the author's website: www.rotman.utoronto.ca/~hull.

11.18 Create an Excel spreadsheet to produce a chart similar to Figure 11.5 showing samples from a bivariate Student t-distribution with four degrees of freedom where the correlation is 0.5. Next suppose that the marginal distributions of V_1 and V_2 are Student t with four degrees of freedom but that a Gaussian copula with a copula correlation parameter of 0.5 is used to define the correlation between the two variables. Construct a chart showing samples from the joint distribution. Compare the two charts you have produced.

11.19 Suppose that a bank has made a large number loans of a certain type. The one-year probability of default on each loan is 1.2%. The bank uses a Gaussian copula for time to default. It is interested in estimating a "99.97% worst case" for the percent of loans that default on the portfolio. Show how this varies with the copula correlation.

11.20 The default rates in the last 15 years for a certain category of loans is 2%, 4%, 7%, 12%, 6%, 5%, 8%, 14%, 10%, 2%, 3%, 2%, 6%, 7%, 9%. Use the maximum likelihood method to calculate the best fit values of the parameters in Vasicek's model. What is the probability distribution of the default rate? What is the 99.9% worst-case default rate?

CHAPTER 12

Basel I, Basel II, and Solvency II

An agreement in 1988, known as the Basel Accord, marked the start of international standards for bank regulation. Since 1988, bank regulation has been an evolutionary process. New regulations have modified previous regulations, but the approaches used in previous regulations have usually been preserved. In order to understand the current regulatory environment, it is therefore necessary to understand historical developments. This chapter explains the evolution of the regulatory environment prior to the 2007 credit crisis. Chapter 13 will cover developments since the crisis.

This chapter starts by reviewing the evolution of bank regulation between the 1980s and 2000. It explains the 1988 Basel Accord (now known as Basel I), netting provisions, and the 1996 Amendment. It then moves on to discuss Basel II, which is a major overhaul of the regulations and was implemented by many banks throughout the world in about 2007. Finally, it reviews Solvency II, a new regulatory framework for insurance companies, which is broadly similar to Basel II and is expected to be implemented by the European Union in 2013.

12.1 THE REASONS FOR REGULATING BANKS

The purpose of bank regulation is to ensure that a bank keeps enough capital for the risks it takes. It is not possible to eliminate altogether the possibility of a bank failing, but governments want to make the probability of default for any given bank very small. By doing this, they hope to create a stable economic environment where private individuals and businesses have confidence in the banking system.

It is tempting to argue: "Bank regulation is unnecessary. Even if there were no regulations, banks would manage their risks prudently and would strive to keep a level of capital that is commensurate with the risks they are taking." Unfortunately, history does not support this view. There is little doubt that regulation has played an important role in increasing bank capital and making banks more aware of the risks they are taking.

As discussed in Section 2.3, governments provide deposit insurance programs to protect depositors. Without deposit insurance, banks that took excessive risks relative to their capital base would find it difficult to attract deposits. However, the impact of deposit insurance is to create an environment where depositors are less discriminating. A bank can take large risks without losing its deposit base.[1] The

---

[1] As mentioned in Chapter 3, this is an example of what insurance companies term moral hazard. The existence of an insurance contract changes the behavior of the insured party.

BUSINESS SNAPSHOT 12.1

Systemic Risk

Systemic risk is the risk that a default by one financial institution will create a "ripple effect" that leads to defaults by other financial institutions and threatens the stability of the financial system. There are huge numbers of over-the-counter transactions between banks. If Bank A fails, Bank B may take a huge loss on the transactions it has with Bank A. This in turn could lead to Bank B failing. Bank C that has many outstanding transactions with both Bank A and Bank B might then take a large loss and experience severe financial difficulties; and so on.

The financial system has survived defaults such as Drexel in 1990, Barings in 1995, and Lehman Brothers in 2008 very well, but regulators continue to be concerned. During the market turmoil of 2007 and 2008, many large financial institutions were bailed out, rather than being allowed to fail, because governments were concerned about systemic risk.

last thing a government wants is to create a deposit insurance program that results in banks taking more risks. It is therefore essential that deposit insurance be accompanied by regulation concerned with capital requirements.

A major concern of governments is what is known as *systemic risk*. This is the risk that a failure by a large bank will lead to failures by other large banks and a collapse of the financial system. The way this can happen is described in Business Snapshot 12.1. When a bank or other large financial institution does get into financial difficulties, governments have a difficult decision to make. If they allow the financial institution to fail, they are putting the financial system at risk. If they bail out the financial institution, they are sending the wrong signals to the market. There is a danger that large financial institutions will be less vigilant in controlling risks because they know that they are "too big to fail" and the government will always bail them out.

During the market turmoil of 2007 and 2008, the decision was taken to bail out many large financial institutions in the United States and Europe. However, Lehman Brothers was allowed to fail in September, 2008. Possibly, the United States government wanted to make it clear to the market that bailouts for large financial institutions were not automatic. However, the decision to let Lehman Brothers fail has been criticized because arguably it made the credit crisis worse.

12.2 BANK REGULATION PRE-1988

Prior to 1988, bank regulators within a country tended to regulate bank capital by setting minimum levels for the ratio of capital to total assets. However, definitions of capital and the ratios considered acceptable varied from country to country. Some countries enforced their regulations more diligently than other countries. Increasingly, banks were competing globally and a bank operating in a country where capital regulations were slack was considered to have a competitive edge over one operating in a country with tighter more strictly enforced capital regulations. In addition, the huge exposures created by loans from the major international banks to less developed countries such as Mexico, Brazil, and Argentina, as well as the accounting games sometimes used for those exposures (see Business Snapshot 2.3) were starting to raise questions about the adequacy of capital levels.

Another problem was that the types of transaction entered into by banks were becoming more complicated. The over-the-counter derivatives market for products such as interest rate swaps, currency swaps, and foreign exchange options was growing fast. These contracts increase the credit risks being taken by a bank. Consider, for example, an interest rate swap. If the counterparty in the interest rate swap transaction defaults when the swap has a positive value to the bank and a negative value to the counterparty, the bank is liable to lose money. Many of these newer transactions were "off-balance-sheet." This means that they had no effect on the level of assets reported by a bank. As a result, they had no effect on the amount of capital the bank was required to keep. It became apparent to regulators that the value of total assets was no longer a good indicator of the total risks being taken. A more sophisticated approach than that of setting minimum levels for the ratio of capital to total balance-sheet assets was needed.

The Basel Committee was formed in 1974. The committee consisted of representatives from Belgium, Canada, France, Germany, Italy, Japan, Luxembourg, the Netherlands, Sweden, Switzerland, the United Kingdom, and the United States. It met regularly in Basel, Switzerland, under the patronage of the Bank for International Settlements. The first major result of these meetings was a document entitled "International Convergence of Capital Measurement and Capital Standards." This was referred to as "The 1988 BIS Accord" or just "The Accord." More recently, it has come to be known as Basel I.

12.3 THE 1988 BIS ACCORD

The 1988 BIS Accord was the first attempt to set international risk-based standards for capital adequacy. It has been subject to much criticism as being too simple and somewhat arbitrary. In fact, the Accord was a huge achievement. It was signed by all 12 members of the Basel Committee and paved the way for significant increases in the resources banks devote to measuring, understanding, and managing risks.

The 1988 BIS Accord defined two requirements that bank capital had to satisfy. The first was that the ratio of a bank's assets to its capital had to be less than 20. (This requirement was similar to that existing prior to 1988 in many countries.) The second requirement involved what is known as the Cooke ratio.[2] For most banks there was no problem in satisfying the capital multiple requirement. The Cooke ratio was the key regulatory requirement.

---

[2] The ratio is named after Peter Cooke from the Bank of England.

TABLE 12.1   Risk Weights for On-Balance-Sheet Items

Risk Weight (%)	Asset Category
0	Cash, gold bullion, claims on OECD governments such as Treasury bonds or insured residential mortgages
20	Claims on OECD banks and OECD public sector entities such as securities issued by U.S. government agencies or claims on municipalities
50	Uninsured residential mortgage loans
100	All other claims such as corporate bonds and less-developed country debt, claims on non-OECD banks

The Cooke Ratio

In calculating the Cooke ratio, both on-balance-sheet and off-balance-sheet items are considered. They are used to calculate what is known as the bank's total *risk-weighted assets* (also sometimes referred to as the *risk-weighted amount*). This is a measure of the bank's total credit exposure.

Consider first on-balance-sheet items. Each on-balance-sheet item is assigned a risk weight reflecting its credit risk. A sample of the risk weights specified in the Accord is shown in Table 12.1. Cash and securities issued by governments of OECD countries (members of the Organisation of Economic Co-operation and Development) are considered to have virtually zero risk and have a risk weight of zero. Loans to corporations have a risk weight of 100%. Loans to banks and government agencies in OECD countries have a risk weight of 20%. Uninsured residential mortgages have a risk weight of 50%. The total risk-weighted assets for N on-balance-sheet items equals

$$\sum_{i=1}^{N} w_i L_i$$

where L_i is the principal amount of the ith item and w_i is its risk weight.

EXAMPLE 12.1

The assets of a bank consist of $100 million of corporate loans, $10 million of OECD government bonds, and $50 million of residential mortgages. The total risk-weighted assets is

$$1.0 \times 100 + 0.0 \times 10 + 0.5 \times 50 = 125$$

or $125 million.

Off-balance-sheet items are expressed as a *credit equivalent amount*. Loosely speaking, the credit equivalent amount is the loan principal that is considered to have the same credit risk. For nonderivatives, the credit equivalent amount is calculated

TABLE 12.2   Add-On Factors as a Percent of Principal for Derivatives

Remaining Maturity (yr)	Interest Rate	Exchange Rate and Gold	Equity	Precious Metals Except Gold	Other Commodities
< 1	0.0	1.0	6.0	7.0	10.0
1 to 5	0.5	5.0	8.0	7.0	12.0
> 5	1.5	7.5	10.0	8.0	15.0

by applying a conversion factor to the principal amount of the instrument. Instruments that from a credit perspective are considered to be similar to loans, such as bankers' acceptances, have a conversion factor of 100%. Others, such as note issuance facilities (where a bank agrees that a company can issue short-term paper on pre-agreed terms in the future), have lower conversion factors.

For an over-the-counter derivative such as an interest rate swap or a forward contract the credit equivalent amount is calculated as

$$\max(V, 0) + aL \tag{12.1}$$

where V is the current value of the derivative to the bank, a is an *add-on factor*, and L is the principal amount. The first term in equation (12.1) is the current exposure. If the counterparty defaults today and V is positive, the contract is an asset to the bank and the bank is liable to lose V. If the counterparty defaults today and V is negative, the contract is an asset to the counterparty and there will be neither a gain nor a loss to the bank. The bank's exposure is therefore $\max(V, 0)$. The add-on amount, aL, is an allowance for the possibility of the exposure increasing in the future. Examples of the add-on factor, a, are shown in Table 12.2.

EXAMPLE 12.2

A bank has entered into a $100 million interest rate swap with a remaining life of four years. The current value of the swap is $2.0 million. In this case, the add-on amount is 0.5% of the principal so that the credit equivalent amount is $2.0 million plus $0.5 million or $2.5 million.

The credit equivalent amount for an off-balance-sheet item is multiplied by the risk weight for the counterparty in order to calculate the risk-weighted assets. The risk weights for off-balance-sheet items are similar to those in Table 12.1 except that the risk weight for a corporation is 0.5 rather than 1.0 when off-balance-sheet items are considered.

EXAMPLE 12.3

Consider again the bank in Example 12.2. If the interest rate swap is with a corporation, the risk-weighted assets are 2.5 × 0.5 or $1.25 million. If it is with an OECD bank, the risk-weighted assets are 2.5 × 0.2 or $0.5 million.

Putting all this together, the total risk-weighted assets for a bank with N on-balance-sheet items and M off-balance-sheet items is

$$\sum_{i=1}^{N} w_i L_i + \sum_{j=1}^{M} w_j^* C_j \qquad (12.2)$$

Here, L_i is the principal of the ith on-balance-sheet item and w_i is the risk weight of the counterparty; C_j is the credit equivalent amount for the jth off-balance-sheet item and w_j^* is the risk weight of the counterparty for the jth off-balance-sheet item.

Capital Requirement

The Accord required banks to keep capital equal to at least 8% of the risk-weighted assets. The capital had two components:

1. *Tier 1 Capital.* This consists of items such as equity and non-cumulative perpetual preferred stock[3]. (Goodwill is subtracted from equity.)
2. *Tier 2 Capital.* This is sometimes referred to as *supplementary capital.* It includes instruments such as cumulative perpetual preferred stock,[4] certain types of 99-year debenture issues, and subordinated debt (i.e., debt subordinated to depositors) with an original life of more than five years.

Equity capital is important because it absorbs losses. Other types of capital are important because they are subordinate to depositors and therefore provide a cushion that protects depositors in the event of a failure by the bank.

The Accord required at least 50% of the required capital (that is, 4% of the risk-weighted assets) to be in Tier 1. Furthermore, the Accord required 2% of risk-weighted assets to be common equity. (The Basel committee has updated its definition of instruments that are eligible for Tier 1 capital and its definition of common equity in Basel III.)

The bank supervisors in some countries require banks to hold more capital than the minimum specified by the Basel Committee and some banks themselves have a target for the capital they will hold that is higher than that specified by their bank supervisors.

12.4 THE G-30 POLICY RECOMMENDATIONS

In 1993, a working group consisting of end-users, dealers, academics, accountants, and lawyers involved in derivatives published a report that contained 20 risk

---

[3] Noncumulative perpetual preferred stock is preferred stock lasting forever where there is a predetermined dividend rate. Unpaid dividends do not cumulate (that is, the dividends for one year are not carried forward to the next year).
[4] In cumulative preferred stock, unpaid dividends cumulate. Any backlog of dividends must be paid before dividends are paid on the common stock.

management recommendations for dealers and end-users of derivatives and four recommendations for legislators, regulators, and supervisors. The report was based on a detailed survey of 80 dealers and 72 end users worldwide. The survey involved both questionnaires and in-depth interviews. The report is not a regulatory document, but it has been influential in the development of risk management practices.

A brief summary of the important recommendations is as follows:

1. A company's policies on risk management should be clearly defined and approved by senior management, ideally at the board of directors level. Managers at all levels should enforce the policies.
2. Derivatives positions should be marked to market at least once a day.
3. Derivatives dealers should measure market risk using a consistent measure such as value at risk. Limits to the market risks that are taken should be set.
4. Derivatives dealers should carry out stress tests to determine potential losses under extreme market conditions.
5. The risk management function should be set up so that it is independent of the trading operation.
6. Credit exposures arising from derivatives trading should be assessed based on the current replacement value of existing positions and potential future replacement costs.
7. Credit exposures to a counterparty should be aggregated in a way that reflects enforceable netting agreements. (We talk about netting in the next section.)
8. The individuals responsible for setting credit limits should be independent of those involved in trading.
9. Dealers and end-users should assess carefully both the costs and benefits of credit risk mitigation techniques such as collateralization and downgrade triggers. In particular, they should assess their own capacity and that of their counterparties to meet the cash flow requirement of downgrade triggers. (Credit mitigation techniques are discussed in Chapter 17.)
10. Only individuals with the appropriate skills and experience should be allowed to have responsibility for trading derivatives, supervising the trading, carrying out back office functions in relation to the trading, and so on.
11. There should be adequate systems in place for data capture, processing, settlement, and management reporting.
12. Dealers and end-users should account for the derivatives transactions used to manage risks so as to achieve a consistency of income recognition treatment between those instruments and the risks being managed.

12.5 NETTING

Participants in the over-the-counter derivatives market have traditionally signed an International Swaps and Derivatives Association (ISDA) master agreement covering their derivatives trades. The word *netting* refers to a clause in the master agreement which states that in the event of a default all transactions are considered as a single transaction. Effectively, this means that, if a company defaults on one transaction that is covered by the master agreement, it must default on all transactions covered by the master agreement.

Netting and ISDA master agreements will be discussed in Chapter 17. At this stage, we note that netting can have the effect of substantially reducing credit risk. Consider a bank that has three swap transactions outstanding with a particular counterparty. The transactions are worth +$24 million, −$17 million, and +$8 million to the bank. Suppose that the counterparty experiences financial difficulties and defaults on its outstanding obligations. To the counterparty the three transactions have values of −$24 million, +$17 million, and −$8 million, respectively. Without netting, the counterparty would default on the first transaction, keep the second transaction, and default on the third transaction. Assuming no recovery, the loss to the bank would be $32 (= 24 + 8) million. With netting, the counterparty is required to default on the second transaction as well. The loss to the bank is then $15 (= 24 − 17 + 8) million.

More generally, suppose that a financial institution has a portfolio of N derivatives outstanding with a particular counterparty and that the current value of the ith derivative is V_i. Without netting, the financial institution's exposure in the event of a default today is

$$\sum_{i=1}^{N} \max(V_i, 0)$$

With netting, it is

$$\max\left(\sum_{i=1}^{N} V_i, 0\right)$$

Without netting, the exposure is the payoff from a portfolio of options. With netting, the exposure is the payoff from an option on a portfolio.

The 1988 Basel Accord did not take netting into account in setting capital requirements. From equation (12.1) the credit equivalent amount for a portfolio of derivatives with a counterparty under the Accord was

$$\sum_{i=1}^{N} [\max(V_i, 0) + a_i L_i]$$

where a_i is the add-on factor for the ith transaction and L_i is the principal for the ith transaction.

By 1995, netting had been successfully tested in the courts in many jurisdictions. As a result, the 1988 Accord was modified to allow banks to reduce their credit equivalent totals when enforceable bilateral netting agreements were in place. The first step was to calculate the net replacement ratio, NRR. This is the ratio of the current exposure with netting to the current exposure without netting:

$$\mathrm{NRR} = \frac{\max(\sum_{i=1}^{N} V_i, 0)}{\sum_{i=1}^{N} \max(V_i, 0)}$$

TABLE 12.3   Portfolio of Derivatives with a Particular Counterparty

Transaction	Principal, L_i	Current Value, V_i	Table 12.2 Add-On Amount, $a_i L_i$
3-year interest rate swap	1,000	−60	5
6-year foreign exchange forward	1,000	70	75
9-month option on a stock	500	55	30

The credit equivalent amount was modified to

$$\max\left(\sum_{i=1}^{N} V_i, 0\right) + (0.4 + 0.6 \times \text{NRR})\sum_{i=1}^{N} a_i L_i$$

EXAMPLE 12.4

Consider the example in Table 12.3, which shows a portfolio of three derivatives that a bank has with a particular counterparty. The third column shows the current mark-to-market values of the transactions and the fourth column shows the add-on amount calculated from Table 12.2. The current exposure with netting is $-60 + 70 + 55 = 65$. The current exposure without netting is $0 + 70 + 55 = 125$. The net replacement ratio is given by

$$\text{NRR} = \frac{65}{125} = 0.52$$

The total of the add-on amounts, $\sum a_i L_i$, is $5 + 75 + 30 = 110$. The credit equivalent amount when netting agreements are in place is $65 + (0.4 + 0.6 \times 0.52) \times 110 = 143.32$. Without netting, agreements of the credit equivalent amount are $125 + 110 = 235$. Suppose that the counterparty is an OECD bank so that the risk weight is 0.2. This means that the risk-weighted assets with netting is $0.2 \times 143.32 = 28.66$. Without netting, it is $0.2 \times 235 = 47$.

12.6   THE 1996 AMENDMENT

In 1995, the Basel Committee issued a consultative proposal to amend the 1988 Accord. This became known as the "1996 Amendment." It was implemented in 1998 and was then sometimes referred to as "BIS 98." The amendment involves keeping capital for the market risks associated with trading activities.

Marking to market is the practice of revaluing assets and liabilities daily. It is also known as *fair value accounting*. Banks are required to use fair value accounting for all assets and liabilities that are held for trading purposes. This includes most derivatives, marketable equity securities, foreign currencies, and commodities. These items constitute what is referred to as the bank's *trading book*. Banks are not required to use fair value accounting for assets that are expected to be held for the whole of their life for investment purposes. These assets, which include loans and some debt securities, constitute what is referred to as the *banking book*. Unless there is reason to believe that repayment of the principal will not be made, they are held at historical cost. (See Section 2.7.)

Under the 1996 Amendment, the credit risk capital charge in the 1988 Accord continued to apply to all on-balance-sheet and off-balance-sheet items in the trading and banking book, except positions in the trading book that consisted of (a) debt and equity traded securities and (b) positions in commodities and foreign exchange. The Amendment introduced a capital charge for the market risk associated with all items in the trading book.[5]

The 1996 Amendment outlined a standardized approach for measuring the capital charge for market risk. The standardized approach assigned capital separately to each of debt securities, equity securities, foreign exchange risk, commodities risk, and options. No account was taken of correlations between different types of instrument. The more sophisticated banks with well-established risk management functions were allowed to use an "internal model-based approach" for setting market risk capital. This involved calculating a value-at-risk measure and converting it into a capital requirement using a formula specified in the 1996 Amendment. Most large banks preferred to use the internal model-based approach because it better reflected the benefits of diversification and led to lower capital requirements.

The value-at-risk measure used in the internal model-based approach is calculated with a 10-day time horizon and a 99% confidence level. It is the loss that has a 1% chance of being exceeded over a 10-day period. The capital requirement is

$$\max(\text{VaR}_{t-1}, m_c \times \text{VaR}_{\text{avg}}) + \text{SRC} \tag{12.3}$$

where m_c is a multiplicative factor, and SRC is a specific risk charge. The variable VaR_{t-1} is the previous day's value at risk and VaR_{avg} is the average value at risk over the last 60 days. The minimum value for m_c is 3. Higher values may be chosen by regulators for a particular bank if tests reveal inadequacies in the bank's value-at-risk model, as will be explained shortly.

The VaR calculation typically reflects movements in broad market variables such as interest rates, exchange rates, stock indices, and commodity prices. It does not include risks related to specific companies such as those concerned with movements in a company's stock price or changes in a company's credit spread. These are captured by the specific risk charge, SRC. One security that gives rise to an SRC is a corporate bond. There are two components to the risk of this security: interest rate risk and credit risk of the corporation issuing the bond. The interest rate risk is captured by VaR; the credit risk is captured by the SRC.[6] The 1996 Amendment proposed standardized methods for assessing a specific risk capital charge, but allowed banks to use internal models for arriving at a capital charge for specific risk.

---

[5] Certain nontrading book positions that are used to hedge positions in the trading book can be included in the calculation of the market risk capital charge.

[6] As mentioned earlier, the 1988 credit risk capital charge did not apply to debt securities in the trading book under the 1996 Amendment.

The internal model for SRC must involve calculating a 10-day 99% value at risk for specific risks. Regulators calculate capital by applying a multiplicative factor (similar to m_c) to the value at risk. This multiplicative factor must be at least 4 and the resultant capital must be at least 50% of the capital given by the standardized approach.

The total capital a bank was required to keep after the implementation of the 1996 Amendment was the sum of (a) credit risk capital equal to 8% of the risk-weighted assets (RWA) and (b) market risk capital as explained in this section. For convenience, a RWA for market risk capital was defined as 12.5 multiplied by the amount given in equation (12.3). This means that the total capital required for credit and market risk is given by

$$\text{Total Capital} = 0.08 \times (\text{credit risk RWA} + \text{market risk RWA}) \qquad (12.4)$$

A bank had more flexibility in the type of capital it used for market risk. It could use Tier 1 or Tier 2 capital. It could also use what is termed Tier 3 capital. This consists of short term subordinated debt with an original maturity of at least two years that is unsecured and fully paid up. (Tier 3 capital was eliminated under Basel III.)

One-Day vs. Ten-Day VaR

Banks almost invariably calculate a one-day 99% VaR in the first instance. Regulators explicitly state that the 10-day 99% VaR can be calculated as $\sqrt{10}$ times the one-day 99% VaR. This means that, when the capital requirement for a bank is calculated as m_c times the average 10-day 99% VaR, it is to all intents and purposes $m_c \times \sqrt{10} = 3.16 m_c$ times the average one-day 99% VaR.

Back-testing

The BIS Amendment requires the one-day 99% VaR that a bank calculates to be back-tested over the previous 250 days. As described in Section 9.10, this involves using the bank's current procedure for estimating VaR for each of the most recent 250 days. If the actual loss that occurred on a day is greater than the VaR level calculated for the day, an "exception" is recorded. Calculations are typically carried out (a) including changes that were made to the portfolio on the day being considered and (b) assuming that no changes were made to the portfolio on the day being considered. (Regulators pay most attention to the first set of calculations.)

If the number of exceptions during the previous 250 days is less than 5, m_c is normally set equal to 3. If the number of exceptions is 5, 6, 7, 8, and 9, the value of the m_c is set equal to 3.4, 3.5, 3.65, 3.75, and 3.85, respectively. The bank supervisor has some discretion as to whether the higher multipliers are used. They will normally be applied when the reason for the exceptions is identified as a deficiency in the VaR model being used. If changes in the bank's positions during the day result in exceptions, the higher multiplier should be considered, but does not have to be used. When the only reason that is identified is bad luck, no guidance is provided for the supervisor. In circumstances where the number of exceptions is 10 or more, the Basel Amendment requires the multiplier to be set at 4. Problem 12.18 considers these guidelines in the context of the statistical tests we discussed in Section 9.10.

12.7 BASEL II

The 1988 Basel Accord improved the way capital requirements were determined, but it does have significant weaknesses. Under the 1988 Basel Accord, all loans by a bank to a corporation have a risk weight of 100% and require the same amount of capital. A loan to a corporation with a AAA credit rating is treated in the same way as one to a corporation with a B credit rating.[7] Also, in Basel I there was no model of default correlation.

In June 1999, the Basel Committee proposed new rules that have become known as Basel II. These were revised in January 2001 and April 2003. A number of Quantitative Impact Studies (QISs) were carried out prior to the implementation of the new rules to test them by calculating the amount of capital that would be required if the rules had been in place.[8] A final set of rules agreed to by all members of the Basel Committee was published in June 2004. This was updated in November 2005. Implementation of the rules began in 2007 after a further QIS. The United States is several years behind the rest of the world in its implementation of Basel II.

The Basel II capital requirements applied to "internationally active" banks. In the United States, there are many small regional banks and the U.S. regulatory authorities decided that Basel II would not apply to them. (These banks are regulated under what is termed Basel IA, which is similar to Basel I.) In Europe, all banks, large or small, were regulated under Basel II. Furthermore, the European Union required the Basel II rules to be applied to securities companies as well as banks.

The Basel II is based on three "pillars":

1. Minimum Capital Requirements
2. Supervisory Review
3. Market Discipline

In Pillar 1, the minimum capital requirement for credit risk in the banking book is calculated in a new way that reflects the credit ratings of counterparties. The capital requirement for market risk remains unchanged from the 1996 Amendment and there is a new capital charge for operational risk. The general requirement in Basel I that banks hold a total capital equal to 8% of risk-weighted assets (RWA) remains unchanged. When the capital requirement for a particular risk is calculated in a way that does not involve RWAs, it is multiplied by 12.5 to convert it into an RWA-equivalent. As a result it is always the case that

$$\text{Total Capital} = 0.08 \times (\text{credit risk RWA} + \text{market risk RWA}$$
$$+ \text{ operational risk RWA}) \qquad (12.5)$$

Pillar 2, which is concerned with the supervisory review process, allows regulators in different countries some discretion in how rules are applied (so that they can

---

[7] Credit ratings are discussed in Section 1.7.

[8] One point to note about the QISs is that they do not take account of changes banks may choose to make to their portfolios to minimize their capital requirements once the new rules have been implemented.

take account of local conditions) but seeks to achieve overall consistency in the application of the rules. It places more emphasis on early intervention when problems arise. Supervisors are required to do far more than just ensuring that the minimum capital required under Basel II is held. Part of their role is to encourage banks to develop and use better risk management techniques and to evaluate these techniques. They should evaluate risks that are not covered by Pillar 1 and enter into an active dialogue with banks when deficiencies are identified.

The third pillar, market discipline, requires banks to disclose more information about the way they allocate capital and the risks they take. The idea here is that banks will be subjected to added pressure to make sound risk management decisions if shareholders and potential shareholders have more information about those decisions.

12.8 CREDIT RISK CAPITAL UNDER BASEL II

For credit risk, Basel II specified three approaches:

1. The Standardized Approach
2. The Foundation Internal Ratings Based (IRB) Approach
3. The Advanced IRB Approach

However, the United States (which, as mentioned earlier applied Basel II only to large banks) decided that only the IRB approach can be used.

The Standardized Approach

The standardized approach is used by banks that are not sufficiently sophisticated (in the eyes of the regulators) to use the internal ratings approaches. The standardized approach is similar to Basel I except for the calculation of risk weights.[9] Some of the new rules here are summarized in Table 12.4. Comparing Table 12.4 with Table 12.1, we see that the OECD status of a bank or a country is no longer considered important under Basel II. The risk weight for a country (sovereign) exposure ranges from 0% to 150% and the risk weight for an exposure to another bank or a corporation ranges from 20% to 150%. In Table 12.1, OECD banks were implicitly assumed to be lesser credit risks than corporations. An OECD bank attracted a risk weight of 20% while a corporation attracted a risk weight of 100%. Table 12.4 treats banks and corporations much more equitably. An interesting observation from Table 12.4 for a country, corporation, or bank that wants to borrow money is that it may be better to have no credit rating at all than a very poor credit rating! Supervisors are allowed to apply lower risk weights (20% rather than 50%, 50% rather than 100%, and 100% rather than 150%) when exposures are to the country in which the bank is incorporated or to that country's central bank.

For claims on banks, the rules are somewhat complicated. Instead of using the risk weights in Table 12.4, national supervisors can choose to base capital

---

[9] Ratios calculated using the new weights are sometimes referred to as McDonough ratios after William McDonough, the head of the Basel Committee.

TABLE 12.4   Risk Weights as a Percent of Principal for Exposures to Countries, Banks, and Corporations Under Basel II's Standardized Approach

	AAA to AA–	A+ to A–	BBB+ to BBB–	BB+ to BB–	B+ to B–	Below B–	Unrated
Country *	0	20	50	100	100	150	100
Banks **	20	50	50	100	100	150	50
Corporations	20	50	100	100	150	150	100

*Includes exposures to the country's central bank.
**National supervisors have options as outlined in the text.

requirements on the rating of the country in which the bank is incorporated. The risk weight assigned to the bank will be 20% if the country of incorporation has a rating between AAA and AA–, 50% if it is between A+ and A–, 100% if it is between BBB+ and B–, 150% if it is below B–, and 100% if it is unrated. Another complication is that, if national supervisors elect to use the rules in Table 12.4, they can choose to treat claims with a maturity less than three months more favorably so that the risk weights are 20% if the rating is between AAA+ and BBB–, 50% if it is between BB+ and B–, 150% if it is below B–, and 20% if it is unrated.

   The standard rule for retail lending is that a risk weight of 75% be applied. (This compares to 100% in the 1988 Accord.) When claims are secured by a residential mortgage, the risk weight is 35%. (This compares with 50% in the 1988 Accord.) Because of poor historical loss experience, the risk weight for claims secured by commercial real estate is 100%.

EXAMPLE 12.5

Suppose that the assets of a bank consist of $100 million of loans to corporations rated A, $10 million of government bonds rated AAA, and $50 million of residential mortgages. Under the Basel II standardized approach, the total risk-weighted assets is

$$0.5 \times 100 + 0.0 \times 10 + 0.35 \times 50 = 67.5$$

or $67.5 million. This compares with $125 million under Basel I (See Example 12.1.)

Adjustments for Collateral

There are two ways banks can adjust risk weights for collateral. The first is termed the *simple approach* and is similar to an approach used in Basel I. The second is termed the *comprehensive approach*. Banks have a choice as to which approach is used in the banking book, but must use the comprehensive approach to calculate capital for counterparty credit risk in the trading book.

   Under the simple approach, the risk weight of the counterparty is replaced by the risk weight of the collateral for the part of the exposure covered by the collateral. (The exposure is calculated after netting.) For any exposure not covered by the collateral, the risk weight of the counterparty is used. The minimum level for the risk weight applied to the collateral is 20%.[10] A requirement is that the collateral must be revalued at least every six months and must be pledged for at least the life of the exposure.

Under the comprehensive approach, banks adjust the size of their exposure upward to allow for possible increases in the exposure and adjust the value of the collateral downward to allow for possible decreases in the value of the collateral.[11] (The adjustments depend on the volatility of the exposure and the collateral.) A new exposure equal to the excess of the adjusted exposure over the adjusted value of the collateral is calculated and the counterparty's risk weight is applied to this exposure. The adjustments applied to the exposure and the collateral can be calculated using rules specified in Basel II or, with regulatory approval, using a bank's internal models. Where netting arrangements apply, exposures and collateral are separately netted and the adjustments made are weighted averages.

EXAMPLE 12.6

Suppose that an $80 million exposure to a particular counterparty is secured by collateral worth $70 million. The collateral consists of bonds issued by an A-rated company. The counterparty has a rating of B+. The risk weight for the counterparty is 150% and the risk weight for the collateral is 50%. The risk-weighted assets applicable to the exposure using the simple approach is

$$0.5 \times 70 + 1.50 \times 10 = 50$$

or $50 million.

Consider next the comprehensive approach. Assume that the adjustment to exposure to allow for possible future increases in the exposure is +10% and the adjustment to the collateral to allow for possible future decreases in its value is −15%. The new exposure is

$$1.1 \times 80 - 0.85 \times 70 = 28.5$$

or $28.5 million and a risk weight of 150% is applied to this exposure to give risk adjusted assets equal to $42.75 million.

The IRB Approach

The model underlying the IRB approach is shown in Figure 12.1. Regulators base the capital requirement on the value at risk calculated using a one-year time horizon and a 99.9% confidence level. They recognize that expected losses are usually covered by

---

[10] An exception is when the collateral consists of cash or government securities with the currency of the collateral being the same as the currency of the exposure.

[11] An adjustment to the exposure is not likely to be necessary on a loan, but is likely to be necessary on an over-the-counter derivative. The adjustment is in addition to the add-on factor.

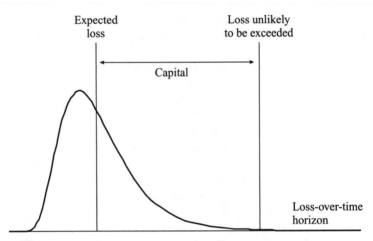

FIGURE 12.1 The Loss Probability Density Function and the Capital Required by a Financial Institution

the way a financial institution prices its products. (For example, the interest charged by a bank on a loan is designed to recover expected loan losses.) The capital required is therefore the value at risk minus the expected loss.

The value at risk is calculated using the one-factor Gaussian copula model of time to default that we discussed in Section 11.5. Assume that a bank has a very large number of obligors and the ith obligor has a one-year probability of default equal to PD_i. The copula correlation between each pair of obligors is ρ.[12] As in Section 11.5, we define

$$\text{WCDR}_i = N\left[\frac{N^{-1}(\text{PD}_i) + \sqrt{\rho}N^{-1}(0.999)}{\sqrt{1-\rho}}\right] \qquad (12.6)$$

where WCDR_i denotes the "worst case probability of default" defined so that the bank is 99.9% certain it will not be exceeded next year for the ith counterparty. Gordy's (2003) research (see Section 11.5) shows that for a large portfolio of instruments (loans, loan commitments, derivatives, etc.) that have the same ρ, the one-year 99.9% VaR is approximately[13]

$$\sum_i \text{EAD}_i \times \text{LGD}_i \times \text{WCDR}_i$$

where EAD_i is the exposure at default of the ith counterparty and LGD_i is the loss given default for the ith counterparty. The variable EAD_i is the dollar amount that is expected to be owed by the ith counterparty at the time of default. If there is a single loan outstanding to the ith counterparty, this is likely to equal the principal

---

[12] Note that the Basel Committee publications use R, not ρ, to denote the copula correlation.
[13] See M. B. Gordy, "A Risk-Factor Model Foundation for Ratings-Based Bank Capital Ratios," *Journal of Financial Intermediation* 12 (2003): 199–232.

TABLE 12.5 Dependence of one-year 99.9% WCDR on PD and ρ

	PD = 0.1%	PD = 0.5%	PD = 1%	PD = 1.5%	PD = 2.0%
$\rho = 0.0$	0.1%	0.5%	1.0%	1.5%	2.0%
$\rho = 0.2$	2.8%	9.1%	14.6%	18.9%	22.6%
$\rho = 0.4$	7.1%	21.1%	31.6%	39.0%	44.9%
$\rho = 0.6$	13.5%	38.7%	54.2%	63.8%	70.5%
$\rho = 0.8$	23.3%	66.3%	83.6%	90.8%	94.4%

amount outstanding on the loan. If there is a single swap or other derivative, a credit equivalent amount must be estimated (see Section 12.3 for the standard ways of doing this in Basel I). When there are several transactions with the ith counterparty, netting calculations similar to those in Section 12.5 can be carried out to determine EAD_i. The variable LGD_i is the proportion of EAD_i that is expected to be lost in the event of default. For example, if a bank expects to recover 30% of the amount owed in the event of default, $LGD_i = 0.7$.

The expected loss from defaults is

$$\sum_i EAD_i \times LGD_i \times PD_i$$

The capital required in Figure 12.1 is the excess of the 99.9% worst-case loss over the expected loss. It is therefore

$$\sum_i EAD_i \times LGD_i \times (WCDR_i - PD_i) \qquad (12.7)$$

We now drop the subscripts and define for a counterparty

PD: The probability that the counterparty will default within one year (expressed as a decimal)

EAD: The exposure at default (in dollars)

LGD: The loss given default or the proportion of the exposure that is lost if there is a default (expressed as a decimal)

Table 12.5 shows how WCDR depends on PD and ρ in the Gaussian copula model. When the correlation ρ is zero, WCDR = PD because in that case there is no default correlation and the percentage of loans defaulting can be expected to be the same in all years. As ρ increases, WCDR increases.

Corporate, Sovereign, and Bank Exposures

In the case of corporate, sovereign, and bank exposures, Basel II assumes a relationship between the correlation parameter, ρ, and the probability of default, PD, based

TABLE 12.6 Relationship between one-year 99.9% WCDR and PD for Corporate, Sovereign, and Bank Exposures

PD	0.1%	0.5%	1%	1.5%	2.0%
WCDR	3.4%	9.8%	14.0%	16.9%	19.0%

on empirical research.[14] The formula is

$$\rho = 0.12 \frac{1 - \exp(-50 \times \text{PD})}{1 - \exp(-50)} + 0.24 \left[1 - \frac{1 - \exp(-50 \times \text{PD})}{1 - \exp(-50)} \right]$$

Because $\exp(-50)$ is a very small number, this formula is to all intents and purposes

$$\rho = 0.12 \left(1 + e^{-50 \times \text{PD}} \right) \tag{12.8}$$

As PD increases, ρ decreases. The reason usually given for this inverse relationship is as follows. As a company becomes less creditworthy, its PD increases and its probability of default becomes more idiosyncratic and less affected by overall market conditions.

Combining equation (12.8) with equation (12.6), we obtain the relationship between WCDR and PD in Table 12.6. WCDR is, as one would expect, an increasing function of PD. However it does not increase as fast as it would if ρ were assumed to be independent of PD.

The formula for the capital required for the counterparty is

$$\text{EAD} \times \text{LGD} \times (\text{WCDR} - \text{PD}) \times \text{MA} \tag{12.9}$$

The meaning of the first three terms in this expression should be clear from our earlier discussion leading to equation (12.7). The variable MA is the maturity adjustment and is defined as

$$\text{MA} = \frac{1 + (M - 2.5) \times b}{1 - 1.5 \times b} \tag{12.10}$$

where

$$b = [0.11852 - 0.05478 \times \ln(\text{PD})]^2$$

and M is the maturity of the exposure. The maturity adjustment is designed to allow for the fact that, if an instrument lasts longer than one year, there is a one-year credit exposure arising from a possible decline in the creditworthiness of the counterparty as well as from a possible default by the counterparty. (Note that, when $M = 1$, MA is 1.0 and has no effect.) As mentioned in Section 12.7 (see Equation (12.5)), the risk-weighted assets (RWA) are calculated as 12.5 times the capital required

$$\text{RWA} = 12.5 \times \text{EAD} \times \text{LGD} \times (\text{WCDR} - \text{PD}) \times \text{MA}$$

so that the capital is 8% of RWA, 4% of which must be Tier 1.

---

[14] See J. Lopez, "The Empirical Relationship Between Average Asset Correlation, Firm Probability of Default and Asset Size," *Journal of Financial Intermediation* 13, no. 2 (2004): 265–283.

Under the Foundation IRB approach, banks supply PD while LGD, EAD, and M are supervisory values set by the Basel Committee. PD is subject to a floor of 0.03% for bank and corporate exposures. LGD is set at 45% for senior claims and 75% for subordinated claims. When there is eligible collateral, in order to correspond to the comprehensive approach that we described earlier, LGD is reduced by the ratio of the adjusted value of the collateral to the adjusted value of the exposure, both calculated using the comprehensive approach. The EAD is calculated in a manner similar to the credit equivalent amount in Basel I and includes the impact of netting. M is set at 2.5 in most circumstances.

Under the advanced IRB approach, banks supply their own estimates of the PD, LGD, EAD, and M for corporate, sovereign, and bank exposures. The PD can be reduced by credit mitigants such as credit triggers. (As in the case of the Foundation IRB approach, it is subject to a floor of 0.03% for bank and corporate exposures.) The two main factors influencing the LGD are the seniority of the debt and the collateral. In calculating EAD, banks can with regulatory approval use their own estimates of credit conversion factors.

The capital given by equation (12.9) is intended to be sufficient to cover unexpected losses over a one-year period that we are 99.9% certain will not be exceeded. (As discussed earlier, the expected losses should be covered by a bank in the way it prices its products.) The WCDR is the probability of default that (theoretically) happens once every thousand years. The Basel committee reserves the right to apply a scaling factor (less than or greater than 1.0) to the result of the calculations in equation (12.9) if it finds that the aggregate capital requirements are too high or low. A typical scaling factor is 1.06.

EXAMPLE 12.7

Suppose that the assets of a bank consist of $100 million of loans to A-rated corporations. The PD for the corporations is estimated as 0.1% and the LGD is 60%. The average maturity is 2.5 years for the corporate loans. This means that

$$b = [0.11852 - 0.05478 \times \ln(0.001)]^2 = 0.247$$

so that

$$MA = \frac{1}{1 - 1.5 \times 0.247} = 1.59$$

From Table 12.6, the WCDR is 3.4%. Under the Basel II IRB approach, the risk-weighted assets for the corporate loans are

$$12.5 \times 100 \times 0.6 \times (0.034 - 0.001) \times 1.59 = 39.3$$

or $39.3 million. This compares with $100 million under Basel I and $50 million under the standardized approach of Basel II. (See Examples 12.1 and 12.5 where a $100 million corporate loan is part of the portfolio.)

TABLE 12.7   Relationship between one-year 99.9% WCDR and PD for Retail Exposures

PD	0.1%	0.5%	1.0%	1.5%	2.0%
WCDR	2.1%	6.3%	9.1%	11.0%	12.3%

Retail Exposures

The model underlying the calculation of capital for retail exposures is similar to that underlying the calculation of corporate, sovereign, and banking exposures. However, the Foundation IRB and Advanced IRB approaches are merged and all banks using the IRB approach provide their own estimates of PD, EAD, and LGD. There is no maturity adjustment, MA. The capital requirement is therefore

$$\text{EAD} \times \text{LGD} \times (\text{WCDR} - \text{PD})$$

and the risk-weighted assets are

$$12.5 \times \text{EAD} \times \text{LGD} \times (\text{WCDR} - \text{PD})$$

WCDR is calculated as in equation (12.6). For residential mortgages, ρ is set equal to 0.15 in this equation. For qualifying revolving exposures, ρ is set equal to 0.04. For all other retail exposures, a relationship between ρ and PD is specified for the calculation of WCDR. This is

$$\rho = 0.03 \frac{1 - \exp(-35 \times \text{PD})}{1 - \exp(-35)} + 0.16 \left[1 - \frac{1 - \exp(-35 \times \text{PD})}{1 - \exp(-35)} \right]$$

Because $\exp(-35)$ is a very small number, this formula is to all intents and purposes

$$\rho = 0.03 + 0.13 e^{-35 \times \text{PD}} \tag{12.11}$$

Comparing equation (12.11) with equation (12.8), we see that correlations are assumed to be much lower for retail exposures than for corporate exposures. Table 12.7 is the table corresponding to Table 12.6 for retail exposures.

EXAMPLE 12.8

Suppose that the assets of a bank consist of $50 million of residential mortgages where the PD is 0.005 and the LGD is 20%. In this case, $\rho = 0.15$ and

$$\text{WCDR} = N \left[\frac{N^{-1}(0.005) + \sqrt{0.15} N^{-1}(0.999)}{\sqrt{1 - 0.15}} \right] = 0.067$$

The risk-weighted assets are

$$12.5 \times 50 \times 0.2 \times (0.067 - 0.005) = 7.8$$

or $7.8 million. This compares with $25 million under Basel I and $17.5 million under the Standardized Approach of Basel II. (See Examples 12.1 and 12.5 where $50 million of residential mortgages is part of the portfolio.)

Guarantees and Credit Derivatives

The approach traditionally taken by the Basel Committee for handling guarantees is the credit substitution approach. Suppose that a AA-rated company guarantees a loan to a BBB-rated company. For the purposes of calculating capital, the credit rating of the guarantor is substituted for the credit rating of the borrower so that capital is calculated as though the loan had been made to the AA-rated company. This overstates the credit risk because, for the lender to lose money, both the guarantor and the borrower must default (with the guarantor defaulting before the borrower).[15] The Basel Committee has addressed this issue. In July 2005, it published a document concerned with the treatment of double defaults under Basel II.[16] As an alternative to using the credit substitution approach, the capital requirement can be calculated as the capital that would be required without the guarantee multiplied by $0.15 + 160 \times PD_g$ where PD_g is the one-year probability of default of the guarantor.

12.9 OPERATIONAL RISK CAPITAL UNDER BASEL II

In addition to changing the way banks calculate credit risk capital, Basel II requires banks to keep capital for operational risk. This is the risk of losses from situations where the bank's procedures fail to work as they are supposed to or where there is an adverse external event such as a fire in a key facility. The impact of the Basel II credit risk calculation is to reduce the credit risk capital requirements for most banks and the capital charge for operational risk has the effect of restoring the total level of capital in the banking system to roughly where it was under Basel I.

There are three approaches to calculating capital for operational risk:

1. The Basic Indicator Approach
2. The Standardized Approach
3. The Advanced Measurement Approach

Which of these is used depends on the sophistication of the bank. The simplest approach is the Basic Indicator Approach. This sets the operational risk capital equal to the bank's average annual gross income over the last three years multiplied by 0.15.[17] The Standardized Approach is similar to the basic indicator approach except

---

[15] Credit default swaps, which we discuss in Chapter 16, provide a type of insurance against default and are handled similarly to guarantees for regulatory purposes.

[16] See Bank for International Settlements, "The Application of Basel II to Trading Activities and the Treatment of Double Defaults," July 2005, available on www.bis.org.

[17] Gross income defined as net interest income plus non-interest income. Net interest income is the excess of income earned on loans over interest paid on deposits and other instruments that are used to fund the loans. Years where gross income is negative are not included in the calculations.

that a different factor is applied to the gross income from different business lines. In the Advanced Measurement Approach, the bank uses its own internal models to calculate the operational risk loss that it is 99.9% certain will not be exceeded in one year. One advantage of the advanced measurement approach is that it allows banks to recognize the risk mitigating impact of insurance contracts subject to certain conditions. The calculation of operational risk is discussed further in Chapter 20.

12.10 PILLAR 2: SUPERVISORY REVIEW

Pillar 2 of Basel II is concerned with the supervisory review process. Four key principles of supervisory review are specified:

1. Banks should have a process for assessing their overall capital adequacy in relation to their risk profile and a strategy for maintaining their capital levels.
2. Supervisors should review and evaluate banks' internal capital adequacy assessments and strategies, as well as their ability to monitor and ensure compliance with regulatory capital ratios. Supervisors should take appropriate supervisory action if they are not satisfied with the result of this process.
3. Supervisors should expect banks to operate above the minimum regulatory capital and should have the ability to require banks to hold capital in excess of this minimum.
4. Supervisors should seek to intervene at an early stage to prevent capital from falling below the minimum levels required to support the risk characteristics of a particular bank and should require rapid remedial action if capital is not maintained or restored.

The Basel Committee suggests that regulators pay particular attention to interest rate risk in the banking book, credit risk, and operational risk. Key issues in credit risk are stress tests used, default definitions used, credit risk concentration, and the risks associated with the use of collateral, guarantees, and credit derivatives.

The Basel Committee also stresses that there should be transparency and accountability in the procedures used by bank supervisors. This is particularly important when a supervisor exercises discretion in the procedures used or sets capital requirements above the minimum specified in Basel II.

12.11 PILLAR 3: MARKET DISCIPLINE

Pillar 3 of Basel II is concerned with increasing the disclosure by a bank of its risk assessment procedures and capital adequacy. The extent to which regulators can force banks to increase their disclosure varies from jurisdiction to jurisdiction. However, banks are unlikely to ignore directives on this from their supervisors, given the potential of supervisors to make their life difficult. Also, in some instances, banks have to increase their disclosure in order to be allowed to use particular methodologies for calculating capital.

Regulatory disclosures are likely to be different in form from accounting disclosures and need not be made in annual reports. It is largely left to the bank to choose disclosures that are material and relevant. Among the items that banks should disclose are:

1. The entities in the banking group to which Basel II is applied and adjustments made for entities to which it is not applied
2. The terms and conditions of the main features of all capital instruments
3. A list of the instruments constituting Tier 1 capital and the amount of capital provided by each item
4. The total amount of Tier 2 capital.
5. Capital requirements for credit, market, and operational risk
6. Other general information on the risks to which a bank is exposed and the assessment methods used by the bank for different categories of risk.
7. The structure of the risk management function and how it operates.

12.12 SOLVENCY II

As discussed in Section 3.11, there are no international standards for the regulation of insurance companies. In the United States, insurance companies are regulated at the state level with some input from the Federal Insurance Office and the National Association of Insurance Commissioners. In Europe, the regulation of insurance companies is handled by the European Union. The long-standing regulatory framework in the European Union, known as Solvency I, is in the process of being replaced by Solvency II. Quantitative Impact Studies are being carried out and it is expected that Solvency II will be implemented in 2013. Whereas Solvency I calculates capital only for underwriting risks, Solvency II will consider investment risks and operational risks as well.

Solvency II has many similarities to Basel II. There are three pillars. Pillar 1 is concerned with the calculation of capital requirements and the types of capital that are eligible. Pillar 2 is concerned with the supervisory review process. Pillar 3 is concerned with the disclosure of risk management information to the market. The three pillars are therefore analogous to the three pillars of Basel II.

Pillar 1 of Solvency II specifies a *minimum capital requirement* (MCR) and a *solvency capital requirement* (SCR). If its capital falls below the SCR level, an insurance company should, at minimum, deliver to the supervisor a plan to restore capital to above the SCR level. The supervisor might require the insurance company to take particular measures to correct the situation. The MCR is regarded as an absolute minimum level of capital. If capital drops below the MCR level, supervisors are likely to prevent the insurance company from taking new business. It might force the insurance company into liquidation, transferring its policies to another company.

There are two ways to calculate the SCR: the standardized approach and the internal models approach. The internal models approach involves a VaR calculation with a one-year time horizon and a 99.5% confidence limit. (The confidence level is therefore less than the 99.9% confidence level used in Pillar 1 of Basel II.) Longer time horizons with lower confidence levels are also allowed when the protection provided is considered equivalent. The SCR involves a capital charge for investment risk, underwriting risk, and operational risk. Investment risk is subdivided into market risk and credit risk. Underwriting risk is subdivided into risk arising from life insurance, non-life insurance (i.e., property and casualty), and health insurance.

Capital should be adequate to deal with large adverse events. Examples of the events considered in quantitative impact studies are:

1. A 32% decrease in global stock markets
2. A 20% decrease in real estate prices
3. A 20% change in foreign exchange rates
4. Specified catastrophic risk scenarios affecting property and casualty payouts.
5. Health care costs increasing by a factor times the historical standard deviation of costs
6. A 10% increase in mortality rates
7. A 25% decrease in mortality rates
8. A 10% increase in expenses

The internal models are required to satisfy three tests. The first is a statistical quality test. This is a test of the soundness of the data and methodology used in calculating VaR. The second is a calibration test. This is a test of whether risks have been assessed in accordance with a common SCR target criterion. The third is a use test. This is a test of whether the model is genuinely relevant to and used by risk managers.

A number of possible approaches for calculating MCR are being considered. One is to set MCR as a percent of SCR. Another is to calculate MCR in the same way as SCR but with a lower confidence level than 99.5%.

There are three types of capital in Solvency II. Tier 1 capital consists of equity capital, retained earnings, and other equivalent funding sources. Tier 2 capital consists of liabilities that are subordinated to policyholders and satisfy certain criteria concerning their availability in wind-down scenarios. Tier 3 capital consists of liabilities that are subordinated to policyholders and do not satisfy these criteria. Similarly to Basel II, the amount of capital that must be Tier 1, Tier 1 plus Tier 2, and Tier 1 plus Tier 2 plus Tier 3 is specified.

SUMMARY

This chapter has provided an overview of capital requirements for banks throughout the world. The way in which regulators calculate the minimum capital a bank is required to hold has changed dramatically since the 1980s. Prior to 1988, regulators determined capital requirements by specifying minimum ratios for capital to assets or maximum ratios for assets to capital. In the late 1980s, both bank supervisors and the banks themselves agreed that changes were necessary. Off-balance-sheet derivatives trading was increasing fast. Also banks were competing globally and it was considered important to create a level playing field by making regulations uniform throughout the world.

The 1988 Basel Accord assigned capital for credit risk both on and off the balance sheet. This involved calculating a risk-weighted asset for each item. The risk-weighted assets for an on-balance-sheet loan were calculated by multiplying the principal by a risk weight for the counterparty. In the case of derivatives such as swaps, banks were first required to calculate credit equivalent amounts. The risk-weighted assets were obtained by multiplying the credit equivalent amount by a risk weight for the counterparty. Banks were required to keep capital equal to 8% of the total risk-weighted assets. In 1995, the capital requirements for credit risk were modified to incorporate netting. In 1996, the Accord was modified to include a capital charge for market risk. Sophisticated banks could base the capital charge on a value-at-risk calculation.

Basel II was proposed in 1999 and implemented by many banks in about 2007. It led to no immediate change to the capital requirement for market risk. Credit risk capital was calculated in a more sophisticated way than previously to reflect either (a) the credit ratings of obligors or (b) a bank's own internal estimates of default probabilities. In addition, there is a capital charge for operational risk.

Solvency II is regulatory framework for insurance companies expected to be implemented by the European Union starting in 2013. It will prescribe minimum capital levels for investment risk, underwriting risk, and operational risk. The structure of Solvency II is broadly similar to Basel II.

FURTHER READING

Bank for International Settlements. "Basel II: International Convergence of Capital Measurement and Capital Standards: A Revised Framework," November 2005, www.bis.org.

Crouhy, M., D. Galai, and R. Mark. *Risk Management.* New York: McGraw-Hill, 2001.

Gordy, M. B. "A Risk-Factor Model Foundation for Ratings-Based Bank Capital Ratios," *Journal of Financial Intermediation* 12 (2003): 199–232.

Lopez, J. A. "The Empirical Relationship Between Average Asset Correlation, Firm Probability of Default, and Asset Size," *Journal of Financial Intermediation* 13, no. 2 (2004): 265–283.

Vasicek, O. "Probability of Loss on a Loan Portfolio." Working Paper, KMV, 1987. (Published in *Risk* in December 2002 under the title "Loan Portfolio Value".)

PRACTICE QUESTIONS AND PROBLEMS
(ANSWERS AT END OF BOOK)

12.1 "When a steel company goes bankrupt, other companies in the same industry benefit because they have one less competitor. But when a bank goes bankrupt other banks do not necessarily benefit." Explain this statement.

12.2 "The existence of deposit insurance makes it particularly important for there to be regulations on the amount of capital banks hold." Explain this statement.

12.3 An interest rate swap involves the exchange of a fixed rate of interest for a floating rate of interest with both being applied to the same principal. The principals are not exchanged. What is the nature of the credit risk for a bank when it enters into a five-year interest rate swap with a notional principal of $100 million? Assume the swap is worth zero initially.

12.4 In a currency swap, interest on a principal in one currency is exchanged for interest on a principal in another currency. The principals in the two currencies are exchanged at the end of the life of the swap. Why is the credit risk on a currency swap greater than that on an interest rate swap?

12.5 A four-year interest rate swap currently has a negative value to a financial institution. Is the financial institution exposed to credit risk on the transaction? Explain your answer. How would the capital requirement be calculated under Basel I?

12.6 Estimate the capital required under Basel I for a bank that has the following transactions with a corporation. Assume no netting.

(a) A nine-year interest rate swap with a notional principal of $250 million and a current market value of −$2 million.

(b) A four-year interest rate swap with a notional principal of $100 million and a current value of $3.5 million.

(c) A six-month derivative on a commodity with a principal of $50 million that is currently worth $1 million.

12.7 What is the capital required in Problem 12.6 under Basel I assuming that the 1995 netting amendment applies?

12.8 All the transactions a bank has with a corporate client are loans to the client. What is the value to the bank of netting provisions in its master agreement with the client?

12.9 Explain why the final stage in the Basel II calculations for credit risk (IRB), market risk, and operational risk is to multiply by 12.5.

12.10 What is the difference between the trading book and the banking book for a bank? A bank currently has a loan of $10 million dollars to a corporate client. At the end of the life of the loan, the client would like to sell debt securities to the bank instead of borrowing. How does this potentially affect the nature of the bank's regulatory capital calculations?

12.11 Under Basel I, banks do not like lending to highly creditworthy companies and prefer to help them issue debt securities. Why is this? Do you expect the banks' attitude to this type of lending to change under Basel II?

12.12 Banks sometimes use what is referred to as regulatory arbitrage to reduce their capital. What do you think this means?

12.13 Equation (12.9) gives the formula for the capital required under Basel II. It involves four terms being multiplied together. Explain each of these terms.

12.14 Explain the difference between the simple and the comprehensive approach for adjusting capital requirements for collateral.

12.15 Explain the difference between the standardized approach, the IRB approach, and the advanced IRB approach for calculating credit risk capital under Basel II.

12.16 Explain the difference between the basic indicator approach, the standardized approach, and the advanced measurement approach for calculating operational risk capital under Basel II.

12.17 Suppose that the assets of a bank consist of $200 million of retail loans (not mortgages). The PD is 1% and the LGD is 70%. What is the risk-weighted assets under the Basel II IRB approach? What are the Tier 1 and Tier 2 capital requirements?

12.18 Section 9.10 discusses how statistics can be used to accept or reject a VaR model. Section 12.6 discusses guidelines for bank supervisors in setting the VaR multiplier m_c. It explains that, if the number of exceptions in 250 trials is five or more, then m_c is increased. What is the chance of five or more exceptions if the VaR model is working well?

FURTHER QUESTIONS

12.19 Why is there an add-on amount in Basel I for derivatives transactions? "Basel I could be improved if the add-on amount for a derivatives transaction depended on the value of the transaction." How would you argue this viewpoint?

12.20 Estimate the capital required under Basel I for a bank that has the following transactions with another bank. Assume no netting.

   (a) A two-year forward contract on a foreign currency, currently worth $2 million, to buy foreign currency worth $50 million

   (b) A long position in a six-month option on the S&P 500. The principal is $20 million and the current value is $4 million.

   (c) A two-year swap involving oil. The principal is $30 million and the current value of the swap is –$5 million.

   What difference does it make if the netting amendment applies?

12.21 A bank has the following transaction with a AA-rated corporation

   (a) A two-year interest rate swap with a principal of $100 million that is worth $3 million

   (b) A nine-month foreign exchange forward contract with a principal of $150 million that is worth –$5 million

   (c) An long position in a six-month option on gold with a principal of $50 million that is worth $7 million

   What is the capital requirement under Basel I if there is no netting? What difference does it make if the netting amendment applies? What is the capital required under Basel II when the standardized approach is used?

12.22 Suppose that the assets of a bank consist of $500 million of loans to BBB-rated corporations. The PD for the corporations is estimated as 0.3%. The average maturity is three years and the LGD is 60%. What is the total risk-weighted assets for credit risk under the Basel II advanced IRB approach? How much Tier 1 and Tier 2 capital is required? How does this compare with the capital required under the Basel II standardized approach and under Basel I?

CHAPTER 13

Basel 2.5, Basel III, and Dodd–Frank

It was perhaps unfortunate for Basel II that its implementation date coincided, at least approximately, with the start of the worst crisis that financial markets had experienced since the 1930s. Some commentators have blamed Basel II for the crisis. They point out that it was a move toward self-regulation where banks, when calculating regulatory capital, had the freedom to use their own estimates of model inputs such as PD, LGD, and EAD. In fact, as explained in Chapter 6, the seeds of the crisis were sown well before Basel II was implemented.[1]

This chapter starts by discussing what has become known as Basel 2.5. This is a collection of changes to the calculation of market risk capital that was put in place by the Basel Committee on Banking Supervision following the large losses experienced by banks during the crisis. The implementation date for Basel 2.5 was December 31, 2011.

The chapter then moves on to consider Basel III, which was a major overhaul of bank regulations, published by the Basel Committee in December 2010. Basel III includes a series of rules concerned with increasing the amount of capital that banks have to keep for credit risk and tightening the definition of capital. An important new feature of Basel III is the specification of liquidity requirements that must be met by banks. Basel III is being phased in over a long period of time ending on December 31, 2019.

The chapter also discusses the Dodd–Frank Act which was signed into law by President Barack Obama in the United States on July 21, 2010. The provisions of the Act include measures designed to change the way derivatives are traded, regulate the activities of rating agencies, ensure that mortgages are granted only to people that can afford to repay, and restrict the extent to which banks can do proprietary trading.

13.1 BASEL 2.5

During the credit crisis, it was recognized that some changes were necessary to the calculation of capital for market risk in the Basel II framework. These changes are

---

[1] In fact, the United States was behind other countries in implementing Basel II. If Basel II had been fully implemented by the start of the crisis, capital levels at U.S. banks would probably have been lower.

referred to as "Basel 2.5" and, as already mentioned, the implementation date for them was December 31, 2011.[2] There are three changes involving:

1. The calculation of a stressed VaR;
2. A new incremental risk charge; and
3. A comprehensive risk measure for instruments dependent on credit correlation.

The measures have the effect of greatly increasing the market risk capital that large banks are required to hold.

Stressed VaR

The 1996 Amendment to Basel I, where capital was first required for market risk, allowed banks to base capital on a 10-day 99% VaR measure. Most banks use a procedure known as historical simulation to calculate VaR. This will be described in Chapter 14. The assumption underlying historical simulation is that the percentage changes in market variables during the next day are a random sample from their percentage daily changes observed during the previous one to four years. The 2003–2006 period was one where the volatilities of most market variables was low. As a result, the market risk VaRs calculated during this period were also low. Furthermore, the VaRs continued to be too low for a period of time after the onset of the crisis.

This led the Basel Committee to introduce what has become known as a "stressed VaR" measure. Stressed VaR is calculated by basing calculations on a 250-day period of stressed market conditions, rather than on the last one to four years. The historical simulation calculations to arrive at a stressed VaR measure assume that the percentage changes in market variables during the next day are a random sample from their percentage daily changes observed during the 250-day period of stressed market conditions.

Basel 2.5 requires banks to calculate two VaRs. One is the usual VaR (based on the previous one to four years of market movements). The other is stressed VaR (calculated from a stressed period of 250 days). The two VaR measures are combined to calculate a total capital charge. The formula for the total capital charge is

$$\max(\text{VaR}_{t-1}, m_c \times \text{VaR}_{\text{avg}}) + \max(\text{sVaR}_{t-1}, m_s \times \text{sVaR}_{\text{avg}})$$

where VaR_{t-1} and sVaR_{t-1} are the VaR and stressed VaR (with a 10-day time horizon and a 99% confidence level) calculated on the previous day. The variables VaR_{avg} and sVaR_{avg} are the average of VaR and stressed VaR (again with a 10-day time horizon and a 99% confidence level) calculated over the previous 60 days. The parameters m_s and m_c are multiplicative factors that are determined by bank supervisors and are at minimum equal to three. As explained in Section 12.6, the capital requirement prior to Basel 2.5 was

$$\max(\text{VaR}_{t-1}, m_c \times \text{VaR}_{\text{avg}})$$

---

[2] See Basel Committee on Bank Supervision, "Revisions to the Basel II Market Risk Framework," February 2011.

Because stressed VaR is always at least as great as VaR, the formula shows that (assuming $m_c = m_s$) the capital requirement must at least double under Basel 2.5.

Originally it was considered that 2008 would constitute a good one-year period for the calculation of stressed VaR. Later it was realized that the one-year period chosen should reflect a bank's portfolio. A bank is now required to search for a one-year period during which its portfolio would perform very poorly. The stressed period used by one bank is therefore not necessarily the same as that used by another bank.

Incremental Risk Charge

In 2005, the Basel Committee became concerned that exposures in the trading book were attracting less capital than similar exposures in the banking book. Consider a bond. If held in the trading book, the capital would be calculated by applying a multiplier to the 10-day 99% VaR, as discussed in Section 12.6. If held in the banking book (and treated like a loan), capital for the bond would be calculated using VaR with a one-year time horizon and a 99.9% confidence level, as discussed in Section 12.8. The trading-book calculation usually gave rise to a much lower capital charge than the banking-book calculation. As a result, banks tended whenever possible to hold credit-dependent instruments in the trading book.[3]

Regulators proposed an "incremental default risk charge" (IDRC) in 2005 that would be calculated for with a 99.9% confidence level and a one-year time horizon for instruments in the trading book that were sensitive to default risk. This meant that the capital requirement for an instrument in the trading book would be similar to the capital requirement if had been in the banking book. In 2008, the Basel Committee recognized that most of the losses in the credit market turmoil of 2007 and 2008 were from changes in credit ratings, widening of credit spreads, and loss of liquidity, rather than solely as a result of defaults. It therefore amended its previous proposals to reflect this and the IDRC became the "incremental risk charge" (IRC).[4]

The IRC requires banks to calculate a one-year 99.9% VaR for losses from credit sensitive products in the trading book. Banks are required to consider rating changes as well as defaults. Because the instruments subject to the IRC are in the trading book, it is assumed that a bank will have the opportunity to rebalance its portfolio during the course of the year so that default risk is mitigated. Banks are therefore required to estimate a liquidity horizon for each instrument subject to the IRC. The liquidity horizon represents the time required to sell the position or to hedge all material risks in a stressed market.

Suppose that the liquidity horizon for a bond with a credit rating of A is three months. For the purposes of the calculation of VaR over a one-year time horizon, the bank assumes that at the end of three months, if the bond's rating has changed

---

[3] If a bank created ABSs from loans in the banking book, as described in Chapter 6, and then bought all the resultant tranches for its trading book, regulatory capital requirements would be lowered even though the bank's risks would be unchanged. This was one reason why banks wanted to securitize loans in the banking book.

[4] Basel Committee on Banking Supervision, "Guidelines for Computing Capital for Incremental Risk in the Trading Book," July 2009.

TABLE 13.1 Standardized Capital Charge for Correlation-Dependent Instruments

External Credit Assessment	AAA to AA−	A+ to A−	BBB+ to BBB−	BB+ to BB−	Below BB− or Unrated
Securitizations	1.6%	4%	8%	28%	Deduction
Resecuritizations	3.2%	8%	18%	52%	Deduction

or if it has defaulted, it is replaced by an A-rated bond similar to that held at the beginning of the period. The same thing happens at the end of six months and at the end of nine months. This is known as the *constant level of risk* assumption.

The impact of the constant level of risk assumption is that it is less likely that there will be a default. Instead, small losses are realized from ratings downgrades when rebalancing takes place. The assumption typically has the effect of reducing the one-year 99.9% VaR.[5] The minimum liquidity horizon for IRC is specified by the Basel Committee as three months.

The IRC therefore provides a measure of the default and credit migration risks of credit products over a one-year horizon at a 99.9% confidence level, taking into account the liquidity horizons of individual positions or sets of positions. Typically banks have to separately calculate a specific risk charge for risks associated with changing credit spreads.

The Comprehensive Risk Measure

The comprehensive risk measure (CRM) is designed to take account of risks in what is known as the "correlation book." This is the portfolio of instruments such as asset-backed securities (ABSs) and collateralized debt obligations (CDOs) that are sensitive to the correlation between the default risks of different assets. These instruments were discussed in Chapter 6. Suppose a bank has a AAA-rated tranche of an ABS. In the normal market environment, there is very little risk of losses from the tranche. However, in stressed market environments when correlations increase, the tranche is vulnerable—as became apparent during the 2007–2009 crisis.

The CRM is a single capital charge replacing the incremental risk charge and the specific risk charge for instruments dependent on credit correlation. A standardized approach for calculating the CRM has been specified and is summarized in Table 13.1. Given the experience of the securitization market during the crisis (see Chapter 6), it is not surprising that capital charges are higher for resecuritizations (e.g., ABS CDOs) than for securitizations (e.g., ABSs). A deduction means than the principal amount is subtracted from capital, which is equivalent to a 100% capital charge.

The Basel Committee allows banks, with supervisory approval, to use their internal models to calculate the CRM for unrated positions. The models developed by banks have to be quite sophisticated to be approved by bank supervisors. For

---

[5] See C. Finger, "CreditMetrics and Constant Level of Risk," MSCI, 2010 for a discussion of the constant level of risk assumption.

example, they must capture the cumulative impact of multiple defaults, credit spread risk, the volatility of implied correlations, the relationship between credit spreads and implied correlations, recovery rate volatility, the risk of hedge slippage, and potential hedge rebalancing costs. A routine and rigorous program of stress testing is also required.

The U.S. is attempting to come up with its own CRM rules because Dodd-Frank does not allow ratings to be used in setting capital requirements.

13.2 BASEL III

Following the 2007–2009 credit crisis, the Basel Committee realized that a major overhaul of Basel II was necessary. Basel 2.5 increased capital requirements for market risk. The Basel Committee wanted to increase capital requirements for credit risk as well. In addition, it considered that the definition of capital needed to be tightened and that regulations were needed to address liquidity risk.

Basel III proposals were first published in December 2009. Following comments from banks, a quantitative impact study, and a number of international summits, the final version of the regulations was published in December 2010.[6] There are six parts to the regulations:

1. Capital Definition and Requirements
2. Capital Conservation Buffer
3. Countercyclical Buffer
4. Leverage Ratio
5. Liquidity Risk
6. Counterparty Credit Risk

The regulations are being implemented gradually between 2013 and 2019.

Capital Definition and Requirements

Under Basel III, a bank's total capital consists of:

1. Tier 1 equity capital
2. Additional Tier 1 capital
3. Tier 2 capital

There is no Tier 3 capital.

Tier 1 equity capital (also referred to as core Tier 1 capital) includes share capital and retained earnings but does not include goodwill or deferred tax assets. It must be adjusted downward to reflect defined benefit pension plan deficits but

---

[6] See Basel Committee for Bank Supervision, "Basel III: A Global Regulatory Framework for More Resilient Banks and Banking Systems," December 2010; and Basel Committee for Bank Supervision, "Basel III: International Framework for Liquidity Risk Measurement Standards and Monitoring," December 2010.

is not adjusted upward to reflect defined benefit plan surpluses. (See Section 3.12 for a discussion of defined benefit plans.) Changes in retained earnings arising from securitized transactions are not counted as part of capital for regulatory purposes. The same is true of changes in retained earnings arising from the bank's own credit risk. (The latter is referred to as DVA and will be discussed in Chapter 17.) There are rules relating to the inclusion of minority interests and capital issued by consolidated subsidiaries. The additional Tier 1 capital category consists of items, such as non-cumulative preferred stock, that were previously Tier 1 but are not common equity. Tier 2 capital includes debt that is subordinated to depositors with an original maturity of five years.

Common equity is referred to by the Basel Committee as "going-concern capital." When the bank is a going concern (i.e. has positive equity capital), common equity absorbs losses. Tier 2 capital is referred to as "gone-concern capital." When the bank is no longer a going concern (i.e., has negative capital) losses have to be absorbed by Tier 2 capital. Tier 2 capital ranks below depositors in a liquidation. While Tier 2 capital remains positive, depositors should in theory be repaid in full.

The capital requirements are as follows:

1. Tier 1 equity capital must be at least 4.5% of risk-weighted assets at all times.
2. Total Tier 1 capital (Tier 1 equity capital plus additional Tier 1 capital) must be at 6% of risk-weighted assets at all times.
3. Total capital (total Tier 1 plus Tier 2) must be at least 8% of risk-weighted assets at all times.

Basel I required Tier 1 equity capital to be at least 2% of risk-weighted assets and total Tier 1 capital to be at least 4% of risk-weighted assets. The Basel III rules are much more demanding because (a) these percentages have been increased and (b) the definition of what qualifies as equity capital for regulatory purposes has been tightened. However, the Tier 1 plus Tier 2 requirement is the same as under Basel I and Basel II.

The transitional arrangements are that Tier 1 equity capital and total Tier 1 capital must be 3.5% and 4.5%, respectively, by January 1, 2013. They must be 4% and 5.5%, respectively, by January 1, 2014. The new capital levels must be in place by January 1, 2015. The new rules for the definition of what constitutes capital are being phased in over a longer period stretching until January 1, 2018.

The Basel Committee also calls for more capital for "systemically important" banks. This term has not been standardized across countries. In the United States, all banks with more than $50 billion in assets are considered systemically important.

Capital Conservation Buffer

In addition to the capital requirements just mentioned, Basel III requires a capital conservation buffer in normal times consisting of a further amount of core Tier 1 equity capital equal to 2.5% of risk-weighted assets. This provision is designed to ensure that banks build up capital during normal times so that it can be run down when losses are incurred during periods of financial difficulties. (The argument in favor of this is that it is much easier for banks to raise capital during normal times than during periods of stressed market conditions.) In circumstances where the

TABLE 13.2   Dividend Restrictions Arising from the Capital
Conservation Buffer

Tier 1 Equity Capital Ratio	Minimum Percent of Earnings Retained
4.000% to 5.125%	100%
5.125% to 5.750%	80%
5.750% to 6.375%	60%
6.375% to 7.000%	40%
> 7%	0%

capital conservation buffer has been wholly or partially used up, banks are required to constrain their dividends until the capital has been replenished. The dividend rules are summarized in Table 13.2. For example, if Tier 1 equity capital is 5.5% of risk-weighted assets, the minimum retained earnings is 80% so that the maximum dividends as a percent of retained earnings is 20%.

The capital conservation buffer means that the Tier 1 equity capital that banks are required to keep in normal times (excluding any extra capital required for systemically important banks) is 7% of risk-weighted assets; total Tier 1 capital is required to be at least 8.5% of risk-weighted assets; Tier 1 plus Tier 2 capital is required to be at least 10.5% of risk-weighted assets. These numbers can decline to 4.5%, 6% and 8% in stressed market conditions (because of losses), but banks are then under pressure to bring capital back up to the required levels. One of the consequences of the increased equity capital requirement is that banks may find it difficult to achieve the returns on equity that they had during the 1990 to 2006 period. However, bank shareholders can console themselves that bank stock is less risky as a result of the extra capital.

The capital conservation buffer requirement will be phased in between January 1, 2016, and January 1, 2019.

Countercyclical Buffer

In addition to the capital conservation buffer, Basel III has specified a countercyclical buffer. This is similar to the capital conservation buffer, but the extent to which it is implemented in a particular country is left to the discretion of national authorities. The buffer is intended to provide protection for the cyclicality of bank earnings. The buffer can be set to between 0% and 2.5% of total risk-weighted assets and must be met with Tier 1 equity capital.

For jurisdictions where the countercyclical buffer is non-zero, Table 13.2 is modified. For example, when the countercyclical buffer is set at its maximum level of 2.5%, it is replaced by Table 13.3. Like the capital conservation buffer, the countercyclical buffer requirements will be phased in between January 1, 2016, and January 1, 2019.

Some countries are requiring greater capital than Basel III, even when the countercyclical buffer is taken into account. Switzerland, for example, requires its two large banks (UBS and Credit Suisse) to have Tier 1 equity capital that is 10% of

TABLE 13.3   Dividend Restrictions Arising from the Capital Conservation Buffer and 2.5% Countercyclical Buffer

Tier 1 Equity Capital Ratio	Minimum Percent of Earnings Retained
4.50% to 5.75%	100%
5.75% to 7.00%	80%
7.00% to 8.25%	60%
8.25% to 9.50%	40%
> 9.50%	0%

risk-weighted assets and total capital which is 19% of risk-weighted assets. One reason for this is that the banks are huge when compared to the economy of Switzerland and a failure by one of the banks would have dire consequences for the country.

Leverage Ratio

In addition to the capital requirements based on risk-weighted assets, Basel III specifies a minimum leverage ratio of 3%. This leverage ratio is the ratio of capital to total exposure. A final decision on the definition of capital for the purposes of calculating the leverage ratio was not made at the time the Basel III rules were published in 2010. Total exposure includes all items on the balance sheet (without any risk weighting) and some off-balance-sheet items such as loan commitments. The leverage ratio is expected to be introduced on January 1, 2018, after a transition period.

Liquidity Risk

Prior to the crisis, the focus of the Basel regulations had been on ensuring that banks had sufficient capital for the risks they were taking. It turned out that many of the problems encountered by financial institutions during the crisis were not as a result of shortage of capital. They were instead a result of liquidity risks taken by the banks.

Liquidity risks arise because there is a tendency for banks to finance long-term needs with short-term funding such as commercial paper. Provided the bank is perceived by the market to be financially healthy, this is usually not a problem.[7] Suppose that a bank uses 90-day commercial paper to fund its activities. When one 90-day issue of commercial paper matures, the bank refinances with a new issue; when the new issue matures, it refinances with another issue; and so on. However, as soon as the bank experiences financial difficulties—or is thought to be experiencing financial difficulties—it is liable to become impossible for the bank to roll over its commercial paper. This type of problem led to the demise to Northern Rock in the United Kingdom and Lehman Brothers in the United States.

---

[7] If the funds are being used to finance long-term fixed-rate loans and interest rates rise, net interest margins are squeezed. But this risk can be hedged with instruments such as interest rate swaps (see Section 8.1).

Basel III has introduced requirements involving two liquidity ratios that are designed to ensure that banks can survive liquidity pressures. The ratios are:

1. Liquidity Coverage Ratio (LCR); and
2. Net Stable Funding Ratio (NSFR)

The LCR focuses on a bank's ability to survive a 30-day period of liquidity disruptions. It is defined as:

$$\frac{\text{High Quality Liquid Assets}}{\text{Net Cash Outflows in a 30-Day Period}}$$

The 30-day period considered in the calculation of this ratio is one of acute stress involving a downgrade of the bank's debt by three notches (e.g., from AA− to A−), a partial loss of deposits, a complete loss of wholesale funding, increased haircuts on secured funding (so that instruments posted as collateral are not valued as highly), and drawdowns on lines of credit. The Basel III regulations require the ratio to be greater than 100% so that the bank's liquid assets are sufficient to survive these pressures.

The NSFR focuses on liquidity management over a period of one year. It is defined as

$$\frac{\text{Amount of Stable Funding}}{\text{Required Amount of Stable Funding}}$$

The numerator is calculated by multiplying each category of funding (capital, wholesale deposits, retail deposits, etc.) by an available stable funding (ASF) factor, reflecting their stability. As shown in Table 13.4, the ASF for wholesale deposits is less than that for retail deposits which is in turn less than that for Tier 1 or Tier 2 capital. The denominator is calculated from the assets and off-balance-sheet items requiring funding. Each category of these is multiplied by a required stable funding (RSF) factor to reflect the permanence of the funding required. Some of the applicable factors are indicated in Table 13.5.

TABLE 13.4 ASF Factors for Net Stable Funding Ratio

ASF Factor	Category
100%	Tier 1 and Tier 2 capital
	Preferred stock and borrowing with a remaining maturity greater than one year
90%	"Stable" demand deposits and term deposits with remaining maturity less than one year provided by retail or small business customers
80%	"Less Stable" demand deposits and term deposits with remaining maturity less than one year provided by retail or small business customers
50%	Wholesale demand deposits and term deposits with remaining maturity less than one year provided by nonfinancial corporates, sovereigns, central banks, multilateral development banks, and public sector entities
0%	All other liability and equity categories

TABLE 13.5   RSF Factors for Net Stable Funding Ratio

RSF Factor	Category
0%	Cash
	Short-term instruments, securities, loans to financial entities if they have a residual maturity of less than one year
5%	Marketable securities with a residual maturity greater than one year if they are claims on sovereign governments or similar bodies with a 0% risk weight
20%	Corporate bonds with a rating of AA− or higher and a residual maturity greater than one year
	Claims on sovereign governments or similar bodies with a risk weight of 20%
50%	Gold, equity securities, bonds rated A+ to A−
65%	Residential mortgages
85%	Loans to retail and small business customers with a remaining maturity less than one year
100%	All other assets

Basel III requires the NSFR to be greater than 100% so that the calculated amount of stable funding is greater than the calculated required amount of stable funding.

EXAMPLE 13.1

A bank has the following balance sheet:

Cash	5	Retail Deposits (stable)	40
Treasury Bonds (> 1 yr)	5	Wholesale Deposits	48
Mortgages	20	Tier 2 Capital	4
Small Business Loans	60	Tier 1 Capital	8
Fixed Assets	10		
	100		100

The Amount of Stable Funding is

$$40 \times 0.9 + 48 \times 0.5 + 4 \times 1.0 + 8 \times 1.0 = 72$$

The Required Amount of Stable Funding is

$$5 \times 0 + 5 \times 0.05 + 20 \times 0.65 + 60 \times 0.85 + 10 \times 1.0 = 74.25$$

The NSFR is therefore

$$\frac{72}{74.25} = 0.970$$

or 97.0%. The bank does not therefore satisfy the NSFR requirement.

The new rules are tough and have the potential to dramatically change bank balance sheets. However, there is a transition period during which the effect of the rules will be monitored. It is possible that the rules will be eased somewhat before they are finally implemented. The LCR requirement is scheduled to be implemented on January 1, 2015. The NSFR requirement is scheduled to be implemented on January 1, 2018.

Counterparty Credit Risk

For each of its derivatives counterparties, a bank calculates a quantity known as the *credit value adjustment* (CVA). This is the expected loss because of the possibility of a default by the counterparty. The way in which the calculation of CVA is carried out is described in Chapter 17. Reported profit is reduced by the total of the CVAs for all counterparties.

As we will see in Chapter 17, the CVA for a counterparty can change because either (a) the market variables underlying the value of the derivatives entered into with the counterparty change or (b) the credit spreads applicable to the counterparty's borrowing change. Basel III requires the CVA risk arising from changing credit spreads to be incorporated into market-risk VaR calculations. As will be explained in Chapter 17, once CVA has been calculated, it is a relatively simple matter to calculate the delta and gamma with respect to a parallel shift in the term structure of the counterparty's credit spread. These can be used to add the counterparty's CVA to the other positions that are considered when market-risk calculations are carried out.

13.3 CONTINGENT CONVERTIBLE BONDS

An interesting development in the capitalization of banks has been what are known as *contingent convertible bonds* (CoCos). Traditionally, convertible bonds have been bonds issued by a company where, in certain circumstances, the holder can choose to convert them into equity at a predetermined exchange ratio. Typically the bond holder chooses to convert when the company is doing well and the stock price is high. CoCos are different in that they automatically get converted into equity when certain conditions are satisfied. Typically, these conditions are satisfied when the company is experiencing financial difficulties.

CoCos are attractive to banks because in normal times the bonds are debt and allow the bank to report a relatively high return on equity. When the bank experiences financial difficulties and incurs losses, the bonds are converted into equity and the bank is able to continue to maintain an equity cushion and avoid insolvency. From the point of view of regulators, CoCos are potentially attractive because they avoid the need for a bailout. Indeed, the conversion of CoCos is sometimes referred to as a "bail-in." New equity for the financial institution is provided from within by private sector bondholders rather than from outside by the public sector.

A key issue in the design of CoCos is the specification of the trigger that forces conversion and the way that the exchange ratio (number of shares received in exchange for one bond) is set. A popular trigger in the bonds issued so far is the ratio of Tier 1 equity capital to risk-weighted assets. Another possible trigger is the ratio of the market value of equity to book value of assets.

Lloyd's Banking Group, Rabobank Nederlands, and Credit Suisse were among the first banks to issue CoCos. Business Snapshot 13.1 provides a description of the bonds issued by Credit Suisse in 2011. These bonds get converted into equity

---

BUSINESS SNAPSHOT 13.1

Credit Suisse's CoCo Bond Issues

Swiss regulators require the two large Swiss banks (UBS and Credit Suisse) to hold Tier 1 equity capital equal to at least 10% of risk-weighted assets and total (Tier 1 plus Tier 2) capital equal to 19% of risk-weighted assets. The deadline for implementation is 2019. Credit Suisse has indicated that it plans to satisfy the extra 9% non-equity capital with contingent convertible capital bonds (CoCos).

On February 14, 2011, Credit Suisse announced that it had agreed to exchange $6.2 billion of existing investments by two Middle Eastern investors, Qatar Holding LLC and the Olayan Group LLC, for CoCos. The bonds automatically convert into equity if either of the following two conditions are satisfied:

1. The Tier 1 equity capital of Credit Suisse falls below 7% of risk-weighted assets.
2. The Swiss bank regulator determines that Credit Suisse requires public sector support to prevent it from becoming insolvent.

Credit Suisse followed this announcement on February 17, 2011, with a public issue of $2 billion of CoCos. These securities have similar terms to ones held to the Middle Eastern investors and were rated BBB+ by Fitch. They mature in 2041 and can be called any time after August 2015. The coupon is 7.875%. Any concerns that the market had no appetite for CoCos were alleviated by this issue. It was 11 times oversubscribed.

Credit Suisse has indicated that it plans to satisfy one-third of the non-equity capital requirement with bonds similar to those just described and two-thirds of the non-equity capital requirement with bonds where the conversion trigger is 5% (rather than 7%) of risk-weighted assets.

---

if either Tier 1 equity capital falls below 7% of risk-weighted assets or the Swiss bank regulators determine that the bank requires public sector support. It has been estimated that over $1 trillion of CoCos will be issued by banks during the decade beginning 2010 as they respond to the new Basel III regulatory requirements on capital adequacy.

13.4 DODD–FRANK ACT

The Dodd–Frank Act in the United States was signed into law in July 2010. Its aim is to prevent future bailouts of financial institutions and protect the consumer. A summary of the main regulations is as follows:

1. Two new bodies, the Financial Stability Oversight Council (FSOC) and the Office of Financial Research (OFR) were created to monitor systemic risk and

research the state of the economy. Their tasks are to identify risks to the financial stability of the United States, promote market discipline, and maintain investor confidence.

2. The orderly liquidation powers of the Federal Deposit Insurance Corporation (FDIC) were expanded. The Office of Thrift Supervision was eliminated.

3. The amount of deposits insured by the FDIC was increased permanently to $250,000.

4. Regulations were introduced requiring large hedge funds and similar financial intermediaries to register with the SEC and report on their activities.

5. A Federal Insurance Office was created to monitor all aspects of the insurance industry and work with state regulators.

6. Proprietary trading and other similar activities of deposit taking institutions were curtailed. This is known as the "Volcker rule" because it was proposed by former Federal Reserve chairman, Paul Volcker. (The main difficulty with this rule is that of distinguishing between hedging and speculative trades.)

7. Some high-risk trading operations were required to be spun off into separately capitalized affiliates.

8. Standardized over-the-counter derivatives were required to be cleared by central clearing parties (CCPs) or by exchanges. Swap execution facilities (SEFs) were mandated to facilitate OTC trading and provide more transparency on prices in the OTC market. The Commodity Futures Trading Commission (CFTC) was given responsibility for monitoring the activities of CCPs and SEFs.

9. The Federal Reserve was required to set risk management standards for systemically important financial utilities engaged in activities such as payment, settlement, and clearing.

10. Protection for investors was increased and improvements were made to the regulation of securities.

11. Rating agencies were required to make the assumptions and methodologies behind their ratings more transparent and the potential legal liabilities of rating agencies were increased. An Office of Credit Ratings was created at the SEC to provide oversight of rating agencies.

12. The use of external credit ratings in the regulation of financial institutions was banned. (This provision of the Act brings Dodd–Frank into direct conflict with the Basel Committee, which as we have seen in this chapter and the last one, does make some use of external credit ratings.)

13. A Bureau of Financial Protection was created within the Federal Reserve to ensure that consumers get clear and accurate information when they shop for financial products such as mortgages and credit cards.

14. Issuers of securitized products were required (with some exceptions) to keep 5% of each product created.

15. Federal bank regulators were required to issue regulations that discourage the use of compensation arrangements that might lead to excessive risk taking (e.g., compensation arrangements based on short run performance). Shareholders were given a non-binding vote on executive compensation. A requirement that board compensation committees be made up of independent directors was introduced.

16. Mortgage lenders were required to make a "reasonable good faith determination" based on verified and documented information that the borrower has the ability to repay a loan. Failure to do this might lead to a foreclosure being disallowed.

17. Large financial firms were required to have board committees where at least one expert has risk management experience at a large complex firm.
18. The FDIC is allowed to take over a large financial institution when it is failing and sell its assets, imposing losses on shareholders and creditors with the costs of failures being paid for by the financial industry.
19. FSOC and OFR, which as mentioned in 1 above have the responsibility of monitoring systemic risk, are charged with identifying systemically important financial institutions (SIFIs). As indicated in Section 13.2, any bank in the United States with assets of more than $50 billion is a SIFI. The criteria for nonbank SIFIs is less clear. FSOC has been given the authority to impose extra capital requirements on SIFIs.
20. The Federal Reserve Board and the FDIC require all SIFIs to prepare what is known as *living wills* mapping out how they can be safely wound up in the event of failure. SIFIs tend to have developed complex organizational structures for tax and regulatory purposes. The living will requirement may result in this being simplified so that the different activities of a SIFI are in separately capitalized legal entities. Regulators have the option of forcing SIFIs to divest certain operations, or even break up entirely, if their living wills are deemed unsatisfactory.

The Dodd–Frank Act did not define a future role for Fannie Mae and Freddie Mac, which were key players in the U.S. mortgage market. These agencies were taken over by the U.S. government in September 2008 in what will undoubtedly prove to be the most expensive part of the credit crisis for U.S. taxpayers.

An important objective of legislators post-crisis is to increase transparency of derivatives markets. One way they are doing this is by creating a trade repository of all derivatives transactions. A key part of this will be the creation of a new Legal Entity Identifier system. In the United States, this will be the responsibility of the Office of Financial Research. AIG's positions in credit derivatives were apparently unknown to financial regulators prior to the bailout in September 2008. A central repository for all derivatives transactions should mean that regulators are never taken by surprise in this way again.

13.5 LEGISLATION IN OTHER COUNTRIES

The large banks are truly global and when regulations vary throughout the world, they are liable to move all or part of their operations from one jurisdiction to another. Although all countries are subject to the same Basel III rules, the extra discretionary capital charged by regulators does vary from country to country. In 2011, the Swiss bank UBS made headlines by suggesting that it might move its investment bank headquarters from Zurich to London, Singapore, or New York to avoid the higher capital requirements imposed by Swiss regulators.

The previous section outlined the rules introduced by legislators in the United States. Legislation in other countries has addressed some of the same issues. Some rules are similar to those in the United States. For example, the Dodd–Frank Act requires originators of securitized products in the United States to keep 5% of all assets created. A similar provision exists in the Capital Requirement Directive 2

(CRD2) of the European Union.[8] But there are some important differences. For example, the Volcker provision of the Dodd–Frank Act restricts proprietary trading by U.S. banks, but most other governments have not introduced similar provisions.

Most national legislators have agreed that standardized over-the-counter derivatives should be cleared through central clearing houses instead of being cleared bilaterally. The rules in different countries are similar, but not exactly the same. A bank may find that it can avoid central clearing rules on some transactions by choosing the jurisdiction governing its transactions carefully.

The central concern of all national legislators is of course the implicit "too-big-to-fail" guarantee. This creates moral hazard, encouraging banks to take risks because, if things work out badly, they will be bailed out. The increases in the Basel capital charges should go some way toward reducing the moral hazard. For systemically important banks, living wills are important. Regulators want banks to be structured so that one part (e.g., one concerned with trading activities) can fail without other parts (e.g., those concerned with deposit-taking) being affected. Most countries with large banks are actively trying to introduce legislation on living wills.

Compensation is an important issue. Pre-crisis, the annual bonus was a large part of the compensation for many traders and other employees and led them to have a relatively short-term horizon in their decision making. If losses were incurred after the payment of a bonus, they did not have to return the bonus. Many banks have recognized the problem and voluntarily moved to bonuses that are deferred by being spread out over three to five years, rather than all being paid in one year. If a trader shows good results in one year and bad results in the next, some of the bonus applicable to the good year will be deferred and then "clawed back" during the bad year. The Dodd–Frank Act restrictions on pay in the financial sector are relatively mild. When financial institutions received funds during the crisis under the Troubled Asset Relief Program (TARP), compensation was restricted. But, as soon as the funds were paid back, banks had much more freedom in their compensation arrangements.[9] Some other countries have restricted compensation, but usually only temporarily. For example, the UK introduced a one-time "supertax" on bonuses in excess of £25,000. Of course, there is a limit to what any one country can do. If it restricts bonuses or taxes them too heavily, banks will simply move key personnel to another jurisdiction.

SUMMARY

The financial crisis that started in 2007 was the worst that many parts of the world had seen since the 1930s. Some financial institutions failed. Others had to be bailed out with taxpayer's money. Not surprisingly, both the Basel Committee and national governments decided that a major overhaul of the regulations affecting financial institutions was required.

The Basel 2.5 regulations increased what the capital banks were required to keep for market risk. They recognized that capital should reflect the volatilities and correlations experienced during stressed market conditions as well as during normal

---

[8] However, Germany has increased the 5% to 10%.

[9] Indeed, this was a major incentive to repay the TARP money as quickly as possible.

market conditions; they eliminated some of the ways banks could reduce regulatory capital by moving items from the banking book to the trading book; and they created a special capital requirement for derivatives dependent on credit correlation, which had been a particular problem during the crisis.

Basel III dramatically increased the amount of equity capital banks were required to keep. It also recognized that many of the problems of banks during the crisis were liquidity problems and imposed new liquidity requirements for financial institutions

National governments have also introduced new regulations for financial institutions. In the United States, the Dodd–Frank Act has many provisions designed to protect consumers and investors, avoid future bailouts, and monitor the functioning of the financial system more carefully.

Exactly how Basel III and national legislation such as Dodd–Frank will be implemented is still uncertain—and this uncertainty is one of the major risks that banks face. How successful will the measures be once they have been implemented? We will not know this for some time. One problem facing regulators is what are referred to as *unintended consequences*. Basel I had the unintended consequence of discouraging loans to high quality corporations because of the 100% risk weight that would be assigned. The 1996 Amendment and the development of the credit derivatives market that came after it encouraged banks to find ways of moving credit risks from the banking book to the trading book in order to reduce capital requirements. There will no doubt be unintended consequences of Basel III and the legislation that is being introduced throughout the world. (For example, the higher equity capital requirements may lead banks to find ways of taking more risks in an effort to maintain their return on equity.) Hopefully, the benefits of the new measures will outweigh any harm to the financial system arising from the unintended consequences.

FURTHER READING

Acharya, V. V., T. F. Cooley, M. P. Richardson, and I. Walter. *Regulating Wall Street: The Dodd–Frank Act and the New Architecture of Global Finance*. Hoboken, NJ: John Wiley & Sons, 2011.

Basel Committee on Bank Supervision. "Revisions to the Basel II Market Risk Framework," February 2011.

Basel Committee on Banking Supervision. "Guidelines for Computing Capital for Incremental Risk in the Trading Book," July 2009.

Basel Committee on Banking Supervision. "Basel III: A Global Regulatory Framework for More Resilient Banks and Banking Systems," December 2010.

Basel Committee on Banking Supervision. "Basel III: International Framework for Liquidity Risk Measurement Standards and Monitoring," December 2010.

Finger, C. "CreditMetrics and Constant Level of Risk," MSCI, 2010.

PRACTICE QUESTIONS AND PROBLEMS
(ANSWERS AT END OF BOOK)

13.1 What are the three major components of Basel 2.5?

13.2 What are the six major components of Basel III?

13.3 What is the difference between VaR as it has been traditionally measured and stressed VaR?

13.4 Explain how the incremental risk charge is calculated. Why was it introduced by the Basel Committee?

13.5 What is the difference between the capital required for a AAA-rated ABS with principal of $100 million and a AAA-rated ABS CDO with a principal of $100 million using the standardized approach?

13.6 By how much has the Tier 1 equity capital (including the capital conservation buffer) increased under Basel III compared with the Tier 1 equity capital requirement under Basel I and II?

13.7 Suppose that the Tier 1 equity ratio for a bank is 6%. What is the maximum dividend, as a percent of earnings, that can be paid if (a) there is no countercyclical buffer and (b) there is a 2.5% countercyclical buffer?

13.8 Explain how the leverage ratio differs from the usual capital ratios calculated by regulators.

13.9 Explain how the Liquidity Coverage Ratio and the Net Stable Funding Ratio are defined.

13.10 How would the Net Stable Funding Ratio in Example 13.1 change if half the wholesale deposits were replaced by stable retail deposits?

13.11 What is CVA? What new regulations concerning CVA were introduced in Basel III?

13.12 Explain how CoCo bonds work. Why are they attractive to (a) banks and (b) regulators?

FURTHER QUESTIONS

13.13 Explain one way that the Dodd–Frank Act is in conflict with (a) the Basel international regulations and (b) the regulations introduced by other national governments.

13.14 A bank has the following balance sheet:

Cash	3	Retail Deposits (stable)	25
Treasury Bonds (> 1 yr)	5	Retail Deposits (less stable)	15
Corporate Bonds Rated A	4	Wholesale Deposits	44
Mortgages	18	Preferred Stock (> 1 yr)	4
Small Business Loans	60	Tier 2 Capital	3
Fixed Assets	10	Tier 1 Capital	9
	100		100

(a) What is the Net Stable Funding Ratio?

(b) The bank decides to satisfy Basel III by raising more retail deposits and keeping the proceeds in Treasury bonds. What extra retail deposits need to be raised?

CHAPTER 14

Market Risk VaR: The Historical Simulation Approach

In this chapter and the next, we cover the two main approaches to calculating VaR for market risk. The approach we consider in this chapter is known as historical simulation and is the one usually used by banks. It involves using the day-to-day changes in the values of market variables that have been observed in the past in a direct way to estimate the probability distribution of the change in the value of the current portfolio between today and tomorrow.

After describing the mechanics of the historical simulation approach, the chapter explains how to calculate the standard error of the VaR estimate, how the procedure can be modified so that recent data are given more weight, and how volatility data can be incorporated into the VaR estimates that are made. Finally, it covers extreme value theory. This is a tool that can be used to improve VaR estimates and deal with situations where the required VaR confidence level is very high.

All the models covered in this chapter are illustrated with a portfolio consisting of an investment in four different stock indices. Historical data on the indices and VaR calculations can be found at: www.rotman.utoronto.ca/~hull/RMFI3e/VaRExample.

14.1 THE METHODOLOGY

Historical simulation involves using past data as a guide to what will happen in the future. Suppose that we want to calculate VaR for a portfolio using a one-day time horizon, a 99% confidence level, and 501 days of data. (The time horizon and confidence level are those typically used for a market risk VaR calculation; 501 is a popular choice for the number of days of data used because, as we shall see, it leads to 500 scenarios being created.) The first step is to identify the market variables affecting the portfolio. These will typically be exchange rates, interest rates, stock indices, and so on. Data are then collected on movements in these market variables over the most recent 501 days. This provides 500 alternative scenarios for what can happen between today and tomorrow. Denote the first day for which we have data as Day 0, the second day as Day 1, and so on. Scenario 1 is where the percentage changes in the values of all variables are the same as they were between Day 0 and Day 1, Scenario 2 is where they are the same as between Day 1 and Day 2, and so on. For each scenario, the dollar change in the value of the portfolio between today and

TABLE 14.1   Investment Portfolio Used for
VaR Calculations

Index	Portfolio Value ($000s)
DJIA	4,000
FTSE 100	3,000
CAC 40	1,000
Nikkei 225	2,000
Total	10,000

tomorrow is calculated. This defines a probability distribution for daily loss (with gains counted as negative losses) in the value of the portfolio. The 99th percentile of the distribution can be estimated as the fifth worst outcome.[1] The estimate of VaR is the loss when we are at this 99th percentile point. We are 99% certain that we will not take a loss greater than the VaR estimate if the changes in market variables in the last 500 days are representative of what will happen between today and tomorrow.

To express the approach algebraically, define v_i as the value of a market variable on Day i and suppose that today is Day n. The ith scenario in the historical simulation approach assumes that the value of the market variable tomorrow will be

$$\text{Value Under } i\text{th Scenario} = v_n \frac{v_i}{v_{i-1}} \qquad (14.1)$$

Illustration

To illustrate the calculations underlying the approach, suppose that an investor in the United States owns, on September 25, 2008, a portfolio worth $10 million consisting of investments in four stock indices: the Dow Jones Industrial Average (DJIA) in the United States, the FTSE 100 in the United Kingdom, the CAC 40 in France, and the Nikkei 225 in Japan. The value of the investment in each index on September 25, 2008, is shown in Table 14.1. An Excel spreadsheet containing 501 days of historical data on the closing prices of the four indices and a complete set of VaR calculations are on the author's website:[2] www.rotman.utoronto.ca/~hull/RMFI3e/VaRExample.

Because we are considering a U.S. investor, the values of the FTSE 100, CAC 40, and Nikkei 225 must be measured in U.S. dollars. For example, the FTSE 100 was 5,823.40 on August 10, 2008, when the exchange rate was 1.8918 USD per GBP.

---

[1] There are alternatives here. A case can be made for using the fifth worst loss, the sixth worst loss, or an average of the two. In Excel's PERCENTILE function, when there are n observations and k is an integer, the $k/(n-1)$ percentile is the observation ranked $k+1$. Other percentiles are calculated using linear interpolation.

[2] To keep the example as straightforward as possible, only days when all four indices traded were included in the compilation of the data. This is why the 501 items of data extend from August 7, 2006, to September 25, 2008. In practice, an attempt might be made to fill in data for days that were not U.S. holidays.

TABLE 14.2 U.S. Dollar Equivalent of Stock Indices for Historical Simulation
Calculation

Day	Date	DJIA	FTSE 100	CAC 40	Nikkei 225
0	Aug. 7, 2006	11,219.38	11,131.84	6,373.89	131.77
1	Aug. 8, 2006	11,173.59	11,096.28	6,378.16	134.38
2	Aug. 9, 2006	11,076.18	11,185.35	6,474.04	135.94
3	Aug. 10, 2006	11,124.37	11,016.71	6,357.49	135.44
...	...	...	...	...	...
...	...	...	...	...	...
499	Sept. 24, 2008	10,825.17	9,438.58	6,033.93	114.26
500	Sept. 25, 2008	11,022.06	9,599.90	6,200.40	112.82

This means that, measured in U.S. dollars, it was $5,823.40 \times 1.8918 = 11,016.71$.
An extract from the data with all indices measured in U.S. dollars is shown in
Table 14.2.

September 25, 2008, is an interesting date to choose in evaluating an equity
investment. The turmoil in credit markets, which started in August 2007, was over
a year old. Equity prices had been declining for several months. Volatilities were
increasing. Lehman Brothers had filed for bankruptcy 10 days earlier. The Treasury
Secretary's $700 billion Troubled Asset Relief Program (TARP) had not yet been
passed by the United States Congress.

Table 14.3 shows the values of the indices (measured in U.S. dollars) on September 26, 2008, for the scenarios considered. Scenario 1 (the first row in Table 14.3)
shows the values of indices on September 26, 2008, assuming that their percentage
changes between September 25 and September 26, 2008, are the same as they were
between August 7 and August 8, 2006; Scenario 2 (the second row in Table 14.3)
shows the values of indices on September 26, 2008, assuming these percentage
changes are the same as those between August 8 and August 9, 2006; and so on.
In general, Scenario i assumes that the percentage changes in the indices between
September 25 and September 26 are the same as they were between Day $i - 1$ and
Day i for $1 \leq i \leq 500$. The 500 rows in Table 14.3 are the 500 scenarios considered.

TABLE 14.3 Scenarios Generated for September 26, 2008, Using Data in Table 14.2

Scenario Number	DJIA	FTSE 100	CAC 40	Nikkei 225	Portfolio Value ($000s)	Loss ($000s)
1	10,977.08	9,569.23	6,204.55	115.05	10,014.334	−14.334
2	10,925.97	9,676.96	6,293.60	114.13	10,027.481	−27.481
3	11,070.01	9,455.16	6,088.77	112.40	9,946.736	53.264
...	...	...	...	...	...	
...	...	...	...	...	...	
499	10,831.43	9,383.49	6,051.94	113.85	9,857.465	142.535
500	11,222.53	9,763.97	6,371.45	111.40	10,126.439	−126.439

(All indices are measured in U.S. dollars.)

The DJIA is 11,022.06 on September 25, 2008. On August 8, 2006, it was 11,173.59, down from 11,219.38 on August 7, 2006. The value of the DJIA under Scenario 1 is therefore

$$11,022.06 \times \frac{11,173.59}{11,219.38} = 10,977.08$$

Similarly the value of the FTSE 100, the CAC 40, and the Nikkei 225 (measured in U.S. dollars) are 9569.23, 6204.55, and 115.05, respectively. The value of the portfolio under Scenario 1 is therefore (in $000s)

$$4,000 \times \frac{10,977.08}{11,022.06} + 3,000 \times \frac{9,569.23}{9,599.90} + 1,000 \times \frac{6,204.55}{6,200.40} + 2,000$$

$$\times \frac{115.05}{112.82} = 10,014.334$$

The portfolio therefore has a gain of $14,334 under Scenario 1. A similar calculation is carried out for the other scenarios. A histogram for the losses (gains are negative losses) is shown in Figure 14.1. (The bars on the histogram represent losses [$000s] in the ranges 450 to 550, 350 to 450, 250 to 350, and so on.)

The losses for the 500 different scenarios are then ranked. An extract from the results of doing this is shown in Table 14.4. The worst scenario is number 494. The one-day 99% value at risk can be estimated as the fifth-worst loss. This is $253,385.

As explained in Section 12.6, the 10-day 99% VaR is usually calculated as $\sqrt{10}$ times the one-day 99% VaR. In this case, the 10-day VaR would therefore be

$$\sqrt{10} \times 253,385 = 801,274$$

or $801,274.

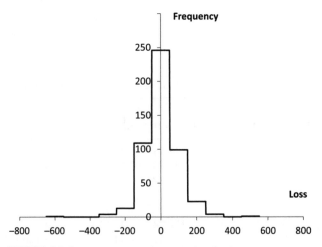

FIGURE 14.1   Histogram of Losses for the Scenarios Considered between September 25 and September 26, 2008

TABLE 14.4 Losses Ranked from
Highest to Lowest for 500 Scenarios

Scenario Number	Loss ($000s)
494	477.841
339	345.435
349	282.204
329	277.041
487	253.385
227	217.974
131	205.256
238	201.389
473	191.269
306	191.050
477	185.127
495	184.450
376	182.707
237	180.105
365	172.224
...	...
...	...
...	...

Each day, the VaR estimate in our example would be updated using the most recent 501 days of data. Consider, for example, what happens on September 26, 2008 (Day 501). We find out new values for all the market variables and are able to calculate a new value for our portfolio. We then go through the procedure we have outlined to calculate a new VaR. Data on the market variables from August 8, 2006, to September 26, 2008 (Day 1 to Day 501), are used in the calculation. (This gives us the required 500 observations on the percentage changes in market variables; the August 7, 2006, Day 0, values of the market variables are no longer used.) Similarly, on the next trading day, September 29, 2008 (Day 502), data from August 9, 2006, to September 29, 2008 (Day 2 to Day 502), are used to determine VaR; and so on.

In practice, a bank's portfolio is, of course, considerably more complicated than the one we have considered here. It is likely to consist of thousands or tens of thousands of positions. Some of the bank's positions are typically in forward contracts, options, and other derivatives. Also, the portfolio itself is likely to change from day to day. If a bank's trading leads to a riskier portfolio, the 10-day 99% VaR typically increases; if it leads to a less risky portfolio, the VaR typically decreases. The VaR on any given day is calculated on the assumption that the portfolio will remain unchanged over the next business day.

The market variables that have to be considered in a VaR calculation include exchange rates, commodity prices, and interest rates. In the case of interest rates, a bank typically needs the Treasury and LIBOR/swap term structure of zero-coupon interest rates in a number of different currencies in order to value its portfolio. The market variables that are considered are the ones from which these term structures are calculated (see Appendix B for the calculations to obtain the zero-coupon term structure of interest rates). There might be as many as ten market variables for each zero curve to which the bank is exposed.

Stressed VaR

As explained in Section 13.1, Basel 2.5 requires banks to calculate a stressed VaR in addition to a VaR based on recent historical data. To calculate a stressed VaR, the bank first searches for a 251-day period during which its current portfolio would perform very badly. The data for that 251-day period then plays the same role as the 501-day period in our example. The changes in market variables between Day 0 and Day 1 of the 251-day period are used to create the first scenario; the changes in market variables between Day 1 and Day 2 of the 251-day period are used to create the second scenario; and so on. In total, 250 scenarios are created and the one-day 99% stressed VaR is the loss that is midway between the loss for the second worst scenario and the loss for the third worst scenario.

14.2 ACCURACY

The historical simulation approach estimates the distribution of portfolio changes from a finite number of observations. As a result, the estimates of percentiles of the distribution are subject to error.

Kendall and Stuart (1972) describe how to calculate a confidence interval for the percentile of a probability distribution when it is estimated from sample data.[3] Suppose that the q-percentile of the distribution is estimated as x. The standard error of the estimate is

$$\frac{1}{f(x)}\sqrt{\frac{(1-q)q}{n}}$$

where n is the number of observations and $f(x)$ is an estimate of the probability density function of the loss evaluated at x. The probability density, $f(x)$, can be estimated approximately by fitting the empirical data to an appropriate distribution whose properties are known.

EXAMPLE 14.1

Suppose we are interested in estimating the 99th percentile of a loss distribution from 500 observations so that $n = 500$ and $q = 0.99$. We can estimate $f(x)$ by approximating the actual empirical distribution with a standard distribution whose properties are known. Suppose that a normal distribution is chosen as the standard distribution and the best-fit mean and standard deviation are zero and $10 million,

---

[3] See M. G. Kendall and A. Stuart, *The Advanced Theory of Statistics, Vol. 1: Distribution Theory*, 4th ed. (London: Charles Griffin and Co., 1972).

respectively. Using Excel, the 99th percentile is NORMINV(0.99,0,10) or 23.26. The value of $f(x)$ is NORMDIST(23.26,0,10,FALSE) or 0.0027. The standard error of the estimate that is made is

$$\frac{1}{0.0027} \times \sqrt{\frac{0.01 \times 0.99}{500}} = 1.67$$

If the estimate of the 99th percentile using historical simulation is \$25 million, a 95% confidence interval is from $25 - 1.96 \times 1.67$ to $25 + 1.96 \times 1.67$, that is, from \$21.7 million to \$28.3 million.

As Example 14.1 illustrates, the standard error of a VaR estimated using historical simulation tends to be quite high. It decreases as the VaR confidence level is decreased. For example, if in Example 14.1 the VaR confidence level had been 95% instead of 99%, the standard error would be \$0.95 million instead of \$1.67 million. The standard error declines as the sample size is increased—but only as the square root of the sample size. If we quadrupled the sample size in Example 14.1 from 500 to 2,000 observations, the standard error halves from \$1.67 million to about \$0.83 million.

Additionally, we should bear in mind that historical simulation assumes that the joint distribution of daily changes in market variables is stationary through time. This is unlikely to be exactly true and creates additional uncertainty about VaR.

In the case of the data considered in Tables 14.1 to 14.4, when the loss is measured in \$000s, the mean is 0.870 and the standard deviation is \$93.698. If a normal distribution is assumed, a similar calculation to that in Example 14.1 gives $f(x)$ as 0.000284 and the standard error of the estimate (in \$000s) is

$$\frac{1}{0.000284} \times \sqrt{\frac{0.01 \times 0.99}{500}} = 15.643$$

The estimate of VaR is \$253,385. This shows that a 95% confidence interval for the VaR is about \$220,000 to \$280,000.

The normal distribution is not a particularly good assumption for the loss distribution, because the losses have heavier tails than the normal distribution. (Excess kurtosis, a measure of the heaviness of tails, is 4.2 for the data in Tables 14.1 to 14.4.) Better standard error estimates can be obtained by assuming a Pareto distribution for $f(x)$, as will be discussed in Section 14.6.

14.3 EXTENSIONS

The key assumption underlying the historical simulation approach is that the history is in some sense a good guide to the future. More precisely, it is that the empirical probability distribution estimated for market variables over the last few years is a good guide to the behavior of the market variables over the next day. Unfortunately, the behavior of market variables is nonstationary. Sometimes the volatility of a market variable is high; sometimes it is low. In this section, we cover extensions of the basic historical simulation approach in Section 14.1 that are designed to adjust for nonstationarity.

Weighting of Observations

The basic historical simulation approach assumes that each day in the past is given equal weight. More formally, if we have observations for n day-to-day changes, each of them is given a weighting of $1/n$. Boudoukh et al. (1998) suggest that more recent observations should be given more weight because they are more reflective of current volatilities and current macroeconomic conditions.[4] The natural weighting scheme to use is one where weights decline exponentially. (We used this in Section 10.6 when developing the exponentially weighted moving average model for monitoring volatility.) The weight assigned to Scenario 1 (which is the one calculated from the most distant data) is λ times that assigned to Scenario 2. This in turn is λ times that given to Scenario 3 and so on. So that the weights add up to 1, the weight given to Scenario i is

$$\frac{\lambda^{n-i}(1-\lambda)}{1-\lambda^n}$$

where n is the number of scenarios. As λ approaches 1 this approaches the basic historical simulation approach where all observations are given a weight of $1/n$. (See Problem 14.2.)

VaR is calculated by ranking the observations from the worst outcome to the best. Starting at the worst outcome, weights are summed until the required percentile of the distribution is reached. For example, if we are calculating VaR with a 99% confidence level, we continue summing weights until the sum just exceeds 0.01. We have then reached the 99% VaR level. The parameter λ can be chosen by experimenting to see which value back-tests best. One disadvantage of the exponential weighting approach relative to the basic historical simulation approach is that the effective sample size is reduced. However, we can compensate for this by using a larger value of n. Indeed, it is not really necessary to discard old days as we move forward in time, because they are given relatively little weight.

Table 14.5 shows the results of using this procedure for the portfolio considered in Section 14.1 with $\lambda = 0.995$. The value of VaR when the confidence level is 99% is now the third worst loss, \$282,204 (not the fifth worst loss of \$253,385). The reason for this result is that recent observations are given more weight and the largest losses have occurred relatively recently. The standard calculation in Section 14.1 gives all observations a weighting of $1/500 = 0.002$. The highest loss occurred on Scenario 494 and this scenario has a weight of

$$\frac{(0.995^6) \times 0.005}{1 - 0.995^{500}} = 0.00528$$

---

[4] See J. Boudoukh, M. Richardson, and R. Whitelaw, "The Best of Both Worlds: A Hybrid Approach to Calculating Value at Risk," *Risk* 11 (May 1998): 64–67.

TABLE 14.5   Losses Ranked from Highest to Lowest for 500 Scenarios with Weights

Scenario Number	Loss ($000s)	Weight	Cumulative Weight
494	477.841	0.00528	0.00528
339	345.435	0.00243	0.00771
349	282.204	0.00255	0.01027
329	277.041	0.00231	0.01258
487	253.385	0.00510	0.01768
227	217.974	0.00139	0.01906
131	202.256	0.00086	0.01992
238	201.389	0.00146	0.02138
473	191.269	0.00476	0.02614
...	...	...	...
...	...	...	...
...	...	...	...

Incorporating Volatility Updating

Hull and White (1998) suggest a way of incorporating volatility, updating into the historical simulation approach.[5] A volatility-updating procedure, such as EWMA or GARCH(1,1) (both of which were described in Chapter 10) is used in parallel with the historical simulation approach for all market variables. Suppose that the daily volatility for a particular market variable estimated at the end of day $i - 1$ is σ_i. This is an estimate of the daily volatility between the end of day $i - 1$ and the end of day i. Suppose that it is now day n. The current estimate of the volatility of the market variable is σ_{n+1}. This applies to the time period between today and tomorrow, which is the time period over which we are calculating VaR.

Suppose that σ_{n+1} is twice σ_i for a particular market variable so that we estimate the daily volatility the variable to be twice as great today as on day $i - 1$. This means that we expect to see changes between today and tomorrow that are twice as big as changes between day $i - 1$ and day i. When carrying out the historical simulation and creating a sample of what could happen between today and tomorrow based on what happened between day $i - 1$ and day i, it therefore makes sense to multiply the latter by 2. In general, when this approach is used, the expression in equation (14.1) for the value of a market variable under the ith scenario becomes

$$\text{Value under } i\text{th Scenario} = v_n \frac{v_{i-1} + (v_i - v_{i-1})\sigma_{n+1}/\sigma_i}{v_{i-1}} \qquad (14.2)$$

Each market variable is handled in the same way.

This approach takes account of volatility changes in a natural and intuitive way and produces VaR estimates that incorporate more current information. The VaR estimates can be greater than any of the historical losses that would have occurred

---

[5] See J. Hull and A. White, "Incorporating Volatility Updating into the Historical Simulation Method for Value at Risk," *Journal of Risk* (Fall 1998): 5–19.

TABLE 14.6   Volatilities (% per Day) Estimated for the Following Day Using EWMA with $\lambda = 0.94$

Day	Date	DJIA	FTSE 100	CAC 40	Nikkei 225
0	Aug. 7, 2006	1.11	1.42	1.40	1.38
1	Aug. 8, 2006	1.08	1.38	1.36	1.43
2	Aug. 9, 2006	1.07	1.35	1.36	1.41
3	Aug. 10, 2006	1.04	1.36	1.39	1.37
...	...	...	...	...	...
...	...	...	...	...	...
499	Sept. 24, 2008	2.21	3.28	3.11	1.61
500	Sept. 25, 2008	2.19	3.21	3.09	1.59

for the current portfolio during the historical period considered. Hull and White produce evidence using exchange rates and stock indices to show that this approach is superior to traditional historical simulation and to the exponential weighting scheme described earlier. More complicated models can in theory be developed, where observations are adjusted for the latest information on correlations as well as for the latest information on volatilities.

For the data in Table 14.2, the daily volatility estimates, calculated using EWMA with a value of λ equal to 0.94, are shown in Table 14.6.[6] The ratios of the volatility estimated for September 26, 2008 (last row of table), to the volatility estimated for August 8, 2008 (first row of table), are 1.94, 2.26, 2.21, and 1.15 for DJIA, FTSE 100, CAC 40, and Nikkei 225, respectively. These are used as multipliers for the actual changes in the indices between August 7 and August 8, 2006. Similarly, the ratios of the volatility estimated for September 26, 2008 (last row of table), to the volatility estimated for August 9, 2008 (second row of table), are 2.03, 2.33, 2.28, and 1.12 for DJIA, FTSE 100, CAC 40, and Nikkei 225, respectively. These are used as multipliers for the actual changes in the indices between August 8 and August 9, 2006. Multipliers for the other 498 daily changes are calculated in the same way.

Because volatilities were highest at the end of the historical period, the effect of the volatility adjustments is to create more variability in the gains and losses for the 500 scenarios. Table 14.7 shows an extract from a table that ranks losses from the highest to the lowest. Comparing this with Table 14.4, we see that the losses are much higher. The one-day 99% VaR is $602,968, over twice as high as the VaR given by the standard calculations.

In this particular case, the volatility of the stock indices remained high for the rest of 2008, with daily changes of between 5% and 10% in the indices being not uncommon. Estimating VaR using the volatility-adjusted approach would have worked better than using the standard approach.

---

[6] A decision must be made on how to start the variance time series. Any reasonable approach can be used. It makes little difference to the results that are obtained. The initial variance in the calculations reported here was the sample variance calculated over the whole time period.

TABLE 14.7   Volatility Adjusted Losses
Ranked from Highest to Lowest for
500 Scenarios

Scenario Number	Loss ($000s)
131	1,082.969
494	715.512
227	687.720
98	661.221
329	602.968
339	546.540
74	492.764
193	470.092
487	458.177
. . .	. . .
. . .	. . .
. . .	. . .

Bootstrap Method

The bootstrap method is a variation on the basic historical simulation approach, aimed at calculating a confidence interval for VaR. It involves creating a set of changes in the portfolio value based on historical movements in market variables in the usual way. We then sample with replacement from these changes to create many new similar data sets. We calculate the VaR for each of the new data sets. Our 95% confidence interval for VaR is the range between the 2.5 percentile point and the 97.5 percentile point of the distribution of the VaRs calculated from the data sets.

Suppose, for example, that we have 500 days of data. We could sample with replacement 500,000 times from the data to obtain 1,000 different sets of 500 days of data. We calculate the VaR for each set. We then rank the VaRs. Suppose that the 25th largest VaR is $5.3 million and the 975th largest VaR is $8.9 million. The 95% confidence interval for VaR is $5.3 million to $8.9 million. Usually, the width of the confidence interval calculated for VaR using the bootstrap method is less than that calculated using the procedure in Section 14.2.

14.4   COMPUTATIONAL ISSUES

Historical simulation involves valuing the whole portfolio of a financial institution many times (500 times in our example). This can be computationally very time consuming. This is particularly true when some of the instruments in the portfolio are valued with Monte Carlo simulation because there is then a "simulation within a simulation" problem: each trial of the historical simulation involves a Monte Carlo simulation.

To reduce computation time, financial institutions sometimes use a delta–gamma approximation. This is explained in Chapter 7. Consider an instrument whose price,

P, is dependent on a single market variable, S. An approximate estimate of the change, ΔP, in P resulting from a change, ΔS, in S is

$$\Delta P = \delta \Delta S + \frac{1}{2}\gamma(\Delta S)^2 \qquad (14.3)$$

where δ and γ are the delta and gamma of P with respect to S. The Greek letters, δ and γ, are always known because they are calculated when the instrument is marked to market each day. This equation can therefore be used as a fast approximate way of calculating the changes in the value of the transaction for the changes in the value of S that are considered by the historical simulation.

When an instrument depends on several market variables, $S_i (1 \leq i \leq n)$, equation (14.3) becomes

$$\Delta P = \sum_{i=1}^{n} \delta_i \Delta S_i + \sum_{i=1}^{n}\sum_{j=1}^{n} \frac{1}{2}\gamma_{ij}\Delta S_i \Delta S_j \qquad (14.4)$$

where δ_i and γ_{ij} are defined as

$$\delta_i = \frac{\partial P}{\partial S_i} \qquad \gamma_{ij} = \frac{\partial^2 P}{\partial S_i \partial S_j}$$

14.5 EXTREME VALUE THEORY

Section 10.4 introduced the power law and explained that it can be used to estimate the tails of a wide range of distributions. We now provide the theoretical underpinnings for the power law and present estimation procedures more sophisticated than those used in Section 10.4. *Extreme value theory* (EVT) is the term used to describe the science of estimating the tails of a distribution. EVT can be used to improve VaR estimates and to help in situations where analysts want to estimate VaR with a very high confidence level. It is a way of smoothing and extrapolating the tails of an empirical distribution.

The Key Result

The key result in EVT was proved by Gnedenko in 1943.[7] It shows that the tails of a wide range of different probability distributions share common properties.

Suppose that $F(v)$ is the cumulative distribution function for a variable v (such as the loss on a portfolio over a certain period of time) and that u is a value of v in the right-hand tail of the distribution. The probability that v lies between u and $u + y$ $(y > 0)$ is $F(u + y) - F(u)$. The probability that v is greater than u is $1 - F(u)$.

---

[7] See D. V. Gnedenko, "Sur la distribution limité du terme d'une série aléatoire," *Ann. Math.* 44 (1943): 423–453.

Define $F_u(y)$ as the probability that v lies between u and $u + y$ conditional on $v > u$. This is

$$F_u(y) = \frac{F(u + y) - F(u)}{1 - F(u)}$$

The variable $F_u(y)$ defines the right tail of the probability distribution. It is the cumulative probability distribution for the amount by which v exceeds u given that it does exceed u.

Gnedenko's result states that, for a wide class of distributions $F(v)$, the distribution of $F_u(y)$ converges to a generalized Pareto distribution as the threshold u is increased. The generalized Pareto (cumulative) distribution is

$$G_{\xi,\beta}(y) = 1 - \left[1 + \xi \frac{y}{\beta}\right]^{-1/\xi} \tag{14.5}$$

The distribution has two parameters that have to be estimated from the data. These are ξ and β. The parameter ξ is the shape parameter and determines the heaviness of the tail of the distribution. The parameter β is a scale parameter.

When the underlying variable v has a normal distribution, $\xi = 0$.[8] As the tails of the distribution become heavier, the value of ξ increases. For most financial data, ξ is positive and in the range 0.1 to 0.4.[9]

Estimating ξ and β

The parameters ξ and β can be estimated using maximum likelihood methods (see Section 10.9 for a discussion of maximum likelihood methods). The probability density function, $g_{\xi,\beta}(y)$, of the cumulative distribution in equation (14.5) is calculated by differentiating $G_{\xi,\beta}(y)$ with respect to y. It is

$$g_{\xi,\beta}(y) = \frac{1}{\beta}\left(1 + \frac{\xi y}{\beta}\right)^{-1/\xi-1} \tag{14.6}$$

We first choose a value for u. (A value close to the 95th percentile point of the empirical distribution usually works well.) We then rank the observations on v from the highest to the lowest and focus our attention on those observations for which $v > u$. Suppose there are n_u such observations and they are v_i $(1 \le i \le n_u)$. The likelihood function (assuming that $\xi \ne 0$) is

$$\prod_{i=1}^{n_u} \frac{1}{\beta}\left(1 + \frac{\xi(v_i - u)}{\beta}\right)^{-1/\xi-1}$$

---

[8] When $\xi = 0$, the generalized Pareto distribution becomes

$$G_{\xi,\beta}(y) = 1 - \exp\left(-\frac{y}{\beta}\right)$$

[9] One of the properties of the distribution in equation (14.5) is that the kth moment of v, $E(v^k)$, is infinite for $k \ge 1/\xi$. For a normal distribution, all moments are finite. When $\xi = 0.25$, only the first three moments are finite; when $\xi = 0.5$, only the first moment is finite; and so on.

Maximizing this function is the same as maximizing its logarithm:

$$\sum_{i=1}^{n_u} \ln \left[\frac{1}{\beta} \left(1 + \frac{\xi(v_i - u)}{\beta} \right)^{-1/\xi - 1} \right] \tag{14.7}$$

Standard numerical procedures can be used to find the values of ξ and β that maximize this expression. Excel's Solver produces good results.

Estimating the Tail of the Distribution

The probability that $v > u + y$ conditional that $v > u$ is $1 - G_{\xi,\beta}(y)$. The probability that $v > u$ is $1 - F(u)$. The unconditional probability that $v > x$ ($x > u$) is therefore

$$[1 - F(u)][1 - G_{\xi,\beta}(x - u)]$$

If n is the total number of observations, an estimate of $1 - F(u)$, calculated from the empirical data, is n_u/n. The unconditional probability that $v > x$ is therefore

$$\text{Prob}(v > x) = \frac{n_u}{n}[1 - G_{\xi,\beta}(x - u)] = \frac{n_u}{n}\left[1 + \xi\frac{x - u}{\beta}\right]^{-1/\xi} \tag{14.8}$$

Equivalence to the Power Law

If we set $u = \beta/\xi$, equation (14.8) reduces to

$$\text{Prob}(v > x) = \frac{n_u}{n}\left[\frac{\xi x}{\beta}\right]^{-1/\xi}$$

This is

$$Kx^{-\alpha}$$

where

$$K = \frac{n_u}{n}\left[\frac{\xi}{\beta}\right]^{-1/\xi}$$

and $\alpha = 1/\xi$. This shows that equation (14.8) is consistent with the power law introduced in Section 10.4.

The Left Tail

The analysis so far has assumed that we are interested in the right tail of the probability distribution of a variable v. If we are interested in the left tail of the probability distribution, we can work with $-v$ instead of v. Suppose, for example, that an oil company has collected data on daily percentage increases in the price of oil and wants to estimate a VaR that is the one-day percentage decline in the price of oil that has a 99.9% probability of not being exceeded. This is a statistic calculated from the left tail of the probability distribution of oil price increases. The oil company would change the sign of each data item (so that the data was measuring oil price decreases rather than increases) and then use the methodology that has been presented.

Calculation of VaR and Expected Shortfall

To calculate VaR with a confidence level of q, it is necessary to solve the equation

$$F(\text{VaR}) = q$$

Because $F(x) = 1 - \text{Prob}(v > x)$, equation (14.8) gives

$$q = 1 - \frac{n_u}{n}\left[1 + \xi\frac{\text{VaR} - u}{\beta}\right]^{-1/\xi}$$

so that

$$\text{VaR} = u + \frac{\beta}{\xi}\left\{\left[\frac{n}{n_u}(1 - q)\right]^{-\xi} - 1\right\} \qquad (14.9)$$

The expected shortfall (see Section 9.3) is given by

$$\text{Expected Shortfall} = \frac{\text{VaR} + \beta - \xi u}{1 - \xi} \qquad (14.10)$$

14.6 APPLICATIONS OF EVT

Consider again the data in Tables 14.1 to 14.4. When $u = 160$, $n_u = 22$ (that is, there are 22 scenarios where the loss in $000s is greater than 160). Table 14.8 shows calculations for the trial values $\beta = 40$ and $\xi = 0.3$. The value of the log-likelihood function in equation (14.7) is –108.37.

When Excel's Solver is used to search for the values of β and ξ that maximize the log-likelihood function, it gives

$$\beta = 32.532$$

$$\xi = 0.436$$

and the maximum value of the log-likelihood function is –108.21.

Suppose that we wish to estimate the probability that the portfolio loss between September 25 and September 26, 2008, will be more than $300,000 (or 3% of its value). From equation (14.8) this is

$$\frac{22}{500}\left[1 + 0.436\frac{300 - 160}{32.532}\right]^{-1/0.436} = 0.0039$$

TABLE 14.8   Extreme Value Theory Calculations for Table 14.4

Scenario Number	Loss ($000s)	Rank	$\ln\left[\frac{1}{\beta}\left(1+\frac{\xi(v_i-u)}{\beta}\right)^{-1/\xi-1}\right]$
494	477.841	1	−8.97
339	345.435	2	−7.47
349	282.204	3	−6.51
329	277.041	4	−6.42
487	253.385	5	−5.99
227	217.974	6	−5.25
131	202,256	7	−4.88
238	201,389	8	−4.86
...	...	...	...
...	...	...	...
...	...	...	...
304	160.778	22	−3.71
			−108.37

Trial Estimates of EVT parameters

ξ	β
0.3	40

The parameter u is 160 and trial values for β and ξ are 40 and 0.3, respectively.

This is more accurate than counting observations. The probability that the portfolio loss will be more than $500,000 (or 5% of its value) is similarly 0.00086.

From equation (14.9), the value of VaR with a 99% confidence limit is

$$160 + \frac{32.532}{0.436}\left\{\left[\frac{500}{22}(1-0.99)\right]^{-0.436} - 1\right\} = 227.8$$

or $227,800. (In this instance, the VaR estimate is about $25,000 less than the fifth-worst loss.) When the confidence level is increased to 99.9%, VaR becomes

$$160 + \frac{32.532}{0.436}\left\{\left[\frac{500}{22}(1-0.999)\right]^{-0.436} - 1\right\} = 474.0$$

or $474,000. When it is increased further to 99.97%, VaR becomes

$$160 + \frac{32.532}{0.436}\left\{\left[\frac{500}{22}(1-0.9997)\right]^{-0.436} - 1\right\} = 742.5$$

or $742,500.

The formula in equation (14.10) can provide a useful application of EVT because it is often difficult to estimate expected shortfall directly with any accuracy. In our example, when the confidence level is 99%, the expected shortfall is

$$\frac{227.8 + 32.532 - 0.436 \times 160}{1 - 0.436} = 337.9$$

or \$348,500. When the confidence level is 99.9%, the expected shortfall is

$$\frac{474.0 + 32.532 - 0.436 \times 160}{1 - 0.436} = 774.8$$

or \$707,700.

EVT can also be used in a straightforward way in conjunction with the volatility-updating procedure in Section 14.3 (see Problem 14.11). It can also be used in conjunction with the weighting-of-observations procedure in Section 14.3. In this case, the terms being summed in equation (14.7) must be multiplied by the weights applicable to the underlying observations.

A final calculation can be used to refine the confidence interval for the 99% VaR estimate in Section 14.2. The probability density function evaluated at the VaR level for the probability distribution of the loss, conditional on it being greater than 160, is given by the $g_{\xi,\beta}$ function in equation (14.6). It is

$$\frac{1}{32.532} \left(1 + \frac{0.436 \times (227.8 - 160)}{32.532} \right)^{-1/0.436 - 1} = 0.0037$$

The unconditional probability density function evaluated at the VaR level is $n_u/n = 22/500$ times this or 0.00016. Not surprisingly, this is lower than the 0.000284 estimated in Section 14.2 and leads to a wider confidence interval for VaR.

Choice of *u*

A natural question is: "How do the results depend on the choice of *u*?" It is often found that values of ξ and β do depend on *u*, but the estimates of $F(x)$ remain roughly the same. (Problem 14.10 considers what happens when *u* is changed from 160 to 150 in the example we have been considering.) We want *u* to be sufficiently high that we are truly investigating the shape of the tail of the distribution, but sufficiently low that the number of data items included in the maximum likelihood calculation is not too low. More data lead to more accuracy in the assessment of the shape of the tail. We have applied the procedure with 500 data items. Ideally, more data would be used.

A rule of thumb is that *u* should be approximately equal to the 95th percentile of the empirical distribution. (In the case of the data we have been looking at, the 95th percentile of the empirical distribution is 156.5.) In the search for the optimal values of ξ and β, both variables should be constrained to be positive. If the optimizer tries to set ξ negative, it is likely to be a sign that either (a) the tail of the distribution is not heavier than the normal distribution or (b) an inappropriate value of *u* has been chosen.

SUMMARY

Historical simulation is a very popular approach for estimating VaR. It involves creating a database consisting of the daily movements in all market variables over a period of time. The first simulation trial assumes that the percentage change in each market variable is the same as that on the first day covered by the database, the second simulation trial assumes that the percentage changes are the same as those on the second day, and so on. The change in the portfolio value is calculated for each simulation trial, and VaR is calculated as the appropriate percentile of the probability distribution of this change. The standard error for a VaR that is estimated using historical simulation tends to be quite high. The higher the VaR confidence level required, the higher the standard error.

There are a number of extensions of the basic historical simulation approach. The weights given to observations can be allowed to decrease exponentially as the observations become older. Volatility updating procedures can be used to take account of differences between the volatilities of market variables today and their volatilities at different times during the period covered by the historical data.

Extreme value theory is a way of smoothing the tails of the probability distribution of portfolio daily changes calculated using historical simulation. It leads to estimates of VaR that reflect the whole shape of the tail of the distribution, not just the positions of a few losses in the tails. Extreme value theory can also be used to estimate VaR when the VaR confidence level is very high. For example, even if we have only 500 days of data, it could be used to come up with an estimate of VaR for a VaR confidence level of 99.9%.

FURTHER READING

Boudoukh, J., M. Richardson, and R. Whitelaw. "The Best of Both Worlds," *Risk* (May 1998): 64–67.

Embrechts, P., C. Kluppelberg, and T. Mikosch. *Modelling Extremal Events for Insurance and Finance.* New York: Springer, 1997.

Hendricks, D. "Evaluation of Value-at-Risk Models Using Historical Data," *Economic Policy Review*, Federal Reserve Bank of New York, vol. 2 (April 1996): 39–69.

Hull, J. C., and A. White. "Incorporating Volatility Updating into the Historical Simulation Method for Value at Risk," *Journal of Risk* 1, no. 1 (1998): 5–19.

McNeil, A. J. "Extreme Value Theory for Risk Managers," in *Internal Modeling and CAD II* (London: Risk Books, 1999). See also www.math.ethz.ch/~mcneil.

Neftci, S. N. "Value at Risk Calculations, Extreme Events and Tail Estimation," *Journal of Derivatives* 7, no. 3 (Spring 2000): 23–38.

PRACTICE QUESTIONS AND PROBLEMS
(ANSWERS AT END OF BOOK)

14.1 What assumptions are being made when VaR is calculated using the historical simulation approach and 500 days of data?

14.2 Show that when λ approaches 1, the weighting scheme in Section 14.3 approaches the basic historical simulation approach.

14.3 Suppose we estimate the one-day 95% VaR (in millions of dollars) from 1,000 observations as 5. By fitting a standard distribution to the observations, the probability density function of the loss distribution at the 95% point is estimated to be 0.01. What is the standard error of the VaR estimate?

14.4 The one-day 99% VaR is calculated in Section 14.1 as $253,385. Look at the underlying spreadsheets on the author's website and calculate (a) the one-day 95% VaR and (b) the one-day 97% VaR.

14.5 Use the spreadsheets on the author's website to calculate a one-day 99% VaR, using the basic methodology in Section 14.1, if the portfolio in Section 14.1 is equally divided between the four indices.

14.6 The "weighting-of-observations" procedure in Section 14.3 gives the one-day 99% VaR equal to $282,204 for the example considered. Use the spreadsheets on the author's website to calculate the one-day 99% VaR when the λ parameter in this procedure is changed from 0.995 to 0.99.

14.7 The "volatility-updating" procedure in Section 14.3 gives the one-day 99% VaR equal to $602,968 for the example considered. Use the spreadsheets on the author's website to calculate the one-day 99% VaR when the λ parameter in this procedure is changed from 0.94 to 0.96.

14.8 In the application of EVT in Section 14.6, what is the probability that the loss will exceed $400,000?

14.9 In the application of EVT in Section 14.6, what is the one-day VaR with a confidence level of 97%?

14.10 Change u from 160 to 150 in the application of EVT in Section 14.6. How does this change the maximum likelihood estimates of ξ and β? How does it change the one-day 99% VaR when the confidence limit is (a) 99% and (b) 99.9%.

14.11 Carry out an extreme value theory analysis on the data from the volatility-updating procedure in Table 14.7 and on the author's website. Use $u = 400$. What are the best fit values of ξ and β? Calculate the one-day VaR with a 99% and 99.9% confidence level. What is the probability of a loss greater than $600,000?

FURTHER QUESTIONS

14.12 Suppose that a one-day 97.5% VaR is estimated as $13 million from 2,000 observations. The one-day changes are approximately normal with mean zero and standard deviation $6 million. Estimate a 99% confidence interval for the VaR estimate.

14.13 Suppose that the portfolio considered in Section 14.1 has (in $000s) 3,000 in DJIA, 3,000 in FTSE, 1,000 in CAC 40, and 3,000 in Nikkei 225. Use the spreadsheet on the author's website to calculate what difference this makes to

(a) The one-day 99% VaR that is calculated in Section 14.1.

(b) The one-day 99% VaR that is calculated using the weighting-of-observations procedure in Section 14.3.

(c) The one-day 99% VaR that is calculated using the volatility-updating procedure in Section 14.3.

(d) The one-day 99% VaR that is calculated using extreme value theory in Section 14.6.

14.14 Investigate the effect of applying extreme value theory to the volatility-adjusted results in Section 14.3 with $u = 350$.

14.15 The "weighting-of-observations" procedure in Section 14.3 gives the one-day 99% VaR equal to \$282,204. Use the spreadsheets on the author's website to calculate the one-day 99% VaR when the λ parameter in this procedure is changed from 0.995 to 0.985.

14.16 The "volatility-updating" procedure in Section 14.3 gives the one-day 99% VaR equal to \$602,968. Use the spreadsheets on the author's website to calculate the one-day 99% VaR when the λ parameter in this procedure is changed from 0.94 to 0.92.

14.17 Values for the NASDAQ composite index during the 1,500 days preceding March 10, 2006, can be downloaded from the author's website. Calculate the one-day 99% VaR on March 10, 2006, for a \$10 million portfolio invested in the index using

(a) The basic historical simulation approach.

(b) The exponential weighting scheme in Section 14.3 with $\lambda = 0.995$.

(c) The volatility-updating procedure in Section 14.3 with $\lambda = 0.94$. (Assume that the volatility is initially equal to the standard deviation of daily returns calculated from the whole sample.)

(d) Extreme value theory with $u = 300$.

(e) A model where daily returns are assumed to be normally distributed. (Use both an equally weighted and the EWMA approach with $\lambda = 0.94$ to estimate the standard deviation of daily returns.)

Discuss the reasons for the differences between the results you get.

CHAPTER 15

Market Risk VaR: The Model-Building Approach

An alternative to the historical simulation approach that is sometimes used by portfolio managers is the *model-building approach*, sometimes also referred to as the *variance–covariance approach*. This involves assuming a model for the joint distribution of changes in market variables and using historical data to estimate the model parameters.

The model-building approach is ideally suited to a portfolio consisting of long and short positions in stocks, bonds, commodities, and other products. It is based on Harry Markowitz's pioneering work in portfolio theory (see Section 1.1). The mean and standard deviation of the value of a portfolio can be calculated from the mean and standard deviation of the returns on the underlying products and the correlations between those returns. If, and it is a big if, daily returns on the investments are assumed to be multivariate normal, the probability distribution for the change in the value of the portfolio over one day is also normal. This makes it very easy to calculate value at risk.

As we shall see, the model-building approach is much more difficult to use when a portfolio involves nonlinear products such as options. It is also difficult to relax the assumption that returns are normal without a big increase in computation time.

15.1 THE BASIC METHODOLOGY

We start by considering how VaR is calculated using the model-building approach in a very simple situation where the portfolio consists of a position in a single stock. The portfolio we consider is one consisting of shares in Microsoft valued at $10 million. We suppose that the time horizon is 10 days and the VaR confidence level is 99% so that we are interested in the loss level over 10 days that we are 99% confident will not be exceeded. Initially, we consider a one-day time horizon.

We assume that the volatility of Microsoft is 2% per day (corresponding to about 32% per year).[1] Because the size of the position is $10 million, the standard

---

[1] As discussed in Section 10.1, in VaR calculations volatility is usually measured per day whereas in option pricing it is measured per year. A volatility per day can be converted to a volatility per year by multiplying by $\sqrt{252}$, or about 16.

deviation of daily changes in the value of the position is 2% of $10 million, or $200,000.

It is customary in the model-building approach to assume that the expected change in a market variable over the time period considered is zero. This is not exactly true, but it is a reasonable assumption. The expected change in the price of a market variable over a short time period is generally small when compared to the standard deviation of the change. Suppose, for example, that Microsoft has an expected return of 20% per annum. Over a one-day period, the expected return is 0.20/252, or about 0.08%, whereas the standard deviation of the return is 2%. Over a 10-day period, the expected return is 0.08 × 10, or about 0.8%, whereas the standard deviation of the return is $2\sqrt{10}$, or about 6.3%.

So far, we have established that the change in the value of the portfolio of Microsoft shares over a one-day period has a standard deviation of $200,000 and (at least approximately) a mean of zero. We assume that the change is normally distributed.[2] Because $N(-2.33) = 0.01$, this means that there is a 1% probability that a normally distributed variable will decrease in value by more than 2.33 standard deviations. Equivalently, it means that we are 99% certain that a normally distributed variable will not decrease in value by more than 2.33 standard deviations. The one-day 99% VaR for our portfolio consisting of a $10 million position in Microsoft is therefore

$$2.33 \times 200,000 = \$466,000$$

Assuming that the changes in Microsoft's stock price on successive days are independent, the N-day VaR is calculated as $\sqrt{N}$ times the one-day VaR. The 10-day 99% VaR for Microsoft is therefore

$$466,000 \times \sqrt{10} = \$1,473,621$$

Consider next a portfolio consisting of a $5 million position in AT&T, and suppose the daily volatility of AT&T is 1% (approximately 16% per year). A similar calculation to that for Microsoft shows that the standard deviation of the change in the value of the portfolio in one day is

$$5,000,000 \times 0.01 = 50,000$$

Assuming that the change is normally distributed, the one-day 99% VaR is

$$50,000 \times 2.33 = \$116,500$$

and the 10-day 99% VaR is

$$116,500 \times \sqrt{10} = \$368,405$$

---

[2] We could assume that the price of Microsoft is lognormal tomorrow. Because one day is such a short period of time, this is almost indistinguishable from the assumption we do make—that the change in the stock price between today and tomorrow is normal.

Two-Asset Case

Now consider a portfolio consisting of both $10 million of Microsoft shares and $5 million of AT&T shares. We suppose that the returns on the two shares have a bivariate normal distribution with a correlation of 0.3. A standard result in statistics tells us that, if two variables X and Y have standard deviations equal to σ_X and σ_Y with the coefficient of correlation between them being equal to ρ, then the standard deviation of $X + Y$ is given by

$$\sigma_{X+Y} = \sqrt{\sigma_X^2 + \sigma_Y^2 + 2\rho\sigma_X\sigma_Y}$$

To apply this result, we set X equal to the change in the value of the position in Microsoft over a one-day period and Y equal to the change in the value of the position in AT&T over a one-day period, so that

$$\sigma_X = 200{,}000 \quad \sigma_Y = 50{,}000$$

The standard deviation of the change in the value of the portfolio consisting of both stocks over a one-day period is therefore

$$\sqrt{200{,}000^2 + 50{,}000^2 + 2 \times 0.3 \times 200{,}000 \times 50{,}000} = 220{,}227$$

The mean change is assumed to be zero. The change is normally distributed. (This is because of the bivariate normal assumption.) So the one-day 99% VaR is therefore

$$220{,}227 \times 2.33 = \$513{,}129$$

The 10-day 99% VaR is $\sqrt{10}$ times this or $1,622,657.

The Benefits of Diversification

In the example we have just considered:

1. The 10-day 99% VaR for the portfolio of Microsoft shares is $1,473,621.
2. The 10-day 99% VaR for the portfolio of AT&T shares is $368,405.
3. The 10-day 99% VaR for the portfolio of both Microsoft and AT&T shares is $1,622,657.

The amount

$$(1{,}473{,}621 + 368{,}405) - 1{,}622{,}657 = \$219{,}369$$

represents the benefits of diversification. If Microsoft and AT&T were perfectly correlated, the VaR for the portfolio of both Microsoft and AT&T would equal the

VaR for the Microsoft portfolio plus the VaR for the AT&T portfolio. Less than perfect correlation leads to some of the risk being "diversified away."[3]

15.2 GENERALIZATION

The examples we have just considered are simple illustrations of the use of the linear model for calculating VaR. Suppose that we have a portfolio worth P consisting of n assets with an amount α_i being invested in asset i ($1 \le i \le n$). Define Δx_i as the return on asset i in one day. The dollar change in the value of our investment in asset i in one day is $\alpha_i \Delta x_i$ and

$$\Delta P = \sum_{i=1}^{n} \alpha_i \Delta x_i \qquad (15.1)$$

where ΔP is the dollar change in the value of the whole portfolio in one day.

In the example considered in the previous section, $10 million was invested in the first asset (Microsoft) and $5 million was invested in the second asset (AT&T) so that (in millions of dollars) $\alpha_1 = 10$, $\alpha_2 = 5$ and

$$\Delta P = 10\Delta x_1 + 5\Delta x_2$$

If we assume that the Δx_i in equation (15.1) are multivariate normal, ΔP is normally distributed. To calculate VaR, we therefore need to calculate only the mean and standard deviation of ΔP. We assume, as discussed in the previous section, that the expected value of each Δx_i is zero. This implies that the mean of ΔP is zero.

To calculate the standard deviation of ΔP, we define σ_i as the daily volatility of the ith asset and ρ_{ij} as the coefficient of correlation between returns on asset i and asset j.[4] This means that σ_i is the standard deviation of Δx_i, and ρ_{ij} is the coefficient of correlation between Δx_i and Δx_j. The variance of ΔP, which we will denote by σ_P^2, is given by

$$\sigma_P^2 = \sum_{i=1}^{n} \sum_{j=1}^{n} \rho_{ij} \alpha_i \alpha_j \sigma_i \sigma_j \qquad (15.2)$$

This equation can also be written as

$$\sigma_P^2 = \sum_{i=1}^{n} \alpha_i^2 \sigma_i^2 + 2 \sum_{i=1}^{n} \sum_{j<i} \rho_{ij} \alpha_i \alpha_j \sigma_i \sigma_j$$

---

[3] As discussed in Section 9.4, VaR does not always reflect the benefits of diversification. For non-normal distributions, the VaR of two portfolios considered jointly can be greater than the sum of their VaRs.

[4] The ρ_{ij} are sometimes calculated using a factor model. See Section 11.3.

The standard deviation of the change over N days is $\sigma_P\sqrt{N}$, and the 99% VaR for an N-day time horizon is $2.33\sigma_P\sqrt{N}$.

In the example considered in the previous section, $\sigma_1 = 0.02$, $\sigma_2 = 0.01$, and $\rho_{12} = 0.3$. As already noted, $\alpha_1 = 10$ and $\alpha_2 = 5$ so that

$$\sigma_P^2 = 10^2 \times 0.02^2 + 5^2 \times 0.01^2 + 2 \times 10 \times 5 \times 0.3 \times 0.02 \times 0.01 = 0.0485$$

and $\sigma_P = 0.220$. This is the standard deviation of the change in the portfolio value per day (in millions of dollars). The 10-day 99% VaR is $2.33 \times 0.220 \times \sqrt{10} = \$1.623$ million. This agrees with the calculation in the previous section.

The portfolio return in one day is $\Delta P/P$. From equation (15.2), the variance of this is

$$\sum_{i=1}^{n}\sum_{j=1}^{n} \rho_{ij} w_i w_j \sigma_i \sigma_j$$

where $w_i = \alpha_i/P$ is the weight of the ith investment in the portfolio. This version of equation (15.2) corresponds to the work of Markowitz and is often used by portfolio managers (see Section 1.1).

15.3 CORRELATION AND COVARIANCE MATRICES

A correlation matrix is a matrix where the entry in the ith row and jth column is the correlation, ρ_{ij}, between variable i and j. It is shown in Table 15.1. Because a variable is always perfectly correlated with itself, the diagonal elements of the correlation matrix are 1. Furthermore, because $\rho_{ij} = \rho_{ji}$, the correlation matrix is symmetric. The correlation matrix, together with the daily standard deviations of the variables, enables the portfolio variance to be calculated using equation (15.2).

Instead of working with correlations and volatilities, analysts often use variances and covariances. The daily variance of variable i, var$_i$, is the square of its daily volatility:

$$\text{var}_i = \sigma_i^2$$

TABLE 15.1 A Correlation Matrix

$$\begin{pmatrix} 1 & \rho_{12} & \rho_{13} & \cdots & \rho_{1n} \\ \rho_{21} & 1 & \rho_{23} & \cdots & \rho_{2n} \\ \rho_{31} & \rho_{32} & 1 & \cdots & \rho_{3n} \\ \cdots & \cdots & \cdots & \cdots & \cdots \\ \cdots & \cdots & \cdots & \cdots & \cdots \\ \rho_{n1} & \rho_{n2} & \rho_{n3} & \cdots & 1 \end{pmatrix}$$

ρ_{ij} is the correlation between variable i and variable j.

TABLE 15.2 A Variance-Covariance Matrix

$$
\begin{pmatrix}
\text{var}_1 & \text{cov}_{12} & \text{cov}_{13} & \cdots & \text{cov}_{1n} \\
\text{cov}_{21} & \text{var}_2 & \text{cov}_{23} & \cdots & \text{cov}_{2n} \\
\text{cov}_{31} & \text{cov}_{32} & \text{var}_3 & \cdots & \text{cov}_{3n} \\
\cdots & \cdots & \cdots & \cdots & \cdots \\
\cdots & \cdots & \cdots & \cdots & \cdots \\
\text{cov}_{n1} & \text{cov}_{n2} & \text{cov}_{n3} & \cdots & \text{var}_n
\end{pmatrix}
$$

cov_{ij} is the covariance between variable i and variable j; diagonal entries are variance: cov_{ii} is the variance of variable i.

The covariance between variable i and variable j, cov_{ij}, is the product of the daily volatility of variable i, the daily volatility of variable j, and the correlation between i and j:

$$
\text{cov}_{ij} = \sigma_i \sigma_j \rho_{ij}
$$

The equation for the variance of the portfolio in equation (15.2) can be written as:

$$
\sigma_P^2 = \sum_{i=1}^{n} \sum_{j=1}^{n} \text{cov}_{ij} \alpha_i \alpha_j \tag{15.3}
$$

In a *covariance matrix* the entry in the ith row and jth column is the covariance between variable i and variable j. As just mentioned, the covariance between a variable and itself is its variance. The diagonal entries in the matrix are therefore variances (see Table 15.2). For this reason, the covariance matrix is sometimes called the *variance-covariance matrix*. (Like the correlation matrix, it is symmetric.) Using matrix notation, the equation for the standard deviation of the portfolio in equation (15.3) becomes

$$
\sigma_P^2 = \boldsymbol{\alpha}^{\mathrm{T}} C \boldsymbol{\alpha}
$$

where $\boldsymbol{\alpha}$ is the (column) vector whose ith element is α_i, C is the variance-covariance matrix, and $\boldsymbol{\alpha}^{\mathrm{T}}$ is the transpose of $\boldsymbol{\alpha}$.

The variances and covariances are generally calculated from historical data. One approach is to calculate them in the standard way by giving equal weight to all data. Another is to use the exponentially weighted moving average method. In this case, the same λ should be used for all calculations in order to ensure a positive-semidefinite matrix (see Section 11.2 for a discussion of the positive-semidefinite condition). GARCH methods can also be used, but ensuring consistency so that a positive-semidefinite matrix is produced is then more complicated.

TABLE 15.3 Correlation Matrix on September 25, 2008, Calculated by Giving the Same Weight to Each of the Last 500 Daily Returns

$$
\begin{pmatrix}
1 & 0.489 & 0.496 & -0.062 \\
0.489 & 1 & 0.918 & 0.201 \\
0.496 & 0.918 & 1 & 0.211 \\
-0.062 & 0.201 & 0.211 & 1
\end{pmatrix}
$$

Variable 1 is DJIA; variable 2 is FTSE 100; variable 3 is CAC 40; variable 4 is Nikkei 225.

Example Involving Four Investments

We now return to the example considered in Chapter 14. This involved a portfolio on September 25, 2008, consisting of a $4 million investment in the Dow Jones Industrial Average, a $3 million investment in the FTSE 100, a $1 million investment in the CAC 40, and a $2 million investment in the Nikkei 225. Daily returns were collected over 500 days ending on September 25, 2008. (Data and calculations presented here are on the author's website: www.rotman.utoronto.ca/~hull/RMFI3e/VaRExample.)

The correlation matrix, when calculations are carried out in the usual way with the same weight for all 500 returns, is shown in Table 15.3. The FTSE 100 and CAC 40 are very highly correlated. The Dow Jones Industrial Average is moderately highly correlated with both the FTSE 100 and the CAC 40. The correlation of the Nikkei 225 with other indices is less high. The covariance matrix is in Table 15.4.

From equation (15.3), this variance-covariance matrix gives the variance of the portfolio losses ($000s) as 8,761.833. The standard deviation is the square root of this, or 93.60. The one-day 99% VaR is therefore

$$2.33 \times 93.60 = 217.757$$

or $217,757. This compares with $253,385, calculated using the basic historical simulation approach in Chapter 14.

Use of EWMA

Instead of calculating variances and covariances by giving equal weight to all observed returns, we now use the exponentially weighted moving average method with

TABLE 15.4 Covariance Matrix on September 25, 2008, Calculated by Giving the Same Weight to Each of the Last 500 Daily Returns

$$
\begin{pmatrix}
0.0001227 & 0.0000768 & 0.0000767 & -0.0000095 \\
0.0000768 & 0.0002010 & 0.0001817 & 0.0000394 \\
0.0000767 & 0.0001817 & 0.0001950 & 0.0000407 \\
-0.0000095 & 0.0000394 & 0.0000407 & 0.0001909
\end{pmatrix}
$$

Variable 1 is DJIA; variable 2 is FTSE 100; variable 3 is CAC 40; variable 4 is Nikkei 225.

TABLE 15.5   Covariance Matrix on September 25, 2008, when EWMA with $\lambda = 0.94$
Is Used

$$
\begin{pmatrix}
0.0004801 & 0.0004303 & 0.0004257 & -0.0000396 \\
0.0004303 & 0.0010314 & 0.0009630 & 0.0002095 \\
0.0004257 & 0.0009630 & 0.0009535 & 0.0001681 \\
-0.0000396 & 0.0002095 & 0.0001681 & 0.0002541
\end{pmatrix}
$$

Variable 1 is DJIA; variable 2 is FTSE 100; variable 3 is CAC 40; variable 4 is Nikkei 225.

TABLE 15.6   Volatilities (% per day) on September 25, 2008, for Equal Weighting and
EWMA approaches

	DJIA	FTSE 100	CAC 40	Nikkei 225
Equal Weighting	1.11	1.42	1.40	1.38
EWMA	2.19	3.21	3.09	1.59

$\lambda = 0.94$. This gives the variance-covariance matrix in Table 15.5.[5] From equation (15.3), the variance of portfolio losses ($000s) is 40,995,765. The standard deviation is the square root of this, or 202.474. The one-day 99% VaR is therefore

$$2.33 \times 202.474 = 471.025$$

or $471,025. This is more than twice as high as the value given when returns are equally weighted. Tables 15.6 and 15.7 show the reasons. The standard deviation of the value of a portfolio consisting of long positions in securities increases with the standard deviations of security returns and also with the correlations between security returns. Table 15.6 shows that the estimated daily standard deviations are much higher when EWMA is used than when data is equally weighted. This is because volatilities were much higher during the period immediately preceding September 25, 2008, than during the rest of the 500 days covered by the data. Comparing Table 15.7 with Table 15.3, we see that correlations had also increased.[6]

15.4 HANDLING INTEREST RATES

It is out of the question to define a separate market variable for every single bond price or interest rate to which a company is exposed. Some simplifications are necessary

---

[5] In the EWMA calculations, the variance is initially set equal to the population variance. But all reasonable starting variances give essentially the same result because in this case all we are interested in is the final variance.

[6] This is an example of the phenomenon that correlations tend to increase in adverse market conditions.

TABLE 15.7 Correlation Matrix on September 25, 2008, when EWMA Method Is Used

$$
\begin{pmatrix}
1 & 0.611 & 0.629 & -0.113 \\
0.611 & 1 & 0.971 & 0.409 \\
0.629 & 0.971 & 1 & 0.342 \\
-0.113 & 0.409 & 0.342 & 1
\end{pmatrix}
$$

Variable 1 is DJIA; variable 2 is FTSE 100; variable 3 is CAC 40; variable 4 is Nikkei 225.

when the model-building approach is used. One possibility is to assume that only parallel shifts in the yield curve occur. It is then necessary to define only one market variable: the size of the parallel shift. The changes in the value of a bond portfolio can then be calculated using the approximate duration relationship in equation (8.6)

$$\Delta P = -DP\Delta y$$

where P is the value of the portfolio, ΔP is the change in P in one day, D is the modified duration of the portfolio, and Δy is the parallel shift in one day. This approach gives a linear relationship between ΔP and Δy, but does not usually give enough accuracy because the relationship is not exact and it does not take account of nonparallel shifts in the yield curve.

The procedure usually followed is to choose as market variables the prices of zero-coupon bonds with standard maturities: 1 month, 3 months, 6 months, 1 year, 2 years, 5 years, 7 years, 10 years, and 30 years. For the purposes of calculating VaR, the cash flows from instruments in the portfolio are mapped into cash flows occurring on the standard maturity dates.

Consider a $1 million position in a Treasury bond lasting 0.8 years that pays a coupon of 10% semiannually. A coupon is paid in 0.3 years and 0.8 years and the principal is paid in 0.8 years. This bond is, therefore, in the first instance, regarded as a $50,000 position in 0.3-year zero-coupon bond plus a $1,050,000 position in a 0.8-year zero-coupon bond. The position in the 0.3-year bond is then replaced by an equivalent position in three-month and six-month zero-coupon bonds, and the position in the 0.8-year bond is replaced by an equivalent position in six-month and one-year zero-coupon bonds. The result is that the position in the 0.8-year coupon-bearing bond is for VaR purposes regarded as a position in zero-coupon bonds having maturities of three months, six months, and one year. This procedure is known as *cash-flow mapping*.

Illustration of Cash-Flow Mapping

We now illustrate how cash-flow mapping works by continuing with the example we have just introduced. It should be emphasized that the procedure we use is just one of several that have been proposed.

Consider first the $1,050,000 that will be received in 0.8 years. We suppose that zero rates, daily bond price volatilities, and correlations between bond returns are as shown in Table 15.8. The first stage is to interpolate between the six-month rate of 6.0% and the one-year rate of 7.0% to obtain a 0.8-year rate of 6.6%. (Annual

TABLE 15.8   Data to Illustrate Cash Flow Mapping Procedure

	3-Month	6-Month	1-Year
Zero rate (% with ann. comp.)	5.50	6.00	7.00
Bond price vol (% per day)	0.06	0.10	0.20

	Correlation between daily returns		
	3-Month Bond	6-Month Bond	1-Year Bond
----------------	--------------	--------------	-------------
3-month bond	1.0	0.9	0.6
6-month bond	0.9	1.0	0.7
1-year bond	0.6	0.7	1.0

compounding is assumed for all rates.) The present value of the $1,050,000 cash flow to be received in 0.8 years is

$$\frac{1,050,000}{1.066^{0.8}} = 997,662$$

We also interpolate between the 0.1% volatility for the six-month bond and the 0.2% volatility for the one-year bond to get a 0.16% volatility for the 0.8-year bond.

Suppose we allocate α of the present value to the six-month bond and $1 - \alpha$ of the present value to the one-year bond. Using equation (15.2) and matching variances, we obtain

$$0.0016^2 = 0.001^2\alpha^2 + 0.002^2(1 - \alpha)^2 + 2 \times 0.7 \times 0.001 \times 0.002\alpha(1 - \alpha)$$

This is a quadratic equation that can be solved in the usual way to give $\alpha = 0.320337$. This means that 32.0337% of the value should be allocated to a six-month zero-coupon bond and 67.9663% of the value should be allocated to a one-year zero-coupon bond. The 0.8-year bond worth $997,662 is therefore replaced by a six-month bond worth

$$997,662 \times 0.320337 = \$319,589$$

and a one-year bond worth

$$997,662 \times 0.679663 = \$678,074$$

This cash-flow mapping scheme has the advantage that it preserves both the value and the variance of the cash flow. Also, it can be shown that the weights assigned to the two adjacent zero-coupon bonds are always positive.

For the $50,000 cash flow received at 0.3 years, we can carry out similar calculations (see Problem 15.7). It turns out that the present value of the cash flow is

TABLE 15.9   The Cash-Flow Mapping Result

	$50,000 Received in 0.3 Years	$1,050,000 Received in 0.8 Years	Total
Position in 3-month bond ($)	37,397		37,397
Position in 6-month bond ($)	11,793	319,589	331,382
Position in 1-year bond ($)		678,074	678,074

$49,189. This can be mapped to a position worth $37,397 in a three-month bond and a position worth $11,793 in a six-month bond.

The results of the calculations are summarized in Table 15.9. The 0.8-year coupon-bearing bond is mapped to a position worth $37,397 in a three-month bond, a position worth $331,382 in a six-month bond, and a position worth $678,074 in a one-year bond. Using the volatilities and correlations in Table 15.9, equation (15.2) gives the variance of the change in the price of the 0.8-year bond with $n = 3$, $\alpha_1 = 37,397$, $\alpha_2 = 331,382$, $\alpha_3 = 678,074$; $\sigma_1 = 0.0006$, $\sigma_2 = 0.001$, and $\sigma_3 = 0.002$; and $\rho_{12} = 0.9$, $\rho_{13} = 0.6$, $\rho_{23} = 0.7$. This variance is 2,628,518. The standard deviation of the change in the price of the bond is, therefore, $\sqrt{2,628,518} = 1,621.3$. Because we are assuming that the bond is the only instrument in the portfolio, the 10-day 99% VaR is

$$1621.3 \times \sqrt{10} \times 2.33 = 11,946$$

or about $11,950.

Principal Components Analysis

As we explained in Section 8.8, a principal components analysis (PCA) can be used to reduce the number of deltas that are calculated for movements in a zero-coupon yield curve. A PCA can also be used (in conjunction with cash-flow mapping) to handle interest rates when VaR is calculated using the model-building approach. For any given portfolio that is dependent on interest rates we can convert a set of delta exposures into a delta exposure to the first PCA factor, a delta exposure to the second PCA factor, and so on. The way this is done is explained in Section 8.8. Consider the data set in Table 15.10, which is the same as that in Table 8.9. In Section 8.8, the exposure to the first factor for this data is calculated as –0.05 and the exposure

TABLE 15.10   Change in Portfolio Value for a One-Basis-Point Rate Move ($ Millions)

3-Year Rate	4-Year Rate	5-Year Rate	7-Year Rate	10-Year Rate
+10	+4	−8	−7	+2

to the second factor is calculated as -3.87. (The first two factors capture over 97% of the variation in interest rates.)

Suppose that f_1 and f_2 are the factor scores. The change in the portfolio value is approximately

$$\Delta P = -0.05 f_1 - 3.87 f_2$$

The factor scores in a PCA are uncorrelated. From Table 8.8 the standard deviations for the first two factors are 17.55 and 4.77. The standard deviation of ΔP is, therefore

$$\sqrt{0.05^2 \times 17.55^2 + 3.87^2 \times 4.77^2} = 18.48$$

The one-day 99% VaR is, therefore, $18.48 \times 2.326 = 42.99$. Note that the portfolio we are considering has very little exposure to the first factor and significant exposure to the second factor. Using only one factor would significantly understate VaR. (See Problem 15.9.) The duration-based method for handling interest rates would also significantly understate VaR in this case as it considers only parallel shifts in the yield curve.

15.5 APPLICATIONS OF THE LINEAR MODEL

The simplest application of the linear model is to a portfolio with no derivatives consisting of positions in stocks, bonds, foreign exchange, and commodities. In this case, the change in the value of the portfolio is linearly dependent on the percentage changes in the prices of the assets comprising the portfolio. Note that, for the purposes of VaR calculations, all asset prices are measured in the domestic currency. The market variables considered by a large bank in the United States are, therefore, likely to include the value of the Nikkei 225 index measured in dollars, the price of a 10-year sterling zero-coupon bond measured in dollars, and so on.

Examples of derivatives that can be handled by the linear model are forward contracts on foreign exchange and interest rate swaps. Suppose a forward foreign exchange contract matures at time T. It can be regarded as the exchange of a foreign zero-coupon bond maturing at time T for a domestic zero-coupon bond maturing at time T. For the purposes of calculating VaR, the forward contract is therefore treated as a long position in the foreign bond combined with a short position in the domestic bond. (As just mentioned, the foreign bond is valued in the domestic currency.) Each bond can be handled using a cash-flow mapping procedure, so that it is a linear combination of bonds with standard maturities.

Consider next an interest rate swap. This can be regarded as the exchange of a floating-rate bond for a fixed-rate bond. The fixed-rate bond is a regular coupon-bearing bond. (See Appendix D.) The floating-rate bond is worth par just after the next payment date. It can be regarded as a zero-coupon bond with a maturity date equal to the next payment date. The interest rate swap, therefore, reduces to a portfolio of long and short positions in bonds and can be handled using a cash-flow mapping procedure.

15.6 LINEAR MODEL AND OPTIONS

We now consider how the linear model can be used when there are options. Consider first a portfolio consisting of options on a single stock whose current price is S. Suppose that the delta of the position (calculated in the way described in Chapter 7) is δ.[7] Because δ is the rate of change of the value of the portfolio with S, it is approximately true that

$$\delta = \frac{\Delta P}{\Delta S}$$

or

$$\Delta P = \delta \Delta S \qquad (15.4)$$

where ΔS is the dollar change in the stock price in one day and ΔP is, as usual, the dollar change in the portfolio in one day. We define Δx as the return on the stock in one day so that

$$\Delta x = \frac{\Delta S}{S}$$

It follows that an approximate relationship between ΔP and Δx is

$$\Delta P = S \delta \Delta x$$

When we have a position in several underlying market variables that includes options, we can derive an approximate linear relationship between ΔP and the Δx_i similarly. This relationship is

$$\Delta P = \sum_{i=1}^{n} S_i \delta_i \Delta x_i \qquad (15.5)$$

where S_i is the value of the ith market variable and δ_i is the delta of the portfolio with respect to the ith market variable. This is equation (15.1):

$$\Delta P = \sum_{i=1}^{n} \alpha_i \Delta x_i \qquad (15.6)$$

with $\alpha_i = S_i \delta_i$. Equation (15.2) can, therefore, be used to calculate the standard deviation of ΔP.

---

[7] In Chapter 7, we denote the delta and gamma of a portfolio by Δ and Γ. In this section and the next one, we use the lower case Greek letters δ and γ to avoid overworking Δ.

EXAMPLE 15.1

A portfolio consists of options on Microsoft and AT&T. The options on Microsoft have a delta of 1,000, and the options on AT&T have a delta of 20,000. The Microsoft share price is $120, and the AT&T share price is $30. From equation (15.5) it is approximately true that

$$\Delta P = 120 \times 1,000 \times \Delta x_1 + 30 \times 20,000 \times \Delta x_2$$

or

$$\Delta P = 120,000\Delta x_1 + 600,000\Delta x_2$$

where Δx_1 and Δx_2 are the returns from Microsoft and AT&T in one day and ΔP is the resultant change in the value of the portfolio. (The portfolio is assumed to be equivalent to an investment of $120,000 in Microsoft and $600,000 in AT&T.) Assuming that the daily volatility of Microsoft is 2% and that of AT&T is 1%, and that the correlation between the daily changes is 0.3, the standard deviation of ΔP (in thousands of dollars) is

$$\sqrt{(120 \times 0.02)^2 + (600 \times 0.01)^2 + 2 \times 120 \times 0.02 \times 600 \times 0.01 \times 0.3} = 7.099$$

Because $N(-1.65) = 0.05$, the five-day 95% VaR is

$$1.65 \times \sqrt{5} \times 7,099 = \$26,193$$

Weakness of Model

When a portfolio includes options, the linear model is an approximation. It does not take account of the gamma of the portfolio. As discussed in Chapter 7, delta is defined as the rate of change of the portfolio value with respect to an underlying market variable and gamma is defined as the rate of change of the delta with respect to the market variable. Gamma measures the curvature of the relationship between the portfolio value and an underlying market variable.

Figure 15.1 shows the impact of a nonzero gamma on the probability distribution of the value of the portfolio. When gamma is positive, the probability distribution tends to be positively skewed; when gamma is negative, it tends to be negatively skewed. Figures 15.2 and 15.3 illustrate the reason for this result. Figure 15.2 shows the relationship between the value of a long call option and the price of the underlying asset. A long call is an example of an option position with positive gamma. The figure shows that, when the probability distribution for the price of the underlying asset at the end of one day is normal, the probability distribution for the option price is positively skewed.[8] Figure 15.3 shows the relationship between the value of a short

---

[8] The normal distribution is a good approximation of the lognormal distribution for short time periods.

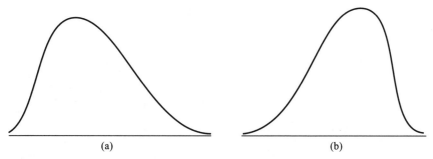

FIGURE 15.1 Probability Distribution for Value of Portfolio
(a) positive gamma, (b) negative gamma

call position and the price of the underlying asset. A short call position has a negative gamma. In this case, we see that a normal distribution for the price of the underlying asset at the end of one day gets mapped into a negatively skewed distribution for the value of the option position.

The VaR for a portfolio is critically dependent on the left tail of the probability distribution of the portfolio value. For example, when the confidence level used is 99%, the VaR is the value in the left tail below which only 1% of the distribution resides. As indicated in Figures 15.1a and 15.2, a positive gamma portfolio tends to have a less heavy left tail than the normal distribution. If the distribution is assumed to be normal, the calculated VaR will tend to be too high. Similarly, as indicated in Figures 15.1b and 15.3, a negative gamma portfolio tends to have a heavier left

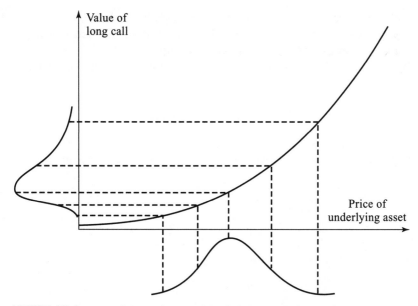

FIGURE 15.2 Translation of Normal Probability Distribution for an Asset into Probability Distribution for Value of a Long Call on the Asset

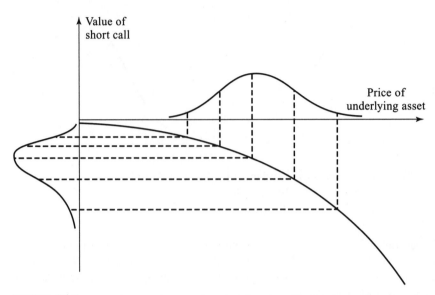

FIGURE 15.3 Translation of Normal Probability Distribution for an Asset into Probability Distribution for Value of a Short Call on the Asset

tail than the normal distribution. If the distribution is assumed to be normal, the calculated VaR will tend to be too low.

15.7 QUADRATIC MODEL

For a more accurate estimate of VaR than that given by the linear model, both delta and gamma measures can be used to relate ΔP to the Δx_i. Consider a portfolio dependent on a single asset whose price is S. Suppose δ and γ are the delta and gamma of the portfolio. As indicated in Chapter 7 and Appendix G, a Taylor Series expansion gives

$$\Delta P = \delta \Delta S + \frac{1}{2} \gamma (\Delta S)^2$$

as an improvement over the linear approximation $\Delta P = \delta \Delta S$.[9] Setting

$$\Delta x = \frac{\Delta S}{S}$$

---

[9] A fuller Taylor series expansion suggests the approximation

$$\Delta P = \Theta \Delta t + \delta \Delta S + \frac{1}{2} \gamma (\Delta S)^2$$

when terms of higher order than Δt are ignored. In practice, the $\Theta \Delta t$ term is so small that it is usually ignored.

reduces this to

$$\Delta P = S\delta\Delta x + \frac{1}{2}S^2\gamma(\Delta x)^2 \tag{15.7}$$

In this case, when Δx is assumed to be normal

$$E(\Delta P) = 0.5S^2\gamma\sigma^2$$

$$E(\Delta P^2) = S^2\delta^2\sigma^2 + 0.75S^4\gamma^2\sigma^4$$

and

$$E(\Delta P^3) = 4.5S^4\delta^2\gamma\sigma^4 + 1.875S^6\gamma^3\sigma^6$$

where σ is the daily volatility of the variable.

For a portfolio with n underlying market variables, with each instrument in the portfolio being dependent on only one of the market variables, equation (15.7) becomes

$$\Delta P = \sum_{i=1}^{n} S_i\delta_i\Delta x_i + \sum_{i=1}^{n}\sum_{j=1}^{n}\frac{1}{2}S_iS_j\gamma_{ij}\Delta x_i\Delta x_j \tag{15.8}$$

where γ_{ij} is a "cross gamma" defined as

$$\gamma_{ij} = \frac{\partial^2 P}{\partial S_i\partial S_j}$$

Cornish–Fisher Expansion

Equation (15.8) is not as easy to work with as equation (15.6), but it can be used to calculate the first few moments of ΔP, when the Δx_i are assumed to be multivariate normal, providing n is not too large.

A result in statistics known as the Cornish-Fisher expansion can be used to estimate quantiles of a probability distribution from its moments. We illustrate this by showing how the first three moments can be used to produce a VaR estimate that takes account of the skewness of ΔP. Define μ_P and σ_P as the mean and standard deviation of ΔP so that

$$\mu_P = E(\Delta P)$$

$$\sigma_P^2 = E[(\Delta P)^2] - [E(\Delta P)]^2$$

The skewness of the probability distribution of ΔP, ξ_P, is defined as

$$\xi_P = \frac{1}{\sigma_P^3}E[(\Delta P - \mu_P)^3] = \frac{E[(\Delta P)^3] - 3E[(\Delta P)^2]\mu_P + 2\mu_P^3}{\sigma_P^3}$$

Using the first three moments of ΔP, the Cornish-Fisher expansion estimates the q-quantile of the distribution of ΔP as

$$\mu_P + w_q \sigma_P$$

where

$$w_q = z_q + \frac{1}{6}(z_q^2 - 1)\xi_P$$

and z_q is q-quantile of the standard normal distribution.

EXAMPLE 15.2

Suppose that for a certain portfolio we calculate $\mu_P = -0.2$, $\sigma_P = 2.2$, and $\xi_P = -0.4$, and we are interested in the 0.01 quantile ($q = 0.01$). In this case, $z_q = -2.33$. If we assume that the probability distribution of ΔP is normal, then the 0.01 quantile is

$$-0.2 - 2.33 \times 2.2 = -5.326$$

In other words, we are 99% certain that

$$\Delta P > -5.326$$

When we use the Cornish-Fisher expansion to adjust for skewness and set $q = 0.01$, we obtain

$$w_q = -2.33 - \frac{1}{6}(2.33^2 - 1) \times 0.4 = -2.625$$

so that the 0.01 quantile of the distribution is

$$-0.2 - 2.625 \times 2.2 = -5.976$$

Taking account of skewness, therefore, changes the VaR from 5.326 to 5.976.

15.8 MONTE CARLO SIMULATION

As an alternative to the approaches described so far, we can implement the model-building approach using Monte Carlo simulation to generate the probability distribution for ΔP. Suppose we wish to calculate a one-day VaR for a portfolio. The procedure is as follows

1. Value the portfolio today in the usual way using the current values of market variables.

2. Sample once from the multivariate normal probability distribution of the Δx_is.[10]
3. Use the sampled values of the Δx_is to determine the value of each market variable at the end of one day.
4. Revalue the portfolio at the end of the day in the usual way.
5. Subtract the value calculated in step one from the value in step four to determine a sample ΔP.
6. Repeat steps two to five many times to build up a probability distribution for ΔP.

The VaR is calculated as the appropriate percentile of the probability distribution of ΔP. Suppose, for example, that we calculate 5,000 different sample values of ΔP in the way just described. The one-day 99% VaR is the value of ΔP for the 50th worst outcome; the one-day 95% VaR is the value of ΔP for the 250th worst outcome; and so on.[11] The N-day VaR is usually assumed to be the one-day VaR multiplied by $\sqrt{N}$.[12]

The drawback of Monte Carlo simulation is that it tends to be computationally slow because a company's complete portfolio (which might consist of hundreds of thousands of different instruments) has to be revalued many times.[13] One way of speeding things up is to assume that equation (15.8) describes the relationship between ΔP and the Δx_is. We can then jump straight from step two to step five in the Monte Carlo simulation and avoid the need for a complete revaluation of the portfolio. This is sometimes referred to as the *partial simulation approach*.

15.9 NON-NORMAL ASSUMPTIONS

The approaches described so far in this chapter have assumed that the underlying market variables have a multivariate normal distribution. This is a serious weakness of the model-building approach. In practice, market variables have heavier tails than the normal distribution so that the model building approach tends to lead to VaR estimates that are too low.

When Monte Carlo simulation is used, there are ways of extending the model building approach so that market variables are no longer assumed to be normal. One possibility is to assume that the variables have a multivariate t-distribution. As indicated by Figures 11.4 and 11.5, this has the effect of giving a higher value to the probability that extreme values for several variables occur simultaneously.

---

[10] One way of doing so is given in Section 11.3.

[11] As in the case of historical simulation, extreme value theory can be used to "smooth the tails" so that better estimates of extreme percentiles are obtained.

[12] This is only approximately true when the portfolio includes options, but it is the assumption that is made in practice for most VaR calculation methods.

[13] An approach for limiting the number of portfolio revaluations is proposed in F. Jamshidian and Y. Zhu, "Scenario Simulation Model: Theory and Methodology," *Finance and Stochastics* 1 (1997): 43–67.

We can assume any set of distributions for the Δx_i in conjunction with a copula model.[14] Suppose, for example, that we assume a one-factor Gaussian copula model. As explained in Chapter 11, this means that when the changes in market variables Δx_i are transformed on a percentile-to-percentile basis to normally distributed variables u_i, the u_i are multivariate normal. We can follow the five steps given earlier except that step 2 is changed and a step is inserted between step 2 and step 3 as follows

2. Sample once from the multivariate probability distribution for the u_is.
2a. Transform each u_i to Δx_i on a percentile-to-percentile basis.

If a financial institution has already implemented the Monte Carlo simulation approach for calculating VaR assuming percentage changes in market variables are normal, it should be relatively easy to implement the approach we describe here. The marginal distributions of the Δx_i can be calculated by fitting a more general distribution than the normal distribution to empirical data.

15.10 MODEL-BUILDING VS. HISTORICAL SIMULATION

In the last chapter and in this one, we have discussed two methods for estimating VaR: the historical simulation approach and the model-building approach. The advantages of the model-building approach are that results can be produced very quickly and can easily be used in conjunction with volatility and correlation updating procedures such as those described in Chapters 10 and 11. As mentioned in Section 14.3, volatility updating can be incorporated into the historical simulation approach—but in a rather more artificial way. The main disadvantage of the model-building approach is that (at least in the simplest version of the approach) it assumes that the market variables have a multivariate normal distribution. In practice, daily changes in market variables often have distributions that are quite different from normal. (See, for example, Table 10.2.) A user of the model building approach is hoping that some form of the central limit theorem of statistics applies so that the probability distribution of daily gains/losses on a large portfolio is normally distributed—even though the gains/losses on the component parts of the portfolio are not normally distributed.

The historical simulation approach has the advantage that historical data determine the joint probability distribution of the market variables. It is also easier to handle interest rates in a historical simulation because, on each trial, a complete zero-coupon yield curve for both today and tomorrow can be calculated. The somewhat messy cash flow mapping procedure described in Section 15.4 is avoided. The main disadvantage of historical simulation is that it is computationally much slower than the model-building approach.

The model-building approach is most often used for investment portfolios. (It is, after all, closely related to the popular Markowitz mean-variance method of portfolio analysis.) It is less commonly used for calculating the VaR for the trading operations of a financial institution. This is because, as explained in Chapter 7,

---

[14] See J. Hull and A. White, "Value at Risk When Daily Changes Are Not Normally Distributed, *Journal of Derivatives* 5, no. 3 (Spring 1998): 9–19.

financial institutions like to maintain their deltas with respect to market variables close to zero. Neither the linear model nor the quadratic model work well when deltas are low and portfolios are nonlinear (see Problem 15.22).

SUMMARY

Whereas historical simulation lets the data determine the joint probability distribution of daily percentage changes in market variables, the model-building approach assumes a particular form for this distribution. The most common assumption is that percentage changes in the variables have a multivariate normal distribution. For situations where the change in the value of the portfolio is linearly dependent on percentage changes in the market variables, VaR can then be calculated exactly in a straightforward way. In other situations, approximations are necessary. One approach is to use a quadratic approximation for the change in the value of the portfolio as a function of percentage changes in the market variables. Another (much slower) approach is to use Monte Carlo simulation.

The model-building approach is frequently used for investment portfolios. It is less popular for the trading portfolios of financial institutions because it does not work well when deltas are low.

FURTHER READING

Frye, J. "Principals of Risk: Finding VAR through Factor-Based Interest Rate Scenarios." In *VAR: Understanding and Applying Value at Risk*. London: Risk Publications, 1997: 275–88.

Hull, J. C., and A. White. "Value at Risk When Daily Changes in Market Variables Are Not Normally Distributed," *Journal of Derivatives* 5 (Spring 1998): 9–19.

Jamshidian, F., and Y. Zhu. "Scenario Simulation Model: Theory and Methodology," *Finance and Stochastics* 1 (1997): 43–67.

Rich, D. "Second Generation VaR and Risk-Adjusted Return on Capital," *Journal of Derivatives*, 10, no. 4 (Summer 2003): 51–61.

PRACTICE QUESTIONS AND PROBLEMS (ANSWERS AT END OF BOOK)

15.1 Consider a position consisting of a $100,000 investment in asset A and a $100,000 investment in asset B. Assume that the daily volatilities of both assets are 1% and that the coefficient of correlation between their returns is 0.3. What is the five-day 99% VaR for the portfolio?

15.2 Describe three ways of handling interest-rate-dependent instruments when the model-building approach is used to calculate VaR.

15.3 Explain how an interest rate swap is mapped into a portfolio of zero-coupon bonds with standard maturities for the purposes of a VaR calculation.

15.4 A financial institution owns a portfolio of options on the U.S. dollar–sterling exchange rate. The delta of the portfolio is 56.0. The current exchange rate is

1.5000. Derive an approximate linear relationship between the change in the portfolio value and the percentage change in the exchange rate. If the daily volatility of the exchange rate is 0.7%, estimate the 10-day 99% VaR.

15.5 Suppose that you know the gamma of the portfolio in Problem 15.4 is 16.2. How does this change your estimate of the relationship between the change in the portfolio value and the percentage change in the exchange rate?

15.6 Suppose that the five-year rate is 6%, the seven-year rate is 7% (both expressed with annual compounding), the daily volatility of a five-year zero-coupon bond is 0.5%, and the daily volatility of a seven-year zero-coupon bond is 0.58%. The correlation between daily returns on the two bonds is 0.6. Map a cash flow of $1,000 received at time 6.5 years into a position in a five-year bond and a position in a seven-year bond. What cash flows in five and seven years are equivalent to the 6.5-year cash flow?

15.7 Verify that the 0.3-year zero-coupon bond in the cash-flow mapping example in Table 15.9 is mapped into a $37,397 position in a three-month bond and a $11,793 position in a six-month bond.

15.8 Suppose that the daily change in the value of a portfolio is, to a good approximation, linearly dependent on two factors, calculated from a principal components analysis. The delta of a portfolio with respect to the first factor is 6 and the delta with respect to the second factor is –4. The standard deviations of the factor are 20 and 8, respectively. What is the five-day 90% VaR?

15.9 The text calculates a VaR estimate for the example in Table 15.10 assuming two factors. How does the estimate change if you assume (a) one factor and (b) three factors?

15.10 A bank has a portfolio of options on an asset. The delta of the options is –30 and the gamma is –5. Explain how these numbers can be interpreted. The asset price is 20 and its volatility is 1% per day. Using the quadratic model, calculate the first three moments of the change in the portfolio value. Calculate a one-day 99% VaR using (a) the first two moments and (b) the first three moments.

15.11 Suppose that in Problem 15.10 the vega of the portfolio is –2 per 1% change in the annual volatility. Derive a model relating the change in the portfolio value in one day to delta, gamma, and vega.

15.12 Explain why the linear model can provide only approximate estimates of VaR for a portfolio containing options.

15.13 Some time ago, a company entered into a forward contract to buy £1 million for $1.5 million. The contract now has six months to maturity. The daily volatility of a six-month zero-coupon sterling bond (when its price is translated to dollars) is 0.06% and the daily volatility of a six-month zero-coupon dollar bond is 0.05%. The correlation between returns from the two bonds is 0.8. The current exchange rate is 1.53. Calculate the standard deviation of the change in the dollar value of the forward contract in one day. What is the 10-day 99% VaR? Assume that the six-month interest rate in both sterling and dollars is 5% per annum with continuous compounding.

15.14 The calculations in Section 15.3 assume that the investments in the DJIA, FTSE 100, CAC 40, and Nikkei 225 are $4 million, $3 million, $1 million, and $2 million, respectively. How does the VaR calculated change if the investment is $2.5 million in each index? Carry out calculations when (a) volatilities and correlations are estimated using the equally weighted model and (b) when they are estimated using the EWMA model with $\lambda = 0.94$. Use the spreadsheets on the author's website.

15.15 What is the effect of changing λ from 0.94 to 0.97 in the EWMA calculations in Section 15.3? Use the spreadsheets on the author's website.

FURTHER QUESTIONS

15.16 Consider a position consisting of a $300,000 investment in gold and a $500,000 investment in silver. Suppose that the daily volatilities of these two assets are 1.8% and 1.2% respectively, and that the coefficient of correlation between their returns is 0.6. What is the 10-day 97.5% VaR for the portfolio? By how much does diversification reduce the VaR?

15.17 Consider a portfolio of options on a single asset. Suppose that the delta of the portfolio is 12, the value of the asset is $10, and the daily volatility of the asset is 2%. Estimate the one-day 95% VaR for the portfolio from the delta.

15.18 Suppose that you know the gamma of the portfolio in Problem 15.17 is −2.6. Derive a quadratic relationship between the change in the portfolio value and the percentage change in the underlying asset price in one day.
(a) Calculate the first three moments of the change in the portfolio value.
(b) Using the first two moments and assuming that the change in the portfolio is normally distributed, calculate the one-day 95% VaR for the portfolio.
(c) Use the third moment and the Cornish–Fisher expansion to revise your answer to (b).

15.19 A company has a long position in a two-year bond and a three-year bond as well as a short position in a five-year bond. Each bond has a principal of $100 million and pays a 5% coupon annually. Calculate the company's exposure to the one-year, two-year, three-year, four-year, and five-year rates. Use the data in Tables 8.7 and 8.8 to calculate a 20-day 95% VaR on the assumption that rate changes are explained by (a) one factor, (b) two factors, and (c) three factors. Assume that the zero-coupon yield curve is flat at 5%.

15.20 A company has a position in bonds worth $6 million. The modified duration of the portfolio is 5.2 years. Assume that only parallel shifts in the yield curve can take place and that the standard deviation of the daily yield change (when yield is measured in percent) is 0.09. Use the duration model to estimate the 20-day 90% VaR for the portfolio. Explain carefully the weaknesses of this approach to calculating VaR. Explain two alternatives that give more accuracy.

15.21 A bank has written a European call option on one stock and a European put option on another stock. For the first option, the stock price is 50, the strike price is 51, the volatility is 28% per annum, and the time to maturity is nine months. For the second option, the stock price is 20, the strike price is 19, the volatility is 25% per annum, and the time to maturity is one year. Neither stock pays a dividend, the risk-free rate is 6% per annum, and the correlation between stock price returns is 0.4. Calculate a 10-day 99% VaR

(a) Using only deltas.

(b) Using the partial simulation approach.

(c) Using the full simulation approach.

15.22 A common complaint of risk managers is that the model-building approach (either linear or quadratic) does not work well when delta is close to zero. Test what happens when delta is close to zero in using Sample Application E in the DerivaGem Application Builder software. (You can do this by experimenting with different option positions and adjusting the position in the underlying to give a delta of zero.) Explain the results you get.

15.23 The calculations in Section 15.3 assume that the investments in the DJIA, FTSE 100, CAC 40, and Nikkei 225 are $4 million, $3 million, $1 million, and $2 million, respectively. How does the VaR calculated change if the investment is $3 million, $3 million, $1 million, and $3 million, respectively? Carry out calculations when (a) volatilities and correlations are estimated using the equally weighted model and (b) when they are estimated using the EWMA model. What is the effect of changing λ from 0.94 to 0.90 in the EWMA calculations? Use the spreadsheets on the author's website.

CHAPTER 16

Credit Risk: Estimating
Default Probabilities

Credit risk arises from the possibility that borrowers, bond issuers, and counterparties in derivatives transactions may default. As explained in Chapter 12, regulators have for a long time required banks to keep capital for credit risk. Under Basel II banks can, with approval from bank supervisors, use their own estimates of default probabilities to determine the amount of capital they are required to keep. This has led banks to search for better ways of estimating these probabilities.

In this chapter, we discuss a number of different approaches to estimating default probabilities and explain the key difference between risk-neutral and real-world estimates. The material we cover will be used in Chapter 17 when we examine how the price of a derivative in the over-the-counter market can be adjusted for counterparty credit risk, and in Chapter 18 when we discuss the calculation of credit value at risk.

16.1 CREDIT RATINGS

As explained in Section 1.7, rating agencies such as Moody's, S&P, and Fitch provide ratings describing the creditworthiness of corporate bonds.[1] A credit rating is designed to provide information about credit quality. As such one might expect frequent changes in credit ratings as positive and negative information reaches the market. In fact, ratings change relatively infrequently. One of the objectives of rating agencies when they assign ratings is ratings stability. For example, they want to avoid ratings reversals, where a company's bonds are downgraded and then upgraded a few weeks later. Ratings therefore change only when there is reason to believe that a long-term change in the company's creditworthiness has taken place. The reason for this is that bond traders are major users of ratings. Often they are subject to rules governing what the credit ratings of the bonds they hold must be. (For example, many bond funds are allowed to hold only investment-grade bonds.) If these ratings

---

[1] In theory, a credit rating is an attribute of a bond issue, not a company. However, in many cases all bonds issued by a company have the same rating. A rating is therefore often referred to as an attribute of a company.

changed frequently, they might have to do a large amount of trading (and incur high transactions costs) just to satisfy the rules.

A related point is that rating agencies try to "rate through the cycle." Suppose that the economy exhibits a downturn and this has the effect of increasing the probability of a company defaulting in the next six months, but makes very little difference to the company's probability of defaulting over the next three to five years. A rating agency would not usually change the company's credit rating in these circumstances.

Companies such as Moody's KMV and Kamakura provide estimates of a company's probability of default that are based on its equity price and other variables. These estimates do not have stability as one of their objectives and tend to respond more quickly to market information than credit ratings. The types of models that are used to produce the estimates will be discussed in Section 16.8.

Internal Credit Ratings

Most banks have procedures for rating the creditworthiness of their corporate and retail clients. This is a necessity. The ratings published by rating agencies are available only for relatively large corporate clients. Many small and medium sized businesses do not issue publicly traded bonds and therefore are not rated by rating agencies. As explained in Chapter 12, the internal-ratings-based (IRB) approach in Basel II allows banks to use their internal ratings in determining the probability of default, PD.

Internal-ratings-based approaches for estimating PD typically involve profitability ratios such as return on assets and balance sheet ratios such as current assets divided by current liabilities (the current ratio) and debt to equity. Banks recognize that it is cash rather than profits that is necessary to repay a loan. They typically take the financial information provided by a company and convert it to a cash flow statement. This allows them to estimate how easy it will be for a company to service its debt.

Altman's Z-Score

Edward Altman has pioneered the use of accounting ratios to predict default. In 1968, he developed what has become known as the Z-score.[2] Using a statistical technique known as discriminant analysis, he attempted to predict defaults from five accounting ratios:

X_1 : Working capital/Total assets

X_2 : Retained earnings/Total assets

X_3 : Earnings before interest and taxes/Total assets

X_4 : Market value of equity/Book value of total liabilities

X_5 : Sales/Total assets

---

[2] See E. I. Altman, "Financial Ratios, Discriminant Analysis, and the Prediction of Corporate Bankruptcy," *Journal of Finance* 23, no. 4 (September 1968): 589–609.

For publicly traded manufacturing companies, the Z-score is calculated as

$$Z = 1.2X_1 + 1.4X_2 + 3.3X_3 + 0.6X_4 + 0.999X_5 \qquad (16.1)$$

If the Z-score is greater than 3.0, the company is unlikely to default. If it is between 2.7 and 3.0 we should be "on alert." If it is between 1.8 and 2.7, there is a good chance of default. If it is less than 1.8, the probability of a financial embarrassment is very high. Equation (16.1) was estimated from a sample of 66 publicly traded manufacturing companies. Of these, 33 failed within one year and 33 did not fail within one year. The model proved to be fairly accurate when tested out of sample (i.e., on a set of firms different from that used to estimate equation 16.1). Both Type I errors (companies that were predicted not to go bankrupt but did do so) and Type II errors (companies that were predicted to go bankrupt, but did not do so) were small.[3] Variations on the model have been developed for manufacturing companies that are not publicly traded and for non-manufacturing companies.

EXAMPLE 16.1

Consider a company for which working capital is 170,000, total assets are 670,000, earnings before interest and taxes is 60,000, sales are 2,200,000, the market value of equity is 380,000, total liabilities is 240,000, and retained earnings is 300,000. In this case, $X_1 = 0.254$, $X_2 = 0.448$, $X_3 = 0.0896$, $X_4 = 1.583$, and $X_5 = 3.284$. The Z-score is

$$1.2 \times 0.254 + 1.4 \times 0.448 + 3.3 \times 0.0896 + 0.6 \times 1.583 + 0.999 \times 3.284 = 5.46$$

The Z-score indicates that the company is not in danger of defaulting in the near future.

16.2 HISTORICAL DEFAULT PROBABILITIES

Table 16.1 is typical of the data that is produced by rating agencies. It shows the default experience through time of companies that started with a certain credit rating. For example, Table 16.1 shows that a bond with an initial Moody's credit rating of Baa has a 0.181% chance of defaulting by the end of the first year, a 0.510% chance of defaulting by the end of the second year, and so on. The probability of a bond defaulting during a particular year can be calculated from the table. For example, the probability that a bond initially rated Baa will default during the second year of its life is $0.510 - 0.181 = 0.329\%$.

Table 16.1 shows that, for investment grade bonds, the probability of default in a year tends to be an increasing function of time. (For example, the probability of a Aa-rated bond defaulting during years one, two, three, four, and five are 0.021%,

---

[3] Clearly Type I errors are much more costly to the lending department of a commercial bank than Type II errors.

TABLE 16.1   Average Cumulative Default Rates (%), 1970–2010

Time (yrs)	1	2	3	4	5	7	10	15	20
Aaa	0.000	0.013	0.013	0.037	0.104	0.244	0.494	0.918	1.090
Aa	0.021	0.059	0.103	0.184	0.273	0.443	0.619	1.260	2.596
A	0.055	0.177	0.362	0.549	0.756	1.239	2.136	3.657	6.019
Baa	0.181	0.510	0.933	1.427	1.953	3.031	4.904	8.845	12.411
Ba	1.157	3.191	5.596	8.146	10.453	14.440	20.101	29.702	36.867
B	4.465	10.432	16.344	21.510	26.173	34.721	44.573	56.345	62.693
Caa	18.163	30.204	39.709	47.317	53.768	61.181	72.384	76.162	78.993

Source: Moody's

0.038%, 0.044%, 0.081%, and 0.089%, respectively.) This is because the bond issuer is initially considered to be creditworthy and the more time that elapses, the greater the possibility that its financial health will decline. For bonds with a poor credit rating, the probability of default is often a decreasing function of time. (For example, the probabilities that a Caa-rated bond will default during years one, two, three, four, and five are 18.163%, 12.041%, 9.505%, 7.608%, and 6.451%, respectively.) The reason here is that, for a bond with a poor credit rating, the next year or two may be critical. If the issuer survives this period, its financial health is likely to have improved.

Hazard Rates

From Table 16.1, we can calculate the probability of a Caa bond defaulting during the third year as $39.709 - 30.204 = 9.505\%$. We will refer to this as the *unconditional default probability*. It is the probability of default during the third year as seen at time zero. The probability that the Caa-rated bond will survive until the end of year two is $100 - 30.204 = 69.796$ %. The probability that it will default during the third year conditional on no earlier default is therefore $0.09505/0.69796$ or 13.62%.

The 13.62% we have just calculated is a conditional default probability for a one-year time period. When we consider a conditional default probability for a short time period of length Δt, we get a measure known as the *hazard rate* or *default intensity*. The hazard rate, $\lambda(t)$, at time t is defined so that $\lambda(t)\Delta t$ is the probability of default between time t and $t + \Delta t$ conditional on no default between time zero and time t. If $V(t)$ is the cumulative probability of the company surviving to time t (i.e., no default by time t), the unconditional default probability between times t and $t + \Delta t$ is $[V(t) - V(t + \Delta t)]$. The probability of default between times t and $t + \Delta t$ conditional on no earlier default is $[V(t) - V(t + \Delta t)]/V(t)$. Hence

$$\frac{V(t) - V(t + \Delta t)}{V(t)} = \lambda(t)\Delta t$$

or

$$\frac{V(t + \Delta t) - V(t)}{\Delta t} = -\lambda(t) V(t)$$

Taking limits

$$\frac{dV(t)}{dt} = -\lambda(t)V(t)$$

from which

$$V(t) = e^{-\int_0^t \lambda(\tau)d\tau}$$

Defining $Q(t)$ as the probability of default by time t, so that $Q(t) = 1 - V(t)$ gives

$$Q(t) = 1 - e^{-\int_0^t \lambda(\tau)d\tau}$$

or

$$Q(t) = 1 - e^{-\bar{\lambda}(t)t} \tag{16.2}$$

where $\bar{\lambda}(t)$ is the average hazard rate between time zero and time t.

EXAMPLE 16.2

Suppose that the hazard rate is a constant 1.5% per year. The probability of a default by the end of the first year is $1 - e^{-0.015 \times 1} = 0.0149$. The probability of a default by the end of the second year is $1 - e^{-0.015 \times 2} = 0.0296$. The probability of a default by the end of the third, fourth, and fifth years are similarly 0.0440, 0.0582, and 0.0723. The unconditional probability of a default during the fourth year is $0.0582 - 0.0440 = 0.0142$. The probability of default in the fourth year, conditional on no earlier default is $0.0142/(1 - 0.0440) = 0.0149$.

16.3 RECOVERY RATES

When a company goes bankrupt, those that are owed money by the company file claims against the company.[4] Sometimes there is a reorganization in which these creditors agree to a partial payment of their claims. In other cases, the assets are sold by the liquidator and the proceeds are used to meet the claims as far as possible. Some claims typically have priorities over other claims and are met more fully.

The *recovery rate* for a bond is normally defined as the price at which it trades about 30 days after default as a percent of its face value. As we saw in Chapter 12, the Basel II formulas are expressed in terms of the loss given default (LGD). The percentage recovery rate is 100 minus the percentage loss given default.

Table 16.2 provides historical data on average recovery rates for different categories of bank loans and bonds in the United States. It shows that bank loans with a

---

[4] In the United States, the claim made by a bond holder is the bond's face value plus accrued interest.

TABLE 16.2   Recovery Rates on Corporate Bonds and Bank
Loans as a Percent of Face Value, 1982 to 2010, Issuer
Weighted

Class	Average Recovery Rate (%)
First lien bank loan	65.8
Second lien bank loan	29.1
Senior unsecured bank loan	47.8
Senior secured bond	50.8
Senior unsecured bond	36.7
Senior subordinated bond	30.7
Subordinated bond	31.3
Junior subordinated bond	24.7

Source: Moody's

first lien on assets had the best average recovery rate, 65.8%. For bonds, the average recovery rate varies from 47.8% for those that are both senior to other lenders and secured to 24.7% for those that rank after other lenders.

Recovery rates are significantly negatively correlated with default rates.[5] This means that a bad year for the default rate is usually doubly bad because it is accompanied by a low recovery rate. For example, when the default rate on non-investment-grade bonds in a year is 1%, we might expect the average recovery rate to be relatively high at about 55%; when this default rate is 10%, we might expect the average recovery rate to be relatively low at about 30%.

16.4 CREDIT DEFAULT SWAPS

An instrument that is very useful for estimating default probabilities is a *credit default swap* (CDS). As indicated in Business Snapshot 16.1, the market for this product has seen huge growth since the late 1990s. The simplest type of CDS is an instrument that provides insurance against the risk of a default by a particular company. The company is known as the *reference entity* and a default by the company is known as a *credit event*. The buyer of the insurance obtains the right to sell bonds issued by the company for their face value when a credit event occurs and the seller of the insurance agrees to buy the bonds for their face value when a credit event occurs.[6] The total face value of the bonds that can be sold is known as the credit default swap's *notional principal*.

---

[5] See E. I. Altman, B. Brady, A. Resti, and A. Sironi, "The Link Between Default and Recovery Rates: Theory, Empirical Evidence, and Implications," *Journal of Business* (November 2005): 2203–2228. The correlation is also discussed in publications by Moody's Investors Service. It finds that the correlation between the average recovery rate in a year and the non investment-grade default rate is about 0.5.

[6] The face value (or par value) of a bond is the principal amount that the issuer will repay at maturity if it does not default.

BUSINESS SNAPSHOT 16.1

The CDS Market

In 1998 and 1999, the International Swaps and Derivatives Association developed a standard contract for trading credit default swaps in the over-the-counter market. Since then, the market has grown very fast. The Bank for International Settlements (BIS) started producing statistics for the size of the credit derivatives market in December 2004. At that time, the total notional principal underlying outstanding contracts was estimated to be about $6 trillion. It peaked at $58 trillion in December 2007 and fell to about $30 trillion in December 2010. Banks and other financial institutions are both buyers and sellers of protection. Banks tend to be net buyers of protection and insurance companies tend to be net sellers of protection. One of the results of the popularity of credit default swaps (and other credit derivatives) is that the financial institution bearing the credit risk of a loan is often different from the financial institution that did the original credit checks.

During the credit turmoil that started in August 2007, regulators became concerned that CDSs were a source of systemic risk. (See Business Snapshot 12.1 for a discussion of systemic risk.) No doubt, their concerns arose in part because of the losses experienced by the insurance company, AIG. This was a big seller of protection on the AAA-rated tranches created from mortgages (see Chapter 6). The protection proved very costly to AIG and a failure of AIG would have led to big losses elsewhere in the financial system. AIG was bailed out by the United States government in September 2008.

CDSs have come under criticism during the European sovereign debt crisis. Some legislators feel that speculative activity in credit default swap markets has exacerbated the debt problems of countries such as Greece and that naked positions (where credit protection is bought without an underlying exposure) should be banned.

During 2007 and 2008, trading ceased in many types of credit derivatives, but CDSs continued to trade actively (albeit with dramatically increased spreads). The advantage of CDSs over other credit derivatives is that the way they work is straightforward. Other derivatives such as ABS CDOs (see Chapter 6) lack this transparency.

There were a huge number of CDS contracts outstanding with a Lehman company as the reference entity when Lehman Brothers declared bankruptcy in September 2008. The recovery rate (determined by the ISDA auction process) was only about eight cents on the dollar, so that the payout to the buyers of protection was equal to about 92% of the notional principal. There were predictions that some sellers of protection would be unable to pay and that further bankruptcies would occur, but on the settlement day (October 21, 2008) everything went smoothly.

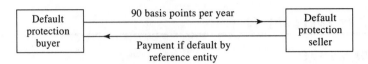

FIGURE 16.1   Credit Default Swap

The buyer of a CDS makes periodic payments to the seller until the end of the life of the CDS or until a credit event occurs. These payments are usually made in arrears every quarter.

An example will help to illustrate how a typical deal is structured. Suppose that two parties enter into a five-year credit default swap on December 20, 2012. Assume that the notional principal is $100 million and the buyer agrees to pay 90 basis points per year (quarterly in arrears) for protection against default by the reference entity.

The CDS is shown in Figure 16.1. If the reference entity does not default (that is, there is no credit event), the buyer receives no payoff and pays approximately $225,000 on March 20, June 20, September 20, and December 20 of each of the years 2013, 2014, 2015, 2016, and 2017.[7] If there is a credit event, a substantial payoff is likely. Suppose that the buyer notifies the seller of a credit event on May 20, 2015 (five months into the third year). If the contract specifies physical settlement, the buyer of protection has the right to sell to the seller of protection bonds issued by the reference entity with a face value of $100 million for $100 million. If, as is now usual, there is a cash settlement, a two-stage auction process is used to determine the mid-market value of the cheapest deliverable bond several days after the credit event. Suppose the auction indicates that the cheapest deliverable bond is worth $35 per $100 of face value. The cash payoff would be $65 million.

The regular payments from the buyer of protection to the seller of protection cease when there is a credit event. However, because these payments are made in arrears, a final accrual payment by the buyer is usually required. In our example, where there is a default on May 20, 2015, the buyer would be required to pay to the seller the amount of the annual payment accrued between March 20, 2015, and May 20, 2015 (approximately $150,000), but no further payments would be required.

The total amount paid per year, as a percent of the notional principal, to buy protection is known as the CDS *spread*. Several large banks are market makers in the credit default swap market. For a five-year credit default swap on a company, a market maker might quote: bid 250 basis points, offer 260 basis points. This means that the market maker is prepared to buy protection by paying 250 basis points per year (i.e., 2.5% of the principal per year) and to sell protection for 260 basis points per year (i.e., 2.6% of the principal per year).

Many different companies and countries are reference entities for the CDS contracts that trade. Contracts with maturities of five years are most popular, but other maturities such as 1, 2, 3, 7, and 10 years are also traded. Usually, contracts mature on the following standard dates: March 20, June 20, September 20, and December 20. The effect of this is that the actual time to maturity of a contract when it is

---

[7] The payments are not exactly $225,000 because of the impact of day count conventions.

BUSINESS SNAPSHOT 16.2

Is the CDS Market a Fair Game?

There is one important difference between credit default swaps and most other over-the-counter derivatives. The other over-the-counter derivatives depend on interest rates, exchange rates, equity indices, commodity prices, and so on. There is no reason to assume that any one market participant has better information than other market participants about these variables.

Credit default swaps spreads depend on the probability that a particular company will default during a particular period of time. Arguably, some market participants have more information to estimate this probability than others. A financial institution that works closely with a particular company by providing advice, making loans, and handling new issues of securities is likely to have more information about the creditworthiness of the company than another financial institution that has no dealings with the company. Economists refer to this as an *asymmetric information* problem.

The importance of asymmetric information in credit default swap markets is debatable. Financial institutions emphasize that the decision to buy protection against the risk of default by a company is normally made by a risk manager and is not based on any special information or analyses that may exist elsewhere in the financial institution about the company.

---

initiated is close to, but not necessarily the same as, the number of years to maturity that is specified. Suppose you call a dealer on November 15, 2012, to buy five-year protection on a reference entity. The contract would probably last until December 20, 2017. Your first payment would be due on December 20, 2012, and would equal an amount covering the November 15, 2012, to December 20, 2012, period.[8] After that, payments would be made quarterly.

A key aspect of a CDS contract is the definition of a credit event (i.e., a default). Usually a credit event is defined as a failure to make a payment as it becomes due, a restructuring of debt, or a bankruptcy. Restructuring is sometimes excluded in North American contracts, particularly in situations where the yield on the company's debt is high. A potential asymmetric information problem in the CDS market is discussed in Business Snapshot 16.2.

The Cheapest-to-Deliver Bond

As explained in Section 16.3, the recovery rate on a bond is defined as the value of the bond immediately after default as a percent of face value. This means that

---

[8] If the time to the first date is less than one month, the first payment is typically on the second payment date, otherwise it is in the first payment date.

the payoff from a CDS is $L(1 - R)$ where L is the notional principal and R is the recovery rate.

Usually a CDS specifies that a number of different bonds can be delivered in the event of a default. The bonds typically have the same seniority, but they may not sell for the same percentage of face value immediately after a default.[9] This gives the holder of a CDS what is known as a *cheapest-to-deliver bond* option. As already mentioned, an auction process is usually used to determine the value of the cheapest-to-deliver bond and, therefore, the payoff to the buyer of protection.

The determination of CDS spreads and the valuation of CDS transactions is discussed in Appendix K.

Credit Indices

Participants in credit markets have developed indices to track credit default swap spreads. In 2004, there were agreements between different producers of indices that led to some consolidation. Two important standard portfolios used by index providers are:

1. CDX NA IG, a portfolio of 125 investment grade companies in North America
2. iTraxx Europe, a portfolio of 125 investment grade companies in Europe

These portfolios are updated on March 20 and September 20 each year. Companies that are no longer investment grade are dropped from the portfolios and new investment grade companies are added.[10]

Suppose that the five-year CDX NA IG index is quoted by a market maker as bid 165 basis points, offer 166 basis points. (This is referred to as the index spread.) Roughly speaking, the quotes mean that a trader can buy CDS protection on all 125 companies in the index for 166 basis points per company. Suppose an investor wants $800,000 of protection on each company. The total cost is $0.0166 \times 800,000 \times 125$ or $1,660,000 per year. (The investor could similarly sell $800,000 of protection on each of the 125 companies for a total of $1,650,000 per annum.) When a company defaults, the investor receives the usual CDS payoff and the annual payment is reduced by $1,660,000/125 = \$13,280$. There is an active market in buying and selling CDS index protection for maturities of 3, 5, 7, and 10 years. The maturities for these types of contracts on the index are usually December 20 and June 20. (This means that a "five-year" contract lasts between $4\frac{3}{4}$ and $5\frac{1}{4}$ years.) Roughly speaking,

---

[9] There are a number of reasons for this. The claim that is made in the event of a default is typically equal to the bond's face value plus accrued interest. Bonds with high accrued interest at the time of default therefore tend to have higher prices immediately after default. Also, the market may judge that in the event of a reorganization of the company some bond-holders will fare better than others.

[10] On September 20, 2011, the Series 16 iTraxx Europe portfolio and the Series 17 CDX NA IG portfolio were defined. The series numbers indicate that by the end of September 2011 the iTraxx Europe portfolio had been updated 15 times and the CDX NA IG portfolio had been updated 16 times.

the index is the average of the CDS spreads on the companies in the underlying portfolio.[11]

The Use of Fixed Coupons

To facilitate trading, the precise way in which CDS and CDS index transactions work is a little more complicated than has been described up to now. In practice, CDS and CDS indices trade like bonds so that the periodic protection payments (analogous to a bond's coupon) remain fixed. For each of the standard transactions that trade, a coupon and a recovery rate is specified. If the quoted spread is greater than the coupon, the buyer of protection pays at the outset to the seller the expected present value of the excess of the spread over the coupon for the remaining life of the contract. If the quoted spread is less than the coupon, the seller of protection pays at the outset to the buyer the expected present value of the excess of the coupon over the spread for the remaining life of the contract. The buyer of protection then pays the coupon times the principal applicable to those companies in the index that have not yet defaulted to the seller.

16.5 CREDIT SPREADS

The credit spread is the extra rate of interest per annum required by investors for bearing a particular credit risk. CDS spreads, which were discussed in Section 16.4, are one type of credit spread. Another is the bond yield spread. This is the amount by which the yield on a corporate bond exceeds the yield on a similar risk-free bond. We now show that the two should be approximately equal.

CDS Spreads and Bond Yields

A CDS can be used to hedge a position in a corporate bond. Suppose that an investor buys a five-year corporate bond yielding 7% per year for its face value and at the same time enters into a five-year CDS to buy protection against the issuer of the bond defaulting. Suppose that the CDS spread is 200 basis points or 2% per annum. The effect of the CDS is to convert the corporate bond to a risk-free bond (at least approximately). If the bond issuer does not default, the investor earns 5% per year (when the CDS spread is netted against the corporate bond yield). If the bond does

---

[11] More precisely, the index is slightly lower than the average of the credit default swap spreads for the companies in the portfolio. To understand the reason for this, consider a portfolio consisting of two companies, one with a spread of 1,000 basis points and the other with a spread of 10 basis points. To buy protection on the companies would cost slightly less than 505 basis points per company. This is because the 1,000 basis points is not expected to be paid for as long as the 10 basis points and should therefore carry less weight. Another complication for CDX NA IG, but not iTraxx Europe, is that the definition of default applicable to the index includes restructuring whereas the definition for CDS contracts on the underlying companies may not.

default, the investor earns 5% up to the time of the default. Under the terms of the CDS, the investor is then able to exchange the bond for its face value. This face value can be invested at the risk-free rate for the remainder of the five years.

This argument shows that the n-year CDS spread should be approximately equal to the excess of the par yield on an n-year corporate bond over the par yield on an n-year risk-free bond.[12] If it is markedly less than this, an investor can earn more than the risk-free rate by buying the corporate bond and buying protection. If it is markedly greater than this, an investor can borrow at less than the risk-free rate by shorting the corporate bond and selling CDS protection. These are not perfect arbitrages as we discuss later, but in normal markets they do give a good guide to the relationship between CDS spreads and bond yields.

The Risk-Free Rate

CDSs provide a direct estimate of the credit spread. To calculate a credit spread from a bond yield, it is necessary to make an assumption about the risk-free rate. When bond yield spreads are quoted by bond traders, the risk-free rate that is used is usually the yield on a Treasury bond of similar maturity. For example, a bond trader might quote the yield on a particular corporate bond as being a spread of 250 basis points over Treasuries.

A number of researchers have compared bond yields to CDS spreads to imply a risk-free rate. This involves matching the maturities of CDSs and bonds and implying a risk-free rate from the arbitrage arguments given above. For example, if the five-year bond yield is 4.7% and the five-year CDS spread is 80 basis points, the implied five-year risk-free rate is 3.9%.

As discussed in Section 8.2, traders have traditionally used LIBOR/swap rates as proxies for risk-free rates when valuing derivatives. The research indicates that this practice has carried over to the credit market. Implied risk-free rates are much closer to the LIBOR/swap rates than to the Treasury rates. One estimate puts implied risk-free rates at about 10 basis points less than the LIBOR/swap rate.[13] This estimate is plausible. As explained in Section 8.2, the credit risk in a swap rate is the credit risk from making a series of short-term loans to AA-rated counterparties and 10 basis points is a reasonable credit spread for a short-term AA-rated instrument.

Asset Swaps

Asset swaps provide a convenient reference point for traders in credit markets because they provide a direct estimate of the excess of a bond yield over the LIBOR/swap rate.

---

[12] The par yield on an n-year bond is the coupon rate per year that causes the bond to sell for its par value (i.e., its face value).

[13] See J. Hull, M. Predescu, and A. White, "The Relationship between Credit Default Swap Spreads, Bond Yields, and Credit Rating Announcements," *Journal of Banking and Finance* 28 (November 2004): 2789–2811.

To explain how asset swaps work, consider the situation where an asset swap spread for a particular bond is quoted as 150 basis points. There are three possible situations

1. The bond sells for its par value of 100. The swap then involves one side (Company A) paying the coupon on the bond and the other side (Company B) paying LIBOR plus 150 basis points.[14]
2. The bond sells below its par value, say, for 95. The swap is then structured so that Company A pays $5 per $100 of notional principal at the outset. After that, Company A pays the bond's coupons and Company B pays LIBOR plus 150 basis points.
3. The underlying bond sells above par, say, for 108. The swap is then structured so that Company B makes a payment of $8 per $100 of principal at the outset. After that, Company A pays the bond's coupons and Company B pays LIBOR plus 150 basis points.

The effect of all this is that the present value of the asset swap spread (150 basis points in our example) is the amount by which the price of the corporate bond is exceeded by the price of a similar risk-free bond where the risk-free rate is assumed to be given by the LIBOR/swap curve (see Problem 16.16).

CDS–Bond Basis

The CDS–bond basis is the excess of the CDS spread over the bond yield spread for a company.

$$\text{CDS-Bond Basis} = \text{CDS Spread} - \text{Bond Yield Spread}$$

The bond yield spread is calculated relative to the LIBOR/swap benchmark. Usually it is assumed to be the asset swap spread.

The arbitrage argument given, relating CDS spreads and bond yields, suggests that the CDS-bond basis should be close to zero. In fact, there are a number of reasons why it deviates from zero. For example

1. The bond may sell for a price that is significantly different from par. (Bond prices above par tend to give rise to a positive basis; bond prices below par tend to give rise to a negative basis.)
2. There is counterparty default risk in a CDS. (This pushes the basis in a negative direction.)
3. There is a cheapest-to-deliver bond option in a CDS. (This pushes the basis in a positive direction.)
4. The payoff in a CDS does not include accrued interest on the bond that is delivered. (This pushes the basis in a negative direction.)

---

[14] Note that it is the promised coupons that are exchanged. The exchanges take place regardless of whether the bond defaults.

5. The restructuring clause in a CDS contract may lead to a payoff when there is no default. (This pushes the basis in a positive direction.)
6. LIBOR is greater than the risk-free rate being assumed by the market. (This pushes the basis in a positive direction.)

Prior to the market turmoil starting in 2007, the basis tended to be positive. For example, De Witt estimates that the average CDS bond basis in 2004 and 2005 was 16 basis points.[15] During the credit crisis that started in August 2007, the basis has tended to be negative. Possibly, counterparty default risk loomed large in the minds of investors. Also, finding the capital to fund the arbitrage might have been a problem for some investors.

16.6 ESTIMATING DEFAULT PROBABILITIES FROM CREDIT SPREADS

We now discuss how default probabilities can be estimated from credit spreads.

Approximate Calculation

Suppose that a five-year credit spread (CDS spread, bond yield spread, or asset swap spread) for a company is 240 basis points and that the expected recovery rate in the event of a default is 40%. The holder of a corporate bond issued by the company must be expecting to lose 240 basis points (or 2.4% per year) from defaults. Roughly speaking, the credit spread can be considered to be an average loss rate. Given the recovery rate of 40%, this leads to an estimate of the average probability of a default per year over the five-year period, conditional on no earlier default, of $0.024/(1 - 0.4)$ or 4%. In general:

$$\bar{\lambda} = \frac{s(T)}{1 - R} \tag{16.3}$$

where $s(T)$ is the credit spread (expressed with continuous compounding) for a maturity of T, R is the recovery rate, and $\bar{\lambda}$ is the average hazard rate between time zero and time T.

If credit spreads are known for a number of different maturities, the term structure of the hazard rate can be bootstrapped (at least approximately) as the following example illustrates.

EXAMPLE 16.3

Suppose that the CDS spread for 3-, 5-, and 10-year instruments is 50, 60, and 100 basis points and the expected recovery rate is 60%. The average hazard rate over three years is approximately $0.005/(1 - 0.6) = 0.0125$. The average hazard rate over five years is approximately $0.006/(1 - 0.6) = 0.015$. The average hazard rate

---

[15] See J. De Witt, "Exploring the CDS-Bond Basis" (Working Paper no. 104, National Bank of Belgium, 2006).

over 10 years is approximately $0.01/(1-0.6)=0.025$. From this we can estimate that the average hazard rate between year 3 and year 5 is $(5 \times 0.015 - 3 \times 0.0125)/2 = 0.01875$. The average hazard rate between year 5 and year 10 is $(10 \times 0.025 - 5 \times 0.015)/5 = 0.035$.

A More Exact Calculation

The calculation we have just given works well for CDS spreads. It also works well for bond yield spreads and asset swap spreads when the underlying bond is selling for close to its par value. We now consider a more exact calculation for situations when the underlying bond's price is not close to par.

Suppose that a five-year corporate bond with a principal of 100 provides a coupon of 6% per annum (paid semiannually) and that the yield on the bond is 7% per annum (with continuous compounding). The yield on a similar risk-free bond is 5% (again with continuous compounding). The yields imply that the price of the corporate bond is 95.34 and the price of the risk-free bond is 104.09. The expected loss from default over the five-year life of the bond is therefore $104.09 - 95.34$, or $8.75. For simplicity, we suppose that the unconditional probability of default per year is the same each year and equal to Q. Furthermore, we assume defaults can happen only at times 0.5, 1.5, 2.5, 3.5, and 4.5 years (immediately before coupon payment dates). Risk-free rates are assumed to be 5% (with continuous compounding) for all maturities and the recovery rate is assumed to be 40%. (The analysis can be extended so that defaults happen more frequently.)

Table 16.3 calculates the expected loss from defaults in terms of Q. To illustrate the calculations, consider the 3.5-year row in Table 16.3. The expected value of the default-free bond at time 3.5 years (calculated using the forward risk-free interest rates) is

$$3 + 3e^{-0.05 \times 0.5} + 3e^{-0.05 \times 1.0} + 103e^{-0.05 \times 1.5} = 104.34$$

Given the definition of recovery rates in Section 16.3, the amount recovered if there is a default is 40 so that the loss given default is $104.34 - 40$ or $64.34. The present value of this loss is 54.01 and the expected loss is therefore $54.01Q$.

TABLE 16.3   Calculation of Loss from Default on a Bond in Terms of the Default Probabilities per Year, Q

Time (yrs)	Def. Prob.	Recovery Amount ($)	Default-Free Value ($)	Loss ($)	Discount Factor	PV of Expected Loss ($)
0.5	Q	40	106.73	66.73	0.9753	$65.08Q$
1.5	Q	40	105.97	65.97	0.9277	$61.20Q$
2.5	Q	40	105.17	65.17	0.8825	$57.52Q$
3.5	Q	40	104.34	64.34	0.8395	$54.01Q$
4.5	Q	40	103.46	63.46	0.7985	$50.67Q$
Total						$288.48Q$

(Notional Principal $= \$100$)

Table 16.3 shows that the total expected loss is 288.48 Q. Setting this equal to the 8.75 expected loss calculated earlier, we obtain a value for Q of 8.75/288.48, or 3.03%. The calculations we have given assume that the default probability is the same in each year and that defaults take place at just one time during the year. We can extend the calculations to assume that defaults take place more frequently. Also, instead of assuming a constant unconditional probability of default, we can assume a constant hazard rate or assume a particular pattern for the variation of the default probability with time. With several bonds, we can estimate several parameters describing the term structure of default probabilities. Suppose, for example, that we have bonds maturing in 3, 5, 7, and 10 years and we assume a step function for the default probability. We could use the first bond to estimate the default probability per year for the first three years, the second bond to estimate the default probability per year for years 4 and 5, the third bond to estimate the default probability per year for years 6 and 7, and the fourth bond to estimate the default probability per year for years 8, 9, and 10 (see Problems 16.15 and 16.24). This approach is analogous to the bootstrap procedure for estimating the term structure of interest rates in Appendix B.

16.7 COMPARISON OF DEFAULT PROBABILITY ESTIMATES

The default probabilities estimated from historical data are much less than those derived from credit spreads.[16] The difference between the two was particularly large during the credit crisis which started in mid-2007. This is because there was what is termed a "flight to quality" during the crisis, where all investors wanted to hold safe securities such as Treasury bonds. The prices of corporate bonds declined, thereby increasing their yields. Calculations such as the one in equation (16.3) gave very high default probability estimates.

Table 16.4 shows that hazard rates calculated from bonds were higher than those calculated from historical data before the crisis. The hazard rates estimated from bonds are based on equation (16.3) and the average yields on bonds lasting about seven years that have been published by Merrill Lynch since December 1996. The results shown are based on average bond yield spreads between December 1996 and June 2007 (i.e., up to the start of the crisis). The recovery rate is assumed to be 40% and the risk-free interest rate is assumed to be the seven-year swap rate minus 10 basis points. For example, for A-rated bonds the average Merrill Lynch yield was 5.995%. The average seven-year swap rate was 5.408% so that the average risk free rate was 5.308%. This gives the average seven-year hazard rate as

$$\frac{0.05995 - 0.05308}{1 - 0.4} = 0.0115$$

or 1.15%.

---

[16] See for example J. Hull, M. Predescu, and A. White, "Bond Prices, Default Probabilities, and Risk Premiums," *Journal of Credit Risk* 1, no. 2 (Spring 2005): 53–60.

TABLE 16.4 Average Seven-Year Hazard Rates

Rating	Historical Hazard Rate	Hazard Rate from Bonds	Ratio	Difference
Aaa	0.03	0.60	17.2	0.57
Aa	0.06	0.73	11.5	0.67
A	0.18	1.15	6.5	0.97
Baa	0.44	2.13	4.8	1.69
Ba	2.23	4.67	2.1	2.44
B	6.09	8.02	1.3	1.93
Caa	13.52	18.39	1.4	4.87

(% per annum)

The historical hazard rate is calculated using the data in the seven-year column of Table 16.1. (We use the seven-year column because the Merrill Lynch data is for bonds which have a life of about seven years.) From equation (16.2) we have

$$\bar{\lambda}(7) = -\frac{1}{7}\ln[1 - Q(7)]$$

where $\bar{\lambda}(t)$ is the average hazard rate up to time t and $Q(t)$ is the cumulative probability of default during this period. The values of $Q(7)$ are taken directly from Table 16.1. Consider, for example, an A-rated company. The value of $Q(7)$ is 0.01239. The average seven-year hazard rate is therefore

$$\bar{\lambda}(7) = -\frac{1}{7}\ln(1 - 0.01239) = 0.0018$$

or 0.18%.

Table 16.4 shows that the ratio of the hazard rate backed out of bond prices to the hazard rate calculated from historical data is high for investment grade bonds and tends to decline as the credit quality declines. By contrast, the difference between the two hazard rates tends to increase as credit quality declines.[17]

Table 16.5 provides another way of looking at these results. It shows the excess return over the risk-free rate (still assumed to be the seven-year swap rate minus 10 basis points) earned by investors in bonds with different credit ratings. Consider again an A-rated bond. The average spread over Treasuries is 111 basis points.

---

[17] The hazard rates calculated from historical data are based on data for the 1970 to 2010 period whereas the credit spread data is from the December 1996 to June 2007 period. This is partly because the Merrill Lynch credit spread data is not available before December 1996 and partly to avoid the credit crisis period when credit spreads ballooned. Other studies have identified a similar difference between the two types of default probability estimates. See, for example, J. S. Fons, "The Default Premium and Corporate Bond Experience," *Journal of Finance* 42, no. 1 (March 1987): 81–97 and E. I. Altman, "Measuring Corporate Bond Mortality and Performance," *Journal of Finance* 44, no. 4 (September 1989): 909–922.

TABLE 16.5 Expected Excess Return on Bonds

	Bond Yield Spread over Treasuries (bp)	Spread of Risk-Free Rate over Treasuries (bp)	Spread for Historical Defaults (bp)	Expected Excess Return (bp)
Aaa	78	42	2	34
Aa	86	42	4	40
A	111	42	11	58
Baa	169	42	26	101
Ba	322	42	132	148
B	523	42	355	126
Caa	1,146	42	759	345

Of this, 42 basis points are accounted for by the average spread between seven-year Treasuries and our proxy for the risk-free rate. A spread of 11 basis points is necessary to cover expected defaults. (This equals the one year probability of default calculated from the historical hazard rate in Table 16.1 multiplied by one minus the assumed recovery rate of 0.4.) This leaves an expected excess return (after expected defaults have been taken into account) of 58 basis points.

Tables 16.4 and 16.5 show that a large percentage difference between default probability estimates translates into a relatively small expected excess return on the bond. For Aaa-rated bonds, the ratio of the two hazard rates is 17.2, but the expected excess return is only 34 basis points. The expected excess return tends to increase as credit quality declines.[18]

The excess return in Table 16.5 does not remain constant through time. Credit spreads, and therefore excess returns, were high in 2001, 2002, and the first half of 2003. After that they were fairly low until the start of the credit crisis in mid-2007 when they started to increase rapidly.

Real World vs. Risk-Neutral Probabilities

The risk-neutral valuation argument is explained in Business Snapshot 16.3. It shows that we can value cash flows on the assumption that all investors are risk neutral (that is, on the assumption that they do not require a premium for bearing risks). When we do this, we get the right answer in the real world as well as in the risk-neutral world.

The default probabilities implied from bond yields are risk-neutral probabilities of default (that is, they are the probabilities of default in a world where all investors are risk-neutral). To understand why this is so, consider the calculations of default probabilities in Table 16.3. The calculations assume that expected default losses can be discounted at the risk-free rate. The risk-neutral valuation principle shows that this is a valid procedure provided the expected losses are calculated in a risk-neutral world. This means that the default probability, Q, in Table 16.3 must be a risk-neutral probability. Risk-neutral default probabilities are sometimes also called *implied default probabilities*.

---

[18] The results for B-rated bonds in Tables 16.4 and 16.5 run counter to the overall pattern.

BUSINESS SNAPSHOT 16.3

Risk-Neutral Valuation

The single most important idea in the valuation of derivatives is risk-neutral valuation. It shows that we can value a derivative by

1. Assuming that all investors are risk neutral.
2. Calculating expected cash flows.
3. Discounting the cash flows at the risk-free rate.

As a simple example of the application of risk-neutral valuation, suppose that the price of a non-dividend-paying stock is $30 and consider a derivative that pays off $100 in one year if the stock price is greater than $40 at that time. (This is known as a binary cash-or-nothing call option.) Suppose that the risk-free rate (continuously compounded) is 5%, the expected return on the stock (also continuously compounded) is 10%, and the stock price volatility is 30% per annum. In a risk-neutral world, the expected growth of the stock price is 5%. It can be shown (with the usual Black–Scholes–Merton lognormal assumptions) that when the stock price has this growth rate, the probability that the stock price will be greater than $40 in one year is 0.1730. The expected payoff from the derivatives is therefore $100 \times 0.1730 = \$17.30$. The value of the derivative is calculated by discounting this at 5%. It is $16.46.

The real-world (physical) probability of the stock price being greater than $40 in one year is calculated by assuming a growth rate of 10%. It is 0.2190. The expected payoff in the real world is therefore $21.90. The problem with using this expected cash flow is that we do not know the correct discount rate. The stock price has risk associated with it that is priced by the market (otherwise the expected return on the stock would not be 5% more than the risk-free rate). The derivative has the effect of "leveraging this risk" so that a very high discount rate is required for its expected payoff. Because we know the correct value of the derivative is $16.46, we can deduce that the correct discount rate to apply to the $21.90 real-world expected payoff must be 28.6%.

By contrast, the default probabilities implied from historical data are real world default probabilities (sometimes also called *physical default probabilities*). The expected excess return in Table 16.5 arises directly from the difference between real-world and risk-neutral default probabilities. If there was no expected excess return, the real-world and risk-neutral default probabilities would be the same.

Why do we see such big differences between real-world and risk-neutral default probabilities? As we have just argued, this is the same as asking why corporate bond traders earn more than the risk-free rate on average.

One reason for the results is that corporate bonds are relatively illiquid and the returns on bonds are higher than they would otherwise be to compensate for this.

But this is a small part of what is going on. In normal markets, it explains perhaps 25 basis points of the excess return in Table 16.5. Another possible reason for the results is that the subjective default probabilities of bond traders are much higher than the those given in Tables 16.1. Bond traders may be allowing for depression scenarios much worse than anything seen in the period covered by their data. However, it is difficult to see how this can explain a large part of the excess return that is observed.[19]

By far the most important reason for the results in Tables 16.4 and 16.5 is that bonds do not default independently of each other. (To put this another way, default correlation is a feature of financial markets.) Evidence for this is that default rates vary markedly from year to year. Moody's statistics (see Table 11.4) show that between 1970 and 2010 the default rate per year for all rated companies ranged from a low 0.087% in 1979 to a high of 5.422% in 2009. This year-to-year variation in default rates gives rise to systematic risk (i.e., risk that cannot be diversified away). Bond traders earn an excess expected return for bearing this risk. In this respect, bond traders are no different from equity traders. The latter earn an excess return that averages around 5% per year for bearing systematic risk. From Table 16.5 we see that the excess return earned by bond traders is much less than this for high quality bonds. However, as the bond's credit quality decreases, it becomes more like equity and the excess return earned tends to increase.

What causes default correlation and the resultant systematic risk? One explanation is the economy. Good macroeconomic conditions decrease the probability of default for all companies; bad macroeconomic conditions increase the probability of default for all companies. (In Vasicek's model, which was discussed in Chapter 11, the factor F can be regarded as representing the overall health of the economy.) Another explanation is what is known as "contagion." This is discussed in Business Snapshot 16.4.

In addition to systematic risk that we have just talked about, there is non systematic (or idiosyncratic) risk associated with each bond. If we were talking about stocks, we would argue that investors can diversify the non systematic risk by choosing a portfolio of, say, 30 stocks. They should not therefore demand a risk premium for bearing nonsystematic risk. For bonds the arguments are not so clear cut. Bond returns are highly skewed with limited upside. (For example, on an individual bond there might be a 99.75% chance of a 7% return in a year, and a 0.25% chance of a –60% return in the year, the first outcome corresponding to no default and the second to default.) This type of risk is difficult to "diversify away."[20] It requires tens of thousands of different bonds to be held. In practice, many bond portfolios are far from fully diversified. As a result, bond traders may earn an extra return for bearing

---

[19] In addition to producing Table 16.1, which is based on the 1970 to 2007 period, Moody's produces a similar table based on the 1920 to 2007 period. When this table is used, historical default intensities for investment grade bonds in Table 16.4 rise somewhat. However, the non-investment-grade historical default intensities decline.

[20] See J. D. Amato and E. M. Remolona, "The Credit Spread Puzzle," *BIS Quarterly Review*, (December 2003): 51–63.

BUSINESS SNAPSHOT 16.4

Contagion

Credit contagion is the process whereby a problem in one sector of the world economy leads to the problems in other unrelated sectors. When Russia defaulted on its debt in 1998, there was a flight to quality and credit spreads on all bonds increased. During the credit crisis that started in 2007, there was a similar flight to quality and again credit spreads increased. The accompanying recession led to a record number of companies defaulting in 2009. In 2011, problems experienced by Greece caused investors to be reluctant to buy the debt of other countries such as Spain, Ireland, Portugal, and Italy. As a result, credit spreads on the debt issued by these countries increased sharply.

The reasons for credit contagion have been debated by researchers. It may be the case that investors become more risk averse when they lose money in one sector. It may be the case that problems in one sector lead investors to become more pessimistic about other unrelated sectors. Whatever the reason, entities in unrelated sectors are liable to find it more difficult to fund their activities and, as a result, may become more likely to default.

---

unsystematic risk as well as for bearing the systematic risk mentioned in the previous paragraph.

Which Estimates Should be Used?

At this stage it is natural to ask whether we should use real-world or risk-neutral default probabilities in the analysis of credit risk. The answer depends on the purpose of the analysis. When valuing credit derivatives or estimating the impact of default risk on the pricing of instruments, we should use risk-neutral default probabilities. This is because the analysis calculates the present value of expected future cash flows and almost invariably (implicitly or explicitly) involves using risk-neutral valuation. When carrying out scenario analyses to calculate potential future losses from defaults we should use real-world default probabilities. For example, the probability of default used to calculate regulatory capital is a real world default probability.

16.8 USING EQUITY PRICES TO ESTIMATE DEFAULT PROBABILITIES

When we use a table such as Table 16.1 to estimate a company's real-world probability of default, we are relying on the company's credit rating. Unfortunately, credit ratings are revised relatively infrequently. This has led some analysts to argue that equity prices can provide more up-to-date information for estimating default probabilities.

In 1974, Merton proposed a model where a company's equity is an option on the assets of the company.[21] Suppose, for simplicity, that a firm has one zero-coupon bond outstanding and that the bond matures at time T. Define

V_0 : Value of company's assets today.

V_T : Value of company's assets at time T.

E_0 : Value of company's equity today.

E_T : Value of company's equity at time T.

D : Amount of debt interest and principal due to be repaid at time T.

σ_V : Volatility of assets (assumed constant).

σ_E : Instantaneous volatility of equity.

If $V_T < D$, it is (at least in theory) rational for the company to default on the debt at time T. The value of the equity is then zero. If $V_T > D$, the company should make the debt repayment at time T and the value of the equity at this time is $V_T - D$. Merton's model, therefore, gives the value of the firm's equity at time T as

$$E_T = \max(V_T - D, 0)$$

This shows that the equity of a company is a call option on the value of the assets of the company with a strike price equal to the repayment required on the debt. The Black–Scholes–Merton formula (see Appendix E at the end of this book) gives the value of the equity today as

$$E_0 = V_0 N(d_1) - De^{-rT} N(d_2) \tag{16.4}$$

where

$$d_1 = \frac{\ln(V_0/D) + (r + \sigma_V^2/2)T}{\sigma_V \sqrt{T}}$$

$$d_2 = d_1 - \sigma_V \sqrt{T}$$

and N is the cumulative normal distribution function.

Under Merton's model, the company defaults when the option is not exercised. The probability of this can be shown to be $N(-d_2)$. To calculate this, we require V_0 and σ_V. Neither of these are directly observable. However, if the company is publicly traded, we can observe E_0. This means that equation (16.4) provides one condition that must be satisfied by V_0 and σ_V. We can also estimate σ_E. From a result in stochastic calculus known as Ito's lemma

$$\sigma_E E_0 = \frac{\partial E}{\partial V} \sigma_V V_0$$

---

[21] See R. Merton "On the Pricing of Corporate Debt: The Risk Structure of Interest Rates," *Journal of Finance* 29 (1974): 449–470.

Here $\partial E / \partial V$ is the delta of the equity. From Appendix E it is $N(d_1)$ so that

$$\sigma_E E_0 = N(d_1)\sigma_V V_0 \qquad (16.5)$$

This provides another equation that must be satisfied by V_0 and σ_V. Equations (16.4) and (16.5) provide a pair of simultaneous equations that can be solved for V_0 and σ_V.[22]

EXAMPLE 16.4

The value of a company's equity is \$3 million and the volatility of the equity is 80%. The debt that will have to be paid in one year is \$10 million. The risk-free rate is 5% per annum. In this case, $E_0 = 3$, $\sigma_E = 0.80$, $r = 0.05$, $T = 1$, and $D = 10$. Solving equations (16.4) and (16.5) yields $V_0 = 12.40$ and $\sigma_V = 0.2123$. The parameter, d_2 is 1.1408 so that the probability of default is $N(-d_2) = 0.127$ or 12.7%. The market value of the debt is $V_0 - E_0$ or 9.40. The present value of the promised payment on the debt is $10e^{-0.05 \times 1} = 9.51$. The expected loss on the debt is therefore $(9.51 - 9.40)/9.51$ or about 1.2% of its no-default value. The expected loss is the probability of default times one minus the recovery rate. The recovery rate (as a percentage of the no-default value) is therefore $1 - 1.2/12.7$ or about 91%.

Extensions of the Basic Model

The basic Merton's model we have just presented has been extended in a number of ways. For example, one version of the model assumes that a default occurs whenever the value of the assets falls below a barrier level. Another allows payments on debt instruments to be required at more than one time. Many analysts have found the implied volatility of equity issued by a company to be a good predictor of the probability of default. (The higher the implied volatility, the higher the probability of default.) Hull et al. (2004) show that this is consistent with Merton's model.[23] They provide a way of implementing Merton's model using two equity implied volatilities and show that the resulting model provides results comparable to those provided by the usual implementation of the model.

Performance of the Model

How well do the default probabilities produced by Merton's model and its extensions correspond to actual default experience? The answer is that Merton's model and its extensions produce a good ranking of default probabilities (risk-neutral or real-world). This means that a monotonic transformation can be estimated to convert the probability of default output from Merton's model into a good estimate of either

---

[22] To solve two non linear equations of the form $F(x, y) = 0$ and $G(x, y) = 0$, we can use the Solver routine in Excel to find the values of x and y that minimize $[F(x, y)]^2 + [G(x, y)]^2$.

[23] See J. Hull, I. Nelken, and A. White, "Merton's Model, Credit Risk, and Volatility Skews," *Journal of Credit Risk* 1, no. 1 (2004): 1–27.

the real-world or risk-neutral default probability. Moody's KMV and Kamakura provide a service that transforms a default probability produced by Merton's model into a real-world default probability. CreditGrades uses Merton's model to estimate credit spreads, which are closely linked to risk-neutral default probabilities. The default probability, $N(-d_2)$, is in theory a risk-neutral default probability because it is calculated from an option pricing model. It may seem strange for Moody's KMV and Kamakura to use it to estimate a real world default probability. Given the nature of the calibration process we have just described, the underlying assumption is that the rank order of risk-neutral default probabilities, real-world default probabilities, and default probabilities produced by Merton's model are the same.

Distance to Default

The term *distance to default* has been coined to describe the output from Merton's model. This is the number of standard deviations the asset price must change for default to be triggered T years in the future. It is

$$\frac{\ln V_0 - \ln D + (r - \sigma_V^2/2)T}{\sigma_V \sqrt{T}}$$

As the distance to default reduces, the company becomes more likely to default. In Example 16.4, the one-year distance to default is 1.14 standard deviations.

SUMMARY

The estimation of default probabilities and recovery rates is an important activity for risk managers. If a company has issued publicly traded debt, credit ratings provide one source of information. Rating agencies such as Moody's provide extensive statistics on default rates for companies that have been awarded particular credit ratings. The recovery rate is the value of a bond shortly after default as a percentage of its face value. Rating agencies provide statistics on recovery rates for different types of bonds.

There are a number of other sources of information for the estimation of default probabilities. The credit default swap (CDS) market is one such source. A CDS is an instrument where one company buys from another company insurance against a third company (or country) defaulting on its obligations. The payoff from the instrument is usually the difference between the face value of a bond issued by the third company and its value immediately after a default. The CDS spread, which can be directly related to the probability of default, is the amount paid per year for protection. Another source of information is the asset swap market. Asset swap spreads provide an estimate of the excess of a bond's yield over the LIBOR/swap rate. A third source of information is the equity market. A model developed by Robert Merton in 1974 can be used to estimate default probabilities from equity prices and equity volatilities.

The default probabilities that are based on historical data, such as those produced by rating agencies, are termed real-world or physical default probabilities.

The default probabilities calculated from the prices of instruments that trade such as credit default swaps, bonds, or asset swaps are termed risk-neutral default probabilities. There are big differences between the two types of probabilities. This is mainly because bonds and related investments have systematic risk which cannot be diversified away. Traders require to be compensated for more than just the real-world expected cost of defaults because of this. The default probabilities calculated from equity prices using Merton's model are in theory risk-neutral default probabilities. However, the output from the model can be calibrated so that either risk-neutral or real world default probability estimates are produced.

Real-world probabilities should be used for scenario analysis and the calculation of credit VaR. Risk-neutral probabilities should be used for valuing credit-sensitive instruments and evaluating price adjustments for counterparty default risk.

FURTHER READING

Altman, E. I. "Measuring Corporate Bond Mortality and Performance," *Journal of Finance* 44 (1989): 902–922.

Duffie, D., and K. Singleton. "Modeling Term Structures of Defaultable Bonds," *Review of Financial Studies* 12 (1999): 687–720.

Fons, J. S. "The Default Premium and Corporate Bond Experience," *Journal of Finance* 42, no. 1 (March 1987): pp. 81–97.

Hull, J., M. Predescu, and A. White. "Relationship Between Credit Default Swap Spreads, Bond Yields, and Credit Rating Announcements," *Journal of Banking and Finance* 28 (November 2004): 2789–2811.

Hull, J., M. Predescu, and A. White. "Bond Prices, Default Probabilities, and Risk Premiums," *Journal of Credit Risk* 1, no. 2 (Spring 2005): 53–60.

Kealhofer S. "Quantifying Credit Risk I: Default Prediction," *Financial Analysts Journal* 59, no. 1 (2003a): 30–44.

Kealhofer, S. "Quantifying Credit Risk II: Debt Valuation," *Financial Analysts Journal* 59, no. 3 (2003): 78–92.

Litterman, R., and T. Iben. "Corporate Bond Valuation and the Term Structure of Credit Spreads," *Journal of Portfolio Management* (Spring 1991): 52–64.

Merton, R. C. "On the Pricing of Corporate Debt: The Risk Structure of Interest Rates," *Journal of Finance* 29 (1974): 449–470.

Rodriguez, R. J. "Default Risk, Yield Spreads, and Time to Maturity," *Journal of Financial and Quantitative Analysis* 23 (1988): 111–117.

PRACTICE QUESTIONS AND PROBLEMS (ANSWERS AT END OF BOOK)

16.1 How many different ratings does Moody's use for investment-grade companies? What are they?

16.2 How many different ratings does S&P use for investment-grade companies? What are they?

16.3 Calculate the average hazard rate for a B-rated company during the first year from the data in Table 16.1.

16.4 Calculate the average hazard rate for a Ba-rated company during the third year from the data in Table 16.1.

16.5 A credit default swap requires a semiannual payment at the rate of 60 basis points per year. The principal is $300 million and the credit default swap is settled in cash. A default occurs after four years and two months, and the calculation agent estimates that the price of the cheapest deliverable bond is 40% of its face value shortly after the default. List the cash flows and their timing for the seller of the credit default swap.

16.6 Explain the two ways a credit default swap can be settled.

16.7 Explain the difference between risk-neutral and real-world default probabilities.

16.8 What is the formula relating the payoff on a CDS to the notional principal and the recovery rate?

16.9 The spread between the yield on a three-year corporate bond and the yield on a similar risk-free bond is 50 basis points. The recovery rate is 30%. Estimate the average hazard rate per year over the three-year period.

16.10 The spread between the yield on a five-year bond issued by a company and the yield on a similar risk-free bond is 80 basis points. Assuming a recovery rate of 40%, estimate the average hazard rate per year over the five-year period. If the spread is 70 basis points for a three-year bond, what do your results indicate about the average hazard rate in years 4 and 5?

16.11 Should researchers use real-world or risk-neutral default probabilities for (a) calculating credit value at risk and (b) adjusting the price of a derivative for defaults?

16.12 How are recovery rates usually defined?

16.13 Verify (a) that the numbers in the second column of Table 16.4 are consistent with the numbers in Table 16.1 and (b) that the numbers in the fourth column of Table 16.5 are consistent with the numbers in Table 16.4 and a recovery rate of 40%.

16.14 A four-year corporate bond provides a coupon of 4% per year payable semi-annually and has a yield of 5% expressed with continuous compounding. The risk-free yield curve is flat at 3% with continuous compounding. Assume that defaults can take place at the end of each year (immediately before a coupon or principal payment) and the recovery rate is 30%. Estimate the risk-neutral default probability on the assumption that it is the same each year using the approach in Table 16.3.

16.15 A company has issued three- and five-year bonds, each of which has a coupon of 4% per annum payable semiannually. The yields on the bonds (expressed with continuous compounding are 4.5% and 4.75%, respectively. Risk-free interest rates are 3.5% with continuous compounding for all maturities. The recovery rate is 40%. Defaults can take place halfway through each year. The unconditional risk-neutral default rates per year are Q_1 for years 1 to and Q_2 for years 4 and 5. Estimate Q_1 and Q_2.

16.16 Suppose that in an asset swap, B is the market price of the bond per dollar of principal, B^* is the default-free value of the bond per dollar of principal, and V is the present value of the asset swap spread per dollar of principal. Show that $V = B^* - B$.

16.17 Show that, under Merton's model in Section 16.8, the credit spread on a T-year zero-coupon bond is $- \ln[N(d_2) + N(-d_1)/L]/T$ where $L = De^{-rT}/V_0$.

16.18 The value of a company's equity is $2 million and the volatility of its equity is 50%. The debt that will have to be repaid in one year is $5 million. The risk-free interest rate is 4% per annum. Use Merton's model to estimate the probability of default. (*Hint*: The Solver function in Excel can be used for this question.)

16.19 A five-year credit default swap entered into on June 20, 2013, requires quarterly payments at the rate of 400 basis points per year. The principal is $100 million. A default occurs after four years and two months. The auction process finds the price of the cheapest deliverable bond to be 30% of its face value. List the cash flows and their timing for the seller of the credit default swap.

16.20 "The position of a buyer of a credit default swap is similar to the position of someone who is long a risk-free bond and short a corporate bond." Explain this statement.

16.21 Why is there a potential asymmetric information problem in credit default swaps?

16.22 Suppose that the LIBOR/swap curve is flat at 6% with continuous compounding and a five-year bond with a coupon of 5% (paid semiannually) sells for 90.00. How much would the bond be worth if it were a risk-free bond? What is the present value expected loss from defaults? How would an asset swap on the bond be structured? What is the asset swap spread that would be calculated in this situation?

FURTHER QUESTIONS

16.23 Suppose that a three-year corporate bond provides a coupon of 7% per year payable semiannually and has a yield of 5% (expressed with semiannual compounding). The yields for all maturities on risk-free bonds is 4% per annum (expressed with semiannual compounding). Assume that defaults can take place every six months (immediately before a coupon payment) and the recovery rate is 45%. Estimate the default probabilities assuming (a) the unconditional default probabilities are the same on each possible default date and (b) the default probabilities conditional on no earlier default are the same on each possible default date.

16.24 A company has issued one- and two-year bonds providing 8% coupons, payable annually. The yields on the bonds (expressed with continuous compounding) are 6.0% and 6.6%, respectively. Risk-free rates are 4.5% for all maturities. The recovery rate is 35%. Defaults can take place halfway through each year. Estimate the risk-neutral default rate each year.

16.25 The value of a company's equity is $4 million and the volatility of its equity is 60%. The debt that will have to be repaid in two years is $15 million. The risk-free interest rate is 6% per annum. Use Merton's model to estimate the expected loss from default, the probability of default, and the recovery rate (as a percentage of the no-default value) in the event of default. Explain why Merton's model gives a high recovery rate. (*Hint*: The Solver function in Excel can be used for this question.)

CHAPTER 17

Counterparty Credit Risk in Derivatives

Assessing the credit risk for a derivatives transaction is much more complicated than assessing the credit risk for a loan because the future exposure (i.e., the amount that could be lost in the event of a default) is not known. If a bank makes a $10 million five-year loan to a client with repayment of principal at the end, the bank knows that its exposure is approximately $10 million at all times during the five-year period. If the bank instead enters into a five-year interest rate swap with the client, the future exposure is much less certain. This is because the future value of the swap depends on movements in interest rates. If the value of the interest rate swap to the bank becomes positive, the exposure is equal to the value of the swap (because this is what the bank could lose in the event of a counterparty default). If the value becomes negative, the exposure is zero (because in that case the bank would not lose anything in the case of a counterparty default).

Derivatives that trade on exchanges entail very little credit risk. This is because, as explained in Chapter 5, the exchange stands between the two parties and has strict rules on the margin to be posted by each side. As mentioned in Chapter 13, legislators throughout the world now require most standardized over-the-counter derivatives transactions to be cleared through central clearing parties (CCPs). Like exchanges, CCPs stand between the two parties in derivatives transactions and have strict rules on margin requirements. Over-the-counter derivatives that are cleared centrally therefore have very little credit risk.

This chapter includes material on central clearing, but focuses on over-the-counter transactions that are cleared bilaterally because these are the transactions where credit risk is greatest. The chapter explains the nature of the agreements that are entered into between market participants, the ways in which credit risk is mitigated, and how counterparty credit risk affects accounting numbers.

17.1 CREDIT EXPOSURE ON DERIVATIVES

We start by quickly reviewing the nature of the exposure created by derivatives transactions. Consider first the simple case where there is only one derivatives transaction outstanding between a derivatives dealer and a counterparty and the derivatives dealer is concerned about the possibility of a default by the counterparty. We assume that no exchange or clearing house is involved.

Three possible situations can be distinguished:

1. The derivative is always a liability to the dealer.
2. The derivative is always an asset to the dealer.
3. The derivative can become either an asset or a liability to the dealer.

An example of a derivative in the first category is a short option; an example in the second category is a long option; an example in the third category is a forward or a swap.

In the first case, the dealer has no credit exposure to the counterparty. If the counterparty declares bankruptcy, it cannot incur a loss.[1] It will not usually gain from a bankruptcy. This is because the derivative is one of the counterparty's assets. It is likely to be retained, closed out, or transferred to a third party in the event that the counterparty declares bankruptcy.

In the second case, the dealer always has credit exposure to the counterparty. If the counterparty goes bankrupt, a loss is liable to be experienced. The amount of the loss depends on any collateral that has been posted and the value of the derivative at the time of the bankruptcy.

The third case is more complicated. The dealer may or may not have credit exposure to the counterparty in the future. If the counterparty declares bankruptcy when the value of the derivative is positive to the dealer, a loss is liable to be experienced. If the counterparty declares bankruptcy when the value is negative to the dealer there will be no loss.

These simple examples illustrate that, in the absence of collateral, the dealer's exposure to the counterparty at any time is

$$\max(V, 0)$$

The variable, V, is the market value of the derivative at the time. It is sometimes referred to as the mark-to-market or MTM value. When there are many derivatives transactions outstanding between the dealer and the counterparty, they are netted (see Section 12.5) and the dealer's exposure is given by this formula with V equal to the net mark-to-market value of all outstanding transactions.

In calculating its credit risk, the dealer is interested in both its credit exposure today and what that exposure might be in the future. (It will be recalled from Chapter 12 that Basel I recognized this by specifying an "add-on" amount for the calculation of capital requirements.) As we will see in this chapter, dealers now have sophisticated procedures for assessing the probability distribution of their exposure to each of their counterparties at future times.

17.2 BILATERAL CLEARING

Traditionally, over-the-counter derivatives transactions have been cleared bilaterally. This usually involves a pair of market participants, A and B, entering into an International Swaps and Derivatives Association (ISDA) Master Agreement that covers all derivatives transactions between them.

---

[1] Because the derivative is an asset to the counterparty, it must be the case that, if the counterparty goes bankrupt, it has run into financial difficulties for reasons unrelated to the derivative.

One important feature of an ISDA Master Agreement, already mentioned, is netting. This is a provision under which all transactions between the two parties are netted and considered as a single transaction when there is an *early termination event*. Early termination events can be declared by one side when there has been an *event of default* by the other side. Examples of events of default are when the other side declares bankruptcy, fails to make payments on outstanding transactions as required, or fails to post collateral as required.[2]

Netting was discussed in Section 12.5. It has now been tested in the courts in most jurisdictions. As pointed out in Section 12.5, it can lead to a big reduction in credit risk. Assuming no collateral, it reduces the potential exposure of market participant B to market participant A, from

$$\sum_{i=1}^{N} \max(V_i, 0)$$

to

$$\max\left(\sum_{i=1}^{N} V_i, 0\right)$$

where N is the number of derivatives transactions between A and B and V_i is the value of the ith transaction to B. The Basel Committee recognized the reduction in credit risk arising from netting in 1995 and reduced capital requirements for credit risk when enforceable bilateral netting agreements were in place (see Section 12.5).

Collateralization

A credit support annex (CSA) of the ISDA Master Agreement specifies collateral arrangements. A typical collateral arrangement requires the net mark-to-market value of outstanding transactions to be calculated periodically (usually every day). This calculation might lead to a request by one side for additional collateral to be posted by the other side. The terminology used is as follows:

1. *Threshold*: The MTM value at which collateral is required. For example, if the threshold applicable to Party A is $5 million in its CSA with Party B, no collateral needs to be posted by Party A until the net MTM value of outstanding transactions to Party B exceeds $5 million. The collateral required is then the excess of the net MTM value over $5 million. The threshold can be regarded as a line of credit provided by Party B to Party A.
2. *Independent Amount*: An initial margin required by one side with the other side. The independent amount is akin to a negative threshold.
3. *Minimum Transfer Amount*: The minimum amount of collateral transferred from one side to the other when MTMs are recalculated for the purposes of the

---

[2] A company is not required to declare an early termination event in these circumstances. Often it chooses not to do so when the net value of its outstanding transactions is negative. This is because early termination would require it to make an immediate cash payment. Furthermore, when there has been an event of default by the counterparty, the company does not have to make any payments due on the transactions. Eventually of course there has to be a settling up.

CSA. The purpose of the minimum transfer amount is to avoid relatively small inconsequential amounts of collateral having to be transferred. If the minimum transfer amount is $1 million, collateral is transferred only if the net MTM calculation shows the extra collateral required is more than $1 million.

4. *Eligible Securities and Currencies*: The securities and currencies that are acceptable as collateral.
5. *Haircut on a Security*: Percentage subtracted from the market value of the security when it is posted as collateral. For example, if a 20% haircut applies to a particular security and the market value of a security is $100 million, it will be counted as providing $80 million of collateral.

Collateral agreements can be one-way or two-way. In a one-way collateral agreement, only one side is required to post collateral when the net MTM value of outstanding transactions to the other side is above the specified threshold. In a two-way collateral agreement, either side may have to post collateral. When a derivatives dealer is considerably more creditworthy than its counterparty, the collateral agreement is likely to be a one-way agreement where only the counterparty is required to post collateral. When the credit standings of the two sides are similar, the collateral agreement is likely to be two-way.

As an example, consider a one-way agreement where Party A is posting collateral and Party B is receiving it. Suppose the threshold is $10 million, transactions are valued daily, and there is no independent amount. If on a particular day the net value of outstanding transactions to Party B is $9 million (so that the net value to Party A is −$9 million), no collateral needs to be posted. If the net value of the transactions to B on the next day moves from $9 million to $12 million, Party B will require $2 million of collateral from Party A. (This assumes that $2 million is greater than the minimum transfer amount.) If on the next day the net value to Party B moves from $12 million to $15 million, Party B will ask for a further $3 million of collateral. If the net value falls to $11 million on the following day, Party A will ask for $4 million of the $5 million collateral that it has already posted to be returned. Interest is usually paid on cash collateral.

Different jurisdictions have different rules about collateral. We continue to suppose that Party A is posting collateral with Party B. In the United States, Party A would retain a security interest in the collateral. In the United Kingdom, ownership of the collateral would be transferred to Party B and, when collateral has to be returned to Party A because the value of outstanding transactions to Party B has declined, different collateral from that originally posted by Party A may be transferred. A complication involving collateral is a practice known as *rehypothecation*, which is discussed in Business Snapshot 17.1.

Early Termination and Settlement

We continue with the example where Party A is posting collateral and Party B is receiving it. If Party B declares an early termination event because of a default event by Party A, Party B must calculate its loss. This is how much a third party would require to be paid to take the position of Party A in the outstanding transactions. If this amount is negative, so that a third party would be prepared to pay to take A's position, the loss to Party B is negative and it owes the liquidators of Party A an amount equal to the negative value. If the amount is positive and greater than

---

BUSINESS SNAPSHOT 17.1

Rehypothecation

A practice in the management of collateral known as rehypothecation can cause problems. If Party A posts collateral with Party B and rehypothecation is permitted, Party B can use the same collateral to satisfy a demand for collateral from Party C; Party C can then use the collateral to satisfy a demand for collateral from Party D; and so on. In 2007, it was estimated that U.S. banks had over $4 trillion of collateral, but that this was created by using $1 trillion of original collateral in conjunction with rehypothecation. Rehypothecation is particularly common in the UK where title to collateral is transferred.

After Lehman declared bankruptcy in September 2008, clients (particularly European hedge fund clients) found it difficult to get a return of the collateral they had posted with Lehman because it had been rehypothecated. As a result of this experience, many market participants are more cautious than they used to be and clauses in CSAs banning or limiting rehypothecation are now common.

---

the collateral posted by A, B is entitled to keep the collateral and claim the excess from A.[3] (However, B will then usually rank equally with other unsecured creditors for the purposes of the claim.) If it is less, B must return some collateral or make a payment to A.

There are two main ways in which the loss is calculated. One is the Market Quotation Method where Party B sends a description of the transactions that are outstanding to other dealers as soon as possible after the early termination event and asks them to quote for taking Party A's position. If more than three quotes are obtained, they are averaged to obtain the loss. If exactly three quotes are obtained, the middle quote is used as an estimate of B's loss. If less than three quotes are obtained, the Market Quotation Method cannot be used and the ISDA Master Agreement then usually requires Party B to estimate its loss itself. Party B then has to calculate the mark-to-market value of the outstanding transactions at the time of the early termination event and adjust for the bid–offer spread that would be incorporated into a quote by a third party.

Downgrade Triggers

A *downgrade trigger* is a clause sometimes included in the CSA between Party A and Party B, stating that if the credit rating of Party A falls below a certain level, Party B has the right to ask for more collateral.

---

[3] It is much easier for derivatives counterparties (even those outside the UK) to obtain ownership of collateral when there is a default than for other counterparties. For example, a bank faces a relatively long process when trying to possess assets that have been posted as collateral for a loan.

AIG provides an example of the operation of a downgrade trigger. Many of AIG's transactions stated that AIG did not have to post collateral provided its credit rating remained above AA. However, once it was downgraded below AA, collateral was required. AIG was downgraded below AA by all three rating agencies on September 15, 2008. This led to collateral calls, which AIG was unable to meet. Its bankruptcy was avoided by a massive government bailout.

Other companies that have run into problems because of downgrade triggers include Enron, Xerox, and Ambac. Downgrade triggers do not provide protection to a company's counterparties from a big jump in a company's credit rating (for example, from AA to default). Also, downgrade triggers work well for a company's counterparties only when the company is making relatively little use of them. If a company has many downgrade triggers in its contracts, an AIG-type situation can arise where a downgrade below a specified credit rating can lead to huge cash demands on the company. If these cash demands cannot be met, immediate bankruptcy follows.

17.3 CENTRAL CLEARING

As discussed in Chapter 13, most jurisdictions now require most standardized over-the-counter derivatives to be cleared centrally. The way this works is as follows. Two companies, A and B, agree to an over-the-counter derivatives transaction. They then present it to a central clearing party (CCP) for clearing. Assuming that the CCP accepts it, the CCP acts as an intermediary and enters into offsetting transactions with the two companies. Suppose, for example, that the transaction is an interest rate swap where company A pays a fixed rate of 5% to company B on a principal of $100 million for five years and company B pays LIBOR to company A on the same principal for the same period of time. Two separate transactions are created. Company A has a transaction with the CCP where it pays 5% and receives LIBOR on $100 million. Company B has a transaction with the CCP where it pays LIBOR and receives 5% on $100 million. The two companies no longer have credit exposure to each other. This is illustrated in Figure 17.1.

The CCP requires an initial margin from both A and B. Each day the deal is valued and this leads to variation margins being required. For example, the CCP

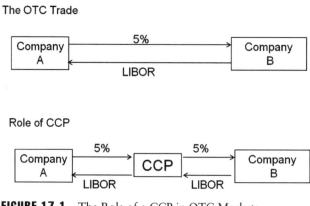

FIGURE 17.1   The Role of a CCP in OTC Markets

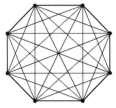 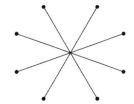

Bilateral clearing   Clearing through a single CCP

FIGURE 17.2 Bilateral vs. Central Clearing

might require an initial margin of $0.5 million from both sides. If, on the first day, interest rates fall so that the value of the swap to A goes down by $100,000, A would be required to pay a *variation margin* equal to this to the CCP and the CCP would be required to pay the same amount to B. If a variation margin is not posted as required by one of the parties, the CCP closes out its transactions with that party. Typically, cash and Treasury instruments are accepted as margin with interest being paid by the CCP on cash balances. The interest rate is close to the overnight federal funds rate for U.S. dollars and close to similar overnight rates for other currencies.

In practice, market participants are likely to have multiple transactions outstanding with the CCP at any given time. The margin required from a participant at any given time reflects the volatility of the value of its total position with the CCP. The role of a CCP in the OTC market is similar to the role of a clearing house in the exchange-traded market. The main difference is that transactions handled by the CCP may be less standard than transactions in the exchange-traded market so that the calculation of margin requirements is more complicated.

The members of the CCP contribute to a guarantee fund. If a member defaults and the margin balances are insufficient to cover the member's obligations, the guarantee fund is used. This means that losses are shared among all the other members.

The difference between bilateral clearing and central clearing in the case where there are eight derivatives dealers is illustrated in Figure 17.2. In the case of central clearing, it is assumed that a single CCP clears all trades. It is easy to see that in this situation the benefits of netting are improved by central clearing. Instead of having seven different netting sets (one with each of the other dealers), a dealer has only one. Suppose for example that one of the dealers has transactions with the other seven dealers that have net MTM values of +10, +15, –20, +5, –10, +10, and +5, respectively. With bilateral clearing, the total exposure (before collateral) would be 45. With central clearing, the exposure after netting would be only 15. Furthermore, this exposure would be to a (hopefully) very-low-risk CCP, rather than to another dealer.

In practice, there are a number of CCPs throughout the world and not all trades are cleared through CCPs. This means that the netting benefits associated with CCPs are not as great as they might otherwise be. Indeed CCPs can make matters worse.[4] This is illustrated by Figure 17.3 which shows the situation where there are three market participants and one CCP. The exposures represented by the dotted lines are

---

[4] See D. Duffie and H. Zhu, "Does Central Clearing Reduce Counterparty Credit Risk?" (Working Paper, Stanford University, 2005), for a discussion of this.

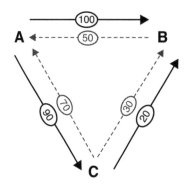
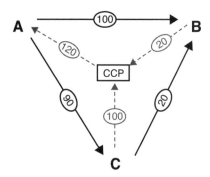

Dealer	Exposure after bilateral netting
A	0
B	100
C	20
Average	40

Dealer	Exposure after netting including CCP	Exposure after netting excluding CCP
A	120	0
B	120	120
C	90	90
Average	110	70

FIGURE 17.3   Example Where There Are Three Market Participants, One CCP, and Two Product Types
One product type can be cleared; the other cannot.

standard transactions that can be cleared centrally. Those represented by the solid line are nonstandard transactions that cannot be cleared centrally. For example, in B's dealings with A, the nonstandard transactions are worth 100 to B and –100 to A; the standard transactions are worth +50 to A and –50 to B. Without central clearing, the average exposure before collateral of the three parties is +40. With central clearing, the average exposure is 110 when the exposure to the CCP is included and 70 when it is not. Central clearing does not improve the collateral requirements of market participants in this simple situation. If transactions are collateralized with a threshold of zero, more collateral is required under central clearing.

Many market participants are likely to have transactions outstanding with most or all of the CCPs. As a result, the margin that has to be posted with CCPs is liable to increase. However, what are termed "interoperability agreements" can develop between CCPs so that the positions of a market participant with different CCPs are netted for the purpose of determining margin requirements.

17.4 CVA

We now return to the situation where there is a bilateral clearing arrangement between a derivatives dealer and a counterparty and consider how the dealer assesses its credit risk.[5]

---

[5] For further reading on CVA and the way it is calculated see J. Hull and A. White, "CVA and Wrong Way Risk," Working Paper, University of Toronto, Canada, 2011; E. Canabarro and

The dealer calculates what has become known as a *credit value adjustment* or CVA for each counterparty with which it has bilaterally cleared OTC derivatives. This is an estimate of its expected loss from a default by the counterparty. The value of outstanding derivatives on the balance sheet of the dealer is reduced by the sum of the CVAs for all counterparties and the change in the total CVA during a period is a charge to the income statement for the period.

Suppose that T is the life of the longest derivative outstanding with a counterparty. To calculate CVA, the period of time between time zero and time T is divided into a number of intervals (e.g., zero to one month, one to three months, etc.).

Suppose that the ith time interval runs from t_{i-1} to t_i ($t_0 = 0$) and there are n intervals. Define

q_i: the risk-neutral probability of a loss from a default by the counterparty during the ith time interval

v_i: the present value of the expected net exposure of the dealer to the counterparty (after collateral) at the midpoint of the ith time interval, conditional on a default

R: the recovery rate of the dealer in the event of a default

Assuming that the net exposure is independent of the probability of default, the present value of the expected loss from a default during the ith interval can be estimated as

$$(1 - R)q_i v_i$$

and the total expected loss is

$$\text{CVA} = \sum_{i=1}^{n}(1 - R)q_i v_i \tag{17.1}$$

The q_i are estimated from the counterparty's credit spreads as discussed in Section 16.6. Suppose that s_i is an estimate of the counterparty's credit spread for a maturity of t_i. From Section 16.6, an estimate of the average hazard rate between time zero and time t_i is

$$\lambda_i = \frac{s_i}{1 - R}$$

and the probability of no default between times zero and t_i is

$$e^{-\lambda_i t_i}$$

D. Duffie, "Measuring and Marking Counterparty Risk," Chapter 9 in *Asset/Liability Management for Financial Institutions*, ed. L. Tilman (New York: Institutional Investor Books, 2003); E. Picault, "Calculating and Hedging Exposure, CVA, and Economic Capital," in *Counterparty Credit Risk Modeling*, ed. M. Pykhtin (London: Risk Books, 2005); and J. Gregory, *Counterparty Credit Risk: the New Challenge for Financial Markets* (Hoboken, NJ: John Wiley & Sons, 2009).

so that

$$q_i = e^{-\lambda_{i-1}t_{i-1}} - e^{-\lambda_i t_i}$$

or

$$q_i = \exp\left(-\frac{s_{i-1}t_{i-1}}{1-R}\right) - \exp\left(-\frac{s_i t_i}{1-R}\right) \tag{17.2}$$

The v_i are usually calculated using Monte Carlo simulation. The market variables determining the future value of the transactions that the dealer has with the counterparty are simulated in a risk-neutral world between time zero and time T. On each simulation trial the exposure of the dealer to the counterparty at the midpoint of each interval is calculated. These exposures are averaged and v_i is set equal to the present value of the average exposure at the midpoint of the ith interval.

In practice some approximations may have to be made to make the computations feasible. The model used to value the portfolio at future times may be less complex than either the model used by the dealer for marking to market the transactions or the model used to simulate the underlying market variables.

Collateral and Cure Periods

Collateral agreements must be incorporated into the calculation of the v_i. Suppose that $w(t)$ is the net mark-to-market value to the dealer at time t of the transactions that it has outstanding with a counterparty today. If there is no collateralization, the net exposure, $E_{NC}(t)$, at time t is given by

$$E_{NC} = \max(w(t), 0)$$

If there is a threshold of K and an early termination event can be declared as soon as the counterparty fails to post collateral, the available collateral at time t is $\max(w(t) - K, 0)$.

In practice, a *cure period* or *margin period at risk* is usually assumed. This is the period of time that elapses between the counterparty ceasing to post collateral and the time when the dealer is able to cover its unhedged risk. The latter is referred to as the "unwind date." Typically the dealer covers its unhedged risk by either replacing the outstanding transactions it had with the counterparty or unwinding the hedges it had for those transactions, or some combination of the two. A cure period of between 10 and 25 business days is commonly assumed.

The cure period means that, even when the CSA between Parties A and B specifies that a zero threshold will apply to Party A, Party B is still subject to some credit risk because the value of outstanding transactions might move in its favor during the cure period creating an uncollateralized exposure.

Suppose that the length of the cure period is c. The collateral available if there is an unwind at time t is

$$C(t) = \max(w(t - c) - K, 0) \tag{17.3}$$

An independent amount I can be treated as a negative threshold so that

$$C(t) = \max(w(t - c) + I, 0) \tag{17.4}$$

The exposure, net of collateral, at time t, $E_{NET}(t)$, is therefore[6]

$$E_{NET}(t) = \max(E_{NC}(t) - C(t), 0) \qquad (17.5)$$

Suppose that the midpoint of the ith interval is t_i^* so that $t_i^* = (t_{i-1} + t_i)/2$. The Monte Carlo simulation to calculate the v_i must be structured so that the value of the derivatives portfolio with the counterparty is calculated at times $t_i^* - c$ as well as at time t_i^* ($i = 1, 2, \ldots, n$). On each simulation trial the value at time $t_i^* - c$ is used to calculate the collateral available at time t_i^* using equations (17.3) and (17.4). The net exposure at time t_i^* is then calculated using equation (17.5).

Peak Exposure

In addition to calculating CVA, dealers usually calculate the *peak exposure* at the midpoint of each interval. This is a high percentile of the exposures given by the Monte Carlo simulation trials. Suppose for example that the percentile chosen is 97.5% and there are 10,000 Monte Carlo simulation trials. The peak exposure at two-months is the 250th highest exposure recorded at that time. The *maximum peak exposure* is the maximum of the peak exposures for all the future times considered.

There is a theoretical issue here (which is usually ignored). To calculate CVA, we simulate the behavior of the market variable in the risk-neutral world and discount at the risk-free rate. (As explained in Chapter 16, it is correct to do this when we are valuing something.) When we calculate peak exposure, we are carrying out a scenario analysis and we should in theory simulate the behavior of market variables in the real world, not the risk-neutral world for this purpose. However, for short maturities this probably does not make too much difference.

17.5 THE IMPACT OF A NEW TRANSACTION

When a new derivatives transaction is being negotiated by a dealer with a counterparty, its incremental effect on CVA may influence the terms offered. If the value of the new transaction is positively correlated with other transactions entered into by the dealer with the counterparty, the incremental effect on CVA is likely to be positive. If this correlation is negative, the new transaction can have the effect of reducing CVA.

Suppose for example that a dealer has one transaction outstanding with a counterparty: a five-year forward foreign currency transaction where the counterparty is buying the currency. If the counterparty then expresses interest in entering into a three-year forward foreign currency transaction, the competitiveness of the dealer's quote might depend on which side of the transaction the counterparty wants to take. If the counterparty wants to buy the currency, the new transaction would have the effect of increasing CVA (which will have a negative impact on the dealer's income). On the other hand, if the counterparty wants to sell the currency, it

---

[6] These equations make the simplifying assumption that collateral is posted continuously and there is no minimum transfer amount. They can be adjusted to relax these assumptions.

would have the effect of reducing CVA (which will have a positive impact on the dealer's income).

CVA considerations suggest that counterparties will often get the most favorable quotes from a dealer with whom they already have large numbers of transactions outstanding rather than from a dealer with whom they have done no previous business. This is because the incremental effect of a transaction on CVA for the first dealer is likely to be less than that for the second dealer. The arguments here assume no collateral is posted and apply only to the transactions that are cleared bilaterally, not to those cleared centrally.

Calculating CVA is computationally intensive. Often dealers have hundreds or thousands of transactions outstanding with a counterparty.[7] Calculating the incremental effect of a new transaction on CVA by recomputing CVA is not usually feasible. Luckily there is a computationally efficient approach for calculating incremental CVA.

When the CVA calculations in Section 17.4 are carried out, the paths followed by market variables on each simulation trial and the value of the portfolio on each simulation trial are stored.[8] When a potential new transaction is being considered, its value at the future times is calculated for the values of the market variables that were obtained on the simulation trials. This gives the incremental impact of the transaction on the future portfolio value for each of the last-used Monte Carlo simulation trials at all future times. The incremental impact on the exposure at each time for each Monte Carlo trial can then be calculated. From this, the incremental effect on the average exposure at each time can be calculated and equation (17.1) can then be used to calculate the incremental effect on CVA.

To illustrate this, suppose that a portfolio with a counterparty depends only on the price of gold and that the price of gold at time 2.5 years on the 545th simulation trial when CVA is calculated is $1,572 with the value of the portfolio to the dealer being $2.4 million. Assuming no collateral is posted, this is also the value of the exposure. If 2.5 years is the midpoint of the 20th time step, this means that v_{20} is the present value of $2.4 million received at time 2.5 years. We suppose that this is $2.3 million.

Suppose that, shortly after CVA is calculated, a potential new transaction with the counterparty, dependent on the price of gold, is contemplated. This transaction is valued at all times for the paths followed by the price of gold on all simulation trials. Suppose that, on the 545th simulation trial, it is calculated that the value of the new transaction will be –$4.2 million at time 2.5 years (when the price of gold is $1,572). This means that the portfolio value reduces from $2.3 million to –$1.9 million at time 2.5 years on the 545th simulation trial as a result of the new transaction. This reduces the exposure to zero so that the new v_{20} is zero. The new transaction therefore has the effect of reducing v_{20} by $2.3 million. Similar calculations are carried out for all simulation trials and all times. The average change, Δv_{20}, in v_{20}

---

[7] Lehman for example had about 1.5 million derivatives transactions with about 8,000 counterparties at the time of its failure.

[8] To be precise, the values of all market variables at the t_i^* and $t_i^* - c$ for $1 \leq i \leq n$ and the MTM portfolio values at these times are stored until the next time CVA is calculated (at which time they can be deleted).

across all the simulation trials is calculated. The other Δv_i are calculated similarly and the incremental effect on CVA of the new transaction is estimated as

$$\sum_{i=1}^{n}(1 - R)q_i \Delta v_i$$

17.6 CVA RISK

A dealer has one CVA for each counterparty. These CVAs can themselves be regarded as derivatives. They are particularly complex derivatives. Indeed, the CVA for a counterparty is more complex than any of the transactions between the dealer and the counterparty because it is contingent on the net value of all the transactions between the dealer and the counterparty.

When CVA increases (decreases), the income reported by a derivatives dealer decreases (increases). For this reason, many dealers consider it prudent to try and hedge CVAs in the same way that they hedge other derivatives. This means that they must calculate the Greek letters (delta, gamma, vega, etc.) discussed in Chapter 7.

The variables affecting the v_i are market variables such as interest rates, exchange rates, commodity prices, and so on. Calculating Greek letters for these is liable to be computationally quite time consuming. For example, to calculate the delta of CVA with respect to an exchange rate, it is necessary to make a small change to the exchange rate and recompute CVA.

The variables affecting the q_i are the credit spreads of the counterparty for different maturities. From equation (17.2)

$$q_i = \exp\left(-\frac{s_{i-1}t_{i-1}}{1 - R}\right) - \exp\left(-\frac{s_i t_i}{1 - R}\right)$$

From equation (17.1)

$$\text{CVA} = \sum_{i=1}^{n}(1 - R)q_i v_i$$

Using a delta/gamma approximation, the change in CVA resulting from a small parallel shift, Δs, in the term structure of credit spreads (with all the market variables determining the v_i being assumed to remain fixed) is therefore

$$\Delta(\text{CVA}) = \sum_{i=1}^{n}\left[t_i \exp\left(-\frac{s_i t_i}{1 - R}\right) - t_{i-1}\exp\left(-\frac{s_{i-1}t_{i-1}}{1 - R}\right)\right]v_i \Delta s$$

$$+ \frac{1}{2(1 - R)}\sum_{i=1}^{n}\left[t_{i-1}^2 \exp\left(-\frac{s_{i-1}t_{i-1}}{1 - R}\right) - t_i^2 \exp\left(-\frac{s_i t_i}{1 - R}\right)\right]v_i(\Delta s)^2$$

$$(17.6)$$

This can be calculated without difficulty once the v_i are known.

Basel III's advanced approach requires dealers to use this equation to incorporate the risks arising from changes in credit spreads into market risk capital calculations. However, risks arising from changes in the market variables affecting the v_i are not included in market risk capital calculations. This is presumably because they are more difficult to calculate.

Sophisticated dealers who are capable of quantifying the v_i risks have complained that, if they hedge these risks, they will be increasing their capital requirements. This is because the hedging trades would be taken into account in determining market risk capital whereas the CVA exposure to the market variables would not.

17.7 WRONG WAY RISK

Up to now we have assumed that the probability of default is independent of the exposure. A situation where there is a positive dependence between the two, so that the probability of default by the counterparty tends to be high (low) when the dealer's exposure to the counterparty is high (low), is referred to as "wrong-way risk." A situation where there is negative dependence, so that the probability of default by the counterparty tends to be high (low) when the dealer's exposure to the counterparty is low (high) is referred to as "right-way risk."

A subjective evaluation of the amount of wrong-way or right-way risk in transactions with a counterparty requires a good knowledge of the counterparty's business, in particular the nature of the risks facing the business. It also requires knowledge of the transactions the counterparty has entered into with other dealers. The latter is difficult to know precisely, but the extra transparency provided by post-crisis legislation may help.

One situation in which wrong-way risk tends to occur is when a counterparty is using a credit default swap to sell protection to the dealer. (AIG and monolines are obvious examples here.) When a dealer buys protection from a counterparty and the credit spread of the reference entity increases, the value of the protection to the dealer becomes positive. However, because the credit spreads of different companies tend to be correlated, it is likely that the credit spread of the counterparty has increased so that the calculated probability of default has also increased. Similarly, right-way risk tends to occur when a counterparty is buying credit protection from the dealer.

A situation in which a company is speculating by entering into many similar trades with one or more dealers is likely to lead to wrong-way risk for these dealers. This is because the company's financial position and therefore its probability of default is likely to be affected adversely if the trades move against the company.

If the company enters into transactions to partially hedge an existing exposure, there should in theory be right-way risk. This is because, when the transactions move against the counterparty, it will be benefiting from the unhedged portion of its exposure so that its probability of default should be relatively low.[9]

A simple way of dealing with wrong-way risk is to use what is termed the "alpha" multiplier to increase v_i in the version of the model where the v_i and q_i are assumed

---

[9] An exception could be when the counterparty is liable to run into liquidity problems. Although the assets being hedged have increased in value, the counterparty might be unable to post collateral when required. An example here is Ashanti Goldfields (see Business Snapshot 21.2).

to be independent. The effect of this is to increase CVA by the alpha multiplier. Basel II rules set alpha equal to 1.4, but allow banks to use their own models, with a floor for alpha of 1.2. This means that, at minimum, the CVA has to be 20% higher than that given by the model where the v_i and q_i are assumed to be independent. If a bank does not have its own model for wrong-way risk, it has to be 40% higher. Estimates of alpha reported by banks range from 1.07 to 1.10.

Some models have been developed to capture the dependence of the probability of default on the exposure. For example, Hull and White (2011) propose a simple model where the hazard rate at time t is a function of variables observable at that time.[10] A positive dependence gives wrong-way risk; a negative dependence gives right-way risk. Their parameter describing the extent of the dependence can be either estimated subjectively or estimated by relating past credit spreads for the counterparty to what the value of the current portfolio would have been in the past. Implementing the model involves relatively minor modifications to the calculations outlined in Section 17.4.

17.8 DVA

Another measure, more controversial than CVA, is debit value adjustment or DVA.[11] The DVA calculated by a dealer for a counterparty is an estimate of the expected cost to the counterparty because the dealer might default. The possibility that it might default is in theory a benefit to the dealer and accounting standards require the book value of the derivatives outstanding with a counterparty to be calculated as their no-default value minus the CVA plus the DVA. The reason why DVA is controversial is that a dealer cannot monetize DVA without actually defaulting.

DVA can be calculated at the same time as CVA. Equation (17.1) gives DVA rather than CVA if R is the recovery rate of the dealer, v_i is the value of a derivative that pays off the counterparty's exposure to the dealer at the mid point of the ith interval, and q_i is the probability of a default by the dealer during the ith interval. The counterparty's net exposure to the dealer, after taking collateral posted by the dealer into account, can be calculated in an analogous way to the dealer's net exposure to the counterparty.

It is interesting to note that when the credit spread of a derivatives dealer increases, DVA increases. This in turn leads to an increase in the reported value of the derivatives on the books of the dealer and a corresponding increase in its profits. Some banks reported several billion dollars of profits from this source in 2008. Not surprisingly, DVA gains and losses have now been excluded from the definition of common equity in determining regulatory capital.

17.9 SOME SIMPLE EXAMPLES

To illustrate the ideas presented in this chapter concerning CVA, we now present some simple examples.

---

[10] See J. Hull and A. White, "CVA and Wrong Way Risk" (working paper, University of Toronto, 2011).

[11] DVA is sometimes also referred to "debt value adjustment."

Single Transaction with Positive Value

Suppose first that a dealer has a single derivatives transaction with a counterparty that is bound to have a positive value to the dealer and a negative value to the counterparty at all future times. (An example would be the situation where the dealer has bought an option from the counterparty.) We suppose that no collateral has to be posted by the counterparty and, for ease of exposition, assume that payoffs on the derivatives transaction occur only on its expiration date.

The exposure of the counterparty to the dealer at a future time is the value of the transaction at that time. The present value of the expected exposure at time t_i, which we have denoted by v_i, is therefore the present value of the expected value of the transaction at time t_i. Because we are assuming no payoffs before maturity, the present value of the expected value of the transaction at time t_i is always equal to its value today.

Equation (17.1) therefore becomes

$$\text{CVA} = (1 - R) f_0 \sum_{i=1}^{n} q_i$$

where f_0 is the value of the derivative today assuming no defaults. If f_0^* is the value after defaults are taken into account:

$$f^* = f_0 - \text{CVA}$$

or

$$f^* = f_0 \left[1 - (1 - R) \sum_{i=1}^{n} q_i \right] \tag{17.7}$$

This means that the effect of defaults is to reduce the value of the derivative by a proportional amount equal to the cumulative risk-neutral probability of default during the life of the derivative times one minus the recovery rate.

Now consider an unsecured zero-coupon bond issued by the counterparty that promises \$1,000 at time T. Define B_0 as the value of the bond assuming no possibility of default and B_0^* as the actual value of the bond. Assuming that the bond ranks equally with the derivative in the event of a default, it will have the same recovery rate. Similarly to equation (17.7)

$$B_0^* = B_0 \left[1 - (1 - R) \sum_{i=1}^{n} q_i \right] \tag{17.8}$$

From equations (17.7) and (17.8)

$$\frac{f_0^*}{f_0} = \frac{B_0^*}{B_0} \tag{17.9}$$

If y is the yield on a risk-free zero-coupon bond maturing at time T and y^* is the yield on a zero coupon bond issued by the counterparty that matures at time T, then $B_0 = e^{-yT}$ and $B_0^* = e^{-y^*T}$ so that equation (17.9) gives

$$f_0^* = f_0 e^{-(y^*-y)T} \qquad (17.10)$$

This shows that the derivative can be valued by discounting the default-free value of the derivative by $y^* - y$.

EXAMPLE 17.1

Consider a two-year over-the-counter option sold by the company with a value, assuming no possibility of default, of $3. Suppose that two-year zero-coupon bonds issued by the company have a yield that is 1.5% greater than a similar risk-free zero-coupon bond. The value of the option is

$$3e^{-0.015\times2} = 2.91$$

or $2.91.

Interest Rate Swaps vs. Currency Swaps

Consider next the situation where the dealer has entered into a pair of interest rate swaps that offset each other with two different counterparties. Figure 17.4 compares the total expected future exposure on the two transactions when they are (a) currency swaps and (b) interest rate swaps. The expected exposure on the interest rate swaps

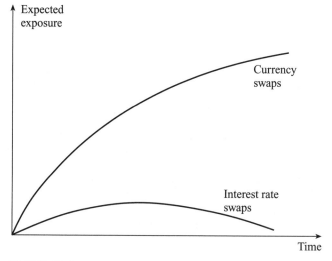

FIGURE 17.4 Expected Exposure on a Matched Pair of Offsetting Interest Rate Swaps and a Matched Pair of Offsetting Currency Swaps

starts at zero, increases, and then decreases. By contrast, expected exposure on the currency swaps increases steadily with the passage of time. The main reason for the difference is that principals are exchanged at the end of the life of a currency swap and there is uncertainty about the exchange rate at that time. The impact of default risk for a dealer in currency swaps is therefore much greater than for a dealer in interest rate swaps.[12]

Single Forward Transaction

For another example, we suppose that a dealer has a single forward transaction with a counterparty giving the dealer the right to buy an asset from the counterparty at time T for a price of K. No collateral has to be posted. Suppose that the forward price of the asset today is F_0 (which is known) and at time t ($t \leq T$) it is F_t (which is unknown). As explained in Appendix C, the value of the transaction at time t is

$$(F_t - K)e^{-r(T-t)}$$

where r is the risk-free interest rate (assumed constant).

The exposure at time t is

$$\max[(F_t - K)e^{-r(T-t)}, 0] = e^{-r(T-t)} \max[(F_t - K), 0] \tag{17.11}$$

The present value of the exposure is therefore $e^{-r(T-t)}$ times the value of a derivative that pays off $\max[(F_t - K), 0]$ at time t. This is an option on a forward price. From Appendix E the value of the derivative is

$$e^{-rt}[F_0 N(d_1) - K N(d_2)]$$

where

$$d_1 = \frac{\ln(F_0/K) + \sigma^2 t/2}{\sigma\sqrt{t}}$$

and

$$d_2 = \frac{\ln(F_0/K) - \sigma^2 t/2}{\sigma\sqrt{t}}$$

and σ is the volatility of the forward price of the asset. It follows from equation (17.11) that the present value of the exposure at time t is

$$e^{-rT}[F_0 N(d_1) - K N(d_2)]$$

---

[12] The q_is for the two counterparties are the same regardless of the transaction, but the v_is are on average greater for currency swaps.

Hence in equation (17.1)

$$v_i = e^{-rT}[F_0 N(d_{1,i}) - KN(d_{2,i})]$$

where

$$d_{1,i} = \frac{\ln(F_0/K) + \sigma^2 t_i/2}{\sigma\sqrt{t_i}}$$

and

$$d_{2,i} = \frac{\ln(F_0/K) - \sigma^2 t_i/2}{\sigma\sqrt{t_i}}$$

EXAMPLE 17.2

Suppose that a bank has entered into a forward contract to buy 1 million ounces of gold from a mining company in two years for $1,500 per ounce. The current forward price for the contract is $1,600 per ounce. The probability of the company defaulting during the first year is 2% and the probability of the company defaulting during the second year is 3%. Defaults are assumed to happen at the mid points of the years. The risk-free rate is 5% per annum. The financial institution anticipates a 30% recovery in the event of a default. The volatility of the forward price of gold when the forward contract expires in two years is 20%.

In this case

$$v_1 = e^{-0.05 \times 2}[1,600 N(d_{1,1}) - 1,500 N(d_{2,1})]$$

where

$$d_{1,1} = \frac{\ln(1,600/1,500) + 0.2^2 \times 0.5/2}{0.2\sqrt{0.5}} = 0.5271$$

$$d_{2,1} = \frac{\ln(1,600/1,500) - 0.2^2 \times 0.5/2}{0.2\sqrt{0.5}} = 0.3856$$

so that $v_1 = 132.38$. Also

$$v_2 = e^{-0.05 \times 2}[1,600 N(d_{1,2}) - 1,500 N(d_{2,2})]$$

where

$$d_{1,2} = \frac{\ln(1,600/1,500) + 0.2^2 \times 1.5/2}{0.2\sqrt{1.5}} = 0.3860$$

$$d_{2,2} = \frac{\ln(1,600/1,500) - 0.2^2 \times 1.5/2}{0.2\sqrt{1.5}} = 0.1410$$

so that $v_2 = 186.65$.

Other variables are: $q_1 = 0.02$, $q_2 = 0.03$, and $R = 0.3$ so that

$$CVA = (1 - 0.3) \times (0.02 \times 132.38 + 0.03 \times 186.65) = 5.77$$

The no-default value of the forward contract is $(1,600 - 1,500)e^{-2 \times 0.05} = 90.48$ or $90.48. The value after the possibility of defaults has been taken into account is therefore

$$90.48 - 5.77 = 84.71$$

or $84.71.

This example can be extended to the situation where the mining company can default more frequently (see Problem 17.18).

SUMMARY

There are three ways in which derivatives can be traded. The first is on an exchange. The second is in the over-the-counter market with a central clearing party being used. The third is in the over-the-counter market with bilateral clearing.

Over-the-counter trades that are cleared bilaterally give rise to the most credit risk for a financial institution. The credit risk is quite difficult to quantify. This is because the future exposure of the financial institution to the counterparty is contingent on movements in market variables.

The over-the-counter market has developed a number of ways of mitigating credit risk. The most important of these is netting. This is a clause in virtually all agreements for derivatives that will be cleared bilaterally. It states that in the event of an early termination, all outstanding derivatives are considered as a single transaction. Another credit mitigation technique is collateralization. This requires a counterparty to post collateral. If the value of its outstanding transactions with the financial institution moves against the counterparty, more collateral is typically required. A third (more questionable) credit mitigation technique is a downgrade trigger. This gives a company the option to require collateral if the credit rating of the counterparty falls below a certain level.

The CVA for a counterparty is the present value of the expected future loss from the possibility of the counterparty defaulting. A derivatives dealer typically has systems in place for calculating on a regular basis the credit value adjustments (CVAs) for its counterparties. The systems must simulate the market variables underlying outstanding transactions with each counterparty so that the expected net exposure at future times conditional on a default can be estimated. The simplest assumption is that the probability of default is independent of the exposure. However, procedures have been developed to incorporate wrong-way risk (where there is positive dependence between the two) and right-way risk (where there is negative dependence between the two).

CVAs are complex derivatives and many dealers hedge them in the same way that they hedge other derivatives. Once a CVA has been calculated, it is a relatively easy step to estimate the sensitivity of the CVA to a small parallel shift in the counterparty's credit spreads. Calculating the sensitivity of CVA to the market variables underlying the transactions with the counterparty is more difficult.

FURTHER READING

Basel Committee on Banking Supervision. "Basel III: A Global Regulatory Framework for More Resilient Banks and Banking Systems," www.bis.org/publ/bcbs189dec2010.pdf, December 2010.

Canabarro, E. and D. Duffie. "Measuring and Marking Counterparty Risk," Chapter 9 in *Asset/Liability Management for Financial Institutions*, edited by L. Tilman. New York: Institutional Investor Books, 2003.

Cepedes, J. C. G., J. A. de J. Herrero, D. Rosen, and D. Saunders. "Effective Modeling of Wrong Way Risk, Counterparty Credit Risk Capital and Alpha in Basel II," *Journal of Risk Model Validation* 4, no. 1 (2010): 71–98.

Duffie, D., and H. Zhu. "Does Central Clearing Reduce Counterparty Credit Risk?" Working Paper, Stanford University, 2009.

Gregory, J. *Counterparty Credit Risk: The New Challenge for Financial Markets.* Hoboken, NJ: John Wiley & Sons, 2009.

Hull, J., and A. White. "The Impact of Default Risk on the Prices of Options and Other Derivative Securities," *Journal of Banking and Finance* 19 (1995): 299–322.

Pengelley, M. "CVA Melee," *Risk* 24, no. 2 (2011): 37–39.

Picault, E. "Calculating and Hedging Exposure, CVA, and Economic Capital for Counterparty Credit Risk," in *Counterparty Credit Risk Modeling*, edited by M. Pykhtin. London: Risk Books, 2005.

Singh, M. and J. Aitken. "The (Sizeable) Role of Rehypothecation in the Shadow Banking System," *IMF*, July 2010.

Sokol, A. "A Practical Guide to Monte Carlo CVA," Chapter 14 in *Lessons From the Crisis*, edited by A. Berd. London: Risk Books, 2010.

PRACTICE QUESTIONS AND PROBLEMS
(ANSWERS AT END OF BOOK)

17.1 Explain why a new transaction by a bank with a counterparty can have the effect of increasing or reducing the bank's credit exposure to the counterparty.

17.2 What is meant by a haircut in a collateral agreement?

17.3 A company offers to post its own equity as collateral. How would you respond?

17.4 Suppose that a financial institution has two derivatives transactions outstanding with different counterparties, X and Y. Which of the following is true?

    (a) The total expected exposure in one year on the two transactions is the sum of the expected exposure on the transaction with X and the expected exposure on the transaction with Y.

    (b) The total present value of the cost of defaults is the sum of the present value of the cost of defaults on the transaction with X plus the present value of the cost of defaults on the transaction with Y.

    (c) The 95 percentile for the total exposure in one year on both transactions is the sum of the 95 percentile for the exposure in one year on the transaction with X and the 95 percentile for the exposure in one year on the transaction with Y.

Explain your answers.

17.5 "In the absence of collateral and other transactions between the parties, a long forward contract subject to credit risk is a combination of a short position in a no-default put and a long position in a call subject to credit risk." Explain this statement.

17.6 Suppose that the spread between the yield on a three-year riskless zero-coupon bond and a three-year zero-coupon bond issued by a corporation is 120 basis points. By how much do standard option pricing models such as Black–Scholes–Merton overstate the value of a three-year option sold by the corporation? Assume there is only this one transaction between the corporation and its counterparty and no collateral is posted.

17.7 Can the existence of default triggers increase default risk? Explain your answer.

17.8 What is the difference between an "Event of Default" and an "Early Termination Event" in an ISDA contract?

17.9 Give two examples of when (a) wrong-way risk and (b) right-way risk can be expected to be observed.

17.10 In Figure 17.3 where the CCP is used, suppose that half of the transactions between A and B that are represented by the solid line are moved to the CCP. What effect does this have on (a) the average exposure of the three parties including their exposures to the CCP and (b) the average exposure of the three parties excluding their exposures to the CCP?

17.11 What credit risks is a company taking when it becomes a member of a CCP and clears transactions through the CCP?

17.12 Explain the terms "threshold," "cure period," and "minimum transfer amount."

17.13 "Netting affects the collateral that has to be posted and the settlement in the event of an early termination." Explain.

17.14 DVA can improve the bottom line when a bank is experiencing financial difficulties." Explain why this is so.

17.15 What part of CVA risk is included in market risk calculations by Basel III?

17.16 A CSA between a dealer and one of its counterparties states that an independent amount of $5 million is required from the counterparty. If the cure period is assumed to be 15 days, under what circumstances will the the dealer's CVA model lead to losses?

17.17 What is rehypothecation?

FURTHER QUESTIONS

17.18 Extend Example 17.2 to calculate CVA when default can happen in the middle of each month. Assume that the default probability per month during the first year is 0.001667 and the default probability per month during the second year is 0.0025.

17.19 Consider a European call option on a non-dividend-paying stock where the stock price is $52, the strike price $50, the risk-free rate is 5%, the volatility is 30%, and the time to maturity is one year. Answer the following questions assuming no recovery in the event of default, that the probability of default is independent of the option valuation, no collateral is posted, and no other transactions between the parties are outstanding.

(a) What is the value of the option assuming no possibility of a default?

(b) What is the value of the option to the buyer if there is a 2% chance that the option seller will default at maturity?

(c) Suppose that, instead of paying the option price up front, the option buyer agrees to pay the forward value of the option price at the end of option's life. By how much does this reduce the cost of defaults to the option buyer in the case where there is a 2% chance of the option seller defaulting?

(d) If in case (c) the option buyer has a 1% chance of defaulting at the end of the life of the option, what is the default risk to the option seller? Discuss the two-sided nature of default risk in the case and the value of the option to each side.

17.20 Suppose that the spread between the yield on a three-year riskless zero-coupon bond and a three-year zero-coupon bond issued by a bank is 210 basis points. The Black-Scholes–Merton price of an option is $4.10. How much should you be prepared to pay for it if you buy it from a bank?

17.21 In Figure 17.3 where the CCP is used, suppose that an extra transaction between A and C which is worth 140 to A is cleared bilaterally. What effect does this have on the tables in Figure 17.3?

CHAPTER 18

Credit Value at Risk

Value at risk is central to the determination of regulatory capital and to much of the risk management carried out by both financial and nonfinancial corporations. Chapters 14 and 15 discussed the calculation of market risk VaR. This chapter covers credit risk VaR.

Credit risk VaR is defined similarly to market risk VaR. It is the credit risk loss over a certain time period that will not be exceeded with a certain confidence level. Some credit risk VaR models consider only losses from defaults; others consider losses from downgrades and credit spread changes as well as from defaults.

Banks calculate credit risk VaR to determine both regulatory capital and economic capital. The regulatory capital requirements for credit risk were discussed in Chapters 12 and 13. Economic capital, which will be discussed in Chapter 23, is a financial institution's own estimate of the capital it requires for the risks it is taking and is used to calculate return on capital measures for its business units. Sometimes the VaR model that a bank chooses to use to determine credit risk economic capital is different from the one it is required to use for the determination of regulatory capital.

In Chapter 16, we explained the important difference between risk-neutral and real-world default probabilities. Risk-neutral default probabilities are used for estimating the present value of future credit losses. The procedure is to estimate expected losses in a risk-neutral world and discount at the risk-free rate. This is what we did when calculating CVA in Chapter 17. Real-world default probabilities are used in scenario analysis. The probability of a particular scenario analysis occurring when credit VaR is calculated should always be a real-world, not a risk-neutral, default probability.[1]

The time horizon for credit risk VaR is often longer than that for market risk VaR. Market risk VaR is usually calculated with a one-day time horizon and then scaled up to 10 days for the calculation of regulatory capital. Credit risk VaR, for instruments that are not held for trading, is usually calculated with a one-year time

---

[1] There is a proviso here. If, when VaR is being calculated, a model involving default probabilities is necessary to value an instrument at the time horizon, T, the default probabilities that are used in the valuation model should be risk-neutral default probabilities. Thus, an analyst might use real-world default probabilities up to time T and then use risk-neutral default probabilities beyond time T to estimate the value of an instrument at time T under the scenarios.

horizon. Historical simulation (see Chapter 14) is the main tool used to calculate market risk VaR, but a more elaborate model is usually necessary to calculate credit risk VaR.

A key aspect of any credit risk VaR model is credit correlation. Defaults (or downgrades or credit spread changes) for different companies do not happen independently of each other. During an economic downturn, most companies are adversely affected and become more likely to default. When the economy is faring well, they are favorably affected and less likely to default. This relationship between default rates and economic factors is what determines credit correlation. Credit correlation increases risks for a financial institution with a portfolio of credit exposures.[2]

18.1   RATINGS TRANSITION MATRICES

The methods used by financial institutions for calculating credit VaR often involve ratings transition matrices. These are matrices showing the probability of a company migrating from one rating category to another during a certain period of time. They are based on historical data. The rating categories can be either those used internally by the financial institution or those produced by rating agencies such as Moody's, S&P, or Fitch. Table 18.1 shows the one-year transition matrix produced by Moody's in 2011 and is based on following the performance of all the companies that Moody's rated between 1970 and 2010. For example, it shows that a company which starts with a rating of A has a 90.88% probability of still being rated A at the end of a year. There is a 2.82% chance that it will be upgraded to Aa by the end of the year, a 5.52% chance that it will be downgraded to Baa, and so on. The probability that it will default during the year is only 0.06%, or 6 chances in 10,000.

Table 18.1 can be used to calculate a transition matrix for periods other than one year. For example, a transition matrix for two years can be calculated by multiplying the matrix by itself. The five-year transition matrix, which is shown in Table 18.2, is calculated as the fifth power of the matrix in Table 18.1. Table 18.2 shows, not surprisingly, that the probability of a company keeping the same credit rating over five years is much less than it is over one year and default probabilities over five years are much higher than over one year.

The credit rating change over a period less than a year is not quite so easy to calculate. For example, estimating a transition matrix for six months involves taking the square root of the matrix in Table 18.1; estimating the transition matrix for three months involves taking the fourth root of the matrix; and so on. The calculation methodology is explained in Appendix J at the end of the book and software for performing the calculations is on the author's website. Table 18.3 shows the rating transition calculated for a period of one month from the data in Table 18.1. As might be expected, the probability that a company's credit rating will stay the same over a period of one month is very high.

---

[2] Credit correlation also sometimes arises from "credit contagion," where a default by one company or country makes default by others more likely (see Business Snapshot 16.4).

TABLE 18.1 One-Year Ratings Transition Matrix, 1970–2010, with Probabilities Expressed as Percentages and Adjustments for Transition to the WR (without rating) Category

Initial Rating	Rating at Year-End								
	Aaa	Aa	A	Baa	Ba	B	Caa	Ca-C	Default
Aaa	90.42	8.92	0.62	0.01	0.03	0.00	0.00	0.00	0.00
Aa	1.02	90.12	8.38	0.38	0.05	0.02	0.01	0.00	0.02
A	0.06	2.82	90.88	5.52	0.51	0.11	0.03	0.01	0.06
Baa	0.05	0.19	4.79	89.41	4.35	0.82	0.18	0.02	0.19
Ba	0.01	0.06	0.41	6.22	83.43	7.97	0.59	0.09	1.22
B	0.01	0.04	0.14	0.38	5.32	82.19	6.45	0.74	4.73
Caa	0.00	0.02	0.02	0.16	0.53	9.41	68.43	4.67	16.76
Ca-C	0.00	0.00	0.00	0.00	0.39	2.85	10.66	43.54	42.56
Default	0.00	0.00	0.00	0.00	0.00	0.00	0.00	0.00	100.00

Source: Moody's.

TABLE 18.2 Five-Year Ratings Transition Matrix Calculated from Table 18.1 with Probabilities Expressed as Percentages

Initial Rating	Rating at Year-End								
	Aaa	Aa	A	Baa	Ba	B	Caa	Ca-C	Default
Aaa	61.12	29.99	7.70	0.89	0.21	0.05	0.01	0.00	0.03
Aa	3.45	61.89	28.70	4.71	0.73	0.25	0.07	0.01	0.19
A	0.44	9.72	65.78	18.88	3.24	1.06	0.24	0.04	0.60
Baa	0.22	1.69	16.38	60.98	12.93	4.64	0.97	0.13	2.06
Ba	0.07	0.44	3.40	18.20	44.69	20.07	3.70	0.52	8.92
B	0.04	0.20	0.83	3.27	13.28	43.05	11.49	1.64	26.21
Caa	0.01	0.08	0.23	0.93	3.52	16.80	18.67	2.93	56.84
Ca-C	0.00	0.02	0.06	0.31	1.39	5.89	6.78	2.40	83.15
Default	0.00	0.00	0.00	0.00	0.00	0.00	0.00	0.00	100.00

TABLE 18.3 One-Month Ratings Transition Matrix Calculated from Table 18.1 with Probabilities Expressed as Percentages

Initial Rating	Rating at Year-End								
	Aaa	Aa	A	Baa	Ba	B	Caa	Ca-C	Default
Aaa	99.16	0.82	0.02	0.00	0.00	0.00	0.00	0.00	0.00
Aa	0.09	99.12	0.77	0.01	0.00	0.00	0.00	0.00	0.00
A	0.00	0.26	99.18	0.51	0.04	0.01	0.00	0.00	0.00
Baa	0.00	0.01	0.44	99.05	0.41	0.06	0.02	0.00	0.01
Ba	0.00	0.00	0.02	0.59	98.46	0.79	0.03	0.01	0.09
B	0.00	0.00	0.01	0.02	0.53	98.32	0.70	0.07	0.36
Caa	0.00	0.00	0.00	0.01	0.02	1.01	96.79	0.67	1.48
Ca-C	0.00	0.00	0.00	0.00	0.04	0.28	1.53	93.23	4.92
Default	0.00	0.00	0.00	0.00	0.00	0.00	0.00	0.00	100.00

The results in Tables 18.2 and 18.3 make the assumption that the credit rating change in one period is independent of that in another period. This is not exactly true. The more recently a company has been downgraded, the more likely it is to be downgraded again in the next short period of time.[3] (This phenomenon is sometimes referred to as ratings momentum.) However, the independence assumption is not too unreasonable for most purposes.[4]

18.2 VASICEK'S MODEL

The Basel II internal-ratings-based (IRB) capital requirements for credit risk in the banking book are based on Vasicek's Gaussian copula model (see Sections 11.5 and 12.8). This is a way of calculating high percentiles of the distribution of the default rate for a portfolio of loans. As in Chapter 11, we define WCDR(T, X) as the Xth percentile of the default rate distribution during a period of length T. (It will be recalled that WCDR is short for worst case default rate.) Vasicek's model relates WCDR(T, X) to the probability of default, PD, and a parameter, ρ, describing credit correlation. The formula, which is proved in Section 11.5, is

$$\text{WCDR}(T, X) = N\left(\frac{N^{-1}(\text{PD}) + \sqrt{\rho}\, N^{-1}(X)}{\sqrt{1 - \rho}}\right) \tag{18.1}$$

For an individual loan, if EAD is the exposure at default and LGD is the loss given default, the Xth percentile of the loss distribution is

$$\text{WCDR}(T, X) \times \text{EAD} \times \text{LGD}$$

As explained in Section 11.5, a result by Gordy (2003) enables us to extend this.[5] If we have a large portfolio of n loans where each loan is a small part of the total portfolio, the Xth percentile of the loss distribution is approximately

$$\sum_{i=1}^{n} \text{WCDR}_i(T, X) \times \text{EAD}_i \times \text{LGD}_i \tag{18.2}$$

providing there is a single ρ where WCDR$_i$(T, X), EAD$_i$, and LGD$_i$ are the values of WCDR, EAD, and LGD for the ith loan in the portfolio.

---

[3] For a discussion of this, see E. Altman and D. Kao, "The Implications of Corporate Bond Rating Drift," *Financial Analysts Journal* (May–June 1992): 64–75; and D. Lando and T. Skodeberg, "Analyzing Rating Transitions and Rating Drift with Continuous Observations," *Journal of Banking and Finance* 26 (2002): 423–444.

[4] When the five-year transition matrix in Table 18.2 is compared with the actual five-year transition matrix published by Moody's, it is found to be reasonably close. The default probabilities in Table 18.2 are a little lower than in the actual transition matrix. This is consistent with ratings momentum.

[5] See M. Gordy, "A Risk-factor Model Foundation for Ratings-Based Capital Rules," *Journal of Financial Intermediation* 12, no. 3 (July 2003): 199–233.

As explained in Chapter 12, regulatory capital for the banking book is set equal to the expression in equation (18.2) with T equal to one year and X equal to 99.9%. Sometimes the expression under the summation sign in equation (18.2) is multiplied by a maturity adjustment factor MA_i, to allow for the fact that, if it lasts longer than one year, the ith loan might deteriorate without defaulting. In the foundation IRB approach, banks estimate PDs, but EADs, LGDs, and MAs are set by the Basel II rules. In the advanced IRB approach, banks estimate PDs, EADs, LGDs, and MAs. But in all cases the parameter ρ is set by Basel II rules.

When Vasicek's model is used to determine economic capital, banks are free to make their own estimates of ρ. Structural models of the type discussed in Section 16.8 can be used to show that ρ for two companies should be roughly equal to the correlation between the returns on the assets of the companies.[6] As an approximation, this is the same as the correlation between the returns on their equities. One way of determining ρ for a portfolio of exposures to companies is therefore to calculate the average correlation between the returns on equities for the companies. If the companies are not publicly traded, the average correlation between representative publicly traded companies can be used instead. Another approach is the maximum likelihood approach described in Section 11.5. Banks can also use alternatives to the Gaussian copula such as those descibed in Section 11.5.

18.3 CREDIT RISK PLUS

In 1997, Credit Suisse Financial Products proposed a methodology for calculating VaR that it termed Credit Risk Plus.[7] It utilizes ideas that are well established in the insurance industry. This section will present one way of implementing the approach.

Suppose that a financial institution has n loans of a certain type and the probability of default for each one during a year is p. The expected number of defaults for the whole portfolio, μ, is given by $\mu = np$. Assuming that default events are independent, the probability of m defaults is given by

$$\frac{n!}{m!(n-m)!}p^m(1-p)^{n-m}$$

If p is small and n large, this can be approximated by the Poisson distribution as

$$\frac{e^{-\mu}\mu^m}{m!}$$

This can be combined with a probability distribution for the losses experienced when there is a counterparty default to obtain a probability distribution for the total

---

[6] See for example, J. Hull, M. Predescu, and A. White, "The Valuation of Correlation Dependent Derivatives Using a Structural Model," *Journal of Credit Risk* 6, no. 3 (Fall 2010): 99–132.
[7] See Credit Suisse Financial Products, "Credit Risk Management Framework" (October, 1997).

loss from defaults. The probability distribution for the loss from a counterparty default can be determined from (a) the probability distribution of exposures to the counterparties and (b) a probability distribution of the recovery rates.

Default rates vary greatly from year to year. This is illustrated by Table 11.4, which shows annual default rates for all rated companies between 1970 and 2010 published by Moody's. The default rate has varied from a low of 0.087% in 1979 to a high of 5.422% in 2009. To account for this year-to-year variation, the probability of default p applicable to a particular year can be sampled from a probability distribution of historical default rates. The default rates used to determine the probability distribution can reflect the financial institution's own default experience or economy-wide data such as that shown in Table 11.4.

One simple approach would be to assume that the overall default rate for the next year is a random sample from the default rates in Table 11.4 (or a similar table) and the probability of default for each counterparty category in a year is proportional to the sampled default rate. For example, one counterparty category might be assumed to have a probability of default equal to 70% of the overall default rate; another might be assumed to have a default rate equal to 120% of the overall default rate; and so on.

An analysis of the data in Table 11.4 shows that the default rate in one year is not independent of the default rate in the previous year. This indicates that randomly sampling a default rate from a table such as Table 11.4 to determine next year's default rate may not be the best approach. It may be preferable to develop a model that relates the default rate in one year to the default rate in the previous year or other economic factors observable in the previous year.

Credit Suisse Financial Products show that, if certain simplifying assumptions are made, the total loss probability distribution can be calculated analytically. To accommodate more general assumptions, Monte Carlo simulation can be used. The procedure is

1. Sample an overall default rate.
2. Calculate a probability of default for each counterparty category.
3. Sample a number of defaults for each counterparty category.
4. Sample an exposure at default for each default.
5. Sample a loss given default for each default.
6. Calculate the total loss from the defaults.
7. Repeat steps 1 to 5 many times to build up a probability distribution for the total loss.
8. Calculate the required VaR from the total loss probability distribution.

If the overall default rate were the same each year, there would be no default correlation between different companies and the loss probability distribution would be roughly symmetrical. The effect of assuming a probability distribution for the overall default rate is to build in default correlation and make the probability distribution of total default losses positively skewed as indicated in Figure 18.1. The default correlation arises because, when a high overall default rate is sampled, all companies have a high probability of default; when a low overall default rate is sampled, all companies have a low probability of default.

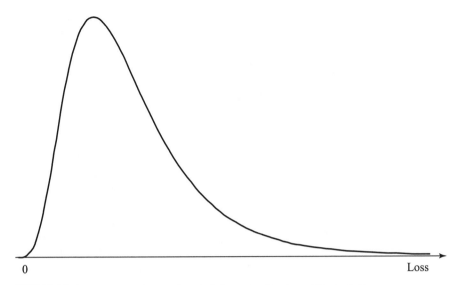

FIGURE 18.1 General Shape of Probability Distribution of Default Losses

18.4 CREDITMETRICS

Vasicek's model and Credit Risk Plus estimate the probability distribution of losses arising only from defaults. The impact of downgrades is not considered.[8]

We now consider the CreditMetrics model which is designed so that it can take account of downgrades as well as defaults. This model was proposed by JPMorgan in 1997. It is based on a rating transition matrix such as the one shown in Table 18.1. The ratings are those used internally or those produced by rating agencies.

Consider a bank with a portfolio of corporate loans. Calculating a one-year VaR for the portfolio using CreditMetrics involves carrying out a Monte Carlo simulation of ratings transitions for loans in the portfolio over a one-year period. The initial rating of each company is known and on each simulation trial a sample from the credit transition matrix gives the final rating. The changes in credit spread over one year can also be calculated. Loans are revalued at the end of the year to determine total credit losses for the year. The results from all simulation trials determine a probability distribution for losses.

It is interesting to note that, if both the CreditMetrics and the Credit Risk Plus models were based on the same set of assumptions, they should in theory predict the same probability distribution for losses over the long term. It is the timing of losses that is different. Suppose, for example, that you hold a certain loan in your portfolio. In year 1 the borrower gets downgraded from A to BBB; in year 2 it gets downgraded from BBB to B; in year 3 it defaults. You could assume that there are no losses in years 1 and 2 and calculate loss in year 3 (the Credit Risk Plus approach). Alternatively, you can calculate separate revaluation losses in years 1, 2, and 3 (the

---

[8] However, the maturity adjustment factor does allow for downgrades in the regulatory implementation of Vasicek's model.

CreditMetrics approach). The losses under the second approach should in theory add up to the losses under the first approach.

The Correlation Model

In sampling to determine credit losses, the credit rating changes for different counterparties are not assumed to be independent. A Gaussian copula model is used to construct a joint probability distribution of rating changes. (See Section 11.4 for a discussion of copula models.) The copula correlation between the rating transitions for two companies is typically set equal to the correlation between their equity returns, with a factor model similar to that in Section 11.3 being assumed for the correlation structure of equity returns.

As an illustration of the credit correlation model, suppose that we are simulating the rating change of an A-rated and a B-rated company over a one-year period using the transition matrix in Table 18.1. Suppose that the correlation between the equity returns of the two companies is 0.2. On each simulation trial we would sample two variables x_A and x_B from standard normal distributions so that their correlation is 0.2. The variable x_A determines the new rating of the A-rated company and variable x_B determines the new rating of the B-rated company. From Table 18.1 the probability of an A-rated company moving to Aaa, Aa, A, ... is 0.0006, 0.0282, 0.9088, ... Because

$$N^{-1}(0.0006) = -3.2389$$

$$N^{-1}(0.0006 + 0.0282) = -1.8987$$

$$N^{-1}(0.0006 + 0.0282 + 0.9088) = 1.5349$$

the A-rated company gets upgraded to Aaa if $x_A < -3.2389$, it becomes Aa-rated if $-3.2389 < x_A < -1.8987$, it stays A-rated if $-1.8987 < x_A < 1.5349$, and so on. Table 18.1 also shows that the probability of a B-rated company moving to Aaa, Aa, A, ... is 0.0001, 0.0004, 0.0014, ... Because

$$N^{-1}(0.0001) = -3.7190$$

$$N^{-1}(0.0001 + 0.0004) = -3.2905$$

$$N^{-1}(0.0001 + 0.0004 + 0.0014) = -2.8943$$

the B-rated becomes Aaa-rated if $x_B < -3.7190$, it becomes Aa-rated if $-3.7190 < x_B < -3.2905$, it becomes A-rated if $-3.2905 < x_B < -2.8943$, and so on. The A-rated company defaults if $x_A > N^{-1}(0.9994)$, that is when $x_A > 3.2389$. The B-rated company defaults when $x_B > N^{-1}(0.9527)$, that is when $x_B > 1.6716$. This example is illustrated in Figure 18.2.

18.5 CREDIT VaR IN THE TRADING BOOK

The trading book consists of instruments that are held for trading while the banking book consists of instruments that are expected to be held to maturity. The approaches for calculating credit VaR we have considered so far have focused on the banking book.

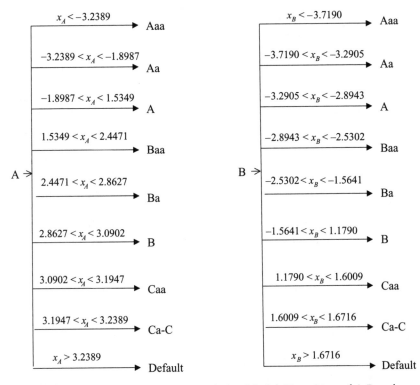

FIGURE 18.2 The CreditMetrics Correlation Model: Transition of A-Rated and B-Rated Companies to a New Rating after One Year (x_A and x_B are sampled from standard normal distributions with the correlation equal to the correlation between the equity returns of A and B.)

Most of a bank's credit exposure has traditionally consisted of loans in the banking book, but instruments such as bonds and credit default swaps, which create credit risk, have now become a significant part of the trading book. The market risk amendment to Basel I which was implemented in 1998 requires a specific risk charge to be calculated for credit risk in the trading book (see Section 12.6). The specific risk charge is, with regulatory approval, calculated by applying a multiplier (whose minimum value is 4) to a 10-day 99% VaR calculated using the bank's own model.

The values of most credit-sensitive products in the trading book depend critically on credit spreads. Calculating credit VaR therefore involves examining potential credit spread changes. One possibility is to use historical simulation to calculate a one-day 99% credit risk VaR in the same way that it is used for market risk VaR. The one-day 99% VaR can then be scaled up by $\sqrt{10}$ to obtain a 10-day 99% VaR. Credit spread changes for each company over the last 500 days (or some other period) are collected. The first historical simulation scenario assumes that the percentage credit spread changes for all companies are the same as they were on the first day; the second scenario assumes that they are the same as they were on the second day; and so on. However, this has an obvious problem. If the company is alive today, it did not default in the past and the calculations carried out therefore assume no probability of default in the future.[9] Another problem is that credit spreads are not updated daily for all companies and so the historical data may not be of high quality.

An alternative approach is to use a version of the CreditMetrics approach. A 10-day rating transitions matrix is calculated as indicated in Section 18.1. The ratings transition matrix defines the probability of a company moving from one rating category to another, or defaulting, during a 10-day period. The historical data on credit rating changes defines a probability distribution for the credit spread changes associated with each rating category at the end of 10 days. A Monte Carlo simulation is carried out. On each trial, the transition matrix is sampled from to determine whether each company stays in the same rating category, changes to a different rating category, or defaults. The probability distribution of credit spread changes is also sampled from to determine the credit spread at the end of the 10 days associated with each rating category. This enables the value of the portfolio at the end of 10 days to be calculated on each trial and a VaR to be obtained.

Credit correlation is introduced by assuming that the credit spread changes for different rating categories are perfectly (or nearly perfectly) correlated so that when the spreads for A-rated instruments move up, those for instruments with other ratings do so as well. A correlation can also be introduced between the rating transitions of different companies as explained in Section 18.4.

EXAMPLE 18.1

For a simple example to illustrate this approach, consider a company that owns a single two-year zero-coupon bond with a principal of $1,000. Suppose that the risk-free rate is 3% and the current credit spread is 200 basis points so that the bond yield is 5%. (Rates are expressed with annual compounding.) The current price of the bond is $1,000/1.05^2 = \$907.03$. Suppose that the bond's current rating is BB and that during the next two weeks (10 business days) there is a 0.3% chance that it will increase to BBB, a 99.2% chance that it will stay the same, a 0.4% chance that it will decrease to B, and a 0.1% chance that it will default. If it defaults, the bond will be worth $400. For each possible rating category there are three equally likely credit spreads. In basis points these are 80, 100, and 120 for BBB; 160, 200, and 240 for BB; and 400, 450, and 500 for B.

The worst outcome is clearly a default. This has a probability of 0.1% and will lead to a loss of $907.03 − 400 = \$507.03$. The next worst outcome involves a transition to a rating of B when the credit spread for that rating category is 500 basis points. This has a probability of $0.4/3 = 0.133\%$. Because the bond will have about 1.96 years to maturity its price will be $1,000/1.08^{1.96} = \$844.59$ for a loss of $907.03 − 844.59 = \$62.44$. A complete list of outcomes with their probabilities are shown in Table 18.4.

The table shows that if the confidence level is higher than 99.9% the VaR is $507.03; if it is between 99.9% and 99.767% it is $62.44; and so on. When the confidence level is 99% (as it is for the calculation of the specific risk charge), VaR is a modest $4.98.

---

[9] One way of dealing with this is to assume that default takes place when the credit spread exceeds a certain level.

TABLE 18.4 Outcomes for Example 18.1

Rating	Spread (bp)	Probability	Bond Value ($)	Loss ($)
Default		0.100%	400.00	507.03
B	500	0.133%	844.59	62.44
B	450	0.133%	867.84	39.19
B	400	0.133%	875.81	31.22
BB	240	33.067%	902.05	4.98
BB	200	33.067%	908.80	−1.77
BB	160	33.067%	915.63	−8.60
BBB	120	0.100%	922.53	−15.50
BBB	100	0.100%	926.01	−18.98
BBB	80	0.100%	929.51	−22.48

As discussed in Section 13.2, Basel III requires the CVA risk arising from credit spread changes to be included in specific risk calculations. This means that among the products considered in calculating the 10-day 99% credit risk VaR are the CVA derivatives associated with each derivatives counterparty. The way in which the value of the CVA for a counterparty depends on a small change in the counterparty's credit spread is given in Section 17.6.

Incremental Risk Charge

As explained in Section 13.1, in the first decade of the twenty-first century, banks found that the capital required for credit sensitive instruments in the trading book was usually much less than that for equivalent instruments in the banking book. (It is easy to see why this might be the case. The 10-day 99% VaR calculated for the simple situation in Example 18.1 is very small because 99% of the time not much changes in 10 days.) As a result, banks preferred transactions that created exposures in the trading book rather than the banking book. This led regulators to introduce the incremental risk charge. This is designed to ensure that the capital charge for credit sensitive instruments in the trading book is at least equal to that of an equivalent-risk instrument in the banking book.

The incremental risk charge requires a bank to calculate a one-year 99.9% VaR. The bank is allowed to use a constant level of risk assumption. This means it can estimate the liquidity horizon for an instrument, X, and assume that its portfolio is rebalanced so that, at the end of the liquidity horizon, instrument X is replaced with a new instrument Y that has the same risk profile that instrument X had originally. Suppose, for example, that the liquidity horizon is three months and a bond in the trading book is initially rated BBB. If, under one scenario that is considered, the bond gets downgraded to B during the three months, it is assumed to be replaced by a new BBB bond at the end of the three months for the calculation of VaR; if this new bond is downgraded to CCC during the following three months, it is replaced by a new BBB bond at the six-month point; and so on.

To illustrate how the VaR calculations might work, suppose again that the liquidity horizon for the instruments in a particular portfolio is three months. A CreditMetrics analysis, similar to that given for specific risk, can be used to produce a probability distribution for the loss in three months. The probability distribution for the loss in one year is obtained by finding the distribution of a variable that is the sum of four independent variables, each of which has the three-month loss distribution.[10] Monte Carlo simulation is one way this can be done.

SUMMARY

Credit VaR is defined similarly to the way VaR is defined for market risk. It is the credit loss that will not be exceeded over some time horizon with a specified confidence level. Basel regulations require credit VaR to be calculated for both the trading book (which consists of items held for trading) and the banking book (which consists of items that are expected to be held to maturity). For items in the trading book, banks, assuming they have received the appropriate regulatory approval, calculate a 10-day 99% VaR to determine the specific risk charge and a one-year 99.9% VaR (with a constant level of risk assumption) to determine the incremental risk charge. For items in the banking book, they determine regulatory capital by calculating a one-year 99.9% VaR.

We have discussed three methods for calculating VaR for the banking book: Vasicek's model, Credit Risk Plus, and CreditMetrics. Vasicek's model is based on a one-factor Gaussian copula model of the time to default for the companies in a portfolio. It is used in the determination of regulatory capital. Credit Risk Plus uses procedures that are similar to those used in the insurance industry to calculate default losses from assumptions about the probabilities of default of individual companies. CreditMetrics is different from the other two methods in that it considers losses from both defaults and downgrades. It uses a Gaussian copula model in conjunction with a ratings transition matrix.

To determine credit risk VaR for the trading book, one approach is to collect historical data on the credit spread changes of companies and use a historical simulation methodology similar to that for market risk. Another is to model the rating transitions of companies and movements in the average credit spreads associated with different rating categories.

FURTHER READING

Credit Suisse Financial Products. "Credit Risk Management Framework" (October, 1997).
Finger, C. C. "The One-Factor CreditMetrics Model in the New Basel Capital Accord," *RiskMetrics Journal*, Summer 2001.
Finger, C. C. "Creditmetrics and Constant Level of Risk." Working paper, RiskMetrics Group-MSCI, September 2010.
Gordy, M. "A Risk-Factor Model Foundation for Ratings-Based Capital Rules," *Journal of Financial Intermediation* 12, no. 3 (July 2003): 199–233.
J. P. Morgan. "CreditMetrics–Technical Document" (April 1997).
Vasicek, O. "Probability of Loss on a Loan Portfolio." Working paper, KMV, 1987. (Published in *Risk* in December 2002 under the title "Loan Portfolio Value.")

---

[10] As a rough approximation, the one-year 99.9% VaR can be assumed to be $\sqrt{4} =$ two times the three-month 99.9% VaR, but may not be accurate in some situations.

PRACTICE QUESTIONS AND PROBLEMS (ANSWERS AT END OF BOOK)

18.1 Explain the difference between the Vasicek's model, Credit Risk Plus model, and CreditMetrics as far as the following are concerned: (a) when a credit loss is recognized and (b) the way in which default correlation is modeled.

18.2 Explain what is meant by the constant level of risk assumption.

18.3 Use the transition matrix in Table 18.1 to calculate a transition matrix for two years. What is the probability of a Aaa-rated company staying Aaa during the two years? What is the probability of it moving to Aa?

18.4 Use the transition matrix in Table 18.1 and software on the author's website to calculate a transition matrix for six months. What is the probability of a Aaa-rated company staying Aaa during the six months? What is the probability of it moving to Aa?

18.5 How can historical simulation be used to calculate a one-day 99% VaR for the credit risk of bonds in the trading book? What are the disadvantages?

18.6 A bank has 100 one-year loans each with a 1% probability of defaults. What is the probability of six or more defaults?

18.7 Repeat Problem 18.6 on the assumption that the probability of default is equally likely to be 0.5% and 1.5%.

18.8 What is the autocorrelation for the default rates in Table 11.4, which can also be found on a spreadsheet on the author's website? What are the implications of this for a Credit Risk Plus model?

18.9 Explain what is meant by (a) the specific risk charge and (b) the incremental risk charge.

FURTHER QUESTIONS

18.10 Explain carefully the distinction between real-world and risk-neutral default probabilities. Which is higher? A bank enters into a credit derivative where it agrees to pay $100 at the end of one year if a certain company's credit rating falls from A to Baa or lower during the year. The one-year risk-free rate is 5%. Using Table 18.1, estimate a value for the derivative. What assumptions are you making? Do they tend to overstate or understate the value of the derivative?

18.11 Suppose that a bank has a total of $10 million of small exposures of a certain type. The one-year probability of default is 1% and the recovery rate averages 40%. Estimate the 99.5% one-year credit VaR using Vasicek's model if the copula correlation parameter is 0.2.

18.12 Use the transition matrix in Table 18.1 and software on the author's website to calculate the transition matrix over 1.25 years.

CHAPTER 19

Scenario Analysis and Stress Testing

Stress testing involves evaluating the impact of extreme, but plausible, scenarios that are not considered by VaR models. If there is one lesson to be learned from the market turmoil that started in the summer of 2007, it is that more emphasis should be placed on stress testing and less emphasis should be placed on the mechanistic application of VaR models. VaR models are useful, but they are inevitably backward looking. Risk management is concerned with what might happen in the future.

This chapter considers the different approaches that can be used to generate scenarios for stress testing and how the results should be used. It explains that the financial crisis of 2007 and 2008 has caused bank supervisors to require banks to conduct more stress testing. Indeed, supervisors themselves have sometimes developed stress tests for financial institutions to determine the ability of the financial sector as a whole to withstand shocks.

19.1 GENERATING THE SCENARIOS

The most popular approach for calculating VaR is the historical simulation approach covered in Chapter 14. This approach assumes that data from the last few years is a good guide to what will happen over the next 1 to 10 days. But if an event has not occurred during the period covered by the data, it will not affect the VaR results when the basic VaR methodology in Section 14.1 is used.

We have discussed a number of ways VaR calculations can be modified so that they reflect more than the simple assumption that the future short term movements in market variables will be a random sample from the recent past. In particular:

1. Volatility updating (see Section 14.3) can lead to more extreme outcomes being considered when the market is highly volatile.
2. Extreme value theory (see Section 14.5) provides a way of extending the tails of the loss distribution obtained from historical data.
3. Calculating stressed VaR (see Section 13.1) considers the impact of a particularly bad period of 250 days that has occurred in the past.

But the nature of a VaR calculation is that it is backward looking. Events that could happen, but are quite different from those that occurred during the period covered by the data, are not taken into account. Stress testing is an attempt to overcome this weakness of the VaR measure.

Stress testing involves estimating how the portfolio of a financial institution would perform under scenarios involving extreme market moves. Sometimes, the extreme market moves are measured in standard deviations, as was the case for our exchange rate example in Table 10.2. If daily changes are normally distributed, a five-standard-deviation daily change in a market variable happens about once every 7,000 years. But in practice, it is not uncommon to see a five-standard-deviation move once or twice every 10 years. (This emphasizes that the assumption that variables are normally distributed is not a good one in risk management.)

A key issue in stress testing is the way in which scenarios are chosen. We now consider alternative procedures.

Stressing Individual Variables

One approach is to use scenarios where there is a large move in one variable and other variables are unchanged. Examples of scenarios of this type that are sometimes considered are:

1. A 100-basis-point parallel shift (up or down) in a yield curve.
2. Increasing or decreasing all the implied volatilities used for an asset by 20% of current values.
3. Increasing or decreasing an equity index by 10%.
4. Increasing or decreasing the exchange rate for a major currency by 6%.
5. Increasing or decreasing the exchange rate for a minor currency by 20%.

The impact of small changes in a variable is measured by its delta, as explained in Chapter 7. The impact of larger changes can be measured by a combination of delta and gamma. Here we are considering changes that are so large that it is likely to be unreliable to estimate the change in the value of a portfolio using Greek letters.

Scenarios Involving Several Variables

Usually, when one market variable shows a big change, others do as well. This has led financial institutions to develop scenarios where several variables change at the same time. A common practice is to use extreme movements in market variables that have occurred in the past. For example, to test the impact of an extreme movement in U.S. equity prices, a company might set the percentage changes in all market variables equal to those on October 19, 1987 (when the S&P 500 moved by 22.3 standard deviations). If this is considered to be too extreme, the company might choose January 8, 1988 (when the S&P 500 moved by 6.8 standard deviations). Other dates when there were big movements in equity prices are September 11, 2001, when terrorists attacked the World Trade Center in New York, and September 15, 2008, when Lehman Brothers declared bankruptcy. To test the effect of extreme movements in UK interest rates, the company might set the percentage changes in all market variables equal to those on April 10, 1992 (when 10-year bond yields moved by 8.7 standard deviations).

Another approach is to magnify what has happened in the past to generate extreme scenarios. For example, we might take a period of time when there were moderately adverse market movements and create a scenario where all variables move by three or five times as much as they did then. The problem with this approach is that correlations increase in stressed market conditions and increasing the movements in all market variables by a particular multiple does not increase correlation.

Some historical scenarios are one-day shocks to market variables. Others, particularly those involving credit and liquidity, involve shocks that take place over several days, several weeks, or even several months. It is important to include volatilities in the market variables that are considered. Typically, extreme movements in market variables such as interest rates and exchange rates are accompanied by large increases in the volatilities of these variables and large increases in the volatilities of a wide range of other variables. Some scenarios are likely to involve big movements in commodity prices. On September 22, 2008, oil posted its biggest one-day price increase ever. On September 27–28, 1999, the price of gold increased by 15.4%. Some scenarios are likely to involve a situation where there is a flight to quality combined with a shortage of liquidity and an increase in credit spreads. This was what happened in August 1998 when Russia defaulted on its debt and in July and August 2007 when investors lost confidence in the products created from the securitization of subprime mortgages (see Chapter 6).

Scenarios Generated by Management

History never repeats itself exactly. This may be partly because traders are aware of past financial crises and try to avoid making the same mistakes as their predecessors. The U.S. mortgage market led to the credit crisis that started in 2007. It is unlikely that future credit crises will be a result of mortgage-lending criteria being relaxed—but it is also likely that there will be credit crises in the future.

In many ways, the scenarios that are most useful in stress testing are those generated by senior management or by the economics group within a financial institution. Senior management and the economics group are in a good position to use their understanding of markets, world politics, the economic environment, and current global uncertainties to develop plausible scenarios that would lead to large losses. Sometimes, the scenarios produced are based on things that have happened in the past, but are adjusted to include key features of the current financial and economic environment.

One way of developing the scenarios is for a committee of senior management to meet periodically and "brainstorm" answers to the simple question: "What can go wrong?" Clemens and Winkler (1999) have done studies to investigate the optimal composition of a committee of this type.[1] Their conclusions are that (a) the committee should have three to five members, (b) the backgrounds of the committee members should be different, and (c) there should be a healthy dialogue between members of the committee. It is important that members of the committee are able step back from their day-to-day responsibilities to consider the big picture.

It is not always the case that senior management's thinking has to be highly innovative in order for it to come up with relevant scenarios. In 2005 and 2006, many commentators realized that the U.S. housing market was experiencing a bubble

---

[1] See R. Clemens and R. Winkler, "Combining Probability Distributions from Experts in Risk Analysis," *Risk Analysis* 19, no. 2 (April 1999): 187–203.

and that sooner or later the bubble would burst. It is easy to be wise after the event, but one reasonable scenario for the stress-testing committee to propose during that period would have been a 10% or 20% decline in house prices in all parts of the country.

It is important that senior management and the board of directors understand and recognize the importance of stress testing. They have the responsibility for taking strategic decisions based on the stress-testing results. One advantage of involving senior management in the development of the scenarios to be used in stress testing is that it should naturally lead to a "buy in" by them to the idea that stress testing is important. The results generated from scenarios that are created by individuals who have middle management positions are unlikely to be taken as seriously.

Core vs. Peripheral Variables

When individual variables are stressed or scenarios are generated by management, the scenarios are likely to be incomplete in that movements of only a few (core) market variables are specified. One approach is to set changes in all other (peripheral) variables to zero, but this is likely to be unsatisfactory. Another approach is to regress the peripheral variables on the core variables that are being stressed to obtain forecasts for them conditional on the changes being made to the core variables. These forecasts (as point forecasts or probability distributions) can be incorporated into the stress test.

This is known as *conditional stress testing* and is discussed by Kupiec (1999).[2] Kim and Finger (2000) carry this idea further by using what they call a "broken arrow" stress test. In this, the correlation between the core variables and the peripheral variables is based on what happens in stressed market conditions rather than what happens on average.[3]

Making Scenarios Complete

Scenarios should be carefully examined in an attempt to make sure that all the adverse consequences are considered. The scenarios should include not only the immediate effect on the financial institution's portfolio of shock to market variables, but also any "knock-on" effect resulting from many different financial institutions being affected by the shock in the same way and responding in the same way. Many people have said that they recognized the real estate bubble in the United States would burst in 2007, but did not realize how bad the consequences would be. They did not anticipate that many financial institutions would experience losses at the same time with the result that there would be a flight to quality with severe liquidity problems and a huge increase in credit spreads.

Another example of knock-on effects is provided by the failure of Long-Term Capital Management (LTCM) in 1998 (see Business Snapshot 19.1). LTCM tended

---

[2] P. Kupiec, "Stress Testing in a Value at Risk Framework," *Journal of Derivatives* 6 (1999): 7–24.

[3] See J. Kim and C. C. Finger, "A Stress Test to Incorporate Correlation Breakdown," *Journal of Risk* 2, no. 3 (Spring 2000): 5–19.

BUSINESS SNAPSHOT 19.1

Long-Term Capital Management's Big Loss

Long-Term Capital Management (LTCM), a hedge fund formed in the mid-1990s, always collateralized its transactions. The hedge fund's investment strategy was known as convergence arbitrage. A very simple example of what it might do is the following. It would find two bonds, X and Y, issued by the same company promising the same payoffs, with X being less liquid (i.e., less actively traded) than Y. The market always places a value on liquidity. As a result, the price of X would be less than the price of Y. LTCM would buy X, short Y, and wait, expecting the prices of the two bonds to converge at some future time.

When interest rates increased, the company expected both bonds to move down in price by about the same amount so that the collateral it paid on bond X would be about the same as the collateral it received on bond Y. Similarly, when interest rates decreased, LTCM expected both bonds to move up in price by about the same amount so that the collateral it received on bond X would be about the same as the collateral it paid on bond Y. It therefore expected that there would be no significant outflow of funds as a result of its collateralization agreements.

In August 1998, Russia defaulted on its debt and this led to what is termed a "flight to quality" in capital markets. One result was that investors valued liquid instruments more highly than usual and the spreads between the prices of the liquid and illiquid instruments in LTCM's portfolio increased dramatically. The prices of the bonds LTCM had bought went down and the prices of those it had shorted increased. It was required to post collateral on both. The company was highly leveraged and found it difficult to make the payments required under the collateralization agreements. The result was that positions had to be closed out and there was a total loss of about $4 billion. If the company had been less highly leveraged it would probably have been able to survive the flight to quality and could have waited for the prices of the liquid and illiquid bonds to become closer.

to have long positions in illiquid securities and short positions in liquid securities. Its failure was caused by a flight to quality following Russia's default on its debt. Many investors were only interested in buying liquid securities. Spreads between liquid and illiquid securities increased. LTCM contends that it had done stress tests looking at the impact of flights to quality similar to those that had occurred pre-1998. What it did not allow for was the knock-on effect. Many hedge funds were following similar trading strategies to those of LTCM in 1998. When the flight to quality started, they were all forced to unwind their positions at the same time. Unwinding meant selling illiquid securities and buying liquid securities, reinforcing the flight to quality and making it more severe than previous flights to quality.

Scenarios should ideally be dynamic so that the response to the shock of the financial institution doing the stress test, as well as the response of other financial institutions, are considered. Consider, for example, the situation where a financial institution has sold options dependent on an underlying asset and maintains delta neutrality. A shock where there is a large increase or decrease in the asset price will lead to an immediate loss on the option position (see Section 7.7). To maintain delta neutrality large amounts of the asset will have to be bought or sold. The cost of subsequent delta hedging is liable to depend on the path followed by the asset price. The worst-case scenario, which should be the one considered by stress testers, is that the asset price experiences wild swings (i.e., large increases and decreases) before it settles down.

Reverse Stress Testing

Reverse stress testing involves the use of computational procedures to search for scenarios that lead to large losses and has become an important tool in risk management.

EXAMPLE 19.1

As a simple example of reverse stress testing, suppose a financial institution has positions in four European call options on an asset. The asset price is $50, the risk-free rate is 3%, the volatility is 20%, and there is no income on the asset. The positions, strike prices, and times to maturity are as indicated in the table below. The current value of the position (in $000s) is −25.90. The DerivaGem Application Builder can be used to search for one-day changes in the asset price and the volatility that will lead to the greatest losses. Some bounds should be put on the changes that are considered. We assume that the asset price will not decrease below $40 or increase above $60. It is assumed that the volatility will not fall below 10% or rise above 30%.

Position (000s)	Strike Price	Life (years)	Position Value ($000s)
+250	50	1.0	1176.67
−125	60	1.5	−293.56
−75	40	0.8	−843.72
−50	55	0.5	−65.30
Total			−25.90

Using the DerivaGem Application Builder in conjunction with Solver, the worst loss is found to be when the volatility decreases to 10% and the asset price falls to $45.99. The loss is $289.38. Reverse stress testing therefore shows that the financial institution is most exposed to a reduction of about 8% in the asset price combined with a sharp decline in volatility.

This might seem to be an unreasonable scenario. It is unlikely that volatility would go down sharply when the asset price declines by 8%. Solver could be run again with the lower bound to volatility being 20% instead of 10%. This gives a worst-case loss occurring when the volatility stays at 20% and the asset price falls to $42.86. The loss (in $000s) is then $87.19.

Searching over all the market variables to which a financial institution is exposed in the way indicated in Example 19.1 is in practice usually not computationally feasible. One approach is to identify 5 to 10 key market variables and assume that changes in other variables are dependent on changes in these variables.

Another way of simplifying the search process is to impose some structure on the problem. A principal components analysis (see Section 8.8) can be carried out on the changes in market variables (ideally using data from stressed market conditions) and then a search can be conducted to determine the changes in the principal components that generate large losses. This reduces the dimension of the space over which the search is conducted and should lead to fewer implausible scenarios.

An alternative approach is for the risk management group to impose a structure on scenarios. For example, management might be interested in a scenario similar to one that has occurred in the past where interest rates rise, stock prices fall, and a particular exchange rate weakens. An analyst could then search to find what multiplier must be applied to the changes observed in the past for a particular loss level to be reached.

Reverse stress testing can be used as a tool to facilitate brainstorming by the stress-testing committee. Prior to a meeting of the stress-testing committee, analysts can use reverse stress testing to come up with several scenarios that would be disastrous to the financial institution. These scenarios, along with others they generate themselves, are then considered by the stress-testing committee. They use their judgment to eliminate some of the analysts' scenarios as implausible and modify others so that they become plausible and are retained for serious evaluation.

19.2 REGULATION

The Basel Committee requires market risk calculations that are based on a bank's internal VaR models to be accompanied by "rigorous and comprehensive" stress testing. Similarly, banks using the IRB approach in Basel II (advanced or foundation) to determine credit risk capital are required to conduct stress tests to determine the robustness of their assumptions.

In May 2009, the Basel Committee issued the final version of its recommendations on stress-testing practices and how stress testing should be supervised by regulators.[4] The recommendations emphasize the importance of stress testing in determining how much capital is necessary to absorb losses should large shocks occur. They make the point that stress testing is particularly important after long periods of benign conditions because such conditions tend to lead to complacency.

The recommendations stress the importance of top management and board involvement in stress testing. In particular, top management and board members should be involved in setting stress-testing objectives, defining scenarios, discussing the results of stress tests, assessing potential actions, and decision making. It makes the point that the banks that fared well in the financial crisis that started in mid-2007 were the ones whose senior management as a whole took an active interest in the

---

[4] See "Principles for Sound Stress-Testing Practices and Supervision," Basel Committee on Banking Supervision, May 2009.

development and operation of stress testing, with the results of stress testing serving as an input into strategic decision making. Stress testing should be conducted across all areas of the bank. It should not be the case that each area conducts its own stress test.

The Basel recommendations make the point that many of the scenarios chosen pre-2007 were based on historical data and much less severe than what actually happened. Specific recommendations for banks are:

1. Stress testing should form an integral part of the overall governance and risk management culture of the bank. Stress testing should be actionable, with the results from stress-testing analyses impacting decision making at the appropriate management level, including strategic business decisions of the board and senior management. Board and senior management involvement in the stress-testing program is essential for its effective operation.

2. A bank should operate a stress-testing program that promotes risk identification and control, provides a complementary risk perspective to other risk management tools, improves capital and liquidity management, and enhances internal and external communication.

3. Stress-testing programs should take account of views from across the organization and should cover a range of perspectives and techniques.

4. A bank should have written policies and procedures governing the stress-testing program. The operation of the program should be appropriately documented.

5. A bank should have a suitably robust infrastructure in place, which is sufficiently flexible to accommodate different and possibly changing stress tests at an appropriate level of granularity.

6. A bank should regularly maintain and update its stress-testing framework. The effectiveness of the stress-testing program, as well as the robustness of major individual components, should be assessed regularly and independently.

7. Stress tests should cover a range of risks and business areas, including at the firm-wide level. A bank should be able to integrate effectively across the range of its stress-testing activities to deliver a complete picture of firm-wide risk.

8. Stress-testing programs should cover a range of scenarios, including forward-looking scenarios, and aim to take into account system-wide interactions and feedback effects.

9. Stress tests should feature a range of severities, including events capable of generating most damage whether through size of loss or through loss of reputation. A stress-testing program should also determine what scenarios could challenge the viability of the bank (reverse stress tests) and thereby uncover hidden risks and interactions among risks.

10. As part of an overall stress-testing program, a bank should aim to take account of simultaneous pressures in funding and asset markets, and the impact of a reduction in market liquidity on exposure valuation.

11. The effectiveness of risk mitigation techniques should be systematically challenged.

12. The stress-testing program should explicitly cover complex and bespoke products such as securitized exposures. Stress tests for securitized assets should consider the underlying assets, their exposure to systematic market factors, relevant

contractual arrangements and embedded triggers, and the impact of leverage, particularly as it relates to the subordination level in the issue structure.

13. The stress-testing program should cover pipeline and warehousing risks.[5] A bank should include such exposures in its stress tests regardless of their probability of being securitized.

14. A bank should enhance its stress-testing methodologies to capture the effect of reputational risk. The bank should integrate risks arising from off-balance-sheet vehicles and other related entities in its stress-testing program.

15. A bank should enhance its stress-testing approaches for highly leveraged counterparties in considering its vulnerability to specific asset categories or market movements and in assessing potential wrong-way risk related to risk-mitigating techniques.

The recommendations for bank supervisors are:

16. Supervisors should make regular and comprehensive assessments of a bank's stress-testing programs.

17. Supervisors should require management to take corrective action if material deficiencies in the stress-testing program are identified or if the results of stress tests are not adequately taken into consideration in the decision-making process.

18. Supervisors should assess and, if necessary, challenge the scope and severity of firm-wide scenarios. Supervisors may ask banks to perform sensitivity analysis with respect to specific portfolios or parameters, use specific scenarios or to evaluate scenarios under which their viability is threatened (reverse stress-testing scenarios).

19. Under Pillar 2 (supervisory review process) of the Basel II framework, supervisors should examine a bank's stress-testing results as part of a supervisory review of both the bank's internal capital assessment and its liquidity risk management. In particular, supervisors should consider the results of forward-looking stress testing for assessing the adequacy of capital and liquidity.

20. Supervisors should consider implementing stress-test exercises based on common scenarios.

21. Supervisors should engage in a constructive dialogue with other public authorities and the industry to identify systemic vulnerabilities. Supervisors should also ensure that they have the capacity and the skills to assess banks' stress-testing programs.

Scenarios Chosen by Regulators

Bank regulators require banks to consider extreme scenarios and then make sure they have enough capital for those scenarios. There is an obvious problem here. Banks want to keep their regulatory capital as low as possible. They therefore have

---

[5] "Pipeline and warehousing" risks refer to risks associated with assets that are awaiting securitization, but might not be securitized if market conditions change. These risks led to losses during the onset of the crisis.

no incentive to consider extreme scenarios that would lead to a bank supervisor telling them that their capital requirements need to be increased. There is therefore a natural tendency for the scenarios they consider to be "watered down" and fairly benign.

One approach to overcoming this problem is for regulators themselves to provide the scenarios (see Recommendations 18 and 20). This creates a lot of additional work for regulators, but it is obviously attractive for them to use the same set of scenarios for all banks. The banks are then compared using a common benchmark and systemic risk problems might be identified (see Business Snapshot 12.1 for an explanation of systemic risk). U.S. regulators used this approach in 2009 when they carried out stress tests of 19 financial institutions and found that 10 of them needed a total of $74.6 billion of additional capital. The European Banking Authority announced the results of a similar stress test in 2011 and found that 9 out of 91 financial insitutions failed the test. (Banks failed the test when their core Tier 1 capital ratio fell below 5%.)

By choosing scenarios themselves, regulators are able to focus the attention of banks on issues that are of concern to regulators. In particular, if regulators see many banks taking positions with similar risks, they could insist that all banks consider a particular set of scenarios that gave rise to adverse results for the positions. The downside of regulators generating scenarios themselves is that part of the reason for the increased focus by supervisors on stress testing is that they want to encourage financial institutions to spend more time generating and worrying about potential adverse scenarios. If supervisors do the work in generating the scenarios, this may not happen. A compromise might be to insist on both management-generated scenarios and supervisor-generated scenarios being evaluated.

Systems put in place by regulators do not always have the results one expects. Business Snapshot 19.2 explains that, when Danish regulators defined key scenarios for life insurance companies and pension funds in Europe, some of those companies responded by hedging against the particular scenarios used by regulators, and only against those scenarios.[6] This is not what regulators intended. Each scenario used in stress testing should be viewed as representative of a range of things that might happen. Financial institutions should ensure that their capital will be in good shape not just for the specified scenarios, but also for other similar or related scenarios. An extreme form of hedging against the red light scenario in Business Snapshot 19.2 would be to buy a security that pays off only if there is a decline in equity prices between 11% and 13% combined with a decline in interest rates between 65 and 75 basis points. This security would presumably cost very little and would be a ridiculous hedge, but could ensure that the financial institution passes the regulator-generated stress tests.

Mechanistic hedging against particular adverse scenarios, whether generated by regulators or in some other way, is not desirable. It is important for the financial institution to understand the range of risks represented by each stress scenario and to take sensible steps to deal with them. Risk management should not be a game between regulators and financial institutions.

---

[6] The information in Business Snapshot 19.2 is from P. L. Jorgensen, "Traffic Light Options," *Journal of Banking and Finance* 31, no. 12 (December 2007): 3698–3719.

BUSINESS SNAPSHOT 19.2

Traffic Light Options

In June 2001, the Danish Financial Supervisory Authority (DFSA) introduced a "traffic light" solvency stress-testing system. This requires life insurance companies and pension funds to submit semiannual reports indicating the impact on them of certain predefined shocks. The "red light scenario" involves a 70-basis-point decrease in interest rates, a 12% decline in stock prices, and an 8% decline in real estate prices. If capital falls below a specified critical level in this scenario, the company is categorized with "red light status" and is subject to more frequent monitoring with monthly reports being required. The "yellow light scenario" involves a 100-basis-point decrease in interest rates, a 30% decline in stock prices, and a 12% decline in real estate prices. If capital falls below the critical level in this scenario, the company is categorized with "yellow light status" and has to submit quarterly reports. When the company's capital stays above the critical levels for the red and yellow light scenarios, the company has a "green light status" and is subject to normal semiannual reporting. Some other countries in Europe have adopted similar procedures.

Investment banks have developed products for helping life insurance and pension funds keep a green light status. These are known as traffic light options. They pay off in the traffic light scenarios so as to give a boost to the financial institution's performance when these scenarios are considered. Rather than hedge against interest rates, equities, and real estate prices in the usual way, the financial institution buys a hedge that pays off only when the traffic light scenario specified for one or more of these variables occurs. This is much less expensive. (In practice, most of the financial institutions being regulated had very little exposure to real estate and the big moves that led to a payoff involved only interest rates and equity prices.)

19.3 WHAT TO DO WITH THE RESULTS

The biggest problem in stress testing is using the results effectively. All too often, the results of stress testing are ignored by senior management. A typical response is, "Yes, there are always one or two scenarios that will sink us. We cannot protect ourselves against everything that might happen." One way of trying to avoid this sort of response is to involve senior management in the development of scenarios, as outlined earlier. A better response on the part of senior management would be, "Are the risks associated with these scenarios acceptable? If not, let's investigate what trades we can put on to make these types of risks more acceptable."

The problem for both senior management and the risk management group is that they have two separate reports on their desks concerning what could go wrong. One report comes from VaR models, the other from stress testing. Which one should they base their decision making on? There is a natural tendency to take the VaR results more seriously because they impact regulatory capital in a direct way.

Integrating Stress Testing and VaR Calculations

Berkowitz (2000) suggests that stress testing will be taken more seriously if its results are integrated into the calculation of VaR.[7] This can be done by assigning a probability to each stress scenarios that is considered. Suppose that a financial institution has considered n_s stress scenarios and the total probability assigned to the stress scenarios is p. Assume further that there are n_v VaR scenarios generated using historical simulation in the usual way. An analyst can assume that there are a total of $n_s + n_v$ scenarios. The n_s stress scenarios have probability p and the n_v historical scenarios have probability $1 - p$.

Unfortunately human beings are not good at estimating a probability for the occurrence of a rare event. To make the task feasible for the stress-testing committee, one approach is to ask the stress-testing committee to allocate each stress scenario to categories with preassigned probabilities. The categories might be:

1. Probability = 0.05%. Extremely unlikely. One chance in 2,000.
2. Probability = 0.2%. Very unlikely, but the scenario should be given about the same weight as the 500 scenarios used in the historical simulation analysis.
3. Probability = 0.5%. Unlikely, but the scenario should be given more weight than the 500 scenarios used in the historical simulation analysis.

EXAMPLE 19.2

Suppose that, in the example in Section 14.1, five stress scenarios are considered. They lead to losses (in $000s) of 235, 300, 450, 750, and 850. The probabilities assigned to the scenarios are 0.5%, 0.2%, 0.2%, 0.05%, and 0.05%, respectively. The total probability of the stress scenarios is, therefore, 1%. This means that the probability assigned to the scenarios generated by historical simulation is 99%. Assuming that equal weighting is used, each historical simulation scenario is assigned a probability of $0.99/500 = 0.00198$. Table 14.4 is therefore replaced by Table 19.1. The probabilities assigned to scenarios are accumulated from the worst scenario to the best.[8] The VaR level when the confidence level is 99% is the first loss for which the cumulative probability is greater than 0.01. In our example this is $282,204.

Rebonato (2010) suggests a more elaborate approach to assessing probabilities of scenarios involving a careful application of a well known result in statistics, Bayes' theorem, and what are known as Bayesian networks.[9] The probability of a scenario consisting of two events is equal to the probability of the first event happening

---

[7] See J. Berkowitz, "A Coherent Framework for Stress Testing," *Journal of Risk* 2, no. 2 (Winter 1999/2000): 5–15.

[8] This is the same procedure that we used when weights were assigned to historical simulation scenarios. (See Table 14.5 in Section 14.3.)

[9] See Riccardo Rebonato, "Coherent Stress Testing: A Bayesian Approach to Financial Stress," (Chichester, UK: John Wiley & Sons, 2010).

TABLE 19.1 Losses Ranked from Highest to Lowest

Scenario	Loss ($000s)	Probability	Cumulative Probability
s5	850.000	0.00050	0.00050
s4	750.000	0.00050	0.00100
v494	477.841	0.00198	0.00298
s3	450.000	0.00200	0.00498
v339	345.435	0.00198	0.00696
s2	300.000	0.00200	0.00896
v349	282.204	0.00198	0.01094
v329	277.041	0.00198	0.01292
v487	253.385	0.00198	0.01490
s1	235.000	0.00500	0.01990
v227	217.974	0.00198	0.02188
v131	205.256	0.00198	0.02386
v238	201.389	0.00198	0.02584
...	...	...	...
...	...	...	...
...	...	...	...

For Example 19.2 s1, s2,... are the stress scenarios; v1, v2,... are the VaR historical simulation scenarios.

times the probability of the second event happening conditional on the first event having happened. Similarly the probability of a scenario consisting of three events is the probability of the first event happening times the probability of the second event happening conditional that the first event has happened times the probability of the third event happening conditional that the first two events have happened. Rebonato's approach provides a way of evaluating the conditional probabilities.

Subjective vs. Objective Probabilities

There are two types of probability estimates: objective and subjective. An *objective probability* for an event is a probability calculated by observing the frequency with which the event happens in repeated trials. As an idealized example of an objective probability, consider an urn containing red balls and black balls in an unknown proportion. We want to know the probability of a ball drawn at random from the urn being red. We could draw a ball at random, observe its color, replace it in the urn, draw another ball at random, observe its color, replace it in the urn, and so on, until 100 balls have been drawn. If 30 of the balls that have been drawn are red and 70 are black, our estimate for the probability of drawing a red ball is 0.3. Unfortunately, most objective probabilities calculated in real life are usually less reliable than the probability in this example, because the probability of the event happening does not remain constant for the observations that are available and the observations may not be independent.

A *subjective probability* is a probability derived from an individual's personal judgment about the chance of a particular event occurring. The probability is not based on historical data. It is a degree of belief. Different people are liable to have different subjective probabilities for the same event.

The probabilities in historical simulation are objective whereas the probabilities assigned to the scenarios in stress testing are subjective. Many analysts are uncomfortable with subjective probabilities because they are not based on data. Also, it is unfortunately the case that political considerations may play a part in a financial institution's decision to focus on historical data. If you use historical data and things go wrong, you can blame the data. If you use subjective judgments that have been provided by a group of people, those people are liable to be blamed.

However, if it is based only on objective probabilities, risk management is inevitably backward looking and fails to capitalize on the judgment and expertise of senior managers. It is the responsibility of those managers to steer the financial institution so that catastrophic risks are avoided.

SUMMARY

Stress testing is an important part of the risk management process. It leads to a financial institution considering the impact of extreme scenarios that are ignored by a traditional VaR analysis, but that do happen from time to time. Once plausible scenarios have been evaluated, the financial institution can take steps to lessen the impact of the particularly bad ones. One advantage of a comprehensive stress-testing program is that a financial institution obtains a better understanding of the nature of the risks in its portfolio.

Scenarios can be generated in a number of different ways. One approach is to consider extreme movements in just one market variable while keeping others fixed. Another is to use the movements in all market variables that occurred during periods in the past when the market experienced extreme shocks. The best approach is to ask a committee of senior management and economists to use their judgment and experience to generate the plausible extreme scenarios. Sometimes financial institutions carry out reverse stress testing where algorithms are used to search for scenarios that would lead to large losses. Scenarios should be as complete as possible and include the impact of knock-on effects as well as the initial shock to market variables. The market turmoil starting in summer 2007 shows that, in some cases, the knock-on effect can be significant and include a flight to quality, an increase in credit spreads, and a shortage of liquidity.

Regulators require financial institutions to keep sufficient capital for stress scenarios. Sometimes regulators themselves develop a common set of stress scenarios to be used by all financial institutions themselves. This helps to identify those financial institutions with insufficient capital and may uncover systemic risk problems.

If subjective probabilities are assigned to the extreme scenarios that are considered, stress testing can be integrated with a VaR analysis. This is an interesting idea, but was not one of the approaches outlined in the Basel Committee consultative document published in January 2009.

FURTHER READING

Alexander, C., and E. A. Sheedy. "Model-Based Stress Tests: Linking Stress Tests to VaR for Market Risk." Working Paper, Macquarie Applied Finance Center, 2008.

Aragonés, J. R., C. Blanco, and K. Dowd. "Incorporating Stress Tests into Market Risk Modeling." *Derivatives Quarterly* 7 (Spring 2001): 44–49.

Aragonés, J. R., C. Blanco, and K. Dowd. "Stress Tests, Market Risk Measures, and Extremes: Bringing Stress Tests to the Forefront of Market Risk Management." In *Stress Testing for Financial Institutions: Applications, Regulations, and Techniques,* edited by D. Rösch and H. Scheule. London: Risk Books, 2008.

Basel Committee on Banking Supervision. "Principles for Sound Stress-Testing Practices and Supervision." May 2009.

Berkowitz, J. "A Coherent Framework for Stress Testing." *Journal of Risk* 2, no. 2 (Winter 1999/2000): 5–15.

Bogle, J. C. "Black Monday and Black Swans." *Financial Analysts Journal* 64, no. 2 (March/April 2008): 30–40.

Clemens, R., and R. Winkler. "Combining Probability Distributions from Experts in Risk Analysis." *Risk Analysis* 19, no. 2 (April 1999): 187–203.

Duffie, D. "Systemic Risk Exposures: A 10-by-10-by-10 Approach." Working Paper, Stanford University, 2011.

Hua, P., and P. Wilmott. "Crash Courses." *Risk* 10, no. 6 (June 1997): 64–67.

Kim, J., and C. C. Finger. "A Stress Test to Incorporate Correlation Breakdown." *Journal of Risk* 2, no. 3 (Spring 2000): 5–19.

Kupiec, P. "Stress Testing in a Value at Risk Framework." *Journal of Derivatives* 6 (1999): 7–24.

Rebonato, R. *Coherent Stress Testing: A Bayesian Approach to the Analysis of Financial Stress.* Chichester, UK: John Wiley & Sons, 2010.

Taleb, N. N. *The Black Swan: The Impact of the Highly Improbable.* New York: Random House, 2007.

PRACTICE QUESTIONS AND PROBLEMS (ANSWERS AT END OF BOOK)

19.1 Explain three different ways that scenarios can be generated for stress testing.

19.2 What is reverse stress testing? How is it used?

19.3 Why might the regulatory environment lead to a financial institution underestimating the severity of the scenarios it considers?

19.4 What are traffic light options? What are their drawbacks?

19.5 Why is it important for senior management to be involved in stress testing?

19.6 What are the advantages and disadvantages of bank regulators choosing some of the scenarios that are considered for stress testing?

19.7 Explain the difference between subjective and objective probabilities.

19.8 Suppose that, in the example in Section 14.1, seven stress scenarios are considered. They lead to losses (in $000s) of 240, 280, 340, 500, 700, 850, and 1,050. The subjective probabilities assigned to the scenarios are 0.5%, 0.5%, 0.2%, 0.2%, 0.05%, 0.05%, and 0.05%, respectively. What is the new one-day 99% VaR that would be calculated using the procedure discussed in Section 19.3?

19.9 Suppose that the positions in the four options in Example 19.1 are changed to 200, −70, −120, and −60. Use the DerivaGem Application Builder and Solver to calculate the worst-case scenario for a daily change. Consider asset prices between $40 and $60 and volatilities between 10% and 30%.

FURTHER QUESTIONS

19.10 What difference does it make to the worst-case scenario in Example 19.1 if (a) the options are American rather than European and (b) the options are barrier options that are knocked out if the asset price reaches $65? Use the DerivaGem Applications Builder in conjunction with Solver to search over asset prices between $40 and $60 and volatilities between 18% and 30%.

19.11 What difference does it make to the VaR calculated in Example 19.2 if the exponentially weighted moving average model is used to assign weights to scenarios as described in Section 14.3?

Operational Risk

In 1999, bank supervisors announced plans to assign capital for operational risk in the new Basel II regulations. This met with some opposition from banks. The chairman and CEO of one major international bank described it as "the dopiest thing I have ever seen." However, bank supervisors persisted. They listed more than 100 operational risk losses by banks, each exceeding $100 million. Here are some of those losses:

Internal fraud: Allied Irish Bank, Barings, and Daiwa lost $700 million, $1 billion, and $1.4 billion, respectively, from fraudulent trading.

External fraud: Republic New York Corp. lost $611 million because of fraud committed by a custodial client.

Employment practices and workplace safety: Merrill Lynch lost $250 million in a legal settlement regarding gender discrimination.

Clients, products, and business practices: Household International lost $484 million from improper lending practices; Providian Financial Corporation lost $405 million from improper sales and billing practices.

Damage to physical assets: Bank of New York lost $140 million because of damage to its facilities related to the September 11, 2001, terrorist attack.

Business disruption and system failures: Salomon Brothers lost $303 million from a change in computing technology.

Execution, delivery, and process management: Bank of America and Wells Fargo Bank lost $225 million and $150 million, respectively, from systems integration failures and transaction processing failures.

Most banks have always had some framework in place for managing operational risk. However, the prospect of new capital requirements has led them to greatly increase the resources they devote to measuring and monitoring operational risk.

It is much more difficult to quantify operational risk than credit or market risk. Operational risk is also more difficult to manage. Financial institutions make a conscious decision to take a certain amount of credit and market risk, and there are many traded instruments that can be used to reduce these risks. Operational risk, by contrast, is a necessary part of doing business. An important part of operational risk management is identifying the types of risk that are being taken and which should be insured against. There is always a danger that a huge loss will be incurred from taking an operational risk that ex ante was not even recognized as a risk.

It might be thought that a loss such as that at Société Générale (SocGen, see Business Snapshot 5.5) was a result of market risk because it was movements in market variables that led to it. However, it should be classified as an operational risk loss because it involved fraud. (Jérôme Kerviel created fictitious trades to hide the big bets he was taking.) Suppose there was no fraud. If it was part of the bank's policy to let traders take huge risks, then the loss would be classified as market risk. But, if this was not part of the bank's policy and there was a breakdown in its controls, it would be classified as operational risk. The SocGen example illustrates that operational risk losses are often contingent on market movements. If the market had moved in Kerviel's favor, there would have been no loss. The fraud and the breakdown in SocGen's control systems might then never have come to light.

There are some parallels between the operational risk losses of banks and the losses of insurance companies. Insurance companies face a small probability of a large loss from a hurricane, earthquake, or other natural disaster. Similarly, banks face a small probability of a large operational risk loss. But there is one important difference. When insurance companies lose a large amount of money because of a natural disaster, all companies in the industry tend to be affected and often premiums rise the next year to cover losses. Operational risk losses tend to affect only one bank. Because it operates in a competitive environment, the bank does not have the luxury of increasing prices for the services it offers during the following year.

20.1 WHAT IS OPERATIONAL RISK?

There are many different ways in which operational risk can be defined. It is tempting to consider operational risk as a residual risk and define it as any risk faced by a financial institution that is not market risk or credit risk. To produce an estimate of operational risk, we could then look at the financial institution's financial statements and remove from the income statement (a) the impact of credit losses and (b) the profits or losses from market risk exposure. The variation in the resulting income would then be attributed to operational risk.

Most people agree that this definition of operational risk is too broad. It includes the risks associated with entering new markets, developing new products, economic factors, and so on. Another possible definition is that operational risk, as its name implies, is the risk arising from operations. This includes the risk of mistakes in processing transactions, making payments, and so on. This definition of risk is too narrow. It does not include major risks such as the risk of a "rogue trader" such as Jérôme Kerviel.

We can distinguish between internal risks and external risks. Internal risks are those over which the company has control. The company chooses whom it employs, what computer systems it develops, what controls are in place, and so on. Some people define operational risks as all internal risks. Operational risk then includes more than just the risk arising from operations. It includes risks arising from inadequate controls such as the rogue trader risk and the risks of other sorts of employee fraud.

Bank regulators favor including more than just internal risks in their definition of operational risk. They include the impact of external events such as natural disasters (for example, a fire or an earthquake that affects the bank's operations), political and regulatory risk (for example, being prevented from operating in a foreign country by that country's government), security breaches, and so on. All of this is reflected in the following definition of operational risk produced by the Basel Committee on Banking Supervision in 2001:

> *The risk of loss resulting from inadequate or failed internal processes, people, and systems or from external events.*

Note that this definition includes legal risk but does not include reputation risk and the risk resulting from strategic decisions.

Some operational risks result in increases in the bank's operating cost or decreases in its revenue. Other operational risks interact with credit and market risk. For example, when mistakes are made in a loan's documentation, it is usually the case that losses result if and only if the counterparty defaults. When a trader exceeds limits and misreports positions, losses result if and only if the market moves against the trader.

20.2 DETERMINATION OF REGULATORY CAPITAL

Banks have three alternatives for determining operational risk regulatory capital. The simplest approach is the *basic indicator approach*. Under this approach, operational risk capital is set equal to 15% of annual gross income over the previous three years. Gross income is defined as net interest income plus noninterest income.[1] A slightly more complicated approach is the *standardized approach*. In this, a bank's activities are divided into eight business lines: corporate finance, trading and sales, retail banking, commercial banking, payment and settlement, agency services, asset management, and retail brokerage. The average gross income over the last three years for each business line is multiplied by a "beta factor" for that business line and the result summed to determine the total capital. The beta factors are shown in Table 20.1. The third alternative is the *advanced measurement approach* (AMA). In this, the operational risk regulatory capital requirement is calculated by the bank internally using qualitative and quantitative criteria.

The Basel Committee has listed conditions that a bank must satisfy in order to use the standardized approach or the AMA approach. It expects large internationally active banks to move toward adopting the AMA approach through time. To use the standardized approach a bank must satisfy the following conditions:

1. The bank must have an operational risk management function that is responsible for identifying, assessing, monitoring, and controlling operational risk.
2. The bank must keep track of relevant losses by business line and must create incentives for the improvement of operational risk.
3. There must be regular reporting of operational risk losses throughout the bank.

---

[1] Net interest income is the excess of income earned on loans over interest paid on deposits and other instruments that are used to fund the loans (see Section 2.2).

TABLE 20.1   Beta Factors in Standardized Approach

Business Line	Beta Factor
Corporate finance	18%
Trading and sales	18%
Retail banking	12%
Commercial banking	15%
Payment and settlement	18%
Agency services	15%
Asset management	12%
Retail brokerage	12%

4. The bank's operational risk management system must be well documented.
5. The bank's operational risk management processes and assessment system must be subject to regular independent reviews by internal auditors. It must also be subject to regular review by external auditors or supervisors or both.

To use the AMA approach, the bank must satisfy additional requirements. It must be able to estimate unexpected losses based on an analysis of relevant internal and external data, and scenario analyses. The bank's system must be capable of allocating economic capital for operational risk across business lines in a way that creates incentives for the business lines to improve operational risk management.

The objective of banks using the AMA approach for operational risk is analogous to their objectives when they attempt to quantify credit risk. They would like to produce a probability distribution of losses such as that shown in Figure 20.1. Assuming that they can convince regulators that their expected operational risk cost

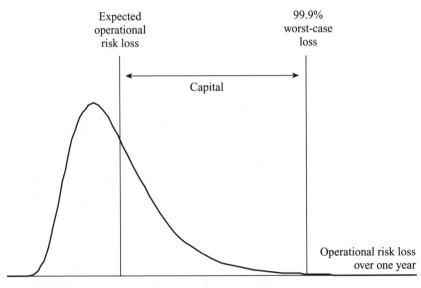

FIGURE 20.1   Calculation of VaR for Operational Risk

is incorporated into their pricing of products, capital is assigned to cover unexpected costs. The confidence level is 99.9% and the time horizon is one year.

20.3 CATEGORIZATION OF OPERATIONAL RISKS

The Basel Committee on Banking Supervision has identified seven categories of operational risk.[2] These are:

1. *Internal fraud*: Acts of a type intended to defraud, misappropriate property, or circumvent regulations, the law, or company policy (excluding diversity or discrimination events which involve at least one internal party). Examples include intentional misreporting of positions, employee theft, and insider trading on an employee's own account.
2. *External fraud*: Acts by third party of a type intended to defraud, misappropriate property, or circumvent the law. Examples include robbery, forgery, check kiting, and damage from computer hacking.
3. *Employment practices and workplace safety*: Acts inconsistent with employment, health, or safety laws or agreements, or which result in payment of personal injury claims, or claims relating to diversity or discrimination issues. Examples include workers compensation claims, violation of employee health and safety rules, organized labor activities, discrimination claims, and general liability (for example, a customer slipping and falling at a branch office).
4. *Clients, products, and business practices*: Unintentional or negligent failure to meet a professional obligation to clients and the use of inappropriate products or business practices. Examples are fiduciary breaches, misuse of confidential customer information, improper trading activities on the bank's account, money laundering, and the sale of unauthorized products.
5. *Damage to physical assets*: Loss or damage to physical assets from natural disasters or other events. Examples include terrorism, vandalism, earthquakes, fires, and floods.
6. *Business disruption and system failures*: Disruption of business or system failures. Examples include hardware and software failures, telecommunication problems, and utility outages.
7. *Execution, delivery, and process management*: Failed transaction processing or process management, and disputes with trade counterparties and vendors. Examples include data entry errors, collateral management failures, incomplete legal documentation, unapproved access given to clients accounts, nonclient counterparty misperformance, and vendor disputes.

There are $7 \times 8 = 56$ combinations of these seven risk types with the eight business lines in Table 20.1. Bank must estimate 1 year 99.9% VaRs for each combination and then merge them to determine a single operational risk VaR measure.

---

[2] See Basel Committee on Bank Supervision, "Sound Practices for the Management and Supervision of Operational Risk," Bank for International Settlements, July 2002.

20.4 LOSS SEVERITY AND LOSS FREQUENCY

There are two distributions that are important in estimating potential operational risk losses for a certain risk type/business line combination. One is the *loss frequency distribution* and the other is the *loss severity distribution*. The loss frequency distribution is the distribution of the number of losses observed during one year. The loss severity distribution is the distribution of the size of a loss, given that a loss occurs. It is usually assumed that loss severity and loss frequency are independent.

For loss frequency, the natural probability distribution to use is a Poisson distribution. This distribution assumes that losses happen randomly through time so that in any short period of time Δt there is a probability $\lambda \Delta t$ of a loss occurring. The probability of n losses in time T years is

$$e^{-\lambda T} \frac{(\lambda T)^n}{n!}$$

The parameter λ can be estimated as the average number of losses per year. For example, if during a 10-year period there were a total of 12 losses, λ would be estimated as 1.2 per year. A Poisson distribution has the property that the mean frequency of losses equals the variance of the frequency of losses.[3]

For the loss-severity probability distribution, a lognormal probability distribution is often used. The parameters of this probability distribution are the mean and standard deviation of the logarithm of the loss.

The loss-frequency distribution must be combined with the loss severity distribution for each risk type/business line combination to determine a loss distribution. Monte Carlo simulation can be used for this purpose.[4] As mentioned earlier, the usual assumption is that loss severity is independent of loss frequency. On each simulation trial, we proceed as follows:

1. We sample from the frequency distribution to determine the number of loss events $(= n)$
2. We sample n times from the loss severity distribution to determine the loss experienced for each loss event $(L_1, L_2, \ldots, L_n)$
3. We determine the total loss experienced $(= L_1 + L_2 + \cdots + L_n)$

When many simulation trials are used, we obtain a total loss distribution for losses of the type being considered.

Figure 20.2 illustrates the procedure. In this example, the expected loss frequency is 3 per year and the loss severity is drawn from a lognormal distribution. The logarithm of each loss ($ millions) is assumed to have a mean of zero and a

---

[3] If the mean frequency is greater than the variance of the frequency, a binomial distribution may be more appropriate. If the mean frequency is less than the variance, a negative binomial distribution (mixed Poisson distribution) may be more appropriate.

[4] Combining the loss severity and loss frequency distribution is a very common problem in insurance. Apart from Monte Carlo simulation, two approaches that are used are Panjer's algorithm and fast Fourier transforms. See H. H. Panjer, "Recursive Evaluation of a Family of Compound Distributions," *ASTIN Bulletin* 12 (1981): 22–29.

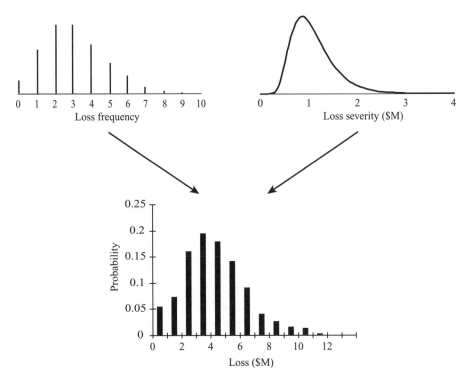

FIGURE 20.2 Calculation of Loss Distribution from Loss Frequency and Loss Severity

standard deviation of 0.4. The Excel worksheet used to produce Figure 20.2 is on the author's website.

20.5 IMPLEMENTATION OF AMA

We now discuss how the advanced measurement approach is implemented in practice. The Basel Committee requires the implementation to involve four elements: internal data, external data, scenario analysis, and business environment and internal control factors.[5] We will consider each of these in turn.

Internal Data

Unfortunately, there is usually relatively little historical data available within a bank to estimate loss severity and loss frequency distributions for particular types of losses. Many banks have not in the past kept records of operational risk losses. They are doing so now, but it may be some time before a reasonable amount of historical data is available. It is interesting to compare operational risk losses with credit risk losses in this respect. Traditionally, banks have done a much better job at documenting

---

[5] See Bank for International Settlements, "Operational Risk: Supervisory Guidelines for the Advanced Measurement Approach," June 2011.

their credit risk losses than their operational risk losses. Also, in the case of credit risks, a bank can rely on a wealth of information published by credit rating agencies to assess probabilities of default and expected losses given default. Similar data on operational risk have not been collected in a systematic way.

There are two types of operational risk losses: high-frequency low-severity losses (HFLSLs) and low-frequency high-severity losses (LFHSLs). An example of the first is credit card fraud losses. An example of the second is rogue trader losses. A bank should focus its attention on LFHSLs. These are what create the tail of the loss distribution. A particular percentile of the total loss distribution can be estimated as the corresponding percentile of the total LFHSL distribution plus the average of the total HFLSL. Another reason for focusing on LFHSLs is that HFLSLs are often taken into account in the pricing of products.

By definition, LFHSLs occur infrequently. Even if good records have been kept, internal data are liable to be inadequate, and must be supplemented with external data and scenario analysis.

External Data

There are two sources of external data. The first is data consortia, which are companies that facilitate the sharing of data between banks. (The insurance industry has had mechanisms for sharing loss data for many years and banks are now beginning to do this as well.) The second is data vendors, who are in the business of collecting publicly available data in a systematic way. External data increases the amount of data available to a bank for estimating potential losses. It also has the advantage that it can lead to a consideration of types of losses that have never been incurred by the bank, but which have been incurred by other banks.

Both internal and external historical data must be adjusted for inflation. In addition, a scale adjustment should be made to external data. If a bank with a revenue of \$10 billion reports a loss of \$8 million, how should the loss be scaled for a bank with a revenue of \$5 billion? A natural assumption is that a similar loss for a bank with a revenue of \$5 billion would be \$4 million. But this estimate is probably too small. For example, research by Shih et al. (2000) suggests that the effect of firm size on the size of a loss experienced is non-linear.[6] Their estimate is

$$\text{Estimated Loss for Bank A} = \text{Observed Loss for Bank B} \times \left(\frac{\text{Bank A Revenue}}{\text{Bank B Revenue}} \right)$$

where $\alpha = 0.23$. This means that in our example the bank with a revenue of \$5 billion would experience a loss of $8 \times 0.5^{0.23} = \$6.82$ million. After the appropriate scale adjustment, data obtained through sharing arrangements with other banks can be merged with the bank's own data to obtain a larger sample for determining the loss severity distribution.

---

[6] See J. Shih, A. Samad-Khan, and P. Medapa, "Is the Size of an Operational Loss Related to Firm Size?" *Operational Risk Magazine*, 2, 1 (January 2000). Whether Shih et al.'s results apply to legal risks is debatable. The size of a settlement in a large lawsuit against a bank can be governed by how much the bank can afford.

The loss data available from data vendors is data taken from public sources such as newspapers and trade journals. Data from vendors cannot be used in the same way as internal data or data obtained through sharing arrangements because they are subject to biases. For example, only large losses are publicly reported, and the larger the loss, the more likely it is to be reported.

Public data are most useful for determining *relative* loss severity. Suppose that a bank has good information on the mean and standard deviation of its loss severity distribution for internal fraud in corporate finance, but not for external fraud in corporate finance or for internal fraud in trading and sales. Suppose that the bank estimates the mean and standard deviation of its loss severity distribution for internal fraud in corporate finance as $50,000 and $30,000. Suppose further that external data indicates that, for external fraud in corporate finance, the mean severity is twice that for internal fraud in corporate finance and the standard deviation of the severity is 1.5 times as great. In the absence of a better alternative, the bank might assume that its own severity for external fraud in corporate finance has a mean of $2 \times 50,000 = $100,000 and a standard deviation of severity equal to $1.5 \times 30,000 = $45,000. Similarly, if the external data indicates that the mean severity for internal fraud in trading and sales is 2.5 times that for internal fraud in corporate finance and the standard deviation is twice as great, the bank might assume that its own severity for internal fraud in trading and sales has a mean of $2.5 \times 50,000 = $125,000 and a standard deviation of $2 \times 30,000 = $60,000.

Scenario Analysis

Scenario analysis has become a key tool for the assessment of operational risk under the AMA. The aim of scenario analysis is to generate scenarios covering the full range of possible LFHSLs. Some of these scenarios might come from the bank's own experience, some might be based on the experience of other banks, some might come from the work of consultants, and some might be generated by the risk management group in conjunction with senior management or business unit managers. The Basel Committee estimates that at many banks the number of scenarios considered that give rise to a loss of greater than 10 million euros is approximately 20 times larger than the number of internal losses of this amount.

An operational risk committee consisting of members of the risk management group and senior management should be asked to estimate loss severity and loss frequency parameters for the scenarios. As explained in Section 20.4, a lognormal distribution is often used for loss severity and a Poisson distribution is often used for loss frequency. Data from other banks may be useful for estimating the loss severity parameters. The loss frequency parameters should reflect the controls in place at the bank and the type of business it is doing. They should reflect the views of the members of the operational risk committee. Similarly to Section 19.3, a number of categories of loss frequency can be defined such as:

1. Scenario happens once every 1,000 years on average ($\lambda = 0.001$)
2. Scenario happens once every 100 years on average ($\lambda = 0.01$)
3. Scenario happens once every 50 years on average ($\lambda = 0.02$)
4. Scenario happens once every 10 years on average ($\lambda = 0.1$)
5. Scenario happens once every 5 years on average ($\lambda = 0.2$)

The committee can be asked to assign each scenario that is developed to one of the categories.

One difference between this scenario analysis and the one in Chapter 19 is that there is no model for determining losses and, if data is not available, the parameters of the loss severity distribution have to be estimated by the committee. One approach is to ask the committee to estimate an average loss and a "high loss" that the committee is 99% certain will not be exceeded. A lognormal distribution can then be fitted to the estimates.

Fortunately, the operational risk environment does not usually change as fast as the market and credit risk environment so that the amount of work involved in developing scenarios and keeping them up to date should not be as onerous. Nevertheless, the approach we have described does require a great deal of senior management time. The relevant scenarios for one bank are often similar to those for other banks and, to lessen the burden on the operational risk committee, there is the potential for standard scenarios to be developed by consultants or by bank industry associations. However, the loss frequency estimates should always be specific to a bank and reflect the controls in place in the bank and the type of business it is currently doing.

As in the case of market and credit risk stress testing, the advantage of generating scenarios using managerial judgment is that they include losses that the financial institution has never experienced, but could incur. The scenario analysis approach leads to management thinking actively and creatively about potential adverse events. This can have a number of benefits. In some cases, strategies for responding to an event so as to minimize its severity are likely to be developed. In other cases, proposals may be made for reducing the probability of the event occurring at all.

Whether scenario analysis or internal/external data approaches are used, distributions for particular loss types have to be combined to produce a total operational risk loss distribution. The correlations assumed for the losses from different operational risk categories can make a big difference to the one-year 99.9% VaR that is calculated, and therefore to the AMA capital. Chapter 23 builds on material in Section 9.9 to explain how correlations can be used to aggregate economic capital requirements across market risk, credit risk, and operational risk. The same approach can be used to aggregate different operational risk capital requirements. It is often argued that operational risk losses are largely uncorrelated with each other and there is some empirical support for this view. If the zero-correlation assumption is made, Monte Carlo simulation can be used in a straightforward way to sample from the distribution of losses for each scenario to obtain a total distribution of risk losses.

Business Environment and Internal Control Factors

Business environment and internal control factors (BEICFs) should be taken into account when loss severity and loss frequency are estimated. These include the complexity of the business line, the technology used, the pace of change, the level of supervision, staff turnover rates, and so on. For example, factors influencing the estimates made for the "rogue trader" scenario might be the level of supervision of traders, the level of trade surveillance, and the strengths or weaknesses of the systems used by the middle and back office.

20.6 PROACTIVE APPROACHES

Risk managers should try to be proactive in preventing losses from occurring. One approach is to monitor what is happening at other banks and try and learn from their mistakes. When a $700 million rogue trader loss happened at a Baltimore subsidiary of Allied Irish Bank in 2002, risk managers throughout the world studied the situation carefully and asked: "Could this happen to us?" Business Snapshot 20.1 describes a situation concerning a British local authority in the late 1980s. It immediately led to all banks instituting procedures for checking that counterparties had the authority to enter into derivatives transactions.

Causal Relationships

Operational risk managers should try to establish causal relations between decisions taken and operational risk losses. Does increasing the average educational qualifications of employees reduce losses arising from mistakes in the way transactions are processed? Will a new computer system reduce the probabilities of losses from

---

BUSINESS SNAPSHOT 20.1

The Hammersmith and Fulham Story

Between 1987 and 1989, the London Borough of Hammersmith and Fulham in Great Britain entered into about 600 interest rate swaps and related transactions with a total notional principal of about six billion pounds. The transactions appear to have been entered into for speculative rather than hedging purposes. The two employees of Hammersmith and Fulham that were responsible for the trades had only a sketchy understanding of the risks they were taking and how the products they were trading worked.

By 1989, because of movements in sterling interest rates, Hammersmith and Fulham had lost several hundred million pounds on the swaps. To the banks on the other side of the transactions, the swaps were worth several hundred million pounds. The banks were concerned about credit risk. They had entered into offsetting swaps to hedge their interest rate risks. If Hammersmith and Fulham defaulted, they would still have to honor their obligations on the offsetting swaps and would take a huge loss.

What actually happened was not a default. Hammersmith and Fulham's auditor asked to have the transactions declared void because Hammersmith and Fulham did not have the authority to enter into the transactions. The British courts agreed. The case was appealed and went all the way to the House of Lords, Britain's highest court. The final decision was that Hammersmith and Fulham did not have the authority to enter into the swaps, but that they ought to have the authority to do so in the future for risk management purposes. Needless to say, banks were furious that their contracts were overturned in this way by the courts.

system failures? Are operational risk losses correlated with the employee turnover rate? If so, can they be reduced by measures taken to improve employee retention? Can the risk of a rogue trader be reduced by the way responsibilities are divided between different individuals and by the way traders are motivated?

One approach to establishing causal relationships is statistical. If we look at 12 different locations where a bank operates and find a high negative correlation between the education of back-office employees and the cost of mistakes in processing transactions, it might well make sense to do a cost-benefit analysis of changing the educational requirements for a back-office job in some of the locations. In some cases, a detailed analysis of the cause of losses may provide insights. For example, if 40% of computer failures can be attributed to the fact that the current hardware is several years old and less reliable than newer versions, a cost-benefit analysis of upgrading is likely to be useful.

RCSA and KRIs

Risk control and self-assessment (RCSA) is an important way in which banks try to achieve a better understanding of their operational risk exposures. It involves asking the managers of business units to identify their operational risks. Sometimes questionnaires and scorecards designed by senior management or consultants are used.

A by-product of any program to measure and understand operational risk is likely to be the development of key risk indicators (KRIs).[7] Risk indicators are key tools in the management of operational risk. The most important indicators are prospective. They provide an early warning system to track the level of operational risk in the organization. Examples of key risk indicators that could be appropriate in particular situations are

1. Staff turnover
2. Number of failed transactions
3. Number of positions filled by temps
4. Ratio of supervisors to staff
5. Number of open positions
6. Percentage of staff that did not take 10 days consecutive leave in the last 12 months

The hope is that key risk indicators can identify potential problems and allow remedial action to be taken before losses are incurred. It is important for a bank to quantify operational risks, but it is even more important to take actions that control and manage those risks.

20.7 ALLOCATION OF OPERATIONAL RISK CAPITAL

Operational risk capital should be allocated to business units in a way that encourages them to improve their operational risk management. Methods for doing this are

---

[7] These are sometimes referred to as Business Environment and Internal Control Factors (BEICFs).

discussed in Sections 9.8 and 23.6. If a business unit can show that it has taken steps to reduce the frequency or severity of a particular risk, it should be allocated less capital. This will have the effect of improving the business unit's return on capital (and possibly lead to the business unit manager receiving an increased bonus).

Note that it is not always optimal for a manager to reduce a particular operational risk. Sometimes the costs of reducing the risk outweigh the benefits of reduced capital so that return on allocated capital decreases. A business unit should be encouraged to make appropriate calculations and determine the amount of operational risk that maximizes return on capital.

The overall result of operational risk assessment and operational risk capital allocation should be that business units become more sensitive to the need for managing operational risk. Hopefully, operational risk management will be seen to be an important part of every manager's job. A key ingredient for the success of any operational risk program is the support of senior management. The Basel Committee on Banking Supervision is very much aware of this. It recommends that a bank's board of directors be involved in the approval of a risk management program and that it reviews the program on a regular basis.

20.8 USE OF POWER LAW

In Section 10.4, we introduced the power law. This states that, for a wide range of variables

$$\text{Prob}(v > x) = Kx^{-\alpha}$$

where v is the value of the variable, x is a relatively large value of v, and K and α are constants. We covered the theoretical underpinnings of the power law and maximum likelihood estimation procedures when we looked at extreme value theory in Section 14.5.

De Fountnouvelle et al. (2003), using data on losses from vendors, found that the power law holds well for the large losses experienced by banks.[8] This makes the calculation of VaR with high degrees of confidence such as 99.9% easier. Loss data (internal or external) and scenario analysis are employed to estimate the power law parameters using the maximum likelihood approach in Chapter 14. The 99.9 percentile of the loss distribution can then be estimated using equation (14.9).

When loss distributions are aggregated, the distribution with the heaviest tails tends to dominate. This means that the loss with the lowest α defines the extreme tails of the total loss distribution.[9] Therefore, if all we are interested in is calculating the extreme tail of the total operational risk loss distribution, it may only be necessary to consider one or two business line/risk type combinations.

---

[8] See P. De Fountnouvelle, V. DeJesus-Rueff, J. Jordan, and E. Rosengren, "Capital and Risk: New Evidence on Implications of Large Operational Risk Losses," Federal Reserve Board of Boston, Working Paper, September 2003.

[9] The parameter ξ in extreme value theory (see Chapter 14) equals $1/\alpha$ so it is the loss distribution with the largest ξ that defines the extreme tails.

20.9 INSURANCE

An important decision for operational risk managers is the extent to which operational risks should be insured against. Insurance policies are available on many different kinds of risk ranging from fire losses to rogue trader losses. Provided that the insurance company's balance sheet satisfies certain criteria, a bank using AMA can reduce the capital it is required to hold by entering into insurance contracts. In Section 3.7 we discussed the moral hazard and adverse selection risks faced by insurance companies. We now review these again in the context of operational risk.

Moral Hazard

One of the risks facing a company that insures a bank against operational risk losses is moral hazard. This is the risk that the existence of the insurance contract will cause the bank to behave differently than it otherwise would. This changed behavior increases the risks to the insurance company. Consider, for example, a bank that insures itself against robberies. As a result of the insurance policy, it may be tempted to be lax in its implementation of security measures—making a robbery more likely than it would otherwise have been.

Insurance companies have traditionally dealt with moral hazard in a number of ways. Typically there is a *deductible* in any insurance policy. This means that the bank is responsible for bearing the first part of any loss. Sometimes there is a *coinsurance provision* in a policy. In this case, the insurance company pays a predetermined percentage (less than 100%) of losses in excess of the deductible. In addition, there is nearly always a *policy limit*. This is a limit on the total liability of the insurer. Consider again a bank that has insured itself against robberies. The existence of deductibles, coinsurance provisions, and policy limits are likely to provide an incentive for a bank not to relax security measures in its branches. The moral hazard problem in rogue trader insurance is discussed in Business Snapshot 20.2.

Adverse Selection

The other major problem facing insurance companies is adverse selection. This is where an insurance company cannot distinguish between good and bad risks. It offers the same price to everyone and inadvertently attracts more of the bad risks. For example, banks without good internal controls are more likely to enter into rogue trader insurance contracts; banks without good internal controls are more likely to buy insurance policies to protect themselves against external fraud.

To overcome the adverse selection problem, an insurance company must try to understand the controls that exist within banks and the losses that have been experienced. As a result of its initial assessment of risks, it may not charge the same premium for the same contract to all banks. As time goes by, it gains more information about the bank's operational risk losses and may increase or reduce the premium charged. This is much the same as the approach adopted by insurance companies when they sell automobile insurance to a driver. At the outset, the insurance company obtains as much information on the driver as possible. As time goes by, it collects more information on the driver's risk (number of accidents, number of speeding tickets, etc.) and modifies the premium charged accordingly.

BUSINESS SNAPSHOT 20.2

Rogue Trader Insurance

A rogue trader insurance policy presents particularly tricky moral hazard problems. An unscrupulous bank could enter into an insurance contract to protect itself against losses from rogue trader risk and then choose to be lax in its implementation of trading limits. If a trader exceeds the trading limit and makes a large profit, the bank is better off than it would be otherwise. If a large loss results, a claim can be made under the rogue trader insurance policy. Deductibles, coinsurance provisions, and policy limits may mean that the amount recovered is less than the loss incurred by the trader. However, potential net losses to the bank are likely to be far less than potential profits making the lax trading limits strategy a good bet for the bank.

Given this problem, it is perhaps surprising that some insurance companies do offer rogue trader insurance policies. These companies tend to specify carefully how trading limits are implemented within the bank. They may require that the existence of the insurance policy not be revealed to anyone on the trading floor. They are also likely to want to retain the right to investigate the circumstances underlying any loss.

From the bank's point of view, the lax trading limits strategy we have outlined may be very shortsighted. The bank might well find that the costs of all types of insurance rise significantly as a result of a rogue trader claim. Also, a large rogue trader loss (even if insured) would cause its reputation to suffer.

20.10 SARBANES-OXLEY

Largely as a result of the Enron bankruptcy, the Sarbanes-Oxley Act was passed in the United States in 2002. This provides another dimension to operational risk management for both financial and nonfinancial institutions in the United States. The act requires boards of directors to become much more involved with day-to-day operations. They must monitor internal controls to ensure risks are being assessed and handled well.

The act specifies rules concerning the composition of the board of directors of public companies and lists the responsibilities of the board. It gives the SEC the power to censure the board or give it additional responsibilities. A company's auditors are not allowed to carry out any significant non-auditing services for the company.[10] Audit partners must be rotated. The audit committee of the board must be made aware of alternative accounting treatments. The CEO and CFO must prepare a statement to accompany the audit report to the effect that the financial statements are accurate. The CEO and CFO are required to return bonuses in the event that financial

---

[10] Enron's auditor, Arthur Andersen, provided a wide range of services in addition to auditing. It did not survive the litigation that followed the downfall of Enron.

statements are restated. Other rules concern insider trading, disclosure, personal loans to executives, reporting of transactions by directors, and the monitoring of internal controls by directors.

SUMMARY

In 1999, bank supervisors indicated their intention to charge capital for operational risk. This has led banks to carefully consider how they should measure and manage operational risk. Bank supervisors have identified seven different types of operational risks and eight different business lines. They encourage banks to quantify risks for each of the 56 risk type/business line combinations.

Operational risk losses of a particular type can be treated in much the same way as actuaries treat losses from insurance policies. A frequency of loss distribution and a severity of loss distribution can be estimated and then combined to form a total loss distribution. When they use the advanced measurement approach (AMA), banks are required to use internal data, external data, scenario analysis, and business environment and risk control factors. The external data comes from other banks via data sharing arrangements or from data vendors. The most important tool is scenario analysis. Loss scenarios covering the full spectrum of large operational risk losses are identified. Loss severity can sometimes be estimated from internal and external data. Loss frequency is usually estimated subjectively by the risk management group in conjunction with senior management and business unit managers and should reflect the business environment and risk control factors at the bank.

Risk managers should try to be forward-looking in their approach to operational risk. They should try to understand what determines operational risk losses and try to develop key risk indicators to track the level of operational risk in different parts of the organization.

Once operational risk capital has been estimated, it is important to develop procedures for allocating it to business units. This should be done in a way that encourages business units to reduce operational risk when this can be done without incurring excessive costs.

The power law introduced in Chapter 10 seems to apply to operational risk losses. This makes it possible to use extreme value theory (see Chapter 14) to estimate the tails of a loss distribution from empirical data. When several loss distributions are aggregated, it is the loss distribution with the heaviest tail that dominates. In principle, this makes the calculation of VaR for total operational risk easier.

Many operational risks can be insured against. However, most policies include deductibles, coinsurance provisions, and policy limits. As a result, a bank is always left bearing part of any risk itself. Moreover, the way insurance premiums change as time passes is likely to depend on the claims made and other indicators that the insurance company has of how well operational risks are being managed.

The whole process of measuring, managing, and allocating operational risk is still in its infancy. As time goes by and data are accumulated, more precise procedures than those we have mentioned in this chapter are likely to emerge. One of the key problems is that there are two sorts of operational risk: high-frequency low-severity risks and low-frequency high-severity risks. The former are relatively easy to quantify, but operational risk VaR is largely driven by the latter.

Bank supervisors seem to be succeeding in their objective of making banks more sensitive to the importance of operational risk. In many ways, the key benefit of an operational risk management program is not the numbers that are produced, but the process that banks go through in producing the numbers. If handled well, the process makes managers more aware of the importance of operational risk and perhaps leads to them thinking about it differently.

FURTHER READING

Bank for International Settlements. "Sound Practices for the Management and Supervision of Operational Risk." February 2003.

Bank for International Settlements. "Operational Risk: Supervisory Guidelines for the Advanced Measurement Approach." June 2011.

Baud, N., A. Frachot, and T. Roncalli. "Internal Data, External Data and Consortium Data for Operational Risk Management: How to Pool Data Properly." Working Paper, Groupe de Recherche Operationelle, Credit Lyonnais, 2002.

Chorafas, D. N. *Operational Risk Control with Basel II: Basic Principles and Capital Requirements*. Elsevier, 2003.

Davis, E., ed. *The Advanced Measurement Approach to Operational Risk*. London: Risk Books, 2006.

De Fountnouvelle, P., V. DeJesus-Rueff, J. Jordan, and E. Rosengren. "Capital and Risk: New Evidence on Implications of Large Operational Risk Losses." Working Paper, Federal Reserve Board of Boston, September 2003.

Dutta, K., and D. Babbel. "Scenario Analysis in the Measurement of Operational Risk Capital: A Change of Measure Approach." Working Paper, Wharton School, University of Pennsylvania, 2010.

Lambrigger, D. D., P. V. Shevchenko, and M. V. Wüthrich. "The Quantification of Operational Risk Using Internal Data, Relevant External Data, and Expert Opinion," *Journal of Operational Risk* 2, no. 3 (Fall 2007), 3–28.

PRACTICE QUESTIONS AND PROBLEMS (ANSWERS AT END OF BOOK)

20.1 What risks are included by regulators in their definition of operational risks? What risks are not included?

20.2 Suppose that external data shows that a loss of $100 million occurred at a bank with annual revenues of $1 billion. Your bank has annual revenues of $3 billion. What is the implication of the external data for losses that could occur at your bank? (Use Shih's result)

20.3 Suppose that there is a 90% probability that operational risk losses of a certain type will not exceed $20 million. The power law parameter, α, is 0.8. What is the probability of losses exceeding (a) $40 million, (b) $80 million, and (c) $200 million?

20.4 Discuss how moral hazard and adverse selection are handled in car insurance.

20.5 Give two ways Sarbanes-Oxley affects the CEOs of public companies.

20.6 When is a trading loss classified as a market risk and when is it classified as an operational risk?

20.7 Discuss whether there is (a) moral hazard and (b) adverse selection in life insurance contracts.

20.8 What is external loss data? How is it obtained? How is it used in determining operational risk loss distributions for a bank?

20.9 What distributions are commonly used for loss frequency and loss severity?

20.10 Give two examples of key risk indicators that might be monitored by a central operational risk management group within a bank.

20.11 The worksheet used to produce Figure 20.2 is on the author's website. What is the mean and standard deviation of the loss distribution? Modify the inputs to the simulation to test the effect of changing the loss frequency from three to four.

FURTHER QUESTIONS

20.12 Suppose that there is a 1% probability that operational risk losses of a certain type exceed $10 million. Use the power law to estimate the 99.97% worst-case operational risk loss when the α parameter equals (a) 0.25, (b) 0.5, (c) 0.9, and (d) 1.0.

20.13 Consider the following two events: (a) a bank loses $1 billion from an unexpected lawsuit relating to its transactions with a counterparty and (b) an insurance company loses $1 billion because of an unexpected hurricane in Texas. Suppose that you have the same investment in shares issued by both the bank and the insurance company. Which loss are you more concerned about? Why?

20.14 The worksheet used to produce Figure 20.2 is on the author's website. How does the loss distribution change when the loss severity has a beta distribution with upper bound of five, lower bound of zero, and the other parameters both one?

CHAPTER 21

Liquidity Risk

The credit crisis that started in the middle of 2007 has emphasized the importance of liquidity risk for both financial institutions and their regulators. Many financial institutions that relied on wholesale deposits for their funding experienced problems as investors lost confidence in financial institutions. Moreover, financial institutions found that many instruments for which there had previously been a liquid market could only be sold at fire-sale prices during the crisis.

It is important to distinguish solvency from liquidity. Solvency refers to a company having more assets than liabilities, so that the value of its equity is positive. Liquidity refers to the ability of a company to make cash payments as they become due. Financial institutions that are solvent can—and sometimes do—fail because of liquidity problems. Consider a bank whose assets are mostly illiquid mortgages. Suppose the assets are financed 90% with deposits and 10% with equity. The bank is comfortably solvent. But it could fail if there is a run on deposits with 25% of depositors suddenly deciding to withdraw their funds. In this chapter we will examine how Northern Rock, a British bank specializing in mortgage lending, failed largely because of liquidity problems of this type.

It is clearly important for financial institutions to manage liquidity carefully. Liquidity needs are uncertain. Financial institutions must assess a worst-case liquidity scenario and make sure that they can survive that scenario by either converting assets into cash or borrowing funds externally. The new Basel III requirements are designed to ensure that banks do this.

Liquidity is also an important consideration in trading. A liquid position in an asset is one that can be unwound at short notice. As the market for an asset becomes less liquid, traders are more likely to take losses because they face bigger bid–offer spreads. For an option or other derivative, it is important for there to be a liquid market for the underlying asset so that the trader has no difficulty in doing the daily trades necessary to maintain delta neutrality (see Chapter 7).

This chapter discusses different aspects of liquidity risk. It considers liquidity trading risk and liquidity funding risk. It also looks at what are termed "liquidity black holes." These are situations where a shock to financial markets causes liquidity to dry up.

21.1 LIQUIDITY TRADING RISK

If a financial institution owns 100, 1,000, 10,000, or even 100,000 shares in IBM, liquidity risk is not a concern. Several million IBM shares trade on the New York

Stock Exchange every day. The quoted price of the shares is very close to the price that the financial institution would be able to sell the shares for. However, not all assets are as readily convertible into cash. For example, a $100 million investment in the bonds of a non-investment-grade U.S. company might be quite difficult to sell at close to the market price in one day. Shares and debt of companies in emerging markets are likely to be even less easy to sell.

The price at which a particular asset can be sold depends on

1. The mid-market price of the asset, or an estimate of its value
2. How much of the asset is to be sold
3. How quickly it is to be sold
4. The economic environment

When there is a market maker who quotes a bid and offer price for a financial asset, the financial institution can sell relatively small amounts of the asset at the bid and buy relatively small amounts at the offer. However, it is usually stated that a particular quote is good for trades up to a certain size. Above that size, the market maker is likely to increase the bid–offer spread. This is because the market maker knows that as the size of a trade increases, the difficulty of hedging the exposure created by the trade also increases.

When there is no market maker for a financial instrument, there is still an implicit bid-offer spread. If a financial institution approaches another financial institution (or an interdealer broker) to do a trade, the price depends on which side of the trade it wants to take. The bid–offer spread for an asset can vary from 0.05% of the asset's mid-market price to as much as 5%, or even 10%, of its mid-market price.

The general nature of the relationship between bid quotes, offer quotes, and trade size is indicated in Figure 21.1. The bid price tends to decrease and the offer

FIGURE 21.1   Bid and Offer Prices as a Function of Quantity Transacted

price tends to increase with the size of a trade. For an instrument where there is a market maker, the bids and offers are the same up to the market maker's size limit and then start to diverge.

Figure 21.1 describes the market for large deals between sophisticated financial institutions. It is interesting to note that bid–offer spreads in the retail market sometimes show the opposite pattern to that in Figure 21.1. Consider, for example, an individual who approaches a branch of a bank wanting to do a foreign exchange transaction or invest money for 90 days. As the size of the transaction increases, the individual is likely to get a better quote.

The price that can be realized for an asset often depends on how quickly it is to be liquidated and the economic environment. Suppose you want to sell your house. Sometimes the real estate market is referred to as a "seller's market." Almost as soon as you put the house on the market, you can expect to get several different offers and the house will be sold within a week. In other markets, it may take six months or more to sell the house. In the latter case, if you need to sell the house immediately, you will have to reduce the asking price well below the estimated market value.

Financial assets are similar to real assets as far as this is concerned. Sometimes liquidity is tight (e.g., after the Russian default of 1998 and after the subprime crisis of 2007). Liquidating even a relatively small position can then be time-consuming and is sometimes impossible. On other occasions, there is plenty of liquidity in the market and relatively large positions can be unwound without difficulty.

One of the problems in the market for financial assets is that, when one financial institution decides for whatever reason that it wants to unwind a position, it is often the case that many other financial institutions with similar positions decide they want to do the same thing. The liquidity normally present in the market then evaporates. This is the "liquidity black hole" phenomenon that will be discussed later in this chapter.

The Importance of Transparency

One thing that the market has learned from the credit crisis of 2007 is that transparency is important for liquidity. If the nature of an asset is uncertain, it is not likely to trade in a liquid market for very long.

As explained in Chapter 6, it had become common practice in the years prior to 2007 to form portfolios of subprime mortgages and other assets and to create financial instruments by securitizing, re-securitizing, and re-re-securitizing the credit risk. Many of the financial instruments were even more complicated than indicated in Chapter 6 because sometimes ABS CDOs included non-mortgage assets or tranches from other ABS CDOs. After August 2007, market participants realized that they knew very little about the risks in the instruments they had traded. Moreover, it was very difficult for them to find out very much about this. Belatedly, they realized they had been using credit ratings as a substitute for an understanding of the instruments.

After August 2007, the instruments created from subprime mortgages became illiquid. Financial institutions had no idea how to mark to market investments that they had been scrambling to buy a few months earlier. They realized that they had purchased highly complicated credit derivatives and that they did not have the tools to value them. They lacked both the necessary models and solid information about the assets in the portfolios underlying the derivatives.

Other well-defined credit derivatives, such as credit default swaps, continued to trade actively after the credit crisis of 2007. The lesson from all this is that the market can sometimes get carried away trading complex products that are not transparent, but, when it comes to its senses, liquidity for the products soon disappears. When the products do trade again, prices are likely to be low and bid–offer spreads are likely to be high. As mentioned in Chapter 6, in July 2008 Merrill Lynch agreed to sell $30.6 billion of ABS CDO tranches (previously rated AAA) to Lone Star Funds for 22 cents on the dollar.

Measuring Market Liquidity

The bid–offer spread for an asset can be measured either as a dollar amount or as a proportion of the asset price. The dollar bid–offer spread is

$$p = \text{Offer price} - \text{Bid price}$$

The proportional bid–offer spread for an asset is defined as

$$s = \frac{\text{Offer price} - \text{Bid price}}{\text{Mid-market price}}$$

where the mid-market price is halfway between the bid and the offer price. Sometimes it is convenient to work with the dollar bid–offer spread, p, and sometimes with the proportional bid–offer spread, s.

In liquidating a position in an asset, a financial institution incurs a cost equal to $p/2 = s\alpha/2$ where α is the dollar (mid-market) value of the position. This reflects the fact that trades are not done at the mid-market price. A buy trade is done at the offer price and a sell trade is done at the bid price.

One measure of the liquidity of a book is how much it would cost to liquidate the book in normal market conditions within a certain time. Suppose that s_i is an estimate of the proportional bid–offer spread in normal market conditions for the ith financial instrument held by a financial institution and α_i is the dollar value of the position in the instrument. Then

$$\text{Cost of liquidation (normal market)} = \sum_{i=1}^{n} \frac{s_i \alpha_i}{2} \qquad (21.1)$$

where n is the number of positions. Note that although diversification reduces market risk, it does not necessarily reduce liquidity trading risk. However, as explained earlier, s_i increases with the size of position i. Holding many small positions rather than a few large positions therefore tends to entail less liquidity risk. Setting position limits is one way of reducing liquidity trading risk.

EXAMPLE 21.1

Suppose that a financial institution has bought 10 million shares of one company and 50 million ounces of a commodity. The shares are bid $89.5, offer $90.5. The commodity is bid $15, offer $15.1. The mid-market value of the position in the shares is $90 \times 10 = \$900$ million. The mid-market value of the position in the commodity is $15.05 \times 50 = \$752.50$ million. The proportional bid–offer spread for the shares is $1/90$ or 0.01111. The proportional bid–offer spread for the commodity is $0.1/15.05$ or 0.006645. The cost of liquidation in a normal market is

$$900 \times 0.01111/2 + 752.5 \times 0.006645/2 = 7.5$$

or $7.5 million

Another measure of liquidity is the cost of liquidation in stressed market conditions within a certain time period. Define μ_i and σ_i as the mean and standard deviation of the proportional bid–offer spread for the ith financial instrument held. Then

$$\text{Cost of liquidation (stressed market)} = \sum_{i=1}^{n} \frac{(\mu_i + \lambda\sigma_i)\alpha_i}{2} \qquad (21.2)$$

The parameter λ gives the required confidence level for the spread. If, for example, we are interested in a considering "a 99% worst case" (in the sense that the bid–offer spreads are exceeded only 1% of the time), and if it is assumed that spreads are normally distributed, then $\lambda = 2.326$.

EXAMPLE 21.2

Suppose that in Example 21.1 the mean and standard deviation for the bid–offer spread for the shares are 1.0 and 2.0, respectively. Suppose further that the mean and standard deviation for the bid–offer spread for the commodity are both 0.1. The mean and standard deviation for the proportional bid–offer spread for the shares are 0.01111 and 0.02222, respectively. The mean and standard deviation for the proportional bid–offer spread for the commodity are both 0.006645. Assuming the spreads are normally distributed, the cost of liquidation that we are 99% confident will not be exceeded is

$$0.5 \times 900 \times (0.01111 + 2.326 \times 0.02222)$$
$$+ 0.5 \times 752.5 \times (0.006645 + 2.326 \times 0.006645) = 36.58$$

or $36.58. This is almost five times the cost of liquidation in normal market conditions.

In practice, bid–offer spreads are not normally distributed and it may be appropriate to use a value of λ that reflects their empirical distribution. For example, if it is found that the 99 percentile point of the distribution is 3.6 standard deviations above the mean for a particular category of financial instruments, λ can be set equal to 3.6 for those instruments.

Equation 21.2 assumes that spreads in all instruments are perfectly correlated. This may seem overly conservative, but it is not. When liquidity is tight and bid–offer spreads widen, they tend to do so for all instruments. It makes sense for a financial institution to monitor changes in the liquidity of its book by calculating the measures in equations (21.1) and (21.2) on a regular basis. As we have seen, the bid–offer spread depends on how quickly a position is to be liquidated. The measures in equations (21.1) and (21.2) are therefore likely to be decreasing functions of the time period assumed for the liquidation.

Liquidity-Adjusted VaR

Market value at risk, which we discussed in Chapters 9, 14, and 15, is designed to calculate an estimate of the "worst change" in the mark-to-market valuation of the trading book. The measures in equations (21.1) and (21.2) are designed to calculate the cost of liquidating a book if market prices do not change. Although VaR and liquidity risk measures deal with different types of risks, some researchers have suggested combining them into a *liquidity-adjusted VaR* measure. One definition of liquidity-adjusted VaR is regular VaR plus the cost of unwinding positions in a normal market. From equation (21.1) this gives

$$\text{Liquidity Adjusted VaR} = \text{VaR} + \sum_{i=1}^{n} \frac{s_i \alpha_i}{2} \tag{21.3}$$

Alternatively it can be defined as regular VaR plus the cost of unwinding positions in a stressed market. From equation (21.2) this gives[1]

$$\text{Liquidity Adjusted VaR} = \text{VaR} + \sum_{i=1}^{n} \frac{(\mu_i + \lambda \sigma_i)\alpha_i}{2}$$

Unwinding a Position Optimally

A trader wishing to unwind a large position in a financial instrument has to decide on the best trading strategy. If the position is unwound quickly, the trader will face large bid–offer spreads, but the potential loss from the mid-market price moving against the trader is small. If the trader chooses to take several days to unwind the position, the bid–offer spread the trader faces each day will be lower, but the potential loss from the mid-market price moving against the trader is larger.

This type of problem is discussed by Almgren and Chriss (2001).[2] Suppose that the size of a position is V units and that a trader has to decide how to liquidate it over an n-day period. In this case, it is convenient to define the bid–offer spread in dollars rather than as a proportion. Define the bid–offer spread when the trader trades q units in one day as $p(q)$ dollars. Define q_i as the units traded on day i and x_i as the size of the trader's position at the end of day i ($1 \leq i \leq n$). It follows that $x_i = x_{i-1} - q_i$ for $1 \leq i \leq n$ where x_0 is defined as the initial position size, V.

---

[1] This was suggested in A. Bangia, F. Diebold, T. Schuermann, and J. Stroughair, "Liquidity on the Outside," *Risk* 12 (June): 68–73.
[2] See R. Almgren and N. Chriss, "Optimal Execution of Portfolio Transactions," *Journal of Risk* 3 (Winter 2001): 5–39.

Each trade costs half the bid–offer spread. The total of the costs related to the bid–offer spread is therefore

$$\sum_{i=1}^{n} q_i \frac{p(q_i)}{2}$$

Suppose that the mid-market price changes are normally distributed with a standard deviation of σ per day and trading takes place at the beginning of a day. The variance of the change in the value of the trader's position on day i is $\sigma^2 x_i^2$. The variance of the price change applicable to the unwind is therefore

$$\sum_{i=1}^{n} \sigma^2 x_i^2$$

A trader might reasonably wish to minimize VaR after trading costs have been considered. This corresponds to minimizing something similar to the liquidity-adjusted VaR measure in equation (21.3). The trader's objective is to choose the q_i so that

$$\lambda \sqrt{\sum_{i=1}^{n} \sigma^2 x_i^2} + \sum_{i=1}^{n} q_i \frac{p(q_i)}{2}$$

is minimized subject to

$$\sum_{i=1}^{n} q_i = V$$

with the x_i being calculated from V and the q_i, as indicated. The parameter λ measures the confidence level in the VaR estimate. For example, when the confidence level is 99%, and daily price changes are assumed to be normally distributed, $\lambda = 2.326$. Once the $s(q)$ function has been estimated, Excel's Solver can be used for the optimization.

EXAMPLE 21.3

A trader wishes to unwind a position of 100 million units in an asset over five days. Suppose that the bid–offer spread p (measured in dollars) as a function of the daily trading volume is

$$p(q) = a + be^{cq}$$

where $a = 0.1$, $b = 0.05$, and $c = 0.03$ and the amount traded, q, is measured in millions of units.

The standard deviation of the price change per day is 0.1. A spreadsheet for calculating the optimal strategy can be downloaded from the author's website. When the confidence level is 95%, the amounts that should be traded on days 1, 2, 3, 4, and 5 are 48.9, 30.0, 14.1, 5.1, and 1.9 million units, respectively. As the VaR confidence level is reduced, the amounts traded per day show less variability. For example, when the confidence level is 90%, they are 45.0, 29.1, 15.6, 7.0, and 3.3 million units, respectively. When the confidence level is 75% they are 36.1, 26.2, 17.7, 11.6, and 8.4 million units, respectively. In the limit when the confidence level is set equal to 50% so that the trader is interested only in expected costs, not in the standard deviation of costs, 20 million units should be traded each day.

As this example illustrates, when a position is to be closed out over n days, more than $1/n$ of the position should be traded on the first day. This is because the longer any part of the position is held, the greater the risk of adverse market moves.

21.2 LIQUIDITY FUNDING RISK

We now move on to consider liquidity funding risk. This is the financial institution's ability to meet its cash needs as they arise. As mentioned at the outset of this chapter, liquidity is not the same as solvency. Financial institutions that are solvent (i.e., have positive equity) can, and sometimes do, fail because of liquidity problems. Northern Rock, a British mortgage lender is a case in point (see Business Snapshot 21.1).

Some cash needs are predictable. For example, if a bank has issued a bond, it knows when coupons will have to be paid. Others, such as those associated with withdrawals of deposits by retail customers and draw-downs by corporations on lines of credit that the bank has granted, are less predictable. As the financial instruments entered into by financial institutions have become more complex, cash needs have become more difficult to predict. For example, downgrade triggers (see Section 17.2), guarantees provided by a financial institution, and possible defaults by counterparties in derivative transactions can have an unexpected impact on cash resources.

Liquidity funding risk is related to liquidity trading risk, considered in the previous section. This is because one way a financial institution can meet its funding requirements is by liquidating part of its trading book.

Sources of Liquidity

The main sources of liquidity for a financial institution are:

1. Holdings of cash and securities such as Treasury bills that can be readily convertible into cash
2. The ability to liquidate trading book positions
3. The ability to borrow money in the wholesale market at short notice
4. The ability to offer favorable terms to attract retail deposits at short notice
5. The ability to securitize assets (such as loans) at short notice
6. Borrowings from the central bank

Liquid Assets

Cash and marketable securities are relatively expensive sources of liquidity. This is because the interest earned on securities that can be readily converted into cash is less

BUSINESS SNAPSHOT 21.1

Northern Rock

Northern Rock, a British bank, was founded in 1997 when the Northern Rock Building Society floated shares on the London Stock Exchange. In 2007, it was one of the top five mortgage lenders in the United Kingdom. It had 76 branches and offered deposit accounts, savings accounts, loans, and house/contents insurance. The bank grew rapidly between 1997 and 2007. Some of its mortgages were securitized through a subsidiary, Granite, that was based in the Channel Islands.

Northern Rock relied on selling short-term debt instruments for much of its funding. Following the subprime crisis of August 2007, the bank found it very difficult to replace maturing instruments. This is because institutional investors became very nervous about lending to banks that were heavily involved in the mortgage business. The bank's assets were sufficient to cover its liabilities so it was not insolvent. To quote from the Financial Services Authority (FSA) in September 2007: "The FSA judges that Northern Rock is solvent, exceeds its regulatory capital requirement, and has a good quality loan book." But Northern Rock's inability to fund itself was a serious problem. It approached the Bank of England for funding on September 12, 2007, and borrowed about £3 billion from the Tripartite Authority (Bank of England, the Financial Services Authority, and HM Treasury) in the following few days.

On September 13, 2007, the BBC business editor Robert Peston broke the news that the bank had requested emergency support from the Bank of England. On Friday, September 14, there was a run of the bank. Thousands of people lined up for hours to withdraw their funds. This was the first run on a British bank in 150 years. Some customers held their funds in an "Internet-only" account, which they were unable to access due to the volume of customers trying to log on. On Monday, September 17, worried savers continued to withdraw their funds. An estimated £2 billion was withdrawn between September 12 and September 17, 2007.

Depositor insurance in the UK guaranteed 100% of the first £2,000 and 90% of the next £33,000. Late on September 17, 2007, the British Chancellor of the Exchequer, Alistair Darling, announced that the British Government and the Bank of England would guarantee all deposits held at Northern Rock. As a result of this announcement and subsequent advertisements in major UK newspapers, the lineups outside Northern Rock's branches gradually disappeared. Northern Rock's shares, which had fallen from £12 earlier in the year to £2.67, rose 16% on Mr. Darling's announcement.

During the months following September 12, 2007, Northern Rock's emergency borrowing requirement increased. The Bank of England insisted on a penalty rate of interest to discourage other banks from taking excessive risks. Northern Rock raised some funds by selling assets, but by February 2008 the emergency borrowing reached £25 billion and the bank was nationalized with the management of the bank being changed. It was split into Northern Rock plc and Northern Rock (Asset Management) with the company's bad debt being put in Northern Rock (Asset Management). In November 2011, Northern Rock plc was bought from the British Government for £747 million by the Virgin Group, which is headed by the colorful entrepreneur, Sir Richard Branson.

The Northern Rock story illustrates just how quickly liquidity problems can lead to a bank spiraling downward.

than the interest earned on other less liquid assets. For example, it is usually more profitable for a bank to allocate assets to loans than to Treasury bills, and more profitable for an insurance company to allocate assets to corporate bonds rather than Treasury bills. There is a trade-off between the liquidity of an asset and the return it provides. We see this in the market for Treasury bonds in the United States. On-the-run bonds are recently issued bonds that trade fairly actively. Off-the-run bonds are bonds that were issued some time ago and are relatively illiquid. The yield on off-the-run bonds is up to 20 basis points higher than the yield on similar on-the-run bonds.

Assessing which assets in the trading book are liquid (readily convertible into cash) and which are not is a key activity for a financial institution. It is important to base this assessment on stressed market conditions, not normal market conditions. When one financial institution is in need of liquidity, many other financial institutions are likely to be in a similar position. Assets that are highly liquid in normal market conditions are liable to become very difficult to sell during stressed market conditions. One result of the credit crisis that started in the summer of 2007 was that the trading books of all financial institutions suddenly became much less liquid.

Wholesale and Retail Deposits

Wholesale deposits are a more volatile source of funding than retail deposits. When markets are unstressed, a creditworthy bank usually has no problem in borrowing money in wholesale markets, but, in stressed market conditions, there is a heightened aversion to risk. This leads to higher interest rates, shorter maturities for loans in the wholesale market, and in some cases a refusal to provide funds at all. Financial institutions should monitor the assets that can be pledged as collateral for loans at short notice. A financial institution can (at a cost) mitigate its funding risks somewhat by arranging lines of credit. For example, Countrywide, an originator of mortgages in the United States, had a syndicated loan facility of $11.5 billion which it was able to use during the credit crisis of 2007. (This helped keep the company afloat, but it still experienced significant problems and was taken over by Bank of America in January 2008.) As Business Snapshot 21.1 shows, Northern Rock, a similar British mortgage lender, did not fare so well.

Deposits from retail clients are a less volatile source of funding than borrowings in the wholesale market. But retail deposits are not as stable as they used to be. Depositors now find it very easy to compare interest rates offered by different financial institutions and make transfers via the Internet. Unfortunately, liquidity problems tend to be market-wide rather than something that affects one or two financial institutions. When one financial institution wants to increase its retail deposit base for liquidity reasons, others usually do as well and the desired increase is likely to be difficult to achieve.

Securitization

As mentioned in Chapter 2, banks have found the "originate-to-distribute" model attractive. Rather than keep illiquid assets such as loans on their balance sheet, they have securitized them. The structures developed for doing this were discussed in Chapter 6. Prior to August 2007, securitization was an important source of liquidity for banks. However, this source of liquidity dried up almost overnight in August 2007 as investors decided that the securitized products were too risky. "Originate-to-distribute" had to be replaced by "originate-and-fund"! Not surprisingly, banks became a lot less willing to lend.

Securitization led to other liquidity problems in August 2007. Banks had entered into liquidity backstop arrangements on the asset-backed commercial paper (ABCP) that was used to fund debt instruments such as mortgages prior to their securitization. When buyers could not be found, they had to buy the instruments themselves. In some cases, in order to avoid their reputations being adversely impacted, they had to provide financial support to conduits and other off-balance-sheet vehicles that were involved in securitization, even though not legally required to do so.

Central Bank Borrowing

Central banks (e.g., the Federal Reserve Board in the United States, the Bank of England in the UK, or the European Central Bank) are often referred to as "lenders of last resort." When commercial banks are experiencing financial difficulties, central banks are prepared to lend money to maintain the health of the financial system. Collateral has to be posted by the banks and the central bank typically applies a haircut (i.e., it lends less than 100% of the value of the collateral) and may charge a relatively high rate of interest. In March 2008, after the failure of Bear Stearns (which was taken over by JPMorgan Chase), the Federal Reserve Board extended its borrowing facility to investment banks as well as commercial banks.[3] Later, it also made the facility available to Fannie Mae and Freddie Mac (which were taken over by the government in September 2008).

Different central banks apply different rules. Following the credit crisis of August 2007, the haircuts used by the European Central Bank (ECB) were lower than those of other central banks. As a result, some British banks preferred to borrow from

---

[3] Central banks are concerned about the failure of investment banks because of systemic risk (see Business Snapshot 12.1). Investment banks have derivatives contracts with other investment banks and with commercial banks. There is a danger that, because of the huge amount of trading between banks, a failure by an investment bank will have a ripple effect throughout the financial sector leading to a failure by commercial banks.

BUSINESS SNAPSHOT 21.2

Ashanti Goldfields

Ashanti Goldfields, a West African gold-mining company based in Ghana, experienced problems resulting from its hedging program in 1999. It had sought to protect its shareholders from gold price declines by selling gold forward. On September 26, 1999, 15 European central banks surprised the market with an announcement that they would limit their gold sales over the following five years. The price of gold jumped up over 25%. Ashanti was unable to meet margin calls and this resulted in a major restructuring which included the sale of a mine, a dilution of the interest of its equity shareholders, and a restructuring of its hedge positions.

the European Central Bank (ECB) rather than the Bank of England. (There are even stories of North American banks contemplating the setting up of subsidiaries in Ireland to access the ECB.) By September 2008, the ECB had lent 467 billion euros and it then announced that it would apply larger haircuts in the future.

Banks try to keep their borrowings from a central bank a secret. There is a danger that the use of central bank borrowings will be interpreted by the market as a sign that the bank is experiencing financial difficulties with the result that other sources of liquidity dry up. As Business Snapshot 21.1 discusses, news that Northern Rock required emergency borrowing led to an immediate run on the bank, exacerbating its liquidity problems.

Hedging Issues

Liquidity problems are liable to arise when companies hedge illiquid assets with contracts that are subject to margin requirements. As indicated in Business Snapshot 7.1, gold-mining companies often hedge their risks by entering into agreements with financial institutions to sell gold forward for two or three years. Often the gold-mining company is required to post margin and the amount of the margin required is calculated every day to reflect the value of its forward agreements. If the price of gold rises fast, the forward agreements lose money and result in big margin calls being made by the financial institution on the gold-mining company. The losses on the forward agreements are offset by increases in the value of the gold in the ground—but this is an illiquid asset. As discussed in Business Snapshot 21.2, Ashanti Goldfields was forced to undertake a major restructuring when it could not meet margin calls after a sharp rise in the price of gold.

Another extreme example of a liquidity funding problem caused by hedging is provided by a German company, Metallgesellschaft that entered into profitable fixed-price oil and gas contracts with its customers (see Business Snapshot 21.3). The lesson from the Ashanti and Metallgesellschaft episodes is not that companies should not use forward and futures contracts for hedging, but rather that they should ensure

BUSINESS SNAPSHOT 21.3

Metallgesellschaft

In the early 1990s, Metallgesellschaft (MG) sold a huge volume of 5- to 10-year heating oil and gasoline fixed-price supply contracts to its customers at six to eight cents above market prices. It hedged its exposure with long positions in short-dated futures contracts that were rolled forward. As it turned out, the price of oil fell and there were margin calls on the futures positions. Considerable short-term cash flow pressures were placed on MG. The members of MG who devised the hedging strategy argued that these short-term cash outflows were offset by positive cash flows that would ultimately be realized on the long-term fixed-price contracts. However, the company's senior management and its bankers became concerned about the huge cash drain. As a result, the company closed out all the hedge positions and agreed with its customers that the fixed-price contracts would be abandoned. The outcome was a loss to MG of $1.33 billion.

that they have access to funding to handle the cash flow mismatches that might arise in extreme circumstances.

Reserve Requirements

In some countries there are *reserve requirements* that require banks to keep a certain percentage of deposits as cash in the bank's vault or on deposit with the central bank. The reserve requirement applies only to transaction deposits (in essence, those made to a checking account). For large banks in the United States, the reserve requirement is currently about 10%. Some countries, such as Canada and the United Kingdom, have no compulsory reserve requirements. Others have higher compulsory reserve requirements than the United States.

In addition to ensuring that banks keep a minimum amount of liquidity, reserve requirements affect the money supply. When the reserve requirement is 10%, a $100 deposit leads to $90 of lending, which leads to a further $90 of deposits in the banking system, which leads to further $81 of lending, and so on. As this process continues, the total money supply (M1) that is created is $90 + 81 + 72.9 + \ldots$ or $900. If the reserve requirement is 20%, a $100 deposit leads to $80 of lending, which leads to $64 of lending, and so on. The total increase in the money supply is $80 + 64 + 51.2 + \ldots$ or $400. Most countries do not use the reserve requirement as a way of controlling the money supply. An exception appears to be China, where the reserve requirement is changed frequently.

Regulation

As explained in Chapter 13, Basel III introduced two liquidity risk requirements: the liquidity coverage ratio (LCR) and the net stable funding ratio (NSFR).

The LCR requirement is

$$\frac{\text{High quality liquid assets}}{\text{Net cash outflows in a 30-day period}} \geq 100\%$$

The 30-day period considered in the calculation of LCR is one of acute stress involving a downgrade of three notches (e.g., from AA+ to A+), a partial loss of deposits, a complete loss of wholesale funding, increased haircuts on secured funding, and drawdowns on lines of credit. This requirement is scheduled to be implemented on January 1, 2015.

The NSFR requirement is

$$\frac{\text{Amount of stable funding}}{\text{Required amount of stable funding}} \geq 100\%$$

The numerator is calculated by multiplying each category of funding (capital, wholesale deposits, retail deposits, etc.) by an available stable funding (ASF) factor, reflecting their stability (see Table 13.4). The denominator is calculated from the assets and off-balance-sheet items requiring funding. Each category of these is multiplied by a required stable funding (RSF) factor to reflect the permanence of the funding (see Table 13.5). This requirement is scheduled to be implemented on January 1, 2018.

Following the liquidity crisis of 2007, bank regulators issued a revised set of principles on how banks should manage liquidity.[4] These are as follows:

1. A bank is responsible for the sound management of liquidity risk. A bank should establish a robust liquidity risk management framework that ensures it maintains sufficient liquidity, including a cushion of unencumbered, high quality liquid assets, to withstand a range of stress events, including those involving the loss or impairment of both unsecured and secured funding sources. Supervisors should assess the adequacy of both a bank's liquidity risk management framework and its liquidity position and should take prompt action if a bank is deficient in either area in order to protect depositors and to limit potential damage to the financial system.

2. A bank should clearly articulate a liquidity risk tolerance that is appropriate for its business strategy and its role in the financial system.

3. Senior management should develop a strategy, policies, and practices to manage liquidity risk in accordance with the risk tolerance and to ensure that the bank maintains sufficient liquidity. Senior management should continuously review information on the bank's liquidity developments and report to the board of directors on a regular basis. A bank's board of directors should review and approve the strategy, policies, and practices related to the management of liquidity at least annually and ensure that senior management manages liquidity risk effectively.

---

[4] See Bank for International Settlements, "Principles for Sound Liquidity Risk Management and Supervision," September 2008.

4. A bank should incorporate liquidity costs, benefits, and risks in the internal pricing, performance measurement, and new product approval process for all significant business activities (both on- and off-balance-sheet), thereby aligning the risk-taking incentives of individual business lines with the liquidity risk exposures their activities create for the bank as a whole.

5. A bank should have a sound process for identifying, measuring, monitoring, and controlling liquidity risk. This process should include a robust framework for comprehensively projecting cash flows arising from assets, liabilities, and off-balance-sheet items over an appropriate set of time horizons.

6. A bank should actively monitor and control liquidity risk exposures and funding needs within and across legal entities, business lines, and currencies, taking into account legal, regulatory, and operational limitations to the transferability of liquidity.

7. A bank should establish a funding strategy that provides effective diversification in the sources and tenor of funding. It should maintain an ongoing presence in its chosen funding markets and strong relationships with funds providers to promote effective diversification of funding sources. A bank should regularly gauge its capacity to raise funds quickly from each source. It should identify the main factors that affect its ability to raise funds and monitor those factors closely to ensure that estimates of fund-raising capacity remain valid.

8. A bank should actively manage its intraday liquidity positions and risks to meet payment and settlement obligations on a timely basis under both normal and stressed conditions and thus contribute to the smooth functioning of payment and settlement systems.

9. A bank should actively manage its collateral positions, differentiating between encumbered and unencumbered assets. A bank should monitor the legal entity and physical location where collateral is held and how it may be mobilized in a timely manner.

10. A bank should conduct stress tests on a regular basis for a variety of short-term and protracted institution-specific and market-wide stress scenarios (individually and in combination) to identify sources of potential liquidity strain and to ensure that current exposures remain in accordance with a bank's established liquidity risk tolerance. A bank should use stress test outcomes to adjust its liquidity risk management strategies, policies, and positions and to develop effective contingency plans.

11. A bank should have a formal contingency funding plan (CFP) that clearly sets out the strategies for addressing liquidity shortfalls in emergency situations. A CFP should outline policies to manage a range of stress environments, establish clear lines of responsibility, include clear invocation and escalation procedures, and be regularly tested and updated to ensure that it is operationally robust.

12. A bank should maintain a cushion of unencumbered, high quality liquid assets to be held as insurance against a range of liquidity stress scenarios, including those that involve the loss or impairment of unsecured and typically available secured funding sources. There should be no legal, regulatory, or operational impediment to using these assets to obtain funding.

13. A bank should publicly disclose information on a regular basis that enables market participants to make an informed judgement about the soundness of its liquidity risk management framework and liquidity position.

    Recommendations for banks supervisors are:
14. Supervisors should regularly perform a comprehensive assessment of a bank's overall liquidity risk management framework and liquidity position to determine whether they deliver an adequate level of resilience to liquidity stress given the bank's role in the financial system.
15. Supervisors should supplement their regular assessments of a bank's liquidity risk management framework and liquidity position by monitoring a combination of internal reports, prudential reports, and market information.
16. Supervisors should intervene to require effective and timely remedial action by a bank to address deficiencies in its liquidity risk management processes or liquidity position.
17. Supervisors should communicate with other supervisors and public authorities, such as central banks, both within and across national borders, to facilitate effective cooperation regarding the supervision and oversight of liquidity risk management. Communication should occur regularly during normal times, with the nature and frequency of the information sharing increasing as appropriate during times of stress.

21.3 LIQUIDITY BLACK HOLES

It is sometimes argued that technological and other developments have led to an improvement in the liquidity of financial markets. This is questionable. It is true that bid–offer spreads have on average declined. But there has also been an increasing tendency for situations to develop where almost everyone wants to do the same type of trade at the same time. The result has been that what are referred to as "liquidity black holes" occur with increasing frequency.[5] A liquidity black hole is a situation where liquidity has dried up in a particular market because everyone wants to sell and no one wants to buy, or vice versa. It is sometimes also referred to as a "crowded exit."[6]

In a well-functioning market, the market may change its opinion about the price of an asset because of new information. However, the price does not overreact. If a price decrease is too great, traders will quickly move in and buy the asset and a new equilibrium price will be established. A liquidity black hole is created when a price decline causes more market participants to want to sell, driving prices well below where they will eventually settle. During the sell-off, liquidity dries up and the asset can be sold only at a fire-sale price.[7]

---

[5] See A. D. Persaud, ed., *Liquidity Black Holes: Understanding, Quantifying and Managing Financial Liquidity Risk* (London: Risk Books, 1999).
[6] See for example J. Clunie, *Predatory Trading and Crowded Exits: New Thinking on Market Volatility* (Petersfield, UK: Harriman House, 2010).
[7] Liquidity black holes tend to be associated with price decreases, but it is in theory also possible for them to occur when there are price increases.

Positive and Negative Feedback Traders

Changes in the liquidity of financial markets are driven by the behavior of traders. There are two sorts of traders in the market: negative feedback traders and positive feedback traders.[8] Negative feedback traders buy when prices fall and sell when prices rise; positive feedback traders sell when prices fall and buy when prices rise.

In liquid markets, negative feedback traders dominate the trading. If the price of an asset gets unreasonably low, traders will move in and buy. This creates demand for the asset that restores the price to a more reasonable level. Similarly, if the price of an asset gets unreasonably high, traders will sell. This creates supply of the asset that also restores the price to a more reasonable level. The result is that the market is liquid with reasonable prices and a good balance of buyers and sellers.

When positive feedback traders dominate the trading, market prices are liable to be unstable and the market may become one-sided and illiquid. A reduction in the price of an asset causes traders to sell. This results in prices falling further, which leads to more selling. An increase in the price of an asset causes traders to buy. This results in the price of the asset increasing further and more buying.

There are a number of reasons why positive feedback trading exists. For example:

1. *Stop-loss rules.* Traders often have rules to limit their losses. When the price of an asset that is owned falls below a certain level, they automatically sell to limit their losses. These rules are known as "stop-loss" rules and are a source of positive feedback trading that is always present in the market.
2. *Dynamic hedging.* Chapter 7 explains how options traders maintain a delta-neutral position using dynamic hedging. In particular, Tables 7.2 and 7.3 show how a trader would hedge a short position in an option over a 20-week period. Hedging a short option position (call or put) involves buying after a price rise and selling after a price decline. This is positive feedback trading that has the potential to reduce liquidity. (By contrast, dynamically hedging a long position in a call or put option involves selling after a price rise and buying after a price decline. This is negative feedback trading and should not interfere with market liquidity.) Any situation where banks have a large short option position has the potential to destabilize the market and cause illiquidity. As discussed in Business Snapshot 3.1, at one point banks sold a huge volume of options on long-term interest rates to British insurance companies. As the banks hedged their risks, the behavior of long-term interest rates in the UK was dramatically affected.
3. *Creating options synthetically.* Hedging a short position in an option is equivalent to creating a long position in the same option synthetically. It follows that a financial institution can create a long option position synthetically by doing the same sort of trading as it would do if it were hedging a short option position. This leads to positive feedback trading that can cause market instability and illiquidity. The classic example here is the stock market crash of October

---

[8] This is a simplification of reality to help understand the dynamics of markets. Some traders follow complicated strategies that cannot be classified as positive feedback or negative feedback.

BUSINESS SNAPSHOT 21.4

The Crash of 1987

On Monday, October 19, 1987, the Dow Jones Industrial Average dropped by more than 20%. Portfolio insurance played a major role in this crash. In October 1987, portfolios involving over $60 billion of equity assets were being managed with trading rules that were designed to synthetically create put options on the portfolios. These trading rules involved selling equities (or selling index futures) when the market declined and buying equity (or buying equity futures) when the market rose.

During the period Wednesday, October 14, 1987, to Friday, October 16, 1987, the market declined by about 10% with much of this decline taking place on Friday afternoon. The portfolio insurance rules should have generated at least $12 billion of equity or index futures sales as a result of this decline. In fact, portfolio insurers had time to sell only $4 billion and they approached the following week with huge amounts of selling already dictated by their models. It is estimated that on Monday, October 19, sell programs by three portfolio insurers accounted for almost 10% of the sales on the New York Stock Exchange, and that portfolio insurance sales amounted to 21.3% of all sales in index futures markets. It is likely that the decline in equity prices was exacerbated by investors other than portfolio insurers selling heavily because they anticipated the actions of portfolio insurers.

Because the market declined so fast and the stock exchange systems were overloaded, many portfolio insurers were unable to execute the trades generated by their models and failed to obtain the protection they required. Needless to say, the popularity of portfolio insurance schemes has declined significantly since 1987. One of the lessons from this story is that it is dangerous to follow a particular trading strategy—even a hedging strategy—when many other market participants are doing the same thing. To quote from the Brady report on the crash, "Liquidity sufficient to absorb the limited selling demands of investors became an illusion of liquidity by massive selling, as everyone showed up on the same side of the market at once. Ironically, it was this illusion of liquidity which led certain similarly motivated investors, such as portfolio insurers, to adopt strategies which call for liquidity far in excess of what the market could supply."

1987. In the period leading up to the crash, the stock market had done very well. Increasing numbers of portfolio managers were using commercially available programs to synthetically create put options on their portfolios. These programs told them to sell part of their portfolio immediately after a price decline and buy it back immediately after a price increase. The result, as indicated in Business Snapshot 21.4, was a liquidity black hole where prices plunged on October 19, 1987. In this case, the liquidity black hole was relatively short-lived. Within four months the market recovered to close to its pre-crash level.

4. *Margins.* A big movement in market variables, particularly for traders who are highly leveraged, may lead to margin calls that cannot be met. This forces traders to close out their positions which reinforces the underlying move in the market variables. It is likely that volatility increases. This may exacerbate the situation because it leads to exchanges increasing their margin requirements.

5. *Predatory trading.* If traders know that a firm is in trouble and must sell large quantities of a certain asset, they know that the price of the asset is likely to decrease. They therefore short the asset. This reinforces the price decline and results in the price falling even further than it would otherwise do. To avoid predatory trading, large positions must usually be unwound slowly.

6. *LTCM.* The failure of the hedge fund, Long-Term Capital Management (LTCM), as outlined in Business Snapshot 19.1 provides an example of positive feedback. One type of LTCM trade was "relative value fixed income." LTCM would take a short position in a liquid bond and a long position in a similar illiquid bond, and wait for the prices to move close together. After the Russian default of 1998, the prices of illiquid instruments declined relative to similar liquid instruments. LTCM (and other companies that were following similar strategies to LTCM) were highly leveraged and unable to meet margin calls. They were forced to close out their positions. This involved buying the liquid bonds and selling the illiquid bonds. This reinforced the flight to quality and made the prices of illiquid and liquid bonds diverge even further.

Leveraging and Deleveraging

A phenomenon in the market is leveraging and deleveraging. This is illustrated in Figures 21.2 and 21.3. When banks are awash with liquidity (e.g., because they have developed ways of securitizing assets or because deposit levels are higher than usual), they make credit easily available to businesses, investors, and consumers. Credit spreads decrease. The easy availability of credit increases demand for both financial and nonfinancial assets and the prices of these assets rise. Assets are often pledged as collateral for the loans that are used to finance them. When the prices

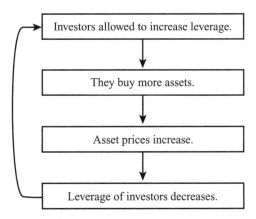

FIGURE 21.2 Leveraging

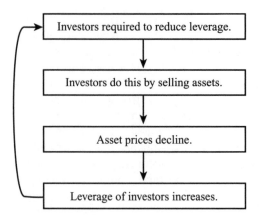

FIGURE 21.3   Deleveraging

of the assets rise, the collateral underlying loans (when measured at market prices) is greater and borrowing can increase further. This leads to further asset purchases and a repeat of the cycle. This cycle is referred to as "leveraging" because it leads to more borrowing throughout the economy.

Deleveraging is the opposite process to leveraging. Banks find themselves less liquid for some reason (e.g., because there is less demand for the products of securitization). They become more reluctant to lend money. Credit spreads increase. There is less demand for both nonfinancial and financial assets and their prices decrease. The value of the collateral supporting loans decreases and banks reduce lines of credit. This leads to asset sales being necessary and a further reduction in asset prices.

The period leading up to 2007 was characterized by leveraging for many of the world's economies. Credit spreads declined and it was relatively easy to borrow money for a wide range of different purposes. From the middle of 2007 onward, the situation changed and the deleveraging process shown in Figure 21.3 started. Credit spreads increased, it became much less easy to borrow money, and asset prices decreased.

Hedge funds are particularly affected by the leveraging–deleveraging cycle. Consider a hedge fund that is able to borrow 20 times its equity during the pre-2007 period. Soon after the middle of 2007, the hedge fund might get a call from its prime broker telling it to reduce leverage to, say, five times equity. It can only do this by selling assets. Asset prices decrease as a result of what the hedge fund, and other hedge funds, are doing. The hedge fund's equity declines and further sales are necessary.

Irrational Exuberance

The term "irrational exuberance" was used by Alan Greenspan, Federal Reserve Board chairman, in a speech in December 1996 when, in reference to the stock market, he said "How do we know when irrational exuberance has unduly escalated asset values?" (The phrase has been remembered because the speech was followed by declines in stock prices worldwide.) Most liquidity black holes can be traced to irrational exuberance of one sort or another. What happens is that traders working for many different financial institutions become irrationally exuberant about a particular asset class or a particular market variable. The balance sheets of financial institutions then become overextended through the accumulation of exposure to this asset class or market variable. Often the process is self-reinforcing. When many financial institutions choose to take a particular position, prices increase, making the position look profitable. This creates extra desire on the part of financial institutions to take the position and yet more profits. Risk managers working for the financial institution should (and probably will) complain about the risks being taken, but in many instances senior management are likely to ignore their concerns because high profits are being made. To quote Chuck Prince, ex-CEO of Citigroup, on July 10, 2007: "When the music stops, in terms of liquidity, things will be complicated. But as long as the music is playing, you've got to get up and dance. We're still dancing."

At some stage the bubble must burst. Many traders then try to get out of their positions at the same time causing illiquid markets and huge losses. Volatility increases and the risk management procedures used within the financial institution (e.g., the calculation of market VaR from historical data) can cause many financial institutions to try to unwind a wide range of risky positions at the same time. This can lead to further losses and more serious illiquidity problems. There may be failures (or rumors of failures) by some banks. Most banks are likely to experience liquidity funding problems and as a result lending may be curtailed.

The classic example of what has been described is the subprime crisis that started in 2007. Other examples are provided by the 1987 stock market crash, the 1994 bond market crash, the 1997–1998 Asian Monetary Crisis, and the 1998 Long-Term Capital Management failure. Irrational exuberance is part of human nature and to some extent is inevitable. As discussed in Chapter 6, it is exacerbated by the way traders are paid. A large part of the compensation comes from a bonus at year-end, which depends on performance during the year. A trader may be savvy enough to know that a market is irrationally exuberant and that there will be a correction. However, if there is a good chance that the correction will be delayed until next year, the trader is motivated to continue building up his or her position to maximize short-term compensation.

The Impact of Regulation

In many ways it is a laudable goal on the part of regulators to seek to ensure that banks throughout the world are regulated in the same way. As explained in Chapter 12, capital requirements and the extent to which they were enforced varied from country to country prior to Basel I. Banks were competing globally and as a result a bank subject to low capital requirements, or capital requirements that were not strictly enforced, found it easier to take risks and was therefore able to be more competitive in the pricing of some products.

However, a uniform regulatory environment comes with costs. All banks tend to respond in the same way to external events. Consider for example market risk. When volatilities and correlations increase, market VaR and the capital required for market risks increase. Banks then take steps to reduce their exposures. Since banks often have similar positions to each other, they try to do similar trades. A liquidity black hole can develop.

There is a similar issue as far as credit risk is concerned. During the low point of the economic cycle, default probabilities are relatively high and capital requirements for loans under the Basel II internal-ratings-based models tend to be high. As a result, banks may be less willing to make loans, creating problems for small and medium-sized businesses. During the high point of the business cycle, default probabilities are relatively low and they may be too willing to grant credit. (This is similar to the phenomenon described in Figures 21.2 and 21.3.) The Basel Committee has recognized this problem and has dealt with it by asserting that the probability of default should be an average of the probability of default through the economic or credit cycle, rather than an estimate applicable to one particular point in time.

Should other financial institutions such as insurance companies, pension funds, and sovereign wealth funds be regulated in the same way as banks? It is tempting to answer "yes" because we do not want to give one financial institution an advantage over others. But the answer should be "no." These financial institutions have longer time horizons than banks. They should not be penalized for investing in illiquid assets. Also, they should not be required to adjust their portfolios when volatilities and correlations increase. These parameters are mean reverting and will eventually decrease again. In Chapter 12 we made the point that Solvency II (the new capital requirements for European insurance companies) has many similarities to Basel II. This may not be appropriate from the perspective of the stability of world financial markets.

The Importance of Diversity

Models in economics usually assume that market participants act independently of each other. We have argued that this is often not the case. It is this lack of independence that causes liquidity black holes. Traders working for financial institutions tend to want to do the same trades at the same time. To solve the problem of liquidity black holes, we need more diversity in financial markets. One way of creating diversity is to recognize that different types of financial institutions have different types of risks and should be regulated differently.

Hedge funds have become important market participants. They are relatively unregulated and can follow any trading strategy they like. To some extent they do add diversity (and therefore liquidity) to the market. But, as mentioned earlier, hedge funds tend to be highly leveraged. When liquidity tightens as it did in the second half of 2007, all hedge funds have to unwind positions accentuating the liquidity problems.

One conclusion from the arguments we have put forward is that a contrarian investment strategy has some merit. If markets overreact, an investor can do quite well by buying when everyone else is selling and there is very little liquidity. However it can be quite difficult for a fund to follow such a strategy if it is subject to short-term VaR-based risk management.

SUMMARY

There are two types of liquidity risk: liquidity trading risk and liquidity funding risk. Liquidity trading risk is concerned with the ease with which positions in the trading book can be unwound. The liquidity trading risk of an asset depends on the nature of the asset, how much of the asset is to be traded, how quickly it is to be traded, and the economic environment. The credit crisis of 2007 emphasizes the importance of transparency. Assets that are not well defined or well understood are unlikely to trade in a liquid market for long. The liquidity of an asset at a particular time can be measured as the dollar bid–offer spread or as the proportional bid–offer spread. The latter is the difference between the bid and offer price divided by the average of the bid and offer price. The cost of unwinding a position in the asset is half of the bid–offer spread. Financial institutions should monitor the cost of unwinding the whole trading book in both normal market conditions and stressed market conditions.

A trader, when faced with the problem of unwinding a large position in an asset, has a trade-off between the bid–offer spread and market risk. Unwinding quickly leads to high bid–offer spreads, but low market risk. Unwinding slowly leads to lower bid–offer spreads, but more market risk. The optimal trading strategy depends on (a) the dollar bid–offer spread as a function of the quantity traded in a day and (b) the probability distribution for daily changes in the asset price. For any particular unwind strategy, the trader can choose a confidence level and calculate the unwind cost that will not be exceeded with the confidence level. The unwind strategy that minimizes this cost can then be determined.

Liquidity funding risk management is concerned with being able to meet cash needs as they arise. It is important for a financial institution to forecast its cash needs in both normal market conditions and stressed market conditions to ensure that they can be met with almost total certainty. Cash needs depend on depositor withdrawals, draw-downs on lines of credit, guarantees that have been made, defaults by counterparties, and so on. Sources of cash are instruments that can be readily converted into cash, borrowings in the wholesale market, asset securitizations, new depositors, cash itself, and (as a last resort) borrowings from a central bank. In June 2008, bank regulators issued a list of 17 principles describing how banks should manage their liquidity and indicated that they would be monitoring the liquidity management procedures of banks more carefully in the future.

The most serious liquidity risks arise from what are sometimes termed liquidity black holes. These occur when all traders want to be on the same side of the market at the same time. This may be because they have similar positions and manage risks in similar ways. It may also be because they become irrationally exuberant, overexposing themselves to particular risks. What is needed is more diversity in the trading strategies followed by market participants. Traders that have long-term objectives should avoid allowing themselves to be influenced by the short-term overreaction of markets.

FURTHER READING

Almgren R., and N. Chriss. "Optimal Execution of Portfolio Transactions." *Journal of Risk* 3 (Winter 2001): 5–39.

Bangia, A., F. Diebold, T. Schuermann, and J. Stroughair. "Liquidity on the Outside." *Risk* 12 (June, 1999): 68–73.

Bank for International Settlements. "Principles for Sound Liquidity Risk Management and Supervision." June 2008.

Bank for International Settlements. "Liquidity Risk Management and Supervisory Challenges." February 2008.

Brunnermeier, M. K., and L. H. Pedersen. "Market Liquidity and Funding Liquidity." *Review of Financial Studies* 22, no. 6 (2009): 2201–2238.

Brunnermeier, M. K., and L. H. Pedersen. "Predatory Trading." *Journal of Finance* 60, no. 4 (2005): 1825–1863.

Clunie, J. *Predatory Trading and Crowded Exits: New Thinking on Market Volatility.* Petersfield, UK: Harriman House, 2010.

Persaud, A. D., ed. *Liquidity Black Holes: Understanding, Quantifying and Managing Financial Liquidity Risk.* London: Risk Books, 1999.

PRACTICE QUESTIONS AND PROBLEMS (ANSWERS AT END OF BOOK)

21.1 What was the transparency problem in the subprime crisis of 2007?

21.2 An asset is quoted bid 50, offer 55. What does this mean? What is the proportional bid–offer spread?

21.3 Suppose that an investor has shorted shares worth $5,000 of Company A and bought shares worth $3,000 of Company B. The proportional bid–offer spread for Company A is 0.01 and the proportional bid–offer spread for Company B is 0.02. What does it cost the investor to unwind the portfolio?

21.4 Suppose that in Problem 21.3 the bid–offer spreads for the two companies are normally distributed. For Company A the bid–offer spread has a mean of 0.01 and a standard deviation of 0.01. For Company B the bid–offer spread has a mean of 0.02 and a standard deviation of 0.03. What is the cost of unwinding that the investor is 95% confident will not be exceeded?

21.5 A trader wishes to unwind a position of 60 million units in an asset over 10 days. The dollar bid–offer spread as a function of daily trading volume q, is $a + be^{cq}$ where $a = 0.2$, $b = 0.1$, and $c = 0.08$ and q is measured in millions. The standard deviation of the price change per day is $0.1. What is the optimal strategy that minimizes the 95% confidence level for the costs?

21.6 Why does a bank need to keep track of the assets it has pledged as collateral as part of its procedures for managing liquidity funding risk?

21.7 Why is it risky to rely on borrowings in the wholesale market for funding?

21.8 What were the nature of the funding risk problems of Ashanti Goldfields and Metallgesellschaft?

21.9 What is meant by (a) positive feedback trading and (b) negative feedback trading? Which is liable to lead to liquidity problems?

21.10 What is meant by liquidity-adjusted VaR?

21.11 Explain how liquidity black holes occur. How can regulation lead to liquidity black holes?

21.12 Why is it beneficial to the liquidity of markets for traders to follow diverse trading strategies?

FURTHER QUESTIONS

21.13 Discuss whether hedge funds are good or bad for the liquidity of markets.

21.14 Suppose that a trader has bought some illiquid shares. In particular, the trader has 100 shares of A, which is bid \$50 and offer \$60, and 200 shares of B, which is bid \$25 offer \$35. What are the proportional bid–offer spreads? What is the impact of the high bid–offer spreads on the amount it would cost the trader to unwind the portfolio? If the bid–offer spreads are normally distributed with mean \$10 and standard deviation \$3, what is the 99% worst-case cost of unwinding in the future as a percentage of the value of the portfolio?

21.15 A trader wishes to unwind a position of 200,000 units in an asset over eight days. The dollar bid–offer spread, as a function of daily trading volume q, is $a + be^{cq}$ where $a = 0.2$, $b = 0.15$, and $c = 0.1$ and q is measured in thousands. The standard deviation of the price change per day is \$1.50. What is the optimal trading strategy for minimizing the 99% confidence level for the costs? What is the average time the trader waits before selling? How does this average time change as the confidence level changes?

CHAPTER 22

Model Risk

Models are approximations to reality. They are necessary for determining the price at which an instrument should be traded. They are also necessary for marking to market a financial institution's position in an instrument once it has been traded.

There are two main types of model risk. One is the risk that the model will give the wrong price at the time a product is bought or sold. This can result in a company buying a product for a price that is too high or selling it for a price that is too low. The other risk concerns hedging. If a company uses the wrong model, the Greek letters it calculates—and the hedges it sets up based on those Greek letters—are liable to be wrong.

The art of building a model for valuing a financial product is to capture the key features of the product without allowing the model to become so complicated that it is difficult to use. This chapter contrasts the way models are used in finance with the way they are used by physicists and other scientists. It discusses how models are used for products that are traded actively and how they are used for customized products for which there are no market prices. It describes different types of model risk and how they can be managed.

22.1 MARKING TO MARKET

We start with a discussion of marking to market. As explained in Sections 2.7 and 12.6, a financial institution is required to mark to market its trading book each day. This means that it has to estimate a value for each financial instrument in its trading portfolio and then calculate the total value of the portfolio. The valuations are used in value-at-risk calculations to determine capital requirements and by accountants to calculate quarterly financial statements. Accountants refer to marking to market as "fair-value accounting."

How is the mark-to-market price of an asset calculated? In practice, a number of different approaches are used. For example:

1. When there are market makers for an asset, or an asset is traded on an exchange, the price of the asset can be based on the most recent quotes. Suppose that a financial instrument has a long position in a particular financial instrument and that a market maker quotes "bid $20, offer $21." (This means that the market maker is prepared to buy at $20 and sell at $21.) In most cases, the financial institution will choose to mark to the mid-market price. This is the average of

the bid price and the offer price, or $20.50 in this case. However, sometimes financial institutions choose to be more conservative and mark a long position to the bid and a short position to the offer.

2. When the financial institution itself has traded the asset in the last day, the price of the asset can be based on the price it paid or received.

3. When interdealer brokers provide information on the prices at which the asset has been traded by other financial institutions in the over-the-counter market, the financial institution can base the price of the asset on this information.

4. When interdealer brokers provide price indications (not the prices of actual trades), the financial institution will (in the absence of anything better) base its prices on this information.

5. For exotic deals and structured products, the price is usually based on a model developed by the financial institution. Using a model instead of a market price for the daily marking to market is sometimes referred to as *marking to model*.

The interdealer brokers being referred to here are intermediaries in the over-the-counter market. Examples are ICAP, Tullett Prebon, and GFI. Instead of approaching other potential counterparties directly to do a trade, a financial institution will often approach an interdealer broker to find a counterparty. (The broker earns a fee for deals it arranges.) One advantage of this is that the identity of the financial institution wanting to do the trade is not disclosed until after the trade has been finalized. Another is that the broker has in many cases more information than the financial institution about who wants to trade what. Brokers collect bid and offer quotes from their clients and relay this price information back to their clients on a regular basis.

When broker quotes are used by a financial institution for marking to market, it is important that the broker be not too closely involved with the financial institution's traders. There have been a few scandals where a trader has managed to conceal losses by persuading a broker to provide favorable quotes to the middle office of a financial institution. The middle office should, whenever possible, try and get quotes from several different brokers.

Financial institutions usually want to be sure that they are pricing deals consistently with the rest of the market. For this reason, they like to periodically obtain a consensus price for a selection of test deals. Markit Group is a company that works in conjunction with large banks to provide consensus pricing. Each month, it presents the banks with a number of over-the-counter deals and asks them to provide quotes. After eliminating outliers, average quotes are calculated and sent back to the banks.

Accounting

The fair-value accounting rules of the Financial Accounting Standards Board in the United States (FAS 157) and the International Accounting Standards Board in Europe (IAS 39) require banks to classify instruments as "held-for-sale" or "held-to-maturity." Those classified as held-to-maturity are in the banking book and their values are not changed unless they become impaired. Those classified as "held-for-sale" are in the trading book and have to be marked to market. Three types of valuations are reported under FAS 157 for instruments that are held-for-sale. Level 1 instruments are those for which there are quoted prices in active markets. Level 2 instruments are those for which there are quoted prices for similar assets in active markets or quoted prices for the same assets in markets that are not active. Level 3 instruments require some valuation assumptions by the bank.

Under the original IAS and FAS proposals, the classification of assets and liabilities could not be changed from held-to-maturity to held-for-sale or vice versa. A financial institution had to decide on how an asset or a liability was to be classified when it was first created. During the credit crisis that started in the summer of 2007, many bankers argued that fair value accounting exacerbated their problems. High market volatility, high credit spreads, and low prices for products created from the securitization of mortgages led to banks having to recognize huge losses on a wide range of instruments that they held. Toward the end of 2008, both the Financial Accounting Standards Board and the International Accounting Standards Board bowed to pressure from bankers and politicians and allowed banks to reclassify "in rare circumstances" some of the instruments in their books from held-for-sale to held-to-maturity. This meant that they did not have to record an immediate loss and equity capital did not decline by as much as it would otherwise have done.

In April 2009, another change was made that allowed financial institutions to use model prices in preference to market prices when they judge that market prices do not represent fair value. This could be because the market prices observed were from distressed sales—but it could be for other less defensible reasons as well. This change was also made in response to pressure from banks and politicians. Many accountants were uncomfortable with these changes. They felt they allowed banks and other financial institutions to use fair value accounting only when it suited them.

The rest of this chapter considers how models are used for marking to market and trading, and looks at the risks that the use of models can entail.

22.2 MODELS FOR LINEAR PRODUCTS

The simplest types of pricing models in finance are the ones used for linear products such as forward contracts and swaps. There is usually very little disagreement in the market on the correct pricing models for these products and the model parameters that are used. The models are accurate and rely on little more than present-value arithmetic. As explained in Section 7.1, hedging linear products is usually straightforward.

However, this does not mean that there is no model risk. Mistakes can be made. As indicated in Business Snapshot 22.1, Kidder Peabody's computer system did not account correctly for funding costs when a linear product was traded. As a result, the system indicated that one of the company's traders was making a large profit when in fact he was taking a huge loss.

Another type of model risk arises when a financial institution makes a faulty assumption in a model. Consider the interest rate swap market. A plain vanilla interest rate swap, such as the one described in Section 5.4, can be valued by assuming that forward interest rates will be realized. This is explained in Appendix D. For example, if the forward interest rate for the period between 2 and 2.5 years is 4.3% per annum, the swap is valued on the assumption that the floating rate that is exchanged for a fixed rate at the 2.5-year point is calculated using this rate. It is tempting to generalize from this and argue that any swap agreement to exchange cash

---

BUSINESS SNAPSHOT 22.1

Kidder Peabody's Embarrassing Mistake

Investment banks have developed a way of creating a zero-coupon bond, called a *strip*, from a coupon-bearing Treasury bond by selling each of the cash flows underlying the coupon-bearing bond as a separate security. Joseph Jett, a trader working for Kidder Peabody, had a relatively simple trading strategy. He would buy strips and sell them in the forward market. The forward price of the strip was always greater than the spot price, and so it appeared that he had found a money-making machine! In fact, the difference between the forward price and the spot price represents nothing more than the cost of funding the purchase of the strip. Suppose for example that the three-month interest rate is 4% per annum and the spot price of a strip is $70. The three-month forward price of the strip is $70e^{0.04 \times 3/12} = \$70.70$.

Kidder Peabody's computer system reported a profit on each of Jett's trades equal to the excess of the forward price over the spot price ($0.70 in our example). By rolling his contracts forward, Jett was able to prevent the funding cost from accruing to him. The result was that the system reported a profit of $100 million on Jett's trading (and Jett received a big bonus) when in fact there was a loss in the region of $350 million. This shows that even large financial institutions can get relatively simple things wrong!

---

flows in the future can be valued on the assumption that forward rates are realized. This is not so. Consider, for example, what is known as a *LIBOR-in-arrears swap*. In this instrument, the floating rate that is observed on a particular date is paid on that date, not one accrual period later as is the case for a plain vanilla swap. A LIBOR-in-arrears swap should be valued on the assumption that the realized interest rate equals the forward interest rate plus a "convexity adjustment." As indicated in Business Snapshot 22.2, financial institutions that did not understand this lost money in the mid-1990s.

22.3 PHYSICS VS. FINANCE

We now move on to consider the models used for nonlinear products. Many individuals who were trained in physics work in the front and middle office of banks and many of the models they use for nonlinear products are similar to those they encountered during their physics training. For example, the differential equation that leads to the famous Black–Scholes-Merton option pricing model is the heat-exchange equation that has been used by physicists for many years. However, as Derman has pointed out, there is an important difference between the models of physics and the models of finance.[1] The models of physics describe physical

---

[1] See E. Derman, *My Life as a Quant: Reflections on Physics and Finance* (Hoboken, NJ: John Wiley & Sons, 2004); and E. Derman, "Model Risk," *Risk* 9, no. 2 (May 1996): 139–145.

BUSINESS SNAPSHOT 22.2

Exploiting the Weaknesses of a Competitor's Model

A LIBOR-in-arrears swap is an interest rate swap where the floating interest rate is paid on the day it is observed, not one accrual period later. Whereas a plain vanilla swap is correctly valued by assuming that future rates will be today's forward rates, a LIBOR-in-arrears swap should be valued on the assumption that the future rate is today's forward interest rate plus a "convexity adjustment."

In the mid-1990s, sophisticated financial institutions understood the correct approach for valuing a LIBOR-in-arrears swap. Less sophisticated financial institutions used the naive "assume forward rates will be realized" approach. The result was that by choosing trades judiciously, sophisticated financial institutions were able to make substantial profits at the expense of their less sophisticated counterparties.

The derivatives business is one where traders do not hesitate to exploit the weaknesses of their competitor's models!

---

processes and are highly accurate. By contrast, the models of finance describe the behavior of market variables. This behavior depends on the actions of human beings. As a result, the models are at best approximate descriptions of the market variables. This is the reason that the use of models in finance entails what is referred to as "model risk."

One important difference between the models of physics and the models of finance concerns model parameters. The parameters of models in physics generally do not change. For example, the gravitational pull on the surface of the earth is always 32 feet per second per second. By contrast, parameters in finance models change daily. The volatility used to price an option might be 20% one day, 22% the next day, and 19% the following day. The parameters used on a day are usually chosen to fit prices observed in the market on that day as closely as possible. The procedure for doing this is known as *calibration*.

The general approach usually used for valuing a financial instrument that is similar to, but not exactly the same as, other financial instruments that trade is illustrated in Figure 22.1. One or more other financial instruments whose prices can be observed in the market are chosen as the "calibrating instruments." These instruments are chosen so that they are as similar as possible to the financial instrument of interest. They are then used to imply model parameters that are appropriate for the instrument being valued.

The approach works particularly well if there is only one unknown model parameter. It is not designed to value a financial instrument in an absolute way. Instead it is designed for relative valuation. The objective is to value the financial instrument consistently with other similar financial instruments whose prices can be observed. The next section illustrates the procedure by showing how it is operationalized for actively traded options.

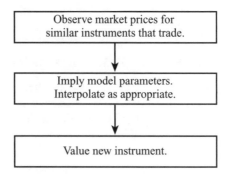

FIGURE 22.1   How Models Are
Usually Used for Valuing a Financial
Instrument

22.4   HOW MODELS ARE USED FOR PRICING STANDARD PRODUCTS

When a financial instrument trades actively, we do not need a model to know what its price is. The market tells us this. Suppose, for example, that a certain option on a stock index trades actively and is quoted by market makers as bid $30, offer $30.50. Our best estimate of its current value is the mid-market price of $30.25.

A situation that is common in the over-the-counter market is one where a financial instrument that has to be valued is a standard product such as an option, but not exactly the same as one that trades in the market. For example, it might be an option with a strike price or time to maturity (or both) different from the options whose prices can be observed. The model is then used as a tool to ensure that the way an instrument is priced is consistent with the observed market prices of other similar instruments. A good example of how this is done is provided by the way the Black–Scholes–Merton model is used in practice. (See Appendix E for a description of the Black-Scholes-Merton model.)

The Black–Scholes–Merton Model

The Black-Scholes-Merton model was published in 1973 and is very widely used in trading rooms throughout the world.[2] The model (and its extensions) relate the price of a European option on an asset to:

1. The price of the asset
2. The strike price
3. The time to option maturity

---

[2] See F. Black and M. Scholes, "The Pricing of Options and Corporate Liabilities," *Journal of Political Economy* 81 (May–June 1973): 637–659; and R. C. Merton, "Theory of Rational Option Pricing," *Bell Journal of Economics and Management Science* 4 (Spring 1973): 141–183.

4. The risk-free interest rate applicable to an investment lasting for the life of the option
5. The asset price volatility
6. The income (if any) expected from the asset during the life of the option

The model is easy to use because most of the inputs are directly observable. The current price of an asset on which an option is written is normally known. The strike price and time to maturity are properties of the option and therefore known. The risk-free interest rates are also known. The income expected from the asset may not be known for certain, but in many instances it can be estimated reasonably accurately. Furthermore, if there are forward contracts trading on the asset, it turns out that the forward price captures everything the model needs to know about the income on the asset.[3] There is only one input that cannot be observed. This is the volatility.

An estimate of volatility can be made from historical data on the price on the underlying asset as described in Chapter 10. If there is no market at all for options on the asset, traders and risk management might base their pricing on such an estimate. But, if there is a market for options on the asset, traders and risk managers follow the practice outlined in Figure 22.1 and calculate the volatilities that match market prices. This does not mean that a trader always agrees with market prices. Traders can (and are paid to) take a view that the market price is too high or too low. But it is important that a financial institution's "official model" for valuing options match the market when market prices are available.

The volatility of an asset that matches an option price is known as the option's *implied volatility*, as explained in Section 10.2. Implied volatilities vary from option to option. We now describe how traders cope with this and choose a volatility for the option being valued.

Volatility Smiles

The variation of implied volatility with strike price for options with a particular maturity on a particular day is known as the *volatility smile*.[4] If the Black–Scholes–Merton model provided an accurate description of the assumptions made by the market, the implied volatility would be the same for all options and the volatility smile would be flat. In fact, this is rarely the case.

The volatility smile used by traders to price foreign currency options has the general form shown in Figure 22.2. The volatility is relatively low for at-the-money options. It becomes progressively higher as an option moves either in-the-money or

---

[3] In practice, the market often uses a variation on the Black–Scholes–Merton model known as Black's model. This was published in 1976. It involves the forward or futures price and the income on the asset is not an input. See F. Black, "The Pricing of Commodity Contracts," *Journal of Financial Economics* 3 (1976): 167–79.

[4] It can be shown that the relationship between strike price and implied volatility should be exactly the same for calls and puts in the case of European options and approximately the same in the case of American options.

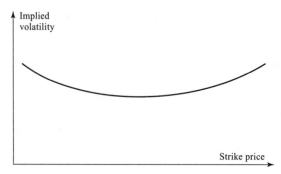

FIGURE 22.2 Volatility Smile for Foreign
Currency Options

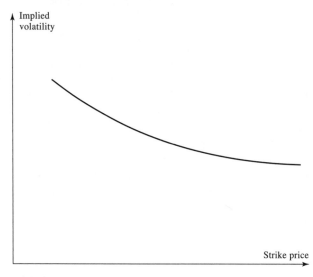

FIGURE 22.3 Volatility Smile for Equity Options

out-of-the-money. The reason for the volatility smile is that Black–Scholes–Merton
assumes

1. The volatility of the asset is constant.
2. The price of the asset changes smoothly with no jumps.

In practice, neither of these conditions is satisfied for an exchange rate. The volatility
of an exchange rate is far from constant, and exchange rates frequently exhibit
jumps.[5] It turns out that the effect of both a nonconstant volatility and jumps is
that extreme outcomes become more likely. This leads to the volatility smile in
Figure 22.2.

   The volatility smile used by traders to price equity options (both those on individual stocks and those on stock indices) has the general form shown in Figure 22.3.

------

[5] Often the jumps are in response to the actions of central banks.

BUSINESS SNAPSHOT 22.3

Crashophobia

It is interesting that the pattern in Figure 22.3 for equities has existed only since the stock market crash of October 1987. Prior to October 1987, implied volatilities were much less dependent on strike price. This has led Mark Rubinstein to suggest that one reason for the equity volatility smile may be "crashophobia." Traders are concerned about the possibility of another crash similar to October 1987 and assign relatively high prices (and therefore relatively high implied volatilities) for deep-out-of-the-money puts.

There is some empirical support for this explanation. Declines in the S&P 500 tend to be accompanied by a steepening of the volatility skew, perhaps because traders become more nervous about the possibility of a crash. When the S&P increases, the skew tends to become less steep.

This is sometimes referred to as a *volatility skew*. The volatility decreases as the strike price increases. The volatility used to price a low-strike-price option (that is, a deep-out-of-the-money put or a deep-in-the-money call) is significantly higher than that used to price a high-strike-price option (that is, a deep-in-the-money put or a deep-out-of-the-money call). One possible explanation for the smile in equity options concerns leverage. As a company's equity declines in value, the company's leverage increases. This means that the equity becomes more risky and its volatility increases. As a company's equity increases in value, leverage decreases. The equity then becomes less risky and its volatility decreases. This argument shows that we can expect the volatility of equity to be a decreasing function of price and is consistent with Figure 22.3. Another explanation is crashophobia (see Business Snapshot 22.3).

Volatility Surfaces

Figures 22.2 and 22.3 are for options with a particular maturity. Traders like to combine the volatility smiles for different maturities into a *volatility surface*. This shows implied volatility as a function of both strike price and time to maturity. Table 22.1 shows a volatility surface for currency options. The table indicates that the volatility smile becomes less pronounced as the time to maturity increases. This is what is usually observed in practice.[6]

---

[6] Some traders choose to define the volatility smile as the relationship between implied volatility and

$$\frac{1}{\sqrt{T}} \ln \frac{K}{F_0}$$

where T is the time to maturity, K is the strike price, and F_0 is the forward price of the asset, rather than as the relationship between the implied volatility and K. The smile is then usually much less dependent on the time to maturity.

TABLE 22.1 Volatility Surface

	Strike Price				
	0.90	0.95	1.00	1.05	1.10
1 month	14.2	13.0	12.0	13.1	14.5
3 month	14.0	13.0	12.0	13.1	14.2
6 month	14.1	13.3	12.5	13.4	14.3
1 year	14.7	14.0	13.5	14.0	14.8
2 year	15.0	14.4	14.0	14.5	15.1
5 year	14.8	14.6	14.4	14.7	15.0

The volatility surface is produced primarily from information provided by brokers in the interdealer market (see Section 22.1). These brokers have more information on the implied volatilities at which transactions are being done on any given day than individual derivatives dealers. Some of the points on a volatility surface such as that in Table 22.1 are calculated from transactions observed by brokers; others are calculated by interpolation between the implied volatilities for observed transactions. Both brokers and option traders develop an understanding of what the volatility surface for a particular underlying asset should look like and how it might change.

When a new option has to be valued, traders look up the appropriate volatility in the table using interpolation. For example, when valuing a nine-month option with a strike price of 1.05, a trader would interpolate between 13.4 and 14.0 in Table 22.1 to obtain a volatility of 13.7%. This is the volatility that would be used in the Black–Scholes–Merton formula. When valuing a 1.5-year option with a strike price of 0.925, a two-dimensional interpolation would be used to give an implied volatility of 14.525%.

Variation through Time

The volatility smiles in Figures 22.2 and 22.3, and the volatility surface in Table 22.1 are at a particular point in time. They are recalculated at least once a day. The volatility smile for an asset tends to retain the same general shape, but the level of the volatility changes through time. The VIX index, which we discussed in Section 10.2, is a measure of the implied volatility of 30-day options on the S&P 500.[7] It can be seen from Figure 10.1 that the index varies from about 10% to about 30% in normal markets and was much higher during the credit crisis that started in 2007.

Why Is Black–Scholes–Merton So Popular?

Many people would argue that any model where the value of a key parameter can easily change by a factor of three (from 10% to 30%) and sometimes by even more is of no use at all. Certainly this would be true for models in physics. But, as explained,

---

[7] For more information on the VIX index, see J. Hull, *Options, Futures, and Other Derivatives*, 8th ed. (Upper Saddle River, NJ: Pearson, 2012) for more information on the VIX index.

models for valuing financial instruments are used in a quite different way from the models of physics. The Black–Scholes–Merton model is popular because

1. It can be used in the way we have described for interpolation in conjunction with a volatility surface and ensures that prices are consistent with observed market prices.
2. It is a communication tool. Traders often prefer quoting implied volatilities to quoting option prices because implied volatilities are more stable than option prices and, as a result, their quotes do not change as frequently. When the price of the underlying asset changes or the interest rate changes, the option price changes but the implied volatility may not.
3. The model is sufficiently simple that a trader can develop intuition about the model and use it to structure his or her thinking about option markets.

But there is nothing unique about the Black–Scholes–Merton model. Another reasonable model, if used in a similar way to Black–Scholes–Merton, would probably lead to similar prices in markets where options trade actively.[8] The fact that the model has only one free (i.e., unobservable) parameter, the volatility, is very appealing to traders because it creates less ambiguity. There is a one-to-one correspondence between an option price and a volatility. If there were two or more free parameters (as there are in some more complicated option pricing models) the model would be less easy to use.

Other Models

Valuing options on assets such as stocks, exchange rates, stock indices, and commodities involves modeling the behavior of a single variable (such as a stock price) and the Black–Scholes–Merton model has become the standard tool. During the 1980s, researchers turned their attention to valuing interest rate derivatives. It turns out that caps, floors, European bond options, and European swap options can be valued with an extension to the Black–Scholes–Merton model and so procedures similar to those we have described can be used to find an appropriate volatility to substitute into the model to value these deals.

Bermudan swap options and other interest rate derivatives are more complicated because they require the behavior of the full term structure of the interest rate to be modeled.[9] Instead of describing the behavior of a single variable, the model has to describe the behavior of the zero-coupon interest rate as a function of maturity (i.e., the term structure of interest rates). Subtle no-arbitrage conditions restrict the assumptions that can be made by the model. Most of the models that have been developed involve more than one parameter. They are designed to match the current

---

[8] This is demonstrated by S. Figlewski, "Assessing the Incremental Value of Option Pricing Theory Relative to an Informationally Passive Benchmark," *Journal of Derivatives* (Fall 2002): 80–96.

[9] A Bermudan swap option is an option to enter into an interest rate swap that can be exercised on two or more payment dates.

term structure of interest rates exactly and the calibration procedure involves finding values for parameters that match observed option prices as closely as possible.

Toward the end of the 1990s, researchers turned their attention to valuing credit derivatives. This involves a challenge different from valuing equity derivatives or interest rate derivatives. The value of a credit derivative depends on whether a particular discrete event (the default of a company) occurs. When the default of only one entity is involved (as is the case with a credit default swap), models are relatively straightforward (see Appendix K). The term structure of the probability of default is estimated from actively traded instruments and this is used to value other deals. When the defaults of several entities are involved (as is the case with a collateralized debt obligation), models are more complicated (see Appendix L). The standard market model is the Gaussian copula model (see Section 11.5). It is used to imply and interpolate between default correlation measures in the same way that Black–Scholes–Merton is used to imply and interpolate between volatilities.

Official vs. Research Models

The models we have been talking about so far are a financial institution's "official models" that are used for valuing trades each day and calculating a trader's profit or loss. It is important that the official model matches the market very closely. A financial institution's external auditors will insist on this. Also, traders could—and probably would—take advantage of situations where the official model deviated from market prices. If the official model gave a price higher (lower) than the market for a product, they could buy (sell) the product in the market to record a profit.

In addition to official models, financial institutions sometimes use research models. These are typically more complicated than the official models and designed to determine trading strategies. When run in parallel with the official models, research models can test whether market prices are too high or too low.

22.5 HEDGING

So far we have focused on the use of models for pricing. Models also have an important role to play in hedging. Traders must manage risks such as delta, gamma, and vega (see Chapter 7). A model is necessary to assess these risks.

We can distinguish between *within-model hedging* and *outside-model hedging*. Within-model hedging is designed to deal with the risk of changes in variables that are assumed to be uncertain by the model. Outside-model hedging deals with the risk of changes in variables that are assumed to be constant (or deterministic) by the model. For the Black–Scholes–Merton model, hedging against movements in the underlying stock price (delta and gamma hedging) is within-model hedging, because the model assumes that stock price changes are uncertain. However, hedging against volatility changes (vega hedging) is outside-model hedging because the model assumes that volatility is constant.

In practice, traders almost invariably do outside-model hedging as well as within-model hedging. This is because, as we have explained, the calibration process results in parameters such as volatilities (which are assumed by a model to be constant) changing daily. A good options trader will monitor the exposure of a trading book to the sorts of shifts in the volatility surface that are typically seen.[10]

A natural assumption is that, if hedging is implemented for all the variables that could change in a day (both those that are assumed to be constant by the model and those that are assumed to be stochastic), the value of the hedger's position will not change. In fact, this is not necessarily the case. If the model used to calculate the hedge is a poor representation of reality, there may be an unexpected gain or loss. The good news here is that, on average, the gain or loss from hedging using the wrong model may be small because there is a good chance that this type of risk is to some extent diversified away across the portfolio of a large financial institution.

Many financial institutions carefully evaluate the effectiveness of their hedging. They find it revealing to decompose the day-to-day change in a portfolio's value into

1. A change resulting from risks that were unhedged
2. A change resulting from the hedging model being imperfect
3. A change resulting from new trades done during the day

This is sometimes referred to as a *P&L decomposition*. If the day-to-day change is unacceptable, the analysis indicates the areas where more effort should be expended.

22.6 MODELS FOR NONSTANDARD PRODUCTS

As we have explained, standard products are valued by observing market prices, implying model parameters, and interpolating as necessary between those parameters. Although the model chosen does have a significant influence on hedging, it does not affect pricing to any great extent.

Nonstandard products are products that are tailored to the needs of specific clients or are not yet sold in sufficient quantity for a standard model to have been established. They are sometimes referred to as exotic products or structured products. Because they do not trade actively, The model used by a financial institution is liable to influence the price it charges a client. Note the important difference between nonstandard products and standard products. A standard product usually trades actively and there is very little uncertainty about its price so that the choice of model primarily affects how hedging is done. In the case of nonstandard products, model risk is much greater because there is the potential for both pricing and hedging being impacted.

A financial institution should not rely on a single model for pricing nonstandard products. Instead it should, whenever possible, use several different models. This leads to a price range for the instrument and a better understanding of the model risks being taken.

---

[10] A principal components analysis, as described in Chapter 8, can be used. If exposure to each of the major principal components is small, the exposure to the shifts that have been observed in practice should also be small.

Suppose that three different models give prices of $6 million, $7.5 million, and $8.5 million for a particular product that a financial institution is planning to sell to a client. Even if the financial institution believes that the first model is the best one and plans to use that model as its standard model for daily repricing and hedging, it should ensure that the price it charges the client is at least $8.5 million. Moreover, it should be conservative about recognizing profits. If the product is sold for $9 million, it is tempting to recognize an immediate profit of $3 million ($9 million less the believed-to-be-accurate price of $6 million). However, this is overly aggressive. A better, more conservative, practice is to put the $3 million into a reserve account and transfer it to profits slowly during the life of the product.[11]

An example of model risk in the pricing of structured products is provided by Business Snapshot 6.1. This makes the point that the assumption that the BBB-rated tranche of an ABS is similar to a BBB bond is not a good one when tranches of an ABS CDO are being priced.

Model Audit Groups

Most large financial institutions have model audit groups as part of their risk management teams. These groups are responsible for vetting new models proposed by traders for particular products. A model cannot usually be used to any significant extent until the model audit group has approved it. Vetting typically includes the following

1. Checking that a model has been correctly implemented
2. Examining whether there is a sound rationale for the model
3. Comparing the model with other models that can accomplish the same task
4. Specifying the limitations of the model
5. Assessing uncertainties in the prices and hedge parameters given by the model

22.7 DANGERS IN MODEL BUILDING

The art of model building is to capture what is important for valuing and hedging an instrument without making the model more complex than it needs to be. Sometimes models have to be quite complex to capture the important features of a product, but this is not always the case.

One danger in model building is *overfitting*. Consider the problem posed by the volatility surface in Table 22.1. We can exactly match the volatility surface with a single model by extending the Black–Scholes–Merton model so that volatility is a complex function of the underlying asset price and time.[12] But, when we do this, we may find that other properties of the model are less reasonable than those of simpler models. In particular, the joint probability distribution of the asset price at two or

---

[11] This is also likely to have sensible implications for the way bonuses are paid.

[12] This is the implied volatility function model proposed by B. Dupire, "Pricing with a Smile," *Risk* 7 (February 1994): 18–20; E. Derman and I. Kani, "Riding on a Smile," *Risk* (February 1994): 32–39; M. Rubinstein, "Implied Binomial Trees," *Journal of Finance* 49, no. 3 (July 1994): 771–818.

more times might be less than ideal and, in some circumstances, future volatility surfaces given by the model might look quite different from those observed in the market today.[13]

Another danger in model building is *overparameterization*. The Black–Scholes–Merton model can be extended to include features such as a stochastic volatility or jumps in the asset price. This invariably introduces extra parameters that have to be estimated. It is usually claimed that the parameters in complex models are more stable than those in simpler models and do not have to be adjusted very much from day to day. This may be true, but we should remember that we are not dealing with physical processes. The parameters in a complex model may remain relatively constant for a period of time and then change, perhaps because there has been what economists refer to as a *regime shift*. A financial institution may find that a more complicated model is an improvement over a simple model until there is a regime change. The more complicated model may not then have the flexibility to cope with changing market conditions.[14]

As we have seen, traders like simple models that have just one unobservable parameter. They are skeptical of more complex models because they are "black boxes" and it is very difficult to develop intuition about them. In some situations, their skepticism is well founded for the reasons we have just mentioned.

22.8 DETECTING MODEL PROBLEMS

The risk management function within a financial institution should carefully monitor the financial institution's trading patterns. In particular, it should keep track of the following

1. The type of trading the financial institution is doing with other financial institutions
2. How competitive it is in bidding for different types of structured transactions
3. The profits being recorded from the trading of different products

Getting too much of a certain type of business, or making huge profits from relatively simple trading strategies, can be a warning sign. If a financial institution finds that its

---

[13] Models that fit the volatility surface at all future times accurately price instruments where there is a payoff at one future time that is dependent only on the asset price at that time. However, it is liable to be less accurate for instruments such as barrier options and compound options that depend on the joint probability distribution of the asset price at two or more times. Hull and Suo find that the implied volatility function model works reasonably well for compound options, but is less accurate for barrier options. See J. C. Hull and W. Suo, "A Methodology for the Assessment of Model Risk and its Application to the Implied Volatility Function Model," *Journal of Financial and Quantitative Analysis* 37, no. 2 (June 2002): 297–318.

[14] The nature of this type of problem in the social sciences is discussed in the famous Lucas Critique, which was propounded by the economist, Robert Lucas, in 1976. See R. Lucas, "Economic Policy Evaluation: A Critique," *Carnegie-Rochester Conference Series on Public Policy* 1 (1976): 19–46.

prices are out of line with the market, it must make adjustments to its mark-to-market procedures to bring them into line.

The high profits being recorded for Joseph Jett's trading at Kidder Peabody (see Business Snapshot 22.1) should have indicated that something was amiss.[15] Likewise, if in the mid-1990s a financial institution's risk management team discovered that traders were entering into a large number of LIBOR-in-arrears swaps with other financial institutions (see Business Snapshot 22.2) where they were receiving fixed and paying floating, they could have alerted modelers to a potential problem and directed that trading in the product be temporarily stopped.

SUMMARY

Since the publication of the Black–Scholes–Merton model in 1973, a huge amount of effort has been devoted to the development of improved models for the behavior of asset prices. It might be thought that it is just a matter of time before the perfect model is produced. Unfortunately, this is not the case. Models in finance are different from those in the physical sciences because they are ultimately models of human behavior. They are always likely to be at best approximations to the way market variables behave. Furthermore, from time to time there are regime shifts where there are fundamental changes in the behavior of market variables.

For products that trade actively, models are used primarily for communicating prices, interpolating between market prices, and hedging. When hedging, traders use both within-model hedging and outside-model hedging. This means that they hedge against movements in variables that the model assumes to be constant (or deterministic) as well as against those movements in variables that are assumed to be stochastic. This type of hedging is imperfect, but hopefully the unhedged risks are largely diversified in a large portfolio.

For products that are highly structured or do not trade actively, models are used for pricing. In this case, choosing the right model is often more of an art than a science. It is a good practice to use several models and assumptions about the underlying parameters in order to obtain a realistic range for pricing and to understand the accompanying model risk.

FURTHER READING

Bates, D. S. "Post '87 Crash Fears in the S&P Futures Market." *Journal of Econometrics* 94 (January/February 2000): 181–238.

Derman, E. "Model Risk." *Risk* 9, no. 5 (May 1996): 139–145.

Derman, E. *My Life as a Quant: Reflections on Physics and Finance.* Hoboken, NJ: John Wiley & Sons, 2004.

Hull, J. C., and W. Suo. "A Methodology for the Assessment of Model Risk and its Application to the Implied Volatility Function Model." *Journal of Financial and Quantitative Analysis* 37, no. 2 (June 2002): 297–318.

---

[15] Barry Finer, risk manager for the government bond desk, did point out the difficulty of making large arbitrage profits from a market as efficient as the U.S. government bond market, but his concerns were dismissed out of hand.

PRACTICE QUESTIONS AND PROBLEMS (ANSWERS AT END OF BOOK)

22.1 Explain what is meant by (a) marking to market and (b) marking to model.

22.2 Give two explanations for the volatility skew observed for options on equities.

22.3 Give two explanations for the volatility smile observed for options on a foreign currency.

22.4 "The Black–Scholes–Merton model is nothing more than a sophisticated interpolation tool." Discuss this viewpoint.

22.5 Using Table 22.1, calculate the volatility a trader would use for an eight-month option with a strike price of 1.04.

22.6 What is the key difference between the models of physics and the models of finance?

22.7 How is a financial institution likely to find that it is using a model different from its competitors for a particular type of derivatives product?

22.8 Distinguish between within-model and outside-model hedging.

22.9 The price of a certain stock is currently $20. Tomorrow, news is expected to be announced that will either increase it by $5 or decrease it by $5. What is the problem in using the Black–Scholes–Merton model to value one-month options on the stock?

22.10 What is meant by "fair-value" accounting? What changes were made to fair-value accounting in 2008 and 2009?

22.11 Suppose that a central bank's policy is to allow an exchange rate to fluctuate between 0.97 and 1.03. What pattern of implied volatilities for options on the exchange rate would you expect to see?

22.12 "For structured products, traders mark to model. They do not mark to market." Explain this remark.

FURTHER QUESTIONS

22.13 Suppose that all options traders decide to switch from the Black–Scholes–Merton model to another model that makes different assumptions about the behavior of asset prices. What effect do you think this would have on (a) the pricing of standard options and (b) the hedging of standard options?

22.14 Using Table 22.1, calculate the volatility a trader would use for an 11-month option with a strike price of 0.98.

22.15 Suppose that a financial institution uses an imprecise model for pricing and hedging a particular type of structured product. Discuss how, if at all, it is likely to realize its mistake.

22.16 A futures price is currently at $40. The risk-free interest rate is 5%. Some news is expected tomorrow that will cause the volatility over the next three months to be either 10% or 30%. There is a 60% chance of the first outcome and a 40% chance of the second outcome. Use the DerivaGem software to calculate a volatility smile for three-month options.

CHAPTER 23

Economic Capital and RAROC

Up to now, we have focused on the development of procedures for evaluating different components of a financial institution's risk (credit risk, market risk, operational risk, liquidity risk, etc.). We now consider how risks can be aggregated and allocated to different business units.

It is important that financial institutions develop a holistic approach to risk management. This involves the specification of a *risk appetite* or level of risk tolerance, the creation of a strong risk management culture throughout the organization, and a sense of risk ownership among senior managers. This process is referred to as *enterprise risk management*. A key aspect of enterprise risk management is the calculation of total economic capital and its allocation to the managers of business units.

Economic capital (sometimes referred to as *risk capital*) is a financial institution's own internal estimate of the capital it needs for the risks it is taking. It is different from regulatory capital, which in the case of banks is based on one-size-fits-all rules determined by the Basel Committee. Economic capital can be regarded as a "currency" for risk-taking within a financial institution. A business unit can take a certain risk only when it is allocated the appropriate economic capital for that risk. The profitability of a business unit is measured relative to the economic capital allocated to the unit.

In this chapter, we discuss the approaches a financial institution uses to arrive at estimates of economic capital for particular risk types and particular business units, and how these estimates are aggregated to produce a single economic capital estimate for the whole financial institution. We also discuss risk-adjusted return on capital, or RAROC. This is the return earned by a business unit on the capital assigned to it. RAROC can be used to assess the past performance of business units. It can also be used to forecast future performance of the units and decide on the most appropriate way of allocating capital in the future. It provides a basis for determining whether some activities should be discontinued and others expanded.

23.1 DEFINITION OF ECONOMIC CAPITAL

Economic capital is usually defined as the amount of capital a financial institution needs in order to absorb losses over one year with a certain confidence level. The confidence level is therefore the probability that the bank will not run out of capital (i.e., become insolvent) in the next year. A common objective for a large international bank is to maintain a AA credit rating. Corporations rated AA have a one-year

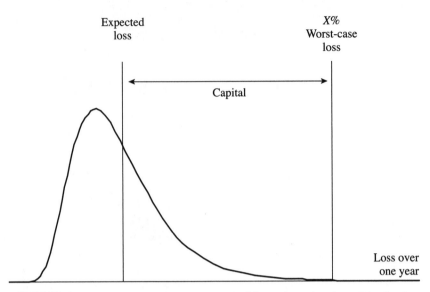

FIGURE 23.1 Calculation of Economic Capital from One-Year Loss Distribution
$X\%$ is the confidence level.

probability of default of about 0.03%. This suggests that the confidence level should
be set as high as 99.97% for economic capital to be a guide as to what is necessary
to maintain a AA rating. For a bank wanting to maintain a BBB credit rating, the
confidence level can be lower. A BBB-rated corporation has a probability of about
0.2% of defaulting in one year, so that a confidence level of 99.98% gives the capital
necessary to maintain a BBB rating.

Capital is required to cover unexpected loss. This is defined as the difference
between the actual loss and the expected loss. As explained in Chapter 12, the
idea here is that expected losses should be taken account of in the way a financial
institution prices its products so that only unexpected losses require capital. As
indicated in Figure 23.1, the economic capital is the difference between expected
losses and the X percentile point on the probability distribution of losses, where
% is the confidence level.

EXAMPLE 23.1

When lending in a certain region of the world, a AA-rated bank estimates its losses
as 1% of outstanding loans per year on average. The 99.9% worst-case loss (i.e.,
the loss exceeded only 0.1% of the time) is estimated as 5% of outstanding loans.
The economic capital required per $100 of loans made is therefore $4. (This is the
difference between the 99.9% worst-case loss and the expected loss.)

Approaches to Measurement

There are two broad approaches to measuring economic capital: the "top-down" and
"bottom-up" approaches. In the top-down approach, the volatility of the financial

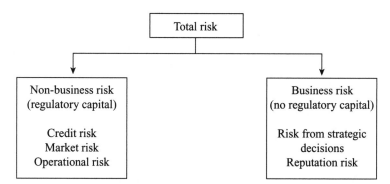

FIGURE 23.2 Categorization of Risks Faced by a Bank and whether Regulatory Capital is Required

institution's assets is estimated and then used to calculate the probability that the value of the assets will fall below the value of the liabilities by the end of the time horizon. A theoretical framework that can be used for the top-down approach is Merton's model which was discussed in Section 16.8.

The approach most often used is the bottom-up approach where loss distributions are estimated for different types of risk and different business units and then aggregated. The first step in the aggregation can be to calculate probability distributions for losses by risk type or losses by business unit. A final aggregation gives a probability distribution of total losses for the whole financial institution.

The various risks facing a bank or other financial institution are summarized in Figure 23.2. As we saw in Chapter 20, bank regulators have chosen to define operational risk as: "The risk of loss resulting from inadequate or failed internal processes, people, and systems or from external events." Operational risk includes model risk and legal risk, but it does not include risk arising from strategic decisions and reputational risk. We will collectively refer to the latter risks as *business risk*. Regulatory capital is not required for business risk, but some banks do assess economic capital for business risk.

23.2 COMPONENTS OF ECONOMIC CAPITAL

In earlier chapters, we covered approaches used to calculate loss distributions for different types of risk. This section reviews some of the key issues.

Market Risk Economic Capital

In Chapters 14 and 15, we discussed the historical simulation and model-building approaches for estimating the probability distribution of losses or gains from market risk. As explained, this distribution is usually calculated in the first instance with a one-day time horizon. Regulatory capital for market risk is calculated as a multiple (at least 3.0) of the 10-day 99% VaR and bank supervisors have indicated that they are comfortable calculating the 10-day 99% VaR as $\sqrt{10}$ times the one-day 99% VaR.

When calculating economic capital, we usually want to use the same time horizon and confidence level for all risks. The time horizon is usually one year and, as already discussed, the confidence level can be as high as 99.97%. The simplest assumptions are (a) that the probability distribution of gains and losses for each day during the next year will be the same as that estimated for the first day and (b) that the distributions are independent. It is then reasonable to assume that the one-year loss or gain distribution is approximately normal. Assuming 252 business days in the year, the standard deviation of the one-year loss or gain equals the standard deviation of the daily loss or gain multiplied by $\sqrt{252}$. The mean loss or gain is much more difficult to estimate than the standard deviation and is usually assumed to be zero. The 99.97% worst-case loss is then 3.43 times the standard deviation of the one-year loss or gain. The 99.8% worst-case loss is 2.88 times the standard deviation of the one-year loss or gain.

EXAMPLE 23.2

Suppose that the one-day standard deviation of market risk losses or gains for a bank is \$5 million. The one-year 99.8% worst-case loss is $2.88 \times \sqrt{252} \times 5 = 228.6$ or \$228.6 million dollars.

Note that we are not assuming that the daily losses or gains are normal. All we are assuming is that they are independent and identically distributed. The central limit theorem of statistics tells us that the sum of many independent identically distributed variables is approximately normal.

Market risk regulatory capital for banks that are assigned the lowest multiplicative factor of 3.0 is

$$3 \times \sqrt{10} \times 99\% \text{ one-day VaR} = 9.49 \times 99\% \text{ one-day VaR}$$

Economic capital when calculated in the way just outlined with a 99.9% confidence level is

$$\sqrt{252} \times 3.09 \times \text{S.D. of Daily Change} = 49.06 \times \text{S.D. of Daily Change}$$

If the daily change in the portfolio value is normal, the 99% one-day VaR is 2.33 times the standard deviation of daily changes and the previous results give the ratio of economic capital to regulatory capital as $49.06/(9.49 \times 2.33) = 2.22$. The non-normality of daily changes is likely to reduce this ratio, but autocorrelation between the daily returns is likely to increase it (see Section 9.6).

Credit Risk Economic Capital

Although Basel II gives banks that use the internal-ratings-based approach for regulatory capital a great deal of freedom, it does not allow them to choose their own credit correlation model and correlation parameters. When calculating economic capital, banks are free to make the assumptions they consider most appropriate for their situation. As explained in Section 18.5, CreditMetrics is often used to calculate the specific risk capital charge and incremental risk charge for credit risk in the trading book. It is also a popular approach for calculating economic capital for the banking book.

Another approach that is sometimes used is Credit Risk Plus, which is described in Section 18.3. This approach borrows a number of ideas from actuarial science to calculate a probability distribution for losses from defaults. Whereas CreditMetrics calculates the loss from downgrades and defaults, Credit Risk Plus calculates losses from defaults only.

In calculating credit risk economic capital, a financial institution can choose to adopt a conditional or unconditional model. In a conditional (cycle-specific) model, the expected and unexpected losses take account of current economic conditions. In an unconditional (cycle-neutral) model, they are calculated by assuming economic conditions that are in some sense an average of those experienced through the cycle. Rating agencies aim to produce ratings that are unconditional. In addition, when regulatory capital is calculated using the internal-ratings-based approach, the PD and LGD estimates should be unconditional. Obviously, it is important to be consistent when economic capital is calculated. If expected losses are conditional, unexpected losses should also be conditional. If expected losses are unconditional, the same should be true of unexpected losses.

Whatever the approach used, a Monte Carlo simulation is usually necessary to calculate the probability distribution of credit losses. Derivatives are difficult to handle because of the uncertainty about the exposure at the time of a default or downgrade.

Operational Risk Economic Capital

Banks are given a great deal of freedom in the assessment of regulatory capital for operational risk under the advanced measurement approach. It is therefore likely that most banks using this approach will calculate operational risk economic capital and operational risk regulatory capital in the same way. As noted in Chapter 20, methods for calculating operational risk capital are still evolving. Some approaches are statistical and some are more subjective.

Business Risk Economic Capital

As mentioned earlier, business risk includes strategic risk (relating to a bank's decision to enter new markets and develop new products) and reputational risk. Business risk is even more difficult to quantify than operational risk and estimates are likely to be largely subjective. However, it is important that senior risk managers within a financial institution have a good understanding of the portfolio of business risks being taken. This enables them to assess the marginal impact on total risk of new strategic initiatives that are being contemplated.

23.3 SHAPES OF THE LOSS DISTRIBUTIONS

The loss probability distributions for market, credit, and operational risk are very different. Rosenberg and Schuermann (2004) used data from a variety of different

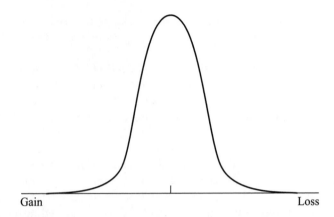

FIGURE 23.3   Loss Probability Density Function for
Market Risk

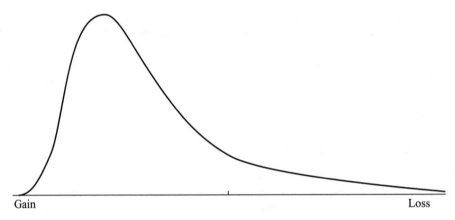

FIGURE 23.4   Loss Probability Density Function for Credit Risk

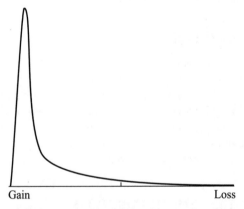

FIGURE 23.5   Loss Probability Density
Function for Operational Risk

TABLE 23.1 Characteristics of Loss Distributions for Different Risk Types

	Second Moment (standard deviation)	Third Moment (skewness)	Fourth Moment (kurtosis)
Market risk	High	Zero	Low
Credit risk	Moderate	Moderate	Moderate
Operational risk	Low	High	High

sources to estimate typical shapes for these distributions.[1] These are shown in Figures 23.3 to 23.5. The market risk loss distribution (see Figure 23.3) is symmetrical but not perfectly normally distributed. A t-distribution with 11 degrees of freedom provides a good fit. The credit risk loss distribution in Figure 23.4 is quite skewed, as one would expect. The operational risk distribution in Figure 23.5 has a quite extreme shape. Most of the time, losses are modest, but occasionally they are very large.

We can characterize a distribution by its second, third, and fourth moments. Loosely speaking, the second moment measures standard deviation (or variance), the third moment measures skewness, and the fourth moment measures kurtosis (i.e., the heaviness of tails). Table 23.1 summarizes the properties of typical loss distributions for market, credit, and operational risk.

23.4 RELATIVE IMPORTANCE OF RISKS

The relative importance of different types of risk depends on the business mix. For a bank whose prime business is taking deposits and making loans, credit risk is of paramount importance. For an investment bank, both credit risk and market risk are important.

For an asset manager, the greatest risk is operational risk. If the asset manager is found to be negligent in some way, there are liable to be expensive investor lawsuits. Business Snapshot 23.1 gives one example of this. Another high profile example is provided by Unilever's pension plan. Mercury Asset Management, owned by Merrill Lynch, pledged not to underperform a benchmark index by more than 3%. Between January 1997 and March 1998, it underperformed the index by 10.5%. Unilever sued Merrill Lynch for $185 million and the matter was settled out of court. The Spanish bank Santander incurred operational risk losses in 2009 on funds it managed for investors and placed with Bernard Madoff, who, it transpired, was running a $50 billion Ponzi scheme.

Interactions between Risks

There are interactions between the different types of risks. For example, when a derivative such as a swap is traded, there are interactions between credit and market risk. If a financial institution's counterparty defaults, credit risk exists only

---

[1] See J. V. Rosenberg, and T. Schuermann, "A General Approach to Integrated Risk Management with Skewed, Fat-Tailed Risks," Federal Reserve Bank of New York, Staff Report no. 185, May 2004.

BUSINESS SNAPSHOT 23.1

The EGT Fund

In 1996, Peter Young was fund manager at Deutsche Morgan Grenfell, a subsidiary of Deutsche Bank. He was responsible for managing a fund called the European Growth Trust (EGT). It had grown to be a very large fund and Young had responsibilities for managing over one billion pounds of investors' money.

Certain rules applied to EGT. One of these was that no more than 10% of the fund could be invested in unlisted securities. Peter Young violated this rule in a way that it can be argued benefited him personally. When the facts were uncovered, he was fired and Deutsche Bank had to compensate investors. The total cost to Deutsche Bank was over 200 million pounds.

---

if market variables have moved so that the value of the derivative to the financial institution is positive. Another interaction is that the probability of default by a counterparty may depend on the value of a financial institution's contract (or contracts) with the counterparty. This is the wrong-way issue discussed in Chapter 17. If the counterparty has entered into the contract for hedging purposes, the dependence should be small. However, if the contract has been entered into for speculative purposes and the contract is large in relation to the size of the counterparty, the dependence is likely to be important.

As the Long-Term Capital Management saga clearly shows, there can be interactions between liquidity risks and market risks (see Business Snapshot 19.1.) There are also interactions between operational risks and market risks. It is unlikely that we would know about the activities of Jérôme Kerviel at Société Générale if he had guessed right about market movements (see Business Snapshot 5.5). Similarly, we are unlikely to hear about a violation of the rules for a fund (such as the one in Business Snapshot 23.1) if the violation leads to a gain rather than a loss.

23.5 AGGREGATING ECONOMIC CAPITAL

A financial institution typically calculates market, credit, operational, and (possibly) business risk loss distributions for a number of different business units. It is then faced with the problem of aggregating the loss distributions to calculate a total economic capital for the whole enterprise.

The simplest approach is to assume that the total economic capital for a set of n different risks is the sum of the economic capital amounts for each risk considered separately, so that

$$E_{\text{total}} = \sum_{i=1}^{n} E_i \tag{23.1}$$

where E_{total} is the total economic capital for the financial institution facing n different risks and E_i is the economic capital for the ith risk considered on its own. This is what the Basel Committee does for regulatory capital. The total regulatory capital a bank is required to keep is the sum of the regulatory capital amounts for credit, market, and operational risks.

Equation (23.1) is clearly a very conservative assumption. It assumes perfect correlation. In the context of economic capital calculations where the confidence level is 99.9%, it would mean that, if a financial institution experiences the 99.9% worst-case loss for market risk, it also experiences the 99.9% worst-case loss for credit risk and operational risk. Rosenberg and Schuermann estimate the correlation between market risk and credit risk to be approximately 50% and the correlation between each of these risks and operational risk to be approximately 20%. They estimate that equation (23.1) when used as a way of aggregating market, credit, and operational risks overstates the total capital required by about 40%.

Assuming Normal Distributions

A simple assumption when aggregating loss distributions is that they are normally distributed. The standard deviation of the total loss from n sources of risk is then

$$\sigma_{\text{total}} = \sqrt{\sum_{i=1}^{n} \sum_{j=1}^{n} \sigma_i \sigma_j \rho_{ij}} \tag{23.2}$$

where σ_i is the standard deviation of the loss from the ith source of risk and ρ_{ij} is the correlation between risk i and risk j. The capital requirement can be calculated from this. For example, the excess of the 99.9% worst-case loss over the expected loss is 3.09 times the number calculated in equation (23.2).

This approach tends to underestimate the capital requirement because it takes no account of the skewness and kurtosis of the loss distributions. Rosenberg and Schuermann estimate that, when the approach is applied to aggregating market, credit, and operational risks, the total capital is underestimated by about 40%.

Using Copulas

A more sophisticated approach to aggregating loss distributions is by using copulas. Copulas were discussed in Chapter 11. Each loss distribution is mapped on a percentile to percentile basis to a standard well-behaved distribution. A correlation structure between the standard distributions is defined and this indirectly defines a correlation structure between the original distributions.

Many different copulas can be defined. In the Gaussian copula, the standard distributions are assumed to be multivariate normal. An alternative is to assume that they are multivariate t. This leads to the probability of two variables both taking extreme values being higher than in the Gaussian copula. This is discussed further in Section 11.4.

The Hybrid Approach

The approach in Section 9.9 for aggregating VaR is also a popular approach for aggregating economic capital estimates. It is sometimes referred to as the *hybrid approach*. It involves calculating the economic capital for a portfolio of risks from the economic capital for the individual risks using

$$E_{\text{total}} = \sqrt{\sum_{i=1}^{n} \sum_{j=1}^{n} E_i E_j \rho_{ij}} \tag{23.3}$$

When the distributions are normal, this approach is exactly correct. When distributions are non-normal, the hybrid approach gives an approximate answer—but one that reflects any heaviness in the tails of the individual loss distributions. Rosenberg and Schuermann find that the answers given by the hybrid approach are reasonably close to those given by copula models.

EXAMPLE 23.3

Suppose that the estimates for economic capital for market, credit, and operational risk for two business units are as shown in Table 23.2. The correlations between the losses are shown in Table 23.3. The correlation between credit risk and market risk within the same business unit is 0.5, and the correlation between operational risk and either credit or market risk within the same business unit is 0.2. (These correspond to the estimates of Rosenberg and Schuermann mentioned earlier.) The correlation between two different risk types in two different business units is zero. The correlation between market risks across business units is 0.4. The correlation between credit risk across business units is 0.6. The correlation between operational risk across business units is zero.

We can aggregate the economic capital using the hybrid approach. The total market risk economic capital is

$$\sqrt{30^2 + 40^2 + 2 \times 0.4 \times 30 \times 40} = 58.8$$

The total credit risk economic capital is

$$\sqrt{70^2 + 80^2 + 2 \times 0.6 \times 70 \times 80} = 134.2$$

TABLE 23.2 Economic Capital Estimates for Example 23.3

	Business Units	
	1	2
Market Risk	30	40
Credit Risk	70	80
Operational Risk	30	90

TABLE 23.3   Correlations between Losses in Example 23.3

	MR-1	CR-1	OR-1	MR-2	CR-2	OR-2
MR-1	1.0	0.5	0.2	0.4	0.0	0.0
CR-1	0.5	1.0	0.2	0.0	0.6	0.0
OR-1	0.2	0.2	1.0	0.0	0.0	0.0
MR-2	0.4	0.0	0.0	1.0	0.5	0.2
CR-2	0.0	0.6	0.0	0.5	1.0	0.2
OR-2	0.0	0.0	0.0	0.2	0.2	1.0

MR, CR, and OR refer to market risk, credit risk, and operational risk; 1 and 2 refer to business units.

The total operational risk economic capital is

$$\sqrt{30^2 + 90^2} = 94.9$$

The total economic capital for business unit 1 is

$$\sqrt{30^2 + 70^2 + 30^2 + 2 \times 0.5 \times 30 \times 70 + 2 \times 0.2 \times 30 \times 30 + 2 \times 0.2 \times 70 \times 30} = 100.0$$

The total economic capital for business unit 2 is

$$\sqrt{40^2 + 80^2 + 90^2 + 2 \times 0.5 \times 40 \times 80 + 2 \times 0.2 \times 40 \times 90 + 2 \times 0.2 \times 80 \times 90} = 153.7$$

The total enterprise-wide economic capital is the square root of

$$30^2 + 40^2 + 70^2 + 80^2 + 30^2 + 90^2 + 2 \times 0.4 \times 30 \times 40 + 2 \times 0.5 \times 30 \times 70$$
$$+ 2 \times 0.2 \times 30 \times 30 + 2 \times 0.5 \times 40 \times 80 + 2 \times 0.2 \times 40 \times 90$$
$$+ 2 \times 0.6 \times 70 \times 80 + 2 \times 0.2 \times 70 \times 30 + 2 \times 0.2 \times 80 \times 90$$

or 203.224.

There are significant diversification benefits. The sum of the economic capital estimates for market, credit, and operational risk is $58.8 + 134.2 + 94.9 = 287.9$ and the sum of the economic capital estimates for two business units is $100 + 153.7 = 253.7$. Both of these are greater than the total economic capital estimate of 203.2.

23.6   ALLOCATION OF ECONOMIC CAPITAL

Suppose that the sum of the economic capital for the business units, $\sum_{i=1}^{n} E_i$, is $2 billion and that the total economic capital for the whole bank, after taking less-than-perfect correlations into account, is $1.3 billion ($= 65\%$ of the sum of the E_is). The $0.7 billion is a diversification gain to the bank. How should the total economic capital be allocated to the business units?

A simple approach is to allocate $0.65 E_i$ to business unit i. However, this is probably not the best approach. Consider a situation where there are 50 business units and that two particular units both have an economic capital of $100 million. Suppose that, when the first business unit is excluded from the calculations, the bank's economic capital decreases by $60 million and that, when the second business unit is excluded from the calculation, the bank's economic capital decreases by $10 million. Arguably, the first business unit should have more economic capital than the second, because its incremental impact on the bank's total economic capital is greater.

The issues here are analogous to those we discussed in Section 9.8 for allocating VaR. One approach is to calculate incremental economic capital for each business unit and then allocate economic capital to business units in proportion to their incremental capital. (Incremental capital is the difference between the total economic capital with and without the business unit.) Another approach is to work with the component economic capital. This involves allocating

$$x_i \frac{\partial E_{\text{total}}}{\partial x_i}$$

to the ith business unit, where x_i is the investment in the ith business unit. As we pointed out in Section 9.8, a result known as Euler's theorem then ensures that the total of the allocated capital is the total economic capital E_{total}.

Define Q_i as the increase in the total economic capital when we increase x_i by a small amount Δx_i. A discrete approximation for the component economic capital for business unit i is

$$\frac{Q_i}{y_i} \tag{23.4}$$

where $y_i = \Delta x_i / x_i$.

EXAMPLE 23.4

Consider again Example 23.3. The total economic capital is 203.2. The economic capital calculated for Business Unit 1 is 100 and that calculated for Business Unit 2 is 153.7.

A simple approach would allocate 100/253.7 of the total economic capital to Business Unit 1 and 153.7/253.7 of the economic capital to Business Unit 2. This would result in 80.1 for Business Unit 1 and 123.1 to Business Unit 2.

The incremental effect of Business Unit 1 on the total economic capital is $203.2 - 153.7 = 49.5$. Similarly, the incremental effect of Business Unit 2 on the total economic capital is $203.2 - 100 = 103.2$. The two incremental capitals do not add up to the total capital (as is usually the case). However, we could use them as a basis for allocating the total capital. We would then allocate $49.5/(49.5 + 103.2)$ of the capital to Business Unit 1 and $103.2/(49.5 + 103.2)$ of it to Business Unit 2. This would result in 65.9 for Business Unit 1 and 137.3 for Business Unit 2.

To apply equation (23.4) and allocate component economic capital to each unit, we could calculate the partial derivative analytically. Alternatively, we can use a numerical calculation. When we increase the size of Business Unit 1 by 1%, its economic capital amounts for market, credit, and operational risk in Table 23.2 increase to 30.3, 70.7, and 30.3, respectively. The total economic capital becomes 203.906 so that $Q_1 = 203.906 - 203.224 = 0.682$.

When we increase the size of Business Unit 2 by 1%, its economic capital amounts for market, credit, and operational risk in Table 23.2 increase to 40.4, 80.8, and 90.9, respectively. The total economic capital becomes 204.577 so that $Q_2 = 204.577 - 203.224 = 1.353$.

In this case, because we are considering 1% increases in the size of each unit, $y_1 = y_2 = 0.01$. From equation (23.4), the economic capital allocations to the two business units are 68.2 and 135.3. (These do not quite add up to the total economic capital of 203.2 because we approximated the partial derivative.)

23.7 DEUTSCHE BANK'S ECONOMIC CAPITAL

Deutsche Bank publishes the results of its economic capital calculations in its annual financial statements. Table 23.4 summarizes the economic capital and regulatory capital reported at the end of 2010. Capital is calculated for credit risk, market risk, operational risk, and business risk. Deutsche Bank calculated a diversification benefit reflecting the lack of perfect correlation between credit, market, and operational risk, but assumed that no diversification benefits were associated with business risk. The total economic capital is about 27.2 billion euros. Table 23.5 shows how this capital was allocated to business units.

The actual capital held is about 30.0 billion euros of core Tier 1 capital (i.e., equity), 12.6 billion euros of additional Tier 1 capital, and about 6.1 billion euros of Tier 2 capital. Table 23.4 shows these capital amounts as a percentage of risk-weighted assets. Deutsche Bank seems to be well capitalized relative to the Basel III regulations, which are explained in Chapter 13. When the capital conservation buffer is included (but not the discretionary countercyclical buffer), a bank is required to have 7% core Tier 1 capital, 8.5% total Tier 1 capital, and 10.5% total Tier 1 and Tier 2 capital. Deutsche Bank has 8.7%, 12.3%, and 14.1%, respectively.

23.8 RAROC

Risk-adjusted performance measurement (RAPM) has become an important part of how business units are assessed. There are many different approaches, but all have

TABLE 23.4 Deutsche Bank's Economic Capital and Regulatory Capital, December 2010 (millions of euros)

Credit risk	12,785
Market risk	13,160
Operational risk	3,682
Diversification benefit across credit, market, and operational risk	(3,534)
Business risk	1,085
Total economic capital	27,178
Total risk-weighted assets	346,204
Core Tier 1 capital (% of risk-weighted assets)	8.7%
Total (core plus additional) capital (% of risk-weighted assets)	12.3%
Total (Tier 1 plus Tier 2) capital (% of risk-weighted assets)	14.1%

TABLE 23.5   Allocation of Deutsche Bank's Economic
Capital, December 2010 (millions of euros)

Corporate banking and securities	14,828
Global transaction banking	1,291
Asset and wealth management	2,717
Private business clients	6,677
Corporate investments	902
Consolidation and adjustments	762
Total	27,178

one thing in common. They compare return with capital employed in a way that incorporates an adjustment for risk.

The most common approach is to compare expected return with economic capital. This is usually referred to as RAROC (risk-adjusted return on capital). The formula is

$$RAROC = \frac{Revenues - Costs - Expected\ losses}{Economic\ capital} \tag{23.5}$$

The numerator may be calculated on a pre-tax or post-tax basis. Sometimes, a risk-free rate of return on the economic capital is calculated and added to the numerator.

EXAMPLE 23.5

When lending in a certain region of the world, a AA-rated bank estimates its losses as 1% of outstanding loans per year on average. The 99.9% worst-case loss (i.e., the loss exceeded only 0.1% of the time) is 5% of outstanding loans. As shown in Example 23.1, the economic capital required per $100 of loans is $4, which is the difference between the 99.9% worst-case loss and the expected loss. (This ignores diversification benefits that would in practice be allocated to the lending unit.) The spread between the cost of funds and the interest charged is 2.5%. Subtracting from this the expected loan loss of 1%, the expected contribution per $100 of loans is $1.50. Assuming that the lending unit's administrative costs total 0.7% of the amount loaned, the expected profit is reduced to $0.80 per $100 in the loan portfolio. RAROC is therefore

$$\frac{0.80}{4} = 20\%$$

An alternative calculation would add the interest on the economic capital to the numerator. Suppose that the risk-free interest rate is 2%. $0.02 \times 4 = 0.08$ is added to the numerator so that RAROC becomes

$$\frac{0.88}{4} = 22\%$$

As pointed out by Matten (2000), it is more accurate to refer to the approach in equation (23.5) as RORAC (return on risk-adjusted capital) rather than RAROC, because it is the capital not the return that reflects risk.[2] In theory, RAROC should involve adjusting the return (i.e., the numerator) for risk. In equation (23.5), it is the capital (i.e., the denominator) that is adjusted for risk.

RAROC can be calculated ex-ante (before the start of the year) or ex-post (after the end of the year). Ex-ante calculations are based on estimates of expected profit. Ex-post calculations are based on actual profit results. Ex-ante calculations are typically used to decide whether a particular business unit should be expanded or contracted. Ex-post calculations are typically used for performance evaluation and bonus calculations.

It is usually not appropriate to base a decision to expand or contract a particular business unit on an ex-post analysis (although there is a natural temptation to do this). It may be that results were bad for the most recent year because credit losses were much larger than average or because there was an unexpectedly large operational risk loss. Key strategic decisions should be based on expected long-term results.

SUMMARY

Economic capital is the capital that a bank or other financial institution deems necessary for the risks it is bearing. When calculating economic capital, a financial institution is free to adopt any approach it likes. It does not have to use the one proposed by regulators. Typically, it estimates economic capital for credit risk, market risk, operational risk, and (possibly) business risk for its business units and then aggregates the estimates to produce an estimate of the economic capital for the whole enterprise. The risks are usually assumed to be less than perfectly correlated. The benefits of diversification are estimated and allocated to business units. Usually the approach used is designed to reflect the contributions of the business units to the total economic capital.

The one-year loss distributions for market risk, credit risk, and operational risk are quite different. The loss distribution for market risk is symmetrical. For credit risk it is skewed, and for operational risk it is highly skewed with very heavy tails.

The total economic capital for a financial institution is allocated to business units so that a return on capital can be calculated. There are a number of possible allocation procedures. The best are those that reflect the incremental impact of the business unit on the total economic capital. The amount of capital allocated to a business unit is generally less than the capital estimated for the business unit as a stand-alone entity because of the diversification benefits.

---

[2] See C. Matten, *Managing Bank Capital: Capital Allocation and Performance Measurement*, 2nd ed. (Chichester, UK: John Wiley & Sons, 2000).

FURTHER READING

Dev, A. *Economic Capital: A Practitioner's Guide*. London: Risk Books, September 2004.

Matten, C. *Managing Bank Capital: Capital Allocation and Performance Measurement*, 2nd ed. Chichester, UK: John Wiley & Sons, 2000.

Rosenberg, J. V., and T. Schuermann. "A General Approach to Integrated Risk Management with Skewed, Fat-Tailed Risks." Federal Reserve Bank of New York, Staff Report no. 185, May 2004.

PRACTICE QUESTIONS AND PROBLEMS (ANSWERS AT END OF BOOK)

23.1 What is the difference between economic capital and regulatory capital?

23.2 What determines the confidence level used by a financial institution in its economic capital calculations?

23.3 What types of risk are included in business risk?

23.4 In what respects are the models used to calculate economic capital for market risk, credit risk, and operational risk likely to be different from those used to calculate regulatory capital?

23.5 Suppose that the credit loss in a year has a lognormal distribution. The logarithm of the loss is normal with mean 0.5 and standard deviation 4. What is the economic capital requirement if a confidence level of 99.97% is used?

23.6 Suppose that the economic capital estimates for two business units are as follows:

	Business Units	
	1	2
Market Risk	20	40
Credit Risk	40	30
Operational Risk	70	10

The correlations are as in Table 23.3. Calculate the total economic capital for each business unit and the two business units together.

23.7 In Problem 23.6, what is the incremental effect of each business unit on the total economic capital? Use this to allocate economic capital to business units. What is the impact on the economic capital of each business unit increasing by 0.5%? Show that your results are consistent with Euler's theorem.

23.8 A bank is considering expanding its asset management operations. The main risk is operational risk. It estimates the expected operational risk loss from the new venture in one year to be $2 million and the 99.9% worst-case loss (arising from a large investor law suit) to be $40 million. The expected fees it will receive from investors for the funds under administration are $12 million per year and administrative costs are expected to be $3 million per year. Estimate the before-tax RAROC.

23.9 RAROC can be used in two different ways. What are they?

FURTHER QUESTIONS

23.10 Suppose that daily gains (losses) are normally distributed with a standard deviation of $5 million.

(a) Estimate the minimum regulatory capital the bank is required to hold. (Assume a multiplicative factor of 4.0.)

(b) Estimate the economic capital using a one-year time horizon and a 99.9% confidence level assuming that there is a correlation of 0.05 between gains (losses) on successive days.

23.11 Suppose that the economic capital estimates for two business units are

	Business Units	
	1	2
Market Risk	10	50
Credit Risk	30	30
Operational Risk	50	10

The correlation between market risk and credit risk in the same business unit is 0.3. The correlation between credit risk in one business unit and credit risk in another is 0.7. The correlation between market risk in one business unit and market risk in the other is 0.2. All other correlations are zero. Calculate the total economic capital. How much should be allocated to each business unit?

23.12 Suppose that a bank's sole business is to lend in two regions of the world. The lending in each region has the same characteristics as in Example 23.5 of Section 23.8. Lending to Region A is three times as great as lending to Region B. The correlation between loan losses in the two regions is 0.4. Estimate the total RAROC.

CHAPTER 24

Risk Management Mistakes to Avoid

Since the mid-1980s, there have been some spectacular losses in financial markets. This chapter explores the lessons we can learn from them and reviews key points made in earlier chapters. The losses that we will consider are listed in Business Snapshot 24.1.

One remarkable aspect of the list in Business Snapshot 24.1 is the number of times huge losses were caused by the activities of a single person. In 1995, Nick Leeson's trading brought a 200-year-old British bank, Barings, to its knees; in 1994, Robert Citron's trading led to Orange County, a municipality in California, losing about $2 billion. Joseph Jett's trading for Kidder Peabody caused losses of $350 million. John Rusnak's losses of $700 million at Allied Irish Bank came to light in 2002. Jérôme Kerviel lost over $7 billion for Société Générale in 2008. Kweku Adoboli lost $2.3 billion for UBS in 2011.

A key lesson from the losses is the importance of internal controls. Many of the losses we will consider occurred because systems were inadequate so that the risky positions being taken were simply not known. It is also important for risk managers to continually "think outside the box" about what could go wrong so that as many potential adverse events as possible are identified.

24.1 RISK LIMITS

The first and most important lesson from the losses concerns risk limits. It is essential that all companies (financial and nonfinancial) define in a clear and unambiguous way limits to the financial risks that can be taken. They should then set up procedures for ensuring that the limits are adhered to. Ideally, overall risk limits should be set at board level. These should then be converted to limits applicable to the individuals responsible for managing particular risks. Daily reports should indicate the gain or loss that will be experienced for particular movements in market variables. These should be checked against the actual gains and losses that are experienced to ensure that the valuation procedures underlying the reports are accurate.

It is particularly important that companies monitor risks carefully when derivatives are used. This is because derivatives can be used for hedging or speculation or arbitrage. Without close monitoring, it is impossible to know whether a derivatives trader has switched from being a hedger to a speculator or switched from being an

BUSINESS SNAPSHOT 24.1

Big Losses

Allied Irish Bank: This bank lost about $700 million from the unauthorized speculative activities of one of its foreign exchange traders, John Rusnak, which lasted a number of years. Rusnak covered up his losses by creating fictitious options trades.

Barings: This 200-year old British bank was wiped out in 1995 by the activities of one trader, Nick Leeson, in Singapore. The trader's mandate was to arbitrage between Nikkei 225 futures quotes in Singapore and Osaka. Instead he made big bets on the future direction of the Nikkei 225 using futures and options. The total loss was close to $1 billion.

Enron's Counterparties: Enron managed to conceal its true situation from its shareholders with some creative contracts. Several financial institutions that allegedly helped Enron do this have each had to settle shareholder lawsuits for over $1 billion.

Hammersmith and Fulham (see Business Snapshot 20.1): This British Local Authority lost about $600 million on sterling interest rate swaps and options in 1988. The two traders responsible for the loss knew surprisingly little about the products they were trading.

Kidder Peabody (see Business Snapshot 22.1): The activities of a single trader, Joseph Jett, led to this New York investment dealer losing $350 million trading U.S. government securities. The loss arose because of a mistake in the way the company's computer system calculated profits.

Long-Term Capital Management (see Business Snapshot 19.1): This hedge fund lost about $4 billion in 1998 carrying out convergence arbitrage strategies. The loss was caused by a flight to quality after Russia defaulted on its debt.

National Westminster Bank: This British bank lost about $130 million from using an inappropriate model to value swap options in 1997.

Orange County (see Appendix B): The activities of the treasurer, Robert Citron, led to this California municipality losing about $2 billion in 1994. The treasurer was using derivatives to speculate that interest rates would not rise.

Procter & Gamble (see Business Snapshot 5.4): The treasury department of this large U.S. company lost about $90 million in 1994 trading highly exotic interest rate derivatives contracts with Bankers Trust. It later sued Bankers Trust and settled out of court.

Société Générale (see Business Snapshot 5.5): Jérôme Kerviel, an equity trader in the Paris office, lost over $7 billion speculating on movements in equity indices in January 2008. He is alleged to have concealed his exposure by creating fictitious trades. Like Leeson at Barings, his mandate was to do arbitrage trades.

Subprime Mortgage Losses (see Chapter 6): In 2007, investors lost confidence in the structured products created from U.S. subprime mortgages. This led to a "credit crunch" with losses of tens of billions of dollars by financial institutions and the worst recession since the 1930s.

UBS: In 2011, Kweku Adoboli lost $2.3 billion taking unauthorized speculative positions in stock market indices.

arbitrageur to being a speculator. The Barings, Société Générale, and UBS losses are classic examples of what can go wrong. In each case, the trader's mandate was to carry out low-risk arbitrage and hedging. Unknown to their superiors, they switched from being arbitrageurs and hedgers to taking huge bets on the future direction of market variables. The systems within the banks were inadequate and did not detect what was going on.

The argument here is not that no risks should be taken. A trader in a financial institution or a fund manager should be allowed to take positions on the future direction of relevant market variables. What we are arguing is that the sizes of the positions that can be taken should be limited and the systems in place should accurately report the risks being taken.

A Difficult Situation

What happens if an individual exceeds risk limits and makes a profit? This is a tricky issue for senior management. It is tempting to ignore violations of risk limits when profits result. However, this is shortsighted. It leads to a culture where risk limits are not taken seriously, and it paves the way for a disaster. The classic example here is Orange County. Robert Citron's activities in 1991–1993 had been very profitable for Orange County, and the municipality had come to rely on his trading for additional funding. People chose to ignore the risks he was taking because he had produced profits. Unfortunately, the losses made in 1994 far exceeded the profits from previous years.

The penalties for exceeding risk limits should be just as great when profits result as when losses result. Otherwise, traders who make losses are liable to keep increasing their bets in the hope that eventually a profit will result and all will be forgiven.

Do Not Assume You Can Outguess the Market

Some traders are quite possibly better than others. But no trader gets it right all the time. A trader who correctly predicts the direction in which market variables will move 60% of the time is doing well. If a trader has an outstanding track record (as Robert Citron did in the early 1990s), it is likely to be a result of luck rather than superior trading skill. As our discussion of mutual fund performance in Chapter 4 shows, it appears that fund managers usually produce superior returns as a result of luck rather than skill.

Suppose that a financial institution employs 16 traders and one of those traders makes profits in every quarter of a year. Should the trader receive a good bonus? Should the trader's risk limits be increased? The answer to the first question is that the trader will inevitably receive a good bonus. The answer to the second question should be no. The chance of making a profit in four consecutive quarters from random trading is 0.5^4 or 1 in 16. This means that just by chance one of the 16 traders will "get it right" every single quarter of the year. We should not assume that the trader's luck will continue and we should not increase the trader's risk limits.

Do Not Underestimate the Benefits of Diversification

When a trader appears good at predicting a particular market variable, there is a tendency to increase the trader's risk limits. We have just argued that this is a bad idea because it is quite likely that the trader has been lucky rather than clever. However, let us suppose that we are really convinced that the trader has special talents. How undiversified should we allow ourselves to become in order to take advantage of the trader's special skills? As indicated in Section 1.1, the benefits from diversification are large. A trader has to be very good for it to be worth foregoing these benefits to speculate heavily on just one market variable.

An example will illustrate the point here. Suppose that there are 20 stocks, each of which has an expected return of 10% per annum and a standard deviation of return of 30%. The correlation between the returns from any two of the stocks is 0.2. By dividing an investment equally among the 20 stocks, an investor has an expected return of 10% per annum and standard deviation of returns of 14.7%. Diversification enables the investor to reduce risks by over half. Another way of expressing this is that diversification enables an investor to double the expected return per unit of risk taken. The investor would have to be very good at stock picking to get a better risk-return trade-off by investing in just one stock.

Carry out Scenario Analyses and Stress Tests

As discussed in Chapter 19, the calculation of risk measures such as VaR should always be accompanied by scenario analyses and stress testing to obtain an understanding of what can go wrong. Without the discipline of stress testing, human beings have an unfortunate tendency to anchor on one or two scenarios when evaluating decisions. In 1993 and 1994, for example, Procter & Gamble was so convinced that interest rates would remain low that it ignored the possibility of a 100-basis-point increase in its decision making.

Once stress-testing results have been produced, they should become inputs to a financial institution's strategic decision making. All too often, particularly when times are good, the results of stress testing are ignored. This happened at a number of financial institutions prior to July 2007.

24.2 MANAGING THE TRADING ROOM

In trading rooms there is a tendency to regard high-performing traders as "untouchable" and to not subject their activities to the same scrutiny as other traders. Apparently Joseph Jett, Kidder Peabody's star trader of Treasury instruments, was often "too busy" to answer questions and discuss his positions with the company's risk managers.

All traders—particularly those making high profits—should be fully accountable. It is important for the financial institution to know whether the high profits are being made by taking unreasonably high risks. It is also important to check that the financial institution's computer systems and pricing models are correct and are not being manipulated in some way.

Separate the Front, Middle, and Back Office

The *front office* in a financial institution consists of the traders who are executing trades, taking positions, and so on. The *middle office* consists of risk managers who are monitoring the risks being taken. The *back office* is where the record keeping and accounting takes place. Some of the worst derivatives disasters have occurred because these functions were not kept separate. Nick Leeson controlled both the front and back office for Barings in Singapore and was, as a result, able to conceal the disastrous nature of his trades from his superiors in London for some time.

Do Not Blindly Trust Models

We discussed model risk in Chapter 22. Some of the large losses experienced by financial institutions arose because of the models and computer systems being used. Kidder Peabody was misled by its own systems. Another example of an incorrect model leading to losses is provided by National Westminster Bank. This bank had an incorrect model for valuing swap options that led to significant losses.

If large profits are reported when relatively simple trading strategies are followed, there is a good chance that the models underlying the calculation of the profits are wrong. Similarly, if a financial institution appears to be particularly competitive on its quotes for a particular type of deal, there is a good chance that it is using a different model from other market participants—which almost certainly means that, before too long, it will have to change its model and report a loss. Getting too much business of a certain type can be just as worrisome to the head of a trading room as getting too little business of that type.

Be Conservative in Recognizing Inception Profits

When a financial institution sells a highly exotic instrument to a nonfinancial corporation, the valuation can be highly dependent on the underlying model. For example, instruments with long-dated embedded interest rate options can be highly dependent on the interest rate model used. In these circumstances, a phrase used to describe the daily marking to market of the deal is *marking to model*. This is because there are no market prices for similar deals that can be used as a benchmark.

Suppose that a financial institution manages to sell an instrument to a client for $10 million more than it is worth—or at least $10 million more than its model says it is worth. The $10 million is known as an *inception profit*. When should it be recognized? There appears to be a lot of variation in what different derivatives dealers do. Some recognize the $10 million immediately, whereas others are much more conservative and recognize it slowly over the life of the deal.

Recognizing inception profits immediately is very dangerous. It encourages traders to use aggressive models, take their bonuses, and leave before the model and the value of the deal come under close scrutiny. It is much better to recognize inception profits slowly, so that traders are motivated to investigate the impact of several different models and several different sets of assumptions before committing themselves to a deal.

Do Not Sell Clients Inappropriate Products

It is tempting to sell corporate clients inappropriate products, particularly when they appear to have an appetite for the underlying risks. But this is shortsighted. A dramatic illustration is provided by the activities of Bankers Trust (BT) in the period leading up to the spring of 1994. Many of BT's clients were persuaded to buy high-risk and totally inappropriate products. A typical product would give the client a good chance of saving a few basis points on its borrowings and a small chance of costing a large amount of money. The products worked well for BT's clients in 1992 and 1993, but blew up in 1994 when interest rates rose sharply. The bad publicity that followed hurt BT greatly. The years it had spent building up trust among corporate clients and developing an enviable reputation for innovation in derivatives were largely lost as a result of the activities of a few overly aggressive salesmen. BT was forced to pay large amounts of money to its clients to settle lawsuits out of court. It was taken over by Deutsche Bank in 1999.

Beware of Easy Profits

Enron provides an example of how overly aggressive deal makers can cost their banks billions of dollars. Doing business with Enron seemed very profitable and banks competed with each other for this business. But the fact that many banks push hard to get a certain type of business should not be taken as an indication that the business will ultimately be profitable. The business that Enron did with banks resulted in many very expensive shareholder lawsuits. In general, transactions where high profits seem easy to achieve should be looked at closely for potential operational, credit, or market risks.

Investing in the AAA-rated tranches of ABSs and ABS CDOs that were created from subprime mortgages (see Chapter 6) seemed like a money-making machine for many banks. The promised returns were higher than the returns normally earned on AAA-rated instruments. Few investors stopped to ask whether this was because there were risks that had not been taken into account.

24.3 LIQUIDITY RISK

We discussed liquidity risk in Chapter 21. Financial engineers usually base the pricing of exotic instruments and other instruments that trade relatively infrequently on the prices of actively traded instruments. For example:

1. A trader often calculates a zero curve from actively traded government bonds (known as on-the-run bonds) and uses it to price bonds that trade less frequently (off-the-run bonds).
2. A trader often implies the volatility of an asset from actively traded options and uses it to price less actively traded options.
3. A trader often implies information about the behavior of interest rates from actively traded interest rate caps and swap options and uses it to price products that are highly structured.

These practices are not unreasonable. However, it is dangerous to assume that less actively traded instruments can always be traded at close to their theoretical prices. When financial markets experience a shock of one sort or another, liquidity black holes may develop (see Section 21.3). Liquidity then becomes very important to investors, and illiquid instruments often sell at a big discount to their theoretical values.

An example of liquidity risk is provided by Long-Term Capital Management (LTCM), which is the subject of Business Snapshot 19.1. This hedge fund followed a strategy known as *convergence arbitrage*. It attempted to identify two securities (or portfolios of securities) that should in theory sell for the same price. If the market price of one security was less than that of the other, it would buy that security and sell the other. The strategy is based on the idea that if two securities have the same theoretical price, their market prices should eventually be the same.

In the summer of 1998, LTCM took a huge loss. This was largely because a default by Russia on its debt caused a flight to quality. LTCM tended to be long illiquid instruments and short the corresponding liquid instruments. (For example, it was long off-the-run bonds and short on-the-run bonds.) The spreads between the prices of illiquid instruments and the corresponding liquid instruments widened sharply after the Russian default. LTCM was highly leveraged. It experienced huge losses and there were margin calls on its positions that it had difficulty meeting.

The LTCM story reinforces the importance of carrying out scenario analyses and stress testing to look at what can happen in extreme scenarios. As discussed in Chapter 19, it is important to consider not only immediate losses but also losses created by knock-on effects.

Beware When Everyone Is Following the Same Trading Strategy

It sometimes happens that many market participants are following essentially the same trading strategy. This creates a dangerous environment where there are liable to be big market moves, liquidity black holes, and large losses for the market participants.

We gave one example of this in Business Snapshot 21.4, which discussed portfolio insurance and the market crash of October 1987. In the months leading up to the crash, increasing numbers of portfolio managers were attempting to insure their portfolios by creating synthetic put options. They bought stocks or stock index futures after a rise in the market and sold them after a fall. This created an unstable market. A relatively small decline in stock prices could lead to a wave of selling by portfolio insurers. The latter would lead to a further decline in the market, which could give rise to another wave of selling, and so on. There is little doubt that, without portfolio insurance, the crash of October 1987 would have been much less severe.

Another example is provided again by LTCM in 1998. Its position was made more difficult by the fact that many other hedge funds were following similar convergence arbitrage strategies. After the Russian default and the flight to quality, LTCM tried to liquidate part of its portfolio to meet margin calls. Unfortunately, other hedge funds were facing similar problems to LTCM and trying to do similar trades. This exacerbated the situation, causing liquidity spreads to be even higher than they would otherwise have been and reinforcing the flight to quality. Consider, for example, LTCM's position in U.S. Treasury bonds. It was long the illiquid off-the-run bonds and short the liquid on-the-run bonds. When a flight to quality caused spreads between yields on the two types of bonds to widen, LTCM had to liquidate its positions by selling off-the-run bonds and buying on-the-run bonds. Other large hedge funds were doing the same. As a result, the price of on-the-run bonds rose relative to off-the-run bonds and the spread between the two yields widened even more.

A further example is provided by British insurance companies in the late 1990s. This is discussed in Business Snapshot 3.1. All insurance companies decided to hedge their exposure to a fall in long-term rates at about the same time. The result was a fall in long-term rates!

The key lesson to be learned from these stories is that it is important to see the big picture of what is going on in financial markets and to understand the risks inherent in situations where many market participants are likely to follow the same trading strategy.

Do Not Make Excessive Use of Short-Term Funding for Long-Term Needs

All financial institutions finance long-term needs with short-term sources of funds to some extent. But a financial institution that relies too heavily on short-term funds is likely to expose itself to unacceptable liquidity risks.

During the period leading up to the credit crisis of 2007, there was a tendency for subprime mortgages and other long-term assets to be financed by commercial paper while they were in a portfolio waiting to be packaged into structured products. Conduits and special purpose vehicles had an ongoing requirement for this type of financing. The commercial paper would typically be rolled over every month. For example, the purchasers of commercial paper issued on April 1 would be redeemed with the proceeds of a new commercial paper issue on May 1; this new commercial paper issue would in turn be redeemed with another new commercial paper issue on June 1; and so on. When investors lost confidence in subprime mortgages in August 2007, it became impossible to roll over commercial paper. In many instances, banks had provided guarantees and had to provide financing. This led to a shortage of liquidity. As a result, the credit crisis was more severe than it would have been if longer-term financing had been arranged.

Many of the failures of financial institutions during the crisis (e.g., Lehman Brothers and Northern Rock) were caused by excessive reliance on short-term funding. Once the market (rightly or wrongly) became concerned about the health of a financial institution, it became impossible to roll over the financial institution's short-term funding. In light of this, it is not surprising that the Basel Committee has introduced liquidity requirements for banks.

Market Transparency is Important

One of the lessons from the credit crisis of 2007 is that market transparency is important. During the period leading up to 2007, investors had been trading highly structured products without any real knowledge of the underlying assets. All they knew was the credit rating of the security being traded. With hindsight, we can say that investors should have demanded more information about the underlying assets and should have more carefully assessed the risks they were taking.

The subprime meltdown of August 2007 caused investors to lose confidence in all structured products and withdraw from that market. This led to a market breakdown where tranches of structured products could only be sold at prices well below their theoretical values. There was a flight to quality and credit spreads increased. If there had been market transparency, so that investors understood the asset-backed securities they were buying, there would still have been subprime losses, but the flight to quality and disruptions to the market would have been less pronounced.

24.4 LESSONS FOR NONFINANCIAL CORPORATIONS

Here are some lessons applicable primarily to nonfinancial corporations.

Make Sure You Fully Understand the Trades You Are Doing

Corporations should never undertake a trade or a trading strategy that they do not fully understand. This is a somewhat obvious point, but it is surprising how often a trader working for a nonfinancial corporation will, after a big loss, admit to not really understanding what was going on and claim to have been misled by investment bankers. Robert Citron, the treasurer of Orange County did this. So did the traders working for Hammersmith and Fulham, who in spite of their huge positions were surprisingly uninformed about how the swaps and other interest rate derivatives they traded really worked.

If a senior manager in a corporation does not understand a trade proposed by a subordinate, the trade should not be approved. A simple rule of thumb is that if a trade and the rationale for entering into it are so complicated that they cannot be understood by the manager, it is almost certainly inappropriate for the corporation. The trades undertaken by Procter & Gamble would have been vetoed under this criterion.

One way of ensuring that you fully understand a financial instrument is to value it. If a corporation does not have the in-house capability to value an instrument, it should not trade it. In practice, corporations often rely on their investment bankers for valuation advice. This is dangerous, as Procter & Gamble found out. When it wanted to unwind its transactions, it found it was facing prices produced by Bankers Trust's proprietary models, which it had no way of checking.

Make Sure a Hedger Does Not Become a Speculator

One of the unfortunate facts of life is that hedging is relatively dull, whereas speculation is exciting. When a company hires a trader to manage foreign-exchange risk, commodity price risk, or interest rate risk, there is a danger that the following happens. At first the trader does the job diligently and earns the confidence of top management. He or she assesses the company's exposures and hedges them. As time goes by, the trader becomes convinced that he or she can outguess the market. Slowly the trader becomes a speculator. At first things go well, but then a loss is made. To recover the loss, the trader doubles up the bets. Further losses are made, and so on. The result is likely to be a disaster.

As mentioned earlier, clear limits to the risks that can be taken should be set by senior management. Controls should be put in place to ensure that the limits are obeyed. The trading strategy for a corporation should start with an analysis of the risks facing the corporation in foreign exchange, interest rate, and other markets. A decision should then be taken on how the risks are to be reduced to acceptable levels. It is a clear sign that something is wrong within a corporation if the trading strategy is not derived in a very direct way from the company's exposures.

Be Cautious about Making the Treasury Department a Profit Center

In the last 20 years, there has been a tendency to make the treasury department within a corporation a profit center. This seems to have much to recommend it. The treasurer is motivated to reduce financing costs and manage risks as profitably as possible. The problem is that the potential for the treasurer to make profits is limited. When raising funds and investing surplus cash, the treasurer is facing an efficient market. The treasurer can usually improve the bottom line only by taking additional risks. The company's hedging program gives the treasurer some scope for making shrewd decisions that increase profits. But it should be remembered that the goal of a hedging program is to reduce risks, not to increase expected profits. The decision to hedge will lead to a worse outcome than the decision not to hedge roughly 50% of the time. The danger of making the treasury department a profit center is that the treasurer is motivated to become a speculator. An Orange County or Procter & Gamble type of outcome is then liable to occur.

24.5 A FINAL POINT

Most of the risks we have considered in this book are what are termed *known risks*. They are risks such as market risks and credit risks that can be quantified using historical data. Two other types of risk are important to financial institutions: *unknown risks* and *unknowable risks*.

Unknown risks are risks where the event that could cause a loss is known, but its probability of occurrence cannot easily be determined. Operational risk includes many different types of unknown risks. What is the probability of a rogue trader loss? What is the probability of a loss from a major lawsuit? What is the probability that operations in an emerging economy will be expropriated? These probabilities cannot usually be estimated using historical data. As discussed in Chapter 19, subjective probabilities are often used. In a widely referenced book, Knight (1921) uses the term "risk" to refer to known risks and the term "uncertainty" to refer to unknown risks.[1]

Unknowable risks are risks where even the event that could cause a loss is not known. Unknowable risks are in many ways the most insidious because they come as a complete surprise and often lead to dramatic losses. An unknowable risk is sometimes referred to as a *black swan*. (Black swans were not considered possible until they were discovered in Australia.) As pointed out by Taleb (2007), once it has occurred, a black swan event is often considered to be obvious.[2] Did the producers

---

[1] See F. H. Knight, *Risk, Uncertainty and Profit* (Boston: Houghton Mifflin Company, 1921).
[2] See N. N. Taleb, *The Black Swan: The Impact of the Highly Improbable* (New York: Random House, 2007).

of multi-volume encyclopedias in 1970 consider the possibility that technological developments would render their product worthless? Probably not, but ex post it seems a fairly obvious risk.

How can companies manage unknown and unknowable risks? A key tool is flexibility. Companies should avoid excessive leverage and try to ensure that their costs are variable rather than fixed as far as possible. Diversification across products and markets also increases flexibility. In the future, insurance companies may well develop more products to handle unknown and unknowable risks. As discussed in Chapter 20, products have already been developed to provide protection against some operational (unknown) risks. Handling unknowable risk is a challenging (but not totally impossible) contract design problem.

FURTHER READING

Diebold, F. X., N. A. Doherty, and R. J. Herring. *The Known, the Unknown, and the Unknowable in Financial Risk Management*. Princeton, NJ: Princeton University Press, 2010.

Dunbar, N. *Inventing Money: The Story of Long-Term Capital Management and the Legends Behind It*. Chichester, UK: John Wiley & Sons, 2000.

Gomory, R. "The Known, the Unknown and the Unknowable," *Scientific American*, June 1995.

Jorion, P. *Big Bets Gone Bad: Derivatives and Bankruptcy in Orange County*. New York: Academic Press, 1995.

Jorion, P. "How Long-Term Lost Its Capital," *Risk* (September 1999): 31–36.

Ju, X., and N. Pearson. "Using Value at Risk to Control Risk Taking: How Wrong Can You Be?" *Journal of Risk* 1 (1999): 5–36.

Persaud, A. D., ed. *Liquidity Black Holes: Understanding Quantifying and Managing Financial Liquidity Risk*. London: Risk Books, 2003.

Sorkin, A. R. *Too Big to Fail*. New York: Penguin, 2009.

Tett, G. *Fool's Gold: How the Bold Dream of a Small Tribe at JPMorgan Was Corrupted by Wall Street Greed and Unleashed a Catastrophe*. New York: Free Press, 2009.

Thomson, R. *Apocalypse Roulette: The Lethal World of Derivatives*. London: Macmillan, 1998.

Zhang, P. G. *Barings Bankruptcy and Financial Derivatives*. Singapore: World Scientific Publishing, 1995.

Compounding Frequencies for Interest Rates

A statement by a bank that the interest rate on one-year deposits is 10% per annum sounds straightforward and unambiguous. In fact, its precise meaning depends on the way the interest rate is measured.

If the interest rate is measured with annual compounding, the bank's statement that the interest rate is 10% means that $100 grows to

$$\$100 \times 1.1 = \$110$$

at the end of one year. When the interest rate is measured with semiannual compounding, it means that we earn 5% every six months, with the interest being reinvested. In this case, $100 grows to

$$\$100 \times 1.05 \times 1.05 = \$110.25$$

at the end of one year. When the interest rate is measured with quarterly compounding, the bank's statement means that we earn 2.5% every three months, with the interest being reinvested. The $100 then grows to

$$\$100 \times 1.025^4 = \$110.38$$

at the end of one year. Table A.1 shows the effect of increasing the compounding frequency further.

The compounding frequency defines the units in which an interest rate is measured. A rate expressed with one compounding frequency can be converted into an equivalent rate with a different compounding frequency. For example, from Table A.1 we see that 10.25% with annual compounding is equivalent to 10% with semiannual compounding. We can think of the difference between one compounding frequency and another to be analogous to the difference between kilometers and miles. They are two different units of measurement.

To generalize our results, suppose that an amount A is invested for n years at an interest rate of R per annum. If the rate is compounded once per annum, the terminal value of the investment is

$$A(1 + R)^n$$

TABLE A.1   Effect of the Compounding Frequency on the
Value of $100 at the End of One Year When the Interest Rate
is 10% per Annum

Compounding Frequency	Value of $100 at End of Year ($)
Annually ($m = 1$)	110.00
Semiannually ($m = 2$)	110.25
Quarterly ($m = 4$)	110.38
Monthly ($m = 12$)	110.47
Weekly ($m = 52$)	110.51
Daily ($m = 365$)	110.52

If the rate is compounded m times per annum, the terminal value of the investment is

$$A\left(1 + \frac{R}{m}\right)^{mn} \tag{A.1}$$

When $m = 1$ the rate is sometimes referred to as the *equivalent annual interest rate*.

Continuous Compounding

The limit as the compounding frequency, m, tends to infinity is known as *continuous compounding*.[1] With continuous compounding, it can be shown that an amount A invested for n years at rate R grows to

$$Ae^{Rn} \tag{A.2}$$

where $e = 2.71828$. The function e^x, which is also written $\exp(x)$, is built into most calculators, so the computation of the expression in equation (A.2) presents no problems. In the example in Table A.1, $A = 100$, $n = 1$, and $R = 0.1$, so that the value to which A grows with continuous compounding is

$$100e^{0.1} = \$110.52$$

This is (to two decimal places) the same as the value with daily compounding. For most practical purposes, continuous compounding can be thought of as being equivalent to daily compounding. Compounding a sum of money at a continuously compounded rate R for n years involves multiplying it by e^{Rn}. Discounting it at a continuously compounded rate R for n years involves multiplying by e^{-Rn}.

---

[1] Actuaries sometimes refer to a continuously compounded rate as the *force of interest*.

Suppose that R_c is a rate of interest with continuous compounding and R_m is the equivalent rate with compounding m times per annum. From the results in equations (A.1) and (A.2), we have

$$Ae^{R_c n} = A\left(1 + \frac{R_m}{m}\right)^{mn}$$

or

$$e^{R_c} = \left(1 + \frac{R_m}{m}\right)^{m}$$

This means that

$$R_c = m\ln\left(1 + \frac{R_m}{m}\right) \tag{A.3}$$

and

$$R_m = m(e^{R_c/m} - 1) \tag{A.4}$$

These equations can be used to convert a rate with a compounding frequency of m times per annum to a continuously compounded rate and vice versa. The function ln is the natural logarithm function and is built into most calculators. It is defined so that if $y = \ln x$, then $x = e^y$.

EXAMPLE A.1

Consider an interest rate that is quoted as 10% per annum with semiannual compounding. From equation (A.3), with $m = 2$ and $R_m = 0.1$, the equivalent rate with continuous compounding is

$$2\ln\left(1 + \frac{0.1}{2}\right) = 0.09758$$

or 9.758% per annum.

EXAMPLE A.2

Suppose that a lender quotes the interest rate on loans as 8% per annum with continuous compounding, and that interest is actually paid quarterly. From equation (A.4), with $m = 4$ and $R_c = 0.08$, the equivalent rate with quarterly compounding is

$$4(e^{0.08/4} - 1) = 0.0808$$

or 8.08% per annum. This means that on a $1,000 loan, interest payments of $20.20 would be required each quarter.

Zero Rates, Forward Rates, and Zero-Coupon Yield Curves

The n-year zero-coupon interest rate is the rate of interest earned on an investment that starts today and lasts for n years. All the interest and principal is realized at the end of n years. There are no intermediate payments. The n-year zero-coupon interest rate is sometimes also referred to as the n-year *spot interest rate*, the n-year *zero rate*, or just the n-year zero. The zero rate as a function of maturity is referred to as the *zero curve*. Suppose a five-year zero rate with continuous compounding is quoted as 5% per annum. (See Appendix A for a discussion of compounding frequencies.) This means that $100, if invested for five years, grows to

$$100 \times e^{0.05 \times 5} = 128.40$$

A forward rate is the future zero rate implied by today's zero rates. Consider the zero rates shown in Table B.1. The forward rate for the period between six months and one year is 6.6%. This is because 5% for the first six months combined with 6.6% for the next six months gives an average of 5.8% for the two ~~years.~~ periods Similarly, the forward rate for the period between 12 months and 18 months is 7.6%, because this rate when combined with 5.8% for the first 12 months gives an average of 6.4% for the 18 months. In general, the forward rate F for the period between times T_1 and T_2 is

$$F = \frac{R_2 T_2 - R_1 T_1}{T_2 - T_1} \qquad (B.1)$$

where R_1 is the zero rate for maturity of T_1 and R_2 is the zero rate for maturity T_2. This formula is exactly true when rates are measured with continuous compounding and approximately true for other compounding frequencies. The results from using this formula on the rates in Table B.1 are in Table B.2. For example, substituting $T_1 = 1.5$, $T_2 = 2.0$, $R_1 = 0.064$, and $R_2 = 0.068$ gives $F = 0.08$ showing that the forward rate for the period between 18 months and 24 months is 8.0%.

Investors who think that future interest rates will be markedly different from forward rates have no difficulty in finding trades that reflect their beliefs. Consider an investor who can borrow or lend at the rates in Table B.1. Suppose the investor thinks that the six-month interest rates will not change much over the next two years. The investor can borrow six-month funds and invest for two years. The six-month

TABLE B.1   Zero Rates

Maturity (years)	Zero Rate (%) (cont. comp.)
0.5	5.0
1.0	5.8
1.5	6.4
2.0	6.8

borrowings can be rolled over at the end of 6, 12, and 18 months. If interest rates do stay about the same, this strategy will yield a profit of about 1.8% per year because interest will be received at 6.8% and paid at 5%. This type of trading strategy is known as a *yield curve play*. The investor is speculating that rates in the future will be quite different from the forward rates shown in Table B.2.

Robert Citron, the Treasurer at Orange County, used yield curve plays similar to the one we have just described very successfully in 1992 and 1993. The profit from Mr. Citron's trades became an important contributor to Orange County's budget and he was re-elected. In 1994, he used the same strategy more aggressively. If short-term interest rates had remained the same or declined, he would have done very well. As it happened, interest rates rose sharply during 1994. On December 1, 1994, Orange County announced that its investment portfolio had lost $1.5 billion and several days later it filed for bankruptcy protection.

Bond Pricing

Most bonds provide coupons periodically. The bond's principal (which is also known as its par value or face value) is received at the end of its life. The theoretical price of a bond can be calculated as the present value of all the cash flows that will be received by the owner of the bond. The most accurate approach is to use a different zero rate for each cash flow. To illustrate this, consider the situation where zero rates are as in Table B.1. Suppose that a two-year bond with a principal of $100 provides coupons at the rate of 6% per annum semiannually. To calculate the present value of the first coupon of $3, we discount it at 5.0% for six months; to calculate the present value of the second coupon of $3, we discount it at 5.8% for one year; and so on. The theoretical price of the bond is therefore

$$3e^{-0.05\times0.5} + 3e^{-0.058\times1.0} + 3e^{-0.064\times1.5} + 103e^{-0.068\times2.0} = 98.39$$

or $98.39.

TABLE B.2   Forward Rates for Zero Rates in Table B.1

Period (years)	Forward Rate (%) (cont. comp.)
0.5 to 1.0	6.6
1.0 to 1.5	7.6
1.5 to 2.0	8.0

TABLE B.3 Rates after Two-year Rate Has Been Determined Using the Bootstrap Method

Maturity (years)	Zero Rate (%) (cont. comp.)
0.5	5.00
1.0	5.80
1.5	6.40
2.0	6.80
2.5	??

Bond Yields

A bond's yield is the discount rate that, when applied to all cash flows, gives a bond price equal to its market price. Suppose that the theoretical price of the bond we have been considering, $98.39, is also its market price (i.e., the market's price of the bond is in exact agreement with the data in Table B.1). If y is the yield on the bond, expressed with continuous compounding, we must have

$$3e^{-y \times 0.5} + 3e^{-y \times 1.0} + 3e^{-y \times 1.5} + 103e^{-y \times 2.0} = 98.39$$

This equation can be solved using Excel's Solver or in some other way to give $y = 6.76\%$.

Treasury Rates

Treasury rates are the rates an investor earns on Treasury bills and Treasury bonds. These are the instruments used by a government to borrow in its own currency. Japanese Treasury rates are the rates at which the Japanese government borrows in yen; U.S. Treasury rates are the rates at which the U.S. government borrows in U.S. dollars; and so on.

Determining Treasury Zero Rates

One way of determining Treasury zero rates such as those in Table B.1 is to observe the yields on "strips." These are zero-coupon bonds that are artificially created by traders when they sell the coupons on a Treasury bond separately from the principal.

Another way of determining Treasury zero rates is from regular Treasury bills and bonds. The most popular approach is known as the *bootstrap method*. This involves working from short maturities to successively longer maturities matching prices. Suppose that Table B.3 gives the Treasury rates determined so far and that a 2.5-year bond providing a coupon of 8% sells for $102 per $100 of principal. We would determine the 2.5-year zero-coupon interest rate as the rate which, when used in conjunction with the rates in Table B.3, gives the correct price for this bond. This involves solving

$$4e^{-0.05 \times 0.5} + 4e^{-0.058 \times 1.0} + 4e^{-0.064 \times 1.5} + 4e^{-0.068 \times 2.0} + 104e^{-R \times 2.5} = 102$$

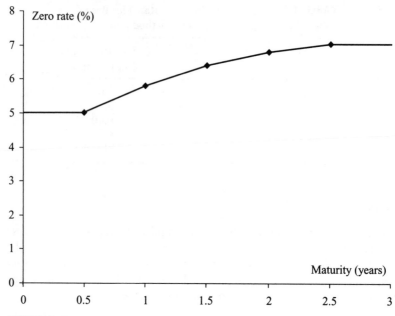

FIGURE B.1 Zero Curve for Data in Table B.3

which gives $R = 7.05\%$. The zero curve is usually assumed to be linear between the points that are determined by the bootstrap method. (In our example, the 2.25-year zero rate would be 6.9025%.) It is also assumed to be constant prior to the first point and beyond the last point. The zero curve for our example is shown in Figure B.1.

LIBOR/Swap Rates

The LIBOR/swap zero curve is determined using a similar bootstrap method to that used for determining the Treasury zero curve. LIBOR deposit rates define the zero curve out to a maturity of one year. Eurodollar futures quotes are sometimes used for the next two or three years of maturities. Swap rates are used after that. The n-year swap rate is the yield on an n-year bond that sells for par.

Valuing Forward and Futures Contracts

The forward or futures price of an investment asset that provides no income is given by

$$S_0 e^{rT}$$

where S_0 is the spot price of the asset today, T is the time to maturity of the forward or futures contract, and r is the continuously compounded risk-free rate for maturity T. When the asset provides income during the life of the contract that has a present value I, this becomes

$$(S_0 - I)e^{rT}$$

When it provides a yield at rate q, it becomes

$$S_0 e^{(r-q)T}$$

A foreign currency can be regarded as an investment asset that provides a yield equal to the foreign risk-free rate, so that the forward or futures price for a foreign currency is

$$S_0 e^{(r-r_f)T}$$

where r_f is the foreign risk-free rate (continuously compounded) and S_0 is the spot exchange rate. The value of a forward contract where the holder has the right to buy the asset for a price of K is, in all cases

$$(F - K)e^{-rT}$$

where F is the forward price. The value of a forward contract where the holder has the right to sell the asset for a price of K is similarly

$$(K - F)e^{-rT}$$

EXAMPLE C.1

Consider a six-month futures contract on the S&P 500. The current value of the index is 1,200, the six-month risk-free rate is 5% per annum, and the average dividend yield on the S&P 500 over the next six months is expected to be 2% per annum (both rates continuously compounded). The futures price is $1,200e^{(0.05-0.02)\times0.5}$ or 1,218.14.

EXAMPLE C.2

The current forward price of a commodity for a contract maturing in nine months is $550 per ounce. A company has a forward contract to buy 1,000 ounces of the commodity for a delivery price of $530 in nine months. The nine-month risk-free rate is 4% per annum continuously compounded. The value of the forward contract is $1,000 \times (550 - 530)e^{-0.04\times9/12}$, or $19,409.

Valuing Swaps

A plain vanilla interest rate swap can be valued by assuming that the interest rates that are realized in the future equal today's forward interest rates. As an example, consider an interest rate swap that has 14 months remaining and a notional principal of $100 million. A fixed rate of 5% per annum is received and LIBOR is paid, with exchanges taking place every six months. Assume that (a) four months ago, the six-month LIBOR rate was 4%, (b) the forward LIBOR interest rate for a six-month period starting in two months is 4.6%, and (c) the forward LIBOR for a six-month period starting in eight months is 5.2%. All rates are expressed with semiannual compounding. Assuming that forward rates are realized, the cash flows on the swap are as shown in Table D.1. (For example, in eight months the fixed-rate cash flow received is $0.5 \times 0.05 \times 100$, or $2.5 million; the floating-rate cash flow paid is $0.5 \times 0.046 \times 100$, or 2.3 million.) The value of the swap is the present value of the net cash flows in the final column.[1]

An alternative approach (which gives the same valuation) is to assume that the swap principal of $100 million is paid and received at the end of the life of the swap. This makes no difference to the value of the swap but allows it to be regarded as the exchange of interest and principal on a fixed-rate bond for interest and principal on a floating-rate bond. The fixed-rate bond's cash flows can be valued in the usual way. A general rule is that the floating-rate bond is always worth an amount equal to the principal immediately after an interest payment. In our example, the floating rate bond is worth $100 million immediately after the payment in two months. This payment (determined four months ago) is $2 million. The floating rate bond is therefore worth $102 million immediately before the payment at the two-month point. The value of the swap today is therefore the present value of the fixed-rate bond less the present value of a cash flow of $102 million in two months.

Currency Swaps

A currency swap can be valued by assuming that exchange rates in the future equal today's forward exchange rates. As an example, consider a currency swap in which 4% will be received in GBP and 6% will be paid in USD once a year. The principals in the two currencies are 10 million USD and 5 million GBP. The swap will last for

---

[1] Note that this is not perfectly accurate because it does not take account of day count conventions and holiday calendars.

TABLE D.1 Valuing an Interest Rate Swap by Assuming Forward Rates Are Realized

Time	Fixed Cash Flow ($ mill.)	Floating Cash Flow ($ mill.)	Net Cash Flow ($ mill.)
2 months	2.5	−2.0	0.5
8 months	2.5	−2.3	0.2
14 months	2.5	−2.6	−0.1

TABLE D.2 Valuing a Currency Swap by Assuming Forward Exchange Rates Are Realized (cash flows in millions)

Time	USD Cash Flow	GBP Cash Flow	Forward Exchange Rate	USD Value of GBP Cash Flow	Net Cash Flow in USD
1	−0.6	0.2	1.8000	0.360	−0.240
2	−0.6	0.2	1.8400	0.368	−0.232
3	−0.6	0.2	1.8800	0.376	−0.224
3	−10.0	5.0	1.8800	9.400	−0.600

another three years. The swap cash flows are shown in the second and third columns of Table D.2. The forward exchange rates are (we assume) those shown in the fourth column. These are used to convert the GBP cash flows to USD. The final column shows the net cash flows. The value of the swap is the present value of these cash flows.

An alternative approach (which gives the same valuation) is to regard the swap as a long position in a GBP bond and a short position in a USD bond. Each bond can be valued in its own currency in the usual way and the current exchange rate can be used to convert the value of the GBP bond from GBP to USD.

Valuing European Options

The Black–Scholes–Merton formulas for valuing European call and put options on an investment asset that provides no income are

$$c = S_0 N(d_1) - K e^{-rT} N(d_2)$$

and

$$p = K e^{-rT} N(-d_2) - S_0 N(-d_1)$$

where

$$d_1 = \frac{\ln(S_0/K) + (r + \sigma^2/2)T}{\sigma\sqrt{T}}$$

$$d_2 = \frac{\ln(S_0/K) + (r - \sigma^2/2)T}{\sigma\sqrt{T}} = d_1 - \sigma\sqrt{T}$$

The function $N(x)$ is the cumulative probability distribution function for a standardized normal distribution (see tables at the end of the book or Excel's NORMSDIST function). The variables c and p are the European call and European put price, S_0 is today's asset price, K is the strike price, r is the continuously compounded risk-free rate, σ is the stock price volatility, and T is the time to maturity of the option.

When the underlying asset provides a cash income, the present value of the income during the life of the option should be subtracted from S_0. When the underlying asset provides a yield at rate q, the formulas become

$$c = S_0 e^{-qT} N(d_1) - K e^{-rT} N(d_2)$$

and

$$p = K e^{-rT} N(-d_2) - S_0 e^{-qT} N(-d_1)$$

where

$$d_1 = \frac{\ln(S_0/K) + (r - q + \sigma^2/2)T}{\sigma\sqrt{T}}$$

$$d_2 = \frac{\ln(S_0/K) + (r - q - \sigma^2/2)T}{\sigma\sqrt{T}} = d_1 - \sigma\sqrt{T}$$

TABLE E.1   Greek Letters for Options on an Asset That Provides a Yield at Rate q

Greek Letter	Call Option	Put Option
Delta	$e^{-qT}N(d_1)$	$e^{-qT}[N(d_1) - 1]$
Gamma	$\dfrac{N'(d_1)e^{-qT}}{S_0\sigma\sqrt{T}}$	$\dfrac{N'(d_1)e^{-qT}}{S_0\sigma\sqrt{T}}$
Theta (per yr)	$-S_0 N'(d_1)\sigma e^{-qT}/(2\sqrt{T})$ $+q S_0 N(d_1)e^{-qT}$ $-r K e^{-rT}N(d_2)$	$-S_0 N'(d_1)\sigma e^{-qT}/(2\sqrt{T})$ $-q S_0 N(-d_1)e^{-qT}$ $+r K e^{-rT}N(-d_2)$
Vega (per %)	$\dfrac{S_0\sqrt{T}N'(d_1)e^{-qT}}{100}$	$\dfrac{S_0\sqrt{T}N'(d_1)e^{-qT}}{100}$
Rho (per %)	$\dfrac{K T e^{-rT}N(d_2)}{100}$	$-\dfrac{K T e^{-rT}N(-d_2)}{100}$

Options on a foreign currency can be valued by setting q equal to the foreign risk-free rate. Options on a futures or forward price can be valued by using these formulas by setting S_0 equal to the current forward or futures price, $r = q$, and σ equal to the volatility of the forward or futures price.

Table E.1 gives formulas for the Greek letters for European options on an asset that provides income at rate q. $N'(x)$ is the standard normal density function:

$$N'(x) = \frac{1}{\sqrt{2\pi}}e^{-x^2/2}$$

EXAMPLE E.1

Consider a six-month European call option on a stock index. The current value of the index is 1,200, the strike price is 1,250, the risk-free rate is 5%, the dividend yield on the index is 2%, and the index volatility is 20%. In this case, $S_0 = 1{,}200$, $K = 1{,}250$, $r = 0.05$, $q = 0.02$, $\sigma = 0.2$, and $T = 0.5$. The value of the option is 53.44, the delta of the option is 0.45, the gamma is 0.0023, the theta is −0.22, the vega is 3.33, and rho is 2.44. Note that the formula in Table E.1 gives theta per year. The theta quoted here is per calendar day.

The calculations in this appendix can be done with the DerivaGem software by selecting Option Type: Black–Scholes European. Option valuation is described more fully in Hull (2012).[1] The implied volatility of an option is defined as the volatility that causes the Black–Scholes–Merton price of the option to be equal to the market price (see Section 10.2).

---

[1] See J. C. Hull, *Options, Futures, and Other Derivatives*, 8th ed. (Upper Saddle River, NJ: Pearson, 2012).

Valuing American Options

To value American-style options, we divide the life of the option into n time steps of length Δt. Suppose that the asset price at the beginning of a step is S. At the end of the time step it moves up to Su with probability p and down to Sd with probability $1 - p$. For an investment asset that provides no income the values of u, d, and p are given by

$$u = e^{\sigma\sqrt{\Delta t}} \quad d = \frac{1}{u} \quad p = \frac{a - d}{u - d}$$

with

$$a = e^{r\Delta t}$$

Figure F.1 shows the tree constructed for valuing a five-month American put option on a non-dividend-paying stock where the initial stock price is 50, the strike price is 50, the risk-free rate is 10%, and the volatility is 40%. In this case, there are five steps so that $\Delta t = 0.08333$, $u = 1.1224$, $d = 0.8909$, $a = 1.0084$, and $p = 0.5073$. The upper number at each node is the stock price and the lower number is the value of the option.

At the final nodes of the tree, the option price is its intrinsic value. For example, at node G, the option price is $50 - 35.36 = 14.64$. At earlier nodes, we first calculate a value assuming that the option is held for a further time period of length Δt and then check to see whether early exercise is optimal. Consider first node E. If the option is held for a further time period, it will be worth 0.00 if there is an up move (probability: p) and 5.45 if there is a down move (probability: $1 - p$). The expected value in time Δt is therefore $0.5073 \times 0 + 0.4927 \times 5.45$ or 2.686, and the 2.66 value at node E is calculated by discounting this at the risk-free rate of 10% for one month. The option should not be exercised at node E as the payoff from early exercise would be zero. Consider next node A. A calculation similar to that just given shows that, assuming it is held for a further time period, the option's value at node A is 9.90. If exercised, its value is $50 - 39.69 = 10.31$. In this case, it should be exercised and the value of being at node A is 10.31.

Continuing to work back from the end of the tree to the beginning, the value of the option at the initial node D is found to be 4.49. As the number of steps on the tree is increased, the accuracy of the option price increases. With 30, 50, and 100 time steps, we get values for the option of 4.263, 4.272, and 4.278, respectively.

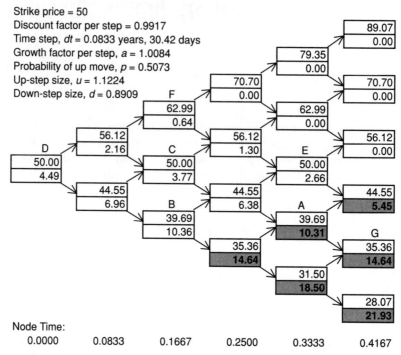

At each node:
 Upper value = Underlying asset price
 Lower value = Option price
 Shading indicates where option is exercised.

Strike price = 50
Discount factor per step = 0.9917
Time step, *dt* = 0.0833 years, 30.42 days
Growth factor per step, *a* = 1.0084
Probability of up move, *p* = 0.5073
Up-step size, *u* = 1.1224
Down-step size, *d* = 0.8909

Node Time:
 0.0000   0.0833   0.1667   0.2500   0.3333   0.4167

FIGURE F.1   Binomial Tree from DerivaGem for American Put on
Non-Dividend-Paying Stock

To calculate delta, we consider the two nodes at time Δt. In our example, as we move from the lower node to the upper node, the option price changes from 6.96 to 2.16 and the stock price changes from 44.55 to 56.12. The estimate of delta is the change in the option price divided by the change in the stock price:

$$\text{Delta} = \frac{2.16 - 6.96}{56.12 - 44.55} = -0.41$$

To calculate gamma we consider the three nodes at time $2\Delta t$. The delta calculated from the upper two nodes (C and F) is −0.241. This can be regarded as the delta for a stock price of $(62.99 + 50)/2 = 56.49$. The delta calculated from the lower two nodes (B and C) is −0.639. This can be regarded as the delta for a stock price of $(50 + 39.69)/2 = 44.84$. The estimate of gamma is the change in delta divided by the change in the stock price:

$$\text{Gamma} = \frac{-0.241 - (-0.639)}{56.49 - 44.84} = 0.034$$

We estimate theta from nodes D and C as

$$\text{Theta} = \frac{3.77 - 4.49}{2 \times 0.08333}$$

or –4.30 per year. This is –0.0118 per calendar day. Vega is estimated by increasing the volatility, constructing a new tree, and observing the effect of the increased volatility on the option price. Rho is calculated similarly.

When the asset underlying the option provides a yield at rate q, the procedure is exactly the same except that $a = e^{(r-q)\Delta t}$ instead of $e^{r\Delta t}$ in the equation for p. When the option is on the forward or futures price, a is set equal to one and the tree shows the forward or futures price at each node. The calculations we have described can be done using the DerivaGem software by selecting Option Type: Binomial American. Binomial trees and other numerical procedures are described more fully in Hull (2012).[1]

---

[1] See J. C. Hull, *Options, Futures, and Other Derivatives*, 8th ed. (Upper Saddle River, NJ: Pearson, 2012).

Taylor Series Expansions

Consider a function $z = F(x)$. When a small change Δx is made to x, there is a corresponding small change Δz in z. A first approximation to the relationship between Δz and Δx is

$$\Delta z = \frac{dz}{dx}\Delta x \tag{G.1}$$

This relationship is exact if z is a linear function of x and approximate in other situations. A more accurate approximation is

$$\Delta z = \frac{dz}{dx}\Delta x + \frac{1}{2}\frac{d^2z}{dx^2}(\Delta x)^2 \tag{G.2}$$

This relationship is exact if z is a quadratic function of x and approximate in other situations. By adding more terms in the series, we can increase accuracy. The full expansion is

$$\Delta z = \frac{dz}{dx}\Delta x + \frac{1}{2!}\frac{d^2z}{dx^2}(\Delta x)^2 + \frac{1}{3!}\frac{d^3z}{dx^3}(\Delta x)^3 + \frac{1}{4!}\frac{d^4z}{dx^4}(\Delta x)^4 + \cdots$$

EXAMPLE G.1

Consider the function $z = \sqrt{x}$ so that

$$\frac{dz}{dx} = \frac{1}{2x^{1/2}} \qquad \frac{d^2z}{dx^2} = -\frac{1}{4x^{3/2}} \qquad \frac{d^3z}{dx^3} = \frac{3}{8x^{5/2}}$$

Suppose that $x = 2$ and $\Delta x = 0.1$ so that $\Delta z = \sqrt{2.1} - \sqrt{2} = 0.034924$. When $x = 2$

$$\frac{dz}{dx} = 0.35355 \qquad \frac{d^2z}{dx^2} = -0.08839 \qquad \frac{d^3z}{dx^3} = 0.06629$$

The first order approximation to Δz, given by equation (G.1), is

$$\Delta z = 0.35355 \times 0.1 = 0.035355$$

The second order approximation, given by equation (G.2), is

$$\Delta z = 0.35355 \times 0.1 + \frac{1}{2} \times (-0.08839) \times 0.1^2 = 0.034913$$

The third order approximation is

$$\Delta z = 0.35355 \times 0.1 + \frac{1}{2} \times (-0.08839) \times 0.1^2 + \frac{1}{6} \times 0.06629 \times 0.1^3 = 0.034924$$

It can be seen that the series expansion quickly converges to the correct answer of 0.034924.

Functions of Two Variables

Consider next a function of two variables, $z = F(x, y)$. Suppose that Δx and Δy are small changes in x and y, respectively, and that Δz is the corresponding small change in z. In this case, the first order approximation is

$$\Delta z = \frac{\partial z}{\partial x} \Delta x + \frac{\partial z}{\partial y} \Delta y \tag{G.3}$$

The second order approximation is

$$\Delta z = \frac{\partial z}{\partial x} \Delta x + \frac{\partial z}{\partial y} \Delta y + \frac{1}{2} \frac{\partial^2 z}{\partial x^2} (\Delta x)^2 + \frac{1}{2} \frac{\partial^2 z}{\partial y^2} (\Delta y)^2 + \frac{\partial^2 z}{\partial x \partial y} (\Delta x \Delta y) \tag{G.4}$$

EXAMPLE G.2

Consider the function $z = \sqrt{xy}$ so that

$$\frac{\partial z}{\partial x} = \frac{y^{1/2}}{2x^{1/2}} \qquad \frac{\partial z}{\partial y} = \frac{x^{1/2}}{2y^{1/2}}$$

$$\frac{\partial^2 z}{\partial x^2} = -\frac{y^{1/2}}{4x^{3/2}} \qquad \frac{\partial^2 z}{\partial y^2} = -\frac{x^{1/2}}{4y^{3/2}} \qquad \frac{\partial^2 z}{\partial x \partial y} = \frac{1}{4(xy)^{1/2}}$$

Suppose that $x = 2$, $y = 1$, $\Delta x = 0.1$, and $\Delta y = 0.1$ so that

$$\Delta z = \sqrt{2.1 \times 1.1} - \sqrt{2 \times 1} = 0.10565$$

When $x = 2$ and $y = 1$

$$\frac{\partial z}{\partial x} = 0.35355 \qquad \frac{\partial z}{\partial y} = 0.70711$$

$$\frac{\partial^2 z}{\partial x^2} = -0.08839 \qquad \frac{\partial^2 z}{\partial y^2} = -0.35355 \qquad \frac{\partial^2 z}{\partial x \partial y} = 0.17678$$

The first order approximation to Δz, given by equation (G.3), is

$$\Delta z = 0.35355 \times 0.1 + 0.70711 \times 0.1 = 0.10607$$

The second order approximation, given by equation (G.4), is

$$\Delta z = 0.35355 \times 0.1 + 0.70711 \times 0.1$$
$$+ \frac{1}{2} \times (-0.08839) \times (0.1)^2 + \frac{1}{2} \times (-0.35355) \times (0.1)^2$$
$$+ 0.17678 \times 0.1 \times 0.1 = 0.10562$$

The series expansion is converging to the correct answer of 0.10565.

General Result

For a function z of n variables, $x_1, x_2, \ldots, x_n$, the Taylor series expansion of Δz is

$$\Delta z = \sum_{m_1=0}^{\infty} \cdots \sum_{m_n=0}^{\infty} \frac{1}{m_1! \cdots m_n!} \frac{\partial^m z}{\partial x_1^{m_1} \cdots \partial x_n^{m_n}} \Delta x_1^{m_1} \cdots \Delta x_n^{m_n}$$

where $m = m_1 + \cdots m_n$ and the term where all m_is are zero is zero.

Eigenvectors and Eigenvalues

Consider an $n \times n$ matrix A and suppose that $\mathbf{x}$ is an $n \times 1$ vector. Consider the equation

$$Ax = \lambda x \tag{H.1}$$

The equation can be written

$$(A - \lambda I)\mathbf{x} = 0$$

where I is the $n \times n$ identity matrix (which is the $n \times n$ matrix with diagonal elements equal to 1 and all other elements equal to zero). Clearly, $\mathbf{x} = 0$ is a solution to equation (H.1). Under what circumstances are there other solutions? A theorem in linear algebra tells us that there are other solutions when the determinant of $A - \lambda I$ is zero. The values of λ that lead to solutions of equation (H.1) are therefore the values of λ that we get when we solve the equation that sets the determinant of $A - \lambda I$ equal to zero. This equation is a nth order polynomial in λ. In general, it has n solutions. The solutions are the *eigenvalues* of the matrix, A. The vector $\mathbf{x}$ that solves equation (H.1) for a particular eigenvalue is an *eigenvector*. In general, there are n eigenvectors, one corresponding to each eigenvalue.

As a simple example, suppose that

$$A = \begin{pmatrix} 1 & -1 \\ 2 & 4 \end{pmatrix}$$

In this case

$$A - \lambda I = \begin{pmatrix} 1 - \lambda & -1 \\ 2 & 4 - \lambda \end{pmatrix}$$

The determinant of this matrix is

$$(1 - \lambda)(4 - \lambda) - (-1) \times 2 = \lambda^2 - 5\lambda + 6$$

The solutions to this equation are $\lambda = 3$ and $\lambda = 2$. These are the two eigenvalues of the matrix.

To determine the eigenvectors corresponding to $\lambda = 3$, we solve equation (H.1):

$$\begin{pmatrix} 1 & -1 \\ 2 & 4 \end{pmatrix} \mathbf{x} = 3\mathbf{x}$$

Setting

$$\mathbf{x} = \begin{pmatrix} x_1 \\ x_2 \end{pmatrix}$$

the equation to be solved becomes

$$\begin{pmatrix} 1 & -1 \\ 2 & 4 \end{pmatrix} \begin{pmatrix} x_1 \\ x_2 \end{pmatrix} = 3 \begin{pmatrix} x_1 \\ x_2 \end{pmatrix}$$

The simultaneous equations corresponding to this are

$$x_1 - x_2 = 3x_1$$

and

$$2x_1 + 4x_2 = 3x_2$$

Both these equations are equivalent to

$$x_2 + 2x_1 = 0$$

It follows that any pair of numbers x_1 and x_2 solve the equation when $\lambda = 3$ providing $x_2 = -2x_1$. By convention, the values of x_1 and x_2 that are reported are those for which the length of the vector $\mathbf{x}$ is 1. This means that $x_1^2 + x_2^2 = 1$. In this case, the solution where $\mathbf{x}$ has a length of 1 is $x_1 = \sqrt{0.2} = 0.447$ and $x_2 = -2\sqrt{0.2} = -0.894$. (An alternative is $x_1 = -0.447$ and $x_2 = 0.894$.) The solution

$$\mathbf{x} = \begin{pmatrix} 0.447 \\ -0.894 \end{pmatrix}$$

is the eigenvector corresponding to the first eigenvalue ($\lambda = 3$).

A similar calculation shows that equation (H.1) is satisfied for $\lambda = 2$ when $x_1 + x_2 = 0$. The solution where $\mathbf{x}$ has a length of 1 is $x_1 = \sqrt{0.5} = 0.707$ and $x_2 = -\sqrt{0.5} = -0.707$. (An alternative is $x_1 = -0.707$ and $x_2 = 0.707$.) The eigenvector corresponding to the second eigenvalue ($\lambda = 2$) is therefore

$$\mathbf{x} = \begin{pmatrix} 0.707 \\ -0.707 \end{pmatrix}$$

For matrices of larger sizes, a numerical procedure must be used to determine eigenvectors and eigenvalues. One such numerical procedure is provided by Press *et al.* (2007).[1]

Applications of eigenvalues and eigenvectors are in Appendices I and J. Software for calculating eigenvectors and eigenvalues is on the author's website.

---

[1] See W. H. Press, S. A. Teukolsky, W. T. Vetterling, and B. P. Flannery, *Numerical Recipes: The Art of Scientific Computing*, 3rd ed. (Cambridge, UK: Cambridge University Press, 2007).

Principal Components Analysis

A principal components analysis is concerned with understanding the structure of data on n correlated variables. The aim of the analysis is to replace the n variables by a smaller number of uncorrelated variables. In the example in Section 8.8, there are 8 variables. These are the daily changes in the 1-year, 2-year, 3-year, 4-year, 5-year, 7-year, 10-year, and 30-year swap rates.

The first step in the analysis is to calculate a covariance matrix from the data. As explained in Section 15.3, this is an $n \times n$ matrix where the (i, j) entry is the covariance between variable i and variable j. The entries on the diagonal (where $i = j$) are variances.

The next step is to calculate the eigenvalues and eigenvectors for this matrix (see Appendix H). The eigenvectors are chosen to have length 1. (As explained in Appendix H this means that the sum of the squares of their elements is 1.) The eigenvector corresponding to the highest eigenvalue is the first principal component; the eigenvector corresponding to the second highest eigenvalue is the second principal component; and so on. The principal components for the example in Section 8.8 are shown in Table 8.7.

The eigenvalue for the ith principal component, as a percentage of the sum of all the eigenvalues, is the percentage of the overall variance explained by the ith principal component. The square root of the ith eigenvalue is the standard deviation of the ith factor score (see Table 8.8).

Software for carrying out a principal components analysis is on the author's website.

Manipulation of Credit Transition Matrices

Suppose that A is an $n \times n$ matrix of credit rating changes in one year. This is a matrix such as the one shown in Table 18.1. Assuming that rating changes in successive time periods are independent, the matrix of credit rating changes in m years is A^m. If m is an integer, this can be readily calculated using the normal rules for matrix multiplication.

Consider next the problem of calculating the transition matrix for $1/m$ years where m is an integer. (For example, when we are interested in one-month changes, $m = 12$.) This is a more complicated problem because we need to calculate the mth root of a matrix. We first calculate eigenvectors $\mathbf{x}_1, \mathbf{x}_2, \ldots, \mathbf{x}_n$ and the corresponding eigenvalues $\lambda_1, \lambda_2, \ldots, \lambda_n$ of the matrix A. These are explained in Appendix H. They have the property that

$$A\mathbf{x_i} = \lambda_i \mathbf{x_i} \tag{J.1}$$

Define X as an $n \times n$ matrix whose ith column is $\mathbf{x}_i$ and Λ as an $n \times n$ diagonal matrix (i.e., a matrix which has zero values everywhere except on the diagonal) where the ith diagonal element is λ_i. From equation (J.1), we have

$$AX = X\Lambda$$

so that

$$A = X\Lambda X^{-1}$$

Define Λ^* as a diagonal matrix where the ith diagonal element is $\lambda_i^{1/m}$. Then

$$(X\Lambda^* X^{-1})^m = (X\Lambda^* X^{-1})(X\Lambda^* X^{-1})(X\Lambda^* X^{-1}) \cdots (X\Lambda^* X^{-1}) = X(\Lambda^*)^m X^{-1}$$
$$= X\Lambda X^{-1} = A$$

showing that the mth root of A, and therefore the transition matrix for time $1/m$ years, is $X\Lambda^* X^{-1}$. Software for carrying out these calculation is on the author's website.

Some authors such as Jarrow, Lando, and Turnbull (1997) prefer to handle this problem in terms of what is termed a *generator matrix*.[1] This is a matrix Γ such that the transition matrix for a short period of time, Δt, is $I + \Gamma \Delta t$ and the transition matrix for a longer period of time, t, is

$$\exp(t\Gamma) = \sum_{k=0}^{\infty} \frac{(t\Gamma)^k}{k!}$$

where I is the identity matrix (with ones on the diagonal and zeroes elsewhere).

---

[1] See R. A. Jarrow, D. Lando, and S. M. Turnbull, "A Markov Model for the Term Structure of Credit Spreads," *Review of Financial Studies* 10 (1997): 481–523.

Valuation of Credit Default Swaps

redit default swaps (CDSs) are described in Chapter 16. They can be valued using (risk-neutral) default probability estimates.

Suppose that the probability of a reference entity defaulting during a year conditional on no earlier default is 2%. Table K.1 shows survival probabilities and unconditional default probabilities (that is, default probabilities as seen at time zero) for each of the five years. The probability of a default during the first year is 0.02 and the probability the reference entity will survive until the end of the first year is 0.98. The probability of a default during the second year is $0.02 \times 0.98 = 0.0196$ and the probability of survival until the end of the second year is $0.98 \times 0.98 = 0.9604$. The probability of default during the third year is $0.02 \times 0.9604 = 0.0192$ and so on.

We will assume that defaults always happen halfway through a year and that payments on a five-year credit default swap are made once a year, at the end of each year. We also assume that the risk-free interest rate is 5% per annum with continuous compounding and the recovery rate is 40%. There are three parts to the calculation. These are shown in Tables K.2, K.3, and K.4.

Table K.2 shows the calculation of the present value of the expected payments made on the CDS assuming that payments are made at the rate of s per year and the notional principal is $1. For example, there is a 0.9412 probability that the third payment of s is made. The expected payment is therefore $0.9412s$ and its present value is $0.9412se^{-0.05 \times 3} = 0.8101s$. The total present value of the expected payments in Table K.2 is $4.0704s$.

Table K.3 shows the calculation of the present value of the expected payoff assuming a notional principal of $1. As mentioned earlier, we are assuming that defaults always happen halfway through a year. For example, there is a 0.0192 probability of a payoff halfway through the third year. Given that the recovery rate is 40%, the expected payoff at this time is $0.0192 \times 0.6 \times 1 = 0.0115$. The present value of the expected payoff is $0.0115e^{-0.05 \times 2.5} = 0.0102$. The total present value of the expected payoffs in Table K.3 is $0.0511.

As a final step, we evaluate in Table K.4 the accrual payment made in the event of a default. These accrual payments arise because the spread payments s are made in arrears so that, when a default occurs, a portion of a spread payment is owed. Consider the third year. There is a 0.0192 probability of a default halfway through the year. An accrual payment of $0.5s$ is due if there is a default. The expected accrual payment halfway through the third year is therefore $0.0192 \times 0.5s = 0.0096s$. Its present value is $0.0096se^{-0.05 \times 2.5} = 0.0085s$. The total present value of the expected accrual payments in Table K.4 is $0.0426s$.

TABLE K.1 Unconditional Default Probabilities and Survival Probabilities

Time (years)	Default Probability	Survival Probability
1	0.0200	0.9800
2	0.0196	0.9604
3	0.0192	0.9412
4	0.0188	0.9224
5	0.0184	0.9039

TABLE K.2 Calculation of the Present Value of Expected Payments (payment = s per annum)

Time (years)	Probability of Survival	Expected Payment	Discount Factor	PV of Expected Payment
1	0.9800	0.9800s	0.9512	0.9322s
2	0.9604	0.9604s	0.9048	0.8690s
3	0.9412	0.9412s	0.8607	0.8101s
4	0.9224	0.9224s	0.8187	0.7552s
5	0.9039	0.9039s	0.7788	0.7040s
Total				4.0704s

TABLE K.3 Calculation of the Present Value of Expected Payoff (notional principal = $1)

Time (years)	Probability of Default	Recovery Rate	Expected Payoff ($)	Discount Factor	PV of Expected Payoff ($)
0.5	0.0200	0.4	0.0120	0.9753	0.0117
1.5	0.0196	0.4	0.0118	0.9277	0.0109
2.5	0.0192	0.4	0.0115	0.8825	0.0102
3.5	0.0188	0.4	0.0113	0.8395	0.0095
4.5	0.0184	0.4	0.0111	0.7985	0.0088
Total					0.0511

TABLE K.4 Calculation of the Present Value of Accrual Payment

Time (years)	Probability of Default	Expected Accrual Payment	Discount Factor	PV of Expected Accrual Payment
0.5	0.0200	0.0100s	0.9753	0.0097s
1.5	0.0196	0.0098s	0.9277	0.0091s
2.5	0.0192	0.0096s	0.8825	0.0085s
3.5	0.0188	0.0094s	0.8395	0.0079s
4.5	0.0184	0.0092s	0.7985	0.0074s
Total				0.0426s

From Tables K.2 and K.4 the present value of the expected payments is

$$4.0704s + 0.0426s = 4.1130s$$

From Table K.3, the present value of the expected payoff is 0.0511. Equating the two, the CDS spread for a new CDS is given by

$$4.1130s = 0.0511$$

or $s = 0.0124$. The mid-market spread should be 0.0124 times the principal or 124 basis points per year. (This is roughly what we would expect from the relationship in equation 16.3: the recovery rate is 40% and the hazard rate is about 2%.)

This example is designed to illustrate the calculation methodology. In practice, we are likely to find that calculations are more extensive than those in Table K.2 to K.4 because (a) payments are often made more frequently than once a year and (b) we want to assume that defaults can happen more frequently than once a year.

Marking to Market a CDS

At the time it is negotiated, a CDS like most other swaps is worth close to zero. At later times it may have a positive or negative value. Suppose, for example, the credit default swap in our example had been negotiated some time ago for a spread of 150 basis points; the present value of the payments by the buyer would be $4.1130 \times 0.0150 = 0.0617$ and the present value of the payoff would be 0.0511. The value of swap to the seller would therefore be $0.0617 - 0.0511$ or 0.0106 times the principal. Similarly, the mark-to market value of the swap to the buyer of protection would be -0.0106 times the principal.

The software DerivaGem that accompanies this book and can be downloaded from the author's website includes a worksheet that carries out the above calculations.

Synthetic CDOs and Their Valuation

Synthetic collateralized debt obligations (CDOs) consist of tranches where one party (Party A) agrees to make payments to another party (Party B) that are equal to those losses on a specified portfolio of debt instruments that are in a certain range. In return, Party B agrees to make payments to Party A that are a certain proportion of the amount of principal that is being insured.

Suppose that the range of losses for a particular tranche is from α_L to α_H. The variables α_L and α_H are known as the attachment point and detachment point, respectively. If α_L is 8% and α_H is 18%, Party A pays to Party B the losses on the portfolio, as they are incurred, in the range 8% to 18% of the total principal of the portfolio. The first 8% of losses on the portfolio does not therefore affect the tranche. The tranche is responsible for the next 10% of losses and its notional principal (initially $18 - 8 = 10\%$ of the portfolio principal) reduces as these losses are incurred. The tranche is wiped out when losses exceed 18%. The payments that are made by Party B to Party A are made periodically at a specified rate applied to the remaining notional tranche principal. This specified rate is known as the *tranche spread*.

The usual assumption is that all the debt instruments in the portfolio have the same probability distribution for the time to default. Define $Q(t)$ as the probability of a debt instrument defaulting by time t. The one-factor Gaussian copula model of time to default presented in Section 11.5 has become the standard market model for valuing a tranche of a collateralized debt obligation (CDO). From equation (11.12)

$$Q(t|F) = N\left\{ \frac{N^{-1}[Q(t)] - \sqrt{\rho}\,F}{\sqrt{1 - \rho}} \right\} \qquad (L.1)$$

where $Q(t|F)$ is the probability of the ith entity defaulting by time t conditional on the value of the factor, F. In the calculation of $Q(t)$ it is usually assumed that the hazard rate for a company is constant. When a CDS spread or other credit spread is available, it can be used to determine the hazard rate using calculations similar to those in Appendix K in conjunction with a search procedure.

Suppose that the hazard rate is λ. Then

$$Q(t) = 1 - e^{-\lambda t} \qquad (L.2)$$

From the properties of the binomial distribution, the probability of exactly k defaults by time t, conditional on F is

$$P(k, T|F) = \frac{n!}{(n-k)!k!} Q(t|F)^k [1 - Q(t|F)]^{n-k} \qquad (\text{L.3})$$

Define

$$n_L = \frac{\alpha_L n}{1 - R} \quad \text{and} \quad n_H = \frac{\alpha_H n}{1 - R}$$

where R is the recovery rate (assumed constant). Also, define $m(x)$ as the smallest integer greater than x. The tranche suffers no losses when the number of defaults, k, is less than $m(n_L)$. It is wiped out when k is greater than or equal to $m(n_H)$. Otherwise the tranche principal at time t is a proportion

$$\frac{\alpha_H - k(1-R)/n}{\alpha_H - \alpha_L}$$

of the initial tranche principal. These results can be used in conjunction with equations (L.1), (L.2), and (L.3) to calculate the expected tranche principal at all times conditional on F. We can then integrate over F to find the (unconditional) expected tranche principal. This integration is usually accomplished with a procedure known as Gaussian quadrature. (The author's website provides the tools for integrating over a normal distribution using Gaussian quadrature.)

It is usually assumed that defaults happen at the midpoint of the intervals between payments. Similarly to Appendix K, we are interested in the following quantities

1. The present value of the expected spread payments received by Party A.
2. The present value of the expected payments for tranche losses made by Party A.
3. The present value of accrual payments received by Party A.

The spread payments received by Party A at a particular time are linearly dependent on the tranche principal at that time. The tranche loss payments made by Party A (assumed to be at the midpoint of an interval) is the change in the principal during the interval. The accrual payment received by Party A is proportional to the tranche loss payments. For any assumption about spreads, all three quantities of interest can therefore be calculated from the expected tranche principal. The breakeven spread can therefore be calculated analogously to the way it is calculated for CDSs in Appendix K.

Derivatives dealers calculate the implied copula correlation, ρ, from the spreads quoted in the market for tranches of CDOs and tend to quote these rather than the spreads themselves. This is similar to the practice in options markets of quoting Black–Scholes–Merton implied volatilities rather than dollar prices. There is a correlation smile phenomenon in CDO markets similar to the volatility smile phenomenon in options markets (see Section 22.4).

The software DerivaGem, which accompanies this book and can be downloaded from the author's website, includes a worksheet for carrying out the above calculations.[1]

---

[1] More details on the calculation can be found in J. C. Hull, *Options, Futures, and Other Derivatives*, 8th ed. (Upper Saddle River, NJ: Pearson, 2012).

Answers to Questions and Problems

CHAPTER 1

1.1 The expected return is 12.5%. The standard deviation of returns is 17.07%.

1.2 From equations (1.1) and (1.2), expected return is 12.5%. SD of return is

$$\sqrt{0.5^2 \times 0.1707^2 + 0.5^2 \times 0.1707^2 + 2 \times 0.15 \times 0.5^2 \times 0.1707^2} = 0.1294$$

or 12.94%.

1.3

w_1	w_2	μ_P	σ_P ($\rho = 0.3$)	σ_P ($\rho = 1$)	σ_P ($\rho = -1$)
0.0	1.0	15%	24.00%	24.00%	24.00%
0.2	0.8	14%	20.39%	22.40%	16.00%
0.4	0.6	13%	17.42%	20.80%	8.00%
0.6	0.4	12%	15.48%	19.20%	0.00%
0.8	0.2	11%	14.96%	17.60%	8.00%
1.0	0.0	10%	16.00%	16.00%	16.00%

1.4 Nonsystematic risk can be diversified; systematic risk cannot. Systematic risk is most important to an equity investor. Either type of risk can lead to the bankruptcy of a corporation.

1.5 We assume that investors trade off mean return and standard deviation of return. For a given mean return, they want to minimize standard deviation of returns. All make the same estimates of means, standard deviations, and coefficients of correlation for returns on individual investments. Furthermore, they can borrow or lend at the risk-free rate. The result is that they all want to be on the "new efficient frontier" in Figure 1.4. They choose the same portfolio of risky investments combined with borrowing or lending at the risk-free rate.

1.6 (a) 7.2%, (b) 9%, (c) 14.4%.

1.7 The capital asset pricing theory assumes that there is one factor driving returns. Arbitrage pricing theory assumes multiple factors.

1.8 In many jurisdictions, interest on debt is deductible to the corporation whereas dividends are not deductible. It can therefore be more tax-efficient for a company to fund itself with debt. However, as debt increases the probability of bankruptcy increases.

1.9 Risk decomposition refers to a procedure where risks are handled one by one. Risk aggregation refers to a procedure where a portfolio of risks is considered.

Risk decomposition requires an in-depth understanding of individual risks. Risk aggregation requires an understanding of the correlations between risks.

1.10 When potential losses are large, we cannot aggregate them and assume they will be diversified away. It is necessary to consider them one by one and handle them with insurance contracts, tighter internal controls, etc.

1.11 This is the probability that profit is no worse than –4% of assets. This profit level is $4.6/1.5 = 3.067$ standard deviations from the mean. The probability that the bank will have a positive equity is therefore $N(3.067)$ where N is the cumulative normal distribution function. This is 99.89%.

1.12 Banks are allowed to accept deposits from the general public. Companies in retailing and manufacturing are not.

1.13 Professional fees ($10 million per month), lost sales (people are reluctant to do business with a company that is being reorganized), and key senior executives left (lack of continuity).

1.14 The return earned by the hedge fund manager with zero alpha would be $0.05 + 0.6 \times (0.10 - 0.05) = 0.08$ or 8%. Because the alpha equals 4%, the hedge fund manager's return was 8% plus 4% or 12%.

CHAPTER 2

2.1 The banking system has become more concentrated, with large banks having a bigger share of the market. The total number of banks reduced from 14,483 to 6,530.

2.2 In the early twentieth century, many states passed laws restricting banks from opening more than one branch. The McFadden Act of 1927 restricted banks from opening branches in more than one state.

2.3 The risk is that interest rates will rise so that, when deposits are rolled over, the bank has to pay a higher rate of interest. The rate received on loans will not change. The result will be a reduction in the bank's net interest income.

2.4 DLC's loss is more than its equity capital and it would probably be liquidated. The subordinated long-term debt holders would incur losses on their $5 million investment. The depositors should get their money back.

2.5 The net interest income of a bank is interest received minus interest paid.

2.6 Credit risk primarily affects loan losses. Noninterest income includes trading gains and losses. Market risk therefore affects noninterest income. It also affects net interest income if assets and liabilities are not matched. Operational risk primarily affects non-interest expenses.

2.7 A private placement is a new issue of securities that is sold to a small number of large institutional investors. A public offering is a new issue of securities that is offered to the general public. In a best efforts deal, the investment bank does as well as it can to place securities with investors, but does not guarantee that they can be sold. In a firm commitment deal, the investment bank agrees to buy the securities from the issuing company for a particular price and attempts to sell them in the market for a higher price.

2.8 The bidders when ranked from the highest price bid to the lowest are: H, C, F, A, B, D, E, and G. Bidders H, C, and F have bid for 140,000 shares. A has bid for 20,000. The price that clears the market is the price that was bid by A or

$100. H, C, and F get their orders filled at this price. Half of A's order is filled at this price.

2.9 A Dutch auction potentially attracts a wide range of bidders. If all interested market participants bid, the price paid should be close to the market price immediately after the IPO. The usual IPO situation where the price turns out to be well below the market price should therefore be avoided. Also, investment banks are not able to restrict purchasers to their best current and potential clients. The Google IPO was different from a standard Dutch auction in that Google reserved the right to choose the number of shares that would be issued, and the percentage allocated to each bidder, when it saw the bids.

2.10 Poison pills can give management a negotiation tool, particularly if the board has the right to overturn a poison pill or make it ineffective. When it is confronted with a potential acquirer, the poison pill can buy the company time to bargain for a better purchase price or find other bidders. However, there is the danger that the poison pill will discourage potential buyers from approaching the company in the first place.

2.11 The brokerage subsidiary of a bank might recommend securities that the investment banking subsidiary is trying to sell. The commercial banking subsidiary might pass confidential information about its clients to the investment banking subsidiary. When a bank does business with a company (or wants to do business with the company), it might persuade the brokerage subsidiary to recommend the company's shares as a "buy." The commercial banking subsidiary might persuade a company to which it has lent money to do a bond issue because it is worried about its exposure to the client. (It wants the investment banking subsidiary to persuade its clients to take on the credit risk.) These conflicts of interest are handled by what are known as Chinese walls. They prevent the flow of information from one part of the bank to another.

2.12 The interest is no longer accrued. The before-tax income will be reduced by 8% of $10 million or $800,000 per year.

2.13 The provision for loan losses reflects the losses the bank expects in the future. It is updated periodically. When the provision is increased in a year by X, there is a charge to the income statement of X. Actual loan losses, when they are recognized, are charged against the balance in the loan loss provision account.

2.14 In the originate-to-distribute model, a bank originates loans and then securitizes them so that they are passed on to investors. This was done extensively with household mortgages during the seven-year period leading up to July 2007. In July 2007, investors lost confidence in the securitized products and banks were force to abandon the originate-to-distribute model, at least temporarily.

CHAPTER 3

3.1 Term life insurance lasts a fixed period (e.g., 5 years or 10 years). The policyholder pays premiums. If the policyholder dies during the life of the policy, the policyholder's beneficiaries receive a payout equal to the principal amount of the policy. Whole life insurance lasts for the whole life of the policy holder. The policy holder pays premiums (usually the same each year) and the policyholder's beneficiaries receive a payout equal to the principal amount of the policy when the policyholder dies. There is an investment element to whole life insurance because the premiums in early years are high relative to the expected payout in those years. (The reverse is true in later years.) Tax on the investment income is deferred until death.

3.2 Variable life insurance is whole life insurance where the policyholder can specify how the funds generated in early years (the excess of the premiums over the actuarial cost of the insurance) are invested. There is a minimum payout on death, but the payout can be more than the minimum if the investments do well. Universal life insurance is whole life insurance where the premium can be reduced to a specified minimum level without the policy lapsing. The insurance company chooses the investments (generally fixed income) and guarantees a minimum return. If the investments do well, the return provided on the policyholder's death may be greater than the guaranteed minimum.

3.3 Annuity contracts have exposure to longevity risk. Life insurance contracts have exposure to mortality risk.

3.4 The lifetime annuity created from an accumulated value was calculated using an interest rate that was the greater of (a) the market interest rate and (b) a prespecified minimum interest rate.

3.5 The probability that the woman will die during the first year is 0.003255. The probability that the woman will die during the second year is $0.003517 \times (1 - 0.003255) = 0.003506$. Suppose that the breakeven premium is X. We must have

$$1,000,000 \times (0.003255 + 0.003506) = X + (1 - 0.003255)X$$

so that $X = 3,386$. The breakeven premium is therefore $3,386.

3.6 The probability of a male surviving to 30 is 0.97147. The probability of a male surviving to 90 is 0.15722. The probability of male surviving to 90 conditional that 30 is reached is therefore $0.15722/0.97147 = 0.16184$. The probability of a female surviving to 90 conditional that 30 is reached is $0.27333/0.98466 = 0.27759$.

3.7 The biggest risks are those arising from catastrophes such as earthquakes and hurricanes and those arising from liability insurance (e.g., claims related to asbestos in the United States). This is because there is no "law of large numbers" working in the insurance company's favor. Either the event happens and there are big payouts or the event does not happen and there are no payouts.

3.8 CAT bonds (catastrophe bonds) are an alternative to reinsurance for an insurance company that has taken on a certain catastrophic risk (e.g., the risk of a hurricane or an earthquake) and wants to get rid of it. CAT bonds are issued by the insurance company. They provide a higher rate of interest than risk-free bonds. However, the bondholders agree to forego interest, and possibly principal, to meet any claims against the insurance company that are within a prespecified range.

3.9 The CAT bond has very little systematic risk. Whether a particular type of catastrophe occurs is independent of the return on the market. The risks in the CAT bond are likely to be largely "diversified away" by the other investments in the portfolio. A B-rated bond does have systematic risk that cannot be diversified away. It is likely therefore that the CAT bond is a better addition to the portfolio.

3.10 In Canada and the United Kingdom, health care is provided by the government. In the United States, publicly funded health care is limited and most individuals buy private health care insurance of one sort or another. In the United Kingdom, a private health care system operates alongside the public system.

3.11 Both moral hazard and adverse selection are potential problems. The insurance might lead to an individual not trying to keep a job as much as he or she otherwise would. Indeed, an individual might purposely lose his or her job to collect the insurance payout! Also, individuals that are most at risk for losing their jobs would be the ones that choose to buy the insurance.

3.12 The payouts of property–casualty insurers show more variability than the payouts of life insurers. This is because of the possibility of catastrophes such as earthquakes and hurricanes and liability insurance claims such as those related to asbestos in the United States.

3.13 The loss ratio is the ratio of payouts to premiums in a year. The expense ratio is the ratio of expenses (e.g., sales commissions and expenses incurred in validating losses) to premiums in a year. The statement is not true because investment income is usually significant. Premiums are received at the beginning of a year and payouts are made during the year or after the end of the year.

3.14 A defined contribution plan is a plan where the contributions of each employee (together with contributions made by the employer for that employee) are kept in a separate account and invested for the employee. When retirement age is reached the accumulated amount is usually converted into an annuity. In a defined benefit plan, all contributions for all employees are pooled and invested. Employees receive a pre-defined pension that is based on their years of employment and final salary. At any given time, a defined benefit plan may be in surplus or in deficit.

3.15 The employee's wages are constant in real terms. Suppose that they are X per year. (The units for X do not matter for the purposes of our calculation.) The pension is $0.75X$. The real return earned is zero. Because employees work for 40 years, the present value of the contributions made by one employee is $40XR$ where R is the contribution rate as a percentage of the employee's wages. The present value of the benefits is $20 \times 0.75X = 15X$. The value of R that is necessary to adequately fund the plan must therefore satisfy

$$40XR = 15X$$

The solution to this equation is $R = 0.375$. The total of the employer and employee contributions should therefore be 37.5% of salary.

CHAPTER 4

4.1 The number of shares of an open-end mutual fund increases as investments in the fund increase and decreases as investors withdraw their funds.

A closed-end fund is like any other corporation with a fixed number of shares that trade.

4.2 The NAV of an open-ended mutual fund is calculated at 4 P.M. each day as the value of the assets held by the fund divided by the number of shares outstanding.

4.3 The investor is deemed to have made capital gains of $300 and $100 in 2012 and 2013, respectively. In 2014, the investor is deemed to have made a capital loss of $200.

4.4 An index fund is a fund that is designed so that its value tracks the performance of an index such as the S&P 500. It can be created by buying all the stocks (or a representative subset of the stocks) that underly the index. Sometimes futures contracts on the index are used.

4.5 The front-end load is the amount an investor pays, as a percentage of his or her investment, when shares of the fund are purchased. The back-end load is the amount an investor pays, as a percentage of his or her investment, when shares of the fund are redeemed.

4.6 An exchange-traded fund (ETF) that tracks an index is created when an institutional investor deposits a portfolio of shares that is designed to track the index and receives shares in the ETF. Institutional investors can at any time exchange shares in the ETF for the underlying shares held by the ETF, or vice versa. The advantage over an open-end mutual fund that tracks the index is that the fund can be traded at any time, the fund can be shorted, and the fund does not have to be partially liquidated to accommodate redemptions. The advantage over a closed-end mutual fund is that there is very little difference between the ETF share price and the net asset value per share of the fund.

4.7 The arithmetic mean of a set of n numbers is the sum of the numbers divided by n. The geometric mean is the nth root of the product of the numbers. The arithmetic mean is always greater than or equal to the geometric mean. The return per year realized when an investment is held for several years is calculated using a geometric, not an arithmetric mean. (The procedure is to calculate the geometric mean of one plus the return in each year and then subtract one.)

4.8 Late trading is the illegal practice of putting in an order to buy or sell an open-end mutual fund at the 4 P.M. price after 4 P.M. Market timing is a practice where favored clients are allowed to buy and sell a mutual fund frequently to take advantage of the fact that some prices used in the calculation of the 4 P.M. net asset value are stale. Front running is the practice of trading by individuals ahead of a large institutional trade that is expected to move the market. Directed brokerage describes the situation where a mutual fund uses a brokerage house for trades when the brokerage house recommends the fund to clients.

4.9 Mutual funds must disclose their investment policies; their use of leverage is limited; they must calculate NAV daily; their shares must be redeemable at any time.

4.10 If a hedge fund is making money out of trading convertible bonds, it must be doing so at the expense of its counterparties. If most of the traders are hedge funds, they cannot all be making money.

4.11 Hurdle rate is the minimum return necessary for an incentive fee to be applicable. High-water mark refers to the previous losses that must be recouped before incentive fees are applicable. Clawback refers to investors being able to apply a percentage of incentive fees against a percentage of future losses.

4.12 If the return is X ($> 2\%$), the investors pay $0.02 + 0.2(X - 0.02)$ in fees. It must therefore be the case that

$$X - 0.02 - 0.2(X - 0.02) = 0.2$$

so that $0.8X = 0.216$ or $X = 0.27$. A return of 27% is necessary.

4.13 Short-term gains and losses do matter if the hedge fund is highly leveraged. Short term losses can lead to margin calls that destroy the hedge fund.

4.14 Prime brokers decide on the amount of leverage that they are prepared to let hedge funds have. This influences the risks that hedge funds can take.

CHAPTER 5

5.1 When a trader enters into a long forward contract, she is agreeing to *buy* the underlying asset for a certain price at a certain time in the future. When a trader enters into a short forward contract, she is agreeing to *sell* the underlying asset for a certain price at a certain time in the future.

5.2 A trader is *hedging* when she has an exposure to the price of an asset and takes a position in a derivative to offset the exposure. In a *speculation*, the trader has no exposure to offset. She is betting on the future movements in the price of the asset. *Arbitrage* involves taking a position in two or more different markets to lock in a profit.

5.3 In the first case, the trader is obligated to buy the asset for $50. (The trader does not have a choice.) In the second case, the trader has an option to buy the asset for $50. (The trader does not have to exercise the option.)

5.4 Selling a call option involves giving someone else the right to buy an asset from you for a certain price. Buying a put option gives you the right to sell the asset to someone else.

5.5 (a) The investor is obligated to sell pounds for 1.7000 when they are worth 1.6900. The gain is $(1.7000 - 1.6900) \times 100,000 = \$1,000$.

   (b) The investor is obligated to sell pounds for 1.7000 when they are worth 1.7200. The loss is $(1.7200 - 1.7000) \times 100,000 = \$2,000$.

5.6 (a) The trader sells for 50 cents per pound something that is worth 48.20 cents per pound. Gain = $(\$0.5000 - \$0.4820) \times 50,000 = \$900$.

   (b) The trader sells for 50 cents per pound something that is worth 51.30 cents per pound. Loss = $(\$0.5130 - \$0.5000) \times 50,000 = \$650$.

5.7 You have sold a put option. You have agreed to buy 100 shares for $40 per share if the party on the other side of the contract chooses to exercise the right to sell for this price. The option will be exercised only when the price of stock is below $40. Suppose, for example, that the option is exercised when the price is $30. You have to buy at $40 shares that are worth $30; you lose $10 per share, or $1,000 in total. If the option is exercised when the price is $20, you lose $20 per share, or $2,000 in total. The worst that can happen is that the price of the stock declines to almost zero during the three-month period. This highly unlikely event would cost you $4,000. In return for the possible future losses, you receive the price of the option from the purchaser.

5.8 The over-the-counter (OTC) market is a telephone- and computer-linked network of financial institutions, fund managers, and corporate treasurers where two participants can enter into any mutually acceptable contract. An exchange-traded market is a market organized by an exchange where traders either meet physically or communicate electronically and the contracts that can be traded have been defined by the exchange.

5.9 One strategy would be to buy 200 shares. Another would be to buy 2,000 options. If the share price does well, the second strategy will give rise to greater gains. For example, if the share price goes up to $40, you gain $[2,000 \times (\$40 - \$30)] - \$5,800 = \$14,200$ from the second strategy and only $200 \times (\$40 - \$29) = \$2,200$ from the first strategy. However, if the share price does badly, the second strategy gives greater losses. For example, if the share price goes down to $25, the first strategy leads to a loss of $200 \times (\$29 - \$25) = \$800$, whereas the second strategy leads to a loss of the whole $5,800 investment. This example shows that options contain built in leverage.

5.10 You could buy 5,000 put options (or 50 contracts) with a strike price of $25 and an expiration date in four months. This provides a type of insurance. If, at the end of four months, the stock price proves to be less than $25, you can exercise the options and sell the shares for $25 each. The cost of this strategy is the price you pay for the put options.

5.11 A stock option provides no funds for the company. It is a security sold by one trader to another. The company is not involved. By contrast, a stock when it is first issued is a claim sold by the company to investors and does provide funds for the company.

5.12 Ignoring the time value of money, the holder of the option will make a profit if the stock price in March is greater than $52.50. This is because the payoff to the holder of the option is, in these circumstances, greater than the $2.50 paid for the option. The option will be exercised if the stock price at maturity is greater than $50.00. Note that, if the stock price is between $50.00 and $52.50, the option is exercised but the holder of the option takes a loss overall.

5.13 Ignoring the time value of money, the seller of the option will make a profit if the stock price in June is greater than $56.00. This is because the cost to the seller of the option is in these circumstances less than the price received for the option. The option will be exercised if the stock price at maturity is less than $60.00. Note that if the stock price is between $56.00 and $60.00 the seller of the option makes a profit even though the option is exercised.

5.14 A long position in a four-month put option can provide insurance against the exchange rate falling below the strike price. It ensures that the foreign currency can be sold for at least the strike price.

5.15 The company could enter into a long forward contract to buy 1 million Canadian dollars in six months. This would have the effect of locking in an exchange rate equal to the current forward exchange rate. Alternatively, the company could buy a call option giving it the right (but not the obligation) to purchase 1 million Canadian dollars at a certain exchange rate in six months. This would provide insurance against a strong Canadian dollar in six months while still allowing the company to benefit from a weak Canadian dollar at that time.

5.16 The payoff from an ICON is the payoff from:
(a) A regular bond
(b) A short position in call options to buy 169,000 yen with an exercise price of 1/169
(c) A long position in call options to buy 169,000 yen with an exercise price of 1/84.5

This is demonstrated by the following table

	Terminal Value of Regular Bond	Terminal Value of Short Calls	Terminal Value of Long Calls	Terminal Value of Whole Position
$S_T > 169$	1,000	0	0	1,000
$84.5 \le S_T \le 169$	1,000	$-169{,}000\left(\frac{1}{S_T} - \frac{1}{169}\right)$	0	$2{,}000 - \frac{169{,}000}{S_T}$
$S_T < 84.5$	1,000	$-169{,}000\left(\frac{1}{S_T} - \frac{1}{169}\right)$	$169{,}000\left(\frac{1}{S_T} - \frac{1}{84.5}\right)$	0

5.17 (a) The trader buys a 180-day call option and takes a short position in a 180-day forward contract.
(b) The trader buys 90-day put options and takes a long position in a 90-day forward contract.

5.18 It enters into a five-year swap where it pays 6.51% and receives LIBOR. Its investment is then at LIBOR minus 1.51%.

5.19 It enters into a five-year swap where it receives 6.47% and pays LIBOR. Its net cost of borrowing is LIBOR +0.53%.

5.20 It enters into a three-year swap where it receives LIBOR and pays 6.24%. Its net borrowing cost for the three years is then 7.24% per annum.

5.21 Suppose that the weather is bad and the farmer's production is lower than expected. Other farmers are likely to have been affected similarly. Corn production overall will be low and as a consequence the price of corn will be relatively high. The farmer is likely to be overhedged relative to actual production. The farmer's problems arising from the bad harvest will be made worse by losses on the short futures position. This problem emphasizes the importance of looking at the big picture when hedging. The farmer is correct to question whether hedging price risk while ignoring other risks is a good strategy.

5.22 It may well be true that there is just as much chance that the price of oil in the future will be above the futures price as that it will be below the futures price. This means that the use of a futures contract for speculation would be like betting on whether a coin comes up heads or tails. But it might make sense for the airline to use futures for hedging rather than speculation. The futures contract then has the effect of reducing risks. It can be argued that an airline should not expose its shareholders to risks associated with the future price of oil when there are contracts available to hedge the risks.

5.23 Microsoft is choosing an option on a portfolio of assets instead of the corresponding portfolio of options. The former is always less expensive because there is the potential for an increase in the price of one asset to be netted off against a decrease in the price of another asset. Compare (a) an option with a strike price of $20 on a portfolio of two assets each worth $10 and (b) a portfolio of two options with a strike price of $10, one on each of the assets. If both assets increase in price or both assets decrease in price, the payoffs are the same. But if one decreases and the other increases, the payoff from (a) is less than that from (b). Both the Asian feature and the basket feature in Microsoft's options help to reduce the cost of the options because of the possibility of gains and losses being netted.

5.24 The two calculations are necessary to determine the initial margin. The first gives

$$500 \times (3.5 + 0.2 \times 57 - 3) = 5,950$$

The second gives

$$500 \times (3.5 + 0.1 \times 57) = 4,600$$

The initial margin is the greater of these, or $5,950. Part of this can be provided by the initial amount of $500 \times 3.5 = \$1,750$ received for the options.

5.25 It means that the price of the energy source can go up or down but will tend over time to get pulled back to its long run average level. Electricity has the highest rate of mean reversion; oil has the lowest.

5.26 As we increase the frequency with which the asset price is observed, the asset price becomes more likely to hit the barrier and the value of a knock-out call goes down.

5.27 The average of the highest and lowest temperature each day is 75° Fahrenheit. The CDD each day is therefore 10 and the cumulative CDD for the month is $10 \times 31 = 310$. The payoff from the call option is therefore $(310 - 250) \times 5,000 = \$300,000$.

5.28 A 5×8 contract for May 2013 is a contract to provide electricity for five days per week during the off-peak period (11 P.M. to 7 A.M.). When daily exercise is specified, the holder of the option is able to choose each weekday whether he or she will buy electricity at the strike price. When there is monthly exercise, he or she chooses once at the beginning of the month whether electricity is to be bought at the strike price for the whole month. The option with daily exercise is worth more.

5.29 The cost of the shares is 500×50 or $25,000. When shares are shorted, the proceeds of the sale form part of the margin. In this case, the total margin required is $1.6 \times 25,000$, or $40,000. The extra margin required is therefore $15,000. This can be in the form of cash or marginable securities. When the share price rises to S, the value of the underlying stock is $500S$. There is a margin call when

$$40,000 < 1.3 \times 500S$$

or $S > 61.54$.

CHAPTER 6

6.1 Mortgages were frequently securitized. The only information that was retained during the securitization process was the applicant's FICO score and the loan-to-value ratio of the mortgage.

6.2 There was a short-term imbalance between supply and demand because many people were persuaded to take out mortgages that they could not afford.

6.3 When the loss rate on the mortgages is 5%, there are no losses on the mezzanine tranche of the ABS and therefore there are no losses on any of the tranches of the ABS CDO. When the loss rate on the mortgages is 12%, the loss on the mezzanine tranche of the ABS is 7/20 or 35%. The loss rate on the equity and mezzanine tranches of the ABS CDO is 100%. The loss rate on the senior tranche of the ABS CDO is $10/75 = 13.333\%$.

6.4 Often a tranche is thin and the probability distribution of the loss is quite different from that on a bond. If a loss occurs, there is a high probability that it will be 100%. A 100% loss is much less likely for a bond.

6.5 An ABS is a set of tranches created from a portfolio of loans, bonds, credit card receivables, etc. An ABS CDO is an ABS created from particular tranches (e.g., the BBB-rated tranches) of a number of different ABSs.

6.6 Investors underestimated how high the default correlations between mortgages would be in stressed market conditions. Investors also did not always realize that the tranches underlying ABS CDOs were usually quite thin so that they were either totally wiped out or untouched. There was an unfortunate tendency to assume that a tranche with a particular rating could be considered to be the same as a bond with that rating. This assumption is not valid for the reasons just mentioned.

6.7 "Agency costs" is a term used to describe the costs in a situation where the interests of two parties are not perfectly aligned. The incentives of traders, originators, valuers, the creators of the structured products, and the rating agencies arguably created agency costs.

6.8 The waterfall defines how the interest and principal cash flows from the underlying portfolio are distributed to the tranches. In a typical arrangement, interest cash flows are first used to pay the most senior tranche its promised return. The cash flows (if any) that are left over are used to provide the next-most-senior tranche with its promised return and so on. Principal cash flows are usually first to repay the most senior tranche, then the next-most-senior tranche, and so on. The equity tranche only receives interest and principal when more senior tranches have been paid.

6.9 Typically an ABS CDO is created from the BBB-rated tranches of an ABS. This is because it is difficult to find investors for these tranches.

6.10 Mian and Sufi showed that regions where mortgage application denials were highest in the United States in 1996 were also regions where mortgage origination grew particularly fast during the 2000 to 2007 period.

6.11 The mezzanine tranche of an ABS or ABS CDO is a tranche that is in the middle as far as seniority goes. It ranks below the senior tranches and therefore absorbs losses before they do. It ranks above the equity tranche (so that the equity tranche absorbs losses before it does).

6.12 As default correlation increases, the senior tranche of an ABS becomes more risky because it is more likely to suffer losses. The equity tranche becomes less risky as the default correlation increases. To understand this second point, note that in the limit when there is perfect correlation (and assuming no recoveries), all tranches have the same losses because either (a) all companies default or (b) no companies default.

6.13 The end-of-year bonus usually reflects performance during the year. Traders and other employees of banks are liable to be always focusing on their next end-of-year bonus and therefore have a short-term time horizon for their decision-making.

CHAPTER 7

7.1 The value of the portfolio decreases by $10,500.

7.2 The value of the portfolio increases by $400.

7.3 In both cases, it increases by $0.5 \times 30 \times 2^2$ or $60.

7.4 A delta of 0.7 means that, when the price of the stock increases by a small amount, the price of the option increases by 70% of this amount. Similarly, when the price of the stock decreases by a small amount, the price of the option decreases by 70% of this amount. A short position in 1,000 options has a delta of -700 and can be made delta neutral with the purchase of 700 shares.

7.5 A theta of -100 per day means that if one day passes with no change in either the stock price or its volatility, the value of the option position declines by $-$100. If a trader feels that neither the stock price nor its implied volatility will change, she should write an option with as big a negative theta as possible so that her position has a high positive theta. Relatively short-life at-the-money options have the biggest negative theta.

7.6 The gamma of an option position is the rate of change of the delta of the position with respect to the asset price. For example, a gamma of 0.1 would indicate that, when the asset price increases by a certain small amount, delta increases by 0.1 of this amount. When the gamma of an option writer's position is large and negative and the delta is zero, the option writer will lose significant amounts of money if there is a large movement (either an increase or a decrease) in the asset price.

7.7 To hedge an option position, it is necessary to create the opposite option position synthetically. For example, to hedge a long position in a put, it is necessary to create a short position in a put synthetically. It follows that the procedure for creating an option position synthetically is the reverse of the procedure for hedging the option position.

7.8 A long position in either a put or a call option has a positive gamma. From Figure 7.9, when gamma is positive, the hedger gains from a large change in the stock price and loses from a small change in the stock price. Hence the hedger will fare better in case (b). When the portfolio contains short option position the hedger will similarly fare better in (a).

7.9 The delta indicates that when the value of the euro exchange rate increases by $0.01, the value of the bank's position increases by $0.01 \times 30,000 = $300.

The gamma indicates that when the euro exchange rate increases by $0.01, the delta of the portfolio decreases by $0.01 \times 80,000 = 800$. For delta neutrality, 30,000 euros should be shorted. When the exchange rate moves up to 0.93, we expect the delta of the portfolio to decrease by $(0.93 - 0.90) \times 80,000 = 2,400$ so that it becomes 27,600. To maintain delta neutrality, it is therefore necessary for the bank to unwind its short position by 2,400 euros so that a net 27,600 have been shorted. When a portfolio is delta neutral and has a negative gamma, a loss is experienced when there is a large movement in the underlying asset price. We can conclude that the bank is likely to have lost money.

7.10 When used in the way described in the text, it does assume volatility is constant. In theory, we could implement a static options replication strategy where there are three dimensions: time, the stock price, and volatility. Prices are then matched on a surface in the three-dimensional space.

7.11 Ten regular options are likely to be needed. This is because there are ten equations to be satisfied, one for each point on the boundary.

7.12 The payoff from an Asian option becomes more certain with the passage of time. As a result, the amount of uncertainty that needs to be hedged decreases with the passage of time.

7.13 Consider a portfolio of options dependent on a single market variable. A single trade is all that is necessary to make the position delta neutral regardless of the number of options in the portfolio.

7.14 The price, delta, gamma, vega, theta, and rho are 0.0217, –0.396, 5.415, 0.00203, –0.0000625, and –0.00119. Delta predicts that the option price should decrease by approximately 0.000396 when the exchange rate increases by 0.001. This is what we find. When the exchange rate is increased to 0.751, the option price decreases to 0.0213.

CHAPTER 8

8.1 In this case, the interest rate mismatch is $10 billion. The bank's net interest income declines by $100 million each year for the next three years.

8.2 If long-term rates were simply a reflection of expected future short-term rates, we would expect the long rates to be less than short rates as often as they are greater than short rates. (This is based on the assumption that half of the time investors expect rates to increase and half of the time investors expect rates to decrease.) Liquidity preference theory argues that long-term rates are high relative to expected future short-term rates. This means that long rates are greater than short rates most of the time. When long rates are less than short rates, the market is expecting a relatively steep decline in rates.

8.3 There are three reasons:

1 Treasury bills and Treasury bonds must be purchased by financial institutions to fulfill a variety of regulatory requirements. This increases demand for these Treasury instruments driving the price up and the yield down.

2 The amount of capital a bank is required to hold to support an investment in Treasury bills and bonds is substantially smaller than the capital required to support a similar investment in other very-low-risk instruments.

3 In the United States, Treasury instruments are given a favorable tax treatment compared with most other fixed-income investments because they are not taxed at the state level.

8.4 In an overnight-indexed swap, the geometric average of the federal funds rate for a period such as three months is exchanged for a prespecified fixed rate

8.5 The LIBOR–OIS spread is a measure of the reluctance of banks to lend to each other.

8.6 Duration provides information about the effect of a small parallel shift in the yield curve on the value of a bond portfolio. The percentage decrease in the value of the portfolio equals the duration of the portfolio multiplied by the amount by which interest rates are increased in the small parallel shift. Its limitation is that it applies only to parallel shifts in the yield curve that are small.

8.7 (a) The bond's price is $86.80, (b) the bond's duration is 4.256 years, (c) the duration formula shows that when the yield decreases by 0.2% the bond's price increases by $0.74, (d) recomputing the bond's price with a yield of 10.8% gives a price of $87.54, which is approximately consistent with (a) and (c).

8.8 (a) The bond's price is $88.91, (b) the bond's modified duration is 3.843 years, (c) the duration formula shows that when the yield decreases by 0.2% the bond's price increases by $0.68, (d) recomputing the bond's price with a yield of 10.8% (annually compounded) gives a price of $89.60, which is approximately consistent with (a) and (c).

8.9 The bond price is $104.80. The duration of the bond is 5.35 years. The convexity is 30.60. The effect of a 1% increase in the yield is estimated by equation (8.4) as

$$104.80 \times (-0.01 \times 5.35 + 0.5 \times 30.60 \times 0.0001) = -5.44$$

The bond price actually changes to $99.36, which is consistent with the estimate.

8.10 We can (a) perturb points on the yield curve (see Figure 8.4), (b) perturb sections of the yield curve (see Figure 8.6), and (c) perturb the market quotes used to create the yield curve.

8.11 The deltas (changes in portfolio value per unit of factor with factor loading being assumed to be in basis points) are −36 and −293.

8.12 The impact on the portfolio, measured as a proportion of the value of the portfolio, is

$$- (0.2 \times 0.001 + 0.6 \times 0.0008 + 0.9 \times 0.0007 + 1.6 \times 0.0006$$
$$+ 2.0 \times 0.0005 - 2.1 \times 0.0003 - 3.0 \times 0.0001) = -0.00234$$

The portfolio decreases by 0.234%.

8.13 Dollar duration is defined as the product of the duration of a portfolio and its price. Dollar convexity is defined as the product of the convexity of a portfolio and its price.

8.14 The partial durations add up to the total duration. The DV01 is the total duration times the portfolio value times 0.0001.

CHAPTER 9

9.1 VaR is the loss that is not expected to be exceeded with a certain confidence level. Expected shortfall is the expected loss conditional that the loss is worse than the VaR level. Expected shortfall has the advantage that it always satisfies the subadditivity (diversification is good) condition.

9.2 A spectral risk measure is a risk measure that assigns weights to the quantiles of the loss distribution. For the subadditivity condition to be satisfied, the weight assigned to the qth quantile must be a non-decreasing function of q.

9.3 There is a 5% chance that you will lose \$6,000 or more during a one-month period.

9.4 Your expected loss during a "bad month" is \$6,000. Bad months are defined as the months where returns are less than the five-percentile points on the distribution of monthly returns.

9.5 (a) \$1 million.

(b) The expected shortfall is $0.9 \times 10 + 0.1 \times 1$ or \$9.1 million.

(c) There is a probability of $0.009^2 = 0.000081$ of a loss of \$20 million, a probability of $2 \times 0.009 \times 0.991 = 0.017838$ of a loss of \$11 million, and a probability of $0.991^2 = 0.982081$ of a loss of \$2 million. The VaR when the confidence level is 99% is therefore \$11 million.

(d) The expected shortfall is $(0.000081 \times 20 + 0.009919 \times 11)/0.01 = \$11.07$ million.

(e) Because $1 + 1 < 11$, the subadditivity condition is not satisfied for VaR. Because $9.1 + 9.1 > 11.07$, it is satisfied for expected shortfall.

9.6 (a) $2 \times 1.96 = \$3.92$ million, (b) $\sqrt{5} \times 2 \times 1.96 = \$8.77$ million, (c) $\sqrt{5} \times 2 \times 2.33 = 10.40$ million.

9.7 (b) becomes \$9.96 million and (c) becomes \$11.82 million.

9.8 Marginal VaR is the rate of change of VaR with the amount invested in the ith asset. Incremental VaR is the incremental effect of the ith asset on VaR (i.e., the difference between VaR with and without the asset). Component VaR is the part of VaR that can be attributed the ith asset (the sum of component VaRs equals the total VaR).

9.9 The probability of 17 or more exceptions is 1-BINOMDIST(16,1000, 0.01, TRUE) or 2.64%. The model should be rejected at the 5% confidence level.

9.10 Bunching is the tendency for exceptions to be bunched rather than occurring randomly throughout the time period considered.

9.11 We are interested in the variance of $\Delta P_1 + \Delta P_2 + \cdots + \Delta P_T$. This is $\sum_{i=1}^{T} \sigma_i^2 + 2 \sum_{i>j} \rho_{ij}\sigma_i\sigma_j$ where σ_i is the standard deviation of ΔP_i and ρ_{ij} is the correlation between ΔP_i and ΔP_j. In this case, $\sigma_i = \sigma$ for all i and $\rho_{ij} = \rho^{i-j}$ when $i > j$. After further algebraic manipulations, this leads directly to equation (9.3).

CHAPTER 10

10.1 $2 \times \sqrt{3}$ or 3.46%.

10.2 The standard deviation of the percentage price change in one day is $25/\sqrt{252}$ or 1.57% and 95% confidence limits are from -3.09% to $+3.09\%$.

10.3 Volatility is much higher when markets are open than when they are closed. Traders therefore measure time in trading days rather than calendar days.

10.4 Implied volatility is the volatility that leads to the option price equaling the market price when Black–Scholes–Merton assumptions are used. It is found by "trial and error." Because different options have different implied volatilities, traders are not using the same assumptions as Black–Scholes–Merton. (See Chapter 22 for a further discussion of this.)

10.5 The normal formula for calculating standard deviation gives 0.547% per day. The simplified approach in equation (10.4) gives 0.530% per day.

10.6 The power law gives $0.01 = K \times 500^{-2}$ so that $K = 2,500$. (a) $2,500 \times 1,000^{-2} = 0.0025$ or 0.25%, (b) $2,500 \times 2,000^{-2} = 0.000625$ or 0.0625%.

10.7 The variance rate estimated, calculated at the end of day $n - 1$ for day n, equals λ times the variance rate calculated at the end of day $n - 2$ for day $n - 1$ plus $1 - \lambda$ times the squared return on day $n - 1$.

10.8 GARCH (1,1) adapts the EWMA model by giving some weight to a long-run average variance rate. Whereas the EWMA has no mean reversion, GARCH (1,1) is consistent with a mean-reverting variance rate model.

10.9 In this case, $\sigma_{n-1} = 0.015$ and $u_n = 0.5/30 = 0.01667$, so that equation (10.8) gives

$$\sigma_n^2 = 0.94 \times 0.015^2 + 0.06 \times 0.01667^2 = 0.0002281$$

The volatility estimate on day n is therefore $\sqrt{0.0002281} = 0.015103$ or 1.5103%.

10.10 Reducing λ from 0.95 to 0.85 means that more weight is given to recent observations of u_i^2 and less weight is given to older observations. Volatilities calculated with $\lambda = 0.85$ will react more quickly to new information and will "bounce around" much more than volatilities calculated with $\lambda = 0.95$.

10.11 With the usual notation $u_{n-1} = 20/1,040 = 0.01923$ so that

$$\sigma_n^2 = 0.000002 + 0.06 \times 0.01923^2 + 0.92 \times 0.01^2 = 0.0001162$$

This gives $\sigma_n = 0.01078$. The new volatility estimate is therefore 1.078% per day.

10.12 The proportional daily change is $-0.005/1.5000 = -0.003333$. The current daily variance estimate is $0.006^2 = 0.000036$. The new daily variance estimate is

$$0.9 \times 0.000036 + 0.1 \times 0.003333^2 = 0.000033511$$

The new volatility is the square root of this. It is 0.00579 or 0.579%.

10.13 The weight given to the long-run average variance rate is $1 - \alpha - \beta$ and the long-run average variance rate is $\omega/(1 - \alpha - \beta)$. Increasing ω increases the long-run average variance rate. Increasing α increases the weight given to the most recent data item, reduces the weight given to the long-run average variance rate, and increases the level of the long-run average variance rate. Increasing β increases the weight given to the previous variance estimate, reduces the weight given to the long-run average variance rate, and increases the level of the long-run average variance rate.

10.14 The long-run average variance rate is $\omega/(1 - \alpha - \beta)$ or $0.000004/0.03 = 0.0001333$. The long-run average volatility is $\sqrt{0.0001333}$ or 1.155%. The equation describing the way the variance rate reverts to its long-run average is

$$E[\sigma_{n+k}^2] = V_L + (\alpha + \beta)^k(\sigma_n^2 - V_L)$$

In this case

$$E[\sigma_{n+k}^2] = 0.0001333 + 0.97^k(\sigma_n^2 - 0.0001333)$$

If the current volatility is 20% per year, $\sigma_n = 0.2/\sqrt{252} = 0.0126$. The expected variance rate in 20 days is

$$0.0001333 + 0.97^{20}(0.0126^2 - 0.0001333) = 0.0001471$$

The expected volatility in 20 days is therefore $\sqrt{0.0001471} = 0.0121$ or 1.21% per day.

10.15 The FTSE expressed in dollars is XY where X is the FTSE expressed in sterling and Y is the exchange rate (value of one pound in dollars). Define x_i as the proportional change in X on day i and y_i as the proportional change in Y on day i. The proportional change in XY is approximately $x_i + y_i$. The standard deviation of x_i is 0.018 and the standard deviation of y_i is 0.009. The correlation between the two is 0.4. The variance of $x_i + y_i$ is therefore

$$0.018^2 + 0.009^2 + 2 \times 0.018 \times 0.009 \times 0.4 = 0.0005346$$

so that the volatility of $x_i + y_i$ is 0.0231 or 2.31%. This is the volatility of the FTSE expressed in dollars. Note that it is greater than the volatility of the FTSE expressed in sterling. This is the impact of the positive correlation. When the FTSE increases, the value of sterling measured in dollars also tends to increase. This creates an even bigger increase in the value of FTSE measured in dollars. Similarly, when FTSE decreases, the value of sterling measured in dollars also tends to decrease, creating an even bigger decrease in the value of FTSE measured in dollars.

10.16 In this case, $V_L = 0.000003/0.02 = 0.00015$ and equation (10.14) gives the expected variance rate in 30 days as

$$0.00015 + 0.98^{30}(0.01^2 - 0.00015) = 0.000123$$

The volatility is $\sqrt{0.000123} = 0.0111$ or 1.11% per day.

10.17 In this case, $V_L = 0.000002/0.02 = 0.0001$. In equation (10.15), $V_L = 0.0001$, $a = 0.0202$, $T = 20$, and $V(0) = 0.000169$ so that the volatility is 19.88%.

CHAPTER 11

11.1 You need the standard deviations of the two variables.

11.2 Loosely speaking, correlation measures the extent of linear dependence. It does not measure other types of dependence. When $y = x^2$, there is perfect dependence between x and y. However, $E(xy) = E(x^3)$. Both of $E(x)$ and $E(x^3)$ are zero when x is normal (or when it has any symmetrical distribution centered at zero). It follows that the coefficient of correlation between x and y is zero.

11.3 In a factor model, the correlation between two variables arises entirely because of their correlation with other variables known as factors. A factor model reduces the number of estimates that have to be made when correlations between large numbers of variables are being produced.

11.4 A positive-semidefinite matrix is a matrix that satisfies equation (11.4) for all vectors **w**. If a correlation matrix is not positive-semidefinite, the correlations are internally inconsistent.

11.5 (a) The volatilities and correlation imply that the current estimate of the covariance is $0.25 \times 0.016 \times 0.025 = 0.0001$.

   (b) If the prices of the assets at close of trading are \$20.50 and \$40.50, the proportional changes are $0.5/20 = 0.025$ and $0.5/40 = 0.0125$. The new covariance estimate is

$$0.95 \times 0.0001 + 0.05 \times 0.025 \times 0.0125 = 0.0001106$$

The new variance estimate for asset A is

$$0.95 \times 0.016^2 + 0.05 \times 0.025^2 = 0.00027445$$

so that the new volatility is 0.0166. The new variance estimate for asset B is

$$0.95 \times 0.025^2 + 0.05 \times 0.0125^2 = 0.000601562$$

so that the new volatility is 0.0245. The new correlation estimate is

$$\frac{0.0001106}{0.0166 \times 0.0245} = 0.272$$

11.6 The most recent returns for X and Y are $1/30 = 0.03333$ and $1/50 = 0.02$, respectively. The previous covariance is $0.01 \times 0.012 \times 0.50 = 0.00006$. The new estimate of the covariance is

$$0.000001 + 0.04 \times 0.03333 \times 0.02 + 0.94 \times 0.00006 = 0.0000841$$

The new estimate of the variance of X is

$$0.000003 + 0.04 \times 0.03333^2 + 0.94 \times 0.01^2 = 0.0001414$$

so that the new volatility of X is $\sqrt{0.0001414} = 0.01189$ or 1.189%. The new estimate of the variance of Y is

$$0.000003 + 0.04 \times 0.02^2 + 0.94 \times 0.012^2 = 0.0001544$$

so that the new volatility of Y is $\sqrt{0.0001544} = 0.01242$ or 1.242%. The new estimate of the correlation between the assets is therefore $0.0000841/(0.01189 \times 0.01242) = 0.569$.

11.7 Continuing with the notation in the answer to Problem 10.15, define z_i as the proportional change in the value of the S&P 500 on day i. The covariance between x_i and z_i is

$$0.7 \times 0.018 \times 0.016 = 0.0002016$$

The covariance between y_i and z_i is

$$0.3 \times 0.009 \times 0.016 = 0.0000432$$

The covariance between $x_i + y_i$ and z_i equals the covariance between x_i and z_i plus the covariance between y_i and z_i. It is

$$0.0002016 + 0.0000432 = 0.0002448$$

The volatility of $x_i + y_i$ is 2.31% from Problem 10.15. The correlation between $x_i + y_i$ and z_i is

$$\frac{0.0002448}{0.016 \times 0.0231} = 0.662$$

Note that the volatility of the S&P 500 drops out in this calculation.

11.8

V_1	V_2		
	0.25	0.5	0.75
0.25	0.095	0.163	0.216
0.50	0.163	0.298	0.413
0.75	0.216	0.413	0.595

11.9 The formulas are

$$\varepsilon_1 = z_1, \quad \varepsilon_2 = \rho_{12}z_1 + z_2\sqrt{1 - \rho_{12}^2}, \quad \varepsilon_3 = \alpha_1 z_1 + \alpha_2 z_2 + \alpha_3 z_3$$

where

$$\alpha_1 = \rho_{13}, \quad \alpha_1\rho_{12} + \alpha_2\sqrt{1 - \rho_{12}^2} = \rho_{23}, \quad \alpha_1^2 + \alpha_2^2 + \alpha_3^2 = 1$$

This means that

$$\alpha_1 = \rho_{13}, \quad \alpha_2 = \frac{\rho_{23} - \rho_{13}\rho_{12}}{\sqrt{1 - \rho_{12}^2}}, \quad \alpha_3 = \sqrt{1 - \alpha_1^2 - \alpha_2^2}$$

11.10 Tail dependence is the tendency for extreme values for two or more variables to occur together. The choice of the copula affects tail dependence. For example, the Student t-copula gives more tail dependence than the Gaussian copula.

11.11 Sample from a bivariate Student t distribution as in Figure 11.5. Convert each sample to a normal distribution on a "percentile-to-percentile" basis.

11.12 The probability that $V_1 < 0.1$ is 0.05. The conditional probability that $V_2 < 0.1$ is $0.006/0.05 = 0.12$. The conditional probability that $V_2 < 0.2$ is $0.017/0.05 = 0.34$, and so on.

11.13 When $V_1 = 0.2$, $U_1 = -0.84$. From the properties of the bivariate normal distribution, the median of U_2 is $-0.5 \times 0.84 = -0.42$. This translates into a median value for V_2 of 0.458.

11.14 In this case

$$WCDR(T, X) = N\left(\frac{N^{-1}(0.015) + \sqrt{0.2}N^{-1}(0.995)}{\sqrt{1 - 0.2}}\right) = 0.127$$

The 99.5% worst case is that there is a loss of $500 \times 0.7 \times 0.127 = 44.62$ or $44.62 million.

11.15 The maximum likelihood estimates for the probability of default and the copula correlation are 4.8% and 11.4%, respectively.

CHAPTER 12

12.1 The removal of a competitor may be beneficial. However, banks enter into many contracts with each other. When one bank goes bankrupt, other banks are liable to lose money on the contracts they have with the bank. Also, other banks will be adversely affected if the bankruptcy reduces the public's overall level of confidence in the banking system.

12.2 Deposit insurance means that depositors are safe regardless of the risks taken by their financial institution. It is liable to lead to financial institutions taking more risks than they otherwise would because they can do so without the risk of losing deposits. This in turn leads to more bank failures and more claims under the deposit insurance system. Regulation requiring the capital held by a bank to be related to the risks taken is necessary to avoid this happening.

12.3 The credit risk on the swap is the risk that the counterparty defaults at some future time when the swap has a positive value to the bank.

12.4 The value of a currency swap is liable to deviate further from zero than the value of an interest rate swap because of the final exchange of principal. As a result, the potential loss from a counterparty default is higher.

12.5 There is some exposure. If the counterparty defaulted now, there would be no loss. However, interest rates could change so that at a future time the swap has a positive value to the financial institution. If the counterparty defaulted at that time, there would be a loss to the financial institution. The capital under Basel I would, from Table 12.2, be 0.5% of the swap's principal.

12.6 The risk-weighted assets for the three transactions are (a) $1.875 million, (b) $2 million, (c) $3 million for a total of $6.875 million. The capital required is 0.08×6.875 or $0.55 million.

12.7 The NRR is $2.5/4.5 = 0.556$. The credit equivalent amount is $2.5 + (0.4 + 0.6 \times 0.556) \times 9.25$ or $9.28 million. The risk-weighted assets is $4.64 million and the capital required is $0.371 million.

12.8 In this case, there is no value to the netting provisions.

12.9 This converts the estimated capital requirement to estimated risk-weighted assets. Capital required equals 8% of risk-weighted assets.

12.10 The trading book consists of instruments that are actively traded and marked to market daily. The banking book consists primarily of loans that are held to maturity and not marked to market daily. The effect of the change is to move the client's borrowings from the banking book to the trading book. This typically reduces capital requirements. (However, the incremental risk charge in Basel 2.5, which is discussed in Chapter 13, brings capital requirements back up to where they were before.)

12.11 Under Basel I, the capital charged for lending to a corporation is the same regardless of the credit rating of the corporation. This leads to a bank's return on capital being relatively low for lending to highly creditworthy corporations. Under Basel II, the capital requirements of a loan are tied much more carefully to the creditworthiness of the borrower. As a result, lending to highly creditworthy companies may become attractive again.

12.12 Regulatory arbitrage involves entering into a transaction or series of transactions solely to reduce regulatory capital requirements.

12.13 EAD is the estimated exposure at default. LGD is the loss given default, that is the proportion of the exposure that will be lost if a default occurs. WCDR is the one-year probability of default in a bad year that occurs only one time in 1,000. PD is the probability of default in an average year. MA is the maturity adjustment. The latter allows for the fact that, in the case of instruments lasting longer than a year, there may be losses arising from a decline in the creditworthiness of the counterparty during the year as well as from a default during the year.

12.14 Under the simple approach, the risk weight of the counterparty is replaced by the risk weight of the collateral for the part of the exposure covered by the collateral. Under the comprehensive approach, the exposure is adjusted for possible increases and the collateral is adjusted for possible decreases in value. The counterparty's risk weight is applied to the excess of the adjusted exposure over the adjusted collateral.

12.15 The standardized approach uses external ratings to determine capital requirements (but in a more sophisticated way than in Basel I). In the IRB approach, the Basel II correlation model is used with PD being determined by the bank. In the advanced IRB approach, the Basel II correlation model is used with PD, LGD, EAD, and M being determined by the bank.

12.16 In the basic indicator approach, total capital is 15% of the average total annual gross income. In the standardized approach, gross income is calculated for different business lines and capital as a percentage of gross income is different for different business lines. In the advanced measurement approach, the bank uses internal models to determine the 99.9% worst case loss in one year.

12.17 $\rho = 0.1216$, WCDR $= 0.0914$, and the capital requirement is $200 \times 0.7 \times 0.0914$ or \$12.79 million. At least half of this must be Tier 1.

12.18 The probability of five or more exceptions is 1-BINOMDIST(4,250,0.01, TRUE) or 10.8%. It could be argued that regulators are using a confidence level of about 10% (rather than the more usual 5%) in choosing to reject a VaR model.

CHAPTER 13

13.1 The three major components of Basel 2.5 are: the calculation of stressed VaR, a new incremental risk charge, and a comprehensive risk measure for instruments dependent on credit correlation.

13.2 The six major components of Basel III are: capital definitions and requirements, the capital conservation buffer, the countercyclical buffer, the leverage ratio, liquidity ratios, and counterparty credit risk.

13.3 VaR, as it is usually defined, is calculated from the most recent one to four years of daily data. Stressed VaR is calculated from a 250-day period in the past that would be particularly bad for the bank's current portfolio.

13.4 The incremental risk charge is calculated as the one-year 99.9% VaR for losses from credit instruments in the trading book. It takes account of rating changes and liquidity horizons. It was introduced because instruments in the trading books often attracted less capital than equivalent instruments in the banking book.

13.5 The capital requirements for the AAA-rated ABS are 1.6% of principal whereas the capital requirements for the AAA-rated ABS CDO are 3.2% of principal.

13.6 Tier 1 equity capital has increased from 2% to 7%, and the definition of equity capital has been tightened.

13.7 (a) 40%, (b) 20%.

13.8 In the leverage ratio, the denominator is not risk-weighted assets. It is total assets on the balance sheet without risk weighting plus some off-balance-sheet items such as loan commitments.

13.9 The liquidity ratio is the ratio of high quality liquid assets to net cash outflows during a stressed period of 30 days. The net stable funding ratio is the ratio of a weighted sum of the items on the "liabilities and net worth" side of the balance sheet divided by a weighted sum of the items on the "assets" side of the balance sheet.

13.10 The amount of stable funding would change to 81.6 and the NSFR would become $81.6/74.25 = 110\%$.

13.11 CVA is a charge to income reflecting expected costs from counterparty defaults in derivatives transactions. The new regulations require the exposure of CVA to credit spreads to be included in the calculation of market risk capital.

13.12 CoCo bonds are automatically converted into equity when a predefined trigger indicates that the bank's capital is low. They are attractive to banks because they do not affect return on equity prior to conversion. They are attractive to regulators because they are a source of capital that can absorb losses in stressed market conditions.

CHAPTER 14

14.1 The assumption is that the statistical process driving changes in market variables over the next day is the same as that over the last 500 days.

14.2

$$\lambda^{i-1}(1-\lambda)/(1-\lambda^n) = \frac{\lambda^{i-1}}{1+\lambda+\lambda^2+\cdots+\lambda^{n-1}}$$

This shows that as λ approaches 1, the weights approach $1/n$.

14.3 The standard error of the estimate is

$$\frac{1}{0.01}\sqrt{\frac{0.05 \times 0.95}{1,000}} = 0.69$$

The standard error of the VaR estimate is $0.69 million.

14.4 The 95% one-day VaR is the 25th worst loss. This is $156,511. The 97% one-day VaR is the 15th worst loss. This is $172,224.

14.5 In the "Scenarios" worksheet, the portfolio investments are changed to 2,500 in cells L2:O2. The losses are then sorted from the largest to the smallest. The fifth worst loss is $238,526. This is the one-day 99% VaR.

14.6 The value of λ in cell F2 of the "Scenarios with Weights" worksheet is changed from 0.995 to 0.99. The losses are then sorted from the largest to the smallest. The cumulative weight for the largest loss (Scenario 494) is 0.00948. The cumulative weight for the second largest loss (Scenario 339) is 0.01147. The one-day 99% VaR is therefore the second worst loss or $345,435.

14.7 The value of λ in cell A2 of the "Data with Vol Ests" worksheet is changed from 0.94 to 0.96. The losses in the "Vol Adjusted Scenarios" worksheet are then sorted from the highest to the lowest. The fifth worst loss is $535,260. This is the new one-day 99% VaR.

14.8 This is

$$\frac{22}{500}\left[1+0.436\frac{400-160}{35.532}\right]^{-1/0.436}$$

or 0.001623.

14.9 The VaR ($000s) is

$$160 + \frac{32.532}{0.436} \left\{ \left[\frac{500}{22}(1 - 0.97) \right]^{-0.436} - 1 \right\} = 173.6$$

or $173,600.

14.10 The maximum likelihood estimates of ξ and β become 0.353 and 34.05. The one-day 99% VaR becomes $230,725 and the one-day 99.9% VaR becomes $452,831.

14.11 The losses from the volatility updating procedure must be transferred to the "Extreme Val Theory" worksheet. With $u = 400$, $n_u = 17$ and the maximum likelihood values of ξ and β are 0.438 and 82.838. The one-day 99% VaR is $534,100. The one-day 99.9% VaR is $1,096,661. The probability of a loss greater than $600,000 is

$$\frac{17}{500} \left[1 + 0.438 \frac{600 - 400}{82.838} \right]^{-1/0.438} = 0.00655$$

CHAPTER 15

15.1 The standard deviation of the daily change in the investment in each asset is $1,000. The variance of the portfolio's daily change is

$$1,000^2 + 1,000^2 + 2 \times 0.3 \times 1,000 \times 1,000 = 2,600,000$$

The standard deviation of the portfolio's daily change is the square root of this or $1,612.45. The five-day 99% value at risk is therefore $2.33 \times \sqrt{5} \times 1,612.45 = \$8,401$.

15.2 The three alternative procedures mentioned in the chapter for handling interest rates when the model building approach is used to calculate VaR involve (a) the use of the duration model, (b) the use of cash flow mapping, and (c) the use of principal components analysis.

15.3 When a final exchange of principal is added in, the floating side is equivalent to a zero-coupon bond with a maturity date equal to the date of the next payment. The fixed side is a coupon-bearing bond, which is equivalent to a portfolio of zero-coupon bonds. The swap can therefore be mapped into a portfolio of zero-coupon bonds with maturity dates corresponding to the payment dates. Each of the zero-coupon bonds can then be mapped into positions in the adjacent standard-maturity zero-coupon bonds.

15.4 $\Delta P = 56 + 1.5\Delta x$. The standard deviation of ΔP is $56 \times 1.5 \times 0.007 = 0.588$. It follows that the 10-day 99% VaR for the portfolio is $0.588 \times 2.33 \times \sqrt{10} = 4.33$.

15.5 The relationship is $\Delta P = 56 \times 1.5\Delta x + 0.5 \times 1.5^2 \times 16.2 \times \Delta x^2$ or $\Delta P = 84\Delta x + 18.225\Delta x^2$.

15.6 The 6.5-year cash flow is equivalent to a position of $48.56 in a five-year zero-coupon bond and a position of $605.49 in a seven-year zero-coupon bond.

The equivalent five-year and seven-year cash flows are $48.56 \times 1.06^5 = 64.98$ and $605.49 \times 1.07^7 = 972.28$.

15.7 A calculation similar to that in the text shows that $37,397 of the value is allocated to the three-month bond worth and $11,793 of the value is allocated to the six-month bond.

15.8 The daily variance of the portfolio is

$$6^2 \times 20^2 + 4^2 \times 8^2 = 15{,}424$$

and the daily standard deviation is $\sqrt{15{,}424} = \$124.19$. Since $N(-1.282) = 0.9$, the five-day 90% value at risk is

$$124.19 \times \sqrt{5} \times 1.282 = \$356.01$$

15.9 (a) 2.0, (b) 43.8.

15.10 The delta of the options is the rate of change of the value of the options with respect to the price of the asset. When the asset price increases by a small amount, the value of the options decreases by 30 times this amount. The gamma of the options is the rate of change of their delta with respect to the price of the asset. When the asset price increases by a small amount, the delta of the portfolio decreases by five times this amount.

In this case, $E(\Delta P) = -0.10$, $E(\Delta P^2) = 36.03$, and $E(\Delta P^3) = -32.415$. The mean change in the portfolio value in one day is -0.1 and the standard deviation of the change in one day is $\sqrt{36.03 - 0.1^2} = 6.002$. The skewness is

$$\frac{-32.415 - 3 \times 36.03 \times (-0.1) + 2 \times (-0.1)^3}{6.002^3} = -\frac{21.608}{216.180} = -0.10$$

Using only the first two moments the one-day 99% value at risk is $14.08. When three moments are considered in conjunction with a Cornish-Fisher expansion, it is $14.53.

15.11 Define σ as the volatility per year, $\Delta \sigma$ as the change in σ in one day, and Δw and the proportional change in σ in one day. We measure in σ as a multiple of 1% so that the current value of σ is $1 \times \sqrt{252} = 15.87$. The delta-gamma-vega model is

$$\Delta P = -30 \Delta S - .5 \times 5 \times (\Delta S)^2 - 2 \Delta \sigma$$

or

$$\Delta P = -30 \times 20 \Delta x - 0.5 \times 5 \times 20^2 (\Delta x)^2 - 2 \times 15.87 \Delta w$$

(where $\Delta x = \Delta S / S$) which simplifies to

$$\Delta P = -600 \Delta x - 1{,}000 (\Delta x)^2 - 31.74 \Delta w$$

The change in the portfolio value now depends on two market variables.

15.12 The change in the value of an option is not linearly related to the changes in the values of the underlying variables. When the changes in the values of underlying variables are normal, the change in the value of the option is non-normal. The linear model assumes that it is normal and is, therefore, only an approximation.

15.13 The contract is a long position in a sterling bond combined with a short position in a dollar bond. The value of the sterling bond is $1.53e^{-0.05 \times 0.5}$, or $1.492 million. The value of the dollar bond is $1.5e^{-0.05 \times 0.5}$, or $1.463 million. The variance of the change in the value of the contract in one day is

$$1.492^2 \times 0.0006^2 + 1.463^2 \times 0.0005^2 - 2 \times 0.8 \times 1.492 \times 0.0006$$

$$\times 1.463 \times 0.0005 = 0.000000288$$

The standard deviation is therefore $0.000537 million. The 10-day 99% VaR is $0.000537 \times \sqrt{10} \times 2.33 = \$0.00396$ million.

15.14 The alphas should be changed to 2,500. This changes the one-day 99% VaR to $226,836 when volatilities and correlations are estimated using the equally weighted model and to $487,737 when EWMA with $\lambda = 0.94$ is used.

15.15 This changes the one-day 99% VaR from $471,025 to $389,291.

CHAPTER 16

16.1 The ten investment grade ratings used by Moody's are: Aaa, Aa1, Aa2, Aa3, A1, A2, A3, Baa1, Baa2, and Baa3.

16.2 The ten investment grade ratings used by S&P are: AAA, AA+, AA, AA−, A+, A, A−, BBB+, BBB, and BBB−.

16.3 From equation (16.2), the average hazard rate, $\bar{\lambda}$ satisfies $0.04465 = 1 - e^{-\bar{\lambda} \times 1}$ so that $\bar{\lambda} = -\ln(0.95535) = 0.0457$. The average hazard rate is 4.57% per year.

16.4 Conditional on no default by year 2, the probability of a default in year 3 is

$$(0.05596 - 0.0.03191)/(1 - 0.03191) = 0.02484$$

Average hazard rate for the third year, $\bar{\lambda}$, satisfies $1 - e^{-\bar{\lambda} \times 1} = 0.02484$. It is 2.52% per year.

16.5 The seller receives $300,000,000 \times 0.0060 \times 0.5 = \$900,000$ at times 0.5, 1.0, 1.5, 2.0, 2.5, 3.0, 3.5, and 4.0 years. The seller also receives a final accrual payment of about $300,000 (= $300,000,000 \times 0.060 \times 2/12$) at the time of the default (four years and two months). The seller pays $300,000,000 \times 0.6 = \$180,000,000$ at the time of the default.

16.6 Sometimes there is physical settlement and sometimes there is cash settlement. In the event of a default when there is physical settlement, the buyer of protection sells bonds issued by the reference entity for their face value. Bonds with a total face value equal to the notional principal can be sold. In the event of a default when there is cash settlement, a calculation agent or an auction determines the value of the cheapest-to-deliver bonds issued by the reference entity a specified number of days after the default event. The cash payoff is then based on the excess of the face value of these bonds over the estimated value.

16.7 Risk-neutral default probabilities are backed out from credit default swaps, asset swaps or bond prices. Real-world default probabilities are calculated from historical data. Risk-neutral default probabilities should be used for valuation. Real-world default probabilities should be used for scenario analysis and credit VaR calculations.

16.8 The payoff is $L(1 - R)$ where L is the notional principal and R is the recovery rate.

16.9 From equation (16.3), the average hazard rate over the three years is $0.0050/(1 - 0.3) = 0.0071$ or 0.71% per year.

16.10 From equation (16.3), the average hazard rate over five years is $0.0080/(1 - 0.4)$ or 1.333% per year. Similarly, the average hazard rate over three years is 1.1667% per year. This means that the average hazard rate for years 4 and 5 is $(5 \times 1.333 - 3 \times 1.1667)/2 = 1.58\%$.

16.11 Real-world probabilities of default should be used for calculating credit value at risk. Risk-neutral probabilities of default should be used for adjusting the price of a derivative for default.

16.12 The recovery rate for a bond is the value of the bond immediately after the issuer defaults as a percent of its face value.

16.13 The first number in the second column of Table 16.4 is calculated from the numbers in the seven-year column of Table 16.1 as

$$-\frac{1}{7} \ln(1 - 0.00244) = 0.0003$$

or 0.03% per year. The second number in the second column of Table 16.4 is calculated from the numbers in the seven-year column of Table 16.1 as

$$-\frac{1}{7} \ln(1 - 0.00443) = 0.0006$$

and so on. The numbers in the fourth column of Table 16.5 are calculated by converting the hazard rates in the second column of Table 16.4 to annual default probabilities and multiplying by 0.6. For Caa this gives $0.6 \times (1 - e^{-0.1352}) = 0.0759$.

16.14 The no-default value of the bond is

$$2e^{-0.03 \times 0.5} + 2e^{-0.03 \times 1.0} + \cdots + 102e^{-0.03 \times 4.0} = 103.66$$

The market price is 96.16. An analysis similar to that in Table 16.3 shows that, if Q is the default probability per year, the loss from defaults is $272.69Q$. The implied probability of default is therefore given by solving $103.66 - 96.16 = 272.69Q$. It is 2.74% per year.

16.15 If Q_1 is the default probability at times 0.5, 1.5, and 2.5 years, an analysis similar to that in Table 16.3 shows that the present value of the loss from defaults for the first bond is $178.31 Q_1$ per \$100 of face value. The default-free value of this bond is

$$4 \times e^{-0.035 \times 1} + 4 \times e^{-0.035 \times 2} + 104 \times e^{-0.035 \times 3} = 101.23$$

and the market value is 98.35. It follows that $178.31 Q_1 = 101.23 - 98.35$ so that $Q_1 = 0.0157$ or 1.57%. If Q_2 is the probability of default at times 3.5 and 4.5, an analysis similar to that in Table 16.3 gives the present value of the loss from default for the second bond to be $180.56 Q_1 + 108.53 Q_2$. The default-free value of the second bond is

$$4e^{-0.035 \times 1} + 4 \times e^{-0.035 \times 2} + \cdots + 104 \times e^{-0.035 \times 5} = 101.97$$

The market value is 96.24. It follows that $180.56 Q_1 + 108.53 Q_2 = 101.97 - 96.24$. Substituting for Q_1, we find that $Q_2 = 0.0260$, or 2.60%.

16.16 We can assume that the principal is paid and received at the end of the life of the swap without changing the swap's value. If the spread were zero, the present value of the floating payments per dollar of principal would be 1. The payment of LIBOR plus the spread therefore has a present value of $1 + V$. The payment of the bond cash flows has a present value per dollar of principal of B^*. The initial payment required from the payer of the bond cash flows per dollar of principal is $1 - B$. (This may be negative; an initial amount of $B - 1$ is then paid by the payer of the floating rate). Because the asset swap is initially worth zero we have

$$1 + V = B^* + 1 - B$$

so that

$$V = B^* - B$$

16.17 The value of the debt in Merton's model is $V_0 - E_0$ or

$$V_0 - V_0 N(d_1) + De^{-rT} N(d_2) = De^{-rT} N(d_2) + V_0 N(-d_1)$$

If the credit spread is s, this should equal $De^{-(r+s)T}$ so that

$$De^{-(r+s)T} = De^{-rT} N(d_2) + V_0 N(-d_1)$$

Substituting $De^{-rT} = LV_0$, we get

$$Le^{-sT} = LN(d_2) + N(-d_1)$$

so that

$$s = -\ln[N(d_2) + N(-d_1)/L]/T$$

16.18 In this case, $E_0 = 2$, $\sigma_E = 0.50$, $D = 5$, $r = 0.04$, and $T = 1$. Solving the simultaneous equations gives $V_0 = 6.80$ and $\sigma_V = 14.82$. The probability of default is $N(-d_2)$ or 1.15%.

16.19 At the end of each quarter for the first four years, the seller receives $1 million. The seller pays $70 million after four years and two months. The seller receives a final accrual payment of $666,667.

16.20 A credit default swap insures a corporate bond issued by the reference entity against default. Its approximate effect is to convert the corporate bond into a risk-free bond. The buyer of a credit default swap has therefore chosen to exchange a corporate bond for a risk-free bond. This means that the buyer is long a risk-free bond and short a similar corporate bond.

16.21 Payoffs from credit default swaps depend on whether a particular company defaults. Arguably some market participants have more information about this than other market participants. (See Business Snapshot 16.2.)

16.22 Suppose that the principal is $100. The present value of the bond if it were risk-free would be

$$2.5e^{-0.06 \times 0.5} + 2.5e^{-0.06 \times 1} + \cdots + 2.5e^{-0.06 \times 5} + 100e^{-0.06 \times 5} = 95.3579$$

The present value of the expected loss from defaults is therefore $95.3579 - 90 = 5.3579$. The asset swap is structured so that the $10 is paid initially. After that, $2.50 is paid every six months. In return, LIBOR plus a spread is received on the principal of $100. The present value of the fixed payments is

$$10 + 2.5e^{-0.06 \times 0.5} + 2.5e^{-0.06 \times 1} + \cdots + 2.5e^{-0.06 \times 5} + 100e^{-0.06 \times 5} = 105.3579$$

The spread over LIBOR must therefore have a present value of 5.3579. The present value of $1 received every six months for five years is 8.5105. The spread received every six months must therefore be $5.3579/8.5105 = \$0.6296$. The asset swap spread is therefore $2 \times 0.6296 = 1.2592\%$ per annum. This problem provides an illustration of the result in Problem 16.16.

CHAPTER 17

17.1 The new transaction will increase the bank's exposure to the counterparty if it tends to have a positive value whenever the existing transactions have a net positive value and a negative value whenever the existing transactions have a negative value. However, if the new transaction tends to offset the existing transactions, it is likely to have the incremental effect of reducing credit risk.

17.2 When securities are pledged as collateral, the haircut is the discount applied to their market value for margin calculations.

17.3 A company's own equity would not be good collateral. When the company defaults on the transactions it has with you, its equity is likely to be worth very little.

17.4 The statements in (a) and (b) are true. The statement in (c) is not. Suppose that v_X and v_Y are the exposures to X and Y. The expected value of $v_X + v_Y$

is the expected value of v_X plus the expected value of v_Y. The same is not true of 95% confidence limits.

17.5 Assume that defaults happen only at the end of the life of the forward contract. In a default-free world, the forward contract is the combination of a long European call and a short European put where the strike price of the options equals the delivery price and the maturity of the options equals the maturity of the forward contract. If the no-default value of the contract is positive at maturity, the call has a positive value and the put is worth zero. The impact of defaults on the forward contract is the same as that on the call. If the no-default value of the contract is negative at maturity, the call has a zero value and the put has a positive value. In this case, defaults have no effect. Again, the impact of defaults on the forward contract is the same as that on the call. It follows that the contract has a value equal to a long position in a call that is subject to default risk and short position in a default-free put.

17.6 The Black–Scholes–Merton price must be multiplied by $e^{-0.012\times3} = 0.964$. Black–Scholes–Merton overstates the price by about 3.6%.

17.7 If many contracts entered into by Company X are subject to the same default trigger, the effect of the default trigger may be to increase risk. If the company is downgraded so that the default trigger is activated, those of its counterparties who have contracts with negative values to Company X will request collateral. As a result, Company X is likely to experience liquidity problems and may be forced into bankruptcy.

17.8 An event of default happens when one side declares bankruptcy or fails to make payments on outstanding transactions as required or fails to post collateral as required. A short period of time after an event of default, the non-defaulting party can declare an early termination event.

17.9 A dealer is likely to have wrong-way risk when the counterparty is entering into a CDS selling credit protection to the dealer or when the counterparty is speculating. The dealer is likely to have right-way risk when the counterparty is entering into a CDS buying credit protection from the dealer or when the counterparty is partially hedging an existing position.

17.10 The exposure of A including its exposure to the CCP is reduced to 70. The exposure of A excluding its exposure to the CCP remains 0. The exposure of B including its exposure to the CCP is reduced to 100. The exposure of B excluding its exposure to the CCP is reduced to 70. The exposures of C are unaffected. The average exposure of the three parties, including the exposures to the CCP, is reduced from 110 to 86.7. The average exposure, excluding the exposures to the CCP, is reduced from 70 to 53.3.

17.11 The company will lose money if (a) the CCP defaults or (b) one of the other members defaults and not enough margin has been posted to cover the defaulting member's obligations.

17.12 Collateral is required when the mark-to-market value of outstanding transactions exceeds the threshold. The cure period is the period that is assumed between an event of default and wind up in CVA calculations. The minimum transfer amount is the minimum amount of collateral that can be requested at any one time.

17.13 Collateral requirements are normally calculated from the net mark-to-market value of all outstanding transactions. In determining settlement amounts, transactions with a positive value are netted against those with a negative value.

17.14 When a bank is experiencing financial difficulties, its probability of default increases. This increases the expected cost to its counterparties from a default by the bank. The latter is known as DVA and is an accounting entry that increases the value of transactions to the bank.

17.15 The part of CVA relating to the credit spread changes of counterparties is included in market risk calculations under Basel III.

17.16 There will be losses in the CVA model if the value of the dealer's transactions with the counterparty is greater than −$5 million and the value increases by more than $5 million during a 15-day period following an event of default.

17.17 Rehypothecation occurs when collateral posted by A with B is used by B to meet collateral demands from a third party, C.

CHAPTER 18

18.1 In Vasicek's model and Credit Risk Plus, a credit loss is recognized when a default occurs. In CreditMetrics, both downgrades and defaults lead to credit losses. In Vasicek's model, a Gaussian copula model of time to default is used. In Credit Risk Plus, a probability distribution is assumed for the default rate per year. In CreditMetrics, a Gaussian copula model is used to define rating transitions.

18.2 The constant level of risk assumption assumes that after a certain period of time, t, an instrument, X, is replaced with an instrument, Y, that has the same risk as X had originally. After a further period of time of length t, Y is replaced by Z that also has the same risk as X had originally, and so on.

18.3 The probability of a Aaa staying Aaa over two years is 81.85%. The probability of it moving to Aa is 16.1%.

18.4 The probability of a Aaa staying Aaa over six months is 95.08%. The probability of it moving to Aa is 4.69%.

18.5 Movements in credit spreads for all companies over the next day could be assumed to be a random sample from their movements over the last 500 days. The disadvantage of this approach is that the companies have zero chance of defaulting and accurate daily credit spread data may not be available for all companies.

18.6 Using the binomial distribution, the probability of six or more losses is 0.0005.

18.7 In this case, we must average the cumulative binomial distributions for 0.5% and 1.5% loss probabilities. The probability of six or more losses is 0.0021. This shows that introducing some correlation increases the tail risk.

18.8 The autocorrelation is 0.54. This suggests that the credit VaR estimate should take account of recent default experience. If the default rate was high last year, it is more likely to be high this year.

18.9 The specific risk charge is a charge for risks in the trading book that are specific to a particular company. The incremental risk charge is a charge reflecting the difference between the capital required for a credit risk in the trading book and the capital required for an equivalent credit risk in the banking book.

CHAPTER 19

19.1 Scenarios can be generated by (a) making large changes to key variables such as interest rates, equity prices, etc., (b) making percentage changes in all market variables that are the same as those that occurred on particular extreme days in the past, and (c) asking a committee of senior management to generate the scenarios.

19.2 Reverse stress testing involves using an algorithm to search for scenarios that lead to big losses. It is used to help identify appropriate scenarios for stress testing.

19.3 Financial institutions might consider that regulators will require more capital if scenarios leading to large losses are considered.

19.4 Traffic light options were options that provided payoffs when the scenarios considered by insurance company regulators occurred. The danger is that, when it buys traffic light options, the financial institution is protecting itself against a too narrow range of adverse scenarios. The financial institution might not be protected against a scenario that is similar to, but not exactly the same as, the scenarios covered by the traffic light options.

19.5 Senior management are in the best position to develop scenarios for stress testing. The involvement of senior management in the development of scenarios makes it more likely that they will take the results of stress testing seriously and incorporate stress testing in their strategic decision making.

19.6 The advantage is that the same scenarios are considered by different banks and systemic risks can be evaluated. The scenarios might be worse than those considered by the banks themselves (see Problem 19.3). The disadvantage is that it might lead to the banks themselves not spending as much time as they should on stress testing.

19.7 An objective probability is calculated from data. A subjective probability is a "degree of belief" and reflects a person's judgment.

19.8 The total probability of the stressed scenarios is 1.5%. The probability associated with the historical simulation scenarios is therefore 98.5%. Each historical simulation scenario has a probability of 0.197. When the scenarios and their probabilities are ranked, we see that the VaR with a 99% confidence limit is $284,204. (For a loss of $340,000, the cumulative probability is 0.00943. For a loss of $284,204, the cumulative probability is 0.01141.)

19.9 In this case, the position values are 941.34, −164.39, −1,349.94, and −78.36. The worst-case scenario is where the asset price is 60 and its volatility is 30%. This leads to a loss of $341.39.

CHAPTER 20

20.1 The definition includes all internal risks and external risks except those related to reputation risk and risks resulting from strategic decisions.

20.2 Based on the results reported by Shih, the loss would be $100 \times 3^{0.23}$ or $128.7 million.

20.3 $\text{Prob}(v > x) = Kx^{-0.8}$. When $x = 20$ the probability is 0.1. This means that $K = 1.0986$. The probability of the specified losses being exceeded are (a) 5.74%, (b) 3.30%, and (c) 1.58%.

20.4 Moral hazard is handled by deductibles and by making premiums dependent on past claims. Adverse selection is handled by finding out as much as possible about a driver before insurance is granted and then modifying premiums as more information on the driver becomes available.

20.5 CEOs must prepare a statement asserting that the financial statements are accurate. They must return bonuses in the event that there is a restatement of financial statements.

20.6 If a trader operates within established risk limits and takes a loss, this is part of market risk. If risk limits are violated, the loss becomes classified as an operational risk.

20.7 (a) It is unlikely that an individual would not look after his or her health because of the existence of a life insurance contract. But it has been known for the beneficiary of a life insurance contract to commit murder to receive the payoff from the contract! (b) Individuals with short life expectancies are more likely to buy life insurance than individuals with long life expectancies.

20.8 External loss data is data relating to the losses of other banks. It is data obtained from sharing agreements with other banks or from data vendors. Vendor data is used to determine relative loss severity. It can be a useful indicator of the ratio of mean loss severity in Business Unit A to mean loss severity in Business Unit B or the ratio of the standard deviation of loss severity in Business Unit A to the standard deviation of loss severity in Business Unit B.

20.9 The Poisson distribution is often used for loss frequency. The lognormal distribution is often used for loss severity.

20.10 Examples of key risk indicators are staff turnover, number of failed transactions, number of positions filled by temps, ratio of supervisors to staff, number of open positions, and percentage of staff that did not take 10 days of consecutive leave in the last 12 months.

20.11 When the loss frequency is three, the mean total loss is about 3.3 and the standard deviation is about 2.0. When the loss frequency is increased to 4, the mean loss is about 4.4 and the standard deviation of the loss is about 2.4.

CHAPTER 21

21.1 Investors did not know very much about the mortgages underlying the tranches that were created and the waterfalls were complex.

21.2 The company or individual providing the quotes is prepared to buy at 50 and sell at 55. The mid-market quote is 52.5. The proportional bid–offer spread is 5.0/52.5 or 0.0952.

21.3 The bid–offer spread for the holding in Company A is $0.01 \times 5,000 = \$50$. The bid–offer spread for the holding in Company B is $0.02 \times 3,000 = \$60$. The cost of unwinding the portfolio is $(50 + 60)/2$ or $55.

21.4 The bid–offer spread for the first holding that we are 95% will not be exceeded is $5,000 \times (0.01 + 1.645 \times 0.01) = \$132.24$. The bid–offer spread for the second holding that we are 95% will not be exceeded is $3,000 \times (0.02 + 1.645 \times 0.03) = \$204.04$. The total cost of unwinding that we are 95% certain will not be exceeded is $(132.24 + 204.04)/2 = \$170.14$.

21.5 The amount traded on successive days should be 15.9, 12.9, 10.0, 7.4, 5.2, 3.4, 2.2, 1.4, 0.9, and 0.7. The bid–offer spread cost is $13.4. The total price variance is 36.6 so that the VaR for the market risk with a 95% confidence level is $1.645 \times \sqrt{36.6} = \$9.90$. (The objective function that is minimized is the sum of these two or $23.30.)

21.6 This is necessary because these assets cannot be converted into cash and cannot be pledged as collateral for additional loans.

21.7 Wholesale deposits are more liable to disappear in stressed market conditions.

21.8 Their hedging led to a loss on the hedge and a gain on the position being hedged. The loss on the hedge gave rise to margin calls. Unfortunately, the position being hedged, although it increased in value to the company, was illiquid.

21.9 Positive feedback trading refers to situations where traders accentuate market movements. They buy when prices increase and sell when prices decrease. Negative feedback trading is when traders do the reverse, that is, they buy when prices decline and sell when prices increase. Positive feedback trading is liable to lead to a liquidity problem.

21.10 This is a VaR measure that includes an adjustment for the bid–offer spread costs that are incurred in a close-out of the position.

21.11 Liquidity black holes occur when most market participants want to be on one side of a market. Regulation is liable to lead to liquidity black holes. This is because, when all financial institutions are regulated in the same way, they tend to want to respond to external economic events in the same way.

21.12 Liquidity black holes are typically caused by too many traders following the same trading strategy. If traders follow diverse trading strategies, liquidity black holes are less likely to occur.

CHAPTER 22

22.1 Marking to market involves valuing a position using the prices at which the same or similar positions are trading in the market. Marking to model occurs when a model plays a key role in determining the price of an instrument.

22.2 Leverage and crashophobia.

22.3 Uncertain volatility and jumps.

22.4 When plain vanilla call and put options are being priced, traders do use the Black–Scholes–Merton model as an interpolation tool. They calculate implied volatilities for the options that are actively traded. By interpolating between strike prices and between times to maturity, they estimate implied volatilities for other options. These implied volatilities are then substituted into Black–Scholes–Merton to calculate prices for these options. Black–Scholes–Merton is more than an interpolation tool when used for hedging.

22.5 13.45%. We get the same answer by (a) interpolating between strike prices of 1.00 and 1.05 and then between maturities six months and one year and (b) interpolating between maturities of six months and one year and then between strike prices of 1.00 and 1.05.

22.6 The models of physics describe the behavior of physical processes. The models of finance ultimately describe the behavior of human beings.

22.7 It might notice that it is getting a large amount of business of a certain type because it is quoting prices different from its competitors. The pricing differences might also become apparent if it decides to unwind transactions and approaches competitors for quotes. Also, it might subscribe to a service where once a month it obtains the average price quotes by dealers for particular transactions.

22.8 Within-model hedging involves hedging against changes in variables that the model assumes to be stochastic. Outside-model hedging involves hedging against parameters that the model assumes to be constant.

22.9 The Black–Scholes–Merton model assumes that the probability distribution of the stock price in one month is lognormal. In this case, it is clearly not lognormal. A reasonable assumption might be that it consists of two lognormal distributions superimposed upon each other and is bimodal. Black–Scholes–Merton is clearly inappropriate.

22.10 Fair-value accounting distinguishes between assets and liabilities that are expected to be held to maturity and assets and liabilities that are held for trading. Assets and liabilities in the second category have to be revalued each time financial statements are produced. In 2008, rules were eased so that financial institutions were, in exceptional cases, allowed to move an item from the "held for trading" to "held to maturity" category or vice versa. In 2009, rules were eased again so that internal models could be used in place of market prices in some situations.

22.11 In this case, the probability distribution of the exchange rate has a thin left tail and a thin right tail relative to the lognormal distribution. We are in the opposite situation to that described for foreign currencies in Section 22.4. Both out-of-the-money and in-the-money calls and puts can be expected to have lower implied volatilities than at-the-money calls and puts.

22.12 The term "marking to market" refers to the practice of revaluing instruments (usually daily) so that they are consistent with the market. The prices calculated for actively traded products do reflect market prices. The model is used merely as an interpolation tool. The term "marking to market" is therefore accurate for these products. The prices for structured products depend on the model being used. Hence the term "marking to model."

CHAPTER 23

23.1 Economic capital is a bank's own estimate of the capital it requires. Regulatory capital is the capital it is required to keep by bank supervisors.

23.2 A company with a AA rating has a 0.03% chance of defaulting in one year.

23.3 Business risk includes risks relating to strategic decisions and reputation.

23.4 The models used for economic capital are likely to be broadly similar to those used to calculate regulatory capital in the case of market risk and operational risk. When calculating credit risk economic capital, a bank may consider it appropriate to use a different credit correlation model and different correlation parameters from those used in regulatory capital calculations.

23.5 The 99.97% worst-case value of the logarithm of the loss is $0.5 + 4 \times 3.43 = 14.23$. The 99.97% worst-case loss is therefore $1.510 million. From the properties of the lognormal distribution, the expected loss is $\exp(0.5 + 4^2/2)$ or \$4,915. The capital requirement is therefore \$1.505 million.

23.6 The economic capital for Business Unit 1 is 96.85. The economic capital for Business Unit 2 is 63.87. The total capital is 124.66.

23.7 The incremental effect of Business Unit 1 on total economic capital is 60.78. The incremental effect of Business Unit 2 on total economic capital is 27.81. This suggests that $60.78/(60.78 + 27.81)$ or 68.61% of economic capital should be allocated to Business Unit 1 and $27.81/(60.78 + 27.81)$ or 31.39% to Business Unit 2. The marginal effect of increasing the size of Business Unit 1 by 0.5% is 0.4182. The marginal effect of increasing the size of Business Unit 2 by 0.5% is 0.2056. Euler's theorem is satisfied because the total economic capital is approximately equal to the sum of 0.4182/0.005 and 0.2056/0.005.

23.8 The capital is \$38 million and the return before tax is \$7 million. The before-tax RAROC is therefore 18.4%. In practice, the allocation of diversification benefits to this venture might reduce capital and increase RAROC.

23.9 RAROC can be used to compare the past performance of different business units or to project the expected future performance of business units.

Glossary

ABS   See Asset-Backed Security.

ABS CDO   Security created from the tranches of different ABSs.

Accrued Interest   The interest earned on a bond since the last coupon payment date.

Additional Tier 1 Capital   Items such as non-cumulative preferred stock that do not qualify as Tier 1 equity capital.

Add-On Factor   When the credit equivalent amount for a derivatives transaction is being calculated, this is the percentage of principal added to the current exposure to allow for possible future changes in the value of the derivative.

Advanced Measurement Approach   The way in which the most sophisticated banks will be allowed to calculate regulatory capital for operational risk under Basel II.

Adverse Selection   The phenomenon that, if an insurance company offers the same premiums to everyone, it tends to end up providing coverage for the worst risks.

Agency Costs   Costs in a business relationship where the interests of the two parties are not perfectly aligned.

Alpha   Return earned on a portfolio in excess of that predicted by the capital asset pricing model.

Alternative Investments   See Hedge Funds.

American Option   An option that can be exercised at any time during its life.

Analytic Result   Result where the answer is in the form of an equation.

Arbitrage   A trading strategy that takes advantage of two or more securities being mispriced relative to each other.

Arbitrage Pricing Theory   A theory where the return from an investment is assumed to depend on several factors.

Arbitrageur   An individual engaging in arbitrage.

ASF Factor   Available stable funding factor, a weighting factor used for sources of funding in the calculation of the Net Stable Funding Ratio.

Asian Option   An option with a payoff dependent on the average price of the underlying asset during a specified period.

Ask Price   The price that a dealer is offering to sell an asset.

Asked Price   See Ask Price.

Asset Swap   Exchanges the promised coupon on a bond for LIBOR plus a spread.

Asset-Backed Security   Security created from the cash flows from bonds, mortgages, credit card receivables, or other instruments.

At-the-Money Option   An option in which the strike price equals the price of the underlying asset.

Autocorrelation   The correlation between the value of a variable and the value of the same variable k days later. (k is referred to as the time lag.)

Average Price Call Option   An option giving a payoff equal to the greater of zero and the amount by which the average price of the asset exceeds the strike price.

Average Price Put Option   An option giving a payoff equal to the greater of zero and the amount by which the strike price exceeds the average price of the asset.

Back-End Load   Fee charged when an investment in a mutual fund is terminated.

Back-Testing   Testing a value-at-risk or other model using historical data.

Back Office   Where record-keeping takes place.

Backwards Induction   A procedure for working from the end of a tree to its beginning in order to value an option.

Banking Book   Part of a bank's portfolio that consists of instruments that are expected to be held to maturity.

Bankruptcy Costs   Costs such as lost sales, loss of key managers, and professional fees arising from a declaration of bankruptcy. These costs are not associated with the adverse events leading to bankruptcy.

Barrier Option   An option whose payoff depends on whether the path of the underlying asset has reached a barrier (i.e., a certain predetermined level).

Basel 2.5   Extra capital charges for items in the trading book, introduced following the credit crisis.

Basel I   The first international agreement on the regulation of banks in 1988.

Basel II   New international regulations for calculating bank capital introduced in 2007.

Basel III   International banking regulations introduced in 2010 involving capital for the banking book and liquidity ratios.

Basic Indicator Approach   The simplest way of calculating regulatory capital for operational risk under Basel II.

Basis   The difference between the spot price and the futures price of a commodity.

Basis Point   When used to describe an interest rate, a basis point is one hundredth of one percent (= 0.01%).

Basis Risk   The risk to a hedger arising from uncertainty about the basis at a future time.

Basket Credit Default Swap   Credit default swap where there are several reference entities.

Basket Option   Option on a portfolio of assets.

Bermudan Option   An option that can be exercised on certain dates during its life.

Best Efforts   Phrase used to describe the situation where an investment bank agrees that it will do the best it can to sell a new issue of securities at a certain price, but does not guarantee that it will be able to sell them.

Beta   A measure of the systematic risk of an asset.

Bid-Ask Spread   The amount by which the ask price exceeds the bid price.

Bid-Offer Spread   See Bid-Ask Spread.

Bid Price   The price that a dealer is prepared to pay for an asset.

Bilateral Clearing   Arrangement between two parties to handle transactions in the OTC market, often involving an ISDA master agreement.

Binary Credit Default Swap   Instrument where there is a fixed dollar payoff in the event of a default by a particular company.

Binary Option   Option with a discontinuous payoff; for example, a cash-or-nothing option or an asset-or-nothing option.

Binomial Model   A model where the price of an asset is monitored over successive short periods of time. In each short period it is assumed that only two price movements are possible.

Binomial Tree   A tree that represents how an asset price can evolve under the binomial model.

BIS Accord   Agreement reached in 1988 between the central banks of 12 countries concerning how banks should be regulated.

Bivariate Normal Distribution   A distribution for two correlated variables, each of which is normal.

Black's Model   An extension of the Black–Scholes–Merton model for valuing European options on futures contracts. It is used extensively in practice to value European options when the distribution of the asset price at maturity is assumed to be lognormal.

Black–Scholes–Merton Model   A model for pricing European options on stocks, developed by Fischer Black, Myron Scholes, and Robert Merton.

Bond Option   An option where a bond is the underlying asset.

Bond Yield   Discount rate which, when applied to all the cash flows of a bond, causes the present value of the cash flows to equal the bond's market price.

Bootstrap Method   A procedure for calculating the zero-coupon yield curve from market data. Also a statistical procedure for calculating confidence levels when distributions are determined empirically.

Bunching   A tendency for days, when the loss is greater than the value at risk, to be bunched close together.

Business Risk   When used for a bank, this refers to strategic risk (related to a bank's decision to enter new markets and develop new products) and reputation risk.

Calendar Days   Includes every day.

Calibration   Method for implying a model's parameters from the prices of actively traded options.

Callable Bond   A bond containing provisions that allow the issuer to buy it back at a predetermined price at certain times during its life.

Call Option   An option to buy an asset at a certain price by a certain date.

Cancelable Swap   Swap that can be canceled by one side on prespecified dates.

Cap   See Interest-Rate Cap.

Capital Adequacy   The adequacy of the capital held by a bank or other financial institution.

Capital Asset Pricing Model   A model relating the expected return on an asset to its beta.

Capital Conservation Buffer   Extra equity capital that, under Basel III, must be kept so that it is available to absorb losses during downturns.

Caplet   One component of an interest rate cap.

Cap Rate   The rate determining payoffs in an interest rate cap.

Case–Shiller Index   Index of house prices in the United States.

Cash-Flow Mapping   A procedure for representing an instrument as a portfolio of zero-coupon bonds for the purpose of calculating value at risk.

Cash Settlement   Procedure for settling a contract in cash rather than by delivering the underlying asset.

CAT Bond   Bond where the interest and, possibly, the principal paid are reduced if a particular category of "catastrophic" insurance claims exceed a certain amount.

CCP   See Central Clearing Party.

CDD   Cooling degree days. The maximum of zero and the amount by which the daily average temperature is greater than 65° Fahrenheit. The average temperature is the average of the highest and lowest temperatures (midnight to midnight).

CDO   See Collateralized Debt Obligation.

CDO Squared   An instrument in which the default risks in a portfolio of CDO tranches are allocated to new securities.

CDS–Bond Basis   The excess of the CDS spread over the asset swap spread.

CDX   An index of the credit quality of 125 North American investment grade companies.

Central Clearing   The use of a clearing house for OTC transactions.

Central Clearing Party   Clearing house for over-the-counter transactions.

Cheapest-to-Deliver Bond   Bond that is cheapest to buy and then deliver in a futures contract or a credit default swap contract.

Chinese Walls   Phrase used to describe the policies in place within a financial institution that prevent information flowing from one part of the financial institution to another when this would be disadvantageous to one or more of the financial institution's clients.

Cholesky Decomposition   Method of sampling from a multivariate normal distribution.

Clawback Clause   Clause where a percentage of previous incentive fees can be recouped to compensate for a percentage of current losses.

Clean Price of Bond   The quoted price of a bond. The cash price paid for the bond (or dirty price) is calculated by adding the accrued interest to the clean price.

Clearing House   A firm that guarantees the performance of the parties in an exchange-traded derivatives transaction. (Also referred to as a clearing corporation.)

Clearing Margin   A margin posted by a member of a clearing house.

Closed End Fund   A mutual fund where there is a fixed number of shares.

Coherent Risk Measure   A risk measure satisfying a number of conditions.

CoCos   See Contingent Convertible Bonds.

Collar   See Interest-Rate Collar.

Collateral   Cash or marketable securities that must be posted by a party to a transaction.

Collateralization   A system for posting collateral by one or both parties in a derivatives transaction.

Collateralized Debt Obligation   A way of packaging credit risk. Several classes of securities (known as tranches) are created from a portfolio of bonds and there are rules for determining how the cost of defaults are allocated to classes.

Commercial Bank   A bank that takes deposits and makes loans.

Component Value at Risk   VaR corresponding to a component of a portfolio. Defined so that the sum of the component VaRs for the components of a portfolio equals the VaR for the whole portfolio.

Compounding Frequency   This defines how an interest rate is measured.

Compounding Swap   Swap where interest compounds instead of being paid.

Compound Option   An option on an option.

Comprehensive Risk Measure   Risk measure that calculates the capital charge for instruments dependent on credit correlation.

Conditional Tail Expectation   See Expected Shortfall.

Conditional Value at Risk (C-VaR)   See Expected Shortfall.

Confirmation   Contract confirming verbal agreement between two parties to a trade in the over-the-counter market.

Consumption Asset   An asset held for consumption rather than investment.

Contingent Convertible Bonds (CoCo)   Bonds that are automatically converted to equity when there is a trigger indicating that the issuer needs more equity capital.

Continuous Compounding   A way of quoting interest rates. It is the limit as the assumed compounding interval is made smaller and smaller.

Convenience Yield   A measure of the benefits from ownership of an asset that are not obtained by the holder of a long futures contract on the asset.

Conversion Factor   Factor multiplied by principal to convert an off-balance-sheet item to its credit equivalent amount.

Convertible Bond   A corporate bond that can be converted by the holder into a predetermined amount of the company's equity at certain times during its life.

Convexity   A measure of the curvature in the relationship between bond prices and bond yields.

Convexity Adjustment   An overworked term. For example, it can refer to the adjustment necessary to convert a futures interest rate to a forward interest rate. It can also refer to the adjustment to a forward rate that is sometimes necessary when instruments are valued.

Cooke Ratio   Ratio of capital to risk-weighted assets under Basel I.

Cooling Degree Days   See CDD.

Copula   A way of defining the correlation between variables with known distributions.

Core Tier 1 Capital   See Tier 1 Equity Capital.

Cornish-Fisher Expansion   An approximate relationship between the fractiles of a probability distribution and its moments.

Correlation   Measure of the extent to which there is a linear relation between two variables.

Correlation Matrix $n \times n$ matrix where the $\{i, j\}$ element is the correlation between variable i and variable j.

Cost of Carry   The storage costs plus the cost of financing an asset minus the income earned on the asset.

Countercyclical Buffer   Extra capital charge, under Basel III, that is left to the discretion of national regulators.

Counterparty   The opposite side in a financial transaction.

Coupon   Interest payment made on a bond.

Covariance   Measure of the linear relationship between two variables (equals the correlation between the variables times the product of their standard deviations).

Covariance Rate   Covariance between daily returns of two variables.

Covered Call   A short position in a call option on an asset combined with a long position in the asset.

Crashophobia   The fear of a stock market crash similar to that in 1987 that some people claim causes market participants to increase the value of deep-out-of-the-money put options.

Credit Contagion   The tendency of a default by one company to lead to defaults by other companies.

Credit Default Swap   An instrument that gives the holder the right to sell a bond for its face value in the event of a default by the issuer.

Credit Derivative   A derivative whose payoff depends on the creditworthiness of one or more companies or countries.

Credit Equivalent Amount   Size of loan that is considered equivalent to an off-balance-sheet transaction in Basel I.

Credit Event   Default or other event that triggers a payout in a credit default swap.

Credit Indices   Indices that track the cost of buying protection for each company in a particular portfolio.

CreditMetrics   A procedure for calculating credit value at risk.

Credit Rating   A measure of the creditworthiness of a bond issue.

Credit Ratings Transition Matrix   A table showing the probability that a company will move from one credit rating to another during a certain period of time.

Credit Risk   The risk that a loss will be experienced because of a default by the counterparty in a derivatives transaction.

Credit Risk Migration   Movement of a company from one rating category to another.

Credit Risk Plus   A procedure for calculating credit value at risk.

Credit Spread   Cost of buying credit protection. Also, the difference between the yield on a bond that might default and the yield on a risk-free bond.

Credit Support Annex   Part of an ISDA Master Agreement specifying collateral arrangements.

Credit Value Adjustment   Adjustment to the value of derivatives transactions made by a dealer to allow for the possibility that the counterparty may default.

Credit Value at Risk   The credit loss that will not be exceeded at some specified confidence level.

CSA   See Credit Support Annex.

Cumulative Distribution Function   The probability that a variable will be less than x as a function of x.

Cure Period   Period of time assumed to elapse between a default event and a wind up in OTC derivatives transactions that are settled bilaterally.

Currency Swap   A swap where interest and principal in one currency are exchanged for interest and principal in another currency.

CVA   See Credit Value Adjustment.

Day Count   A convention for quoting interest rates.

Day Trade   A trade that is entered into and closed out on the same day.

Debit Value Adjustment   Adjustment to the value of derivatives transactions made by a dealer to allow for the possibility that the dealer may default.

Debt Value Adjustment   See Debit Value Adjustment.

Default Correlation   Measures the tendency of two companies to default at about the same time.

Default Intensity   See Hazard Rate.

Deferred Annuity   Annuity where time elapses between the payment of the funds that will provide the annuity and the start of the annuity.

Defined Benefit Plan   Pension plan where there is a formula defining the pension that will be received. Typically, the formula depends on the number of years of service and the salary during the final years of service.

Defined Contribution Plan   Pension plan where an employee's contributions plus the contributions made for the employee by the employer are kept in a separate account and invested. On retirement the funds in the account are usually converted into an annuity. Sometimes, they can be taken out as a lump sum.

Deleveraging   Individuals and companies reducing their borrowings.

Delivery Price   Price that will be paid or received in a forward contract.

Delta   The rate of change of the price of a derivative with the price of the underlying asset.

Delta Hedging   A hedging scheme that is designed to make the price of a portfolio of derivatives insensitive to small changes in the price of the underlying asset.

Delta-Neutral Portfolio   A portfolio with a delta of zero so that there is no sensitivity to small changes in the price of the underlying asset.

Dependence   Variable A is dependent on variable B if knowing the value of B affects the probability density function of A.

Deposit Insurance   Government programs for providing restitution to the depositors of a bank in the event that the bank fails.

DerivaGem   Software for valuing options; available on the author's website.

Derivative   An instrument whose price depends on, or is derived from, the price of another asset.

Deterministic Variable   A variable whose future value is known.

Directed Brokerage   Phrase used to describe the situation where a fund directs its trades to a brokerage house in return for the brokerage house advising its clients to buy the fund.

Dirty Price of Bond   Cash price of bond.

Discount Bond   See Zero-Coupon Bond.

Discount Instrument   An instrument, such as a Treasury bill, that provides no coupons.

Discount Rate   The annualized dollar return on a Treasury bill or similar instrument expressed as a percentage of the final face value.

Distance to Default   The number of standard deviations that the value of a company's assets must move for a default to be triggered.

Diversification   Reducing risk by dividing a portfolio between many different assets.

Dividend   A cash payment made to the owner of a stock.

Dividend Yield   The dividend as a percentage of the stock price.

Dodd-Frank Act   An act in the United States that was introduced following the credit crisis and is designed to protect consumers and investors, avoid future bailouts, and monitor the functioning of the financial system more carefully.

Dollar Convexity   The convexity of an interest rate dependent portfolio multiplied by the value of the portfolio.

Dollar Duration   The duration of an interest rate dependent portfolio multiplied by the value of the portfolio.

Down-and-In Option   An option that comes into existence when the price of the underlying asset declines to a prespecified level.

Down-and-Out Option   An option that ceases to exist when the price of the underlying asset declines to a prespecified level.

Downgrade Trigger   A clause in a contract that states that the contract can be terminated by one side if the credit rating of the other side falls below a certain level.

Duration   A measure of the average life of a bond. It is also an approximation of the ratio of the proportional change in the bond price to the absolute change in its yield.

Duration Matching   A procedure for matching the durations of assets and liabilities.

Dutch Auction   A process where investors provide bids indicating the number of shares they are prepared to buy and the price they are prepared to pay. Suppose there are N shares on offer. The price that clears the market is the highest price, P, which is such that investors are prepared to buy more than N shares at either P or a higher price than P. The investors who have bid more than P get their orders filled at a price of P. The investors who have bid P get part of their orders filled at P.

DVA   See Debit Value Adjustment.

DV01   The impact of a one-basis-point increase in all interest rates.

Dynamic Hedging   A procedure for hedging an option position by periodically changing the position held in the underlying asset. The objective is usually to maintain a delta-neutral position.

Dynamic Scenarios   Scenarios involving adverse movements in market variables that consider the way companies will respond to the adverse movements.

EAD   See Exposure at Default.

Early Exercise   Exercise prior to the maturity date.

Early Termination Event   The early termination of OTC derivative transactions by one side because of an event of default by the other side.

Economic Capital   The capital that a bank's own calculation indicates it needs.

Efficient Frontier   The optimal trade-offs for an investor between expected return and standard deviation of return.

Efficient Market Hypothesis   A hypothesis that asset prices reflect relevant information.

Electronic Trading   System of trading where a computer is used to match buyers and sellers.

Embedded Option   An option that is an inseparable part of another instrument.

Empirical Research   Research based on historical market data.

Endowment Life Insurance   Insurance that pays out a predetermined amount on maturity of the contract or on the policyholder's death, whichever is earlier.

Enterprise Risk Management   A holistic approach to risk management.

Equity Swap   A swap where the return on an equity portfolio is exchanged for either a fixed or a floating rate of interest.

Equity Tranche   Tranche which is first to be affected by losses on the underlying portfolio.

Eurocurrency   A currency that is outside the formal control of the issuing country's monetary authorities.

Eurodollar   A dollar held in a bank outside the United States.

Eurodollar Futures Contract   A futures contract written on a Eurodollar deposit.

Eurodollar Interest Rate   The interest rate on a Eurodollar deposit.

European Option   An option that can be exercised only at the end of its life.

Event of Default   Bankruptcy or failure to make payments as they become due or failure to post collateral as it becomes due.

EWMA   Exponentially weighted moving average.

Exception   Situation where realized loss exceeds the value-at-risk estimate.

Excess Cost Layers   The costs for an insurance company on a particular type of business that are within a certain range.

Excess Kurtosis   Measure of the extent to which the tails of a probability distribution are fatter than those of a normal distribution.

Excess Spread   Situation where the aggregate return promised to the tranches is less than the promised return on the underlying assets.

Exchange-Traded Fund   Fund that is created in such a way that units can be exchanged for the underlying shares and vice versa by institutional investors.

Exchange-Traded Market   Market organized by an exchange such as the New York Stock Exchange or Chicago Board Options Exchange.

Ex-Dividend Date   When a dividend is declared, an ex-dividend date is specified. Investors who own shares of the stock just before the ex-dividend date receive the dividend.

Exercise Price   The price at which the underlying asset may be bought or sold in an option contract. (Also called the strike price.)

Exotic Option   A nonstandard option.

Expectations Theory   The theory that forward interest rates equal expected future spot interest rates.

Expected Shortfall   Expected loss during N days conditional on being in the $(100 - X)\%$ tail of the distribution of losses. The variable N is the time horizon and $X\%$ is the confidence level.

Expected Tail Loss   See Expected Shortfall.

Expected Value of a Variable   The average value of the variable obtained by weighting the alternative values by their probabilities.

Expense Ratio   Ratio of expenses to value of assets under management for a fund.

Expiration Date   The end of life of a contract.

Exponentially Weighted Moving Average Model   A model where exponential weighting is used to provide forecasts for a variable from historical data. It is sometimes applied to variances and covariances in value at risk calculations.

Exponential Weighting   A weighting scheme where the weight given to an observation depends on how recent it is. The weight given to an observation t time periods ago is λ times the weight given to an observation $t - 1$ time periods ago where $\lambda < 1$.

Exposure at Default   The maximum amount that could be lost (assuming no recovery) when a default occurs.

Extreme Value Theory   A theory enabling the shape of the tails of a distribution to be estimated from data.

Factor   Source of uncertainty.

Factor Analysis   An analysis aimed at finding a small number of factors that describe most of the variation in a large number of correlated variables. (Similar to a principal components analysis.)

Factor Copula   A copula involving several variables where a factor model describes the correlation structure of the transformed variables.

Factor Loadings   The values of variables in a factor model when we have one unit of a particular factor and no units of other factors.

Factor Model   Model where a set of correlated variables are assumed to depend linearly on a number of uncorrelated factors.

Factor Score   In a factor model, this is the amount of a factor present in a particular observation on the variables.

Fair Value Accounting   Involves showing financial instruments on the balance sheet at their market value.

FICO   A credit score developed by Fair Isaac Corporation.

Financial Intermediary   A bank or other financial institution that facilitates the flow of funds between different entities in the economy.

Firm Commitment   Phrase used to describe the situation where an investment bank guarantees that a new issue of securities will be sold at a certain price. If investors do not want to buy the securities, the investment bank will have to do so.

Fixed Annuity   Lifetime annuity where payments that will be received by the policyholder are fixed in advance.

Floor   See Interest Rate Floor.

Floor-Ceiling Agreement   See Collar.

Floorlet   One component of a floor.

Floor Rate   The rate in an interest rate floor agreement.

Foreign Currency Option   An option on a foreign exchange rate.

Forward Contract   A contract that obligates the holder to buy or sell an asset for a predetermined delivery price at a predetermined future time.

Forward Exchange Rate   The forward price of one unit of a foreign currency.

Forward Interest Rate   The interest rate for a future period of time implied by the rates prevailing in the market today.

Forward Price   The delivery price in a forward contract that causes the contract to be worth zero.

Forward Rate   Can refer to a forward interest rate or a forward exchange rate.

Forward Rate Agreement (FRA)   Agreement that a certain interest rate will apply to a certain principal amount for a certain time period in the future.

Front-End Load   Fee charged when mutual fund is purchased.

Front Office   Where trading takes place.

Front Running   Trading a stock on a personal account before a fund trades a large volume of the stock.

Fund of Funds   A fund that invests in a portfolio of different hedge funds.

Futures Contract   A contract that obligates the holder to buy or sell an asset at a predetermined delivery price during a specified future time period. The contract is settled daily.

Futures Option   An option on a futures contract.

Futures Price   The delivery price currently applicable to a futures contract.

G-30 Policy Recommendations   A set of recommendations concerning derivatives issued by nonregulators in 1993.

Gamma   The rate of change of delta with respect to the asset price.

Gamma-Neutral Portfolio   A portfolio with a gamma of zero.

GAP Management   Procedure for matching maturities of assets and liabilities.

GARCH Model   A model for forecasting volatility where the variance rate follows a mean-reverting process.

Gaussian Copula Model   A copula model based on the multivariate normal distribution.

Glass–Steagall Act   An act passed in the United States separating commercial and investment banks.

Greek Letters   See Greeks.

Greeks   Hedge parameters such as delta, gamma, vega, theta, and rho.

Group Life Insurance   Life insurance arranged for a group of people, usually by an employer.

Haircut   Discount applied to the value of an asset when it is used as collateral.

Hazard Rate   Measures probability of default in a short period of time conditional on no earlier default.

HDD   Heating degree days. The maximum of zero and the amount by which the daily average temperature is less than 65° Fahrenheit. The average temperature is the average of the highest and lowest temperatures (midnight to midnight).

Heating Degree Days   See HDD.

Hedge   A trade designed to reduce risk.

Hedge Funds   Funds that are subject to less restrictions and less regulation than mutual funds. They can take short positions and use derivatives, but they cannot publicly offer their securities.

Hedger   An individual who enters into hedging trades.

Hedge Ratio   The ratio of the size of a position in a hedging instrument to the size of the position being hedged.

High-Water mark Clause   Clause stating that gains equal to previous losses must be made before incentive fees apply.

Historical Default Probability   Default probability estimated from historical default experience.

Historical Simulation   A simulation based on historical data.

Historical Volatility   A volatility estimated from historical data.

Holiday Calendar   Calendar defining which days are holidays for the purposes of determining payment dates in a financial transaction.

Hurdle Rate   Return that must be earned by a hedge fund before the incentive fee applies.

Hybrid Approach   Approach to aggregating different types of economic capital.

Implied Default Probability   See Risk-Neutral Default Probability.

Implied Volatility   Volatility implied from an option price using the Black–Scholes–Merton or a similar model.

Inception Profit   Profit created by selling a derivative for more than its theoretical value.

Incremental Risk Charge   Extra capital charge for credit sensitive instruments in the trading book. The charge reflects the fact that capital requirements for credit instruments in the banking book are often higher than for equivalent-risk instruments in the trading book.

Incremental Value at Risk   The difference between the value at risk with and without a particular component of the portfolio.

Independence   Variable A is independent of variable B if knowing the value of variable B does not affect the probability density function for variable A.

Independent Amount   Collateral required by a dealer in bilateral OTC trading that is independent of the value of outstanding transactions.

Index Fund   A fund that is designed to match the performance of a particular stock index.

Initial Margin   The cash required from a futures trader at the time of the trade.

Initial Public Offering   See IPO.

Instantaneous Forward Rate   Forward rate for a very short period of time in the future.

Interest-Rate Cap   An option that provides a payoff when a specified interest rate is above a certain level. The interest rate is a floating rate that is reset periodically.

Interest-Rate Collar   A combination of an interest-rate cap and an interest-rate floor.

Interest-Rate Derivative   A derivative whose payoffs are dependent on future interest rates.

Interest-Rate Floor   An option that provides a payoff when an interest rate is below a certain level. The interest rate is a floating rate that is reset periodically.

Interest-Rate Option   An option where the payoff is dependent on the level of interest rates.

Interest-Rate Swap   An exchange of a fixed rate of interest on a certain notional principal for a floating rate of interest on the same notional principal.

Internal Credit Rating   Credit rating produced by a financial institution rather than by an outside agency such as Moody's or S&P.

In-the-Money Option   Either (a) a call option where the asset price is greater than the strike price or (b) a put option where the asset price is less than the strike price.

Intrinsic Value   For a call option, this is the greater of the excess of the asset price over the strike price and zero. For a put option, it is the greater of the excess of the strike price over the asset price and zero.

Investment Asset   An asset held by a significant number of individuals for investment purposes.

Investment Bank   A bank that helps companies issue debt and equity securities.

Investment Grade   Bond or other instrument with a credit rating of BBB (Baa) or above.

IPO   Initial Public Offering. An offering to investors of shares in a company for the first time. Prior to an IPO, shares are typically held only by the company's founders, its employees, and the providers of venture capital.

IRB Approach   Internal Ratings Based approach for assessing credit risk capital in Basel II.

IRC   See Incremental Risk Charge.

ISDA   International Swaps and Derivatives Association.

ISDA Master Agreement   Agreement between two parties governing their OTC derivatives trades.

ITraxx   An index of the credit quality of 125 European investment grade companies.

Junk Bond   Noninvestment-grade bond.

Key Risk Indicators   Indicators to track the level of operational risk.

Kurtosis   A measure of the heaviness of the tails of a distribution.

Late Trading   Trading a mutual fund after 4 P.M. at the 4 P.M. price.

Leveraging   Individuals and companies increasing their borrowings.

LGD   See Loss Given Default.

Liar Loan   Loan where the borrower does not tell the truth on the application form.

LIBID   London interbank bid rate. The rate bid by banks on Eurocurrency deposits (i.e., the rate at which a bank is willing to borrow from other banks).

LIBOR   London interbank offered rate. The rate offered by banks on Eurocurrency deposits (i.e., the rate at which a bank is willing to lend to other banks).

LIBOR-in-Arrears Swap   Swap where the interest paid on a date is determined by the interest rate observed on that date (not by the interest rate observed on the previous payment date).

LIBOR/Swap Zero Curve   Zero rates that are calculated from LIBOR rates, eurodollar futures, and swap rates.

LIBOR Zero Curve   See LIBOR/Swap Zero Curve.

Life Insurance   Insurance where payouts depend on when a person dies.

Linear Model   A model where the change in the portfolio value depends linearly on the returns of the underlying market variables.

Linear Product   Derivative product whose price depends linearly on one or more underlying variables.

Liquidity-Adjusted VaR   A value at risk calculation that takes account of the impact of the bid–offer spread when positions are unwound.

Liquidity Black Holes   The risk that liquidity will dry up because everyone wants to be on the same side of the market.

Liquidity Coverage Ratio   Ratio of high quality liquid assets to cash outflows during a stressed period of 30 days.

Liquidity Funding Risk   The risk that sources of funding will dry up.

Liquidity Preference Theory   A theory leading to the conclusion that forward interest rates are above expected future spot interest rates.

Liquidity Premium   The amount that forward interest rates exceed expected future spot interest rates.

Liquidity Trading Risk   The risk that it will not be possible to unwind positions in financial instruments at their theoretical price.

Living Will   A plan for winding up a financial institution so that some parts survive.

Lognormal Distribution   A variable has a lognormal distribution when the logarithm of the variable has a normal distribution.

Longevity Bond   Bond where a population is defined and the coupon paid at a particular time is proportional to the number of people in the population that are still alive at that time.

Longevity Risk   Risk that people will live longer than expected.

Long Position   A position involving the purchase of an asset.

Long-Tail Risk   Risk in property–casualty insurance that there will be claims made well after the end of the life of a policy.

London Interbank Bid Rate   See LIBID.

London Interbank Offered Rate   See LIBOR.

Lookback Option   An option whose payoff is dependent on the maximum or minimum of the asset price achieved during a certain period.

Loss Given Default   The percentage of the exposure to a counterparty that is lost when a default by the counterparty occurs.

Macaulay's Duration   The weighted average of the times when cash flows are received where the weight applied to a cash flow is proportional to the present value of the cash flow.

Maintenance Margin   When the balance in a trader's margin account falls below the maintenance margin level, the trader receives a margin call requiring the margin account to be topped up.

Margin   Amount of collateral required in cash or marketable securities from a trader.

Marginal Value at Risk   The rate of change of the value at risk with the size of one component of the portfolio.

Margin Call   A request for extra margin when the balance in the margin account falls below the maintenance margin level.

Marginal Distribution   The unconditional distribution of a variable.

Market Maker   A trader who is willing to quote both bid and offer prices for an asset.

Market Model   A model most commonly used by traders.

Market Portfolio   A portfolio consisting of the universe of all possible investments.

Market Risk   Risk relating to movements in market variables.

Market Timing   Frequent trading of a mutual fund to benefit from stale prices or to do late trading.

Marking to Market   The practice of revaluing a financial instrument to reflect the current values of the relevant market variables.

Marking to Model   Use of a model to determine the current value of a financial instrument.

Maturity Date   The end of the life of a contract.

Maximum Likelihood Method   A method for choosing the values of parameters by maximizing the probability of a set of observations occurring.

Mean Reversion   The tendency of a market variable (such as a volatility or an interest rate) to revert back to some long-run average level.

Merton's Model   Model using equity prices to estimate default probabilities. (Other models developed by Merton are also sometimes referred to as Merton's model.)

Mezzanine Tranche   Tranche which experiences losses after the equity tranche but before the senior tranche.

Middle Office   Where risk management takes place.

Minimum Transfer Amount   Minimum amount transferred in a collateralization agreement.

Model Building Approach   The use of a model to estimate value at risk.

Model Risk   The risk relating to the use of models to price derivative products.

Modified Duration   A modification to the standard duration measure so that it more accurately describes the relationship between proportional changes in a bond price and actual changes in its yield. The modification takes account of the compounding frequency with which the yield is quoted.

Money Center Banks   Banks with a global presence that fund themselves to a significant extent in wholesale markets.

Monte Carlo Simulation   A procedure for randomly sampling changes in market variables.

Moral Hazard   The possibility that the behavior of an insured entity will change because of the existence of an insurance contract.

Mortality Risk   Risk that people will die earlier than expected.

Multibank Holding Company   A holding company owning several banks. This structure was used in the United States for getting around some bank regulations.

Multivariate Normal Distribution   The joint distribution of many variables, each of which is normal.

Mutual Fund   A vehicle for investing the funds of many small investors.

Naked Position   A short position in a call option that is not combined with a long position in the underlying asset.

National Association of Insurance Commissioners   National body that provides services to the insurance regulators in each state in the United States.

Negative Feedback Trading   Trading where assets are sold after a price increase and bought after a price decrease.

Net Asset Value   Value of a fund's investments divided by the number of shares in the fund.

Net Interest Income   The excess of interest earned over interest paid for a bank.

Net Replacement Ratio   The ratio of current exposure with netting to current exposure without netting.

Net Stable Funding Ratio   Weighted average of funding available divided by weighted average of funding required.

Netting   The ability to offset contracts with positive and negative values in the event of a default by a counterparty.

NINJA   Term used to describe a poor credit risk: no income, no job, no assets.

Noninvestment Grade   Bond or other instrument with a credit rating below BBB (Baa).

Nonlife Insurance   See Property–Casualty Insurance.

Nonlinear product   Derivative product that is not linearly dependent on the underlying variables.

Nonperforming Loan   A loan where interest is more than 90 days overdue.

Nonsystematic risk   Risk that can be diversified away.

Normal Distribution   The standard bell-shaped distribution of statistics.

Normal Market   A market where futures prices increase with maturity.

Notional Principal   The principal used to calculate payments in a derivatives transaction. The principal is "notional" because it is neither paid nor received.

Numerical Procedure   A method of calculation when no formula is available.

Objective Probability   Probability based on data.

Offer Price   See Ask Price.

OIS   See Overnight Indexed Swap.

Open End Fund   Mutual fund where the number of shares outstanding increases and decreases as investors deposit and withdraw funds.

Open Interest   The total number of long positions outstanding in a futures contract (equals the total number of short positions).

Open Outcry   System of trading where traders meet on the floor of the exchange.

Operational Risk   The risk of loss arising from inadequate or failed internal processes, people, and systems or from external events.

Option   The right to buy or sell an asset.

Originate-to-Distribute Model   Phrase use to describe the practice where a bank originates loans, credit card receivables, and so on, and securitizes them so that the credit risks are distributed to other investors.

OTC Market   See Over-the-Counter Market.

Out-of-the-Money Option   Either (a) a call option where the asset price is less than the strike price or (b) a put option where the asset price is greater than the strike price.

Outside-Model Hedging   Hedging against parameters that are constant in the model as well as against variables that are stochastic in the model.

Overcollateralization   Situation where total principal of the underlying assets is greater than the sum of the principals of the tranches that are created from the assets.

Overnight Indexed Swap   An agreement to exchange the geometric average of overnight rates during a certain period for a fixed rate.

Over-the-Counter Market   A market where traders deal by phone. The traders are usually financial institutions, corporations, and fund managers.

Parallel Shift A movement in the yield curve where each point on the curve changes by the same amount.

Partial Duration Percentage change in value of a portfolio for a small change in one point on the zero-coupon yield curve.

Partial Simulation Approach Approach for calculating value at risk where Greek letters and Taylor series expansions are used to approximate the change in the portfolio value.

Par Value The principal amount of a bond.

Par Yield The coupon on a bond that makes its price equal the principal.

Payoff The cash realized by the holder of an option or other derivative at the end of its life.

PD Probability of default.

Peak Exposure A high percentile (e.g., 97.5) of the estimated exposure distribution at a particular future time.

Performing Loan A loan where interest is not more than 90 days overdue.

Permanent Life Insurance See Whole Life Insurance.

Physical Default Probability See Historical Default Probability.

Plain Vanilla A term used to describe a standard deal.

Poison Pill Action taken by a company to make a takeover of the company more difficult.

Poisson Distribution Distribution for number of events in a certain time period in a Poisson process.

Poisson Process A process describing a situation where events happen at random. The probability of an event in time Δt is $\lambda \Delta t$ where λ is the intensity of the process.

Policyholder Holder of an insurance policy.

Portfolio Immunization Making a portfolio relatively insensitive to interest rates.

Portfolio Insurance Entering into trades to ensure that the value of a portfolio will not fall below a certain level.

Positive Feedback Trading Trading where assets are sold after a price decline and bought after a price increase.

Positive Semi-Definite Condition that must be satisfied by a variance–covariance matrix for it to be valid.

Power Law Law describing the tails of many probability distributions that are encountered in practice.

Premium The price of an option.

Prime Broker A bank that clears a hedge fund's trades, provides it with borrowings, and provides other services.

Principal The par or face value of a debt instrument.

Principal Components Analysis An analysis aimed at finding a small number of factors that describe most of the variation in a large number of correlated variables. (Similar to a factor analysis.)

Private Placement Selling a new issue of securities to a small number of large financial institutions without offering it to the general public.

Property–Casualty Insurance Property insurance provides a payout in the event of loss of property or damage to property. Casualty insurance provides protection against legal liabilities or damage to the property of others.

Proprietary Trading Trading for a financial institution's own account rather than the account of one of the financial institution's clients.

Public Offering Attempting to sell a new issue of securities to the general public.

Put-Call Parity The relationship between the price of a European call option and the price of a European put option when they have the same strike price and maturity date.

Put Option An option to sell an asset for a certain price by a certain date.

Puttable Bond A bond where the holder has the right to sell it back to the issuer at certain predetermined times for a predetermined price.

Puttable Swap A swap where one side has the right to terminate early.

Quadratic Model   Quadratic relationship between change in portfolio value and percentage changes in market variables.

Quantitative Impact Studies   Studies by the Basel committee of the effect of proposed new regulations.

RAROC   Risk-adjusted return on capital.

RCSA   Risk control and self assessment. An approach to assessing operational risk.

Rebalancing   The process of adjusting a trading position periodically. Usually the purpose is to maintain delta neutrality.

Recovery Rate   Amount recovered in the event of a default as a percent of the face value.

Reference Entity   Company or country whose default is being insured against in a credit default swap.

Regulatory Arbitrage   Transactions designed to reduce the total regulatory capital of the financial institutions involved.

Regulatory Capital   Capital a financial institution is required by regulators to keep.

Rehypothecation   Use of collateral posted by one counterparty to satisfy the collateral requirements of another counterparty.

Reinsurance   Situation where an insurance company passes on some of its risks to another company. Of course, it has to pay the other company for taking on the risks.

Repo   Repurchase agreement. A procedure for borrowing money by selling securities to a counterparty and agreeing to buy them back later at a slightly higher price.

Repo Rate   The rate of interest in a repo transaction.

Reserve Requirement   Percentage of deposits that must be kept in cash or on deposit with the central bank.

Reset Date   The date in a swap or cap or floor when the floating rate for the next period is set.

Retail Banking   Taking relatively small deposits from retail customers and making relatively small loans to them.

Reverse Stress Testing   Using an algorithm to search for scenarios that lead to large losses.

Reversion Level   The level to which the value of a market variable (e.g., a volatility) tends to revert.

Rho   Rate of change of the price of a derivative with the interest rate.

Right Way Risk   Situation where a counterparty becomes less likely to default as the dealer's exposure to the counterparty increases.

Risk Appetite   A statement by a financial institution describing the level of risk that can be tolerated.

Risk-Free Rate   The rate of interest that can be earned without assuming any risks.

Risk-Neutral Default Probability   Default probability implied from a credit spread.

Risk-Neutral Valuation   The valuation of an option or other derivative assuming the world is risk neutral. Risk-neutral valuation gives the correct price for a derivative in all worlds, not just in a risk-neutral world.

Risk-Neutral World   A world where investors are assumed to require no extra return on average for bearing risks.

Risk-Weighted Amount   See Risk-Weighted Assets.

Risk-Weighted Assets   Quantity calculated in Basel I and Basel II. Total capital must be at least 8% of risk-weighted assets.

Roll Back   See Backwards Induction.

RSF Factor   Required stable funding factor, a weighting factor applied to funding requirements in the calculation of the Net Stable Funding Ratio.

Sarbanes–Oxley   Act passed in the United States in 2002 increasing the responsibilities of directors, CEOs, and CFOs of public companies.

Scenario Analysis   An analysis of the effects of possible alternative future movements in market variables on the value of a portfolio. Also used to generate scenarios leading to operational risk losses.

Scorecard Approach   An assessment procedure used for operational risk.

SEC   Securities and Exchange Commission.

Securitization   Process whereby securities are created from future cash flow streams.

Senior Tranche   Tranche which is the last to experience losses because of defaults on the underlying assets.

Short Position   A position assumed when traders sell shares they do not own.

Short Selling   Selling in the market shares that have been borrowed from another investor.

Simulation   See Monte Carlo Simulation.

Skewness   Measure of the lack of symmetry in a probability distribution.

Solvency I   Current regulatory framework for insurance companies in the European Union.

Solvency II   A new regulatory framework for insurance companies proposed by the European Union.

Solvency Risk   The risk that liabilities will be greater than assets.

Sovereign Wealth Funds   Funds set up to make investments for a country.

Specific Risk Charge   Capital requirement for idiosyncratic risks in the trading book.

Spectral Risk Measure   Risk measure that assigns weights to the quantiles of the loss distribution.

Speculative Grade   See Non-Investment-Grade.

Speculator   An individual who is taking a position in the market. Usually the individual is betting that the price of an asset will go up or that the price of an asset will go down.

Spot Interest Rate   See Zero-Coupon Interest Rate.

Spot Price   The price for immediate delivery.

Spot Volatilities   The volatilities used to price a cap when a different volatility is used for each caplet.

Static Hedge   A hedge that does not have to be changed once it is initiated.

Static Options Replication   A procedure for hedging a portfolio that involves finding another portfolio of approximately equal value on some boundary.

Stochastic Variable   Variable whose future value is uncertain.

Stock Index   An index monitoring the value of a portfolio of stocks.

Stock Index Futures   Futures on a stock index.

Stock Index Option   An option on a stock index.

Stock Option   Option on a stock.

Stop–Loss Rule   A trading rule where a position is unwound when losses on the position reach a certain level.

Storage Costs   The costs of storing a commodity.

Stressed VaR   Value at risk calculated from a 250-day period of stressed market conditions that would be particularly bad for the financial institution.

Stress Testing   Testing of the impact of extreme market moves on the value of a portfolio.

Strike Price   The price at which the asset may be bought or sold in an option contract. (Also called the exercise price.)

Structured Product   Derivative designed by a financial institution to meet the needs of a client.

Student t-Copula   Copula based on the multivariate Student t-distribution.

Student t-Distribution   Distribution with heavier tails than the normal distribution.

Subjective Probability   Probability that reflects a person's opinion, rather than data.

Subprime Mortgage   Mortgages that are more risky than the average mortgage.

Supplementary Capital   See Tier 2 Capital.

Survivor Bond   See Longevity Bond.

Swap   An agreement to exchange cash flows in the future according to a prearranged formula.

Swap Rate   The fixed rate in an interest rate swap that causes the swap to have a value of zero.

Swaption An option to enter into an interest rate swap where a specified fixed rate is exchanged for floating.

Swap Zero Curve See LIBOR/Swap Zero Curve.

Synthetic CDO A CDO created by selling credit default swaps.

Synthetic Option An option created by trading the underlying asset.

Systematic Risk Risk that cannot be diversified away.

Systemic Risk Risk that a default by one financial institution will lead to defaults by other financial institutions.

Tail Correlation Correlation between the tails of two distributions. Measures the extent to which extreme values tend to occur together.

Tail Dependence Measure of the frequency with which extreme outcomes occur at the same time for two variables.

Tail Loss See Expected Shortfall.

Taylor Series Expansion For a function of several variables, this relates changes in the value of the function to changes in the values of the variables when the changes are small.

Teaser Rate A low interest rate offered for the first two or three years on a mortgage.

Temporary Life Insurance See Term Life Insurance.

Terminal Value The value at maturity.

Term Life Insurance Life insurance that pays off if death occurs before a certain date.

Term Structure of Interest Rates The relationship between interest rates and their maturities.

Theta The rate of change of the price of an option or other derivative with the passage of time.

Threshold Value of outstanding transactions that leads to collateral being required in bilateral OTC trading.

Tier 1 Equity Capital Equity capital, redefined under Basel III (also called Tier 1 Core Capital).

Tier 2 Capital Subordinated debt (life greater than five years) and similar sources of capital.

Tier 3 Capital Short-term subordinated debt (life between two and five years).

Time Decay See Theta.

Time Value The value of an option arising from the time left to maturity (equals an option's price minus its intrinsic value).

Total Expense Ratio Ratio of total expenses to premiums for a property–casualty insurance company.

Total Return Swap A swap where the return on an asset such as a bond is exchanged for LIBOR plus a spread. The return on the asset includes income such as coupons and the change in value of the asset.

Tracking Error A measure of the error in a trading strategy designed to track a stock index.

Trading Book Part of a bank's portfolio that consists of instruments that are held for resale.

Trading Days Days when markets are open for trading.

Tranche One of several securities that have different risk attributes. Examples are the tranches of a CDO.

Transaction Costs The cost of carrying out a trade (commissions plus the difference between the price obtained and the midpoint of the bid-offer spread).

Treasury Bill A short-term non-coupon-bearing instrument issued by the government to finance its debt.

Treasury Bond A long-term coupon-bearing instrument issued by the government to finance its debt.

Treasury Note Treasury bond lasting less than 10 years.

Tree Representation of the evolution of the value of a market variable for the purposes of valuing an option or other derivative.

Underlying Variable A variable that the price of an option or other derivative depends on.

Unit Trust   See Mutual Fund.

Universal Life Insurance   A form of whole life insurance where the premium payments can be varied from year to year. The final payout is determined from the premiums, the performance of the investment, and costs.

Unsystematic Risk   See Nonsystematic Risk.

Up-and-In Option   An option that comes into existence when the price of the underlying asset increases to a prespecified level.

Up-and-Out Option   An option that ceases to exist when the price of the underlying asset increases to a prespecified level.

Value at Risk   A loss that will not be exceeded at some specified confidence level.

Variable Annuity   A typical arrangement wherein the policy holder deposits a lump sum with an insurance company and chooses from a number of options on how it is to be invested. At some future time (the maturity date), the accumulated value is converted into an annuity. If the policy holder dies before the maturity date, his or her beneficiaries receive the accumulated value.

Variable Life Insurance   A form of whole life insurance where the policy holder decides how funds will be invested. If the investments do well, the proceeds can be used to reduce premiums. There is a guaranteed minimum payout on death, but the payout may be higher if the investments do well.

Variance-Covariance Matrix   A matrix showing variances of, and covariances between, a number of different market variables.

Variance Rate   The square of volatility.

Variation Margin   Extra margin required to bring balance in the margin account up to the required level.

Vasicek's Model   Model of default correlation based on the Gaussian copula. (Other models developed by Vasicek are also sometimes referred to as Vasicek's model.)

Vega   The rate of change in the price of an option or other derivative with volatility.

Vega-Neutral Portfolio   A portfolio with a vega of zero.

VIX Index   Index of the implied volatilities of options on the S&P 500.

Volatility   A measure of the uncertainty of the return realized on an asset.

Volatility Skew   A term used to describe the volatility smile when it is nonsymmetrical.

Volatility Smile   The variation of implied volatility with strike price.

Volatility Surface   A table showing the variation of implied volatilities with strike price and time to maturity.

Volatility Term Structure   The variation of implied volatility with time to maturity.

Waterfall   Rules for determining how principal and interest cash flows from an underlying portfolio are distributed to tranches. In a typical arrangement, interest cash flows are first used to pay the senior tranche its promised return. The cash flows (if any) that are left over are used to provide the next-most-senior tranche with its promised return, and so on. Principal cash flows are usually used first to repay the senior tranche, then the next-most-senior tranche, and so on. The equity tranche is the last to receive both interest and principal cash flows.

Weather Derivative   Derivative where the payoff depends on the weather.

Whole Life Insurance   Life insurance that lasts for the whole life of the insured and so is certain to provide a payout.

Wholesale Banking   Taking large deposits and making large loans.

Within-Model Hedging   Hedging only against those variables that the model considers as stochastic. (cf., Outside-Model Hedging).

Writing an Option   Selling an option.

Wrong Way Risk   Situation where a counterparty becomes more likely to default as the dealer's exposure to the counterparty increases.

Yield   A return provided by an instrument.

Yield Curve   See Term Structure of Interest Rates.

Zero-Coupon Bond   A bond that provides no coupons.

Zero-Coupon Interest Rate   The interest rate that would be earned on a bond that provides no coupons.

Zero-Coupon Yield Curve   A plot of the zero-coupon interest rate against time to maturity.

Zero Curve   See Zero-Coupon Yield Curve.

Zero Rate   See Zero-Coupon Interest Rate.

Z-Score   A number indicating how likely a company is to default.

DerivaGem Software

There are a number of new features of DerivaGem. The software has been simplified by eliminating the *.dll files. Source code is included with the functions and functions are now accessible to Mac and Linux users. CDSs and CDOs can now be valued. The software can be downloaded from the author's website.

GETTING STARTED

The most difficult part of using software is getting started. Here is a step-by-step guide to valuing an option using DerivaGem Version 2.01.

1. Open the Excel file DG201.xls
2. If you are using Office 2007, click on *Options* at the top of your screen (above the F column) and then click *Enable this content*. If you are not using Office 2007, make sure that your security for Macros is set at medium or low. (You can do this by clicking *Tools*, followed by *Macros*, followed by *Security*.)
3. Click on the *Equity_FX_Index_Futures* worksheet tab at the bottom of the page.
4. Choose *Currency* as the Underlying Type and *Binomial American* as the Option Type. Click on the *Put* button. Leave *Imply Volatility* unchecked.
5. You are now all set to value an American put option on a currency. There are seven inputs: exchange rate, volatility, risk-free rate (domestic), foreign risk-free rate, time to expiration (yrs), exercise price, and time steps. Input these in cells D6, D7, D8, D9, D19, D20, and D21 as 1.61, 12%, 8%, 9%, 1.0, 1.60, and 4, respectively.
6. Hit *Enter* on your keyboard and click on *Calculate*. You will see the price of the option in cell D25 as 0.07099 and the Greek letters in cells D26 to D30. The screen you should have produced is shown in the graphic following.
7. Click on *Display Tree*. You will see the binomial tree used to calculate the option.

NEXT STEPS

You should now have no difficulty valuing other types of options on other underlyings with this worksheet. To imply a volatility, check the *Imply Volatility* box and input the option price in cell D25. Hit *Enter* and click on *Calculate*. The implied volatility is displayed in cell D7.

Many different charts can be displayed. To display a chart, you must first choose the variable you require on the vertical axis, the variable you require on the horizontal

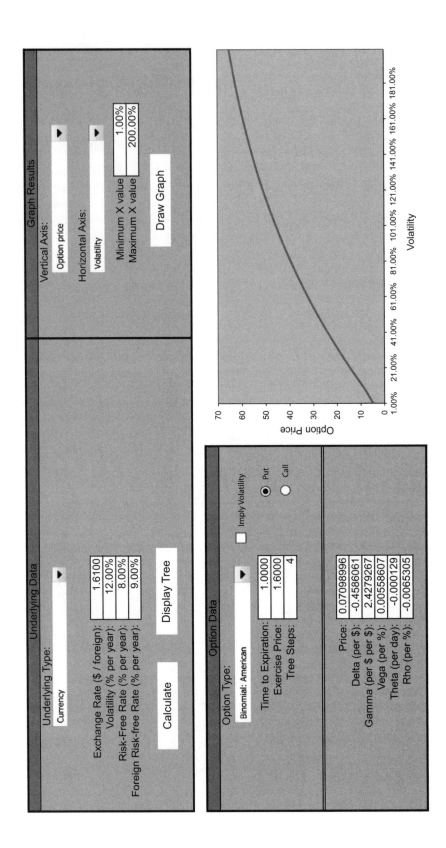

axis, and the range of values to be considered on the horizontal axis. Following that, you should hit *Enter* on your keyboard and click on *Draw Graph*.

Other points to note about this worksheet are:

1. For European and American equity options, up to 10 dividends on the underlying stock can be input in a table that pops up. Enter the time of each dividend (measured in years from today) in the first column and the amount of the dividend in the second column. Dividends must be entered in chronological order.
2. Up to 500 time steps can be used for the valuation of American options, but only a maximum of 10 time steps can be displayed.
3. Greek letters for all options other than standard calls and puts are calculated by perturbing the inputs, not by using analytic formulas.
4. For an Asian option, the *Current Average* is the average price since inception. For a new deal (with zero time to inception) the current average is irrelevant.
5. In the case of a lookback option, *Minimum to Date* is used when a call is valued and *Maximum to Date* is used when a put is valued. For a new deal these should be set equal to the current price of the underlying asset.
6. Interest rates are continuously compounded.

BOND OPTIONS

The general operation of the *Bond_Options* worksheet is similar to that of the *Equity_FX_Index_Futures* worksheet. The alternative models are Black's model, the normal model of the short rate, and the lognormal model of the short rate. (These models are described in my book *Options, Futures, and Other Derivatives*.) The first model can be applied only to European options. The other two can be applied to European or American options. The coupon is the rate paid per year and the frequency of payments can be selected as *Quarterly*, *Semi-Annual*, or *Annual*. The zero-coupon yield curve is entered in the table labeled *Term Structure*. Enter maturities (measured in years) in the first column and the corresponding continuously compounded rates in the second column. The maturities must be in chronological order. DerivaGem assumes a piecewise linear zero curve similar to that in Figure B.1 of Appendix B. The strike price can be quoted (clean) or cash (dirty). The quoted bond price, which is calculated by the software, and the strike price, which is input, are per \$100 of principal.

CAPS AND SWAPTIONS

The general operation of the *Caps_and Swap_Options* worksheet is similar to that of the *Equity_FX_Index_Futures* worksheet. The worksheet is used to value interest rate caps/floors and swap options. (The alternative models are explained in my book *Options, Futures, and Other Derivatives*.) The term structure of interest rates is entered in the same way as for bond options. The frequency of payments can be selected as *Monthly*, *Quarterly*, *Semi-Annual*, or *Annual*. The software calculates payment dates by working backward from the end of the life of the instrument. The initial accrual period for a cap/floor may be a nonstandard length between 0.5 and 1.5 times a normal accrual period.

CDSs

The CDS worksheet is used to calculate hazard rates from CDS spreads and vice versa. Users must input a term structure of interest rates (continuously compounded) and either a term structure of CDS spreads or a term structure of hazard rates. The initial hazard rate applies from time zero to the time specified; the second hazard rate applies from the time corresponding to the first hazard rate to the time corresponding to the second hazard rate; and so on. The hazard rates are continuously compounded so that a hazard rate $\lambda(t)$ at time t means that the probability of default between times t and $t + \Delta t$, conditional on no earlier default is $\lambda(t)\Delta t$. The calculations are carried out assuming that default can occur only at points midway between payment dates. This corresponds to the calculations for the example in Appendix K. (Note that, in this example, the hazard rate is 2% with annual compounding or 2.02% with continuous compounding.)

CDOs

The CDO worksheet calculates quotes for the tranches of CDOs from tranche correlations input by the user (see Appendix L). The attachment points and detachment points for tranches are input by the user. The quotes can be in basis points or involve an upfront payment. In the latter case, the spread in basis points is fixed and the upfront payment, as a percent of the tranche principal, is either input or implied. (For example, the fixed spread for the equity tranche of iTraxx Europe or CDX NA IG is 500 basis points.) The number of integration points defines the accuracy of calculations and can be left as 10 for most purposes. (The maximum is 30.) The software displays the expected loss as a percent of the tranche principal (ExpLoss) and the present value of expected payments (PVPmts) at the rate of 10,000 basis points per year. The spread is ExpLoss*10,000/PVPmts. The upfront payment is ExpLoss–(Spread*PVPmts/10,000). The worksheet can be used to imply either tranche (compound) correlations or base correlations from quotes input by the user. For base correlations to be calculated, it is necessary for the first attachment point to be 0% and the detachment point for one tranche to be the attachment point for the next tranche.

HOW GREEK LETTERS ARE DEFINED

In the *Equity_FX_Index_Futures* worksheet, the Greek letters are defined as follows.

Delta: Change in option price per dollar increase in underlying asset.

Gamma: Change in delta per dollar increase in underlying asset.

Vega: Change in option price per 1% increase in volatility (e.g., volatility increases from 20% to 21%).

Rho: Change in option price per 1% increase in interest rate (e.g., interest increases from 5% to 6%).

Theta: Change in option price per calendar day passing.

In the *Bond_Options* and *Caps_and_Swap_Options* worksheets the Greek letters are defined as follows:

DV01: Change in option price per one-basis-point upward parallel shift in the zero curve.

Gamma01: Change in DV01 per one-basis-point upward parallel shift in the zero curve, multiplied by 100.

Vega: Change in option price when volatility parameter increases by 1% (e.g., volatility increases from 20% to 21%).

THE APPLICATIONS BUILDER

Once you are familiar with the Options Calculator (DG201.xls), you may want to start using the Application Builder. This consists of most of the functions underlying the Options Calculator with source code. It enables you to create tables of option values, create your own charts, or develop applications. Excel users should load DG201 functions.xls and Open Office users should load Open Office DG201 functions.ods. Below are some sample applications that have been developed. If any reader wishes to distribute other applications to colleagues, I would be pleased to do this (with full acknowledgements) via my website and the next release of the software.

A. Binomial Convergence. This investigates the convergence of the binomial model in Appendix F.
B. Greek Letters. This provides charts showing the Greek letters in Chapter 7.
C. Delta Hedge. This investigates the performance of delta hedging as in Tables 7.2 and 7.3.
D. Delta and Gamma Hedge. This investigates the performance of delta plus gamma hedging for a position in a binary option.
E. Value at Risk. This calculates Value at Risk for a portfolio using three different approaches.
F. Barrier Replication. This carries out calculations for static options replication (see Section 7.9).
G. Trinomial Convergence. This investigates the convergence of a trinomial tree model (not covered in this book).

Table for $N(x)$ when $x \leq 0$

This table shows values of $N(x)$ for $x \leq 0$. The table should be used with interpolation. For example, $N(-0.1234) = N(-0.12) - 0.34[N(-0.12) - N(-0.13)] = 0.4522 - 0.34 \times (0.4522 - 0.4483) = 0.4509$.

x	0.00	0.01	0.02	0.03	0.04	0.05	0.06	0.07	0.08	0.09
−0.0	0.5000	0.4960	0.4920	0.4880	0.4840	0.4801	0.4761	0.4721	0.4681	0.4641
−0.1	0.4602	0.4562	0.4522	0.4483	0.4443	0.4404	0.4364	0.4325	0.4286	0.4247
−0.2	0.4207	0.4168	0.4129	0.4090	0.4052	0.4013	0.3974	0.3936	0.3897	0.3859
−0.3	0.3821	0.3783	0.3745	0.3707	0.3669	0.3632	0.3594	0.3557	0.3520	0.3483
−0.4	0.3446	0.3409	0.3372	0.3336	0.3300	0.3264	0.3228	0.3192	0.3156	0.3121
−0.5	0.3085	0.3050	0.3015	0.2981	0.2946	0.2912	0.2877	0.2843	0.2810	0.2776
−0.6	0.2743	0.2709	0.2676	0.2643	0.2611	0.2578	0.2546	0.2514	0.2483	0.2451
−0.7	0.2420	0.2389	0.2358	0.2327	0.2296	0.2266	0.2236	0.2206	0.2177	0.2148
−0.8	0.2119	0.2090	0.2061	0.2033	0.2005	0.1977	0.1949	0.1922	0.1894	0.1867
−0.9	0.1841	0.1814	0.1788	0.1762	0.1736	0.1711	0.1685	0.1660	0.1635	0.1611
−1.0	0.1587	0.1562	0.1539	0.1515	0.1492	0.1469	0.1446	0.1423	0.1401	0.1379
−1.1	0.1357	0.1335	0.1314	0.1292	0.1271	0.1251	0.1230	0.1210	0.1190	0.1170
−1.2	0.1151	0.1131	0.1112	0.1093	0.1075	0.1056	0.1038	0.1020	0.1003	0.0985
−1.3	0.0968	0.0951	0.0934	0.0918	0.0901	0.0885	0.0869	0.0853	0.0838	0.0823
−1.4	0.0808	0.0793	0.0778	0.0764	0.0749	0.0735	0.0721	0.0708	0.0694	0.0681
−1.5	0.0668	0.0655	0.0643	0.0630	0.0618	0.0606	0.0594	0.0582	0.0571	0.0559
−1.6	0.0548	0.0537	0.0526	0.0516	0.0505	0.0495	0.0485	0.0475	0.0465	0.0455
−1.7	0.0446	0.0436	0.0427	0.0418	0.0409	0.0401	0.0392	0.0384	0.0375	0.0367
−1.8	0.0359	0.0351	0.0344	0.0336	0.0329	0.0322	0.0314	0.0307	0.0301	0.0294
−1.9	0.0287	0.0281	0.0274	0.0268	0.0262	0.0256	0.0250	0.0244	0.0239	0.0233
−2.0	0.0228	0.0222	0.0217	0.0212	0.0207	0.0202	0.0197	0.0192	0.0188	0.0183
−2.1	0.0179	0.0174	0.0170	0.0166	0.0162	0.0158	0.0154	0.0150	0.0146	0.0143
−2.2	0.0139	0.0136	0.0132	0.0129	0.0125	0.0122	0.0119	0.0116	0.0113	0.0110
−2.3	0.0107	0.0104	0.0102	0.0099	0.0096	0.0094	0.0091	0.0089	0.0087	0.0084
−2.4	0.0082	0.0080	0.0078	0.0075	0.0073	0.0071	0.0069	0.0068	0.0066	0.0064
−2.5	0.0062	0.0060	0.0059	0.0057	0.0055	0.0054	0.0052	0.0051	0.0049	0.0048
−2.6	0.0047	0.0045	0.0044	0.0043	0.0041	0.0040	0.0039	0.0038	0.0037	0.0036
−2.7	0.0035	0.0034	0.0033	0.0032	0.0031	0.0030	0.0029	0.0028	0.0027	0.0026
−2.8	0.0026	0.0025	0.0024	0.0023	0.0023	0.0022	0.0021	0.0021	0.0020	0.0019
−2.9	0.0019	0.0018	0.0018	0.0017	0.0016	0.0016	0.0015	0.0015	0.0014	0.0014
−3.0	0.0014	0.0013	0.0013	0.0012	0.0012	0.0011	0.0011	0.0011	0.0010	0.0010
−3.1	0.0010	0.0009	0.0009	0.0009	0.0008	0.0008	0.0008	0.0008	0.0007	0.0007
−3.2	0.0007	0.0007	0.0006	0.0006	0.0006	0.0006	0.0006	0.0005	0.0005	0.0005
−3.3	0.0005	0.0005	0.0005	0.0004	0.0004	0.0004	0.0004	0.0004	0.0004	0.0003
−3.4	0.0003	0.0003	0.0003	0.0003	0.0003	0.0003	0.0003	0.0003	0.0003	0.0002
−3.5	0.0002	0.0002	0.0002	0.0002	0.0002	0.0002	0.0002	0.0002	0.0002	0.0002
−3.6	0.0002	0.0002	0.0001	0.0001	0.0001	0.0001	0.0001	0.0001	0.0001	0.0001
−3.7	0.0001	0.0001	0.0001	0.0001	0.0001	0.0001	0.0001	0.0001	0.0001	0.0001
−3.8	0.0001	0.0001	0.0001	0.0001	0.0001	0.0001	0.0001	0.0001	0.0001	0.0001
−3.9	0.0000	0.0000	0.0000	0.0000	0.0000	0.0000	0.0000	0.0000	0.0000	0.0000
−4.0	0.0000	0.0000	0.0000	0.0000	0.0000	0.0000	0.0000	0.0000	0.0000	0.0000

Table for N(x) when x ≥ 0

This table shows values of $N(x)$ for $x \geq 0$. The table should be used with interpolation. For example, $N(0.6278) = N(0.62) + 0.78[N(0.63) - N(0.62)] = 0.7324 + 0.78 \times (0.7357 - 0.7324) = 0.7350$.

x	0.00	0.01	0.02	0.03	0.04	0.05	0.06	0.07	0.08	0.09
0.0	0.5000	0.5040	0.5080	0.5120	0.5160	0.5199	0.5239	0.5279	0.5319	0.5359
0.1	0.5398	0.5438	0.5478	0.5517	0.5557	0.5596	0.5636	0.5675	0.5714	0.5753
0.2	0.5793	0.5832	0.5871	0.5910	0.5948	0.5987	0.6026	0.6064	0.6103	0.6141
0.3	0.6179	0.6217	0.6255	0.6293	0.6331	0.6368	0.6406	0.6443	0.6480	0.6517
0.4	0.6554	0.6591	0.6628	0.6664	0.6700	0.6736	0.6772	0.6808	0.6844	0.6879
0.5	0.6915	0.6950	0.6985	0.7019	0.7054	0.7088	0.7123	0.7157	0.7190	0.7224
0.6	0.7257	0.7291	0.7324	0.7357	0.7389	0.7422	0.7454	0.7486	0.7517	0.7549
0.7	0.7580	0.7611	0.7642	0.7673	0.7704	0.7734	0.7764	0.7794	0.7823	0.7852
0.8	0.7881	0.7910	0.7939	0.7967	0.7995	0.8023	0.8051	0.8078	0.8106	0.8133
0.9	0.8159	0.8186	0.8212	0.8238	0.8264	0.8289	0.8315	0.8340	0.8365	0.8389
1.0	0.8413	0.8438	0.8461	0.8485	0.8508	0.8531	0.8554	0.8577	0.8599	0.8621
1.1	0.8643	0.8665	0.8686	0.8708	0.8729	0.8749	0.8770	0.8790	0.8810	0.8830
1.2	0.8849	0.8869	0.8888	0.8907	0.8925	0.8944	0.8962	0.8980	0.8997	0.9015
1.3	0.9032	0.9049	0.9066	0.9082	0.9099	0.9115	0.9131	0.9147	0.9162	0.9177
1.4	0.9192	0.9207	0.9222	0.9236	0.9251	0.9265	0.9279	0.9292	0.9306	0.9319
1.5	0.9332	0.9345	0.9357	0.9370	0.9382	0.9394	0.9406	0.9418	0.9429	0.9441
1.6	0.9452	0.9463	0.9474	0.9484	0.9495	0.9505	0.9515	0.9525	0.9535	0.9545
1.7	0.9554	0.9564	0.9573	0.9582	0.9591	0.9599	0.9608	0.9616	0.9625	0.9633
1.8	0.9641	0.9649	0.9656	0.9664	0.9671	0.9678	0.9686	0.9693	0.9699	0.9706
1.9	0.9713	0.9719	0.9726	0.9732	0.9738	0.9744	0.9750	0.9756	0.9761	0.9767
2.0	0.9772	0.9778	0.9783	0.9788	0.9793	0.9798	0.9803	0.9808	0.9812	0.9817
2.1	0.9821	0.9826	0.9830	0.9834	0.9838	0.9842	0.9846	0.9850	0.9854	0.9857
2.2	0.9861	0.9864	0.9868	0.9871	0.9875	0.9878	0.9881	0.9884	0.9887	0.9890
2.3	0.9893	0.9896	0.9898	0.9901	0.9904	0.9906	0.9909	0.9911	0.9913	0.9916
2.4	0.9918	0.9920	0.9922	0.9925	0.9927	0.9929	0.9931	0.9932	0.9934	0.9936
2.5	0.9938	0.9940	0.9941	0.9943	0.9945	0.9946	0.9948	0.9949	0.9951	0.9952
2.6	0.9953	0.9955	0.9956	0.9957	0.9959	0.9960	0.9961	0.9962	0.9963	0.9964
2.7	0.9965	0.9966	0.9967	0.9968	0.9969	0.9970	0.9971	0.9972	0.9973	0.9974
2.8	0.9974	0.9975	0.9976	0.9977	0.9977	0.9978	0.9979	0.9979	0.9980	0.9981
2.9	0.9981	0.9982	0.9982	0.9983	0.9984	0.9984	0.9985	0.9985	0.9986	0.9986
3.0	0.9986	0.9987	0.9987	0.9988	0.9988	0.9989	0.9989	0.9989	0.9990	0.9990
3.1	0.9990	0.9991	0.9991	0.9991	0.9992	0.9992	0.9992	0.9992	0.9993	0.9993
3.2	0.9993	0.9993	0.9994	0.9994	0.9994	0.9994	0.9994	0.9995	0.9995	0.9995
3.3	0.9995	0.9995	0.9995	0.9996	0.9996	0.9996	0.9996	0.9996	0.9996	0.9997
3.4	0.9997	0.9997	0.9997	0.9997	0.9997	0.9997	0.9997	0.9997	0.9997	0.9998
3.5	0.9998	0.9998	0.9998	0.9998	0.9998	0.9998	0.9998	0.9998	0.9998	0.9998
3.6	0.9998	0.9998	0.9999	0.9999	0.9999	0.9999	0.9999	0.9999	0.9999	0.9999
3.7	0.9999	0.9999	0.9999	0.9999	0.9999	0.9999	0.9999	0.9999	0.9999	0.9999
3.8	0.9999	0.9999	0.9999	0.9999	0.9999	0.9999	0.9999	0.9999	0.9999	0.9999
3.9	1.0000	1.0000	1.0000	1.0000	1.0000	1.0000	1.0000	1.0000	1.0000	1.0000
4.0	1.0000	1.0000	1.0000	1.0000	1.0000	1.0000	1.0000	1.0000	1.0000	1.0000

401(k) plans, 60

AAA-rated tranches, 130, 353
Abraham, Ann, 47
ABCP. *See* Asset-backed commercial paper
ABS. *See* Asset-backed security
ABS CDOs, 127–134, 353, 449–450, 595
Abu Dhabi Investment Authority, 38
Accounting, 34–35, 474–475
Accrual accounting, 34
Accrual payments, 551–553
Accrued interest, 595
Accumulated value, 46
Acharya, V. V., 300
Additional Tier 1 capital, 595
Add-on factor, 261, 595
Adjustable rate mortgage (ARM), 122
Adoboli, Kweku, 71, 114, 509, 510
ADR. *See* American Depository Receipt
Advanced IRB approaches, 275–276
Advanced measurement approach (AMA), 277–278, 431–433, 435–438, 444, 595
Adverse selection, 55–56, 63, 442, 595
Advisory services, 29, 31–32
Agency costs, 132, 595
Aggregating VaRs, 197
AIG, 353, 380, 388
Aitken, J., 395
Alexander, C., 426
Allied Irish Bank, 1, 114, 509, 510
Almgren, R., 452, 469
Alpha, 10–13, 72, 388–389, 595
negative, 13
Alternative investments. *See* Hedge funds
Altman, Edward, 348, 352, 363, 371, 402
AMA. *See* Advanced measurement approach
Amato, J. D., 366
Amaranth, 78
Ambac, 380
Ambachtsheer, K. P., 64
American Depository Receipt (ADR), 82
American option, 100, 535–537, 595

Analytic result, 595
Annual renewable term insurance, 42
Annuity contract, 45–46, 50, 63
Appaloosa Management, 76
Aragonés, J. R., 427
Arbitrage, 359, 595
Arbitrage pricing theory, 13, 595
Arbitrageur, 595
ARCH*(m)* model, 205, 216
ARM. *See* Adjustable rate mortgage
Arthur Andersen, 443
Artzner, P., 188, 201
ASF factor. *See* Available stable funding factor
Ashanti Goldfields, 458
Asian option, 111, 112, 154, 595
Ask price, 595. *See also* Offer price
Asset-backed commercial paper (ABCP), 457
Asset-backed security (ABS), 125–133, 287, 288, 595
Asset-liability management, 159–161
Asset pricing, 473
Asset swap, 358–359, 595
Asymmetric information, 355
At-the-money option, 100, 148, 595
Autocorrelation, 192–103, 595
Auto insurance, 51, 54, 55–56
Autoregressive conditional heteroscedastity (ARCH) model, 205, 216
Available stable funding (ASF) factor, 293, 595
Average price call options, 111, 595
Average price put options, 595

Babbel, D., 445
Back-end load, 69, 595
Back office, 137, 513, 596
Back-testing, 83, 188, 197–201, 267, 595
Backwards induction, 596
Bail-in, 295
Bangia, A., 452, 469
Bankers Trust, 113, 510, 514, 517
Bank failures, 26–27, 258, 457

Bank for International Settlements (BIS), 92–93, 353
Bank holding companies, 23, 33
Bank Holding Company Act, 23
Banking book, 35, 132, 266, 287, 596
Bank of America, 33, 456
Bank capital
  economic, 491–505
  regulatory, 257–300
Bank of England, 455
Bankruptcy costs, 14–16, 18, 596
Banks and banking, 21–38
  accounting, 34–25
  conflicts of interest in, 34
  consolidation of, 23
  large, 34–37
  originate-to-distribute model, 35–37
  potential conflicts of interest in, 33–34
  regulation of, 257–300
  risks, 37–38
  services, 34
  size distribution of, 22
  systemic risk, 258
Barings Bank, 1, 114, 258, 509–511, 513
Barrier options, 111, 154, 596
Basak, S., 201
Basel 2.5, 285–289, 299–300
Basel Accord, 257, 264, 280–281
Basel Amendment, 265–267
Basel Committee on Banking Supervision, 259, 262, 265, 268, 274, 285–288, 297, 299, 377, 426, 431, 435, 437, 467, 468, 491, 499, 516
Basel I, 257, 300, 407, 596
Basel 1A, 268
Basel II, 257, 268–280, 285, 389, 467, 596
  adjustments for collateral, 270–271
  corporate, sovereign, and bank exposures, 272–275
  guarantees and credit derivatives, 277
  internal ratings based (IRB) approach, 271–272
  market discipline, 269, 278–279
  operational risk capital, 277–278
  retail exposures, 275–276
  Standardized Approach, 269–270, 277
  stress testing, 419–421
  supervisory review, 268–269, 278
Basel III, 285, 289–295, 300, 388, 409, 459–462, 503, 596
  capital conservation buffer, 290–291
  capital requirements, 289–290

countercyclical buffer, 291–292
  counterparty credit risk, 295
  leverage ratio, 292
  liquidity risk, 292–295
Basic indicator approach, 277, 431, 596
Basis, 596
Basis points, 166, 596
Basis risk, 596
Basket credit default swaps, 596
Basket options, 111, 596
Bates, D. S., 488
Baud, N., 445
Beaglehole, D. R., 52, 64
Bear Stearns, 23, 33, 161, 457
Beder, T., 201
Berkowitz, J., 424, 427
Berkshire Hathaway, 56, 75
Bermudan swap options, 483, 596
Best efforts, 27, 28, 596
Beta, 8–10, 13, 596
Bid-ask-spread, 596. *See also* Bid-offer spread
Bid-offer spread, 32, 448, 450–453, 462, 469
Bid price, 89, 448–449, 596
Bilateral clearing, 376–380, 596
Binary cash-or-nothing call option, 36
Binary credit default swaps, 596
Binary options, 111, 596
Binomial model, 535–537, 596
Binomial tree, 535–537, 596
BIS. *See* Bank for International Settlements
BIS Accord, 259–262, 596
BIS Amendment, 184, 267
Bivariate normal distribution, 238–239, 241–242, 245, 596
Bivariate Student t-distribution, 244–247
Black, F., 478, 479
Black-Scholes-Merton model, 141, 144, 210, 365, 368, 476, 478–483, 486, 488, 533–534, 596
Black's model, 479, 596
Black swan, 518
Blanco, C., 427
Bogle, John, 69, 427
Bollerslev, T., 218, 230
Bond convexity, 168–169, 171
Bond duration, 164–168
Bond mutual funds, 67
Bond option, 597
Bond pricing, 526
Bond ratings, 18

Bond yield, 357–358, 527, 597
Bonuses, 132–133, 299
Bootstrap method, 597
   for VaR confidence intervals, 313
   for zero rates, 527
Bottom-up measurement approach, 492–493
Boudoukh, J., 201, 310, 320
Box, G. E. P., 224
Boyle, F., 115
Boyle, P., 115
Brady, B., 352
Brady bonds, 82, 455–456
Branson, Richard, 456
Break-even premium, 49–50
Brent index, 109
Bridgewater Associates, 76
Brin, Sergei, 30
British Bankers Association (BBA), 162
Broken arrow stress testing, 416
Brokerage services, 32
Brunnermeier, M. K., 470
Buckets, 174
Buffett, Warren, 56, 75
Bunching, 200, 597
Bureau of Financial Protection, 297
Business days, 206
Business disruption, 429, 433
Business environment and internal control
   factors (BEICFs), 438, 440
Business risk, 493, 503, 597
Business risk economic capital, 495
Buying on margin, 104–105

CAC 40, 304–306, 312
Calendar days, 597
Calibration, 477, 597
Callable bond, 597
Call options, 85, 100, 140–144, 597
Canabarro, E., 382, 395
Cancelable swap, 597
Canter, M. S., 64
Cap. *See* Interest-rate cap
Capital adequacy, 25–26, 597
Capital asset pricing model, 7–13, 597
Capital conservation buffer, 290–291, 597
Capital gains taxes, 10
Capital Requirement Directive 2 (CRD2),
   298–299
Capital requirements, 56–57, 279, 289–290
   bankruptcy and, 16
   Basel Accord, 262
   Basel II, 268

Basel III, 289–295
Basel 2A, 285–289
   in commercial banking, 24–26
   insurance companies, 56–57, 279–281
   liquidity impacts, 466–467
   small banks, 24–26
Caplet, 597
Cap rate, 597
Caps, 102
Case-Shiller index, 597
Cash-flow mapping, 331–333, 597
Cash settlement, 597
Casualty insurance, 51–53
Catastrophic risks, 51
CAT bond, 52, 597
Causal relationships, 439–440
CBOE. *See* Chicago Board Options
   Exchange (CBOE)
CCP. *See* Central clearing parties (CCPs)
CDD (cooling degree days), 108–109, 597
CDO. *See* Collateralized debt obligation
CDO squared, 597
CDS. *See* Credit default swap
CDS-bond basis, 359–360, 597
CDS spread, 354
CDX, 356, 357, 597
CDX NA IG, 356, 357
Central banks, 164, 457–458
Central clearing, 380–382, 597
Central clearing parties (CCPs), 104, 297,
   375, 380–382, 597
Central limit theorem, 494
Cepedes, J. C. G., 395
Chase Bank, 23
Cheapest-to-deliver bond, 355–356, 597
Chemical Bank, 23
Cherubini, U., 253
Chicago Board of Trade (CBOT), 89
Chicago Board Options Exchange (CBOE),
   89, 101, 102, 208
Chicago Mercantile Exchange, 109
Chief Risk Officer, 1
Chinese walls, 34, 597
Chi-square, 200
Cholesky decomposition, 240, 597
Chorafas, D. N., 445
Chriss, N., 452, 469
Christoffersen, P. F., 200
Citicorp, 36, 517
Citigroup, 1, 22, 36, 38, 131, 467
Citron, Robert, 509, 511, 526
Clawback clause, 76, 597

Clean price of bond, 597
Clearing houses, 103–104, 598
Clearing margin, 598
Clemens, R., 415, 427
Clients, products, and business practices, 429, 433
Cliff risk, 130
Closed-end funds, 70, 85, 598
Clunie, J., 462, 470
CoCo. *See* Contingent convertible bond
Coefficient of correlation, 233, 234
Cohen, Steve, 76
Coherent risk measure, 190, 191, 598
Coinsurance provision, 55, 442
Cole, J. B., 64
Collar, 604
Collateral, 107, 270–271, 384–384, 457, 598
Collateralization, 377–378, 598
Collateralized debt obligation (CDO), 127, 129–130, 288, 598
  synthetic, 555–557, 611
  valuation, 555–557
Combined ratio, 53
Combined ratio after dividends, 53
Commercial banking, 21, 22–27, 598
  capital requirements, 24–26
  conflicts of interest in, 33–34
  investment banking and, 33–34
  limitations on, 33
  regulation of, 22–23
  services, 34
Commercial paper, 516
Commodities Futures Trading Commission (CFTC), 297
Community banks, 22, 23
Companies
  risk *vs.* return for, 13–16
Compensation, 132–133, 299
Component value at risk, 195–196, 201, 598
Compounding frequency, 521–523, 598
Compounding swap, 598
Compound options, 111, 598
Comprehensive approach for collateral, 270
Comprehensive risk measure (CRM), 288–289, 598
Conditional default probability, 190–191, 350
Conditional stress testing, 416
Conditional tail expectation. *See* Expected shortfall

Conditional value at risk (C-VaR). *See* Expected shortfall
Confidence interval for VaR, 308, 313, 319
Confidence level for VaR, 191, 194–196, 200, 279, 317, 491–493
Confirmation, 598
Conflicts of interest, 33–34
Constant level of risk assumption, 288
Consumption asset, 598
Continental Illinois, 161
Contingency funding plan (CFP), 461
Contingent convertible bond (CoCo), 295–296, 598
Continually refreshed rate, 163
Continuous compounding, 522, 598
Contributory group life insurance, 45
Control areas, 110
Convenience yield, 598
Convergence arbitrage, 515
Conversion factor, 261, 598
Convertible arbitrage, 81–82
Convertible bonds, 598
Convexity, 168–169, 171, 598
Convexity adjustment, 476, 598
Cooke ratio, 259–260, 598
Cooley, T. F., 300
Cooling degree day, 108–109, 597
Copula correlation, 243, 250, 406
Copulas, 233, 240–252, 499, 598
  factor model, 246, 247, 252
  Gaussian model, 241–244, 246, 247, 251, 252, 272
  multivariate, 246
  Student t-copulas, 244–246
  Vasicek's model, 246–252
Core Tier 1 capital, 289–290, 503. *See also* Tier 1 equity capital
Core variables, 416
Cornett, M. M., 38
Cornish-Fisher expansion, 339–340, 598
Corporate bonds, 18, 61
Corporate exposures, 273–275
Correlation matrix, 327–330, 598
Correlations, 233–240, 598
  defined, 233–234
  dependence *vs.*, 234
  model, 406
  monitoring, 235–238
  multivariate normal distributions, 238–240
Cost of carry, 599
Countercyclical buffer, 291–292, 599

Counterparty, 261, 599
Counterparty credit risk, 295, 375–394
Countrywide, 456
Coupon, 599
Covariance, 233–234, 237–238, 252, 599
Covariance matrix, 327–330
Covariance rates, 235–236, 599
Covered call, 107, 599
Crashophobia, 481, 599
Creation units, 71
Credit card losses, 436
Credit contagion, 366, 367, 400, 599
Credit correlation, 246–252, 400–410
Credit default swap (CDS), 352–357, 370,
    450, 551–553, 599
Credit derivatives, 17, 353, 599
Credit equivalent amount, 260–261, 599
Credit events, 352, 355, 599
Credit exposure, 375–376
Credit indices, 356–357, 599
CreditMetrics, 184, 405–410, 494–495, 599
Credit ratings, 18, 347–349, 368, 599
    economic capital and, 491–492
    internal, 348
    transition matrices, 400–403, 549, 550
Credit ratings transition matrices, 400–402,
    549, 550, 599
Credit risk, 24, 37, 104, 599
    advanced IRB approach, 269–277
    Basel I, 259–262
    Basel II, 269–277
    Basel III, 289–295
    counterparty, 375–394
    credit value at risk, 399–410
    default probability, 342–371
    economic capital, 494–495, 500
    foundation IRB approach, 269, 275
    migration, 400–402
    risk aggregation and, 17
    standardized approach, 269, 270
Credit risk economic capital, 494–495, 500
Credit risk loss distribution, 497
Credit risk migration, 400–402, 599
Credit Risk Plus, 403–405, 495, 599
Credit spreads, 357–362, 599
Credit substitution, 277
Credit Suisse, 291–292, 295–296
Credit Suisse Financial Products, 403, 404,
    410
Credit Suisse First Boston, 30
Credit support annex (CSA), 377–379, 599
Credit transition matrices, 549–450

Credit trigger. *See* Downgrade trigger
Credit value adjustment (CVA), 295,
    382–389, 394, 599
Credit value at risk, 399–410, 599
    CreditMetrics, 404–405
    Credit Risk Plus, 403–404
    ratings transition matrices, 400–402
    time horizon, 399–400
    trading book, 406–410
    Vasicek's model, 402–403
CRM. *See* Comprehensive risk measure
Cross gamma, 339
Crouhy, M., 281
Crowded exit, 462
CSA. *See* Credit support annex
Cumby, R., 230
Cumulative bivariate normal distribution,
    242–243
Cumulative distribution function, 250,
    314–315, 599
Cumulative loss distribution, 186
Cumulative preferred stock, 262
Cure periods, 384–384, 599
Currency swaps, 391–392, 531–532, 599
Current ratio, 348
Curvature, 145
CVA. *See* Credit value adjustment
C-VaR. *See* Expected shortfall

Daily volatility, 206–207, 209–211,
    213–216, 229, 311–312
Dalio, Ray, 76
Danish Financial Supervisory Authority
    (DFSA), 423
Data consortia, 436
Data mining, 83
Data vendors, 436
Davis, E., 445
Day count, 599
Day trade, 599
Debit value adjustment (DVA), 389, 599
Debt financing, 27
Debt repudiation, 36
Debt rescheduling, 36
Debt value adjustment. *See* Debit value
    adjustment
Decay rate, 220
Dedicated short funds, 80
Deductible, 55, 442
Default correlation, 246–252, 400–410,
    600
Default intensity. *See* Hazard rate

Default probability. *See* Probability of default (PD)
Default rates, 247, 351, 403–404
Deferred annuity, 45–46, 600
Defined benefit plan, 59–63, 600
Defined contribution plan, 59–60, 63, 600
De Fountnouvelle, P., 441, 445
De Jesus-Rueff, V., 441, 445
Delbaen, F., 188, 201
Deleveraging, 465–466, 600
Delivery price, 600
Delta, 137–144, 150, 178–179, 534, 536, 600
    interest rate, 174–176
Delta hedging, 138–146, 151–156, 600
Delta-neutral portfolios, 138, 144, 147, 149, 151–152, 156, 600
Demarta, S., 253
Dependence, 234, 600
Deposit insurance, 26–27, 257, 600
DerivaGem, 150, 418–419, 534, 537, 553, 556, 600, 615–619
Derivatives, 92–93, 375–394, 600
Derman, E., 156, 476, 476, 486, 488
Deterministic variable, 600
Deutsche Bank, 498, 503, 514
Deutsche Morgan Grenfell, 498
Dev, A., 506
DeWitt, J., 360
Diebold, F., 452, 469, 519
Directed brokerage, 74, 600
Discount bonds. *See* Zero-coupon bonds
Discount brokers, 32
Discount instruments, 600
Discount rate, 600
Distance to default, 370, 600
Distressed securities, 80–81
Diversifiable risk, 13
Diversification, 17, 67, 325–326, 366, 461, 468–469, 512, 519, 600
Dividends, 600
Dividend yield, 600
Dodd-Frank Act, 58, 131, 285, 296–297, 299, 300, 600
Doff, R., 64
Doherty, N. A., 519
Dollar convexity, 169, 179, 600
Dollar duration, 167–168, 171, 174–176, 600
Douglas Amendment to the Bank Holding Company Act, 23
Dow Jones Credit Suisse, 79, 84

Dow Jones Industrial Average (DJIA), 208, 304–306, 312, 464
Dowd, K., 201, 427
Down-and-in option, 600
Down-and-out option, 600
Downgrade trigger, 379–380, 601
Drexel, 258
Duffie, D., 180, 201, 371, 381, 383, 395, 427
Dunbar, N., 519
Dupire, B., 486
Duration, 164–168, 170–171, 180, 601
Duration matching, 601
Dutch auction, 29, 30, 601
Dutta, K., 445
DV01, 174–175
DVA. *See* Debit value adjustment
Dynamic hedging, 463, 601
Dynamic scenarios, 418, 601

EAD. *See* Exposure at default (EAD)
Early exercise, 601
Early termination event, 377, 378, 601
Earth Satellite Corporation, 109
Eber, J.-M., 188, 201
Economic capital, 37–38, 491–503, 505, 601
    aggregating, 498–501
    allocating, 501–503
    components of, 493–495
    defined, 491–493
    Deutsche Bank, 503
    relative importance of risk, 497–498
    shapes of the loss distributions, 495–497
Efficient frontier, 5–8, 601
Efficient market hypothesis, 601
Eigenvalues, 177, 543–545, 547
Eigenvectors, 177, 543–545, 547
Electricity derivatives, 110–111
Electronic trading, 89, 601
Embedded option, 601
Embrechts, P., 320
Emerging markets hedge funds, 82
Empirical research, 601
Employment practices and workplace safety, 429, 433
Endowment life insurance, 44–45, 601
Energy derivatives
    Electricity, 110
    Natural gas, 109
    Oil, 109
Engle, R. F., 216, 219, 223, 230, 238, 253

Enron, 380, 443, 510, 514
Enterprise risk management, 491, 601
Eonia (Euro OverNight Index Average), 164
Equitable Life, 47
Equity capital, 16, 24, 25–26, 262, 289–292
Equity financing, 27
Equity mutual funds, 68
Equity prices and default probabilities, 367–370
Equity swap, 601
Equity tranches, 125–127, 601
Ergener, D., 156
ESL Investments, 76
ETF. *See* Exchange traded fund
Euler, Leonhard, 196
Euler's theorem, 196–197
Eurobonds, 82
Eurocurrency, 601
Eurodollar, 601
Eurodollar futures contracts, 163, 601
Eurodollar interest rate, 601
European Banking Authority, 422
European Central Bank, 457–458
European Growth Trust (EGT), 498
European options, 100, 533–534, 601
European Union, 59, 257, 299
Event of default, 377, 601
EVT. *See* Extreme value theory
EWMA model, 205, 216–218, 220, 221, 224, 229, 234, 236, 238, 311, 329–330, 601, 602
Ex-ante calculations, 505
Exceptions, 196, 197, 601
Excess cost layers, 56, 601
Excess kurtosis, 309, 601
Excess-of-loss reinsurance contracts, 56
Excess return on bonds, 363–364
Excess spread, 601
Exchange rate heavy tails, 209–213
Exchange-traded fund (ETF), 71, 85, 602
Exchange-traded markets, 89–90, 92, 94–95, 102, 103, 115, 602
Ex-dividend date, 602
Exercise price, 100, 602
Exotic options, 111–113, 153–154, 602
Expectations theory, 602
Expected loss from defaults, 273
Expected return, 2–5, 7–13
Expected shortfall, 186–188, 191, 200, 317, 602
Expected tail loss. *See* Expected shortfall
Expected value, 3, 602

Expense ratio, 52–53, 69, 602
Expiration date, 100, 602
Exponentially weighted moving average (EWMA) model. *See* EWMA model
Exponential spectral risk measure, 191
Exponential weighting, 602
Exposure at default (EAD), 264, 273, 275, 276, 602
External data, 436–437
External fraud, 429, 433
External risks, 430
Extreme value theory (EVT), 194, 314–320, 413, 602

Fabozzi, F. J., 180
Face value, of bonds, 352
Factor, 602
Factor analysis, 602
Factor copula model, 246, 252, 602
Factor loadings, 177, 602
Factor models, 240, 247, 602
Factor score, 177, 602
Fair-value accounting, 265, 473, 602
Fama, E. F., 207, 229
Fannie Mae, 35–36, 298
FAS. *See* Financial Accounting Standards Board
FDIC. *See* Federal Deposit Insurance Corporation
FDIC Improvement Act, 27
"Fear index," 209
Federal Deposit Insurance Corporation (FDIC), 26–27, 297, 298
Federal Home Loan Mortgage Corporation (FHLMC), 35–36, 298
Federal Insurance Office, 58, 279
Federal National Mortgage Association (FNMA), 35–36, 298
Federal Reserve Board, 33, 131, 298, 457, 467
Fed funds rate, 164
FICO, 125, 602
Fiduciary accounts, 33
Figlewski, S., 230, 483
Financial Accounting Standards Board (FAS), 474–475
Financial bailouts, 16
Financial crisis of 2007, 121–135, 367, 413, 460, 466
  causes of, 130–133
  consequences, 130
  housing market, 121–124

Financial crisis of 2007 (*Continued*)
  lessons from, 133–134
  securitization, 124–130
Financial instruments, 89–115
Financial intermediary, 602
Financial Services Authority (FSA), 92, 455
Financial Services Modernization Act, 33
Financial Stability Oversight Council
    (FSOC), 296–298
Financial Times, 15
Finer, Barry, 488
Finger, C. C., 228, 300, 410, 416, 427
Firm commitment, 27, 28, 602
First-order autocorrelation, 192–193
Fitch, 18, 347
Fixed annuity, 45, 602
Fixed assets, 24
Fixed benefits, 45
Fixed coupons, 357
Fixed income arbitrage, 82
Fixed-income hedge fund managers, 82
Fixed-rate loans, 99
Flannery, B. P., 545
Flavell, R., 115
Flight to quality, 131, 362, 417
Floating-rate loans, 99
Fons, J. S., 363, 371
Floor, 102–103, 604
Floorlet, 603
Floor rate, 603
Force of interest, 522
Foreign currency options, 210, 603
Foreign currency risk, 93–94, 112
Forward contracts, 93–94, 96–97, 100, 334,
    529–530, 603
  and credit risk, 392–394
Forward exchange rate, 603
Forward interest rates, 180, 603
Forward price, 603
Forward quotes, 93
Forward rate, 603
Forward rate agreement (FRA), 603
Foundation Internal Ratings Based (IRB)
    approach, 269, 271–272, 274–276
Frachot, A., 445
Fractile, 191
Freddie Mac, 35–36, 298
French, K. R., 207, 230
Front-end load, 69, 603
Front office, 137, 513, 603
Front running, 74, 603
Froot, K. A., 64

Frye, J., 180, 343
FSA. *See* Financial Services Authority
FTSE 100, 69, 304–306, 312
Full-service brokers, 32
Fund of funds, 75, 603
Futures contracts, 94–96, 100, 529–530,
    603
  margins for, 105
Futures option, 534, 537, 603
Futures price, 529, 603

G-30 policy recommendations, 262–263,
    603
Galai, D., 281
Gamma, 144–146, 150, 151–155, 336–338,
    534, 536, 603
  interest rate, 179
Gamma-neutral portfolios, 145–146, 148,
    603
GAO. *See* Guaranteed Annuity Option
GAP management, 174, 603
GARCH (1,1) model, 205, 218–220,
    225–229, 234–237, 311, 603
GARCH (*p,q*) model, 218
Gaussian copula model, 241–244, 246, 247,
    251, 252, 272, 406, 499, 603
Gaussian quadrature, 555
Geczy, C., 115
Generator matrix, 550
Ginnie Mae, 35–36
Glass-Steagall Act of 1933, 33, 603
Global macro hedge funds, 83
Gnedenko, D. V., 314–315
Going-concern capital, 290
Gold, 39, 137, 458
Goldman Sachs, 33–34, 78–79, 153
Gold mining companies, 140, 458
Gomory, R., 519
Google, 29, 30
Gordy, M. B., 249, 253, 272, 281, 402, 410
Gorton, G., 129, 135
Government National Mortgage Association
    (GNMA), 35–36
Greek letters (Greeks), 137, 147, 150, 152,
    156, 187, 534, 603, 618–619
Greenspan, Alan, 131, 466
Gregory, J., 383, 395
Gross income, 277
Group health insurance, 54–55
Group life insurance, 45, 603
Guaranteed Annuity Option (GAO), 47
Guaranteed interest rate, 47

Haircut, 378, 603
Hammersmith and Fulham, 439, 510, 517
Hasbrook, J., 230
Hazard rates, 350–351, 362–363, 603
HDD (heating degree days), 108–109, 603
Health insurance, 53–55, 63
Heath, D., 188, 201
Heating degree days. *See* HDD
Heavy tailed distribution, 210, 211
Hedge, 139, 603
Hedge and forget property, 139
Hedge fund managers, 77–78, 83
Hedge funds, 67, 74–85, 603
    fees, 75–77
    leveraging and deleveraging cycle, 466
    liquidity and, 469
    performance, 83–84
    strategies, 79–83
Hedger, 603
Hedge ratio, 603
Hedging, 137–156
    calculating, 150
    calculating deltas, 175–176
    delta, 137–144, 151–156
    exotic options, 153–154
    gamma, 144–146, 153, 156
    guidelines, 517
    liquidity and, 458
    models, 484–485
    realities of, 152–153
    rho, 149–150
    scenario analysis, 154–155
    Taylor series expansion, 151–152
    theta, 148–149
    vega, 146–148, 153, 156
Hedging errors, 145
Held-for-sale instruments, 474–475
Held-to-maturity instruments, 474–475
Hendricks, D., 320
Herrero, A. de J., 395
Herring, R. J., 519
High denial zip codes, 123
High-frequency low-severity losses
    (HFLSLs), 436
High-watermark clause, 76, 604
Historical default probability, 366, 604
Historical scenarios, 414–415
Historical simulation, 303–320, 604
    accuracy, 308–309
    computational issues, 313–314
    extensions, 309–313
    extreme value theory, 314–319

    methodology, 303–308
    model building approach *vs.*, 341–342
Historical volatility, 604
Holding companies, 23
Holiday calendar, 604
Homogeneity, 188
Homogeneous expectations, 10
Hopper, G., 201
Housing market, 121–124, 134–135,
    415–416, 449
Hua, P., 201, 427
Hull, J. C., 135, 209, 252, 311, 320, 342,
    358, 362, 369, 371, 382, 389, 395,
    403, 482, 487, 534, 537, 557
Hunter, Brian, 78
Hurdle rate, 76, 604
Hurricane damage, 51, 56
Hybrid approach, 499–500, 604
Hybrid mutual funds, 68

IAS. *See* International Accounting Standards
    Board
Iben, T., 371
IDRC. *See* Incremental default risk charge
    (IDRC)
Implied default probability, 364. *See also*
    Risk-neutral default probabilities
Implied risk-free rates, 358
Implied volatility, 208–209, 479, 481, 604
Inception profit, 513, 604
Incremental capital, 502
Incremental default risk charge (IDRC), 287
Incremental risk charge (IRC), 287–288,
    409–410, 604
Incremental value at risk, 195–196, 201, 604
Independence, 604
Independent amount, 377, 604
Indexation, 60
Index funds, 69, 70, 604
IndyMac, 27
Initial margin, 104–106, 604
Initial public offerings (IPOs), 28–30, 604
Instantaneous forward rate, 604
Insurance, 41–59, 62–63, 67, 279, 436, 516
    annuity contracts, 45–46
    capital requirements, 56–57
    health insurance, 53–55
    life insurance, 41–45
    longevity and mortality risk, 50–51
    moral hazard and adverse selection, 55–56
    mortality tables, 46–50
    operational risk and, 442–443

Insurance (*Continued*)
  property-casualty insurance, 51–53
  regulation, 58–59
  reinsurance, 56
  risk aggregation, 17
  risks, 58
Intel, 101
Interdealer brokers, 474
Interest-rate cap, 102–103, 604
Interest-rate collar, 102–103, 604
Interest-rate deltas, 174–176
Interest-rate-dependent securities, 170–171
Interest-rate derivatives, 102–103, 604
Interest-rate floor, 102–103, 604
Interest-rate options, 46, 102–103, 604
Interest-rate risk, 26, 112, 159–180
Interest rates, 330–334, 521–523
Interest-rate swaps, 259, 261, 334,
  391–382, 439, 604
Internal controls, 509
Internal credit ratings, 348, 604
Internal data, 435–436
Internal fraud, 429, 433
Internal ratings based (IRB) approach,
  271–272, 274–276, 348
Internal risks, 430
International Accounting Standards Board
  (IAS), 474–475
International Petroleum Exchange (IPE),
  109
International Swaps and Derivatives
  Association (ISDA), 100, 263–264, 353
Master Agreement, 376–377, 379
Interstate banking, 23
In-the-money option, 100, 148, 604
Intrinsic value, 604
Investment asset, 604
Investment banking, 21, 27–32, 34, 604
  advisory services, 29, 31–32
  commercial banking and, 33–34
  conflicts of interest in, 33–34
  Dutch auction approach, 29
  initial public offerings (IPOs), 28–30
  limitations on, 33
Investment-grade bonds, 18, 349–350, 604
IPOs, 28–30, 604
IRB approach. *See* Internal ratings based
  approach
IRC. *See* Incremental risk charge
Irrational exuberance, 467–468
ISDA. *See* International Swaps and
  Derivatives Association

ISDA master agreement, 605
ITraxx, 356, 357, 605

Jackson, P., 201
Jamshidian, F., 341, 343
Japanese Treasury rates, 527
Jarrow, R. A., 550
Jensen, M. C., 71, 72, 85
Jett, Joseph, 476, 488, 510, 512
Joint distribution, 243–244, 486–487
Jones, Alfred Winslow, 75, 79
Jones, A. W., & Co., 75
Jones, F. J., 116
Jordan, J., 441, 445
Jorgensen, P. L., 422
Jorion, P., 180, 201, 519
JPMorgan Chase, 22, 23, 33, 67, 183, 184,
  405, 410, 457
Ju, X., 519
Junk bonds, 18, 605

Kane, A., 230
Kamakura, 348, 369–370
Kani, I., 156, 486
Kao, D., 402
Kealhofer, S., 371
Kendall, M. G., 308
Kerviel, Jêrome, 114, 115, 430, 498, 509,
  510
Key risk indicators (KRIs), 440, 605
Keys, B. J., 125, 135
Khorana, A., 69, 85
Kidder Peabody, 475, 476, 488, 509, 510,
  512, 513
Kim, J., 416, 427
Kluppelberg, C., 320
KMV, 348, 369–370
Knight, F. H., 518
Knock-out call options, 154
Known risk, 518–519
KRI. *See* Key risk indicator
Krinsman, A. N., 135
Kupiec, P., 199, 416, 427
Kurtosis, 210, 605

Lambrigger, D. D., 445
Lampert, Eddie, 76
Lando, D., 402, 550
Late trading, 74, 605
Law of large numbers, 51
LCR. *See* Liquidity coverage ratio
Leeson, Nick, 114, 509, 510, 513

Legal Entity Identifier system, 298
Lehman Brothers, 15, 33, 131, 161, 209, 258, 292, 305, 353, 379, 386, 414, 516
Leptokurtic distribution, 210
Leverage ratio, 292
Leveraging, 465–466, 605
Lewis, M., 135
LGD. *See* Loss given default
Lhabitant, F.-S., 85
Liar loans, 123, 605
LIBID, 162, 605
LIBOR, 98–99, 103, 122, 162–164, 180, 380, 531, 605
LIBOR-in-arrears swaps, 476, 477, 605
LIBOR-OIS spread, 164
LIBOR/swap rates, 358–359, 370
LIBOR/swap yield curve, 163, 175
LIBOR/swap zero curve, 528, 605
Life assurance, 41–42
Life expectancy, 46–50
Life insurance, 41–45, 56–57, 62–63, 605
Linear homogeneity, 196
Linear model, 334–338, 605
Linear products, 138–140, 475–476, 605
Liquid assets, 454
Liquidation costs, 451
Liquidity
    black holes, 449, 462–470, 605
    defined, 447
    funding risk, 454–462, 469, 605
    risk requirements, 459–462
    sources, 454
    trading risk, 447–454, 469, 605
    unwinding positions, 452, 469
Liquidity-adjusted VaR, 452, 605
Liquidity coverage ratio (LCR), 293, 295, 459–460, 605
Liquidity horizon, 287–288
Liquidity mismatch, 161–162
Liquidity preference theory, 161, 605
Liquidity premium, 605
Liquidity ratios, 131
Liquidity risk, 292–295, 447–470, 514–515
Liquid position, 447
Litterman, R., 371
Litzenberger, R. H., 52, 64, 116
Living wills, 298, 605
Ljung, G. M., 224
Ljung-Box statistic, 224–225
Lloyd's Banking Group, 295
Loan losses, 24, 35, 36
Loan-to-value ratio, 125

Local currency bonds, 82
Lognormal distribution, 605
London interbank bid rate. *See* LIBID
London interbank offered rate. *See* LIBOR
Longevity bond, 50, 605
Longevity derivatives, 50–51
Longevity risk, 50, 62, 605
Long position, 93, 95, 96, 102, 150, 605
Long/short equity strategies, 79–80
Long-tail risk, 51–52, 605
Long-Term Capital Management (LTCM), 78, 84, 416–417, 465, 498, 510, 515–516
Long-term variance rate, 223
Long-term volatility, 223
Longin, F. M., 201
Lookback options, 111, 606
Loomis, Carol, 75
Lopez, J., 274, 281
Loss adjustment expense, 53
Loss data, 437
Loss distributions, 438
Losses, 509–519
Loss frequency distribution, 434–435
Loss given default (LGD), 273, 275, 351, 606
Loss probability distributions, 495–497
Loss ratio, 52–53
Loss severity distribution, 434–435
Low-frequency high-severity losses (LFHSLs), 436, 437
Lucas, Robert, 487
Lucas Critique, 487
Luciano, E., 253

MA. *See* Maturity adjustment
Macaulay, Frederick, 166–167
Macaulay's duration, 166–167, 606
Madoff, Bernard, 497
Maintenance margin, 104–106, 606
Mark, R., 281
Margin account, 91, 104–107
Marginal distribution, 240–241, 252, 606
Marginal value at risk, 195–196, 200–201, 606
Margin calls, 104, 105, 606
Margin, 104–107, 464–465, 606
    buying on, 104
    for futures contracts, 106
    for options trading, 106–107
    for OTC derivatives, 107
    for short sales, 105–106

Market discipline, 268, 269, 278–279
Market liquidity measurements, 450–452
Market makers, 32, 606
Market model, 606
Market-neutral strategy, 82
Market portfolio, 7–13, 606
Market price, 35
Market Quotation Method, 379
Market risk, 16–17, 37, 266, 606
   capital, 267
   economic capital, 493–494, 500
   loss distribution, 497
Market risk VaR
   calculations, 295
   historical simulation approach, 303–320
   model-building approach, 323–343
Market timing, 10–11, 74, 606
Market transparency. *See* transparency
Marking to market (MTM), 35, 265, 376,
   378, 381, 473–475, 606
Marking to model, 35, 474, 513, 606
Markit Group, 474
Markowitz, H., 2, 19, 323, 327
Markowitz portfolio theory, 184, 342
Marshall, C., 201
Matten, C., 505, 506
Maturity adjustment (MA), 274, 403
Maturity date, 100, 606
Maude, D. J., 201
Maximum likelihood methods, 220–225,
   250–251, 315, 606
Maximum peak exposure, 385
McCarran-Ferguson Act of 1945, 58
McDonough, William, 269
McDonough ratios, 269
McFadden Act, 23
McNeil, A. J., 253, 320
MCR. *See* Minimum capital requirement
Mean reversion, 220, 606
Medapa, P., 436
Medicaid, 54
Mercury Asset Management, 497
Merger arbitrage, 81
Mergers and acquisitions, 29, 31–32
Merrill Lynch, 1, 33, 128–129, 131, 362,
   450, 497
Merton, Robert, 368, 370, 371, 478
Merton's model, 368, 369–371, 493, 606
Mesokurtic distribution, 210
Metallgesellschaft (MG), 458, 459
Mezrich, J., 223, 230, 238, 253
Mezz ABS CDOs, 127, 129, 134

Mezzanine tranche, 125–127, 606
Mian, A., 123, 135
Microsoft, 112, 153, 324–325, 336
Middle office, 17, 137, 513, 606
Mid-market value, 450–453
Mikosch, T., 320
Miller, M. H., 116
Minimum capital requirement (MCR),
   279–280
Minimum transfer amount, 377–378, 606
Minton, B. A., 115
Model audit groups, 486
Model building approach, market risk VaR,
   323–343, 606
   correlation and covariance matrices,
     327–330
   generalization, 326–327
   historical simulation *vs.*, 341–342
   interest rates, 330–334
   linear model, 334–338
   methodology, 323–326
   Monte Carlo simulation, 340–342
   quadratic model, 338–340
Model risk, 473–488, 513, 606
   accounting, 474–475
   hedging, 484–485
   linear products, 475–476
   marking to market, 473–475
   model-building dangers, 486–487
   model problems, 487–488
   nonlinear products, 476–477
   nonstandard products, 485–486
   physics *vs.* finance models, 476–477
   standard products, 477–484
Modified duration, 166–167, 606
Money center banks, 21–23, 606
Money market funds, 68
Monotonicity, 188
Monte Carlo simulation, 313–314,
   340–341, 385, 386, 404, 405, 408,
   438, 495, 606
Moody's, 18, 347–348, 366, 369–370, 400,
   404
Moody's Investors Service, 352
Moral hazard, 27, 55, 63, 257, 299, 442,
   606
Morgan Stanley, 30, 33–34, 79
Mortality risk, 50, 606
Mortality tables, 46–50, 63
Mortgage defaults, 131
Mortgage foreclosures, 123–124, 135
Mortgage market, 35–37, 42, 121–124

MTM. *See* Marking to market
Mukherjee, T., 125, 135
Multibank holding companies, 23, 606
Multibranch banks, 23
Multivariate normal distribution, 238–240, 606
Mutual funds, 67–74, 84–85, 607

Naked position, 607
NASDAQ 100, 208
National Association of Insurance Commissioners, 58, 279, 607
National Westminster Bank, 510, 513
Natural gas derivatives, 109–110
NAV. *See* Net asset value
Neftci, S. N., 320
Negative alpha, 13
Negative equity homeowner, 123
Negative feedback trading, 462–463, 607
Negative skewness, 10
Negotiated ratings, 127
Nelkin, I., 369
Nelson, D., 218, 230
Net asset value (NAV), 68, 70, 74, 607
Net interest income, 24, 159–162, 179–180, 277, 431, 607
Net interest margin, 159, 161
Net replacement ratio (NRR), 264–265, 607
Net stable funding ratio (NSFR), 293–295, 459–460, 607
Netting, 263–265, 377, 607
New York Mercantile Exchange (NYMEX), 109, 110
New York Stock Exchange (NYSE), 89, 464
Ng, V., 219, 230
Nikkei 225, 304–306, 312, 334, 510
NINJA, 123, 607
Noh, J., 230
Non-business days, 206
Noncontributory group life insurance, 45
Noncumulative perpetual preferred stock, 262
Nonfinancial corporations, 517–518
Non-interest expense, 24
Non-interest income, 24
Noninvestment grade bonds, 18, 607
Nonlife insurance, 41, 607
Nonlinear products, 140–144, 607
    models for, 476–477
Non-normal assumptions, 341–342
Nonparallel yield curve shifts, 172–174

Nonperforming loans, 35, 607
Non-recourse mortgages, 124
Nonstandard products, models for, 485–486
Nonsystematic risk, 8, 13–14, 366, 607
Non-traditional derivatives, 107–111
Normal distribution, 210, 211, 239–240, 308–309, 336, 499, 607
Normal market, 607
Northern Rock (United Kingdom), 161, 292, 447, 454, 455–456, 516
Notice of intention to deliver, 96
Notional principal, 352, 607
NRR. *See* Net replacement ratio
NSFR. *See* Net stable funding ratio
Numerical procedure, 607

Obama, Barack, 54, 285
Objective probability, 425, 607
Observation, weighting, 310
OECD. *See* Organisation of Economic Co-operation and Development (OECD)
Off-balance-sheet derivatives, 259, 260–261, 280–281
Offer price, 89–90
Office of Credit Ratings, 297
Office of Financial Research (OFR), 296–297
Official models, 484
Oil derivatives, 109
OIS. *See* Overnight indexed swap
OIS rate, 164
Olayan Group LLC, 296
One-bank holding companies, 23
One-factor copula models, 251–252
One-factor correlation models, 240
Open-end funds, 68, 71, 85, 607
Open interest, 607
Open outcry, 607
Operating ratio, 53
Operational risk, 25, 37, 277–278, 429–445, 518, 607
    AMA approach, 431, 435–438
    capital allocation, 440–441
    defined, 430–431
    insurance, 442–443
    loss severity and loss frequency, 434–435
    power law, 441
    proactive approaches, 439–440
    regulatory capital, 431–433
    Sarbanes-Oxley Act, 443–444
    types of, 429–430, 433

Operational risk capital, 277–278, 440–441, 444
Operational risk economic capital, 495, 501
Operational risk loss distribution, 497
Option premium, 101
Options, 100–103, 140–144, 607
  linear model and, 335–338
  margins for, 106–107
  synthetic, 463
Oracle, 31
Orange County, 509, 510, 517, 526
Organisation of Economic Co-operation and
    Development (OECD), 260, 265, 269
Originate-to-distribute model, 35–37, 457, 607
OTC markets. *See* Over-the-counter (OTC) markets
Out-of-the-money options, 100, 143, 148, 607
Outside-model hedging, 484, 607
Overcollateralization, 130, 607
Overfitting, 486–487
Overnight borrowing rate, 164
Overnight indexed swap (OIS), 163–164, 607
Overparameterization, 487
Over-the-counter (OTC) markets, 32, 90, 92, 102, 104, 107–110, 115, 261, 263–265, 271, 355, 375, 607
  central clearing parties and, 380–382
  pricing models, 479–484

Page, Larry, 30
Pan, J., 201
Panjer, H. H., 434
Panjer's algorithm, 434
Parallel shift, 170–171, 608
Pareto distribution, 309, 315–316
Partial duration, 172–173, 608
Partial simulation approach, 341, 608
Par value, 352, 608
Par yield, 608
Patient Protection and Affordable Care Act, 54
Paulson, John, 76
Paulson and Co., 76
Payoff, 608
PCA. *See* Principal components analysis
PD. *See* Probability of default (PD)
Peak exposure, 385, 608
Pearson, N., 519
Pedersen, L. H., 470

Penalty-free withdrawals, 46
Pengelley, M., 395
Pension Benefit Guarantee Corporation (PBGC), 62
Pension plans, 41, 59–63, 192
PeopleSoft, Inc., 31
Percentile, 191
Perfect storm, 61
Performing loan, 608
Peripheral variables, 416
Permanent life insurance, 42. *See also* Whole life insurance
Perraudin, W., 201
Persaud, A. D., 462, 470, 519
Philippines, 36
Physical assets damage, 429, 433
Physical default probability, 365. *See also* Historical default probability
Picault, E., 383, 395
Pillar 1, Basel II, 268–278
Pillar 2, Basel II, 268–269, 278, 421
Pillar 3, Basel II, 269, 278–279
Pipeline risks, 421
Plain vanilla derivatives, 93–103, 608
Plain vanilla interest rate swaps, 97, 531
Platykurtic distribution, 210
P&L Decomposition, 485
Poison pills, 31, 608
Poisson distribution, 403, 434, 608
Poisson process, 608
Policyholder, 41, 42–43, 54, 59, 608
Policy limit, 55, 442
Portfolio immunization, 171, 608
Portfolio insurance, 608
Portfolios
  delta of, 137–144
  expected return, 4–5
  pension plans, 62
  probability distribution of gain or loss in value, 183–185, 187
  value at risk, 183–184
Positive feedback trading, 462–465, 608
Positive-semidefinite property, 237–238, 240, 608
Positive skewness, 10
Power law, 211–213, 316, 441, 444, 608
Predatory lending, 123
Predatory trading, 465
Predescu, M., 358, 362, 371, 403
Premium, 41, 43, 45, 49–50, 54, 608
Prepayment risk, 36
Press, W. H., 545

Pricing models, 478–484
Prime broker, 78–79, 608
Prince, Chuck, 467
Principal, 608
Principal components analysis (PCA), 176–179, 333–334, 485, 547, 608
Private placement, 27, 608
Probability density function, 250, 308
Probability of default (PD), 17, 189–191, 273–276, 347–371, 403–404, 608
   Altman's Z-score, 348–349
   comparison of estimates, 362–367
   copulas, 249–251
   estimating from credit spreads, 360–362
   estimating from equity prices, 367–370
   historical, 349–351
   real world vs. risk-neutral, 364–367
   Vasicek's model of, 246–252
   WCDR (worst cast default rate), 249
Process management disruption, 429, 433
Procter and Gamble, 113, 510, 512, 517
Property-casualty insurance, 41, 51–53, 57, 62–63, 608
Property damage, 51
Property insurance, 51–53
Proportional adjustment, 76
Proportional bid-offer spread, 450–451
Proprietary (prop) trading, 32, 297, 608
Prospectus, 27
Public data, 437
Public offerings, 27, 608
Purchase of shares, 91
Put-call parity, 608
Put options, 100, 124, 608
Puttable bonds, 608
Puttable swaps, 608

Qatar Holding LLC, 296
Quadratic model, 338–340, 609
Quantile, 191
Quantitative impact studies (QIS), 268, 609
Quantum Fund, 83
Quiet period, 30

Rabobank Nederlands, 295
RAPM. *See* Risk-adjusted performance measurement
RAROC, 609
Rating agencies, 347–348
Rating transition matrices, 400–402
RCSA. *See* Risk Control and Self Assessment
Real-world default probabilities, 365, 369

Rebalancing, 141–142, 156, 609
Rebonato, R., 424–425, 427
Recovery account, 76
Recovery rates, 133, 351–352, 355–356, 362, 609
Reference entity, 352, 609
Regime shift, 487
Regional banks, 22, 23
Regulation. *See also* Dodd-Frank Act
   of banks, 16, 22–23, 257–279, 285–300
   of hedge funds, 74–75
   of insurance companies, 279–280
   and liquidity, 459–462, 467–468
   of mutual funds, 73–74
   and stress testing, 419–423
Regulatory arbitrage, 132
Regulatory capital, 257–300, 609
Regulatory disclosures, 278–279
Rehypothecation, 378, 379, 609
Reinsurance, 56, 609
Reitano, R., 172, 180
Relative loss severity, 437
Relative value strategy, 82
Remolona, E. M., 366
Renaissance Technologies Corp., 76
Repo (repurchase agreement), 609
Repo rate, 609
Required stable funding (RSF) factor, 293–294, 460, 609
Re-securitization, 134
Reserve requirements, 459, 609
Reset date, 609
Resti, A., 352
Retail banking, 21, 609
Retail deposits, 456–457
Retail exposures, 275–276
Return on equity (ROE), 25
Reverse stress testing, 418–419, 609
Reversion level, 609
Reynolds, C. E., 52, 64
Rho, 149–150, 534, 537, 609
Rich, D., 343
Richardson, M., 201, 300, 310, 320
Riegel-Neal Interstate Banking and Branching Efficiency Act, 23
Right-way risk, 388–389, 609
Risk-adjusted performance measurement (RAPM), 503
Risk-adjusted return on capital (RAROC), 491, 503–505
Risk-adverse investors, 4–5
Risk aggregation, 16–17, 19

Risk appetite, 491, 609
Risk-based premiums, 27
Risk capital. *See* Economic capital
Risk control and self-assessment (RCSA), 440, 609
Risk decomposition, 16–17, 19
Risk-free investments, 5–7
Risk-free rate, 358, 609
Risk management
  challenges, 114–115
  defined, 1
  by financial institutions, 16–17
  holistic approach to, 491
RiskMetrics, 184, 218
Risk-neutral default probabilities, 364–371, 609
Risk-neutral valuation, 364–365, 609
Risk-neutral world, 369–370, 609
Risk premium, 366
Risk-return tradeoffs, 1–5, 13–16, 18
Risk tolerance, 491
Risk-weighted amount, 260–262, 270, 609
Risk-weighted assets (RWA), 260–262, 267, 268, 271, 280, 609
Road shows, 27
Robertson, Julian, 75
Rodriguez, R. J., 371
Rogue trader insurance, 443
Rogue trader risk, 1, 114, 436, 438, 509
Roll, R., 207, 230
Roll back, 535–537, 609
Rolling over, 161
Roncalli, T., 445
Rosen, D., 395
Rosenberg, J. V., 495, 497, 499, 500, 506
Rosengren, E., 441, 445
Ross, S., 2, 17, 70, 85
RSF factor. *See* Required stable funding factor
Rubinstein, Mark, 481, 486
Rusnak, John, 114, 509, 510
Russia, 417, 465, 510, 515
RWA. *See* Risk weighted assets

SAC Capital Partners, 76
Samad-Khan, A., 436
Sandor, R. L., 64
Santander, 497
Sarbanes-Oxley Act, 443–444, 609
Saunders, A., 38
Saunders, D., 395

Scenario analysis, 154–155, 413–426, 437–438, 444, 512, 609
Schloss, Walter J., 75
Scholes, M., 478
Schmidt, Eric, 30
Schrand, C., 115
Schuermann, T., 452, 469, 495, 497, 499, 500, 506
Scorecard approach, 610
SEC, 67, 71, 73, 74, 91, 610
Securities and Exchange Commission (SEC), 30
Securities trading, 27, 32, 33–34
Securitization, 37, 124–130, 135, 457, 610
Seller's market, 449
Selling expenses, 53
Senior tranche, 125–127, 610
Seru, A., 125, 135
Servaes, H., 69, 85
Shapiro, A., 201
Share-for-share exchange, 32
Sharpe, W., 2, 19
Sheedy, E. A., 426
Shevchenko, P. V., 445
Shih, J., 436
Short forward contracts, 94
Short position, 93, 95, 96, 102, 139, 150, 463, 610
Short selling, 90–92, 105–106, 610
Short-squeezed, 90–92
Short-term funding, 161–162, 516
Siegel, M., 201
Simons, Jim, 76
Simple approach (adjustment for collateral), 270
Simulation. *See* Historical simulation and Monte Carlo simulation
Singh, M., 395
Singleton, K., 371
Sironi, A., 352
Skewness, 10, 610
Skodeberg, T., 402
Smith, C. W., 19
Smith, D. J., 113
Société Générale (Soc Gen), 1, 114, 115, 430, 498, 509–511
Sokol, A., 395
Solvency, 447
Solvency capital requirement (SCR), 279–280
Solvency I, 59, 279, 610

Solvency II, 59, 257, 279–280, 610
Solver, 222, 224
SONIA (Sterling OverNight Index Average), 164
Sorkin, A. R., 135, 519
Soros, George, 75, 83
Sovereign bonds, 18
Sovereign exposures, 273–275
Sovereign wealth funds, 38, 610
SOX. *See* Sarbanes Oxley
S&P, 18, 123, 347
S&P 500, 46, 61, 69, 71, 84, 113, 414
Special purpose vehicle (SPV), 125
Specific risk charge (SRC), 266–267, 610
Spectral risk measure, 191, 610
Speculative grade (junk) bonds, 18, 610
Speculator, 610
Spider, 71
Spinning, 28
Spot exchange rate, 94
Spot interest rate, 610
Spot price, 610
Spot quotes, 93
Spot trades, 90
Spot volatility, 610
SRC. *See* Specific risk charge
Standard deviation of loss, 499
Standard deviation of portfolio return, 4–5, 194
Standard deviation of return, 3–7
Standardized approach
  credit risk, 269–270
  operational risk, 277, 431–432
Standard error of VaR, 308
Standard normal distribution, 241–242
State Farm, 67
Static hedge, 610
Static options replication, 154, 155, 610
Stochastic variable, 610
Stock index futures, 610
Stock index option, 610
Stock indices, 304–306, 610
Stock market crash (1987), 463–464, 481, 515
Stock option, 610
Stop-loss rules, 463, 610
Storage costs, 610
Stressed VaR, 286–287, 308, 413, 610
Stress testing, 413–426, 461, 512, 610
  conditional, 416
  regulation, 419–423

results, 423–426
reverse, 418–419
scenarios, 413–418
variables, 414–415
Strike price, 100, 479, 610
Strips, 476
Stroughair, J., 452, 469
Structured products, 112, 516, 610
Stuart, A., 308
Student t-copulas, 244–246, 610
Student t-distribution, 244, 245, 610
Stulz, R. M., 19
Subadditivity, 188, 191
Subjective probability, 424, 425, 610
Subordinated long-term debt, 24, 26
Subprime crisis, 1, 16, 121–135, 514, 516–517
Subprime mortgages, 121, 134, 510, 610
Sufi, A., 123, 135
Suo, W., 487, 488
Supervisory review, 268–269, 278, 279
Supplementary capital. *See* Tier 2 capital
Surplus premium, 43
Survivor bond, 50, 605
Swap execution facilities (SEFs), 297
Swap options (swaptions), 102, 611
Swap rates, 99, 162–164, 610
Swaps, 96–100, 531–532, 610
Swaptions, 102, 611
Swap zero curve. *See* LIBOR/swap zero curve
Swing options, 111
Swiss Re, 56
Synthetic CDOs, 555–557, 611
Synthetic options, 463–464, 611
Synthetic risk, 611
System failures, 429, 433
Systemically important financial institutions (SIFIs), 298
Systematic risk, 8, 13–14, 50, 371, 611
Systemic risk, 258, 298, 611

Tail correlation, 611
Tail dependence, 244–246, 611
Tail loss. *See* Expected shortfall
Tail of distribution, 316–317
Tail value, 244, 246
Take-and-pay options, 111
Takeovers, 29, 31–32
Taleb, N. N., 156, 427, 518
Tass hedge funds database, 83

Taxes
 capital gains, 10
 life insurance and, 43–44
 mutual funds and, 68
Taylor series expansion, 151–152, 338,
 539–541, 611
Teaser rate, 122, 124, 611
Temporary life insurance. *See* Term life
 insurance
Tepper, David, 76
Terminal value, 611
Term life insurance, 42, 62–63, 611
Term structure of interest rates, 159, 611
Tett, G., 135, 519
Teukolsky, S. A., 545
Teweles, R. J., 116
Theta, 148–150, 534, 537, 611
Thomson, R., 519
Threshold, 107, 377, 611
Tier 1 capital, 26, 262, 280, 289–291, 503
Tier 1 equity capital, 289–292, 295, 611
Tier 2 capital, 26, 262, 280, 289–290, 611
Tier 3 capital, 280, 611
Time decay, 148, 611
Time horizon, 191–193, 195, 200
Time value, 611
"Too big to fail," 258, 299
Top-down measurement approach, 492–493
Total expense ratio, 69, 292, 611
Total money supply (M1), 459
Total return swap, 611
Tracking error, 69, 611
Traders, 462–465, 512
Trades, 90, 517
Trading book, 35, 132, 265–266, 287,
 406–410, 456, 611
Trading days, 611
Trading rules, 83
Tranches, 125–127, 353, 611
Tranche spread, 555
Transaction costs, 144, 611
Translation invariance, 188
Transparency, 133, 449–450, 469, 516–517
Treasury bills, 104, 163, 527, 611
Treasury bonds, 163, 527, 611
Treasury department, within corporations,
 518
Treasury rates, 163, 527
Treasury yield, 113
Treasury yield curve, 159
Treasury zero rates, 527–528

Tree, 535–536, 611
Tripartite Authority, 455
Troubled Asset Relief Program (TARP),
 299, 305
Tufano, P., 69, 85
Turnbull, S. M., 550

UBS, 1, 71, 129, 131, 291–292, 296,
 509–511
Uncertainty (vs. risk), 518
Unconditional default probabilities, 350,
 551–552
Unconditional distribution, 240–241, 252,
 316
Underlying variable, 611
Unilever, 497
Unintended consequences, 300
United States Energy Information
 Administration, 109
Unit trust. *See* Mutual funds
Univariate standardized normal distribution,
 239
Universal life insurance, 44, 612
Unknowable risks, 518–519
Unknown risk, 518–519
Unsystematic risk. *See* Nonsystematic risk
Unwinding positions, 452, 469
Up-and-in option, 612
Up-and-out option, 612
Uptick rule, 91
U.S. Department of Social Security, 46

Value at risk (VaR), 183–201, 266, 279, 612
 aggregating, 197
 back-testing, 197–200
 calculating, 185–186
 capital and, 188–190
 coherent risk measures, 190–191
 component, 195–196
 defined, 183–185
 Euler's theorem and, 196–197
 expected shortfall *vs.*, 186–188
 incremental, 195–196
 liquidity-adjusted, 452
 marginal, 195–196
 market risk, historical simulation,
 303–320
 operational risk estimates, 433
 parameters, 191–195
 stressed, 286–287, 308, 413
Vanguard 500 Index Fund, 69

VaR. *See* Value at risk
Variable annuities, 45, 612
Variable life insurance, 44, 612
Variable-universal life insurance, 44
Variance-covariance approach. *See* model
    building approach, market risk VaR
Variance-covariance matrix, 238, 328,
    612
Variance rates, 206, 213, 223, 612
Variance targeting, 223
Variation margin, 104, 381, 612
Vasicek, O., 249, 253, 281, 410
Vasicek's model, 246–252, 366, 402–403,
    405, 612
Vecchiato, W., 253
Vega, 146–148, 150, 153–155, 534, 537,
    612
    interest rate, 179
Vega-neutral portfolios, 147–148, 612
Vetterling, W. T., 545
Vig, V., 125, 135
Virgin Group, 455–456
VIX index, 208–209, 482, 612
Volatility, 146, 150, 205–229, 309, 369,
    413, 612
    causes of, 207
    daily, 209–211, 213–216, 229, 311–312
    defined, 205–207
    EWMA model, 205, 216–218, 220, 229
    forecasting, 225–229
    GARCH (1,1) model, 205, 218–220,
    225–229
    implied, 208–209, 479, 481
    long-term, 223
    market risk VaR and, 311–312
    maximum likelihood methods, 220–225
    power law, 211–213
    skew, 481, 612
    smile, 479, 481, 612
    surfaces, 481–482, 612
    term structures, 227–228, 612
    updating, 311–312
    weighting schemes, 215–216
Volcker, Paul, 297
Volcker rule, 297, 299
VXN index, 208

Walter, I., 300
Warehousing risks, 421
Warwick, B., 116
Washington Mutual, 23
Waterfall, 126–127, 612
WCDR (worst cast default rate), 249, 272,
    273, 275, 276, 402
Weather derivatives, 108–109, 612
Weather risk, 108
Weatherstone, Dennis, 184
Weighting observations, 310
White, A., 135, 209, 252, 311, 320, 342,
    358, 362, 369, 371, 382, 389, 395, 403
Whitelaw, R., 201, 310, 320
Whole life insurance, 42–44, 63, 612
Wholesale banking, 21, 612
Wholesale deposits, 456
Wilmot, P., 201, 427
Winkler, R., 415, 427
Within-model hedging, 484, 612
With-profits endowment life insurance, 45
Workplace safety, 429, 433
Worst cast default rate. *See* WCDR
Writing an option, 102, 612
Wrong-way risk, 388–389, 612
Wüthrich, M. V., 445

Xerox, 380

Yield, 612
Yield curve, 159, 162, 163, 176, 613
Yield curve play, 526
Young, Peter, 498

Zero-coupon bonds, 165, 175, 476,
    525–528, 613
Zero-coupon interest rate, 525–528, 613
Zero-coupon yield curve, 82, 170–175, 180,
    613
Zero curve, 176, 179, 528, 613
Zero rate, 525–528, 613
Zhang, P. G., 519
Zhu, H., 381, 395
Zhu, Y., 341, 343
Zimmerman, T., 123, 135
Z-score, 348–349, 613